Shakespeare's Medical Language

A Dictionary

ARDEN SHAKESPEARE DICTIONARY SERIES

Series Editor

Sandra Clark (Birkbeck College, University of London)

Class and Society in Shakespeare	(Paul Innes)
Military Language in Shakespeare	Charles Edelman
Shakespeare and the Language of Food	(Joan Fitzpatrick)
Shakespeare's Books	Stuart Gillespie
Shakespeare's Demonology	(Marion Gibson)
Shakespeare's Legal Language	B.J. Sokol & Mary Sokol
Shakespeare's Medical Language	(Sujata Iyengar)
Shakespeare's Non-Standard English	N.F. Blake
Shakespeare's Plants and Gardens: A Dictionary	(Vivian Thomas and Nicki Faircloth)
Shakespeare's Political and Economic Language	(Vivian Thomas)
Shakespeare's Religious Language	R. Chris Hassel Jr.
Shakespeare's Theatre	Hugh Macrae Richmond
Women in Shakespeare	Alison Findlay

Forthcoming:

Shakespeare's Insults	(Nathalie Vienne-Guerrin)
Shakespeare and National Identity	(Christopher Ivic)

ARDEN SHAKESPEARE DICTIONARIES

Shakespeare's Medical Language

A Dictionary

SUJATA IYENGAR

BLOOMSBURY

LONDON · NEW DELHI · NEW YORK · SYDNEY

Bloomsbury Arden Shakespeare

An imprint of Bloomsbury Publishing Plc

50 Bedford Square   1385 Broadway
London   New York
WC1B 3DP   NY 10018
UK   USA

www.bloomsbury.com

Bloomsbury is a registered trade mark of Bloomsbury Publishing Plc

This edition of Shakespeare's Medical Language by Sujata Iyengar, first
published 2011 by the Continuum International Publishing Group

© Sujata Iyengar, 2011
This paperback edition © Sujata Iyengar, 2014

British Library Cataloguing-in-Publication Data
A catalogue record for this book is available from the British Library.

ISBN: PB: 978-1-4725-2040-1

Library of Congress Cataloging-in-Publication Data
A catalogue record for this book is available from the Library of Congress.

Typeset by Newgen Imaging Systems Pvt Ltd, Chennai, India
Printed and bound in Great Britain

Contents

Acknowledgments   viii

Series Editor's Preface   ix

List of Medical Terms   x

List of Abbreviations   xv

Introduction   1

A–Z   11

Bibliography   365

Index   399

To my parents,
Dr. Eshwar Narayan Iyengar and Dr. Mythili Iyengar,
who have spent their working lives
caring for patients on the NHS

Acknowledgments

Many people have helped me during the long process of researching and writing this book. I thank the following persons and institutions: at the University of Georgia, the University of Georgia Research Foundation, my department head Doug Anderson (who offered support both intellectual and practical, arguing with me about the provenance of "mummy" and generously taking over my administrative responsibilities himself so that I could finish this project), Valerie Babb (another kind department head who allowed me the necessary flexibility to take care of my own intervening medical concerns), Kris Boudreau, Christy Desmet (co-editor extraordinaire), Fran Teague (who filled my mailbox with apposite articles), Roxanne Eberle, Nelson Hilton (who as department head allowed me to travel to Edinburgh to begin research on this project), my administrative coordinator Laurie Norris (who fielded endless phone calls from students as I wrestled with the manuscript), Hugh Ruppersburg, my Dean; at other institutions, David Riggs (who said, "Great idea!") and Bruce Smith (who said, "You are just the person to do it"); at Continuum, my extremely patient and helpful series editor, Sandra Clark, and the long-suffering production managers Anna Fleming and Colleen Coalter; and Murali and the team at Newgen Imaging in Chennai. I acknowledge the Folger Shakespeare Library, for fellowship in all its senses, and the thoughtful staffs of the Radcliffe Science Library, the Bodleian, the Edinburgh University Library and the Wellcome, and my astonishing graduate and undergraduate students, especially Erin Christian, Victoria Farmer, Corey Goergen, Katie Grubbs, Christopher Holmes, Josh King, Allison Lenhardt, Sonya Loftis, Lian Peters, Polly Reid, Casey Westerman, Nikki Williamson, and Lauren Byrd (with whom I had especially lively and memorable discussions about purging, sex, deformity, death, epilepsy, Paracelsus, perturbation, skin, brains, apoplexy, melancholy, kidneys, and herbal medicines, respectively). I was lucky enough to be able to correspond with many scholars via email as well as at conferences, and to receive "virtual" encouragement from around the world from my "Facebook friends," for which I am very grateful: you know who you are! I extend special thanks to Maria Chappell and Sara Amis, for heroic alphabetizing and cite-checking and to Mollie Barnes and Amber Shaw for proof-reading assistance.

Finally, I thank my husband, Richard Menke, my children, Kavya Iyengar Menke and Kartik Iyengar Menke, my parents, Dr. Mythili Iyengar and Dr. E. N. Iyengar (to whom this volume is dedicated), and my in-laws, Karen Menke and Bruce Menke, and Doug Menke, Anna Lau, and Avery Menke, all of whom tolerated a great deal of abstraction in me (and several research trips) as I was completing the manuscript.

Any remaining absurd omissions, vulgar errors, or egregious impostures are, unfortunately, my own.

Series Editor's Preface

Arden Shakespeare Dictionaries aim to provide the student of Shakespeare with a series of authoritative guides to the principal subject-areas covered by the plays and poems. They are produced by scholars who are experts both on Shakespeare and on the topic of the individual dictionary, based on the most recent scholarship, succinctly written and accessibly present. They offer readers a self-contained body of information on the topic under discussion, its occurrence, and significance in Shakespeare's works, and its contemporary meanings.

The topics are all vital ones for understanding the plays and poems; they have been selected for their importance in illuminating aspects of Shakespeare's writings where an informed understanding of the range of Shakespeare's usage, and of the contemporary literary, historical, and cultural issues involved, will add to the reader's appreciation of his work. Because of the diversity of the topics covered in the series, individual dictionaries may vary in emphasis and approach, but the aim and basic format of the entries remain the same from volume to volume.

Sandra Clark
Birkbeck College
University of London

List of Medical Terms

1. Abhorson [abortion]
2. Abortive *See also* Abhorson [abortion], Hare-lip, Legs forward, Mole
3. Ache *See also* Bone-ache; Tooth-ache
4. Aconitum
5. Aesculapius
6. Agony
7. Ague
8. Alchemist, Alchemy, Alcumist *See also* Med'cine Potable, Paracelsus, Tincture
9. Allicholy, Allycholly *see* Melancholy
10. Almshouse *see* Hospital
11. Anatomy, Atomy
12. Angelica
13. Apoplexy
14. Apothecary
15. Apple *See also* Eye
16. Aqua Vitae
17. Artery
18. Ashy
19. Atomy *see* Anatomy
20. Bald *see* Hair
21. Balm, Balsam, Balsamum
22. Barley-broth
23. Baths *See also* Tub-fast
24. Bedlam *See also* Crazed, Ecstasy, Frenzy, Hospital, Insane, Lunacy, Madness
25. Belch
26. Belly
27. Bladder
28. Blain *See also* Carbuncle, Itch, Kibe, Plague
29. Blind *See also* Eye, Eye-string, Pearl, Sand-blind, Web and Pin
30. Blood *See also* Artery, Heart, Liver, Spirit, Vein
31. Bone-ache *See also* Pox
32. Bowels
33. Brain *See also* Fume, Vapour
34. Brawn
35. Breast *See also* Dug, Pap, Milk-pap, Nipple
36. Brimstone
37. Bruise *see* Parmaceti
38. Bubukle *See also* Carbuncle
39. Bunch-backed *see* Crookback
40. Burdock, Bur-dock, Bur, Burr
41. Burnet
42. Burning fever *see* Tertian
43. Buttock
44. Caduceus
45. Caius
46. Canker
47. Carbuncle *See also* Bubukle
48. Carduus Benedictus
49. Cataplasm *See also* Plaster, Poultice
50. Catarrhs
51. Cheek
52. Childbed *See also* Midwife
53. Choler, Choleric *See also* Complexion, Gall, Humor
54. Cicatrice *See also* Skin
55. Civet *See also* Perfume
56. Clapperclaw
57. Close-stool *see* Jakes
58. Cloves
59. Clyster *see* Clyster-pipes
60. Clyster-pipes

61. Cod, Cods, Cod-piece
62. Cold
63. Colic *See also* Guts-griping
64. College
65. Coloquintida
66. Complexion *See also* Humor, Race
67. Compound
68. Consumption
69. Contagion
70. Copper nose
71. Corns *See also* Warts
72. Cough
73. Cowslip
74. Cramp
75. Crazed, Crazy *See also* Bedlam, Ecstasy, Frenzy, Lunacy, Madness
76. Crookback *See also* Legs forward, Monster
77. Cure
78. Cyme
79. Darnel
80. Dead men's fingers *see* Long purples
81. Deaf *See also* Ear, Earwax
82. Death
83. Decoct *See also* Barley-broth
84. Deform, Deformed, Deformity *See also* Hare-lip, Mole, Monster, Prodigy, Stigmatical
85. Diet *See also* Excrement, Humor, Purge, Stomach, Surfeit
86. Disease
87. Distemper
88. Distil, Distilled, Distillation *See also* Alchemy, Limbeck
89. Distraction *see* Lunacy, Madness
90. Dizzy, Giddy *See also* Apoplexy, Epilepsy
91. Dock *See also* Burdock, Burr
92. Doctor She
93. Dozy *see* Dizzy
94. Dram
95. Dropsies, Dropsy
96. Drug, Drugs *See also* Medicine, Physic
97. Dry, Dryness *See also* Heat, Cold, Complexion, Moisture
98. Dug *See also* Breast
99. Ear
100. Earwax
101. Ecstasy *See also* Bedlam, Crazed, Frenzy, Lunacy, Madness
102. Element
103. Empirics *See also* Alchemist, Apothecary, Herb-Woman, Mountebank, Midwife, Paracelsus, Physician, Surgeon
104. Empiricutic
105. Epilepsy, epileptic
106. Erection
107. Eringoes
108. Eunuch
109. Evil
110. Excrement
111. Eye, eyne
112. Eyebrow
113. Eyelid
114. Eye-string
115. Faint *See also* Swoon
116. Falling sickness *see* Epilepsy
117. Femiter *see* Fumiter
118. Fennel
119. Fever
120. Fistula
121. Flax
122. Flux
123. Folly *see* Madness, Natural
124. Frantic *see* Frenzy
125. Frenzy
126. Fume
127. Fumiter, Fumitory, Fumitor
128. Galen, Galenic
129. Gall
130. Gangrened
131. Geld, Gelded *See also* Eunuch, Glib, Splay, Unseminar'd
132. Giddy *see* Dizzy
133. Glib *see* Geld
134. Goose of Winchester

135. Gore
136. Gout
137. Gravel
138. Gravel-blind
139. Green-sickness *See also* Love-sick
140. Groin
141. Gum, Gums
142. Gut
143. Guts-griping
144. Hair
145. Hare-brain'd *See also* Brain
146. Hare-lip *See also* Mole, Monster, Deformed
147. Headache *see* Ache
148. Heart
149. Heart-string
150. Heat, Hot
151. Hebona
152. Hebenon *see* Hebona
153. Hectic
154. Hem! *see* Cough
155. Hemlock
156. Herb-grace
157. Herb-woman
158. Hibocrates
159. High-gravel-blind *see* sand-blind
160. Hip-gout *see* Sciatica
161. Hippocrates *see* Hibocrates
162. Hor-dock *see* Burdock
163. Horse-leech
164. Hospital
165. Hot *see* Heat
166. Humor
167. Hymen
168. Hyssop
169. Hysterica passio
170. Illness
171. Imposthume
172. Incision
173. Indigested
174. Infect, Infection
175. Inflammation
176. Insane *See also* Bedlam, Crazed, Ecstasy, Frenzy, Lunacy, Madness
177. Insanie
178. Jakes
179. Jaundice
180. Kecksies
181. Kibe *See also* Blain
182. Kidney
183. Lavender
184. Lazar *see* Leprosy
185. Leech
186. Legs forward *See also* Childbed, Midwife
187. Leprosy
188. Lethargy, Lethargies *see* Apoplexy
189. Lettuce
190. Lice *see* Louse
191. Lily-livered
192. Limbeck
193. Lime-kills i'th'palm *see* Lime-kilns i'th'palm
194. Lime-kilns i'th' palm
195. Linen
196. Lisp
197. Liver
198. Liver-vein
199. Long purples
200. Louse, Lousy, Nit
201. Love-in-idleness
202. Love-sick
203. Lucina
204. Lunacy, Lunatic *See also* Bedlam, Crazed, Ecstasy, Frenzy, Insane, Madness
205. Lungs
206. Madness *See also* Bedlam, Crazed, Ecstasy, Frenzy, Insane, Lunacy
207. Maidenhead *see* Hymen
208. Malady *see* Disease
209. Malady of France *see* Pox
210. Mallicholy *see* Melancholy
211. Mandragora
212. Mandrake *see* Mandragora
213. Mare *see* Sleep
214. Marjoram
215. Marrow
216. Measles
217. Medicine

218. Medicinable, Med'cinable
219. Med'cine Potable
220. Melancholy
221. Mercury *see* quicksilver
222. Mettle
223. Midwife
224. Milk
225. Milk-liver'd *see* Lily-liver'd, Pigeon-liver'd
226. Milk-pap *see* Pap
227. Mistempered *see* Distemper
228. Moist, Moisture
229. Mole
230. Monster
231. Mother *see* Hysterica Passio
232. Mountebank
233. Mummy
234. Nail
235. Natural *See also* Madness
236. Navel
237. Neeze
238. Neopolitan bone-ache *see* bone-ache
239. Nerve *See also* sinew
240. Nettle
241. Night-mare *see* Sleep
242. Nipple *See also* Breast, Dug
243. Nit *see* Louse
244. Nose
245. Nose-herb *see* Pomander
246. Nurse
247. O'ercharged
248. Organ
249. Palsy
250. Pap *See also* Breast, Dug
251. Paracelsus, Paracelsian
252. Parmaceti
253. Parti-ey'd
254. Patient
255. Pearl
256. Perfume
257. Perturbation
258. Pestilence *See also* Plague
259. Phlegm *see* Phlegmatic
260. Phlegmatic
261. Physic
262. Physical
263. Physician
264. *Pia Mater*
265. Pigeon-liver'd
266. Pill, Pills
267. Pin and Web *see* Web and Pin
268. Piss *see* Urine
269. Plague
270. Plague-sore *see* Plague
271. Planet
272. Plantain
273. Plaster
274. Plurisy
275. Pomander
276. Poppy
277. Potato
278. Potion
279. Poultice
280. Powdering-tub *see* Tub-fast
281. Pox *See also* Tub-fast
282. Pregnant
283. Prescription
284. Prodigy
285. Prunes *See also* Abhorson, Abortive
286. P's *see* Urine
287. Puking
288. Pulse
289. Pulsidge
290. Purgation, Purge *See also* Blood, Clyster-pipe, Humor, Potion, Puking, Sweat, Vomit
291. Qualm *See also* Stomach-qualmed
292. Quat
293. Quick
294. Quicksilver
295. Quintessence
296. Quotidian
297. Race *See also* Complexion
298. Ratsbane
299. Raw eyes
300. Receipt *See also* Prescription
301. Reins *See also* Kidney
302. Rheum, rheumatic

303. Rhubarb
304. Ripp'd *see* Untimely Ripp'd
305. Rue
306. Ruptures
307. Salt *See also* Tub-fast
308. Salve
309. Sand-blind
310. Sanguine
311. Sapego
312. Saturn
313. Scab
314. Scar *see* Cicatrice, Skin
315. Sciatica
316. Scruple
317. Scurvy
318. Searchers *see* Pestilence, Plague
319. Sea-sick
320. Seed *See also* Sex
321. Senna *see* Cyme
322. Serpigo *see* Sapego
323. Sex
324. Sexual, Sexuality *see* Sex
325. Sickness
326. Simple
327. Sinew
328. Sinows, Sinow *see* Sinew
329. Skin
330. Sleep
331. Sound *see* Swoon
332. Spear-grass
333. Spital, Spital-house *see* Hospital
334. Splay *see* Geld
335. Spleen
336. Squint *see* Web and Pin
337. Staggers *see* Dizzy
338. Stale *see* Urine
339. Stammer *See also* Tongue-tied
340. Star *see* Planet
341. Stigmatical *See also* Deformed, Hare-lip, Mole, Monster
342. Stomach
343. Stomach-qualmed
344. Strangle, Strangled
345. Strings *see* Heart-strings
346. Sulphur *see* Brimstone
347. Suppeago *see* Sapego
348. Surfeit
349. Surgeon
350. Surgeon's Box
351. Sweat
352. Swoon
353. Syrup
354. Taurus *See also* Planet
355. Tawny
356. Teeth
357. Temperality
358. Tent
359. Tertian
360. Tetter
361. Tincture
362. Tisick
363. Tongue-tied
364. Tongue
365. Tooth-ache
366. Tooth-drawer
367. Tub-fast
368. Ulcer, Ulcerous
369. Unpaved *See also* Unseminar'd
370. Unseminar'd *See also* Unpaved
371. Untimely ripp'd
372. Urinal, Jordan
373. Urine
374. Vapor, Vapour
375. Ventricle
376. Vial
377. Viol
378. Virgin-knot *see* Hymen
379. Vomit *See also* Puking, Purge
380. Wall-eyed
381. Wappen'd
382. Wart
383. Web and pin
384. Wet-nurse *see* Nurse
385. Wezand
386. Whites of Egg *see* Flax
387. Womb
388. Wormwood
389. Wound
390. Yew
391. Zany *see* Natural

List of Abbreviations

Abbreviations are consistent with those used by the *Harvard Concordance to Shakespeare*, edited by Marvin Spevack, and by the Modern Language Association of America.

ADO	*Much Ado About Nothing*
ANT	*Antony and Cleopatra*
AWW	*All's Well That Ends Well*
AYL	*As You Like It*
COR	*Coriolanus*
CYM	*Cymbeline*
ERR	*The Comedy of Errors*
F	*The First Folio*
F2, F3 etc.	The Second, Third Folios etc.
HAM	*Hamlet*
1H4	*King Henry IV*, Part 1
2H4	*King Henry IV*, Part 2
H5	*King Henry V*
1H6	*King Henry VI*, Part 1
2H6	*King Henry VI*, Part 2
3H6	*King Henry VI*, Part 3
H8	*King Henry VIII, or All is True*
JC	*Julius Caesar*
JN	*King John*
LC	*A Lover's Complaint*
LLL	*Love's Labour's Lost*
LR	*King Lear*
LUC	*The Rape of Lucrece*
MAC	*Macbeth*
MM	*Measure for Measure*
MND	*Midsummer Night's Dream*
MV	*The Merchant of Venice*
OED	*Oxford English Dictionary Online*
OTH	*Othello*
PER	*Pericles*
PHT	*The Phoenix and the Turtle*
PP	*The Passionate Pilgrim*

Q	A play in quarto edition
Qq	Several quartos
Q1, Q2 etc.	The first published quarto, the second published quarto, etc.
R2	*King Richard II*
R3	*King Richard III*
ROM	*Romeo and Juliet*
SHR	*The Taming of the Shrew*
SON	*Sonnets*
TGV	*The Two Gentlemen of Verona*
TIM	*Timon of Athens*
TIT	*Titus Andronicus*
TMP	*The Tempest*
TN	*Twelfth Night*
TNK	*The Two Noble Kinsmen*
TRO	*Troilus and Cressida*
VEN	*Venus and Adonis*
WIV	*The Merry Wives of Windsor*
WT	*The Winter's Tale*

Introduction:
Shakespeare's Bodies

Physicians and general readers have long been fascinated by Shakespeare's medical language and the presence or mentioning of healers, wise women, surgeons, physicians, and unlicensed practitioners in his writing. Victorian and early-twentieth-century writers drew on the published diaries of Shakespeare's son-in-law, physician John Hall, to speculate that Shakespeare conversed with Hall about diseases, patients, and cures, and that much of this information appeared in the plays. The mid-twentieth century saw many attempts to diagnose Shakespearean characters, according to both early modern ailments (the humoral source of the ills of the tragic hero, discussed by Campbell 1962) and then-contemporary medical developments (the diagnosis of Shakespearean green-sickness as "biliousness" in the 1950s [quoted in Starobinski 1981]). The past thirty years, however, have seen an explosion of work suggesting that, if we are interested in early modern embodiment, we have to consider not only the pathological body but the healthy one, and to historicize the early modern body. That is to say, the body and its processes, diseases and appearances are not themselves immutable and unchanging, but are themselves formed by different social, historical, and political forces. Two of the strongest influences propelling this kind of work are Michel Foucault's *Discipline and Punish* (1975) on the one hand and, although more elliptically, Judith Butler's *Gender Trouble* (1990), both of which argue in very different ways that the body (for Butler, the *sexed* body) can and should be located historically.

Studies of the early modern body have since attempted to coax the body out of hiding, as it were, offering us Francis Barker's "tremulous private body," Thomas Laqueur's "one-sex" body, Gail Kern Paster's "embarrassed" body, Michael Schoenfeldt's and Katherine Maus's studies of inwardness and physiological interiority, and Carla Mazzio and David Hillman's "dismembered" body. The pioneering work of Francis Barker (1984) suggested that the process by which the early modern body becomes "private," secret, or shameful parallels the emergence of subjectivity into textuality—a movement comparable not to the benign "civilizing process" discussed by Norbert Elias (1939) but to the need to "discipline and punish" both body and mind as outlined by Foucault. Schoenfeldt (1999) connects the discourses of seemingly purely mindful or spiritual activity and shows how such activities necessarily involved the body of the early modern thinker, while Maus (1995) takes what seems the most exterior

1

of forms—early modern stage play—and suggests that physical movement and the expression of bodily feeling work in the Renaissance to figure interiority in its most modern sense. Mazzio and Hillman's collection, *The Body in Parts* (1997), continued this process of historicism, suggesting that even the notion of a single, human body, or of discrete organs and products within it, is itself historically determined.

As the body changes historically, so do its attributes, such as sex. Thomas Laqueur (1990) asserts that the sexed body is a modern invention, secondary in the early modern period to an Aristotelian or (some argue) Galenic "one-sex" model in which both men's and women's bodies existed not as binary, gendered opposites but as points on a wide continuum of sexual difference. Women were "imperfect" men, incomplete because of insufficient heat at the time of conception, according to Aristotelians. Galen argues that they were "inverted" men, and anatomical drawings from the sixteenth century illustrate homology or sameness. Early modern medical men averred that men and women possessed the same sexual organs: yard (penis or clitoris), stones (testicles or ovaries), belly (stomach or uterus), vessels (seminal vesicles or Fallopian tubes), but in women, these organs had retreated further inside the body, while in men, they remained the "right" way round. But Gail Kern Paster (1993) argues that, despite the one-sex model, women's bodies and their products were particularly gendered, "disciplined" or made to disappear, through the workings and development of "shame" toward bodily functions. And still others argue for a Galenic medicine that was proto-feminist in its insistence that both men and women were, *contra* Aristotle, "perfect" or complete—each in his or her own sex (Maclean 1980), or for a two-sex Hippocratic model that became newly popular in the late sixteenth century because of a crisis in masculinity triggered by the presence of strong female rulers such as Elizabeth I of England or Mary of Guise (King 2007).

Others have investigated gender and medicine in a less theoretical way by uncovering the surprisingly large and varied world of female medical practitioners in early modern England (Pelling and Webster 1979; Hunter and Hutton 1997; Pelling and White 2003; Fissell 2004 and 2008; Leong 2008; Harkness 2008). Despite the anxiety of the Royal College of Physicians surrounding such healers, women appear to have worked as plague-searchers, diagnosing and quarantining patients during the outbreak in London in 1578 in what one scholar has called the first public health campaign in the world; as midwives who turned and delivered babies (performing what we now call episiotomies where necessary, in direct defiance of the prohibition against the use of knives or instruments by women, weavers, smiths, and others who did not belong to the Company of Barber-Surgeons); as herbalists or wise-women whose right to prescribe simples (single-source plant remedies) was defended in court by Queen Elizabeth's minister Francis Walsingham himself; as midwife-apothecaries who carried not just clean linens and birthing-stools with them on home-visits but also proprietary powders; as domestic compounders of medicines for their families, households, and communities.

We have learned from recent work on the early modern body that the healthy early modern body was—of necessity—imaginary. The warm, sanguine, impermeable and, crucially, male idealized humoral body appears in Shakespeare's *corpus* only when fighting for its survival. Furthermore, if the ideal body is hot, sanguine, and impenetrable, women are necessarily, inherently, pathological in their cold, phlegmatic, moist impressionability. Furthermore, human beings living in torrid or frigid zones had to overcome greater environmental obstacles than those in temperate Europe in order to achieve and maintain a healthy mind in a healthy body. We have also learned, from work such as Mary Floyd-Wilson's (2004); Douglas Trevor's (2004); and Paster's most recent volume (2005) that it is impossible, in Shakespeare's day as in our own, to separate entirely the realm of the medical or somatic from metaphysical, emotional, geographical, and other factors. Humoral theory was flexible enough to account for subtle variations in "clime, complexion, and degree" (*OTH* 3.3.260), each of which (geography; skin color or personality—two sides of the same humoral coin; or rank) explained, complicated or even obviated a straightforward humoral conclusion, diagnosis, or cure. "Race," then, joins "sex," "humor," "complexion," and our other medical words as part of the process of historicizing and fleshing out Shakespeare's bodies.

Pathological Bodies

On Shakespeare and medicine in particular, twentieth-century commentaries include F. David Hoeniger's *Medicine and Shakespeare in the English Renaissance* (1992), which provides an overview of Galenic and early modern medicine (a subject previously covered in helpful detail by Nancy Siraisi, 1990); an abbreviated guide to medical concepts, illnesses, and therapies within the plays; and detailed readings of *Macbeth* (the king's evil, or scrofula), *All's Well That Ends Well* (the fistula), and *King Lear* (madness). More recently, Kerwin (2005) lays the discourses of medicine alongside other genres (antitheatrical tracts, anti-cosmetic diatribes, and stage-plays in particular) in order to explore the variation within particular medical cultures during the early modern period, such as the two competing "drug cultures" he identifies, the deployment of cosmetic surgery, or the rise of the showy mountebank or mysterious virtuoso. Pettigrew (2007) concentrates more narrowly on Shakespeare's plays, looking at each practitioner and commenting on the absence of Shakespearean surgeons.

Conservative Galenism held that all disease stemmed from internal imbalances of the body's fluids and processes and required allopathic treatment, that is, correction by opposites. The body presented a complex ecosystem in which the four humors—sanguine humor or blood, melancholy or black bile, choler or gall or yellow bile, and phlegm, were fungible and could transform into other humors as required by the body or as triggered by environmental or even emotional circumstances. Hippocrates had argued for the transmission of disease through *miasma* or bad air or foul water, and for the existence of four fluids in the body responsible for its health and vigor. Galen added the notion of complexion or temperament, that is, humoral personality. One's humoral personality was both innate and contingent, subject to one's natural complexion and to the effects of the Galenic "non-naturals": diet (the food and drink one consumed); sleep (where, how, and when one slept or woke); exercise (how much and what kind of physical activity one took, and where and in what position one stood or sat when at rest); air (what one breathed, smelt, or felt upon the skin); fullness and voiding (how much one ate, how quickly it was digested, and how often one defecated or urinated); and perturbations and passions (what one experienced as an emotion, for how long, and how intensely). Plants, animals, and bodily organs each had their own complexion or humoral constitution, and even without the "unnatural" triggers of pathological disease, a body disordered or distempered in any one of the six non-naturals might become ill or weak.

The concept of "contagion" existed in early modern Galenic medicine, but only as a kind of mirroring effect: exposure to a person with an infectious disease, or to foul air, water, or food, might stimulate the same disease in other persons, and exposure to certain atmospheric conditions might trigger a particular ailment, but only if the patient's body were already humorally predisposed to these contaminating influences. The body always tried to restore equilibrium. Thus a choleric person exposed to the damp, cool atmosphere of a fen might overcompensate by producing too much hot, dry choler and thereby suffering a fever. Or a constitutionally cold and phlegmatic person might be encouraged by the cool, damp conditions of the fen to produce more mucus and suffer what we still call a "cold." The feverish patient might then be treated with cooling medicines and foods such as lettuce or sorrel, and bled by a surgeon, again in order to reduce the bodily heat that was causing the fever, while the sniffling one might be prescribed chicken broth and encouraged to wrap up warmly. Or one might contract syphilis through sexual immorality (since it was clearly transmitted by sexual intercourse), or plague through moral turpitude (since, again, it was clearly contagious among people). Since all symptoms proceeded from humoral imbalance, correcting the distemper by prescribing materials of the opposite composition would cure the disease.

Most work on Shakespeare and medicine prior to the twenty-first century, such as Hoeniger's, sees the plays as engaging with traditional, Galenic humoralism, and herbal therapies (and of being generally unaware of the discoveries of Paracelsus). More recent work by scholars such as Jonathan Gil Harris (2004); Margaret Healy (1991); Stephanie Moss and Kaara Peterson (2004); and Lynnette Hunter (2004) has argued, however, that the germ-theory and chemical medicines of Paracelsus exist in Shakespeare alongside the humoral model. This newer Paracelsian trend in Shakespearean criticism explains why Paracelsus himself merits such a lengthy entry in this dictionary despite Shakespeare's invoking his name only once—and that to his discredit, since both the skills of both "Galen and Paracelsus" have proven unable to cure the sickly King of France where Helena, "Doctor She!" has been successful.

4

Paracelsus, in contrast to Galen, argued that diseases were specific to processes or organs, not general; that symptoms belonged to particular diseases, each of which had its own specific remedy; and, most importantly, that infections originated outside the body, in "seeds" or germs of disease mingled in everything. Such diseases should be treated homeopathically, with the refined or chemically purified part of the substance that had caused them. Chemical refinement could separate the germs of disease from the curative element within the material. Ague was a disease of sulphur, and could thus be cured by a purified extract of sulphur; syphilis was a disease of mercury, and was treated with the topical application of mercury to the skin or by inhaling the smoke from burning mercury ore, or cinnabar.

Civic authorities and lay-people could see the effectiveness of the mercury cure; they could also testify to the usefulness of quarantine in treating leprosy (eradicated by Shakespeare's time, though often confused with the so-called new disease of syphilis because both produced skin lesions) and in delaying or preventing the transmission of bubonic plague, as the Elizabethan "plague orders" from 1578 (mandating the employment of "searchers" to diagnose deaths from plague, the sealing up of houses with infected persons, and the removal of waste) show. And yet the College of Physicians endorsed these measures—some of which are still used today to help control epidemic disease—while insisting that person-to-person transmission could only take place if both sufferers were humorally vulnerable. How could infection be both intrinsic and extrinsic, idiosyncratic and universal? Allen Debus (1965) argues convincingly that, whatever the learned College might claim, practitioners "on the ground" comfortably employed effective Paracelsian therapies (such as the mercury treatment for syphilis) without concerning themselves about the controversial theories underlying them. The casebook of John Hall, Shakespeare's son-in-law, might be a case in point: Hall regularly prescribes chemical medicines (including body products) alongside Galenic simples or single-source herbal remedies, integrating the two competing medical philosophies with little difficulty (Lane 1996).

Harris, Healy, and others similarly argue for a breakdown between theory and practice, an ambiguous status given to infectious disease that they find in Shakespeare's own references to infection, contagion, pox, leprosy, and other communicable disorders. Paracelsian homeopathy and chemical treatments likewise appear in Shakespeare. Moreover, it is certainly possible to detect in Shakespeare's aristocratic physician in *Pericles*, Cerimon, the type of the "good" Paracelsian physician who refines chemical medicines from nature (and in Cymbeline's wicked queen, the "bad" Paracelsian mountebank who feeds animals poisons distilled from minerals before attempting the lives of her enemies); to wonder whether Paracelsian harmonies inform the therapeutic music that restores Pericles and, in *The Winter's Tale*, Hermione to vitality; and to note that Shakespeare frequently imagines female flesh weighed in apothecary's measure such as "drams" and "scruples," as if it is the controversial Paracelsian compound known as "mummy," reportedly consisting of mummified maidens' flesh. Scholarship currently in press and forthcoming on Shakespeare and medicine will almost certainly continue to investigate these less-explored Paracelsian qualities in Shakespeare's works.

Methods, Intents, and Sources

Since this book maintains that the experience of health and disease in the early modern world is experiential, phenomenological, embedded in everyday life rather than restricted to a sector designated discretely "medical," the (A) entries of the dictionary are a little fuller than is usual in this series. In some cases (most notably the top-heavy entry on Paracelsus, mentioned above), the (A) sections overshadow the Shakespearean "guided tour." There are several reasons for this emphasis.

First, this dictionary serves several groups with different interests: those wishing to understand specific references in the plays, in particular, archaic diagnoses or therapies ("choleric," "tub-fast") and words that have changed their meanings ("diet," "urinal"), and who need or want technical explanations of those terms within the plays; those who want to learn more about early modern medical concepts ("spirit," "humors"); and those who might have questions about the embodied experience of living in Shakespeare's England (see for instance "childbed," "eye"). Moreover, I strongly believe that the full descriptions, including the etiology and recommended therapies for certain disorders, are necessary in order fully to understand the wonderful aptness of many of Shakespeare's medical or bodily metaphors and even his stagings. The apoplexy of King Henry IV figures the partial paralysis and stasis of the kingdom and also its reliance upon the very organs rendered insensible by the disorder, the ear and the tongue (Reid 2010). Having read about the operation of "couching" for cataract and the application of "flax and whites of eggs" as a poultice to the bleeding eyes, one imagines the blinding of Gloucester in *King Lear* as a grotesque parody of that therapeutic ocular surgery. And after one reads a surgeon's request for a servant to be present to catch the blood in a basin during a phlebotomy, the entrance of Titus Andronicus with a sharp knife (like a lancet or "lancelet," as the tool was first known?) and of Lavinia with a basin in *Titus Andronicus* presents Titus not just as a cook and his assistant (as the stage directions tell us) but also as a surgeon letting the corrupted blood of a toxic empire. Scholars and students of Shakespeare will see that there is much more work to be done on the plays to investigate the full extent of their material, medical, metaphorical world.

In all cases I have returned to primary materials from the late sixteenth and seventeenth centuries, uncovering in a few instances (such as the phrase "caesarian section" under "untimely ripp'd") medical usages that antedate by a few years the first reference in the *Oxford English Dictionary*. Where there exists a single "definitive" or very well-known primary source on a particular disease or therapy (such as Gyer's *English Phlebotomy* on bloodletting [1592], or Caius' treatise on the sweating sickness [1552]), I have consulted that text specifically, and where there are half-a-dozen or more sources (such as dietaries or herbals), I have focused upon three or four that went through multiple editions in Shakespeare's lifetime or that provided the basis for later authors with relatively little change. Occasionally I cite a lesser-known text purely in order to direct readers toward a source they might not otherwise discover. Given the literary focus of this project, I favored writers with a certain rhetorical vigor or flourish over those whose prose is more difficult to read (both Banister and Crooke wrote anatomies, for example, but Crooke's prose is interesting in itself, as Eve Keller has argued, 2006). I do not always cite the earliest edition of a text, preferring to stay within Shakespeare's lifetime, unless subsequent editions offer little change or additions to the first. I have also attended to medical literature in English (or translated into English), by surgeons, physicians, noblemen, apothecaries, journalists attempting to expose mountebanks, and so on rather than to the Latin texts that college-educated physicians would have read. While medical men trained at the university would keep up with the Latin scholarship, there is a vast increase in vernacular medical literature in this period, as Nutton, King, and others have documented. Surgeons, unlicensed provincial healers, nobly-born women, and literate lay-folk (including Shakespeare), would have read this growing, relatively inexpensive, and widely available literature in English and French. Occasionally where an important source exists only in Latin or Greek (such as Tooker's account of Queen Elizabeth's ability to cure the "King's Evil" in *Charisma*, 1597), I have supplemented my own small Latin and no Greek with the standard translation, where available.

This dictionary does not purport to diagnose Shakespeare's characters with present-day ailments, nor to evaluate the effectiveness of early modern versus current treatments, since I am neither qualified nor eager to do so. For this reason, present-day physicians will find this volume very different from a "medical dictionary," and will encounter few entries that overlap with present-day medical terms. I have not, for example, cross-referenced the present-day term "enema" in the "List of Medical Terms" at the beginning of the volume with an injunction to "see Clyster," because it would be misleading to treat early modern therapies as if they were akin in procedural terms, intents, and consequences to present-day ones (as, for example, the *Wikipedia* entry on "Enema" currently does). The experience of a laxative administered rectally in a hospital ward by a trained professional with a fountain or bulb syringe (that is, an enema) differs experientially, institutionally, and ontologically from an early modern "clister" put in with a pipe by a family member or physician at home. In another example, it seems reasonable to comment under "ague" that this was a common term for malaria, rife in sixteenth-century England, but we cannot assume that every time Shakespeare says "ague," he means "malaria." For ease of cross-referencing, however, the "List of Medical Terms" often includes adjectival and noun forms of words even if these are not used in the plays and poems, only in the entries; and some present-day medical terms (including "enema") are cross-referenced in the index at the end of the volume. Several entries provide references for readers who wish to learn more about possible real-world origins for Shakespearean illnesses and therapies, but for the most part, even these entries are more concerned with what references to bodies, body-parts, body-fluids, bodily functions, diseases, and therapies might mean in the context of Shakespeare's plays, and the particular significance that these have in individual plays and in the Shakespearean *corpus* at large. At the same time, I do hope that physicians and other healers among the book's readership will enjoy "running a differential" on Shakespearean characters and speculating on the therapeutic value or futility of treatments prescribed.

In a larger sense, I urge readers not to patronize early modern medical cultures and their practitioners. Medicine, therapy, and bodily awareness informed sixteenth- and seventeenth-century life in all its aspects, something that can seem to be at odds with twenty-first-century medicine, with its MRI scans, laboratory tests, specialists, titrated doses, and checklist protocols. A book about a very different way of life and era helped my thinking on the early modern cultures of medicine in unexpected ways. Anne Fadiman's *The Spirit Catches You and You Fall Down: A Hmong Child, Her American Doctors, and the Collision of Two Cultures* (1998) describes the preliterate and highly artistic culture of the mountain people of Laos who helped American troops in the Vietnam War and were promised a home in the United States to protect them from retaliation. The displaced Hmong whom Fadiman interviewed subscribed to a world-view that was at once highly medicalized and yet completely at odds with Western medicine. Every aspect of human life affected embodiment, for the Hmong, and yet this intense awareness of the body and its material parts coexisted with a profound and affecting spirituality. But Western medicine, Fadiman observes, traditionally separates body and soul. The conflict between the two cultures of therapy—Hmong shamanism and American empiricism—reached a crisis in the treatment of Lia, the young girl whose story Fadiman recounts at length in her book. Without treating the "spirit," and addressing the family's concerns and apprehensions, it proved impossible for even the best pediatricians in the country to save Lia from what her American doctors call a persistent vegetative state and her parents call the loss of her soul.

Fadiman's analysis is instructive not because I am comparing Shakespeare's world to that of the Hmong (it would be foolish to do so) but because it reminds us that it would be equally foolish to mock as purely misguided medical cultures that are distant from our own in time, space, and ethos. For whatever reason, keen and honest sixteenth-century observers did see ugly, swollen lumps or sores on patients' necks diminish at the Queen's royal touch; elderly men die from grief or joy; incurable cankers suddenly enter remission. They did not know why, nor (yet) do we. Even scientific cultures of medicine are sometimes themselves subject to practices that continue only because of tradition rather than proven effectiveness. Consider the long resistance of the medical establishment to accepting that stomach ulcers were triggered not by one's spicy diet or poor stress-management but by a bacterium. Until the mid-1990s, peptic ulcers were treated by essentially humoral means (bland food, antacids, and stress-reduction) because it was thought impossible for bacteria to survive in the stomach's acid, even though scientists had seen the spiral-shaped bacteria in stomach ulcers as early as 1875; Susumu Ito had grown *Helicobacter pylori* from his own stomach in 1967, and Warren and Marshall had demonstrated a bacterial trigger for stomach ulcers in the early 1980s (Marshall 2002, 18). The story of Marshall's drinking a batch of *Helicobacter pylori* himself in frustration (much to the ire of his wife), succumbing to acute gastritis, and writing up his sufferings for the *Medical Journal of Australia* has now passed into legend (Marshall 2002, 194–8). Consider also the discovery of the so-called brain in the gut or enteric nervous system, which demonstrated that "gut feelings" could indeed both cause and cure disease (Hadhazy 2010). Or consider the current controversy over whether or not Chronic Fatigue Syndrome (myalgic encephalopathy) is triggered by a retrovirus or is "only" a psychosocial disease, as if the answer had to be one or the other—or as if the "psychological" and the "neurological" results of the disorder could be neatly separated (Boseley 2010). The persistence of humoralism in early modern England is unremarkable given the resistance of any highly developed medical culture to countenance radical change.

Doctors often comment that medicine is both an art and a science, and that both physicians and patients are storytellers. The body has a story, too, one that develops through time and space and that can be dramatized as an ongoing conversation. Shakespeare's bodies come to life through the actors who play them on stage and through the words that can reconfigure for us what it means to be an embodied being in a still-mysterious material and metaphysical world.

Abhorson [abortion] (A) As in present-day medical language, abortion or, in the more common early modern spelling, abhorsion, refers both to the spontaneous or involuntary loss of pregnancy and to the deliberate termination of a pregnancy through artificial means. Women might suffer miscarriages, especially in the first trimester, by **vomiting** after eating spoiled or too-spicy food, breathing bad air, or drinking impure water; by any kind of violent accident or agitation, such as falling downstairs, or riding in coaches or wagons; by lifting a heavy weight; by experiencing a strong passion or emotion, such as fear at exposure to loud thunder or gunfire; by engaging in excessive sexual intercourse; or by taking strong **medicines** or laxatives. Alternatively, if the child were unable to draw enough nourishment from the mother, if the child were too large or the mother too small, too fat, too lean, or too full of the watery **humors** associated with women, the child might be born dead before its time. In such cases, the mother was often counseled to take bed-rest and to remain cheerful, with the aid of opiates if necessary. Many lay-people, and certainly wise-women, **physicians**, and **apothecaries**, knew about herbal abortifacients (such as **rue** or pennyroyal), or emmenagogues (such as rosemary), which brought on menstrual periods, or prolactin reducers (such as sage), which decreased **milk** supply.

(B) Mario DiGangi argues convincingly that the name of the character Abhorson in *Measure for Measure* is a homonym for "abortion," the culmination of a series of references to abortion throughout the play, and that the dish of "stewed **prunes**" in the window of Mistress Overdone's house signals that she is not only a procuress

11

or but also an abortionist. Prunes were both an aphrodisiac and a laxative, and thus particularly dangerous for the heavily **pregnant** Mistress Elbow.

(C) Guillemeau (C1v–D1v, 1612) cautions women and their midwives about the delicate nature of an early pregnancy. He distinguishes between a "shift" occurring as a "flow" before the fetus had taken shape, and an abortment or abhorsion, occurring with "violent expulsion" after the fortieth day, or after the fetus was recognizable (Guillemeau 1612, I3v). Rüff (1637, E6r–E7r) imagines young women using several different means to end an unwanted pregnancy: lacing themselves tightly, then visiting a "witch" to drink a potion, visiting apothecaries to procure strong herbs, washing their feet and legs in a **decoction**, and finally opening the veins in the feet, a strategy used to induce menstruation by drawing the retained humors downwards, as Fissell points out (2004, 69). On abortion in *MM*, see DiGangi (1993); for speculation on "Ophelia's Herbal" as known abortifacients, see Newman (1979). Dobranski (1998) reads *ADO* as haunted by the ghosts of miscarried or dead children. Riddle (1992) and McLaren (1984) find evidence that herbal contraceptives and abortifacients were widely available in the early modern period. On women's vernacular knowledge of abortifacients, see also Fissell (2004).

abortive See also **Abhorson [abortion], deformed, hare-lip, legs forward, mole**
(A) Abortive fetuses, ideas, and plans are untimely, brought forth before they are ready. Abortive acts and offspring are simultaneously incomplete, and monstrous or deformed, a reflection of the belief that untimely births and birth defects were God's punishment vested on a community of sinners, or, from the seventeenth century onwards, the result of monstrous **sicknesses** engendered in the womb. Infants with birth defects were often called **monsters** or "**prodigies**," the first from the belief that they demonstrated an unholy mixture (of genders or species), the second for their imagined worth as spectacular omens. In general, monsters were infants born with variations such as extra limbs, marks, scars, swellings, and so on, and prodigies were creatures unrecognizable as human (for example, dogs or snakes born to women).
(B) Shakespeare uses the term abortive in both its literal and figurative senses. Figuratively, suggests Cardinal Panulph, the people shall interpret bad weather as "Abortives, presages and **tongues** of heaven" calling down vengeance upon wicked King John for his foul intent to murder Arthur (*JN* 3.4.158). Biron sarcastically calls the King's plan to abjure the company of women a "barren task" and questions what we might now call a "half-baked" plan: "Why should I joy in any abortive birth?" (*LLL* 1.1.104).

The figurative and literal meanings of abortive, as both "untimely" and as "deformed," culminate in the "abortive, rooting hog" that is Richard III, in the first tetralogy (*R3* 1.1.227). Suffolk describes the usurpers' "abortive" pride (*2H6* 4.1.60), as part of a sustained metaphor of birth ("coming forth" and "voiding") within his speech. Anne curses Richard over her husband's corpse with words that come back to haunt her and that reflect the accounts of Richard's own birth:

> If ever he have child, abortive be it,
> Prodigious, and untimely brought to light,
> Whose ugly and unnatural aspect
> May fright the hopeful mother at the view.
>
> (*R3* 1.2.21–4)

"Unnatural" and "untimely" describe at once Richard's seizing the crown and his impudent wooing of Anne over Henry's bier. The frightened mother predicts the Duchess of York's spoken regret over having borne and nourished Richard, himself born abortively or too early, and with "prodigious" or direful omens such as his being "born with teeth" and presenting as a breech ("legs forward") birth (*3H6* 5.6.75).

(C) Fissell (2004) identifies a dramatic change in vernacular attitudes toward the **womb**, and toward monstrous or miscarried births, beginning in the early seventeenth century, a transformed vision of the womb from a healthy, even miraculous generative space into a dangerous pit of disorder and **disease**. The terror of mothers on seeing their deformed offspring appears frequently in the literature (Fissell 65–7). Paré's account of "Monsters and Prodigies" participates in this shift from wonder to disgust (1634); Daston and Park's *Wonders and the Orders of Nature* meticulously examines the aesthetic, cultural, and social meanings of awe and the natural world (of which abortive or monstrous births formed a part) in early modern and Enlightenment Europe (1998).

ache See also **bone-ache, tooth-ache** (A) Aches proceeded from any number of ailments within the body: old age, **wounds**, the great **pox**, fatigue. **Heart**-aches and headaches might indicate emotional distress. Headaches came from evil **fumes** from incorrectly digested food, an excess of **heat** or of **cold** or of **moisture** or of aridity, drunkenness, **fevers**, too much **choler** or **phlegm**, and could also indicate a diagnosis of **melancholy**, often caused by too much study, or an imminent **epileptic** attack. Headaches should be treated by allopathic means: those caused by heat required cooling medicines such as rose-water, those caused by cold required hot materials such as pepper, those caused by dryness required a **moist diet** including, say, egg yolks, and those caused by an excess of moisture, desiccants and placement in cold, **dry** air. Some sufferers succumbed to headaches from the heat of the sun, especially those who were young, healthy, hot-complexioned, and who took "overmuch businesse in hand" (Barrough 1583, A4r). A headache caused by too much **blood** or plethora (such as a migraine) required evacuation or purging, including bloodletting from the arm vein on the side of the migraine. External remedies included chafing the forehead, with a **linen** cloth or with the fingers, until the **skin** was red and hot, ideally before the attack had reached its climax.

(B) Shakespeare's characters ache in their bones, their heads, their **teeth,** shoulders, and their wounds, but only Hamlet's heart aches (*HAM* 3.1.61). They ache from exposure and fatigue, like Juliet's Nurse, who complains of her throbbing brows, "Lord, how my head aches! What a head have I! It beats as it would fall in twenty pieces" (*ROM* 2.5.48–9). They ache from fighting, like Alicibiades, whose "wounds ache" (*TIM* 3.5.95) from injury, and as a man threatens the Porter in *H8*, "I'll make your head ache" (5.3.88), presumably by hitting him. Hamlet argues that physical pain is an essential part of being human and embodied, much as Claudio does when he imagines life after death not as eternal Paradise but potentially worse than life's ills, "age, ache, penury and imprisonment" (*MM* 3.1.129). Desdemona compares Othello's jealousy to the nagging ache in a finger, which consumes the entire body even though the suffering part is small (*OTH* 3.4.146–8); compare also Leonato's figure for impossibility, "to charm ache with air," which attests to the often hopeless nature of the ailment (*ADO* 5.1.26).

Othello's headache in 3.3 might be the migrainous aura that sometimes precedes an epileptic attack, especially since the therapy that Desdemona offers, chafing his temples with a linen cloth and offering to bind his brow, was standard practice in such situations. Hubert appears to suffer from what **physicians** called inveterate or long-lasting headache, or perhaps migraine. Arthur reminds Hubert of his gentle therapy to try to dissuade the latter from blinding him:

> when your head did but ache,
> I knit my handercher about your brows,
> The best I had, a princess wrought it me,
> And I did never ask it you again;
> And with my hand at midnight held your head,
> And like the watchful minutes to the hour,
> Still and anon cheer'd up the heavy time,
> Saying, "What lack you?" and "Where lies your grief?"
> Or "What good love may I perform for you?"
> Many a poor man's son would have lien still
> And ne'er have spoke a loving word to you;
> But you at your **sick** service had a prince.

(*JN* 4.1.41–52)

Hubert's headache may come from "heavy" melancholy, a disorder that King John has taxed him with before. Arthur follows the standard recommendations of binding his brows, holding his head (perhaps if he **vomits** from inveterate headache; it is unclear what Arthur's "sick service" exactly means) and attempting to dispel the throbbing melancholy.

(C) Barrough (1583) offers several chapters on headache and on the categories of sufferers. He classifies different sorts of headache (from cold, from phlegm, from heat, from fatigue, from "migrime" or migraine, and so on) and recommends chafing the brow with a linen cloth for headaches proceeding from cold in particular (B1v). Gesner (1576) offers **distilled** remedies to be taken internally, and Batman connects headache to certain kinds of wine and to sleeplessness (1582, P2v, P4v).

14

aconitum The plant aconitum or aconite (monkshood or wolfsbane) is a deadly poison that "killeth out of hand" through **cold** and putrefaction (Dodoens 1595, 2i7v). In *2H4*, the dying King urges Thomas of Clarence to bind himself to his brother Harry with a "hoop of gold" indissoluble by "the venom of suggestion," even by suggestion "strong /As aconitum or rash gunpowder" (4.4.47–8). The King mixes his metaphors, so that Clarence is both an antidote to the poison of rumor and a structural reinforcement against explosions. For a description, see Bullein (1579); for its working, Banister (1575).

Aesculapius (A) The classical deity presiding over medicine and healing, Aesculapius or Asclepius was the son of Apollo and the nymph Coronis, and had been taught the arts of hunting and healing by the centaur Chiron. So skilled was Aesculapius that he could even revive the dead, but Zeus killed him with a thunderbolt at the height of his powers, either because he was worried that human beings would seek to live forever or because Hades coveted more **dead** souls for his realm. Since he was half divine, however, Zeus hearkened to Apollo's request that the divine **physician** be placed among the stars. For this reason, his emblem was a staff entwined with a single serpent (often confused, however, with the **caduceus** of the god Hermes, which bears two twining snakes and a pair of wings at the top).
(B) Shakespeare's characters invoke Aesculapius twice, once to comic and once to serious effect. *WIV* mocks Doctor Caius and his traditional tools, such as **urinals**, both in his characterization as a buffoon and through the comments of the Host, who teasingly compliments **Caius** before his duel with Sir Hugh Evans as "my Aesculapius? My **Galen**? . . . bully-**stale**?" (2.3.29–30). The play opposes the parson and the physician, "the soul-curer and body-curer" (3.1.98), but both are proven foolish. We can detect the insincerity of the Host's extravagant comparisons of Caius to the renowned ancient physicians Aesculapius and Galen by the phrase "bully-stale" that follows it, which equates the doctor with the **urine** or stale that he collects and uses to diagnose ailments, sometimes without even seeing the patient who produced it. In *Pericles*, on the other hand, the model medical man Cerimon prays sincerely, "Aesculapius guide us!" (3.2.110), calling to the divine healer for his skill in resuscitating the dead. Having drawn the supposed corpse of Thaisa from the ocean, Pericles pronounces her not dead but comatose, reviving her with warmth, air, chafing, and either a **vial** of **medicine** (as in Shakespeare's source) or music from a **viol**.
(C) Pindar's third Pythian Ode tells the story of Aesculapius' birth (Verity and Instone 2007, 50–3).

agony In Shakespeare, agony is the painful struggle of the soul with death. Gloucester gleefully gloats, "Sprawl'st thou? Take that, to end thy agony," as he dispatches Prince Edward, jokingly turning a political murder into a mercy killing (*3H6* 5.5.39). The Duke of Buckingham fights anger at his trial in favor of fortitude:

15

> Stirr'd
> With such an agony, he **sweat** extremely,
> And something spoke in **choler**, ill, and hasty
> But he fell to himself again, and sweetly
> In all the rest show'd a most noble patience.
>
> (*H8* 2.1.32–6)

Moved by too much **heat**, the duke sweats and breeds choler or anger, but his temperament is naturally well-composed and moves from bitter **gall** to "sweet" acceptance. Berowne comments on the impossibility of his assignment from Rosaline "to jest a twelvemonth in a **hospital**" that death is no laughing matter, and "Mirth cannot move a soul in agony" (*LLL* 5.2.857), a sentiment reiterated by Leonato, who urges the futility of charming "agony with words" (*ADO* 5.1.26). Clarence's dream of his death by drowning prefigures his "sore agony" (*R3* 1.4.42), and the Duchess of York describes her labor with her son "in anguish, pain and agony," like death-throes (*R3* 4.4.164).

ague See also **fever, quotidian, tertian** (A) There were several different sorts of ague, a **disease** that made one feverish, chilled, achy, pale, and tired, and that produced rigors or fits of shivering so intense that patients' **teeth** chattered. Quotidian agues manifested a fever that spiked once a day; tertian agues spiked once every thirty-six hours, on days one and three of an illness; and quartan agues spiked on days one and four. **Patients** were unable to leave their bedchambers because of the intense shaking, bodyache, and fever; they frequently lost weight from the **illness** and became spare and lean, as if consumed from within. One might catch an ague from **cold**, wet, or unseasonable weather (such as warm sunshine in March), especially if one's body became chilled or wet through. Winds at sea or by the shore could also provoke agues, and even warm, sunny places could be dangerous if the air itself were contaminated. Fens, marshes, and standing water were also known to be full of miasma or foul, **infected** air that might trigger an ague. In such circumstances, the climate or the foul air encouraged the body to produce too much or too little of **choler**, **melancholy**, or phlegm, depending on an individual's own **complexion** or humoral temperament and particular humoral response to weather, location, **diet**, and other circumstances.

A **physician**'s first step was to **purge** the **humors** that had become corrupted by the atmosphere and thus caused the disease. Patients might take oral emetics such as fly agaric to encourage vomiting, and endure **clysters** administered rectally to empty out the **bowel**. Should the fever remain high, a **surgeon** should bleed the patient, ideally from the basilic or **liver-vein** (see **fever**).

(B) Shakespeare alludes both to the supposed climatic origins of the ague and to its most distinctive symptoms, the severe shivering, pallor, and the rapid weight-loss of patients. Hotspur evidently believes that damp, cool, or unseasonable weather, and inadequate protection from it, induces agues: "Home without boots, and in foul weather too! How 'scapes he agues, in the devil's name?" (*1H4* 3.1.67–8), he wonders, and comments that sycophancy nourishes **illness** in the body politic because it is out of place, like warm weather in the wintertime: "worse than the sun in March, /This praise doth nourish agues" (*1H4* 4.1.111–12). Buckingham suffers "An untimely ague /[that] Stay'd [him] a prisoner in [his] chamber" (*H8* 1.1.4–5), an ague that might have been politically opportune, since it kept him out of court—well-timed, in fact, rather than untimely or unseasonal or inappropriate. King Lear, "wet" by the rain, made to "chatter" by the wind, and deafened by the thunder, faces the constraints of his mortal, feeble, human body: "they told me I was everything; 'tis a lie, I am not ague-proof" (*LR* 4.6.101–5). Breezes and draughts, in- and outdoors, chilled the body suddenly and brought on **disease**. Salarino believes that even the thoughts of inopportune weather can trigger ill-health; he explains Antonio's sadness as anxiety for his venture capital, speculating that if he had as many ships at sea, "My wind cooling my broth /Would blow me to an ague" (*MV* 1.1.22–3). Ague lurked invisibly even in fine weather, undetectable to those breathing the poisoned air: "danger, like an ague, subtly taints /Even then when we sit idly in the sun" (*TRO* 3.30.232–3).

Caliban's fearful shivering leads Stephano to diagnose him with "an ague" and to offer him "all the wine in [his] bottle . . . [to] help his ague" (*TMP* 2.2.66, 92–3); *TIM* also associates convulsive shaking, "strong shudders" with "heavenly agues" (4.3.138). "This ague fit of fear is over-blown," scoffs Richard II, who believes that he can easily conquer his cousin Bolingbroke (*R2* 3.2.190). Fear also made the skin pale, and Sir Andrew Aguecheek in *TN* is named for his quaking cowardice. Shakespeare's Venus lists "agues pale and faint" (739) as part of a litany of ills that besiege humankind, her argument for consummating their love while Adonis is still young and healthy.

The fever for power, suggests Caesar, is "that same ague which hath made [the conspirators'] lean"; no wonder he prefers to "have about [him] men that are fat" and already replete (*JC* 2.2.113, 1.2.192). "Famine and the ague eat . . . up" the besieged English in *Macbeth* (5.5.4), and Constance worries that even if she reunites with her son after death, "he will look as hollow as a ghost, /As dim and meagre as an ague's fit" (*JN* 3.4.84–5). Old age shrinks shanks and renders one susceptible to agues because of the increased coldness of the elderly body. Richard II ignores John of Gaunt's warnings as the ramblings of "A lunatic lean-witted fool, /Presuming on an ague's privilege" (*R2* 2.1.115–16).

(C) Gesner recommends hops as good for taking away quartan ague (1576, I3r). M. J. Dobson (1994) and Reiter (2000) identify agues with malarial illness and comment upon the prevalence of the disease in sixteenth-century England.

alchemist, alchemy, alcumist See also **med'cine potable, Paracelsus, tincture**
(A) Present-day usage distinguishes between the alchemist, who attempted to transmute base metals into gold, and the chemist, who attempts to separate out basic **elements**. But alchemy and "chemistry" do not become distinct words or concepts until the early eighteenth century; for Shakespeare, the alchemist and the chemist are one and the same. All (al)chemists were engaged in the process

of purification, although some wished to transmute metals, and others to refine medicines. Every metal contained a kernel of pure gold, surrounded by dross or waste matter. The alchemist's task was to separate these parts, helped by the catalyst known as the "elixir" or "philosopher's stone" or sometimes as the **quintessence**, the most fundamental or elemental part of matter. The Paracelsian revolution in seventeenth-century **medicine** encouraged **physicians** to become alchemists who would extract and purify medicinal elements from raw materials, for therapeutic use. Paracelsians saw God as a divine alchemist, separating or refining pure substances from dross, and the Paracelsian physician as his representative on earth, attempting to purify true medicines out of corrupted earthly matter.

(B) Shakespeare's figurative alchemists are concerned with metallurgy rather than medicine. King Philip rejoices at his daughter's marriage by calling the sun an "alchemist" whose gaze turns "cloddy earth" to "glittering gold" (*JN* 3.1.70). Since the sun's rays merely gild or cover the land with gold temporarily, however, the alchemical reference is unflattering: all that the alchemist can effect is a superficial coating of gold, not a fundamental transmutation. The misanthropic Timon of Athens offers the "rascal dogs," the venal Poet and Painter, beatings in lieu of the "gold" they are expecting, crying, "You are an alcumist; make gold of that" (*TIM* 5.1.114). Casca complains that Caesar is like the legendary elixir or philosopher's stone that can turn base metals into gold, so that even when he misbehaves, his actions seem noble: "that which would appear offence in us, / His countenance, like richest alchemy, / Will change to virtue and to worthiness" (*JC* 1.3.158–60). Sonnet 33 imagines the sun's rays turning water into liquid gold "with heavenly alchemy" before "basest clouds" or, in the figure, dross covers up the gold. Liquid or potable gold was a known and expensive remedy (see **med'cine potable**). Sonnet 114 more closely represents a Paracelsian refinement process. It asks whether the poet's love is base "flattery" that lies about his beloved's attributes, or a magical alchemy that purifies and refines the "**monsters** and things indigest**," **abortive** or misshapen births, into perfect infantine angels, "cherubins." Chemical refinement worked by "Creating every bad a perfect best," by separating out the bad "seeds" of creation and extracting the "best" or purest, therapeutic elements (see **Paracelsus**). The sonneteer concludes that his love is flattery: he knows that he is seeing "monsters" and consuming "poison," but gazes, and drinks it nonetheless.

(C) Early modern alchemical texts are notoriously abstruse. The verse exposition of Ripley (1591) is perhaps the least opaque account of the theory, but is still rhapsodic, mystical, and obscure. Gesner (1576) is perhaps the most useful early modern source on the (al)chemical process and offers detailed instructions for **distillation**, refinement, evaporation, and so on, along with labeled diagrams of the apparatus. Many alchemical texts circulated in manuscript, as Kassell argues in her essay on the well-known astrologer, unlicensed but successful healer and "self-appointed nemesis of the Royal College of Physicians" Simon Forman (2001, 345); she also points out that Forman, at least, seems to have kept his chemical endeavors separate from his medical practice, treating

patients with astrology and natural magic but continuing his quest for the elixir or philosopher's stone as a distinct venture. Standard secondary sources on the alchemical tradition in early modern England were for many years Yates (1979); Debus (1977) and, popularly and widely disseminated, Carl Jung's essays on alchemy (1953). Newman and Grafton's collection (2001), however, demonstrates the separation among different types of so-called occultic philosophies in the early modern period and historicizes the distinction we have inherited from the eighteenth century—not from Shakespeare's time—between supposedly misguided alchemy versus supposedly scientific chemistry (Principe and Newman 2001). Moreover, it challenges Yates's conflation of alchemy and astrology under the general rubric of "the occult"; the extremely limited dissemination of Paracelsianism seen by Debus; and criticizes the notion of "spiritual alchemy" that claimed that early modern practitioners were interested not in the material processes of transmuting metals but in religious or psychological transformation (Newman and Grafton 2001). Nonetheless, "spiritual alchemy" proves popular and illuminating among literary critics, for obvious reasons. Gray (2006) contextualizes early modern alchemy with the long-standing and persistent Platonic tradition. Healy (2007) traces spatial imagery in Shakespeare's sonnets as part of a nexus of spiritual, mystical, personal alchemical figures in Shakespeare's sonnets. Simonds integrates both approaches, accurately describing alchemy as the early modern process of distillation, and reproducing illustrations from Gesner, but in the service of a convincing argument about the alchemical hermaphrodite in Shakespeare's Sonnet 20 (1999).

allicholy, allycholly *see* **melancholy**

almshouse see **hospital**

anatomy, atomy (A) The anatomy was properly the act of dissecting a dead body and the body itself as prepared for dissection, and by extension the body itself. Anatomical dissection did take place in Shakespeare's London; the foundation of the united Guild of Barber-**Surgeons** in 1540 allowed members of the company four bodies of convicted felons for dissection and study. Popular sixteenth-century use, however, employed both anatomy and atomy as synonyms for skeleton, a body made of bones or a body emaciated to skin and bones. It is possible that the meaning of the word "atomy" was confused or collapsed with its sense of "atom" or "small object."
(B) Shakespeare uses anatomy or atomy in each of these recognized senses: skeleton, dissecting corpse, and living but doomed body. Some of Shakespeare's references may denote a particular actor, John Sincklo, notorious for his cadaverous visage. Sincklo moved from the Lord Pembroke's Men to the Lord Chamberlain's Men in 1598, and Shakespeare seems to have written him into parts as a creepy-comic, living *memento mori* or harbinger of death. Mistress Quickly and Doll Tearsheet, chided off the stage by beadles, tease one of them unremittingly about his skeletal appearance. "Goodman death, Goodman bones"

is a "thin thing," an "atomy" (*2H4* 5.4.29–30); stage directions indicate that this walking corpse was Sincklo, who might also have played the **apothecary** in *ROM* and served as a mental model for Pinch, the **mountebank** in *ERR* 5.1.238–42:

> a hungry lean-faced villain,
> A mere anatomy, a mountebank,
> A threadbare juggler and a fortune-teller,
> A needy, hollow-eyed, sharp-looking wretch,
> A living dead man.

Skin and bones, Pinch looks like a corpse with **eyes** sunk in their sockets, his face drawn as if famished from poverty and his very clothes worn from use.

Queen Constance, **crazed** with grief, calls on **death**, personified as a skeleton lover, after the disappearance of her son Arthur. She offers to kiss death's reeking mouth, to place her own eyes in the empty eye-sockets of a skull, to wear carrion worms on her fingers as wedding rings, in order to "rouse from **sleep** that fell anatomy," to awaken death itself to take her, so that she may reunite with her dead son (*JN* 3.4.40).

After Romeo kills Tybalt, he fantasizes about self-dissection to remove his hated name of Montague, asking, "In what vile part of this anatomy /Doth my name lodge?" (*ROM* 3.3.106). Sir Toby Belch, however, imagines dissecting Sir Andrew Aguecheek to comic effect. "For Andrew, if he were opened, and you find so much **blood** in his **liver** as will clog the foot of a flea, I'll eat the rest of the anatomy," he gibes (*TN* 3.2.60–3). Andrew is such a **lily-liver'd** coward that his liver contains hardly any blood; if there were any blood in him at all, Sir Toby would venture to eat the rest of his corpse.

(C) Vesalius' germinal *De Humani Corporis Fabrica* (1543) popularized illustrations of active anatomies or corpses displaying their innards. Crooke's *Microcosmographia* (1615) was the first "anatomy" or anatomical textbook to be published in England by a physician, rather than a surgeon. J. Dobson and R.M. Walker's history of the Barbers and Barber-Surgeons of London (1979) reproduces an illustration of medical man John Banister presiding over a dissection in 1581 at the Barber-Surgeons' Hall (41). Sawday (1996) historicizes and theorizes the culture of dissection in Shakespeare's England. Pesta's dissertation discusses references to anatomies and skeletons in Shakespeare's plays (1999); both he and Belling (2000) have detailed chapters on *HAM*'s use of skeletal and anatomical imagery. Nunn (2005) considers bodies maimed or torn apart in *LR* and *COR*. Cregan's erudite and readable *The Theater of the Body* (2009) investigates dissection, anatomy, illustration, performance, and other forms of bodily knowledge in the early modern period; most relevant to Shakespeareans are her chapters on the early seventeenth century (1–134).

angelica Either the name of Juliet's nurse, used by old Capulet as he demands, "Look to the baked meats, good Angelica!" before the marriage-feast (*ROM* 4.4. 5), or, as Ferguson and Yachnin argue, the name of a herb known as a prophylactic against, ironically, **pestilence** or **plague** (1981), the very ailment that prevents

Friar Laurence's urgent letter from reaching Romeo. Ferguson and Yachnin point out that Q1 gives "Enter nurse with hearbes" and punctuate Capulet's lines thus: "good Angelica /Spare not for cost." Brasbridge (1578, *The Poor Man's Jewel*) recommends both angelica and *carduus benedictus* against plague.

apoplexy See also **epilepsy, fit, swoon** (A) The sudden loss of motion and sensory perception in the entire body (as distinguished from **palsy**, which affected only one half of the body), apoplexy came from an excess of **phlegm** in the **brain**. Cold air, a fall, old age, a **melancholy** constitution and, most frequently, drunkenness could lead to such an excess. Apoplexies both imitated and predicted **death**, rendering sufferers mute, **blind, deaf,** and still; most cases were considered incurable. Treatments for mild cases included letting small amounts of **blood** frequently from both temples; applying strong **clysters** and suppositories to encourage excretion; putting strong-smelling herbs under the **nose**; provoking sneezes; chafing the extremities with a **decoction** of lily-roots and cupping or scarifying the shoulders (see **surgeon's box**); and forcing an oiled feather or a finger down the throat to induce **vomiting**. Apoplexy was related to epilepsy (also known as "little apoplexy") as well as to swoons, giddiness, *hysterica passio*, and general paralysis.
(B) Apoplexy in *2H4* mimics death to such an extent that Prince Hal, fooled by his father's stillness, takes the crown from his bedside and places it on his own head. Falstaff has earlier diagnosed the King's illness as a "whoreson apoplexy," "a kind of lethargy . . . a tingling" (1.2.108–13), and even speculates as to its causes: "It hath its original from much grief, from study and **perturbation** of the brain: I have read the cause of his effects in **Galen**: it is a kind of deafness" (1.2.115–17). Whether or not the fat knight "read . . . Galen," his diagnosis is on the mark: King Henry is known to be melancholic (racked by guilt over his unlineal grasp of the crown and the deposition of his cousin Richard II, and anxious about his madcap, unprincely son Hal), he is elderly and thus predisposed to disorders of phlegm and melancholy, such as apoplexy; and he has always been of a cold **complexion** (hence his distaste for both Richard II's histrionics in *R2* and for Hal's tavern acquaintances in *1H4*). A servingman in *COR* compares peace to "a very apoplexy, lethargy; mulled, deaf, sleepy, insensible," comforting but torpid, ignorant, and dangerously unobservant (*COR* 4.5.223). Hamlet accuses Gertrude of having sense that is "apoplex'd," made senseless, although still able to move; only such an infirmity, he argues, could have allowed her to marry Claudius (*HAM* 3.4.73).
(C) For a detailed description of symptoms, causes, and treatments, see Barrough (1583, chapter 21). Both Barrough and Gyer (1592, D6v) caution that excessive bloodletting, particularly in the elderly, can in fact cause apoplexy, and Barrough suggests that bloodletting will either kill or **cure** the patient; thus if bloodletting is unsuccessful, there is little point in trying other remedies. **Paracelsus** diagnoses the syndrome as a subset of **falling sickness**, like palpitations, **cramps**, giddiness, and "suffocation of the matrix," and offers a vivid description of the patient as one whose "mouth bee drawn aside, and his speech and senses taken from him" (1596, E4r, H4r).

21

apothecary (A) Apothecaries mixed **drugs** prescribed by physicians and then sold them to **patients,** or to physicians themselves. Until 1590, it was against the rules of the Royal **College** of Physicians for a **physician** to **compound** his own cures without the help of a trusted apothecary. Apothecaries ranked lower than physicians, their duties strictly circumscribed: the law prevented them from compounding and prescribing drugs that had not been prescribed by a physician, although many did so nonetheless. They were thus the source of some anxiety in early modern England, along with **empirics** or unlicensed practitioners. Nonetheless, an act for the toleration of irregular practitioners in London in 1543 included apothecaries among those who had a right to practice freely. In Shakespeare's time, apothecaries were struggling for recognition as a legitimate medical profession. They asked Elizabeth I (though they were denied) to prevent physicians from compounding and selling their own **medicines.** In 1606, King James I incorporated apothecaries into the Grocers' company, and they developed their own charter and separated from the Grocers' company in 1617. One year later, the physicians struck back with their own pharmacopoeia, or list of allowed ingredients, restricting the independence of apothecaries to make their own medicines and increasing the freedom of physicians to compound and dispense their own medicaments.

(B) Beaufort's brief reference in *2H4* identifies the apothecary with the toxin he provides (3.3.17–18), but King Lear turns to him for "comfort" (*LR* 4.6.130–1). Lear's reference, however, implies that the "good apothecary" who will provide "an ounce of **civet** . . . to sweeten my imagination" does so for "money," turning the apothecary into a liar, like his daughters, one who covers up the reek of **death** with **perfume.** The association of the apothecary in *Romeo and Juliet* with death extends not only to the toxins he provides but also to the contents of his shop. The seller's "tatter'd weeds" are both his threadbare clothing and the raw materials he uses, his **simples** or herbs. The stuffed creatures in his shop are "ill-shaped," his merchandise "beggarly," "musty," "empty," "old . . . remnants." The shop also contains apothecary jars, to store herbs and seeds, "**bladders**" to store liquids, and both "musty" smells and the sweet fragrance of the rose, a great variety of items, but only in small amounts, and evidently in infrequent demand: "Green earthen pots, bladders and musty seeds, /Remnants of packthread and old cakes of roses, /Were thinly scatter'd, to make up a show" (5.1.46–9). As Romeo consumes the poison, he conflates it with its seller, the "true apothecary" whose "drugs are quick" (5.3.119). The late plays contrast well-meaning dispensing doctors such as Cornelius in *CYM* or Cerimon in *PER* with their scheming, compounding counterparts, who learn merely the skills of **distillation** without the art of healing (the Queen in *CYM,* Dionyza in *PER*). Cleopatra is likewise a rogue apothecary, "pursu[ing] conclusions infinite /Of easy ways to die," studying **physic** for criminal purposes (*ANT* 5.2.355).

(C) Bullein (1562, I4r) provides a list of "Apoticaries rules" including the injunctions to eschew bribery, to maintain a clean shop and flourishing physic-garden, to use pure ingredients and clean vessels, to read in Dioscorides and other herbals, to invent new medicines, to return true bills to the physician and patient employing him, to submit to the authority of the physician, to use true measure, and to trust in God (see also Pettigrew 2007, 99 for other rules). Interestingly, the phrase "true apothecary" appears in the 1595 edition of Elyot's *Castel of Helthe*, which describes such a man as one "that hath alway drugs vncorrupted, and whom the Phisition may surely trust to dispense his things truly" (1595, M4v). Kerwin (2005) analyzes the "drug cultures" of early modern England and suggests that Shakespeare presents in *ROM* the consequences of medical conflict in the persons of the "stumbling" cleric Friar Laurence and the mercenary apothecary (in contrast to the physicians Cerimon in *PER*, who insists on supervising his own apothecary, or Cornelius in *CYM*, who mistrusts his apothecary-apprentice the queen). Pettigrew (2007) suggests that Shakespeare's plays refer "equivocal[ly]" to the apothecary as both a source of illicit poison or bad treatment and of legitimate succor in time of need. For the history of apothecary-jars (usually tin-glazed earthenware in the late sixteenth and early seventeenth century in England), see Drey (1978, esp. chapter 6, 129–39).

apple See also **eye** The pupil of the eye, which in Shakespearean usage (though no longer generally accepted in philosophical circles by the late sixteenth century) both sent out eye-spirit or rays or beams and received them from objects in the world. The pupil or black of the eye in early modern **anatomy** was an orb, like an apple, or like one of the solid, crystalline Ptolemaic spheres of the classical universe; Robert Boyle is the first to suggest that the pupil or apple is more like a window or aperture than a globe (1686, X4v). Berowne accuses Boyet of betraying the young men in favor of the ladies, to "laugh upon the apple of [the princess's] eye" (*LLL* 5.2.475). Oberon wishes the juice of the enchanted **love-in-idleness** to "Sink in apple of [Demetrius'] eye" and compel him to love Helena (*MND* 3.2.104).

aqua vitae (A) Literally "the water of life"; **distilled** or strong spirits, used as a restorative and (quite effective) disinfectant, *aqua vitae* became in the seventeenth century an important part of the **Paracelsian** chemical purification process for refining medicines.
(B) Shakespeare, however, refers to *aqua vitae* as a first-aid tool in *ERR* (4.1.89, where it is listed along with **balsamum** and oil as an essential component of a ship's medical kit), *WT* (4.4.786, in Autolycus's extravagant mock-curse), and *ROM* (3.2.88, when the Nurse feels **faint** at men's dissembling and calls for *aqua vitae* to revive herself, and 4.5, in which her unwitting pun on *vitae* or "of life" emphasizes the dramatic irony of Juliet's supposed **death**). Master Ford in *WIV* and Sir Toby Belch in *TN* refer to its high alcohol level in order to reinforce early stereotypes of those who, supposedly, cannot remain sober: "a drunken Irishman" (*WIV* 3.2.304) and a sottish "**midwife**" (*TN* 2.5.196).
(C) For the distillation process and recipes, see esp. Gesner (1559).

artery See also **heart, vein** (A) Arteries, along with the heart, manufactured vital spirit and diffused it, along with **blood**, around the body. Arterial blood was lighter than venous blood because of the presence of vital spirit. The arteries expanded and contracted just as the heart did. When they expanded in the heart, they created a vacuum and attracted surrounding liquid, especially that which was thin and light, such as **vapors**, spirituous blood, and the vital spirit. Sooty vapors were sweated off through the skin, and spirituous blood and vital spirit went on to nourish and sustain the parts of the body. One **artery** brought blood and vital spirit to the **lungs** to nourish them, and took air from the lungs in order to aerate the blood before sending it to the extremities.

(B) Shakespeare refers to the arteries' role in spreading vital spirit in *LLL*, when Biron complains that "universal plodding poisons up / The nimble spirits in the arteries" (4.3.302); too much study thickens and cools the blood (presumably engendering **melancholy** in the student). Shakespeare's other usage both emphasizes the strength of the arteries and their relative weakness in human beings. Summoned by his father's Ghost, Hamlet vows that his "petty arter[ies]" (the strongest blood vessels in the body) will henceforth be "As hardy as the Nemean lion's **nerve**" (*HAM* 1.4.82).

(C) Vicary (1587, C1v) and Lowe (1634, C4r) describe the function and appearance of the arteries.

ashy See also **blood, cheek** (A) In **death** or under extreme duress, **blood** was thought to flow away from the face and the extremities, in order to sustain the **heart** in its struggle to maintain equilibrium.

(B) The word ashy appears three times in Shakespeare to evoke an unnatural, grey pallor connoting death, anger, decay, or fear, in contrast to the rosy cheeks of the living or the "black" cheeks of a murdered man, the red blush of "shame" or "guilt" or the vigorous burning of desire. In *2H6*, Warwick explains this mechanism, and cites Gloucester's face, "full of blood" even in death, as evidence that he has been **strangled**. Warwick contrasts Gloucester's "black face" to the "ashy semblance, meagre, pale and bloodless" of ghosts of men who have died peacefully (3.2.162). In *Venus and Adonis*, stanza 12, the narrator explains the changing hues of Adonis as reflections of his inconstant emotions, "crimson shame and anger ashy-pale," associating shame with the color red because of the tendency for light-skinned people to blush when embarrassed. The question of whether an embarrassed blush was a sign of innocence or guilt is so vexed in Elizabethan England that the foreboding and cynical *Lucrece* dismisses both "red" and "pale" as signs of "guilty instance" on the one hand and the "fear that false hearts have" on the other (stanza 216). *Lucrece*'s cynicism extends to art, whose inability to represent life it compares to the dwindling embers of a fire; just as the artist can present only "dry drops" for tears, so the "dying eyes" he paints can shine only "ashy lights," only fading reminders of the burning torches of Tarquin's.

(C) Wright (1604) or Coeffeteau (1621) are the most useful early modern sources on emotions and the face, detailing the processes of **perturbation** or emotional disturbance and its effects on the heart and blood flow. Fernie (2002) argues that shame and its associated blushing take on added importance in early modern culture because of heightened personal and intellectual expectations; Iyengar (2005) discusses the association of blushing and pallor with race in *ADO*; Royster (2000) helpfully points out the negative attribution of pallor to ethnic groups such as the Goths in early modern England.

atomy see **anatomy**

bald see **hair**

balm, balsam, balsamum (A) In general, balm refers to any soothing ointment applied to a **wound**, but specifically to any treatment made from any tree of the Balsamodendrum genus (balsam). True balsam was a renowned panacea or cure-all. It countered snake- and dog-bites, salved and cleansed wounds, soothed sore muscles, sanitized houses, anointed kings, and opened the **blood** vessels and passages. Its **heat** made it useful in treating those of **cold** or **moist complexions** and also in curing illnesses from too much **phlegm**, such as head colds, **consumptions**, or **imposthumes**; it also helped in curing **fistula,** loss of appetite, **palsy,** joint pain, haemorrhoids, bruising, halitosis, non-**dropsical** swellings, sores, a wet **cough,** and served as a prophylactic against **plague** and food poisoning. **Patients** could take it in water or wine, as a **simple,** or apply it as a **poultice** or ointment to the offending body part or wound. Balm was often applied after a hot **bath,** which softened the **skin** and allowed the ointment to penetrate the body. Along with *aqua vitae* (refined alcohol), it often formed part of a rudimentary first-aid kit at sea. Finally, balm was used to preserve and fragrance corpses after **death** in the process of embalming.

(B) Shakespeare uses the words balm, balsam, and balsamum interchangeably, although only the word balm is used to refer to royal tears that both heal and consecrate (and, given the use of body products or **mummy** or putrefied human flesh as **medicine** in the period, and the function of the king as a healer of **the evil**, we cannot assume that such allusions to medicinal body fluids are purely figurative). King Henry VI, lamenting his lost kingdom, mourns, "Thy place is fill'd, thy sceptre wrung from thee /Thy balm wash'd off wherewith thou wast anointed" (*3H6* 3.1.16–17). The play establishes him as a saintly, royal healer, albeit one who is unappreciated by his subjects. "My pity hath been balm to heal their wounds, /My mildness hath allay'd their swelling griefs," (4.8.41–2), he comments, figuring his tears as a soothing **salve** that not only helps wounds to unite but also reduces swollen impostumes or sores. The noble tears of Lady Anne, however, cannot bring her dead husband back to life: "Lo, in these windows that let forth thy life /I pour the helpless balm of my poor **eyes**" (*R3* 1.2.12–13). Richard II insists that "Not all the water in the rough rude sea / Can wash the balm off from an anointed king" (3.2.55), and indeed, the only thing that can unking a ruler is his own resignation: when Richard resigns his crown, he performs his unthroning piece by piece, including the cleansing of the oil that anointed him: "With mine own tears I wash away my balm" (*R2* 4.1.207). Henry IV bitterly castigates his son, "Let all the tears that should bedew my hearse /Be drops of balm to sanctify thy head" (*2H4* 4.5.114) when Hal, thinking his father is dead, removes the crown. In Henry's imagined transformation, the tears of sorrow that Hal should shed become the unction that anoints a crowned king. Balm is again that which anoints a king when Henry V (*HV* 4.1.260) observes that " 'Tis not the balm, the sceptre and the ball" that makes a king, but the support of his subjects.

Balm sanctifies, but also soothes. Cominius offers Martius, **faint** from blood-loss, a "gentle bath" and "balms" for his wounds (*COR* 1.6.64). Cordelia is the "balm of [Lear's] age" until she fails the love-test (1.1.215). **Sleep** is "the balm of hurt minds," lost to both Macbeth and his lady (2.2.36). Cleopatra's death approaches "as sweet as balm, as soft as air, as gentle," a suicidal wound healed in the making (5.2.311). True balsam or balm countered snakebite, but here death itself is the panacea for pain.

Troilus accuses Pandarus of enlarging, rather than salving, the "open **ulcer** of [his] **heart**": "instead of oil and balm, /Thou lay'st in every gash that love hath given me /The knife that made it" (*TRO* 1.1.61–3). Alcibiades bitterly complains that he ought to be receiving balsam to salve his wounds, not banishment (*TIM* 3.5.109). Dromio of Syracuse includes balsamum in a list of shipboard first-aid essentials (*ERR* 4.1.89), because of its cleansing properties, and *WIV* evokes both its sanitizing and consecrating qualities when Quickly orders the fairies to "scour /With juice of balm" the chairs of Windsor Castle (5.5.62).

(C) Turner claims that the true balsam grows only in Germany, not in England, where it is called "gentle balm" (1551, D4r). On its heat and natural origin, see Banister (Nr, 1575); on making arti cial balsam, see Bullein (fo. 3, 1579). Bullein has another treatise entirely devoted to the virtues of balsam (1585). Gerard (1597) distinguishes between balm and balsam; the former, when stamped in wine, can **cure** the king's evil and counter venom, but the latter has "marvelous effects on green wounds" and can calm the rigors of a **quotidian ague** (4R6r–8r). Guibert (1639, T2v–V3v) offers detailed instructions on how to embalm an entire corpse and individual body parts, together with recipes for various aromatic balms with which to fill the body.

barley-broth (A) An English grain, barley was cultivated for both food and **medicine**, used therapeutically as a **poultice** applied externally and drunk as

"ptisane" or barley-broth (also called "barley-water"), especially where cooling medicines were required. It was considered **cold** and **dry**, and particularly effective against **pleurisy** or **fever**.
(B) Shakespeare's French soldiers are astonished at the martial **heat** of the English and their national medicine: "Can . . . their barley-broth, /Decoct their cold **blood** to such valiant heat?" (*H5* 3.5.18–20). Since barley-water was consumed to cool down hot disorders such as fever, the French employ it as a metonymy for the "cold blood" of the English, chilled by the climate into cowardice. A decoction activated an ingredient through boiling it in water, so in this instance English barley-broth has warmed and literally encouraged the soldiers.
(C) For a description, see Gerard (70, 1633); on its mildness, see Langton (I5v, 1545); on its usefulness as a poultice, see Vigo (fol. Xxix, 1543); on its use in pleurisy, see Bullein (1562, passim); on its use as a water or **syrup**, see Woodall (1617); on its association with English medicine, and the French contempt for it, see Estienne (Book 5, chapter 18, 1616).

baths See also **tub-fast** (A) Physicians recommended hot baths for soldiers after battle, to soften the **skin**, relax the muscles, and make the **wounds** ready for the application of soothing **balms**. **Patients** should visit hot springs only under a **physician**'s advice, however, and should exhaust other remedies and confess themselves to God before venturing in, since the springs were hot enough that some bathers were scalded. After walking for half an hour, then **purging** and voiding (with the aid of **pills** or **clysters** if necessary), patients were to rest in the bath, eating **lettuce** or purslane to cool themselves if they overheated.
(B) Shakespeare alludes to the use of mercury baths for venereal **disease** (see **tub-fast**) but also to warm baths for warriors, hot springs, and what Turner (1587) calls a *balneum Mariae* or double-boiler. Cominius wishes the war-weary Martius could be "conducted to a gentle bath /And balms applied to" (*COR* 1.6.63–4), and Macbeth speaks longingly of **sleep** as "sore labour's bath" (*MAC* 2.2.35). Sonnet 153 imagines Cupid putting down his fire-brand to take a nap. One of Diana's nymphs, discovering the "love-kindling fire," plunged it into a cold stream that consequently turned into a healing "seething bath . . . /Against strange maladies." Alas, the **illness** the bath cannot **cure** is the speaker's own; he needs a still-hotter spring, the fiery pools in his mistress' **eyes**. Sonnet 154 retells the same tale, but this time the speaker argues that his "disease" is incurable, because "Love's fire heats water, water cools not love." Just as Cupid's brand turned a chaste fountain hot instead of quenching it as the nymph intended, so love's fire will warm the water instead of being cooled by it. Finally, an outraged Falstaff complains of "stew[ing]" in the buckbasket full of laundry to escape the jealous Master Ford: "And in the height of this bath, when I was more than half stewed in grease, like a Dutch dish, to be thrown into the Thames, and cooled, glowing hot, in that surge, like a horse-shoe; think of that,—hissing hot,—think of that, Master Brook" (*WIV* 3.5.118–22). Falstaff's "bath" is clearly a *balneum Mariae* or *bain-marie*, as if he is **distilled** (see **kidney**).

(C) Physician and herbalist William Turner lauded hot springs or spas and recommended the English springs, such as the ones at Bath because of their **brimstone**. His *Book of Baths* (1587) went into several editions and may have sparked a new fashion in the sixteenth century for visiting spas.

Bedlam See also **hospital, insane, lunacy, madness** (A) Bedlam, the abbreviation of "St. Mary of Bethlehem Hospital," became a byword for chaos or disorder. Founded in 1247 for the general care of the **sick** and infirm, by the reign of Richard II the hospital had come to be used primarily as an insane asylum. Bedlam was originally funded by charitable donations (the brothers were authorized to beg for alms), and the city of London, later funded (stingily) by the Crown. Corrupt treasurers (including **physician** Helkiah Crooke in the early seventeenth century), however, demanded fees from **patients** and their families. By Shakespeare's lifetime, both truly ill wanderers and counterfeit "Bedlam beggars" wandered the countryside demanding charity. Bedlam was also notorious for the harsh treatment meted out to its inmates; scourgings, whippings, and shackling were commonplace, although some recent scholars have argued that its cruelty has been overstated and that it was common to tie physical restraints upon poor people who were delirious or **crazed** for their own protection rather than as a punitive measure (see **frenzy**).
(B) Edgar disguises himself as a Bedlam beggar, Tom o' Bedlam, in *King Lear*, in a dramatic counterpoint to Lear's genuine madness. His great soliloquy (2.3.1–21) offers us a useful description of Bedlam beggars true and false, with **hair** caked into "knots" by neglect or design (the so-called elf-locks, from the folk belief that such tangles were supernatural in origin); flesh "mortified" or **wounded** by pins; the "roaring" voice of one hounded by demons or feigning insanity to make money; the "blanket" or loincloth of extreme penury, naked frenzy, or deliberately "presented nakedness." Moreover, his authentic misery opposes the counterfeiting of his half-brother Edmund, whose "sigh[s] like Tom o' Bedlam" signal not genuine grief but his deception of their father (1.2.136). *2H6* associates Bedlam with rebellion against the crown (3.1.51; 5.1.131, 132). Other direct references in Shakespeare associate Bedlam with madness, in particular, with the sound of howling or shrieking, while indirect references (such as Rosalind's comment that lovers deserve "a dark house and a whip" as much as madmen do [*AYL* 3.2.401]) evoke the cruelties of the asylum.
(C) For contemporary descriptions of Bedlam, the best sources are the Jacobean dramas: *The Duchess of Malfi* (Webster 1993); *The Changeling* (Middleton 2007); *Honest Whore, Part I* (Dekker 1998); *Lover's Melancholy* (Ford 1995); and *The Pilgrim* (Beaumont and Fletcher 1905). Documentary accounts appear in Lupton (1632) and More (1522). On counterfeit Bedlam beggars, see Harman (1567). On the history of Bethlehem Hospital, see O'Donoghue (1914) and Andrews (1997). Reed (1952) and MacDonald (1981) maintain that Londoners regarded the insane much as the characters in Jacobean tragedy do—as a comic turn—but Neely (2004), Jackson (2005), and McBride (2002) argue that the

practice of viewing the lunatics in Bedlam also encouraged charity and compassion toward Bedlam's inmates. On Bedlam in Shakespeare, see also Peat (2004); Neely (2004). On Edgar's disguise, see Carroll (1987). Kallendorf (2003) argues that the pin-pricks refer to the test inflicted on those thought to be possessed by demons, who were "commonly believed to feel only numbness when pierced with sharp objects" (137).

belch (A) To eructate, emit excess gas from the mouth, especially after consuming a **surfeit** or too much rich food or alcohol and becoming **o'ercharged** or overfull. Belches rid the body of the noxious **vapors** produced by excess food that the body could not concoct, or digest, and that putrefied or corrupted instead of being used for nutrition.
(B) In Shakespeare its use is sometimes jocular, as in the name of Sir Toby Belch in *Twelfth Night*, who presumably eructates after eating too much cake and ale. Emilia's famous proto-feminist complaint about men imagines women as food that men "eat hungerly, and when they are full, they belch us" (*OTH* 3.4.106); women are at first necessary nourishment, and then waste. Sometimes, however, there is a drowning urgency to belch out air, as in Clarence's nightmare of drowning (*R3* 1.4.41). The Shakespearean sea, personified as a monster hungry for wrecks, belches out human flotsam, including treasure, as in *PER* 3.2.54–5: "If the sea's **stomach** be o'ercharged with gold, /'Tis a good constraint of fortune it belches upon us," suggests Cerimon. In contrast, Ariel argues that the sea cannot be overloaded or replete, and that the three men of sin, Alonso, Sebastian, and Alonso, have been cast on the island as the waste products of a **diseased** body politic: "Destiny . . . the never-surfeited sea /Hath caused to belch up you" (*TMP* 3.3.55–6). Belches can figuratively **purge** the body of unpleasant emotions, as when Cloten, planning the murder of Posthumus, comments about Imogen's refusal of his advances, "the bitterness of it I now belch from my **heart**" (*CYM* 3.5.134).
(C) Johannes de Mediolano's *Regimen Sanitatem Salerni* (1528, G3r, F2v, V3r) blames rotten meat, radishes, and too much **choler** for belching.

belly (A) Belly referred to either the **stomach** or the **womb**, paralleled by their ability to store and process nutrition, turning food into chyle through the process of concoction, in the case of the stomach, and turning maternal **blood** into fetal matter, in the case of the womb. After the stomach concocted or digested food into chyle, it sent the chyle to the **liver** for the so-called second concoction, in which the liver converted chyle into nutritive blood to sustain the **organs** of the body. Nutritive blood then went to the **heart** where it partly nourished that important organ but also received air from the **lungs** that it used to generate pure blood and spirituous blood, to make vital spirit and warmth for the body. Some of this spirit traveled to the **brain** where it was further refined into animal spirit (named for the Latin word *anima* or soul, since it was the vehicle of the rational soul, which distinguished human beings from animals and guided reason).

(B) Large bellies in men indicate advancing age, as in the cases of Falstaff (*2H4* 1.2.146) or Jaques' justice with his "fair round belly" (*AYL* 2.7.154). Women with children in their bellies include Jacquenetta (*LLL* 5.2.677), young Gobbo's "negro" lover (*MV* 3.5.39), and the imaginary love-child described by Celia if Rosalind puts a "man in [her] belly" (*AYL* 3.2.204). The fullest treatment of the belly in Shakespeare, however, is the parable that Menenius tells the plebeians in order to convince them not to riot for corn. Menenius describes the parts of the body agitating against the belly because it consumes all the food, in an analogy that equates the plebeians to the lower organs of the body politic (including a leader who is the "great toe," *COR* 1.1.155) and the patricians to the seemingly "cormorant belly" (*COR* 1.1.121). The belly responds to the charges calmly:

> "True is it, my incorporate friends," quoth he,
> "That I receive the general food at first,
> Which you do live upon; and fit it is,
> Because I am the store-house and the shop
> Of the whole body: but, if you do remember,
> I send it through the rivers of your blood,
> Even to the court, the heart, to the seat o' the brain;
> And, through the cranks and offices of man,
> The strongest nerves and small inferior veins
> From me receive that natural competency
> Whereby they live."
>
> (*COR* 1.1.130–40)

Direct access to food would do the plebeians no good, claims Menenius; the belly, like the senators, distributes nutrition around the body according to the needs and abilities of both strong and weak parts. Menenius' analogy is weakened, however, by his asserting the power of the belly over the heart and the brain. To be ruled by the belly was proverbially to be gluttonous and selfish, a devouring "cormorant," as the citizen suggests. The parable risks casting the senators as usurpers who have ignored the natural hierarchies of the body politic.

(C) Hale (1971) argues that Menenius' knowledge of physiology is incorrect and that Shakespeare uses his errors to demonstrate the difficulty of applying political theory to praxis. Riss (1992) argues that Menenius' fable fails to convince its internal hearers as a sign of not just the difficulty but the entire failure of the political theory of the body politic in early modern England. Holstun (1983) likewise criticizes the model, but this time on specifically humoral grounds.

bladder See also **imposthume** (A) A bladder was an **ulcer** filled with a watery fluid, thought to be **choler** that the body had not concocted sufficiently and so was finer or more subtle than the properly concocted or digested **humor**. This sharp and piercing fluid broke through the flesh but became trapped by the thick epidermis. The **cure** was regulation of **diet** (in particular, reducing choler by eating **cold** foods), purging the excess choler, and applying **poultices**; **barley** was considered especially useful. "Bladder" can also refer to the animal bladders that were inflated and used for storage, or children's play (as balloons or floats).

(B) Falstaff complains (*1H4* 2.4.333) that "Sighing and grief" have blown him up "like a bladder," and Romeo notes that the **apothecary**'s shop is furnished with all manner of miscellaneous merchandise, including "bladders" (*ROM* 5.1.46). Shakespeare gives us our best documentary evidence for how Elizabethan children learned to swim when Cardinal Wolsey compares his ambition to "little wanton boys that swim on bladders" (*H8* 3.2.359). But the clearest medical reference comes from Thersites, who wishes "bladders of imposthume," hugely swollen, pustulous sores, upon Patroclus (*TRO* 5.1.21).

(C) For a description of imposthumes and bladders, and treatment, see Vigo (1543), Book Two. For a description of the anatomical bladder, see Crooke (1615).

blain See also **carbuncle, kibe, plague** A blain can be any kind of sore or **ulcer**, or "chilblains," painful ulcers, usually in the extremities, from prolonged exposure to **cold** and humidity, although Shakespeare uses the word kibe for this sense. Blain commonly refers to the pustules of plague, and occasionally to a carbuncle. Timon curses the Athenians with "Itches and blains" (*TIM* 4.1.28), which could refer either to the tendency of chilblains to itch painfully when the sufferer enters a warm room, or to the pruritus of plague symptoms. For pestilential blains, see Woodall (1617, 3D4v–3E); for blain as carbuncle, see Pliny (1601, Book 37, chapter 7).

blind See also **eye, eye-string, pearl, pin and web, sand-blind** (A) **Blind** people lacked the faculty of vision, either congenitally or as the result of a temporary or permanent disorder. Since Plato had declared that sight was the highest of all the senses, through which one might encounter the Ideal form of things, such a loss was catastrophic. Temporary blindness might be triggered by darkness, or by looking on brightly polished or sunlit objects. Conditions such as sand-blindness interfered with the vision but did not altogether destroy it. Permanent blindness might be the result of maiming or injury, weeping, or untreated ophthalmia or inflammation of the eye. At the same time, churchmen preached "the vanity of the eye" and attributed a greater spirituality or divine vision to the blind. Such persons, like those who were lame, counted among the "worthy poor" who deserved alms, in contrast to the "sturdy beggars" or able-bodied poor, some of whom allegedly feigned poor vision in order to elicit sympathy from well-wishers; nonetheless, the association of blindness and beggary was taken for granted. By the 1630s, glass eyes appear to be in regular use among the wealthy—presumably for cosmetic reasons, since they served no functional purpose, unlike the ivory teeth and wooden legs to which they were sometimes compared.

(B) Blindness in Shakespeare is emblematic; the result of willful injury or maiming; a temporary condition caused by weeping or sand-blindness or bright light or darkness; part of a disguise, as in hoodman-blind; or a figurative condition caused by too much fear, anger, or love afflicting the reason. Shakespeare's characters describe Fortune and Cupid as blind, in the terms of traditional emblem-books; both are often figures for chance or luck, good or bad, and both may be cruel. "Love looks not with the eyes, but with the mind; /And therefore is wing'd Cupid painted blind," philosophizes Helena (*MND* 1.1.234–5). Morocco and Aufidius call on "blind fortune" (*MV* 1.2.36; *COR* 5.6.117); Fluellen explains the emblem to Pistol somewhat repetitively: "Fortune is painted blind, with a muffler afore her eyes, to signify to you that Fortune is blind" (*H5* 3.6.31–2).

Tears could destroy the vision by parching the eye. **Phlegm** and pure, spirituous **blood** nourished the **brain**, which refined it further into animal or soul-enlivening spirits, including eye-spirit. Tears interfered with this process, since these precious, highly refined optical **humors** were used up when they were turned into tears. The corrosive quality of salty tears added to their danger, hence Hamlet's expostulation, "O **heat**, **dry** up my brains! Tears seven times **salt**, /Burn out the sense and virtue of mine eye!" (*HAM* 4.5.155–6). Eyes dried out enough by tears might crack their eye-strings or optic nerves.

Berowne (albeit obscurely) explains both blindness caused by too much reading, especially in the dark, and that caused by too much sunshine:

> Light seeking light doth light of light beguile:
> So, ere you find where light in darkness lies,
> Your light grows dark by losing of your eyes.
> Study me how to please the eye indeed
> By fixing it upon a fairer eye,
> Who dazzling so, that eye shall be his heed
> And give him light that it was blinded by.
>
> (*LLL* 1.1.77–83)

If one seeks intellectual or moral illumination in a book, one sits reading in the dark, away from the outdoors and healthy sunlight; such intellectual insight can only be earned by "losing of your eyes," becoming blind from too much study. On the other hand, turning one's eyes to gaze upon something brighter than itself would "dazzle" or blind the eye from too much light. Fortunately, lovers can exchange eyes, so the blinded lover can learn to see again by taking the eyes of the beloved as his concern or heed, and see with his lover's eyes.

In *JN*, the cooling of the braziers Hubert has heated to put out Arthur's eyes corresponds to the warming of Hubert's affection and his determination not to carry out his orders to maim the child. For his part, Arthur pleads: "O, save me, Hubert, save me! my eyes are out /Even with the fierce looks of these bloody men" (4.1.72–3). Just as lovers claimed to receive **wounds** from cruel ladies (a fancy Phebe mocks in *AYL*; "if mine eyes can wound, now let them kill thee," 3.5.16), so Arthur feels the beams or eye-spirit of the ruffians poke his own eyes as if to remove them utterly. It is telling that, although John does not wish the stigma of killing Arthur altogether, he believes that blinding him will render him equally unable to rule, or will kill him indirectly.

Blindness in *LR*, as many have observed, is both literal and figurative. Glouces-ter's and Lear's moral blindness to their faults of lewdness and rashness trigger the events that lead to Gloucester's literal blinding at the hands of Regan and Cornwall. Goneril's claim to love her father "Dearer than eye-sight, space, and liberty" (1.1.56) cruelly predicts the fates of fathers and their loyal servants in the play (blinded, bound, imprisoned), and "the dark and vicious place /Where" Gloucester begot Edmund "cost [him his] eyes" (5.3.173–4). Regan removes Gloucester's eyes with the celebrated phrase, "Out, vild jelly!" an anatomical reference to the thick, translucent, vitreous humor of the eyeball (3.7.83). Through its vivid tactile detail, the comparison of the eye's humor to jelly forces the audience to become complicit in the mutilation. The servant who in the first Quarto (1608) brings the suffering Gloucester "**flax** and **whites of eggs** /To apply to his bleeding face" (3.7.106–7) follows a then-standard **prescription** after a cataract operation; the restraints tying Gloucester to the chair may grotesquely parody surgical practice, although both **Hippocrates** (1610) and Baley (1616) recommend that the surgeon ask an onlooker to hold the patient's head still, and that the patient himself hold open his eye-lid.

Hamlet disgustedly compares his mother's taste in selecting Claudius to a child playing a game of blind-man's buff:

> What devil was't
> That thus hath cozen'd you at hoodman-blind?
> Eyes without feeling, feeling without sight,
> **Ears** without hands or eyes, smelling sans all,
> Or but a sickly part of one true sense
> Could not so mope.
>
>   (*HAM* 3.4.76–81)

In hoodman-blind, the sense of vision is removed, but Hamlet takes the analogy further. Gertrude has been so deluded that if she had vision without sensation, sensation without vision, only smell, taste, and hearing, or even smell alone, or even an etiolated single sense, she could not have chosen worse.

(C) On the association of blindness and beggary, see the rogue literature, for example Chapman's comedy *The Blinde Beggar of Alexandria* (1598). Both Hippoc-rates (1610) and Baley (1616) recommend flax and egg-white for a post-cataract plaster. Hakewill's *Vanity of the Eie* (1608) comforts a gentlewoman on the loss of her sight with the argument that seeing persons rarely enter heaven, but the blind have access to a purer spirituality and connection with God. Secondary sources on blindness and poverty include S. Clark's account of theories of vision in early modern England (2007), and Woodbridge's exhaustive investigation of early modern beggary (2001). Colie treats the motif of blindness and insight in *LR* as part of the "Renaissance tradition of paradox" (1966), while Nunn inter-prets the blinding of Gloucester as a moral dissection that enables him to experi-ence the world without the physical distractions of his material eyes (2005). B. Smith (1999) observes that for Bacon, hearing, not sight, is the highest sense, because it has the most direct access to the animal spirits or the rational soul (see **ear**). Wheatley (2009) finds a source for Edgar's deception of Gloucester in the medieval French farce or "street theater" *The Boy and the Blind Man*, in which a servant-boy assaults and tricks his blind master (see also **parti-ey'd**).

blood See also **artery, heart, liver, vein** (A) Early modern blood comprised not only the **sanguine humor** or pure blood, but also the other humors, **melancholy** or black bile; **choler** or yellow bile; and **phlegm**. Each of these humors was in turn made up of the four **elements**, air, earth, fire, and water, in different proportions, and each humor corresponded to a particular element and had particular qualities (pure blood corresponded to air, and was warm and **moist**; melancholy corresponded to earth, and was **cold** and **dry**; choler corresponded to fire, and was warm and dry; phlegm corresponded to water, and was cold and moist). These humors were not present in the blood in equal proportions, however. The blood of a temperate man contained less choler than melancholy; less melancholy than phlegm; and less phlegm than pure blood. The body manufactured blood in the liver, from chyle, which was in turn concocted in the **stomach** from the food and drink that a person consumed. Veins carried nutritive blood from the liver to the rest of the body, while arteries carried pure blood to the heart, where it was refined into spirituous blood.

Blood nourished the body in several ways. Pure blood fed the **heart** and formed the basis of the vital, natural, and animal spirits that allowed each of the body's parts to complete its functions. Phlegm nourished the **brain, lungs**, and other moist **organs** such as the **tongue**. Melancholy built up the heavier parts of the body such as the bones. Choler maintained the body's **heat** and enabled digestion and evacuation. Blood also transported the spirits around the body; spirit was the connection between body and soul, or, **Paracelsian physicians** argued, the soul itself. Although blood could ebb and flow between the heart and the body's extremities, especially under the duress of strong emotion or **perturbation**, it did not "circulate"; physicians of Shakespeare's lifetime envisioned the heart as the throne-room or hearth of the body, warming and sustaining it, rather than as a pump or engine that pushed blood around the body. Since it did not recirculate, blood was used up by the body, eventually turning into **vapors** and diffusing out through the body's extremities as **excrements** such as **hair** and **nails** or **sweat**. Strong emotion might consume the body's store of blood faster than the liver could manufacture it or the heart could enspirit it. Passions might first **o'ercharge** the heart with too much blood, blanching the face and extremities as blood left them for the seat of emotion. The only respite was to vent or release the sigh, the groan, or the rage, but in so doing, the body used up precious blood.

Bloodletting was one of several means to **purge** the body, or to reduce a particular humor in order to restore balance and health to the body (see **incision** for details of the procedure). The body evacuated or purged itself naturally (for example, through producing mucus, **urine**, or other bodily fluids), and the **surgeon**'s task was to assist nature, taking care to avoid emptying the body of necessary or good humors while reducing the dangerous ones. Phlebotomy or bloodletting was only one method of purging the body; most authorities advised surgeons to bleed patients in conjunction with other therapies. Blood might need to be let or drawn therapeutically in cases where a particular body part was disordered because the patient suffered from repletion or fullness, either plethora (too much blood in the body) or cachochymia (too much of one particular humor in the blood). Patients might also become ill if the quality of a particular humor were too sharp, hot, cold, or heavy for a person's body to sustain, or if a humor had become corrupted or had settled in the wrong place. Under such circumstances, bleeding would draw away the ill-placed humor, allowing healthier blood, with a proportion of humor more appropriate for its location, to take its place. For example, one might relieve amenorrhea by bleeding a woman on the ankle to draw down the menstrual blood.

Phlebotomy also proved useful in **fever** reduction, especially in cases of quartan or **quotidian agues**, fevers that spiked every fourth day or every night respectively. Where fever accompanied pustules or sores, however, such as in the **pox** or the **plague**, phlebotomists ought to abstain, unless the fever ran so high that no other option was possible. In such a case, the phlebotomist ought to fasten cupping-glasses or **surgeon's boxes** over the papules, in order to prevent the pus from being drawn into the body by the bloodletting. It was best to bleed patients a small amount on a regular basis, rather than by taking a large quantity at once, although unskilled practitioners ignored this advice and believed that patients should be bled until they fainted. Some careless operators even cut into an artery rather than a vein, which would kill the patient. Certain times of year (such as Spring) were best for bloodletting, and certain times of day, depending on one's humoral temperament or **complexion**. Moreover, certain persons ought not to be bled at all. **Pregnant** women, especially in the first trimester, ran the risk of miscarriage **(abortion)** if they were bled, because phlebotomy might draw away from the uterus the pure blood out of which the fetus was developing. Young children ought not to be bled, because blood nourished children and enabled them to grow; children were weak; finally, their skins were tender and moist enough that humors could pass through them without phlebotomy's being necessary for evacuation. Menstruating women ought to be bled only to relieve high fevers, since the body was naturally purging itself through menstrual blood. The very elderly ought not be bled, either, because older people produced less pure blood over the course of their lifetime, even though the overall volume of blood in the body remained constant throughout a person's life. Drawing a witch's blood, on the other hand, either with a weapon or by "scratching" with one's nails, a bramble-bush, or needles, was a sure way of breaking any spell she held over you.

Human and animal blood or body parts could also be used in **medicines** (see **mummy**). During the sixteenth and seventeenth centuries, the new Paracelsian anthropophagy or medicinal cannibalism combined with the ancient Hippocratic tradition of cacophagy or the therapeutic ingestion of "dirty" substances (see **Paracelsus**). Human blood might be drunk, warm, by sufferers of **epilepsy**, and treated blood was an ingredient in many medicines in the London pharmacopoeia of 1618. A very few Paracelsians considered menstrual blood medicinal or magical by itself, and a few authorities may have believed an ancient myth that men's hemorrhoidal **flux** or bloody flux, especially in Jews, was "menstrual," the product of male menstruation.

Most authorities and lay-people, however, distinguished between women's monthly periods and other kinds of unisex, anal bleeding. Female menstruation explained in part women's coldness, since they lost vital blood and its associated heat each month, yet at the same time, menses—or flowers, to use the common early modern word—indicated female fertility and health. Menstrual blood came from all parts of the female body to the uterus, where it would either nourish a developing fetus (in a pregnant woman) or naturally purge the female body of its excessive humors (in one who had not conceived). Retained menses in a non-pregnant woman could become an **excrement** or waste product of the body, and cause disorders such as *hysterica passio* or the suffocation of the mother, in which the womb, overburdened with bad or putrefying blood, might wander up to the throat or heart. Menstrual blood was healthily retained during pregnancy (though some women might bleed every month, into the fourth or fifth month, without harming the fetus); after the baby was born, menstrual blood was refined into breast milk, considered one of the purest fluids in the human body and a medicine in its own right, especially for **eye** disorders (see **milk**).

(B) Shakespeare alludes to blood in all of its common senses: as a nourishing fluid whose components were essential to the body and its functions; as the sanguine humor responsible for cheer and well-being; as the source of spirit in the body; as a sign of life when within the body, and of **death** when outside it; as a symbol of lineage, especially royalty; as an indication of murder; and so on. He also alludes to the practice of phlebotomy and (once, directly) to menstruation.

Since blood transported nutrition around the body, Shakespeare imagines a conflict-ridden kingdom, and the warlords who rule it, as hungry for the blood of fighting men, especially in the English history plays of the first tetralogy. Richard Plantagenet identifies himself with the ravenous body politic whose "blood-drinking hate" will blanch the white rose and make it his emblem in a quarrel that, he ominously observes, "will drink blood another day" (*1H6* 2.4.108, 133). Margaret of Anjou claims that she would mourn Duke Humphry with "blood-consuming" and "blood-drinking" groans and sighs, if such sacrifice could only protect her from the slander of having had him murdered (*2H6* 3.2.63). Queen Anne calls for the earth to "drink" the blood of Richard III as it absorbs the blood from the freshly-weeping **wounds** of the dead Henry VI (*R3* 1.2.63), and Pomfret Castle has the "guiltless blood to drink" of Rivers, just as it had imbibed the blood of Richard II (*R3* 3.3.14).

Blood is explicitly that which permits life, or "life-blood," in political or financial metaphor and physiological fact. Hotspur laments "the very life-blood of our enterprise" in the failed attempt to fight Bolingbroke (*1H4* 4.1.29) and Bassanio sees in the letter telling of the loss of Antonio's venture "every word . . . a gaping wound, /Issuing life-blood," a literal death-sentence on Antonio since the latter has guaranteed a "pound of flesh" as surety to Shylock (*MV*

3.2.265–6). Young Talbot tells his father, "These words of yours draw life-blood from my heart," a statement that is physiologically true for an early modern body, in which regret and other strong emotions used up the store of pure blood in the heart and brought one closer to death (*1H6* 4.6.43). York imagines Queen Margaret a "tiger's heart wrapt in a woman's hide," a tiger who "could . . . drain the life-blood of the child," suck out the life of young Rutland and taunt his father with the child's blood (*3H6* 1.4.137–8). Suffolk threatens Wolsey with a weapon-thrust in the heart: "thou shouldst feel /My sword I' the life-blood" (*H8* 3.2.227). Tamora's use of the phrase is both literal and figurative. "Titus, I have touched the to the quick, /Thy life-blood out," she gloats, referring to her vicious sons' assault on Lavinia and to her bloody trick in convincing (via Aaron) Titus to maim himself (*TIT* 4.4.37).

Malvolio refers to blood as the vehicle for spirit as he fantasizes about marriage with Olivia and speaks aloud to himself, "Thy Fates open their hands; let thy blood and spirit embrace them" (*TN* 2.5.147). Iachimo, finally remorseful, finds his "heart drops blood, and [his] false spirits /Quail to remember" the wrong he has done Imogen; regret draws blood from his heart and uses up his store of vital spirit (*CYM* 5.5.148–9). King John calls melancholy a "surly spirit" that has "baked thy blood and made it heavy-thick, /Which else runs tickling up and down the veins," in one of the references to the movement of blood that misleads some into believing that Shakespeare discovered the principle of circulation (*JN* 3.3.43–4). The lines actually mean that the heavy, cold, dry humor of melancholy (which nourished hard, thick parts of the body such as bone, and thickened the blood so that it stayed in the body long enough for the members to derive nourishment from it) has parched the blood to such an extent that it is clotted or too sluggish to travel to the extremities or to the heart, where it is needed. Blood normally "runs tickling up and down the veins" only in the sense that it can rush to the heart or the face under extreme emotion; under normal circumstances it travels from the liver to the heart and then to the outside of the body, where it is dissipated as **vapor**, sweat, hair, nails, and other waste products. Brutus' lines in *JC* 2.1.167–8, "We all stand up against the spirit of Caesar; /And in the spirit of men there is no blood," are also confusing, in part because Brutus relies on the multiple meanings of spirit (in our present-day sense of "mind"; in its technical sense of one of the three functions of the classical, tripartite soul; in its supernatural sense of "ghost"; in its political sense of "ideas"; in its personal sense of "identity") in order to make blood and spirit seem intrinsically connected. Brutus argues that they need to shed Caesar's blood but ought to do so with as little "butcher[y]" as possible. They need to kill Caesar even though they stand against his spirit, not his body, because the only way they can reach Caesar's spirit is to "dismember" his body. Spirit is thus the natural, vital, and animal energy responsible for growth, sensation, and thought in the body respectively, energy that enters the blood through air taken into the lungs and that enspirits the blood in the heart. There is therefore no way to separate spirit from blood without shedding blood and to "carve" up Caesar's body.

The phrase "blood and death" appears several times in Shakespeare, some-times associated with warfare, sometimes with murder. The Bastard connects "blows, blood and death!" (*JN* 2.1.360); Hector, weary of battle, urges his sword to "Rest . . . ; thou hast thy fill of blood and death" (*TRO* 5.8.4). Macduff calls the trumpets of battle "clamorous harbingers of blood and death" (*MAC* 5.6.10). Macbeth himself sees a dagger with "gouts of blood" (2.1.46) on the handle pointing the way to Duncan's chamber, and Lady Macbeth cannot remove the stench of blood from her **nostrils** nor the imagined bloodstains from her hands as she walks in her sleep (see discussion under **sleep**). Martius calls the body of the murdered Bassanius a "fearful sight of blood and death" (*TIT* 2.3.216). The first tetralogy, especially *3H6* and *R3*, connect blood and death, both through the figures of the white and red roses (discussed below), and through "bloody Clifford" "who thunders to his captives blood and death" (*3H6* 2.1.127). Glouces-ter himself kills King Henry and mocks the drops of blood on his sword as the weapon "weep[ing] for the poor king's death"; he feigns surprise that Henry's blood "sink[s] in the ground" instead of "aspiring" to the skies (*3H6* 5.6.63, 61). Queen Anne bitterly retorts to Richard, "I have no moe sons of the royal blood/ For you to murder" (*R3* 4.4.200–1). A hymeneal metaphor in the second tetral-ogy, however, describes the death of Suffolk as a consummation between him and the King: "espoused to death, with blood he seal'd /A testament of noble-ending love" (*H5* 4.6.26–7).

Blood distinguishes royal from commoner, although Lady Anne castigates Richard III as but its dregs, a "bloodless remnant of that royal blood!" (*R3* 1.2.7). Aaron's protection of his son, "Touch not the boy; he is of royal blood" (*TIT* 5.1.49) startlingly reveals to the Andronici both Aaron's own capacity for affec-tion and the child's parentage. Fittingly for a monarch so concerned with rank, blood appears associated with royalty most frequently in *R2*. Mowbray taunts Bolingbroke with "his high blood's royalty" and his kinship to the king, which Bolingbroke determines to "lay aside" so that they may fight (1.1.58, 71). King Richard accuses John of Gaunt of making him pale and "chasing the royal blood/ With fury from his native residence," in a change to the familiar equation of the heart with the body's throne-room (2.1.118–19). The seat of Richard's blood is instead his kingly countenance, from which anger has forced the royal blood away, presumably to the liver. When Richard finally dies, his murderer, Exton, regrets the death of one "as full of valour as of royal blood" (5.5.113).

Shakespeare's references to bloodletting allude both to the efficacy of the prac-tice to reduce excesses brought on by too much food, emotion, or other causes and to its inadequacy in cases of poison. The Archbishop of York refers to the practice of letting blood to reduce a "burning fever" brought on by "surfeiting and wanton hours" (*2H4* 4.1.55–6). King Richard II attempts to make peace between Boling-broke and Mowbray through an extended metaphor in which they are diseased organs suffering from an excess of wrathful **choler** in a delicate body politic:

> Wrath-kindled gentlemen, be ruled by me;
> Let's purge this choler without letting blood:

> This we prescribe, though no physician;
> Deep malice makes too deep incision;
> Forget, forgive; conclude and be agreed;
> Our doctors say this is no month to bleed.
>
> (1.1.152–7)

The royal would-be healer agrees that the kingdom needs a purge to cure its excess of choler, but argues that bloodletting is too extreme an evacuation, because the parties involved might cut too deeply and bleed the kingdom dry out of spite. Furthermore, it is the wrong time of year for bloodletting. Instead, he recommends a moral cure: forgiveness and therapeutic memory loss. Mowbray retorts that an allopathic cure will not suffice; he requires a homeopathic cure, since he is "Pierced to the soul with slander's venom'd spear, / The which no balm can cure but his heart-blood / Which breathed this poison" (1.1.171–3).

Soothing **balm** will not relieve the sore; the only remedy is pure blood from the heart of the offender. Heart-blood can both "breathe" and cure poison because it is in the heart that blood becomes refined, through the action of air, into spirit, the bond between soul and body. War is a kind of bloodletting to the Duke in *AWW*, who justifies the "great decision [that] hath much blood let forth / And more thirsts after" (3.1.3–4), a reference to the raging thirst experienced by patients after surgeons had bled them. Gleeful Gloucester tells Catesby that "dangerous adversaries . . . / Tomorrow are let blood at Pomfret-castle," turning mortal **wounds** into therapeutic phlebotomies (*R3* 3.1.183–4). Arviragus mourns for Fidele's illness and wishes he could "let a parish of such Clotens' blood" if only it could return the pinkness to Fidele's **cheeks** (*CYM* 4.2.168).

Titus Andronicus overwhelms us with its **gore**, but enhances its horror (and grotesque humor) by parodying medical practice. In 5.2, Titus enters with a knife and Lavinia with a basin, as if they are surgeons about to open a vein. The bonds imprisoning Demetrius and Chiron mimic the tourniquets used by surgeons. Titus and Lavinia do indeed perform a phlebotomy, but one that is therapeutic only to them. The play also emphasizes the connections between medicine and cookery through a kind of medical cannibalism; not only doctors might enter a room with a knife and a basin, but also butchers and cooks.

Shakespeare's only direct reference to menstruation is an off-color joke by Gonzalo in *TMP*, who claims that they cannot drown, because the ship's captain is destined to hang instead. "I'll warrant him for drowning, though the ship were . . . as leaky as an unstanched wench" (1.1.46–8), he adds, comparing the sinking ship to a young girl menstruating without adequate protection (women used rags or cloths to absorb their monthly flow).

(C) Harward (1601) and Gyer (1592) provide accounts of the theory and practice of bloodletting in Shakespeare's England. Harward quotes Avicenna to argue against letting the blood of those suffering from **"infectious" disease**: "seeing that this venome doth not consist in the bloud, but comming from out-wardly doth sodainely possesse the heart, [. . .] we do not thinke that it can be expelled or drawne out from it by Phlebotomy" (1601, C5r). Gyer defends blood-letting in verse translated from the *Regimen* of Salerno: "It swageth wrath, and cheeres the sad: /Preserues loue-sick, from being mad" (1592, D2v). Berkeley (1984) identifies a class-hierarchy in Shakespeare that he argues is closely related to a character's blood. A. Smith's dissertation (1994) ranges exhaustively through the meanings of blood in early modern culture, including a helpful chapter on **perturbation** and emotion. Paster (1993) has provided one of the most influen-tial recent accounts of early modern blood. Taking issue with Laqueur's argu-ment that a one-sex model or continuum of gender difference predominated in the early modern period, Paster argues that binary sexual difference manifested itself in early modern culture through differing attitudes toward blood. Where Laqueur (1990) adduced male menstruation or bloody flux as an analogue to female terms or courses, Paster argues that female menstruation is distinct from both hemorrhoidal flux and from the laudable, voluntary bloodshed that occurs to men in war and during medical treatment. Hindson (2009) agrees with Paster that early modern English accounts regard menstruation as definitively female, and dismisses Laqueur's account as overstated, but argues that menstrual blood was rarely shameful or "embarrassing." On menstruation, see also Balizet (2005); Hindson (2009); on blood-loss from the **hymen**, see Jankowski (2003); Balizet (2007), who lays to rest the persistent but unfounded myth that the bedsheets of a newly wed couple were hung outside the house to display bloodstains proving the new wife's virginity. Many of the essays in Moss and Peterson (2004) consider blood and bloodletting in both Galenic and Paracelsian terms. Phillis (2001) discusses Lucrece's blood as tainted by her rape, as does Belling (2004), who reads the deaths of Lucrece and Lavinia as therapeutic phlebotomies performed upon the body politic to purge the infection of rape. On the proto-racial and geohumoral logic of early modern blood lore, see esp. Neely (2004); Habib (2004); Bovilsky (2008); and Adelman (2008). On medicinal cannibalism, see Noble (2004); Gordon-Grube (1988). On the invention of the lancet, see Parker (2008). On "scratching" a witch, see Roberts (1983). Roland Greene's forthcoming *Five Words* will include a detailed examination of blood in early modern culture and language.

bone-ache See also **pox** Shakespeare distinguishes between old bones that **ache** from infirmity, such as the Nurse's in *Romeo and Juliet* (2.5.26, 63), Gonzalo's in *The Tempest* (3.3.2), the "weary bones" of Cardinal Wolsey (*H8* 4.2.22) and the bone-ache or "Neopolitan bone-ache" (*TRO* Q1, Thersites' catalog, 2.3.19, 5.1.22, 5.3.105), another name for the great pox (syphilis), from its tertiary symptoms of joint pain. Sometimes the two categories overlap: when Pandarus complains of his "aching bones" (*TRO* 5.10.35, 50), we know that the **disease** he plans to "bequeath" to the audience must be sexually transmitted, and it is also a reminder of mortality. Hamlet similarly associates ageing, **death**, and aching bones with "breeding," complaining of a sympathetic "ache" in his own in the graveyard (*HAM* 5.1.91–3), and when Falstaff rails against those who never felt "the ache in [their] shoulders" (*2H4* 5.1.83), he may allude to his own venereal ills.

bowels (A) The internal **organs** of the body. Like the **guts**, which formed a part of the bowels, the bowels formed a kind of "stuffing" in between major organs and glands, as well as serving the particular functions associated with their constituents: the **spleen** (purifying the **melancholy** or thickest part of the **blood**), the **kidney** (separating out the **urine** from the blood), the **liver** (producing blood from the chyle coming from digested food in the **stomach**), and the **lungs** (aerating the blood that came from the **heart**).
(B) Shakespeare uses bowels in both its literal sense (the inside of the body, the intestines) and figuratively to mean the inside of the sea or the earth; courage or valor; compassion; and, once, male **seed** or offspring. Titus mourns with words and tears, comparing his effluvia to **vomit**: "For why my bowels cannot hide her woes, /But like a drunkard must I vomit them" (*TIT* 3.1.230–1). Poison makes the "bowels suddenly burst out" of the Monk who poisons King John (*JN* 5.6.30), whose "bowels" in turn "crumble up to dust" (5.7.31). A "treacherous blade" pierces "the bowels of thy sovereign's son," remarks the murderer in *R3* (1.4.207), and Aaron threatens, "this sword shall plough thy bowels up" (*TIT* 4.2.87). Cassius, proud of his role in the assassination, boasts, "this good sword /. . . ran through Caesar's bowels" (*JC* 5.3.42). Falstaff comments that he "need[s] no more weight than [his] own bowels" (*1H4* 5.3.35), and quick-tempered Pistol employs "bowels" as a curse-word (*H5* 2.1.51).

Hastings describes the "fatal bowels of the deep" (*R3* 3.4.101); the sea swallows things into its "brinish bowels" (*TIT* 3.1.97). The "bowels of the harmless earth" (*1H4* 1.3.61) or "the bowels of the land" (*R3* 5.2.3) may be wounded by battle, especially by civil wars such as the broils that tear "the bowels of ungrateful Rome" (*COR* 4.5.130), the "country's bowels out" (*COR* 5.3.103), "the bowels of the commonwealth" (*1H6* 3.1.73). Tearing out "the bowels of the French," however, is admirable in the English (*1H6* 4.7.42).

Hector calls himself a "lady of . . . softer bowels . . . spongy to suck in the sense of fear," full of compassion and apt to absorb **phlegm** or peaceability (*TRO* 2.2.11–12). Exeter's plea to the French King to abjure further bloodshed "in the bowels of the Lord" refers to God's compassion (2.4.102). Thersites curses Ajax, who is beating him, as a "thing of no bowels," a cruel wretch (*TRO* 2.1.49). In contrast, the cannons in *JN* "have their bowels full of wrath . . . ready . . . to spit forth" (2.1.210).

Shakespeare's most unusual usage appears in *MM*. Vincentio, urging Claudio to "Be absolute for **death**," includes among his arguments the suggestion that "Thine own bowels, which do call thee sire, /The mere effusion of thy proper loins, /Do curse thee" (3.1.29–31). Here bowels appear to connote children (extended from the seminal fluid or "effusion" produced in the bowels or innards of the body and expelled from the loins).

(C) Maus (1995) argues in *Inwardness and Theater* for the specific effects that internal organs, including the bowels, have upon early modern psychological and emotional life. Schoenfeldt (1999) discusses the profound early modern connection between self-control and morality, and bodily control over fluids and processes. Hillman (2007) identifies a tension between Cartesian and pre-Cartesian beliefs about soul and body, inward and outward senses of selfhood.

brain See also **fume** (A) The early modern brain controlled judgment (reason), recall (memory), and imagination (fantasy), each attribute housed in its own cell or ventricle, joined with passages. Information traveled through these passages along the vehicle of **spirit,** refined from **blood** through a series of concoctions. The **stomach** concocted or cooked food into chyle; then the **liver** concocted chyle into blood, then aeration in the **lungs** produced spirituous or pure blood. Some said that the pure blood went through another refinement or purification process in the brain, when it was concocted into the animal spirit that was the vehicle of the rational soul. The brain also dried **humors** into fumes that could, like a fog, confuse reason or the senses. Sources vary on the layout of the ventricles or compartments; some arrange them alongside each other, with reason in the middle, while others imagine them to progress from front to back and still others appear to imagine a house or library with three levels. Vicary (1587) subdivides each ventricle into two, so that the first compartment, that of fantasy, includes the five senses and the imagination, which took sensory information from the senses (the "common wits") and shaped them into recognizable objects and perceptions. The ventricle for reason then decided what to make of the objects and sensations presented to it by the fantasy. Finally, the memory chamber kept track of the imagination's impressions and the reason's conclusions in a system variously compared to a "treasury" or, most frequently, a "library."

The early modern brain was nourished both on phlegm (since the brain itself was cool, white, and **moist**, like the **phlegmatic** humor) and on the refined blood that came to it from the **heart** and which it refined further into animal spirit (from *anima*, meaning soul). The brain housed the rational soul (part of the early modern tripartite soul), which was responsible for reason, judgment, and morality. This part of the soul was unique to humans, and some argued that the brain therefore housed the divine soul that would return to God upon **death**, and that the brain ruled the body. Others countered that the vital spirit generated in the heart—the seat of the sensible or sensitive soul—enabled **heat**, movement, and life, and that the heart therefore ruled the body. Ideas or "conceits" were thus begotten in the brain from the combination of fantasy and reason, sense-data taken in by the body, shaped by reason in the brain, and committed to memory. The early modern brain can thus be **pregnant** with ideas (Shakespeare uses the word pregnant only in this sense).

(B) Shakespeare's brains are organs of fantasy, reason, memory, and the soul. Theseus famously declares:

> Lovers and madmen have such seething brains,
> Such shaping fantasies, that apprehend
> More than cool reason ever comprehends.
> . . .
> And as imagination bodies forth
> The forms of things unknown, the poet's pen
> Turns them to shapes and gives to airy nothing
> A local habitation and a name.
>
> (*MND* 5.1.4–17)

Heat makes the brains of lunatics and lovers "seeth[e]" with the vapors of hot blood, which makes the ventricle of fantasy within the brain more active than the cooler compartment of reason. Sense-data comes in through the "five wits" housed in the brain, but instead of using "common sense" to reach a rational conclusion about the meaning of that data, the strong fantasy of the madman and the lover notices and "shapes" sense-data in unaccustomed ways. The poet can temper fantasy with reason, however, so that fantastical creatures never known upon the earth now have a location on paper or in an imagined literary world. Mercutio, another visionary, describes "dreams" as

> the children of an idle brain,
> Begot of nothing but vain fantasy,
> Which is as thin of substance as the air
> And more inconstant than the wind.
>
> (*ROM* 1.4.97–100)

The brain is "idle" in **sleep**, closed to the impressions of the five senses, so that dreams come only from fantasy in the brain, not from reason's conclusions about the material world and the body. Fantasy in the brain flows freely, like animal spirit, a creation of the human, rational soul but not rational in itself. Mercutio blames idleness or relaxation for dreams, but Brutus comments that the boy Lucius has no anxieties or worries and therefore sleeps soundly, with "no figures nor no fantasies, /Which busy care draws in the brains of men" (*JC* 2.1.232). Death, too, makes the brain "idle." The "idle comments" of King John show Prince Henry that he is near death. "Some suppose the soul's frail dwelling-house" to be the "pure brain," comments Prince Henry (*JN* 5.7.3, 2). The brain is "pure" because it is nourished on the most refined part of the blood, turned into animal or animating spirit, the vehicle of the rational soul, ruler of all three parts of the early modern tripartite soul.

Imprisoned, Richard II imagines his conceits or ideas to be the offspring of his brain and his soul. He extends the common analogy between the king's mortal body and the immortal political body of the realm:

> My brain I'll prove the female to my soul,
> My soul the father; and these two beget
> A generation of still-breeding thoughts,

And these same thoughts people this little world,
In humors like the people of this world,
For no thought is contented.

$(R2\ 5.5.6–11)$

Like the **womb**, the brain was nourished on phlegm; both **seed** or seminal humor
and animal spirit were multiply-concocted or refined. Phlegm was cool; animal
spirit and seed, hot.

Heat from fumes (from poorly concocted food or humors) might overwhelm
the brain's capacity for reason. Octavius hopes that Cleopatra will "keep [Antony's]
brain fuming," and conquer his reason with the lavish **diet** from his "feasts" (*ANT*
2.1.24). Enobarbus determines to leave Antony when he believes that the "dimi-
nution in [Antony's] brain /Restores his heart: when valour preys on reason, /It
eats the sword it fights with" (*ANT* 3.13.197–9). Antony's heart is enlarged with
love for Cleopatra and foolish bravado to fight Octavius; he uses up all his blood
to produce vital spirit in the heart rather than animal spirit (the vehicle of the
rational soul) in the brain. Horatio warns Hamlet that the Ghost "might deprive
[his] sovereignty of reason" by drawing him up to the cliff that "put[s] toys of
desperation, /Without more motive, into every brain" by the roaring of the sea
beneath (*HAM* 1.4.73, 76). The noise and sight of the raging sea overwhelms the
senses in the rational part of the brain so that reason can no longer rule the
impulses of imagination. Fumes might also **dry** the brain, which required **cold**
and moisture in order to generate—or conceive, in the metaphor of pregnancy
often applied to the brain—ideas. Nestor mocks Achilles for his "brain as barren
as banks of Libya," and as "dry" (*TRO* 1.3.327–9). Jaques argues that although
Touchstone's "brain / . . . is as dry as the remainder biscuit /After a voyage" (so
that he cannot conceive new ideas), his memory allows him still to "vent" or release
jokes from "strange places cramm'd /With observation" (*AYL* 2.7.38–40, 41–3).

Shakespeare appears to share the common visualization of memory in the
brain as a chamber or library, as in *MAC* 1.7.65 (see **limbeck**). Macbeth imagines
Lady Macbeth's memory as a register with "written troubles of the brain," perhaps printed in a heavy tome that "weighs upon the heart" or as scraps of paper
collected in a "stuff'd bosom of . . . perilous stuff" (5.3.42). The sonnet-writer
recommends that his lover write down everything he cannot remember: "what
thy memory cannot contain /Commit to these waste blanks." Ideas gestate in
the brain but can only be "deliver'd from [the] brain" and "nursed" to youth
after they have been given permanent form on paper (*SON* 77.11). "[L]asting
memory within [the] brain" comprises "tables" or tablets "character'd," printed,
carved, inscribed, or written upon (*SON* 122.1); so marked, they will

remain
Beyond all date, even to eternity;
Or at the least, so long as brain and heart
Have faculty by nature to subsist.

$(SON\ 122.3–6)$

Hamlet aggressively vows to wipe out his memory, to erase

> all trivial fond records,
> All saws of books, all forms, all pressures past,
> That youth and observation copied there;
> And thy commandment all alone shall live
> Within the book and volume of my brain,
> Unmix'd with baser matter.
>
> (*HAM* 1.5.101–6)

Hamlet imagines his memory to resemble a commonplace book (the journal-like notebooks many early modern men kept and in which they noted quotations, observations, mnemonics, jokes, accounts, and anything they liked). Now only the ghost's words will linger there, his brain a single volume with a single text. But Othello's mind is a prison, and Iago holds the key to the fantasy of adultery. Iago frowns "As if [he] . . . had . . . shut up in [his] brain /Some horrible conceit" (*OTH* 3.3.114–15). The chamber of fantasy contains the monster of jealousy, wandering into the ventricle of memory to plant falsehood there so that Othello imagines he has "ocular proof" of Desdemona's crime.

(C) See Crooke (1615) on the substance of the brain as cool, moist, thick, slimy, white **marrow**; Vicary on the three ventricles (1587). Crane (2001) was one of the first extended treatments of Shakespeare and cognition, pointing out the prevailing metaphor of birth to describe the generation of ideas and paralleling Shakespeare knowledge-production to twenty-first-century neuroscience. On sense-perception, see Vinge (1975) for a philosophical overview, and B. R. Smith (1999 and 2008). More recent studies include Daigle's dissertation on the "Galenic brain" (which she argues unites flesh and spirit, 2010); and the essays in Bassi and Cimarosti (2006). The special section of *The Shakespeare International Yearbook* edited by Graham Bradshaw, Tom Bishop, and Mark Turner (2004) on "Shakespeare in the Age of Cognitive Science" contains useful essays by Crane on atomism and nothingness in LR; Sweetser on vertical and horizontal spatial awareness in MM; and Freeman on blended metaphors of light/darkness, knowledge/ignorance in OTH. There is a rich and growing literature on Shakespeare and brain imaging that is beyond the scope of this project; see, for example, Matthews and McQuain (2003); Davis (2007). Ackerman (2005) and Ramachandran (1999) independently single out Shakespeare's use of metaphor for what it can teach us about the human brain.

brawn A synonym for muscle in Elizabethan English. Aufidius gives up his previous desire to "hew [Martius'] target from [his] brawn," to tear his enemy's shield from his strong arm, when Martius joins the Volscian side against the Romans (*COR* 4.5.120). Shakespeare sometimes uses the word in our contemptuous modern sense, to refer to mindless former strength, as in "Harry Monmouth's brawn" (*2H4* 1.1.19), or to thoughtless bulk, as in Falstaff's "damned brawn" (*1H4* 2.4.110) or Nestor's self-deprecating "withered brawn" (*TRO* 1.3.297).

Imogen uses the term adoringly as she blazons Posthumus and his "brawns of Hercules," but the praise is necessarily ironic to an audience that knows that the corpse she lauds is not her husband's at all (*CYM* 4.2.311).

breast See also **dug, pap, milk-pap, nipple** (A) The breast in Shakespeare is a gender-neutral metonym for the **heart** (understood as the seat of emotions, life-**blood**, or physical strength), the highly eroticized site of sexual difference, and, rarely, the source of infant nutrition (unlike the dug, which is exclusively lactating). Early modern anatomists attempt to bring opposing ancient theories of sexual similarity (and of secondary sex-organs such as the breasts) into harmony (see **sex**). The **Hippocratic** writings claim that the breasts, in both men and women, serve primarily to protect the heart in both women and men, and to draw away waste products of the body. Women's bodies would normally **purge** their pathological excess of **phlegm** through menstruation, but during times at which they do not menstruate, such as after childbirth, they needed an additional vent for evacuation. Aristotle emphasized the protective function of the breasts, and **Galen** their use for lactation in women. Crooke attempts to reconcile Aristotelianism and feminist Galenism by claiming that women's breasts do indeed have a sex-specific "use," that is to say, they are capable not merely of synthesizing or converting fluids from elsewhere in the body but of making **milk** by themselves through the process of concoction. Crooke reconciles his two authorities by combining Aristotle's belief that the breast's primary function is as a "buckler or Target" (shield) for the heart and Galen's, that it is lactation:

> You shall therefore reconcile *Galen* and *Aristotle,* if you say, that the Dugges were created originally for the generation of Milke, and secondarily for the strengthning & defence of the heart. And againe, that the originall cause of their scituation in the breast was for the defence of the heart, and the secondary for the generation of milke. (Crooke 1615, Sr)

In other words, Aristotle is correct about the purpose of the *location* of the breasts (in front of the heart, as opposed to on the **belly** as in other mammals) and Galen about their function (milk-making, rather than drawing away evil **humors**).
(B) The breasts protected the heart, the **organ** most closely associated with blood; moreover, women's blood could be transformed into breast milk, in a continuation of the process by which maternal blood nourished the fetus *in utero.* Thus blood and breast appear frequently together in Shakespeare, as life-blood drains away from the heart through the breast (in the case of a chest-**wound**) or as blood nourishes a new life (in the case of the nursing infant). Volumnia characteristically transforms breast milk into blood when she exhorts her fainting daughter-in-law: "the breasts of Hecuba /When she did suckle Hector, look'd not lovelier /Than Hector's forehead when it spit forth blood" (*COR* 1.3.40–2).

The maternal, the erotic, and the martial are for her equally stimulating. Similarly, Cleopatra calls the asp that poisons her "my baby at my breast /That sucks the nurse asleep," a poisonous infant that leaves the "vent of blood" observed by later witnesses (5.2.309–10, 349).

Examples of the neutral use of breast to mean chest or heart (and by extension, the emotions therein, such as courage, fear, kindness, or vengefulness) abound throughout the canon. "[T]he breast of civil peace" (*1H4* 4.3.43) uses breast as a synecdoche for the people; forgiveness appears in "Volscian breasts" (*COR* 5.2.85), "pain" in the breast of an unrequited lover (*LLL* 4.3.170); affection in the "loving breast" of a fond grandfather (*TIT* 5.3.163); "a bold spirit in a loyal breast" (*R2* 1.1.183), and a range of feeling in the speaker's "breast" in Sonnets 22–24. Biron, however, includes the breast as part of his ironic blazon of women's parts:

> When shall you hear that I
> Will praise a hand, a foot, a face, an **eye**,
> A gait, a state, a brow, a breast, a waist,
> A leg, a limb?
>
> (*LLL* 4.3.181–4)

Iachimo clearly fetishizes the female breast as a proxy for sexual contact when he describes, twice, his sight of the "**mole** cinque-spotted" (*CYM* 2.2.37) on Imogen's left breast. Hidden in the trunk, he sees it from a distance, and compares the mark to the spots on a **cowslip**'s petals (evoking beauty, delicacy, and the natural world). Salaciously recounting his supposed conquest of Imogen to her husband, however, he turns the breast into a figure for enthusiastic and bawdy coupling rather than a sign of feminine elegance. The breast is now important as a marker of sex-difference, understood not as feminine vulnerability and innocence (as in the marks on a flower) but as the erotic availability of women; the breast is "worthy the pressing" (2.4.135), worthy only as an object that can be fondled. He moves still closer in his imagined encounter when he claims not only to have touched the mole but also to have "kissed" it, the assertion that finally drives Posthumus mad with jealous rage.

(C) Crooke (1615, Sr) describes the function and working of the breast (as a shield in men, and as a milk-producing gland in women). Yalom (1997) argues that the Western European Renaissance eroticized women's breasts, transforming it from a sacred, sustaining, maternal force to a sexualized icon of social control. Vickers (1985) discusses the breast in the blazon of Elizabethan love-poetry and Shakespeare's deployment of it in *LC*. Schwarz (2000) analyzes the myth, popular in Shakespeare's day, that the legendary warrior women the Amazons cut off one breast in order better to shoot their arrows.

brimstone Hot and **dry,** brimstone or **sulphur** ignited almost instantly. It burned away **cold, moist humors** and **scabs, warts**, whelks, and running sores on the **skin**. Combined with theriac or treacle, brimstone was especially valuable against poison. Shakespeare uses brimstone twice as an expletive and once figuratively. Both Othello and Sir Toby Belch cry, "Fire and brimstone!" the imagined hellfire of Christian tracts, when they imagine a young woman's illicit sexuality, Othello as he imagines Desdemona favoring Cassio, and Sir Toby as he hears Malvolio fantasize about Olivia (*OTH* 4.1.234; *TN* 2.5.50). Fabian maintains that Olivia ignores Aguecheek in favor of Cesario only "to awaken your dormouse valour, to put fire in your **heart** and brimstone in your **liver**," to inflame the naturally pusillanimous Aguecheek to courage, which required valiant heat (*TN* 3.2.20).

bruise *see* **parmaceti**

burning fever *see* **tertian**

bubukle See also **carbuncle** Fluellen confuses two medical terms, bubo and carbuncle, with his nonce-word, bubukle. A carbuncle was a raised pimple that could appear anywhere on the body and that might have several causes; it began as a blackhead, but developed into a red, swollen mass. A bubo was a red or **sanguine** swelling that appeared in the armpits or between the **buttocks**, and might be associated with the **plague** (hence our modern term for *Yersinia pestis*, bubonic plague). Fluellen describes Bardolph's face as "all bubukles, and whelks, and knobs, and flames o' Fire" (*H5* 3.6.102) as part of the play's sustained mockery of Bardolph's flushed appearance. On the usual locations of the bubo, see Batman (1582, S2v); on its association with the plague, see Paré's treatise on the plague (1630).

bunch-backed *see* **crookback**

burdock, bur-dock, bur, burr A thistle-like weed producing thorny flower-heads called **burrs** (although "burr" is also generally used to refer to other flower-heads that cling to one's clothes). Cordelia measures how far Lear has fallen by comparing his lost kingly crown to his crown of weeds (implicitly, one of thorns, like Christ's), of

> Rank **femiter** and furrow-weeds,
> With burdocks, **hemlock**, **nettles**, cuckoo-flowers,
> **Darnel**, and all the idle weeds that grow
> In our sustaining corn.
>
> (4.4.3–6)

The Duke of Burgundy similarly calls burrs useless or idle plants (*H5* 5.2.52). Characters compare themselves or others to tenacious burrs when, like Lucio (*MM* 4.3.179), Helena (*MND* 3.2.260), or, falsely, like Cressida (*TRO* 3.2.111), they "will stick" (*MM* 4.3.179), although spritely Rosalind and Celia vow to shake the burrs of love from their petticoats (*AYL* 1.3.13, 17). Culpeper (1649) claims that a **simple** of burdock root "Helps such as spit **blood** and matter," "expels wind," relieves **tooth-ache**, "strengthens the back," aids the **kidneys**, dries leucorrhea in women, and that a **poultice** "helps the bitings of mad dogs" (C3r). Pechey (1694) adds asthma and "gouty **diseases**" to its uses (p. 31).

burnet So-called because of its brown flowers, **burnet** was prescribed as a cooling medicine for the **bloody flux**, nausea, pain in the side, **pleurisy** and **womb infection**, the **plague**, **wound** healing, and the **tertian ague**. The unique reference in Shakespeare comes from the Duke of Burgundy's speech in *Henry V* (5.2.42–52); see discussion under **kecksies**. For its uses, see Ascham (Bvr–v, 1561), Moore (1564, 17), Ruscelli (1569, C2v), Cartwright (1579, B3r), Kellwaye (1593, D2r), Bullein (1562, G4r).

buttock The flesh covering the sitting-bones, serving as a "stoole" or a "cushion" for the body (La Primaudaye, 1594, C8v, p. 48). The Clown in *AWW* offers us a taxonomy of buttocks: the "pin-buttock," "quatch-buttock," and "**brawn** buttock." Pin- and brawn- clearly refer to slender and muscular buttocks respectively, but "quatch" remains obscure; many commentators conjecture it means "squat" or broad, but the word quatch in early modern English means to speak or make a sound (2.2.18–19), so there may be a pun on breaking wind. Dromio of Syracuse associates the buttocks of his fat girlfriend with the "bogs" (presumably genitals) close by (*ERR* 3.2.117). Menenius, describing his own propensity for night-carousing, calls himself "one that converses more with the buttock of the night than with the forehead of the morning," continuing the obscenity with a complaint that he "finds the ass in compound" with most of Sicinius' words (*COR* 2.1.52, 58).

caduceus There currently exists confusion between the ancient symbol of **physicians,** the staff of the ancient healer, and god of **medicine, Aesculapius,** entwined by a single snake, and the caduceus or the staff of Mercury, topped with wings and entwined by two serpents. Mercury was the presiding deity of communication, travel, and intelligence; he became linked with medicine through his connection with **alchemy** or hermeticism (from the Roman name for him, Hermes). Shakespeare's Thersites is probably praying to Mercury as the god of mind, rather than confusing his caduceus with Aesculapius' staff, when he prays that the former may "lose all the serpentine craft of [his] caduceus" (*TRO* 2.3.12) if he does not curse Ajax and Achilles with stupidity.

Caius Shakespeare's comic French physician in *WIV* appears to be named after John Caius (1510–73), the first **physician** to perform anatomical dissection in England. One of the founders of Gonville and Caius College in Cambridge, Caius was a learned and skilful man, unlike his namesake. Hoeniger (1992) suggests that Shakespeare made his Dr. Caius French to reflect the influx of French Huguenot refugees entering Britain after the St. Bartholomew's Day massacre in Paris in 1572 (39, 60–1). Pettigrew (2007) suggests that Shakespeare's Caius is a quack who has deliberately adopted the name of a notable physician in order to defraud his patients. Given Caius' own expressed desire to write clearly in English from "good wyl to my countrie, frendes, & acquaintance" (1552, A7r, fol.7r), the humor of such identity theft would be enhanced by the solecisms of *WIV*'s Caius.

canker (A) Cankers (also called "cancerous **imposthumes**" or "tumors") were either round, uneven, hard tumors that ached and sometimes throbbed, or chronic **wounds** or **ulcers** that refused to heal and that extended deep into surrounding tissue, sometimes invisibly to the naked **eye**. Some writers contrast cankers, some of which could be benign and potentially curable, to "cancer," which was mortal, but healers could not readily distinguish between the two categories. The most dangerous cankers, or "carcinomas," might begin as lumps the size of a pea or a bean that were easily ignored by the common man, but grew to large, immovable masses that even a child could discern on the body. Nourished by large **veins**, such cankers were swollen with **blood** that had been thickened by the **cold, dry** fluid **melancholy**, and resisted pressure when touched. They could be pale and livid, or black. They gnawed away at the body from within and were sometimes called "cancer" because, like a crab, they clung tight to the body part where they were found. Some cankers produced ulcers on the outer body; these tumors were considered **hot**, even though they came from melancholy. Tumors that did not produce ulcers were considered hidden cancers. Corresponding signs included sorrow; throbbing in the affected **organ** at night, and oozing from the sore, which might smell foul. If tumors appeared in the legs or thighs, the **disease** was called lupus and treated by phlebotomy and **purging** to draw down the blood, especially from the genital area (using emmenagogues to induce menstruation in women and **clysters** to encourage hemorrhoidal bleeding in men). If excision were possible, the **surgeon** must be sure to remove the tumor from the "roots," but this was only possible when cankers appeared in the extremities. After removing a tumor, the surgeon cauterized the wound with arsenic or some other "defensative" **compound** against **infection**. If cankers appeared in the **stomach**, the **breasts**, the shoulders, the neck, or the armpits, however, they were incurable, because they could not be removed surgically without killing the patient. Under such circumstances, all the healer could do was to hinder the growth of the tumor through **diet** and purgations to reduce the patient's superfluous melancholy. Melancholy caused cankers because patients followed a diet that produced too much melancholy for their **complexions** or humoral temperaments, or because the **spleen** was collecting melancholy from the **liver**, as was its function, but the body could not expel the melancholy; or because the melancholy itself collected and became "adust" or burned in a particular organ. In the latter case, when the melancholy itself became heated or corrupted in the veins, the patient's diet ought to include both cold and humid foods, such as salted meat and spice, and cheese; **physicians** and family members also ought to encourage patients to good cheer, and to avoid hard work, sadness, or anger. A desperate remedy that sometimes worked was the **urine** of a girl about five or six years old, or asses' milk, but surgeons had to beware promising more than they could offer, since the prognosis for canker was so bleak.

(B) Shakespearean cankers gnaw **hearts**, minds, and flowers. Even Shakespeare's many references to the plant-blight known as canker connote the figurative implications of canker in humans: a disease that kills or corrupts from within, sometimes unseen from the outside. The history plays and the tragedies present canker as political corruption, an unseen threat to true kingship. In the first tetralogy, the civil broils known as the Wars of the Roses naturally lend themselves to horticultural metaphors. Somerset chaffs the Duke of York with his white rose's "thorn" and earns the riposte, "thy consuming canker eats his falsehood" (*1H6* 2.4.71). York's rose bears a "sharp and piercing" thorn to prick his enemies, but Somerset's red rose is bitten or corrupted from within. "The canker of ambitious thoughts" gnaws unseen at the white rose, too, in the mind of the Duchess of Gloucester (*2H6* 1.2.18). In the second tetralogy, Hotspur compares Richard II to "that sweet, lovely rose" and Bolingbroke to "this thorn, this canker" that will erode the kingdom from within when all seems healthy on the outside (*1H4* 1.3.175–6). Later in the play Falstaff compares the younger sons and ragged rascals who make up his recruits to "the cankers of a calm world and a long peace," the men who would under normal circumstances have been killed in battle or accident but who now remain in the commonwealth to undermine existing political structures and loyalties (4.2.29). Salisbury perhaps alludes to a last-ditch remedy for lupus when he suggests they "heal the inveterate canker of one wound /By making many" (*JN* 5.2.14–15); the surgeon might make multiple wounds to bleed the patient, a small amount each time. In this instance, alliance with the Dauphin is an unwelcome **"plaster"** because it will harm his own troops. Hamlet compares political intrigue to the "canker [that] galls the infants of the spring, /Too oft before their buttons be disclosed," but it is unclear—perhaps to Hamlet himself—whether "this canker of our nature" (1.3.39, 5.2.69) is Claudius' evil, or Hamlet's justifiable urge to revenge. Edgar is likewise "By treason's **tooth** bare-gnawn and canker-bit" when he returns to fight (*LR* 5.3.122). Out-of-place in a comedy, the political malcontent Don John claims he "had rather be a canker in a hedge than a rose in his [brother's] grace" (*ADO* 1.3.27–8).

The sonnets both praise the young man's **cheek** as a damask rose (a relatively recent import to England), and fantasize his **consumption** by a physical canker that corresponds to both his exquisite bodily beauty and his hidden moral corruption. "[L]oathsome canker lives in sweetest bud" (Sonnet 135); "canker vice the sweetest buds doth love," (Sonnet 70); and "canker-blooms have full as deep a dye /As the perfumed **tincture** of the roses" (Sonnet 54). Flowers with worms or rotting matter at their hearts appear as fragrantly beautiful as those that do not, paradoxically making even corruption benevolent: "How sweet and lovely dost thou make the shame /Which, like a canker in the fragrant rose, /Doth spot the beauty of thy budding name!" (Sonnet 95). Often the canker's progress resembles a literal consuming or eating. In Sonnet 99, a blossom succumbs to "A vengeful canker [that] eat him up to **death**"; Proteus defends "eating love" by comparing it to "The eating canker" that lives in "the sweetest bud," only to evoke from Valentine the contradictory response that

> as the most forward bud
> Is eaten by the canker ere it blow,
> Even so by love the young and tender wit
> Is turned to **folly**, blasting in the bud.

> (*TGV* 1.1.45–8)

Timon, too, imagines a toothed "canker [to] gnaw" the heart of those who attempt to reconcile him with humanity (4.3.50). "So [Caliban's] mind cankers," becomes "uglier" as does his body, concludes Prospero (*TMP* 4.1.192).

Friar Laurence, collecting **simples**, mixes horticultural and medical metaphors in his description of the human mind:

> Within the infant rind of this small flower
> Poison hath residence and **medicine** power:
> For this, being smelt, with that part cheers each part;
> Being tasted, slays all senses with the heart.
> Two such opposed kings encamp them still
> In man as well as herbs, grace and rude will;
> And where the worser is predominant,
> Full soon the canker death eats up that plant.
>   (*ROM* 2.3.23–30)

The Friar's focus upon discrete floral ingredients might seem to suggest an interest in the new chemical or refined **Paracelsian** remedies, but even die-hard **Galenic** herbalists knew that one part of a plant might be fatal, another therapeutic. Human bodies, argues the Friar, contain similarly opposing virtues: "Grace and rude will," the control of human passions and their uncontrolled expression. "Canker death," initially invisible to the eye, will consume minds whose strong desires are immediately gratified with no regard to consequences. Immediately after this homily, Romeo enters, determined to enlist the Friar's help in marrying Juliet; the Friar will eventually offer Juliet a **drug** that "slays all senses with the heart," and the "canker death" of the Capulet-Montague feud will "eat up" the lovers.

(C) Banister (1575) describes ulcerated and tumored cankers; Barrough (1583) uses the word "carcinoma" in English for the first time (Z5v), and distinguishes at length among different sorts of tumors deriving from melancholy. Lowe (1597) is the least optimistic, and treats canker and cancer as the same ailment; he warns young surgeons that canker is usually fatal, painful, and incurable, and ranks the treatment of canker as a lesson in humility for any would-be healer. Hunter (2004) discusses canker treatments in light of early modern conflicts about infection and quarantine; see also Harris's discussions of infectious disease (1998, 2004). Duncan-Jones explores the botanical elements of the figure at length (1995).

carbuncle See also **bubukle** Originally a word for ruby, **carbuncle** refers to a hard, black, raised sore upon the body that quickly becomes red and burning, thought to be caused by too much **blood** pooling and becoming too thick and **hot**. A **cold** and **moist diet** would counteract the hot, **dry** blood, while **clysters** and bleeding, and deep scarification with salt water, might alleviate the symptoms. Healers might also apply **plasters** of coriander powder. Shakespeare uses the word both to mean simply a jewel (as in *COR* 1.4.55 or *CYM* 5.5.189) but also to compare the boils on a woman's face to "rubies, carbuncles, sapphires" (*ERR* 3.2.135) and the torture that Goneril imposes on Lear to "a **plague**-sore, an embossed carbuncle" in his side (2.4.224).

carduus benedictus Holy or blessed thistle, *carduus benedictus* was **hot** and **dry**, thus a good **cure** for **diseases** caused by an excess of **phlegm** or mucus, and also against the **plague** and **melancholy**. Astrologers also prescribed holy thistle for the new disease of syphilis, because, as a herb of Mars, it was opposed to Venus, the ruler of venereal disease. When Beatrice is "stuffed . . . [with] **cold**" in *ADO*, Margaret mischievously prescribes "**distilled** *carduus benedictus*," punning on the name of Benedick. Her joke thus complies with established early modern therapy for upper respiratory congestion and sustains the bawdy joke about a maid being "stuffed" or **pregnant** (3.4.65–6). Brasbridge (1578) writes at length about the virtues of *carduus benedictus* and **angelica** against plague. Drouet (1578, G2r–H4v), and Bright (1615, I7r) also recommend *carduus benedictus* for the plague; Burton (1621, Pt. 2, section 4, p. 440) recommends it for melancholy, and Gerard for cleansing and opening (because it was a hot, dry herb) and against the "French disease" or syphilis (1633, 5Fr–v). Dodoens (1595, 614–15, RR3v–4r) recommends it as an emmenagogue, a **medicine** that "moves women's flowers." Dobranski collects references in *ADO* to **pregnancy, wombs**, and miscarriage (including Margaret's reference to *carduus benedictus*) and compares the "miscarried" love affair between Benedick and Beatrice prior to the play's opening to the structure of the play itself (1998).

cataplasm See also **plaster, poultice** In modern English, a cataplasm is a poultice, but in early modern usage it can be either a poultice or a plaster. In Shakespeare's unique reference it appears to mean a dressing applied to an open **wound** in order to close it and to draw out poison, that is, a plaster. Laertes boasts that the poison that he has obtained for his fencing foil is of such power that

> Where it draws **blood** no cataplasm so rare,
> Collected from all **simples** that have virtue
> Under the moon, can save the thing from **death**
> That is but scratch'd withal.
>
> (*HAM* 4.7.143–6)

The poison is so strong that dressings (cataplasm), herbal **medicine** taken internally (simples), and astrological medicine (the influence of the moon) cannot save the victim. Early modern **surgeons** use the terms cataplasm and plaster interchangeably; see Guillemeau (E1r, 1597), although Pope John XXI distinguishes a cataplasm as a dressing made from fresh or dried herbs sodden in water (1553, f3v).

catarrhs Thersites curses Patroclus with, among other items, catarrhs or **rheums** (*TRO* 5.1.19). A catarrh could mean either an **apoplexy** caused by thickened

phlegm in the **brain**, or phlegm itself, running down from the brain (which it nourished) and out of the **eyes, nose**, and mouth. Thersites probably means "apoplexy," given the severity of the other ills listed in his speech; see, for example, Holinshed, "a catarrh, which the physicians call an apoplexie" (1586, p. 795).

cheek See also **ashy, complexion, humor, perturbation, tawny** (A) The color, corpulence, and firmness of the cheeks provided evidence of a person's temperament or humoral personality, and of sudden changes in emotion. Full, red-and-white, firm cheeks indicated a **sanguine** complexion; white, soft, fat cheeks, a **phlegmatic**; sallow, thin, and lean, a **choleric**; and brown and wrinkled, a **melancholic**. Sudden joy or fear could render the face either pale or red, while a blush might indicate either chaste modesty or brazen shamelessness. At moments of great emotional upheaval, **blood** either rushed to the **heart** to sustain it and to give it the vital spirit it needed for sense and motion (making the face pale, as it lost blood), or rushed to the face, to provide material for the **brain** to refine into additional animal spirit to refresh the soul and provide succor.

Blushing cheeks bore an ambiguous status as both public marker of erotic innocence and scarlet badge of shame, since the helpless rush of blood to the face from the heart could indicate righteous indignation, ingenuous incomprehension, or shameful sexual knowledge. Anti-cosmetic writers complained that women who made themselves up with fucus or face-paint were thus denying one of their natural functions—blushing—by covering their cheeks so that observers could not see them change color. Women's faces functioned as cultural signposts, so if women could not be seen to blush, they could no longer serve as examples to others. Moral philosophers argued, further, that women who were not seen to blush visibly were not blushing at all, an argument extended to apply to dark-skinned peoples. Since brown- and black-skinned persons could not be seen to blush, averred Thomas Wright and others, they could not experience shame: first, since their blood was not rushing to the face away from the heart, and second, since their response was invisible to others—and the reaction of others was an important trigger for shame. (Darwin would demolish this argument three hundred years later, observing that dark-skinned peoples did indeed blush, even if the blood-flow was invisible to an untrained **eye**.) Brown, black, or "tawny" cheeks (by birth, or by tanning) thus signified shamelessness or moral hardness, leading to an ethnocentric argument in which the very blushing of the English indicated their superior moral fiber and capacity for shame.
(B) Moth summarizes the problem with using women's cheeks as indicators of their moral states. The ideal beauty bore cheeks like red-and-white roses. But

> If she be made of white and red,
> Her faults will ne'er be known,
> For blushing cheeks by faults are bred
> And fears by pale white shown:

> Then if she fear, or be to blame,
> By this you shall not know,
> For still her cheeks possess the same
> Which native she doth owe.
>
>   (*LLL* 1.2.99–106)

A beautiful woman's chastity is undetectable, as is her lewdness; her face is already colored red and white, together, so the pallor of fear and the red of shame are indistinguishable from her "native" or natural hue. Perhaps the best-known Shakespearean example of this conundrum appears in *ADO* 4.1.34–42, in which Claudio repudiates Hero at the altar, believing her to be unchaste. "Behold how like a maid she blushes here!" he begins, only to conclude, "Her blush is guiltiness, not modesty." The Friar who defends Hero does so on the grounds that "angel whiteness" vanquishes her blushes; her pallor signifies not guilty fear but saintly virtue (4.1.161).

So associated are pale cheeks with chaste femininity and dark ones with erotic misadventure that Pisanio advises Imogen that, if she is to disguise herself as a man, she "must /Forget that rarest treasure of your cheek," her whiteness, and consent to the embraces of "common-kissing Titan," the sun, as if tanning were equivalent to sexual libertinism (3.4.159–60, 163). Brutus bitterly complains about Martius' popularity with the same metaphor of a lustful sun kissing the chaste red-and-white complexions of ladies into a brown lasciviousness:

> Veil'd dames
> Commit the war of white and damask in
> Their nicely gawded cheeks to the wanton spoil
> Of Phoebus' burning kisses.
>
>   (*COR* 2.1.215–18)

Eager to see Martius, ladies brave the sun's rays and risk a tan that will darken and harden cheeks that are pink and soft as the "damask" roses reportedly introduced to England by Henry VIII's physician (and founder of the College of Physicians), Thomas Linacre. Phebe's admiring blazon of Ganymede includes praise of the "mingled damask" "mixed in his cheek," in comparison to the "riper . . . red" of his lip (*AYL* 3.5.121–3). The damask rose was carnation-pink, rather than scarlet-red. Ganymede does not return the favor, accusing Phebe of bearing a "cheek of cream," an unfashionably sallow face to go with her "inky brows" (*AYL* 3.5.47). A "damask" cheek felt soft, like a rose, as a woman's body was supposed to be. Iachimo salaciously fantasizes about Imogen's "cheek /To bathe [his] lips upon" (*CYM* 1.6.99–100) and so, in a very different register, does Romeo of Juliet: "See, how she leans her cheek upon her hand! /O, that I were a glove upon that hand /That I might touch that cheek!" (*ROM* 2.2.23–5).

Pallor might also indicate ill-health, grief, anxiety, or **death**. Lady Percy expresses concern that Hotspur has "lost the fresh blood in [his] cheeks" (*1H4* 2.3.44); "Calpurnia's cheek is pale" with worry (*JC* 1.2.185); the "damask cheek" of Cesario's imagined sister turns "green and yellow [with] melancholy" (*TN* 2.4.112–13). Extreme pallor, of course, indicates imminent or actual death. Henry VI laments the son who has been killed by his father in the Wars of the Roses, his "purple blood" like the "red rose" and "pale cheeks" like "the white" (*3H6* 2.5.97–100). Romeo believes Juliet cannot be dead, since her face is still pink: "beauty's ensign yet /Is crimson in thy lips and in thy cheeks, /And death's pale flag is not advanced there" (*ROM* 5.3.94–6). "The dead man's earthy cheeks" in *TIT* 2.3.229 are so both because they are literally covered with dirt in the pit but also because the body returned to cold, **dry** earth in death.

In the first tetralogy and *TIT*, the cheeks of warriors are wet with tears at the loss of a child. Queen Margaret savagely taunts the Duke of York with "A napkin steeped in the harmless blood /Of sweet young Rutland," his youngest son, "to dry [his] cheeks," a phrase repeated twice in the play (*3H6* 1.4.83, 2.1.61). Titus laments Lavinia's mutilation and assault, the murder of his son-in-law, and the false accusation of his sons with "bitter tears, which now you see /Filling the aged wrinkles in my cheeks," his "cheeks . . . stain'd, as meadows, yet not dry, /With miry slime left on them by a flood" (*TIT* 3.1.6–7, 12–46). But the future Richard III swears to "wet [his] cheeks with artificial tears" (*3H6* 3.2.184); we see him do this as he woos Lady Anne, claiming that she alone has made him weep although he remained dry-eyed at his own father's death when others "wet their cheeks / Like trees bedash'd with rain" (*R3* 1.2.162–3).

As persons aged, they became cooler and drier, more prone to melancholy, and their cheeks became lank and wrinkled. Adriana complains that not only "homely age" but also her errant husband "hath wasted" her "poor cheek" (*ERR* 2.1.90), and the comedy of Petruchio's insistence that Katharina greet the aged Vincentio as a "young budding virgin, fair and fresh and sweet" is emphasized by his praise of the "war of white and red within her cheeks!" when Vincentio is really "a man, old, wrinkled, faded, wither'd" (*SHR* 4.5.30–7, 43). Age has turned Falstaff sallow, with "a yellow cheek," says the Lord Chief Justice (*2H4* 1.2.181). Flute's Thisby eulogizes Bottom/Pyramus's "yellow **cowslip** cheeks" (*MND* 5.1.332), a reference that is more likely to be jocular than a serious indication of temperament or age.

Starvation and hardship, as well as advancing years, can waste cheeks. It is a mark of Mark Antony's superhuman stoicism that on a military campaign in the desert he can "drink /The **stale** of horses," and yet his "cheek so much as lanked not"; he remained strong and vital even when malnourished (*ANT* 1.4.61–2, 70). "Lank-lean" soldiers' "cheeks and war-worn coats" turn them into "horrid ghosts" by virtue of their skeletal pallor (*H5* 4.pr.26, 28).

(C) Vicary (1587, E1r) describes the function and significance of the cheeks. Wright (1604) connects blushing with the modesty and humoral temperance of the English, and blames dark-skinned southerners for their inability to blush and thus, he says, to experience shame. Fernie connects blushing to the experience of shame in Shakespeare's works (2002); Baumbach offers a detailed semiotics of Shakespearean physiognomy, arguing that Shakespearean faces can literally be read like books (2008). Harkness' illustrated history of the rose (2003) includes several beautiful images of the damask rose.

childbed See also **midwife** (A) Only women attended births, with the exception of posthumous Caesarean sections, which were performed by **surgeons** or barbers (see **untimely ripp'd**). It was important that women in labor, or travail, as it was then known, be kept quiet, in a room with a warm fire but not too much light, and certainly not open to the outside air. Parturient women might give birth lying in a bed, sitting on a birthing stool, or standing or leaning while supported by one or two strong attendants, or they might lie upon a pallet near the fire, with a strong block of wood or a heap of pillows near their feet so that they could push against something during labor. It was important that women not sink down deep into the bed, however, since it was known to make labor more difficult. Several women attendants were necessary, not only to support the mother physically as she labored but also to hold her hands during contractions, to massage her **belly**, to stroke her forehead and otherwise comfort her. Midwives and surgeons alike recommended that women alternated walking about the room with lying down to rest in bed, to open the **womb** by motion but also to give them the chance of **sleep** if they could take it. They ought not to eat heavily, but could drink wine with water, or broth, and, if they had any appetite, they could try an egg or bread and butter. As the contractions grew stronger, the midwife oiled her hand with fresh butter or pig fat and checked to see whether the mouth of the womb was open (we might now say, "to check the mother's cervix"). Three successive **fluxes** or flows of **humors** (fluids) indicated an imminent birth: the first was slimy, the second, **bloody**, and the third watery. Some midwives, impatient to attend another birth or to relieve a woman's suffering, broke the waters manually by tearing the membrane with their **nails**, but most did not recommend this practice because of the danger of infection, and also because the fetus might not have yet turned into position for labor. After the watery discharge, the woman entered the second stage of labor. The midwife then took up her position, ideally in a chair slightly below the birthing mother, and made sure that the baby was presenting head-first. If the fetus was correctly placed, travail could go ahead, and the midwife urged the woman to push, encouraging her with thoughts of her new baby. The midwife anointed the woman's vulva with butter or fat to lubricate the passage of the child, placing her hands beneath the infant's shoulders and drawing out the body slowly so as not to injure the mother. If the umbilical cord were wrapped around the baby's neck, she gently unwound it, and if the baby did not cry, she spritzed a little wine into its mouth, **ears**, and **nose** to trigger a breath. The midwife or another attendant massaged the mother's uterus to bring down the "secondine" (the afterbirth or placenta), which some placed on the newborn's body and swaddled along with the child.

Both mother and baby were then cleansed with fine **linen**, and the infant was moisturized with butter or almond oil (some used rose oil, too), to firm up the still semi-solid infant **skin**. The infant might be given a little honey on a fingertip, or treacle, and the mother given a sustaining drink (such as white wine with ***carduus benedictus***) and her vulva and lower abdomen anointed with "strengthening medicines" to help the womb close, such as oils of St. John's Wort and roses mixed with whole eggs and applied on a **flax plaster**. Her lower belly might be swaddled to prevent air from entering the womb and giving her postpartum pangs.

Difficult deliveries could be caused by a woman's fear; by someone in the room with hands clasped or fingers locked (which might shut the womb); by **cold** air, which constricted the uterus; by pleasant **perfumes**, which drew the womb upwards; by the mother's own body-shape, her age, or state of health, or pain threshold; premature or late delivery; if the waters broke before the child had turned; if the child itself were malformed or presented **legs forward** (breech presentation); if the afterbirth covered the neck of the womb (the condition we now call *placenta previa*); or if the woman had a **mole** or tumor. Cases where the mother's or the baby's body, or the baby's position, presented difficulties called for an expert midwife.

After birth, the mother needed to rest for a month during her "lying-in" time (also called childbed). The lying-in room needed to be quiet, dark, and very warm, since air—especially cold air—was extremely dangerous to the womb. At this time, the birth-attendants massaged the mother's **breasts** and belly with almond oil, butter, and other **medicines** to restore their strength, and she was encouraged to eat moderately foods that were easily digested, such as chicken broth, barley-water, eggs, and jelly. After about a week, she could introduce meat and maybe a little wine into her **diet**, and after about three weeks, she could bathe.

(B) Shakespeare's Thaisa suffers what her husband Pericles calls "A terrible childbed," at sea, with "No light, no fire" (*PER* 3.1.56). Exposed to the "unfriendly **elements**," Thaisa is at risk for the excess cold so dangerous to parturient women (an exposure that puts her into a **swoon** so deep that her husband and the sailors believe "At sea in childbed died she," 5.3.5). It is a little surprising that Pericles singles out the absence of "light" as part of the "terrible childbed," since birthing-rooms were usually dark and cave-like, to protect the mother's **brain** from becoming overstimulated and to protect the newborn's eyes from being dazzled immediately after it was born. Not only is the parturient mother, but also the newborn infant at risk from her "blustrous birth," blown by sea-breezes when she should be safely swaddled and laid warmly with her mother. In her "chiding . . . nativity" the infant Marina is exposed to the five classical elements in turn: lightning ("fire"), wind ("air"), sea-spray ("water"), hailstones ("earth"), and darkness ("heaven," referring to the ether or invisible, crystalline substance of which the spheres and celestial bodies were made). *WT* marks Leontes' cruelty to Hermione by his dragging her to trial immediately after she delivers Perdita,

> The child-bed privilege denied, which 'longs
> To women of all fashion; lastly, hurried

> Here to this place, i' the open air, before
> [She has] got strength of limit.
>
> (*WT* 3.2.103–6)

Women of all ranks, remarks Hermione, are granted their month of recovery after childbirth. "Strength of limit" would be the mother's ability to stand and walk unsupported by her friends and attendants. Moreover, all books and lore commented on the dangers of "the open air" for new mothers, and upon their feeble powers after delivery. Hermione's swooning collapse is unsurprising, and nor is Leontes' belief that she dies because of her exposure to the air before her body was ready.

Other dangers to women in childbed included, of course, **death** in parturition itself or from blood-loss or puerperal **fever** ("childbed fever") afterwards. Messala in *JC* describes Cassius' willed death at the hands of Pindarus as a childbed ending in maternal fatality:

> Mistrust of good success hath done this deed.
> O hateful error, melancholy's child,
> Why dost thou show to the apt thoughts of men
> The things that are not? O error, soon conceived,
> Thou never comest unto a happy birth,
> But kill'st the mother that engender'd thee!
>
> (*JC* 5.3.65–70)

Here, the monstrous child, Cassius' error, is begotten of Cassius' fears for the future and his own melancholy **complexion** or temperament, which always fears the worst. Cassius himself is the mother, mortally wounded by the birth. However dangerous for the mother, though, birth liberates the Shakespearean infant from a womb that entraps them as a gaol does a captive. Both Paulina in *WT* and Aaron in *TIT* describe the babies whose legitimacy they assert to reluctant relatives (Perdita's jealous father Leontes, in the first case, and half-brothers Demetrius and Chiron in the second) as manumitted prisoners or even freedmen. Aaron mocks,

> Look, how the black slave smiles upon the father,
> As who should say "Old lad, I am thine own."
> He is your brother, lords, sensibly fed,
> Of that self-blood that first gave life to you,
> And from that womb where you imprison'd were
> He is enfranchised and come to light.
>
> (*TIT* 4.2.120–5)

The baby and his half-brethren are united in their joint sufferings in Tamora's womb and sustenance upon her blood. "Black slave," like "Old lad," is here a term of endearment but also a sharp reminder of the practice of taking prisoners

61

in battle (as indeed Aaron, Demetrius, Chiron, and even Tamora have been captured by the Andronici at the beginning of the play), the nascent African slave trade, and absolute power that fathers have over children in this world (compare Titus' sentencing of his own son to death). The consummation of Tamora's and Aaron's affair "comes[s] to light" in the literal body of the dark-skinned baby. Aaron emphasizes almost grotesquely the physical space or prison cell that all three male children inhabited, but Paulina's diction in *WT* returns from the prison cell to the law court:

> This child was prisoner to the womb and is
> By law and process of great nature thence
> Freed and enfranchised, not a party to
> The anger of the king nor guilty of,
> If any be, the trespass of the queen.
>
> (*WT* 2.2. 57–61)

"[G]reat nature" itself has liberated the infant from the slightest contact with its mother, so that even if she has sinned, the child bears no blame. "Trespass" suggests movement, but the child was trapped, physically unable to participate in a trespass or boundary-breach while it was enwombed in its mother. Paulina's legal dyads ("law and process"; "Freed and enfranchised") turn Leontes from all-powerful judge (as in his mock-trial of Hermione) into subordinate and plaintiff. God or "great nature" outranks him and dismisses his claim against the baby, if not against his wife.

King Henry VIII uses Katherine's ill-fated childbirths to justify his claim that his conscience no longer permits him to remain as her husband. His speech is worth quoting at length because of the way in which it figures his scruples as a gestating birth waiting to emerge from his mind, as a counterweight to Katharine's own reminder to him of the many childbeds she has endured as his wife, and for his figuration of conscience as a kind of male hysteria:

> This respite shook
> The bosom of my conscience, enter'd me,
> Yea, with a splitting power, and made to tremble
> The region of my breast; which forced such way,
> That many mazed considerings did throng
> And press'd in with this caution. First, methought
> I stood not in the smile of heaven; who had
> Commanded nature, that my lady's womb,
> If it conceived a male child by me, should
> Do no more offices of life to't than
> The grave does to the dead; for her male issue
> Or died where they were made, or shortly after
> This world had air'd them: hence I took a thought,
> This was a judgment on me; that my kingdom,

Well worthy the best heir o' the world, should not
Be gladded in't by me: then follows, that
I weigh'd the danger which my realms stood in
By this my issue's fail; and that gave to me
Many a groaning throe.

(*H8* 2.4.)

Henry's diction imagines his mind as if raped by the scruples or "respite" of his conscience, violated with a "splitting power" that "forced [its] way" into his **heart** like a throng of attendants at court demanding his attention. The crowding of passions or emotions around his heart mimics the condition of *hysterica passio* in women, in which gross or unconcocted humors from the womb send **fumes** to the brain that overpower the senses and the mind. Both Henry's figurative womb and Katherine's real one are tombs to infants, suffocating potential "heirs" with the foul "air" or **vapor** of **sickness** and sin. The awareness of his imagined sin, unrepented and unrevoked, putrefied in Henry's conscience just as a dead fetus, or undigested humors, might corrupt *in utero*, "weigh[ing]" him down as a heavy pregnancy would and inducing "many a groaning throe," many a pang of labor. The emphasis that the play puts upon Anne's successful childbed—together with the choosing of godparents by Henry himself at an elaborately staged christening— belies, argues Jeanne Addison Roberts, the historical truth that would have been known to any Jacobean audience member: Anne's "delivery of a still-born son a few months later and her own subsequent trial and execution" (1992, 129).

(C) Primary printed sources may not reflect the actual practices of childbirth attendants, as Cressy (1997) observes. Nonetheless, we know that *The Birth of Mankynde* (Raynalde 1565), Guillemeau (1612), and Jacob Rüff's *Expert Midwife* (1637) were read avidly by lay- and medical men (and perhaps a few women). Cressy's chapters on birth usefully discuss evidence from printed sources, diaries, letters, and lore about the darkened chamber, the use of the birthing stool, and the importance of warm air and of freedom from draughts. Eccles offers a history of both obstetrics and gynecology in the era (1982). Adrian Wilson (1995) discusses the growing importance of the "man-midwife" in the later seventeenth and early eighteenth centuries. Roberts' excellent essay, "Shakespeare's Maimed Birth Rites," identifies all Shakespeare's birth scenes as **deformed**, interrupted, or imperfect rituals (which often exclude the mother and her female attendants) and suggests that such disruptions "in patriarchal creations reflect the fears and tensions of the father when faced with birth" (1992, 124). Murphy-Lawless (1998), while not addressing early modern obstetric practices in itself, is invaluable reading on the risk-benefit analysis (the imagined risk of maternal death) that underlines present-day medicalized birth in the Western world. Keller (2006) analyzes the rhetoric of early modern reproduction, especially in Crooke's *Microcosmographia* (1615). Becker (2003) discusses death in childbirth in the context of early modern women and death (40–3). Howard (2003) estimates the death risk to an early modern parturient woman to be about six or seven percent, that is, much less than the rhetoric of morbid fear in the woman's

own writings might suggest; she sensitively reads the concerns of early modern
mothers alongside present-day anxieties surrounding birth rather than (as an
earlier generation of historians had done) as evidence for higher death-rates
among early modern women. King (2007) argues for a science of gynecology
(the study of the **diseases** of women as a sex distinct from men) rather than
obstetrics (the study of childbirth and the reproductive organs) in **Hippocratic**
texts and argues for the revival of this tradition in the late sixteenth century.

choler, choleric See also **complexion, gall, humor** (A) **Choler**, also called gall or
yellow bile, nourished the gallbladder (and in some accounts, the **spleen**), made
heavy foods and drink digestible, thinned the **blood**, warmed the body, and
aided the body in defecation. Choler was hot, **dry**, light, notoriously bitter, yellow
or green in color, and associated with the masculine; its **element** was fire, its
season, summer, and its ruling planet, Mars. Choleric persons were rash, hasty,
impulsive, brave, and (in classical accounts, but not necessarily in Shakespeare)
quick-witted. They were often red-faced (if English), from the rush of blood
to the extremities from the **heart** and **liver** during a fit of anger, or sallow (if
Italian), from the excess of bile in the veins. Choleric persons were often lean
and hungry, and needed to eat moderate amounts of beef, bacon, and venison
to satisfy their appetites. Extremely heating foods such as sack, garlic, onions,
and mustard should be taken only in moderation, however, and frequent bloodletting, either in battle or by a surgeon, could prevent **diseases** of **heat** such as
fevers or "costiveness" (constipation, from which both choleric and **melancholic**
types tended to suffer). Drastic or uncontrollable fits of choler could be controlled by applying cooling medicines and foods such as **lettuce**, sorrel, small ale,
cold water, or **milk**, but when in good health and temper, choleric persons ought
to consume items that were temperamentally appropriate for them.
(B) While Shakespeare's characters are rarely humoral types in the manner of
Jonson's, several of his characters are called choleric by others within their respective plays. Warriors are particularly apt to choler, because, as Shakespeare and
others recognized, military prowess to a certain extent depended upon the
ability to become violently enraged. Fluellen is "valiant /And . . . touched with
choler" (*H5* 4.7.179–80), and the Duke of York in the first tetralogy is twice
deprived of speech by his anger. "[B]oiling choler chokes /The hollow passage
of my poison'd voice," he cries (*1H6* 5.4.120–1), as if bile is bubbling up his
windpipe and burning his throat, and in *2H6* he splutters, "Scarce can I speak,
my choler is so great" (5.1.23). Timon is similarly choked by his own anger:
"Choler does kill me that thou art alive!" (*TIM* 4.3.367). In contrast, Henry
Lancaster, no warrior but a man of "church-like humors," urges the brawling
English to make peace among themselves and "digest /[their] angry choler on
[their] enemies" (*1H6* 1.1.247, 4.1.167–8). Hotspur's very name identifies
him as a fiery warrior, "drunk with choler" at his military misfortunes (*1H4*
1.3.129). According to Fluellen, however, even Hotspur's former nemesis, Harry
Monmouth, resembles Alexander the Great both in military prowess and in
temperament, in "his rages, and his furies, and his wraths, and his cholers, and

his moods, and his displeasures, and his indignations, and also being a little intoxicates in his prains" (*H5* 2.7.34–7). The Duke of Norfolk urges Buckingham, "let your reason [contend] with your choler," but Buckingham does not heed him; even at his execution he "something spoke in choler, ill, and hasty" (*H8* 1.1.130, 2.1.34). One **cure** for choler was cold water and a calm mind, as the Host suggests to Caius: "throw cold water on thy choler" (*WIV* 2.3.85). Quickly mixes up her therapies and diction and urges Pistol to "aggravate [his] choler," when she intends to calm him down (*2H4* 2.4.162). Martius Coriolanus is so often called choleric that he may be correct to claim that any blood he loses in battle is "physical" (*COR* 1.5.18) that is, therapeutic, to his constitution. Sicinius tells Brutus that the latter "should have ta'en the advantage of [Martius'] choler" to lose him the vote (*COR* 2.3.198). Menenius and Martius both scoff "Choler!" at Sicinius' self-righteous advocacy of "the people" against Martius (*COR* 3.1.83–4). "Put him to choler straight . . . he speaks /What's in his heart," advises Brutus once more (*COR* 3.3.25–6). Grumpy warriors frequently cool down as quickly as they heat up, however. The Duchess of Gloucester complains to her testy husband, "Are you so choleric /With Eleanor, for telling but her dream?" and earns the sheepish response, "Nay, be not angry; I am pleased again" (*2H6* 1.2.51–2, 55).

We are never sure whether Cassio is really "rash and very sudden in choler" or whether that is merely Iago's invention (*OTH* 2.1.272), but Cassius does seem full of "rash choler," as Brutus complains (*JC* 4.3.39):

> Go show your slaves how choleric you are,
> And make your bondmen tremble. . . .
> . . .
> . . . By the gods
> You shall digest the venom of your spleen,
> Though it do split you; for, from this day forth,
> I'll use you for my mirth, yea, for my laughter,
> When you are waspish.
>
> (4.3.43–50)

"Choleric" masters beat their servants with sticks for a "dry basting," according to Dromio of Syracuse (*ERR* 2.2.62–3), and Cassius vents his "spleen" on his slaves. Brutus insists, however, that Cassius needs to "digest" his choler, which has become adust or burned, and turned into vengeful melancholy. The spleen removed heavy or sorrowful feelings from the body and so a working spleen rendered the body light and happy. Cassius is so irritable that, Brutus suggests, he can serve as the spleen for other people, keeping them joyful while he himself is miserably "waspish." Lear is another "rash" man; old age tended to cool down the body, but Lear becomes "infirm and choleric" with age (1.1.299).

Isabella observes that what is merely **distemper** or inappropriate anger in one of high rank can have criminal consequences for those lower in station: "That in the captain's but a choleric word, /Which in the soldier is flat blasphemy" (*MM* 2.2.130–1). *1H4* 2.4.324–5 puns on choler and the word "collar." Bardolph claims his red face denotes "Choler, my lord, if rightly taken," to which Hal retorts, "No, . . . halter," meaning that the petty theft in which Bardolph engages is a hanging offence. *ROM* begins with a series of puns on choler, the passion of rashness and violence that so greatly shapes the action of the play. Gregory refuses to "carry coals," to take insults, lest, Sampson suggests, they become "colliers" or laborers. Gregory explains, "an we be in choler, we'll fight," rather than suppress their anger peaceably, and Sampson responds with a warning that they may be hanged for fighting: "draw your neck out of collar" (*ROM* 1.1.1–5). At Romeo and Juliet's first meeting, Tybalt seethes at Romeo's unlicensed presence at the Capulet ball:

> Patience perforce with willful choler meeting
> Makes my flesh tremble in their different greeting.
> I will withdraw: but this intrusion shall
> Now seeming sweet convert to bitter gall.
> (*ROM* 1.5.89–92)

His whole body shakes at the violent encounter between the opposition of mild, cool patience and sharp, hot, choler; the choler, retained by force in the body and not permitted a vent by word or deed, becomes putrid or corrupted, causing the trembling characteristic of **ague** or fever to which choleric persons were prone. Romeo's encounter seems "sweet" like wholesome blood, but Tybalt's disease will infect Romeo with the "bitter gall" of anger or vengeance. Marina similarly imagines both choler and lust as infections that can spread to those in contact. Boult the pandar is liable "To the choleric fisting of every rogue," the impulsive punches of everyone who comes there, and his "food is such /As hath been belch'd on by infected **lungs**," his nourishment has been tainted by air that will encourage the production of evil humors in his body (*PER* 4.6.167–9).

Finally, Petruchio employs humoral theory, and specifically advice about **diet**, in order to tame Katharina. He diagnoses both himself and Kate as "choleric," angry, rash, and witty, but claims that the beef is "burnt and dried away," "over-roasted" and thus forbidden them in case it "engenders choler, planteth anger" (*SHR* 4.1.174, 170–2). Burned choler or choler adust was a type of melancholy that could trigger false laughter or merriment. Petruchio thus identifies his and Katharina's verbal sparring into pathology; witty wordplay between the two of them signifies distemper, a world out of sorts. Petruchio's wit needs to trump Katharina's. Petruchio's servant Grumio follows through his orders in 4.3.17–22, teasing Katharina with the promise of a "neat's foot" or a "fat tripe" (good for **phlegmatic** or melancholic persons) and then denying her even that sustenance by claiming it, too, is "choleric."

(C) Elyot (1539) outlines the four temperaments and the dietary and behavioral management of each. Lemnius (1576) and Wright (1604) explore the physiological mechanisms that connect human emotion or passion to individual humoral constitution. Bright (1586) and Burton (1621) explain the relationships among the various humors, which when rendered "adust" or blackened could become

cicatrice

the thick, sluggish, saturnine, melancholy humor; both identify melancholy that springs from choler adust as vengeful. Draper (1964) identifies Coriolanus as a choleric hero and Lear as one who moves from rash choler to mad melancholy. Hoeniger (1992) summarizes the theory of the four temperaments and expertly investigates the confusion surrounding the **spleen** (associated with both choler and melancholy). Paster (1993) connects the physiological humors and their control with the social enforcement of gender in early modern England, in particular the associations of "laudable blood[shed]" with angry, fighting, choleric men and of shameful menstruation and micturition with embarrassed, furtive, phlegmatic women. Floyd-Wilson (2003) deftly historicizes the transmission of **Galenic** humoral theory and its deployment by nationalistic early modern English writers to valorize the **sanguine** temperament (associated with England) over the choleric or the melancholy. Fitzpatrick (2007) offers specific dietary recommendations prescribed to various humoral types.

cicatrice See also **skin** (A) The scar left behind by a healed **wound**. The formation of scar tissue was understood to be necessary for wounds to heal, and surgeons' manuals include instruction on how to minimize cicatrices, for example on the face, by keeping wounds **moist** with plasters and covered with **linen** cloth. Inducing a "strong" cicatrice often required applying a "black plaster" made of lead, white wax, alum, fat of some kind (chicken grease or tallow) and rose or violet oil.
(B) Shakespeare's cowardly soldier Parolles aptly calls the cicatrice, and the ability to inflict it, an "emblem of war" (*AWW* 2.1.43). Unfortunately we do not believe his boast of having given a cicatrice to an enemy both because of the name of the allegedly wounded soldier—Captain Spurio—and the scar's location, "on the sinister cheek" (*AWW* 2.1.4). Coriolanus' cicatrices mark both his military prowess and his arrogance, the height of his triumph and the depth of his downfall. His mother boasts on his return from Corioles, "There shall be large cicatrices to show the people, when he shall stand for his place" (*COR* 2.1.148). But Coriolanus' refusal to show off these marks of valor in public provokes his banishment from Rome and defection to the enemy camp of Aufidius. Sealing up letters to England that demand Hamlet's **death**, Claudius thinks of another seal, "raw and red," the cicatrice or newly healed scar in the body politic of England, which is just recovering from battle with Denmark (*HAM* 4.3.60).
Shakespeare uses the word cicatrice in *As You Like It* figuratively to mean the temporary mark left upon skin by pressure from an object. Phebe complains that, since all injuries leave marks upon the body, were her scornful glances truly killing the love-lorn Silvius, he would have a wound or a scar to show. After all, even a rush leaves a momentary red mark upon the skin, a "cicatrice and capable impressure" (*AYL* 3.5.23).
(C) Banister has a recipe for a "black plaster" to induce a cicatrice or heal an **ulcer** (1575, K1r–v). Bullein recommends "water of planten [**plantain**], rose water, hony of roses, & a little Allume . . . wt a soft Sponge to moyst the place" (1579, 2C2r). Lowe describes a method to minimize scarring on the face by sewing not the wound or the skin but cloth laid closely over the wound and plastered

67

(1597, S2r). Crooke argues that, since cicatrices form when skin is removed, skin must be made of **"seed"** and **blood**, not from dried flesh as Aristotle suggests, "since . . . it can never be restored." He argues that cicatrices are "not a true skin but illegitimate, ingendred of a substance of another kind" (1615, Iv).

civet See also **perfume** Shakespeare's Touchstone offers us the pithiest description of civet, a glandular secretion from the anal pouch of the African civet-cat, still used in perfumery: "the very uncleanly **flux** of a cat" (*AYL* 3.2.68). We learn that Benedick is in love not just from "the loss of a beard" but also from the odor of civet that, Don Pedro announces, now perfumes him (*ADO* 3.2.50). Courtiers used civet to scent their hands (*AYL* 3.2.64), and Lear claims that the poverty-stricken are better off than the wealthy because they "[owe] the cat no perfume" (3.4.105). Later Lear imagines an **apothecary** vainly dispensing him some civet to "sweeten his imagination" (*LR* 4.6.130–1). Paré recommends inserting civet or musk into the cervix to stimulate the ejaculation of female **seed** (1634, 4Fr, p. 889), and Gesner recommends its use in an "odoriferous" water to ward off **plague** (1576, M9r, p. 88).

clapperclaw Possibly the so-called claw-hand **deformed** by **leprosy**, and used for scratching the sores of leprosy or for ringing the bell or *clapper* that warned passersby that a leper was approaching. Since the word *clap* is current in Shakespeare's time for a sexually transmitted **infection**, the references in *WIV* (2.3.65–8) and *TRO* (5.4.1) may allude to the confusion between syphilis and leprosy in early modern medical practice. See Fox (1973).

close-stool see **jakes**

cloves These aromatic spices were used to **perfume pomanders** such as the "lemon . . . stuck with cloves" that Berowne and Longaville imagine (*LLL* 5.2.647–8). Pedestrians carried pomanders to relieve the odors of the unsanitary early modern streets and to protect against **disease**. Oil of cloves was also used to relieve **tooth-ache**.

clyster see **clyster-pipes**

clyster-pipes A **clyster** is a liquid treatment, usually of water, **milk**, oil, or wine, or some **compound** of herbs, roots, seeds, and so on, inserted into the anus through the clyster-pipe in order to **purge** extraneous **humors** by forcing the **patient** to defecate. Such a treatment was called purgation by siege (by seat). Clyster-pipes were made of gold, silver, ivory, or wood. Iago reveals his contempt for Cassio in an aside to the audience in which, observing Desdemona and Cassio kissing hands in the courtly fashion of the time, he wishes Cassio's fingers were "clyster-pipes" (*OTH* 2.1.177). Iago fantasizes that Cassio's courtly kissing could administer a laxative to Desdemona that would force her to lose her love for Othello violently and quickly. Elyot (1539) describes both the clyster and the pipe used to administer it. Saunders

(2004) contextualizes the image alongside early modern discourses of purgation and argues that the clyster-pipe forms part of a larger pattern of scatological imagery throughout *Othello*, in particular, associations between feces, dirt, and blackness.

cod, cods, codpiece (A) Vicary describes the cods as a "purse" with "two pockets" to store and "comfort" the testicles safely, that is the scrotum (1587, H3v). Thus the codpiece began its life in the 1530s as a triangular pocket to conceal the cods, but rapidly transcended its practical function to become a decorative, often exaggerated or stuffed packet.
(B) In Shakespeare's lifetime, however, the codpiece was falling out of fashion, the subject of jokes and sexual innuendo, such as Byron's epithet on Cupid as "king of codpieces" (*LLL* 3.1.184). Borachio jokes obscenely about the outmoded fashion of Hercules in the worm-eaten tapestry, his codpiece "as massy as his club" (*ADO* 3.3.137). Touchstone's mock reminiscence of "Jane Smile" includes his memory of wooing a squash and giving Jane "two cods" as a gift, a joke both absurd because of the substitution of vegetables for flowers in the currency of love but also obscene because of the innuendo in cods (*AYL* 2.4.52). Lear's fool uses codpiece as a synonym for the cods it conceals, comparing his master's **folly** in giving up his kingdom to that of the beggar who wants to "house" his "cod-piece," to engage in sexual intercourse, before his "head has any [house]" (*LR* 3.2.28). In response to Kent's query, "Who's there?" the Fool replies, "grace and a cod-piece; that's a wise man and a fool" (3.2.40). The aged Lear may stubbornly wear the fashions of his youth, including the outdated codpiece, just as, perhaps, the insistence of Julia's maid in *TGV* that the cross-dressed girl wear a "codpiece to stick pins on" (2.7.53, 56) helps to date the play very early in Shakespeare's career. Autolycus reminds us of the codpiece's earliest function, as a pocket, when he gloats about "geld[ing] a codpiece," cutting the strings of purses and picking pockets with impunity (*WT* 4.4.611). Lucio, however, identifies the codpiece with the penis, not the scrotum, as he complains about the **death** sentence meted out to Claudio for begetting a child out of wedlock, "for the rebellion of a codpiece to take away the life of a man!" (*MM* 3.2.115). Finally, Iago's imagined "fair, and witty" wench at the landing at Cyprus knows not to "change the cod's head for the salmon's tail," a reference that sounds vulgar to most editors but that seems to defy glossing (*OTH* 2.1.155). Clearly the woman will keep something valuable (the cod's head) rather than trading it for something worthless (the salmon's tail), and both cod and tail suggest obscenity. It might mean that the woman will remain faithful to her husband (the head of the cod) rather than adulterously trading her "tail"—or Iago might be enjoying the vague smuttiness of the words rather than fleshing out a metaphor.
(C) Fisher (2006) narrates the history of codpieces and costume. Vicary (1587) and Crooke (1615) include the cods in their descriptions of the **organs** of generation.

cold (A) One of the four qualities of the **elements** and **humors** (the others were **moisture**, aridity, and **heat**), cold was a temperature, a state of being, and an ailment. Cold, including the cold elements of earth and water and the cold humors of **melancholy** and **phlegm**, enabled the body to retain food long enough to extract nutrition (by thickening the blood and slowing its flow), to maintain strong bones and **teeth** (by nourishing thick or solid parts of the body), to keep the **brain** cool (both literally and metaphorically), and to control strong passions such as lust and anger (by tempering the heat and volume of blood produced in the **liver**). Just as heat was necessary for human life, however, its absence, cold, indicated **death**. **Simples** such as henbane were poisonous by virtue of their extreme chill, which stopped the production and movement of **blood** (and thus of spirit) altogether and seemed to freeze the body. Serious ailments of cold, to which the elderly were particularly prone, included **apoplexy** and **palsy**.

Some of the more common and certainly more minor ills associated with too much chill were the highly **contagious** rhinoviruses that we still call "colds." Humoral theory held that colds came from an excess of cold and moist humors, or phlegm, in the head or the brain. **Patients** were advised to avoid draughts, open windows, foul air or lodging, lying on the floor, and to rest near a warm fire and apply heat to their feet. Patients "caught" colds, however, not through what we today understand as **infection**; no external germ or agent was responsible. Instead, inopportune circumstances such as draughts or travel on fens or in the fog, and so on encouraged a humoral body already predisposed to make too much phlegm (by heredity, by the climate, wind patterns, or circumstances of one's birth, by one's **diet**, and so on) to produce even more in response to the immediate stimulus. Patients should avoid known triggers, but if they succumbed, they should eat plenty of hot, nourishing food to counteract the humoral chill (hence the aphorism, "Starve a **fever**, feed a cold"), and take hot, drying **medicines** such as *carduus benedictus*.

(B) Shakespeare's characters catch cold, or joke about catching it, in many of the ways that wise-women and physicians predicted. Bullcalf catches "A whoreson cold, sir, a **cough**" from ringing the coronation bells outdoors (*2H4* 3.2.181). Lucetta jokes that the scraps of paper that Julia has flung on the ground to "kiss, contend . . . do what you will" should not lie on the ground, "for catching cold" (*TGV* 1.2.133), and Dromio of Syracuse worries lest a companion "catch cold on's feet" from getting wet (*ERR* 3.1.37). Troilus complains that Cressida "will catch cold" from her interrupted **sleep** the night after they consummate their love: "You will catch cold, and curse me" (*TRO* 4.2.15). Grumio, Petruchio's servant, points out the various ways in which he, his master, and mistress might catch "extreme cold": the house is unheated, they have been traveling a long way, and they are "weary," and however "hot" a shrew his mistress, her heat alone cannot protect them from becoming "frozen to death" unless they have a fire (*SHR* 4.1.38–45). "Poor Tom's a-cold," repeats the naked Edgar in *LR* 3.4.147 and 4.1.52, a vivid evocation of the plight of **Bedlam** beggars and other wanderers. Another noble nomad, the Duke in *AYL*, "shrink[s] with cold" (2.1.9). Shakespearean symptoms include Beatrice's "stuffed" **nose**, to Margaret's bawdy joy (see discussion under *carduus benedictus*).

Figuratively, to catch cold of a person or an agreement means to become unwelcome or unwanted. Iachimo reverses the common belief that one should "Starve a fever, feed a cold," when he asks for a legally witnessed agreement with

Posthumus "lest the bargain should catch cold and starve" (*CYM* 1.4.166), and Lear's fool predicts, "an thou canst not smile as the wind sits, thou'lt catch cold shortly" (*LR* 1.4.101), alluding to the belief that a draught encouraged a cold and to Lear's impending exile on the heath after falling out of favor with his daughters. The **choleric** Hotspur, temperamentally unapt to catch cold, mocks those who shun the dangers of insurrection and those who fear illness alike: " 'tis dangerous to take a cold, to sleep, to drink" (*1H4* 2.3.8).

Cold as a state of body or mind denominates death, chastity, cruelty, and political or bodily **sickness**. Quickly realizes Falstaff is dead by his chill: "[his feet] were as cold as any stone; then I felt to his knees, and they were as cold as any stone, and so upward and upward, and all was as cold as any stone" (*H5* 2.3.24–5). Juliet's "cold" convinces Capulet that she is indeed dead (*ROM* 4.5.25). "Must our mouths be cold?" cries the desperate Boatswain (*TMP* 1.1.53). Othello laments, "Cold, cold, my girl!" over the corpse he himself has murdered (*OTH* 5.2.275). To die is "to lie in cold obstruction, and to rot" (*MM* 3.1.118) to return to the cold, dry element of earth out of which the Biblical Adam was originally formed. The blood in corpses contained "cold congealed blood" (*3H6* 5.2.37) that, immobilized, could no longer carry the essential human spirits (which connected mortal body and immortal soul) to various organs of the body. "Cold **hearts**" (*1H4* 4.3.7; *ANT* 3.13.159; *H8* 1.2.61) were such because blood abandoned them, together with the vital spirits that were necessary for sensation and action. Lucio worries that the chaste Isabella is "too cold" or chaste to convince Angelo to pardon her brother (*MM* 2.2.45); her heart and liver lack the warm blood necessary for love, lust, and, in Angelo's case, courage. Angelo himself is so coldly passionless that, Lucio reports, he was not begotten in the ordinary way but from cold, watery creatures, a "sea-maid and two stock-fishes"; his very "**urine** is congealed ice" (*MM* 3.2.108–10). "Cold meats" or cold food indicate cooling affections as well as slovenly housekeeping. Cloten dismisses Imogen's contract with the lower-born Posthumus as an alliance "foster'd with cold dishes," and seeks to win her for himself (*CYM* 2.3.114). "The funeral baked meats /Did coldly furnish forth the marriage-table," sardonically comments Hamlet of Gertrude and Claudius' wedding-banquet (*HAM* 1.2.180–1). *HAM* begins with "bitter cold" that indicates a biting sickness (1.1.8). Ophelia mourns her father laid "in the cold ground" (4.5.70) and is herself mourned as one of the "cold maids" who call the "long purple" wild orchids "dead men's fingers" (4.7.171). Lear's "wits begin to turn" at the moment he sympathizes with the Fool's chill: "Come on, my boy: how dost, my boy? art cold? /I am cold myself" (*LR* 3.2.68–9). The frigid air marks the callousness of his daughters, his own foolish cruelty in banishing Cordelia, and, paradoxically, his renewed humanity and fellow-feeling with the Fool and all the poor wanderers on the heath.

(C) Bullein (1579) prescribes chicken broth to warm a phlegmatic or melancholic (cold) person, an ancient folk-remedy recently proven efficacious against rhinoviruses (at least, in the laboratory; see Rennard et al., 2000). Barrough (1583) recommends winding a handkerchief soaked in oil of chamomile or dill around the forehead of one who suffers from a headache with a cold.

colic See also **guts-griping** (A) Colic, or windy colic, afflicted the **stomachs** of those who retained too much wind or gas in the **belly**. Their pains could be extreme, and their stomachs rumbled loudly as the griping pains moved around the lower body. **Fennel**, **marjoram**, mallows, beets, or honey and water, eased their suffering, especially if taken as a **clyster** or suppository. Colic from too much **phlegm** required a drink of **wormwood**; from too much **choler**, a clyster of violets and perhaps a drink of **prunes**. Windy colic might require a drink of new **milk** and egg yolk, and a **plaster** laid upon the belly. Children were especially prone to the colic, because they had worms; frequent **colds**; or had received bad milk from their nurses. A colicky child could not **sleep** for crying and sometimes could not urinate; baby boys suffering from colic had enlarged and erect penises. Babies could not be **purged**, so in such cases, the **wet-nurse** needed to avoid any gas-producing foods, such as beans, peas, butter, and boiled eggs, and to wash the baby's belly with a **decoction** of cumin, dill and fennel seed before plastering it with oil and wax, or with ale and fresh butter boiled with cumin and put into a tightly fastened pig-bladder—always taking care not to burn the baby with the hot plasters.
(B) Colic in Shakespeare is always windy. Hotspur questions Glendower's supernatural account of the events at his birth, arguing instead that earthquakes sometimes happen because "the teeming earth /Is with a kind of colic pinch'd and vex'd /By the imprisoning of unruly wind within her womb" (*1H4* 3.1.27–30). Menenius mocks the plebeian tribunes by implying that they lack the stoic courage of their social betters in both physical and judicial matters. When they are required to adjudicate, "if you chance to be pinched with the colic, you make faces like mummers; set up the bloody flag against all patience; and, in roaring for a chamber-pot, dismiss the controversy bleeding the more entangled by your hearing" (*COR* 2.1.74). They grimace like dumb-show players, and wage war (the bloody flag) against their decision-making. There may be a suggestion of the belly **flux** with the two figurative references to **blood** and the urgent cry for the chamber-pot; the tribunes act as though they have the serious condition of dysentery when they suffer from the childish colic. Ajax orders the trumpet to "Blow, villain, till thy sphered bias **cheek** /Outswell the colic," imagining the trumpeter's cheek puffed outward to sound his note as the belly distends with painful wind (*TRO* 4.5.9).
(C) Goeurot (1550, Y6v–7v) describes the travails and **cures** of colicky children. Ruscelli (1569, E2r) recommends a tisane of strained **rue**, camomile, dill, aniseed, fennel, and other herbs that dissolve the trapped wind or gases thought to cause the pain of colic.

college See also **physician**, **surgeon** King Henry VIII founded the College of Physicians in 1518, during an epidemic of **plague**, in response to a request from Thomas Linacre. Its charter granted it the right to license physicians first in London, and then (from 1523) in the whole of England. Its purpose was two-fold: to supervise the education of medical practitioners and to standardize their practice (those seeking licenses were required to undergo an oral examination in front of the other fellows), and to challenge the authority of the trades-guilds of the Barber-Surgeons (who had their own guild) and the **apothecaries**. Among the first healers licensed by the College were several surgeons and so-called **empirics**. The college gained a coat of arms in 1546. Although the college brought proceedings against some women who practiced medicine, women retained the right to make **simples**, and the college mostly refrained from pursuing **midwives** licensed by the Bishop of London or the Archbishop of Canterbury. Shakespeare uses the term **college** to refer to an august body of learned men. The King, skeptical of Helena's prowess, wonders why he should trust his health to "empirics,"

> When our most learned doctors leave us and
> The congregated college have concluded
> That labouring art can never ransom nature
> From her inaidible estate.
>
> (*AWW* 2.1.116–19)

The term "college" deliberately separated the physicians from the trades'-guilds; "congregated" alludes to the fact that many doctors were also ordained as ministers. Benedick determines that "a college of wit-crackers cannot flout me out of my **humor**" (*ADO* 5.4.100), happy to be incurable even by a college of learned men, or the butt of jokes by his friends. For the history of the College of Physicians, see G. Clark (1966).

coloquintida The vine-like colocynth or coloquintida (bitter apple, bitter cucumber), **hot** and **dry** to the second or third degree, was known as an acerbic, strong, dangerous, laxative (Dodoens 1595; Gerard 1597). Iago observes of the newly jealous Othello that "the food that to him now is as luscious as locusts, shall be to him shortly as bitter as coloquintida" (1.3.349). Locusts or grasshoppers were proverbially delicious, although not generally consumed in England. Dodoens recommends colocynth for the **falling sickness** and its administration via **clysters**. Moss (2004) suggests that Desdemona herself, as virgin **mummy**, becomes a homeopathic, **Paracelsian**, consumable or cannibalistic **medicine**, and in this speech, she transforms from delicacy into **purge**.

complexion See also **humor, race** (A) Complexion is both the early modern medical term for the Greek *crasis* (temperament, or humoral personality) and the manifestation of that temperament in the **skin** of the face, through its color. Complexion varied according to body-type and also according to geographical origin, climate (including humidity, temperature, wind direction, air, and water), **diet** and exercise, waking and **sleep** habits, parentage, rank, sexual activities and desires, age, and many other variables. English humoralism, however, developed from the ancient ideals (in which, for example, the warlike, quick-witted **choleric** man, or the introspective, scholarly, **melancholic** man might have served as models for civilized life) into a nationalistic system that lauded the **sanguine** temperament of England as the cheerful, good-hearted pattern for behavior (earlier writers had dismissed the sanguine fellow as a buffoon). The table below summarizes some of the humoral associations at work in Shakespeare's England, in descending order of perceived accuracy:

Complexion or Temperament (Greek *crasis*)	Choleric (angry, rash, valiant, quick-witted)	Melancholic (fearful, sorrowful, malicious, whimsical, witty)	Sanguine (cheerful, valiant, rational, just, short-tempered)	Phlegmatic (dull, torpid, slow, cowardly)
Humor predominating in the body	Choler Yellow bile (Gall)	Melancholy Black Bile	Blood Sanguine fluid	Phlegm Phlegm or Urine
Element	Fire	Earth	Air	Water
Season	Summer	Autumn	Spring	Winter
Planet	Mars	Saturn	Jupiter, the Sun	The Moon
Qualities	Hot Dry Masculine Yellow Bitter	Cold Dry Feminine Black Sour	Hot Moist Masculine Red Sweet	Cold Moist Feminine White Watery
Organ(s)	Gallbladder or Spleen	Spleen or Bones	Liver or Heart	Lungs or Kidneys or Brain
Function(s)	Thins the blood; aids digestion; provokes sweat and other excrements	Thickens blood; nourishes spleen and "heavy" organs such as bone	Nourishes heart, liver; vehicle for spirit	Nourishes brain and "moist" parts of the body; evacuates solid waste
Dreams	Battle, anger, wounds	Frightening things; shame or disgrace	Blood, or pleasant activities	Fish, or water
Urine	Clear and high-colored (yellow)	Thin and watery	Thick and reddish, abundant	Thick, white or pale
Age at which it predominates	Young adulthood, adolescence	Old age	Middle age	Infancy; or all women
Skin-color (also called complexion)	Fire-red, or sallow	Dusky or livid	White and red; pink	Pale
Hair-color or -type	Black or auburn; curled	Straight and thin, or tightly curled	Red or blonde; Abundant	Flaxen; Long and straight
Geographical regions loosely associated with it	Turkish, Arabian, Italian	Italian, Spanish, African	English, French	Scandinavian, Gothic, Danish

Thus it was certain that a man of a choleric temperament abounded in yellow bile; very likely that his **urine** was yellow; probable that he was sallow-skinned; and possible that he was Italian or had recently traveled in Italy. As the table indicates, complexion also denotes skin-tone, the sense in which we use the word today. There is some overlap between the social category that we call "race" or "ethnicity" in contemporary English, and the early modern term, complexion. At the same time, climatological and emotional variables meant that none of these categories was fixed, but rather contingent upon environmental circumstances.

(B) Sometimes complexion can be connected with the **elements** of the atmosphere and the humors of the body. Cassius suggests that "the complexion of the element /In favour's like the work we have in hand, /Most bloody, fiery, and most terrible" (*JC* 1.3.128–30). The weather is, like the planned assassination, "bloody, fiery, and . . . terrible," in other words, of a choleric complexion or temperament. The weather in *HAM* is **cold**, but "very sultry and hot for my complexion," remarks Hamlet, who is determined to be opposite to whatever the unfortunate Osric suggests (5.2.99). The sonnets famously pun on "black" as a reference to coloring, mood, sinfulness, and other qualities. Complexion in Sonnet 132 can mean the dark **hair**, **eyes**, or skin of the poet's mistress: "I will swear beauty herself is black /And all are foul who thy complexion lack."

Shakespeare puns frequently on complexion as temperament and complexion as skin-color. Hal comments that it "discolours the complexion of [his] greatness to acknowledge" a "desire [for] small beer" (*2H4* 2.2.5–7). Just as he seems less princely in his character for spending time with low-born tapsters or cowardly knights, so drinking weak ale might thin his **blood** and make him pale. Moth deliberately confuses Armado on the subject of complexion:

Armado: Who was Samson's love . . . ?
Moth: A woman.
Armado: Of what complexion?
Moth: Of all the four, or the three, or the two, or one of the four.
Armado: Tell me precisely of what complexion.
Moth: Of the sea-water green, sir.
Armado: Is that one of the four complexions?
Moth: As I have read, sir; and the best of them too.
Armado: Green indeed is the colour of lovers; but to have a love of that colour, methinks Samson had small reason for it. He surely affected her for her wit.
Moth: It was so, sir; for she had a green wit.
Armado: My love is most immaculate white and red.

(*LLL* 1.2.76–90)

Armado means "what temperament?" but mischievous Moth first mocks the idea of humoral personality, suggesting that the number of categories is random;

second, he interprets complexion to mean skin-color; third, he suggests that her complexion might have been green (from **green-sickness**); finally, he puns on green, meaning unready or sophomoric. Armado takes him utterly seriously in his response, admiring the "white and red" of his mistress' face. The other lords, with the notable exception of Biron, agree white and red (the sanguine complexion) to be the ideal of feminine beauty. When Biron admires Rosaline's face as the "fair **cheek**" where "Of all complexions the cull'd sovereignty /Do meet, as at a fair," the fairground where the choicest monarchs meet (4.3.230–1), Ferdinand counters him by arguing that the dark-skinned "Ethiopes of their sweet complexion crack" next to Rosaline; Rosaline is so dark that the maligned complexion or skin-tone of black Africans appears fair in comparison (4.3.264). (Rosaline perhaps gets her revenge in 5.2, when she taunts the Princess for her pock-marked skin; see discussion under **pox**.)

MV employs the word complexion to connote both racial and generational difference. Even before Morocco enters, Portia expects him to have "the condition of a saint and the complexion of a devil" (1.2.130), and Morocco describes his "complexion" as "The shadow'd livery of the burnished sun" (*MV* 2.1.2), skin tanned by the sun's rays (in the most commonly cited early modern explanation for dark skin). Having dismissed him, Portia retorts: "Let all of his complexion choose me so," an overt comment on his skin-tone but an indirect comment on his choice of the silver casket and his vanity (2.7.79). "It is the complexion of them all to leave the dam," conclude Shylock's friends about Jessica's flight; like a fledgeling leaving the nest, grown children are bound to part from their parents, even the kindest and most nurturing (3.1.29). *OTH* refers only twice to complexion, but both instances indicate a connection between geographical origin and climate and develop the play's imagery of elemental qualities such as **heat** and **moisture** and its association of blackness with the devil. Iago fuels Othello's fears by suggesting Desdemona herself has abnormal desires because she sought to marry out of "her own clime, complexion, and degree" (3.3.230). "Clime" is the climate that can determine temperament; complexion puns on skin-tone and on humoral personality; "degree" refers to rank and also to her qualities relative to Othello. Othello later characterizes "Patience" as a "young and rose-lipped cherubin" whom he asks to "turn [its] complexion" to "look grim as hell," where the cultural associations of hell with darkness explain the figure: the young, sanguine, pink, healthy angel, patience, must change its personality to a mature, vengeful, melancholic, black devil that will wait to damn Desdemona (4.2.62–4).

Women's complexions—both their temperaments and their faces—are more delicate than men's. *MM*'s Isabella defines women as "soft as our complexions are," with tender skins and feelings (2.4.129). Like children's skins, women's skin was more porous and susceptible to outside influence, "credulous to false prints," as Isabella says. Her phrase also alludes to the often-quoted but false early modern etymology of the Latin word *mulier,* woman; it was thought to derive from *mollis aer,* soft air, because women were inherently impressionable, providing only the formless matter for conception, for example, while men conferred the shape or form of the fetus. Orsino in *TN* 2.4.25–7 is surprised to learn that Cesario loves "a woman . . . of [his] complexion"; such a woman, he tells the supposed youth, is "not worth [him]" (presumably because of her masculine appearance) (2.4.26–7). Vincentio alludes to the belief that planetary movements influenced **disease** and personality when he tells Claudio that human life is by its very nature prone to unsettling change: "thy complexion shifts to strange effects /After the moon" (*MM* 3.1.24). Isabella herself can transcend the bodily or emotional constraints of human complexion because she channels the divine: "grace, being the soul of your complexion, shall keep the body of it ever fair" (3.1.183–4). No matter how sordid the Duke's plan, Isabella remains free from taint, "fair."

Complexion in *AYL* reveals the ability to love. Corin interprets the exchange between the love-lorn Silvius and the heartless Phebe as a humoral struggle "Between the pale complexion of true love /And the red glow of scorn and proud disdain" (3.4.53–4). True love makes blood flow to the **heart**, blanching the face as the blood leaves it; arrogance and wrath force blood to the **liver** and the face. Phebe comments of Ganymede/Rosalind, "the best thing in him /Is his complexion," his pink-and-white skin (3.5.115–16). Ganymede's sudden pallor on learning of Orlando's injury belies his claim that he was merely pretending to **faint**; Oliver observes, "there is too great testimony in your complexion that it was a passion of earnest" (4.3.170). Ganymede's sudden fear drives his blood away from his face, toward his heart, depriving him of the animal **spirits** required for voluntary sensation and understanding (making him **swoon**).

(C) The bibliography on this topic is extensive. Early modern sources include Elyot (1539); Bodin (1566, trans. 1966); Lemnius (1576); Wright (1604); Burton (1621); see also introductions to Galen's complexion-theory (as opposed to early modern England's), Johnston's translation of **Galen** (2006), and the *Cambridge Companion to Galen* (ed. Hankinson 2008). Recent secondary sources on medieval and early modern humoralism include Siraisi (1990) and Hoeniger (1992), who helpfully offer an overview of Galenic humoral theory. Floyd-Wilson (2003), however, expertly traces a specific early modern version of what she calls "geohumoralism" in England (see **race**). Arikha's popular history of the four humors is engaging and well-researched (2007). On complexion, race, and skin-color, see esp. Wheeler (2000), whose *Complexion of Race* considers humoralism and emerging racial categories in the eighteenth century; Royster (2000), who looks at Gothicism and white skin as humoral and racial markers in the sixteenth century; Iyengar (2005), who explores the challenge that exploration presented to existing theories of race and complexion, and Bovilsky (2008), who addresses what we might call secondary race-characteristics (hair, features) in addition to skin-color. The idea of four temperaments or complexions persists in "popular" psychology. Works that claim to apply humoral theory to contemporary life include Williams (1996) and Rolfe (2002). Perhaps more reliable are present-day four-part psychological schema such as Keirsey, D. and Bates, M. (1984) or Myers-Briggs (1995).

compound (A) **Medicine** made by mixing several ingredients, not necessarily by pounding or mashing them (although this is the origin of the word). While **physicians** and wise-women could collect and prescribe **simples**, or single-source herbal remedies, only apothecaries could compound, **distil**, and mix diverse and multiple ingredients. So identified was the **apothecary** with the process of compounding that the apothecary's recognized sign was the mortar and pestle, used to powder ingredients.

(B) Shakespeare refers to compounds and compounding as the process and product of sophisticated medicine, to **humoral** mixing, to making up a quarrel (by pounding the source of disagreement into powder) and political negotiation. Compounds may have tasted—and smelled—vile. Stuffed in the buckbasket of dirty laundry, fat Falstaff complains of the "rankest compound of villanous smell that ever offended **nostril**" (*WIV* 3.5.92) Shakespeare's clinical compounders are dangerous. The wicked queen in Cymbeline develops the "most poisonous compounds, /Which are the movers of a languishing **death**" (*CYM* 1.5.8–9) that Cornelius unwillingly fetches for her in order to attempt Imogen's life, although she claims she will try her luck on animals first and that she is just practicing skills that the doctor himself taught her in order to investigate "their several virtues and effects," in other words, to develop her skills as a **Paracelsian empiric**:

> Hast thou not learn'd me how
> To make **perfumes**? distil? preserve? yea, so
> That our great king himself doth woo me oft
> For my confections?
>
> (1.5.12–15)

Luckily, Cornelius suspects her plans and "did compound for her" instead a **potion** that creates the illusion of death, rather than death itself (5.5.254). Shakespeare's sonnets likewise contrast "simple" virtue to "compound" vice. Sonnet 76 bemoans the poet's reluctance to innovate:

> Why with the time do I not glance aside
> To new-found methods and to compounds strange?
> Why write I still all one, ever the same,
> And keep invention in a noted weed,
> That every word doth almost tell my name,
> Showing their birth and where they did proceed?

"Weed" puns once more on recognizable clothing and the single-source herbal origins of simples, in contrast to the obscure origins of compounds. "Strange" alludes to the foreign ingredients found in many compounds, and "new-found methods" to the practice of newly popular Paracelsian chemistry (refinement and distillation). Sonnet 118 argues at greater length in favor of old, familiar medicines over newer ones:

> Like as, to make our appetites more keen,
> With eager compounds we our palate urge,
> As, to prevent our **maladies** unseen,
> We sicken to shun **sickness** when we **purge**,
> Even so, being full of your ne'er-cloying sweetness,
> To bitter sauces did I frame my feeding
> And, sick of welfare, found a kind of meetness
> To be **diseased** ere that there was true needing.
> Thus policy in love, to anticipate
> The **ills** that were not, grew to faults assured
> And brought to medicine a healthful state
> Which, rank of goodness, would by **ill** be cured:
> But thence I learn, and find the lesson true,
> **Drugs** poison him that so fell sick of you.

Just as sated people try new dishes or "compounds," just as **patients** purge or evacuate their bodies in order to restore a balanced state of health and to correct the invisible balance of the humors, so the poet was stuffed or over-full of his lover's sweetness and tried, prophylactically, to consume something bitter, something harmful to the body. "Sick of welfare," wanting a change, the speaker found a novelty and appropriateness in wilfully seeking out illness instead of waiting to fall ill naturally, or to fall out of love with the passage of time. His deliberate plan, to avoid future boredom or dissatisfaction by seeking new loves before stasis or "ills" set in, applied "medicine" to a healthy relationship because he himself was "rank," foul or rotten, and sought a **cure** not in goodness or honesty but in lies and illness. But other lovers—the compound drugs that he has taken in preference to his wholesome, sweet love—have poisoned him rather than purging or cleansing him. In *ROM*, however, Romeo assuages the conscience of the impoverished apothecary who sells him his poison by arguing that "gold [is] worse poison to men's souls, /Doing more murders in this loathsome world, /Than these poor compounds that thou mayst not sell" (5.1.80–2).

Hal and Falstaff each call the other a humoral compound, the former a "whoreson mad compound of majesty" (*2H4* 2.4.294), the latter a "compound" of butter and sack (*1H4* 2.4.123). King Henry IV himself bitterly tells his son, "Only compound me with forgotten dust" (*2H4* 4.5.115), referring to the mashing or pummeling process of making a compound with a mortar and pestle. *H5* presents compounding as both determined negotiations for peace and the humoral mixing of different personalities in an army or in a marriage. Bardolph,

Pistol, and Nym make friends "As manhood shall compound" (*H5* 2.1.98) over Falstaff's reported deathbed; Montjoy warns Harry against "compound[ing]" for a ransom (4.3.80); the King mysteriously comments "I must perforce compound /With mistful **eyes**" right before giving the order to kill all the prisoners— perhaps compound here means both strategic planning and humoral control, the tempering or compounding of **phlegmatic** sadness, watery tears, with **choleric** fury (4.6.33). Finally, the king woos Katherine of France by offering to "compound a boy, half French, half English" (5.2.207). Baptista in *SHR* asserts "I will compound this strife" (make up this quarrel), by offering his daughter Bianca to the highest bidder (2.1.341).

(C) Elyot (1539) explains the difference between simple and compound **humors**, simple and compound members of the body, and simple and compound temperaments or complexions. Pope John XXI (1553, f2r) includes a table of the measurements for different kinds of compound medicines and for what purpose each formulation is commonly prescribed, such as juleps, mixtures, electuaries, **syrups**, **decoctions**, collyriums, **cataplasms**, and so on.

consumption See also **hectic, tisick** (A) Consumption was the name given to a wasting **disease** such as the tisick that appeared to consume the sufferer from within (hence its name) often appearing with a hectic **fever**. Consumptives remained lean and shivering, no matter how much food they ate or how warm they kept themselves, losing precious bodily **humors** and **blood** until they were completely **dry**, the **heart** like a burnt-out candle. Their faces and bodies were distinctive—skeletal, pale, and, if they suffered from the hectic, flushed in their **cheeks**. The rapid weight-loss and cadaverousness of the disease could resemble the wasting of advanced syphilis, or **pox**. Breathing **moist** air and eating meat might help, or drinking woman's **milk**, if it could be obtained, but the disorder was usually fatal, although sufferers might linger with their symptoms for many months. In the eighteenth and nineteenth centuries the word consumption became a synonym for tuberculosis, but in Shakespeare's time it is the general term for any sort of "cachexia" or wasting disease.

(B) Shakespeare's references to consumption all emphasize the deadly nature of the disorder. Falstaff puns on the **illness** called consumption and his own inordinate ability to consume food, liquor, and money: "I can get no remedy against this consumption of the purse: borrowing only lingers and lingers it out, but the disease is incurable" (*2H4* 1.2.236). Beatrice claims she only agreed to wed Benedick "to save [his] life" because she had been told he was "in a consumption" (*ADO* 3.2.2). In a serious register, both *TIM* and *LR* curse human beings with consumptions at the height of their mad misanthropies. Timon rails, "Consumptions sow /In hollow bones of man; strike their sharp shins," alluding to the disease's ability to sap the very **marrow** from the bones and associating it with the joint-pain of syphilis (*TIM* 4.3.151). He curses Apemantus again with "consumption" (4.3.201) again later in the scene, for good measure. Lear in his

madness compares women's bodies to hell and disgustedly connects them with the "Burning, scalding /Stench, consumption" of venereal disease (4.6.129).

(C) Barrough (1583, P1v) compares the consumptive heart to a guttering candle, distinguishing between the hectic and the "absolute" consumption on the grounds that, if there are any moist humors left in the body, the patient suffers from a hectic, but if the patient's body is entirely used up, the patient has fallen into a consumption, and the prognosis is dire. Bullein (1579) comments on the disorder's tenacity, but recommends hemp, chicken broth, powdered and **decocted** hedgehog-skins, **breast milk**, and the herb crows-foot as remedies.

contagion (A) Contagion in Shakespeare's England could refer to the transmission of **disease** through contact with an infected body or object, as in present-day usage (see **infection**), but also to disease itself, especially **plague**, and to air or water thought to induce illness. A crucial difference between our understanding of contagion and the early moderns', however, is that for us disease comes from external agents or germs, but early modern **patients** caught contagions and infections only if they were already vulnerable to illness by humoral imbalance. Contagions spread by encouraging humoral imbalances in the patient's body in response to environmental cues and actions such as lust (in venereal disease), **cold** and damp weather (in colds), poison, bad smells, foul water or food, and so on. What **Hippocrates** had long ago called "airs, waters, places" were perhaps the greatest source of contagion. Cold and damp air, especially in a fog or on a fen, encouraged the body to produce the cold, moist humor of **phlegm** and might cause one to catch cold; the body sneezed, **coughed**, and produced mucus from the **nose** in an attempt to purge this excessive phlegm. Lust might heat the **liver** to such an extent that it produced too much **blood** from the nutrition consumed; the blood might corrupt any one of the four **humors** in the body (depending on the **complexion** or humoral personality of the patient) and result in a **fever**, **skin** blotches, joint pains, or other ills. The **cure** for contagions of all kinds was therefore restoring the humoral balance of the body, usually by **purging** by mouth (through emetics) or by siege or seat (through **clysters** or laxatives); sometimes phlebotomy or bloodletting was necessary. Prophylaxis was much to be preferred: patients ought to avoid excesses of **heat**, cold, **moisture**, and aridity, strong emotion (**perturbation**), too much food and drink (or the wrong kind of food and drink), bad smells, and dirty places such as graveyards and dung-heaps.

At the same time, folk wisdom, and newer **Paracelsian** learning, especially in the face of epidemics such as plague and the new disease of syphilis, held that certain disorders did indeed move from person to person and seemed to have an external cause. Paracelsian healers argued that there were multiple diseases, that the diagnostician needed to distinguish between external symptoms and underlying disorder, and that each disease had its own, separate origin and its own particular cure. Moreover, civic and church authorities had long treated diseases thought to be transmissible from person to person (such as **leprosy** or plague) by sequestering the victims, enforcing basic sanitation, and burying the dead promptly. In other words, regardless of the technical, humoral reasons underlying an outbreak of contagion, practical measures treated the disease as if an external agent were to blame rather than the moral or humoral failings of those who succumbed to it.

(B) Sexual relations, poison, bad air, water, and places, and the smell of dead bodies spread contagious disease in Shakespeare, who also appears to understand the power of what Christakis and Fowler, writing about present-day social networks, call "social contagion" (2009) or the power of behaviors (suicide, falling in love, conspiracy) to be transmitted across a social network. An anguished Adriana refuses to believe that Antipholus of Syracuse is not her husband, accusing him of infidelity and then arguing that, if he has proven false, he has "strumpeted" her (since they are one flesh, as man and wife) by his "contagion" (*ERR* 2.2.144). Both his travels and his sexual activity threaten to contaminate him, as Harris (2004) observes.

Martius wishes all the "Contagions of the south" upon the Romans who have betrayed him–both the sexually transmitted infections thought to originate in Southern Europe and the ill-effects of the warm, moist climate (*COR* 1.4.30). Warm Southern air bred disease by encouraging putrefaction (of food), and because of the insects that lived there, but cold air is troublesome, too; Portia fears "the vile contagion of the night" (*JC* 2.1.265) will encourage the "sickness" with which she diagnoses the treacherous Brutus, in a sensitive exposition that suggests that Brutus himself is the source of disease and that he infects the air (see discussion under **physical**). Hamlet characterizes "the witching time" of midnight as one "When churchyards yawn and hell itself breathes out /Contagion to this world," connecting the cold night air to the foul odor of decaying bodies (3.2.389–90). Friar Lawrence similarly urges Juliet away from the tomb, "that nest /Of **death**, contagion, and unnatural **sleep**" (5.3.151–2). Laertes calls the poison with which he anoints his foil "this contagion" (*HAM* 4.7.147); however counterintuitive it seems to us to call a toxin a contagion, it is technically true that the poison is spread by touch, by contact, and hence is literally a contagion.

The plays also present the "social contagion" of love, suicide, and rebellion. *AYL* 5.2 parodies the mass **love-sickness** of Silvius, Phebe, and Orlando through the repeated refrain, "so am I for Phebe . . . for Ganymede . . . for Rosalind," ending with Ganymede's equivocal, "And I for no woman" (85–107). Olivia in *TN* makes the comparison explicit with her comment, "Even so quickly may one catch the plague?" (1.5.295) when she falls in love at the first sight of Viola/Cesario. Poole (2002) suggests that violence becomes contagious in *HAM* and *JC*, and we might consider Ophelia infected by Hamlet's suicidal thoughts. Given the language of contagion and political infection in *JC*, we can also revisit Caesar's famous wish to

> have men about me that are fat;
> Sleek-headed men and such as sleep o' nights:

> Yond Cassius has a lean and hungry look;
> He thinks too much: such men are dangerous.
>
> (1.2.192–5)

In humoral terms, the lean and hungry Cassius is choleric and perhaps therefore malicious or splenetic, consuming his food in spite and an excess of bodily **heat**. He may suffer from the non-natural **melancholy** that came from **choler** "adust" or burned black into the melancholy humor, a condition particularly dangerous to others since it combined the angry irritability of the choleric man with the wit and malice of the melancholic. Fat men would be **phlegmatic**, calm, and peaceable, unlikely to revolt. Cassius' humoral excesses prove socially contagious, infecting his co-conspirators as Caesar has feared.

(C) Hippocrates' "Airs, Waters, Places" outlines the so-called *miasma* theory, that infections were transmitted through foul air, water, or food (1983). Early modern uses often discuss the contagion of sin in the Church of England (Foxe's *Acts and Monuments* comments on the "contagion of original sin" and of heresy; 3A3r, 3G6r, 1583), but Goeurot (1550); Drouet (1578); Kellwaye (1593) and others apply the term to disease. Goeurot singles out **measles**, chicken pox, and scarlet fever as contagions most commonly suffered by children. Drouet assumes that the plague is transmitted through foul air and the breath of others, in other words, through *miasma*. Kellwaye, however, appears both to characterize the air itself as contagious, and the plague as the result of disorder or disease hiding within a superficially healthy but humorally imbalanced body, and yet also to imagine bubonic plague as a contagion that lives *within* the air, independent from it, and that can be communicated to other, concluding: "yt it is not only the venemous and contagious ayre which we receiue that doth kill vs, but it is the present communicating of that contagion" (D1v). Jonathan Gil Harris (2004) and Margaret Healy (2004) suggest that early modern patients and healers of syphilis and plague respectively had some awareness of person-to-person transmission of disease, especially through sexual contact, and argue convincingly for a Paracelsian or proto-microbial early modern theory of contagious disease. Qualtiere and Slights (2003) historicize infectious disease, particularly syphilis, in early modern Europe through a detailed reading of the etiology of venereal disease in *TIM*. Poole (2002) presciently identifies the concept of contagion in Shakespeare as the imbibing of shared air and of shared, random risk—specifically, in *JC* and *TN*, the "blind, indiscriminate, unconscious, a-moral" directions of "love and violence" (102). Louise Noble interprets medicinal cannibalism as practiced in *TA* as a Paracelsian homeopathy that uses cacophagy, the ingestion of a contaminated or disgusting body product, to immunize and treat a diseased body politic (2003).

copper nose Sufferers from tertiary syphilis (**pox**) might lose the bridges of their **noses** to the **disease** and resort to copper prosthetics. Cressida slyly imputes venereal disease to Helen when she suggests that "Helen's golden

tongue had commended Troilus for a copper nose" (*TRO* 1.1.105–6), that is, he would contract syphilis from Helen if he had sex with her. The astronomer Tycho Brahe is known to have worn a copper prosthesis, although he lost his own nose to injury (in a brawl in 1566 or '67) rather than to disease (Thoren 1990, 25).

corns See also **warts** (A) White, round, callous warts that grew on the toes and the soles of the feet and made walking painful, usually as the result of thickened **phlegm**. Since corns were deeply rooted in the flesh, the best **cure** involved resolving or opening medicines (to thin the thick phlegmatic **humor**) combined with two kinds of surgery, cutting and burning (**incision** and scarification). As in other kinds of wart removal, after the **patient** had **purged** with laxatives, the **surgeon** took an iron plate with a hole in it, made to fit snugly around the offending area so that the healthy skin around it would not be burned during the cauterization, applied **heat** to burn and scar the area, then anointed the area with butter or "**Galen**'s wax" and dressed it as any other **wound** or **ulcer**. Patients who feared cautery could try ointments of slaked lime instead, to burn off the corn by chemical means; and then, as now, some determined souls, or those who could not afford a surgeon, pared their corns as they did their **nails**, with a sharp knife and a deal of courage, and dressed them with fig pulp and perhaps ground-up snail- or oyster-shell.
(B) Both Shakespeare's references allude to the pain of untreated corns. The jocular Lord Capulet urges the ladies "that have their toes /Unplagued with corns" to dance with him; he will brook no excuse: "she that makes dainty, /She, I'll swear, hath corns" (*ROM* 1.5.16–20). Lear's fool sings, "The man that makes his toe /What he his **heart** should make /Shall of a corn cry woe" (*LR* 3.2.31–3). The fool alludes to the ancient hierarchy of the human body and its parts, in which the foot and the toe should be subservient to the heart and the head. Lear has allowed subordinate members of his family—his daughters, the toes—to rule his emotions and his experience, rather than continuing to rule them as the heart or monarch of both family and kingdom, so that now he suffers mortally from the pain of what should have been a minor annoyance (the displeasure of his daughters).
(C) Wecker (L4v–L8r, 1585) details the procedure for the surgical removal of corns. Newton (P5r, M5v, 1580) recommends willow for warts and corns, and excision and binding with a **linen** cloth and fig rind for a corn in the toe. "A.T." (P4r–v, 1596) also outlines the home remedy for those who could not afford a surgeon, and is equally convinced that "it hath been proven" that the rind of a fig will corrode an ingrown corn; if that fails, he recommends stamped marigold, or snail shell (P5r).

cough, coughing, Hem! (A) Coughing expelled **fumes** or **vapors** from the mouth that had been drawn up from the **heart** by the **lungs**, or **phlegm** from the lungs themselves, if they were **diseased**, or excessive **rheums** and thin

humors drawn from the **brain** by the lungs for expulsions. The elderly were particularly susceptible to coughs because of their greater chill, which encouraged the production of excess phlegm. Early moderns cried "Hem!" (we now might represent the sound, "Ahem!") to clear their throats of mucus or to cough.

(B) Puck mocks old ladies for coughing (*MND* 2.1.54), Ulysses, old gentlemen who "cough and spit," like Pandarus, who cries, "hem!" (*TRO* 1.3.73, 1.2.228). He imitates Nestor by crying "hem! And strok[ing his] beard" (1.3.165). Both the **cold** of wintertime and a cold in the head can induce "coughing" (*LLL* 5.2.992; *2H4* 3.2.181; *AYL* 1.3.19). Octavius describes the nauseated "cough" of beasts compelled to drink the **stale urine** or "gilded puddle" that Mark Antony imbibes unshrinkingly on campaign (*ANT* 1.4.62–3). Characters feign coughs to alert each other to approaching constables or beadles, crying "hem! If anybody come[s]" (*OTH* 4.2.29; *2H4* 2.4.30, 3.2.218); the drinking games of Eastcheap employ "hem!" as the signal to drink deeply again (*1H4* 2.4.17), and Benvolio has used "coughing in the street" as an excuse to pick a quarrel, according to Mercutio (*ROM* 3.1.25).

(C) Cough medicines were usually called **hot** and **dry** in order to thin secretions and dilute phlegm. They were usually formulated in a **syrup**. Common ingredients in several sources include figs, licorice, aniseed, **fennel**, elecampane root (known to be an expectorant), and white sugar or sugar candy; another frequent recommendation is for the patient to consume dry toast with "sweete sallet oil" (olive oil), or to "seeth[e]" (simmer) figs in white wine or ale before drinking it. Cartwright (Fr–F2r, 1579) suggests pounding garlic into pig fat, using it to anoint the feet, and keeping the feet very warm with bedclothes and a heated plate. A. T. devotes several pages to cough remedies (O3v–P5r, 1596). *A Closet for Ladies and Gentlewomen* recommends mustard seeds and figs, simmered in ale, which is then to be drunk (M2v, 1608).

cowslip (A) The name cowslip is used in early modern herbal medicine to refer to the various delicate, yellow-flowering plants of the genus *primula*, including the *primula veris* (cowslip), *primula elatior* (oxlip), and *primula vulgaris* (primrose), although Shakespeare appears to distinguish among these flowers. Cowslip, **dry** in the third degree, was considered helpful in treating the **bloody flux**, inflamed **eyes**, **ulcers**, snakebite or wasp-sting, **fistula**, the king's **evil**, **gout**, **palsy**, convulsions, **cramps**, the stone, scalds, as an abortifacient, and, **compounded**, against bad dreams.

(B) Cowslips appear in Shakespeare to evoke utility, as in the Duke of Burgundy's lament for France (*H5* 5.2.49), or beauty and delicacy, as in Ariel's Song (*TMP* 5.1.89) or *MND* (2.1.10, 2.1.15); in these latter instances it also establishes the fairies' and Ariel's tiny size. It appears twice in *CYM*, both times in a perversion of its rightful function. The wicked queen, known for her skill in compounding, sends her ladies out to gather healthful herbs, "violets, cowslips, and primroses" (1.5.83) while she obtains a secret poison from Cornelius, and Iachimo compares the "mole cinque-spotted" on Imogen's **breast** to the "crimson drops /i'the bottom of a . . . cowslip" (2.2.38–9), a detail that tricks her husband into thinking that she has committed adultery.

(C) Dodoens (1595) accounts these plants "no great account" in medicine (K4v), but according to Bullein (1562), cowslip is one of the "giftes of God" (f4r; fo. 34). Gerard (1633; 782–3) and Burton (1621, p. 480) also include them in their lists of helpful plants. Gesner (1576) mentions its usefulness in expelling a fetus from the womb and bringing on menses (I4v).

cramp (A) Cramp sometimes came from the **dropsy**, from too much **moisture** settling in the joints. Like the dropsy, cramps were a **disease** of **melancholy** or **phlegm**; children, the elderly, or those exposed to **cold** air or water (such as in swimming) were particularly vulnerable. Children suffered from cramp because their **nerves** were weak and still developing, or because of thick **humors** preventing spirit from reaching the **sinews** and joints. The **cure** was massage, or ointments that would dissolve the obstruction on the nerves, or (for a child) a **bath** of chamomile oil, fenugreek and melilot (sweet clover), or of betony, **wormwood**, vervain, and thyme. Adults could rub their afflicted limbs with *aqua vitae* or sage oil.

(B) Parolles' cowardice is detectable by his speed in running away and in his reluctance in beginning an assay "in a retreat he outruns any lackey; . . . in coming on he has the cramp" (*AWW* 4.3.291). Ganymede facetiously blames Leander's drowning in the Hellespont not on love but on "being taken with a cramp" (*AYL* 4.1.104). Perhaps because of his own advancing age, Prospero likes to afflict his enemies with the spasmodic pain of cramps, threatening Caliban, "thou shall have cramps" and "I'll rack thee with old cramps" (*TMP* 1.2.325, 369), and averring of Stephano and Trinculo, "I'll shorten up their sinews /With aged cramps" (4.1.259–66). He makes good his threat, leading the racked Stephano to complain, "I am not Stephano, but a cramp" (5.1.287).

(C) *Regimen* blames cramp on dropsy (1528, C3v); Goeurot (1550) identifies cramps as a disease of children and offers recipes (U5r; mis-signed). Gesner's *Treasure of Euonymus* recommends rubbing the legs with alcohol (1559, M3v).

crazed, crazy See also **Bedlam, ecstasy, frenzy, lunacy, madness** Mad, **insane**, deprived of reason. The word originally means "broken" or "cracked" (*OED* adj. 1), like a piece of pottery, and Shakespeare's usages imply a falling-off or departure from a prior state of affairs in which an institution, rule, or person was intact and sound. Thus Demetrius calls Lysander's claim to Hermia's affection a "crazed title" (*MND* 1.1.32) a right broken by the withdrawal of her father's approval; Gloucester believes that sorrow has "crazed" his wits (*LR* 3.4.170); Macbeth tries to convince the murderers that even "a notion crazed," a madman's reason, would find Banquo guilty of harming them (*MAC* 3.1.82); Richard III and his allies impugn Edward's son as the bastard of his brother and a "care-crazed mother of many children," driven from righteousness by penury (*R3* 3.7.184); and in the same play, the Duchess of York complains that her voice has been "crazed" or cracked by "miseries" (4.4.17). Talbot contemptuously dismisses the Duke of Bedford to a place "fitter for sickness and for crazy age" (*1H6* 3.2.89). Anderson (2006) connects fragmentation or dismemberment in Shakespeare's plays (for example, the mutilations of *TIT*) to madness triggered by "trauma" or sudden shock.

crookback See also **legs forward, monster** Crookbacks or hunchbacks often inherited their **deformity** from a diseased parent, either because the father himself was crook-backed or because one or both progenitors suffered from a **disease** such as the French pox (syphilis). Prince Edward calls his uncle Richard (the future Richard III) a "Crookback" in *3H6* (5.5.30). Olivier's film makes this insult one of the moments at which Richard resolves to murder his nephews (1955). Queen Margaret castigates Richard as a "poisonous, bunch-backed toad" (*R3* 1.3.245), alluding to his shape and to the poison the toad was supposed to bear in its **skin**. Earlier she calls him a "bottled spider," suggesting that his hunch resembles the convex swelling of a leathern bottle. More's *History* (1564) is responsible for the persistent legend of Richard's deformity. Hill (1571, 2G5r) identifies a crookback as "a niggard and ill-conditioned." Torrey (2000) describes the classical and early modern association between physical deformity and moral corruption. Rhodes (1977) summarizes modern **physicians**' attempts to diagnose Richard. Detective-story writer Aird and general practitioner McIntosh (1978) point out the associations among Richard's reported symptoms, his abnormal birth presentation, and his being toothed at birth, and speculate that Shakespeare hints at the sexual insufficiency linked to the disorder. Overton recounts the experience of performing Richard as a hunchback (2006).

cure (A) Present-day medical usage imagines a cure to entail the disappearance of **disease** altogether, without recurrence, but historians of medicine suggest that we should consider an early modern "cure" more in the sense of a remission or a respite from symptoms, or in its earliest sense in *OED*, "care" or concern. Early modern healers diagnosed and treated symptoms of **humoral** imbalance, rather than diseases caused by specific organisms or morbid processes within the body, for the most part, and a cure was whatever practice or medicament alleviated that particular symptom, usually by allopathic means (curing by opposites). Such cures might depend for their efficacy upon external treatments such as fomentations, **plasters**, **poultices** and **salves**, as well as upon the timing of the administration of internal elixirs such as **potions** to be taken orally or **clysters** to be inserted rectally. Cure can refer both to the effects of therapy and to the means used for that effect.

Paracelsian cures, however, treated the patient homeopathically—like curing like—by chemical or magical rather than herbal remedies. Key concepts for **Paracelsus** included the belief that the human body formed a microcosm or smaller version of the larger universe, the macrocosm. The human microcosm was the new-created world after Lucifer's fall from Grace, a body that could be redeemed, however, through faith and virtue. Moreover, all earthly objects contained the "signature" or metaphysical sign of their counterparts in heaven. Each disease therefore had its own specific cure, one that shared a correspond-ence or signature with the ailment. Thus **quicksilver** or mercury cured syphilis, because the disease was spread by meretrices who sold their bodies in the marketplace and whose ruling deity was Mercury. Similarly, liverwort and kidneywort cured ailments in the organs that their foliage resembled, and mithridatum, made from, among other things, viper's venom, cured almost any snakebite through its intrinsic virtue. In addition, each patient possessed an *arcanis* or astral body that should be treated through Christian faith, so that the Paracelsian healer worked a spiritual as well as a material cure. The belief in signatures and in the astral body sometimes led to the use of magical amulets to treat or protect the sick and, in the 1630s, to controversial therapies such as the "weapon-salve," in which anointing the weapon that had inflicted the **wound** would cure the sore itself.

(B) Shakespeare puns on "care" and "cure" frequently. "Care is no cure," pronounces Joan of Arc (*1H6* 3.3.3). "Past cure I am, now reason is past care," writes the sonneteer (147.9); medicines for **fever** are useless once the **brain** or rational soul is affected. The saying may be proverbial; "Past cure is still past care," jokes Rosaline (*LLL* 5.2.28). *AWW* uses the phrase or compound-word "past-cure" and the phrase, "past cure" to indicate the seriousness of the King's condition and Helena's miraculous intervention (*AWW* 2.1.121, 158). In *JN* "past cure" is a euphemism for Arthur's **death** (*JN* 4.2.86). Juliet wails, "past hope, past cure, past help!" at the news of her arranged marriage to Paris (*ROM* 4.1.45). Alonso fears that his grief at his son's supposed death is "past cure," until Prospero miraculously produces him (*TMP* 5.1.141). Indeed Prospero's art, like Helena's in *AWW*, can perform magical remedies, "cur[ing] deafness" by the tale of Prospero's exile (*TMP* 1.2.106), and producing "cures" or medicaments out of human flesh, as Prospero imagines: "A solemn air and the best comforter /To an unsettled fancy cure thy brains, Now useless, boil'd within thy skull!" (5.1.58–60)

To **cure** meat is to preserve it for later **consumption** by smoking it. The brains of the Neapolitans have been "boiled" by their frightening experiences and by Prospero's spells, like **mummy** cured or preserved from condemned felons. Prospero, however, will re-cure or refresh their boiled brains with their own remorse and a "solemn air," with a pun on the music that he can provide and the fresh air that will reach their brains and blow away the vapors or **fumes** that confuse them.

H8 presents the old religion as a **sickness** from which the kingdom must be cured; the word cure is applied both in favor of and against Cardinal Wolsey, who turns out to be playing a double game (supporting Henry to his face but working against him behind his back). Lord Sands calls Anne Bullen his "little cure" (punning on cure as concern, or financial charge) right before King Henry dances with her for the first time (*H8* 1.4.33). While Norfolk and others blame "the bold, bad man" Wolsey, the King calls him "a cure fit for a king" (2.2.75). Wolsey himself disingenuously disavows any **spleen** or malice against Katharine, claiming, "in him /It lies to cure me: and the cure is, to /Remove these thoughts from you" (2.4.101), and, later, "We are to cure such sorrows, not to sow them" (3.1.158). When his letter to Rome is discovered, he rages, "Is there no way to cure this?" (3.2.216)—but such sickness is mortal. Wolsey falls out of favor and the kingdom recovers its (Protestant) health. In *MM*, while waiting too long might leave one "past cure" (2.1.111), cures at any time might kill the patient as it attempts to "cure" the **ruptures** between affianced lovers (*MM* 3.1.236). Vincentio is fond of justifying his absence—and Angelo's inhuman and hypocritical rigor—by arguing that "severity must cure" the **poxy** wickedness of the kingdom (*MM* 3.2.100), which suffers in a **fever** whose "dissolution" itself "must cure it" (3.2.223). Benvolio similarly urges Romeo to take on a new **infection**, arguing that he needs a homeopathic cure, a new love to drive out the old (*ROM* 1.2.48), and Cardinal Panulph in *JN* suggests that "falsehood falsehood cures, as fire cools fire /Within the scorched **veins** of one new-burn'd," as a **surgeon** might apply heating medicines and salves to burn that risked infection (3.1.277). A cure might also be a **diet** to remedy **surfeit** or an overdose of a particular food (*MM* 2.1.111); Iago seeks to "diet [his] revenge" by inducing in Othello "a jealousy so strong /That judgment cannot cure" (*OTH* 2.1.302).

MAC, however, appears to employ cure in its modern medical sense, the utter banishment of disease. Macbeth urges the doctor to "cure" his wife of her sorrow, an impossible task (5.3.39). In contrast, the king of England, the saintly Edward, successfully cures his subjects of the "King's Evil" or scrofula (see **evil**; 4.3.142, 152), and Malcolm urges Macduff to "make medicines of our great revenge /To cure this deadly grief" (4.3.215).

(C) Joan Lane helpfully writes, "A successful cure for [John] Hall [Shakespeare's son-in-law] was the freedom from symptoms and in most cases the patient's history ends at this point" (1996, xxxix–xl). The case-histories of other physicians and surgeons follow a similar pattern—the cessation, even if temporary, of the presenting symptom is taken for a "cure"—one of the reasons why surgeon Peter Lowe's acknowledgment of the then-incurable nature of **canker** or cancer stands out for its unmitigated honesty (1597).

cyme Generally taken to be a misreading of *cynne*, or senna, a common early modern purgative or laxative. Taken internally, senna is a laxative so powerful that its effects were (and are still) usually tempered with cinnamon, aniseed, or

rhubarb, with which Macbeth couples it in his prescription for Scotland (see discussion under **urine** and **purge**). Dodoens (1595) describes it as **hot** in the second degree, and **dry** in the first, and recommends it for **melancholy** with the warning that it can cause griping pain in the **belly** (2F3v). Gerard (1597) calls it dry to the third degree, and suggests mixing it with ginger or rhubarb (4C4r).

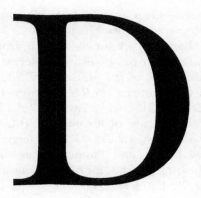

D

darnel Easily confused with wheat, **darnel** is a common weed, although in the seventeenth century it is used to treat **ulcers**, the itch, **leprosy**, the King's **Evil**, **gangrene**, and hip-gout, or **sciatica**. It appears in *LR* as one of "idle weeds" that take sustenance from needful corn (4.4.5). The meadows of France are overgrown with darnel and other wild plants (*H5* 5.2.45); and when Joan La Pucelle tricks the Duke of Burgundy into letting her troops into Rouen by pretending they are selling corn, she mockingly asks him if he liked their wares: " 'Twas full of darnel; do you like the taste?" (*1H6* 3.2.44). For its therapeutic value, see Pechey (1694).

dead men's fingers see **long purples**

deaf See also **ear, earwax** (A) The rarefied air in the inner ear, which mingled with **spirit** and carried sound to the **brain** and its animal or rational spirit, was consumed with old age, and by loud sounds that exhausted the spirit and wore out the tympanum or eardrum. Young persons might be deaf from birth, or become deaf through an excess of **choler** (which should be **purged** appropriately) or, conversely, from thick, clammy, **moist humors** in the **ears** (cured by purging **phlegm** from the brain). **Apoplexies**, **swoons**, lethargies, **palsies**, and other **diseases** of **cold** and old age could also deprive the body of its senses, including hearing, since it deprived the brain (and hence the five senses) of the rational spirit it required in order to process sense-data. The adder was proverbially deaf to the voice or sound of the snake-charmer; hence the deafness of adders alluded to those who were willfully deaf out of self-interest, as in Psalm 63:4–5. Some of the remedies—such as dropping warmed almond oil and onion-juice in one ear at a time, or inserting drops of vinegar in the ear, after which the patient was to hop up and down upon one leg and tilt the head on one side to let moisture run out—suggest that at least one common cause of temporary deafness might have been excessive earwax.

(B) Shakespeare's deaf characters are unable to hear, from physiological weakness, from willful ignorance, or from excessive choler or wrath. Loud clamors such as the "ear-deafening voice of the oracle" (*WT* 3.1.9), or the "deaf'ning, dreadful thunders" of a storm at sea (*PER* 3.1.5) overwhelm the ear. Aegeon is deaf from old age (*ERR* 5.1.317), as is Titus (*TIT* 4.4.98); Caesar's left "ear is deaf," perhaps as a consequence of his **epilepsy** (which was also popularly known as the "little apoplexy"; *JC* 1.2.213). Falstaff feigns deafness in order to avoid paying a bill (*2H4* 1.2.67), and Tamora praises the woods as "ruthless, dreadful, deaf, dull" unhearing grounds for her evil sons whose "deaf ears" there ignore Lavinia's pleas (*TIT* 2.1.128, 2.3.160).

The first tetralogy presents King Henry VI as a pious but ineffectual king who is deaf to his wife's villainy and to the plots against him. "Art thou, like the adder, waxen deaf? /Be poisonous too and kill thy forlorn queen," cries Margaret (*2H6* 3.2.76). Henry mourns over the "dumb, deaf trunk" of Duke Humphrey (3.2.144), but does not realize who has murdered him. "Wrath makes [Clifford] deaf," suggests Margaret (presumably from the choleric humors that have filled his ears; *3H6* 1.4.53). Richard II accuses Mowbray and Bolingbroke of a similar hardness of hearing from choler: "High-stomach'd are they both, and full of ire, /In rage deaf as the sea, hasty as fire" (*R2* 1.1.19). Tybalt is similarly "deaf to peace" and the prince "deaf to pleading and excuses" (*ROM* 3.1.158, 192).

(C) For the humoral origins of deafness, and remedies, see Barrough (1583, E1v); A.T. (1596). Brunschwig's "homish apothecarye" recommends both the **surgeon's box** (wet- or dry-cupping) behind the ears and leaping up and down on one leg after the insertion of ear-drops (1561, B5r).

death (A) The cessation of life, movement, and awareness in the body; the separation of the soul from the body. Onlookers knew death was imminent by certain signs, noted by **Hippocrates** since antiquity: the dying plucked imaginary specks from the bedclothes, spoke hoarsely, and their faces became pinched, their **eyes** sunken, their **noses** sharp, lips loose, forehead **dry**, **skin ashy**-pale or black. Other signs of impending death included **cold**, steadily creeping up the body; a faint and thready **pulse** that gradually grew feebler until it ceased altogether; shallow breath; pallor throughout the body; gradually stiffening limbs; unseeing and then closed eyes; the failure of the other senses; and skin stretched over the face as in a death-mask, as the whole body contracted. Death was final once the soul had parted from the body; some believed that the soul departed through the body's **wounds** or orifices at the moment of death. But then, as indeed now, death might be difficult to diagnose. **Apoplexies, swooning**, "the mother" (*hysterica passio*), and all sorts of falling sicknesses or **epilepsies** could mimic death, as could non-natural poisons that put the consumer into a deep **sleep**. For this reason, some authorities recommended that women who suffered from "the mother" be left unburied for three days after supposed death, in case they were still alive but under a particularly prolonged fit. The standard test for whether breath and life remained in the body was to place downy feathers or threads of cotton at the patient's **nostrils** or mouth; if they moved, the patient was still breathing, no matter how shallowly, and was still alive, even if the **physician** could not detect a faint pulse.

(B) The feather-test, however, fools both King Lear, who thinks Cordelia is alive ("This feather stirs; she lives!" *LR* 3.5.266–7) and Prince Hal, who thinks his father is dead:

> By his gates of breath
> There lies a downy feather which stirs not:
> Did he suspire, that light and weightless down
> Perforce must move.
>
> (*2H4* 4.5.31–4)

The King soon rouses from what turns out to have been the stupor of apoplexy, not death, and accuses his son of wishing, rather than observing, him dead. King Henry VI tries to convince the keepers that he is still sovereign by proving that he is alive, and able to blow a feather, not realizing that proving the vitality of his physical body ("body mortal," in medieval political theory) cannot resuscitate his allegorical, kingly body ("body politic"), which has been taken over by Edward: "Why, am I dead? do I not breathe a man? /Ah, simple men, you know not what you swear! /Look, as I blow this feather from my face . . . !" (*3H6* 3.1.82–4).

Mistress Quickly famously outlines the Hippocratic signs of death in her account of Falstaff's passing away:

> After I saw him fumble with the sheets and play with flowers and smile upon his fingers' ends, I knew there was but one way; for his nose was as sharp as a pen, and a' babbled of green fields. "How now, sir John!" quoth I "what, man! be o' good cheer." So a' cried out "God, God, God!" three or four times. Now I, to comfort him, bid him a' should not think of God; I hoped there was no need to trouble himself with any such thoughts yet. So a' bade me lay more clothes on his feet: I put my hand into the bed and felt them, and they were as cold as any stone; then I felt to his knees, and they were as cold as any stone, and so upward and upward, and all was as cold as any stone.
>
> (*H5* 2.3.14–25)

"Babbled" is the traditional editorial emendation to the Folio's "table," although Fleissner (1983) argues that keeping "table" suggests Falstaff's livid **complexion** and thus adheres more closely to Hippocratic tradition. Quickly's not to think about God is of course, deeply ironic, as is the fact that one of our best descriptions of what happens in early modern death comes from Friar Laurence's description to Juliet of the false death he will induce in her through his **drug**:

> presently through all thy veins shall run
> A cold and drowsy **humor**, for no pulse
> Shall keep his native progress, but surcease:
> No warmth, no breath, shall testify thou livest;
> The roses in thy lips and **cheeks** shall fade
> To paly ashes, thy eyes' windows fall,
> Like death, when he shuts up the day of life;
> Each part, deprived of supple government,
> Shall, stiff and stark and cold, appear like death:
> . . . [a] borrow'd likeness of shrunk death.
>
> (*ROM* 4.1.95–104)

The drug will make her **blood** cold and slow, so that the **heart** constricts and remains still and the **arteries** have no corresponding pulse, since they do not have fresh, spirituous blood to send to the extremities. In the absence of blood and the presence of the cold poison, her body's warmth will cool down and the blood in her face and lips will be used up and not replaced. Her eyes will close and she will be unable to move her limbs, because she will have no blood coming to her **brain** from the heart and thus no vital spirit to warm her nor animal spirit for the rational brain and the five senses to experience sense-data. Even the **liver** will cease producing nutritive blood or natural spirit, so the body will stop growing and become "shrunk."

(C) Lowe (1597, A4v) and others include the Hippocratic prognostics. There is an excellent and extremely full current bibliography on early modern death, dying, and burial. Ariès's brilliantly pithy *Western Attitudes toward Death from the Middle Ages to the Present* (1976; trans. and repr. 1994) is essential reading, but the fullest and more up-to-date treatment of early modern religious traditions surrounding death and the widest array of sources is in Cressy (1997). Countering the assertion of Stone (1983) that high infant mortality rates weakened family ties between parents and children, Cressy amasses evidence from letters, epitaphs, and literature to argue for the deep attachments within the early modern family and the extent of mourning for a lost child or parent or partner. Gittings (1988) surveys historical evidence (including parish records and personal letters) in order to argue for an increasingly alienated view of death in the twentieth century. She contrasts the present time to an imagined early modern past (similar to Ariès's account) in which death, preparations for death, mortal illness, infant loss, and funerals formed a regular part of life and in which such topics were not taboo or discouraged from discussion. Unlike Cressy, however, Gittings agrees with Stone that sixteenth- and seventeenth-century mourners grieved their lost ones less profoundly than the present-day bereaved because of this constant awareness of death and mortality. Doebler (1994) discusses both visual icons such as woodcuts and written accounts of the *ars moriendi* or art of dying, the notion of the "good death" in early modern culture; Becker (2003) considers with sophistication the extent to which early modern women had to mimic supposedly masculine virtues such as stoicism in order to endure a "good death" as part of her excellent study, *Death and the Early Modern Englishwoman*. Dollimore (2001, 102–10) includes a chapter about desire and death in Shakespeare's sonnets in his larger treatment of death and eros in Western culture. Phillippy (2002) helpfully investigates the material work of women in preparing bodies for burial and women's increasing reluctance for their own bodies to be embalmed (opened and filled with balm to preserve the corpse from putrefaction) and the gendering of women's grief and mourning rituals in early modern literature and culture. Dobson (2003) provides useful tables of mortality from disease in various parishes and of the mortal illnesses thought to proceed from different kinds of foul air or *miasma*. Cregan revisits the well-known story of the opened, embalmed, and finally exploding corpse of Queen Elizabeth I in order to make a large epistemological argument about the gradual systematizing of bodily knowledge (and the gendering of that knowledge) in early modern England (2009). Turner's essay on cognitive science and Shakespearean "blended metaphors" of death (Death as a French Warrior in the history plays; the Ghost as a blended space of an enlivened but dead human body in *HAM*) offers many new ways of looking at Shakespeare's enacted and figurative deaths (2004).

decoct See also **barley-broth** Shakespeare's single use of this technical term is figurative. A decoction was a medicament made by boiling leaves, roots, or other plant parts in water that was then drunk. The French Constable complains that the English climate itself breeds **diseases** because of its cold, and that the English are therefore pallid and cowardly. Their barley-broth is fit food for old horses, mostly "sodden water," and so he wonders whence they get their courage:

> Can sodden water,
> A drench for sur-rein'd jades, their barley-broth,
> Decoct their cold **blood** to such valiant **heat**?
> And shall our quick blood, spirited with wine,
> Seem frosty?
>
> (*H5* 3.5.18–22)

Wine encouraged production of **spirit**, especially of the animal spirit necessary for action. Yet despite their warm wine, the French seem "frosty," cold and pusillanimous, in comparison to the "valiant" English, whose meager barley-broth boils in their veins as if to decoct or activate their blood and courage.

deform, deformed, deformity See also **hare-lip, mole, monster, prodigy, stigmatical** (A) Misshapen, usually from birth, though also from humoral excesses, from **disease**, or from witchcraft. Infants were born with supernumerary digits, moles, hare-lips, scales, fur, and other variations because of impurities in the seminal **humor** or **seed** of either parent. The mother provided the matter or stuff of which the infant was made, the father its shape or form, so that a deformed infant demonstrated in its shape the failure of its parents properly to conceive a child.

(B) Medical treatises blamed ill-composed parental seed for deformities in the offspring, but Shakespeare's characters may be deformed by witchcraft, time, beauty, love, and fashion. Richard III is deformed in the standard sense, "Deform'd, unfinish'd, sent before my time /Into this breathing world, scarce half made up," the process of physical shaping in the womb incomplete because of his premature birth (R3 1.1.20–1). Antipholus of Syracuse is convinced that Ephesus is a den of sorcery, full of "soul-killing witches that deform the body" (1.2.100). Jealous Adriana complains that the man whom she thinks is her husband—the hapless Antipholus of Syracuse, whom she has taken to be his twin of Ephesus—is "deformed, crooked, old and sere." Her sister, courted by Antipholus of Syracuse, very reasonably retorts, "Who would then be jealous of such a one?" (*ERR* 4.2.19). Adriana here implies that her husband has been "deformed" and made stigmatical (branded) by a malignant external agent. The father of both Antipholuses, Aegeon, blames the "deformed hand" of time, rather than witchcraft, for the failure of Antipholus and Dromio of Ephesus to recognize him.

Holofernes, the pedantic schoolmaster in *LLL*, expostulates, "monster Ignorance, how deformed dost thou look!" (4.2.23, see discussion under **monster**). Berowne compares the beauty of the Princess and her Ladies to a defective eye-spirit that, "Varying in subjects as the **eye** doth roll /To every varied object in his glance" has "much deform'd us, fashioning our humors /Even to the opposed end of our intents" (*LLL* 5.2.757). Vision in Shakespeare—especially that of lovers—adheres to a classical model in which the eye emits spirit or rays that mingle with the rays or *pneuma* sent out by an object and then return to the eye. In this instance, the ladies' beauty has convinced the scholars to forego their vow of celibate study in favor of courtship and has thus deformed their intentions. Speed teases Valentine by suggesting that Sylvia has been deformed by his love for her, before which she was beautiful (*TGV* 2.1.63). Sonnet 113 reverses the metaphor:

> For if it see the rudest or gentlest sight,
> The most sweet favour or deformed'st creature,
> The mountain or the sea, the day or night,
> The crow or dove, it shapes them to your feature:
> Incapable of more, replete with you,
> My most true mind thus makes mine eye untrue.
>
> (9–14)

The sight of the beautiful beloved can make even deformed or ugly or frightening creatures handsome, reformed and recreated by eye-beams that come directly from the lover's **brain** after touching the beautiful form of the lover. His eye-spirit is completely used up by gazing upon his lover and he has literally no eyes for anything else (see **eye**). Rejected, as he believes, by Sebastian, Antonio suggests that "None can be call'd deform'd but the unkind: /Virtue is beauty," and the handsome Sebastian has deformed himself by his treachery (*TN* 3.4.368).

ADO features a series of excruciating puns on the word as the watchmen over-hear Conrade and Borachio triumphing at the success of their plot to sully Hero's reputation but are unable to make sense of their conversation. When Borachio calls "fashion" a "deformed thief" (3.3.124, 130), the first watchman misunderstands the metaphor to refer to a real gentleman-thief by the name of "Deformed" (3.3.125, 169, 172). The second, however, understands the plan to be a "piece of lechery" and arrests the malefactors, only for Leonato to dismiss the interrogation to the incompetent Dogberry and Verges in 3.5 because he is in haste to attend his daughter's wedding. The imaginary thief Deformed reappears as Dogberry finally reveals the plot to Leonato and Claudio is seized with remorse (5.1.308). The puns on deformed implicitly present the plot as a monstrous birth, a connection made by the second watchman as he threatens the schemers, "You'll be made bring Deformed forth" (3.3.172).

(C) *Two Remarkable and True Histories* (1620) recounts how "a maruellous deformed monster was found in the belly of a cow" in 1619. Paré (1634) writes at length about "Monsters and Prodigies" in Chapter 25 of his *Workes*, concluding that most monsters or deformed infants are born to persons with defective seed. Lucking (1997) discusses the puns on Deformed in *ADO*.

diet See also **complexion, excrement, humor, purge, stomach, surfeit** (A) Diet referred to the food and drink appropriate for one's complexion or humoral temperament and consumed on a regular basis, to the fasting or special regimens undertaken in response to **disease** (especially diseases of surfeit or overeating), and to food and board at an inn or lodging. Food and drink formed an essential part of humoral medicine. Like air, water, soil, and human bodies, comestibles too partook of qualities such as moistness, **dryness**, **heat**, or chill and must be taken accordingly. Thus **lettuce** was a cooling food and so often prescribed to **choleric** persons or those recovering from **fevers**; women suffering from an excess of **cold, moist** phlegm might be encouraged to eat warming foods such as lamb. It was particularly important to diet oneself after surfeit, or overeating, to restore the body's natural balance. By extension, diet can serve as a shorthand for an entire way of life, including exercise, **sleep** habits, and sexual activity.

(B) Diet refers to mere subsistence for the mercenaries employed by Fortinbras — lawless (in the quartos) or landless (in the Folio)—soldiers who have nothing to lose and who therefore fight for him in return for "food and diet" (*HAM* 1.1.99). The Hostess charges Falstaff for his "diet and by-drinkings," his regular food and the extra sack he sips on the side (*1H4* 3.3.73). Antonio requests and pays for his and Sebastian's "diet at the inn" where they stay in Illyria (*TN* 3.3.40).

Richard of Gloucester establishes Edward's ill-health and bad habits in order to lay the ground for possibly murdering him, and to blame him for self-indulgence: "he hath kept an evil diet long, /And overmuch consumed his royal person" (*R3* 1.1.139). Cleopatra worries that inhaling the foul breath of common people when she is led in triumph through Rome will make her **sick**, because their breath, "rank of gross diet," stinking from the coarse and unrefined food they eat, contains the "vapour" of undigested food that could trigger a humoral reaction in one exposed to it (*ANT* 5.2.212). The Archbishop of York prescribes for the English a course of military action "to diet rank minds sick of happiness" (*2H4* 4.1.64), arguing that too much good fortune or peace creates the gross or "rank" **vapors** that cause disease. Yet a healthy diet might not necessarily indicate temperance and morality: the conspirators in *H5* are "spare in diet, /Free from gross passion or of mirth or anger, /Constant in spirit, not swerving with the **blood**," and yet betrayed their king (*H5* 2.2.131), and Iago feeds upon misinformation "to diet [his] revenge" (*OTH* 2.1.294); the food appropriate for the complexion of his vengeance is Cassio's dismissal. Cassio fears that keeping his distance from Othello, as Desdemona recommends, is too "nice and waterish [a] diet," too careful and **phlegmatic** a food for his warlike commander, who will forget about him altogether (*OTH* 3.3.15). Dieting or fasting was integral to the working of certain **cures**, such as the sweating-tub or tub-fast for syphilis or **pox** (*TIM* 4.3.88; see **tub-fast**); hence Lucio explains that "one . . . past cure" might still recover if "they kept very good diet" (*MM* 2.1.112). Even undiseased love might make one "fast, like one that takes diet" (*TGV* 2.1.24). Adriana describes one of the duties of a noble wife to "diet [her husband's] sickness" (*ERR* 5.1.99). Therapeutic diets may also be punitive in intention. Timon's misanthropy leads him to see all men as equally corrupt, and their habits as equivalent. "Your diet shall be in all places alike," he remarks at the mock-banquet. The stones and lukewarm, "reeking" water he serves have scatological analogues (feces and **urine**) that evoke the distasteful bodily products of real banquets (*TIM* 3.6.66). Diana interprets Bertram's refusal to acknowledge her as his attempt to "diet" her, to starve her of love and recognition (*AWW* 5.3.221). "Thou art all the comfort /The gods will diet me with" says Imogen of Pisanio's plan for her; she has surfeited on Posthumus' love and must now undergo the remedial dieting or fasting in banishment from him (*CYM* 3.4.180).

In one instance Shakespeare puns on "diet" to mean a meeting, alluding to the famous "Diet of Worms" or the meeting of the Holy Roman Empire at Worms in 1521 to discuss Martin Luther and the Reformation. Hamlet describes the decomposition of Polonius' body as the work of "a certain convocation of politic worms" (*HAM* 4.3.20) concluding, "Your worm is your only emperor for diet" (4.3.21); human bodies end up as the diet of worms, whether they are emperors or servants. (C) Dietaries are tremendously popular in the period, often going through multiple editions. The famous "School of Salerno" offered a guide published in English as the *Regimen Sanitatem Salerni* (1528), or the Salernian Regimen of Health. Elyot (1539) outlines the basic theory of the four temperaments and specific guidelines on the kinds of diet each ought to follow, as does Boorde (1542). Furnivall's edition (1870) helpfully collects and abstracts the various dietaries and regimens of Andrew Boorde (1547–48). Appleby (1979) investigates "diet" in its modern sense—what people in the period actually ate—in sixteenth-century

England, noting the contrast between the widespread malnutrition of the poor and the overindulgence of the wealthy. Fitzpatrick (2007) offers both a general overview of dietary advice in the period and specific readings of the plays, such as Jaques' compassion for the deer in *AYL* in the context of early modern vegetarianism; see also Fitzpatrick (2011), *Shakespeare and the Language of Food*.

disease (A) An ailment, **malady**, **illness**, caused by **distemper** or the imbalance of **humors** within the whole body or part of the body.
(B) Such ills are sometimes political, "foul disease[s]" (*HAM* 4.1.21; *LR* 1.1.174) within "the body of [the] kingdom" (*2H4* 3.1.38) that can be cured only by **purge** (*MAC* 5.3.51–2) or "bleed[ing]" (*2H4* 4.1.57). Occasionally the political rebel is a **canker** or tumor, "a disease that must be cut away" (*COR* 3.1.293), or boils, "diseases in our bodies" such as "We do lance" (*ANT* 5.1.37–8). Literal diseases or illnesses include "the King's disease," cured by Helena (*AWW* 1.1.23, 228), the "**rheumatic** diseases" visited upon the earth by the quarrels of the fairies (*MND* 2.1.105), the venereal "Diseases . . . sold dearer than **physic**" in the brothel where Marina is trapped (*PER* 4.6.98), or mental troubles, such as the sleepwalking disorder that is a "disease . . . beyond [his] practice," a malady of the mind, not the body, that the Doctor cannot **cure** (*MAC* 5.1.59). For Shylock, the capacity to be "subject to the same diseases" renders Christian and Jew equally human (*MV* 3.1.62). Pandarus at first accuses his audience of suffering from sexually transmitted **infections** and then offers to seek a cure and then to visit his ailments upon his admirers and critics alike: "Till then I'll **sweat** and seek about for eases, /And at that time bequeath you my diseases" (*TRO* 5.10.55–6). Venus lists several distinct "maladies" (*VEN* 745) or diseases from which human beings suffer as part of her campaign to convince Adonis to consummate their love before his beauty fades:

> As burning **fevers**, **agues** pale and faint,
> Life-poisoning **pestilence** and **frenzies** wood,
> The **marrow**-eating **sickness**, whose attaint
> Disorder breeds by heating of the **blood**:
> **Surfeits**, **imposthumes**, grief, and damn'd despair,
> Swear nature's **death** for framing thee so fair.
> (*VEN* 739–44)

Burning fevers, unlike **tertians** or **quotidians**, did not remit, heating the patient's body throughout the day and night. Agues rendered sufferers pale, trembling, and cadaverous, in what is for Venus a grotesque parody of the pallor and flush of erotic love. Pestilence or **plague** attacked both individual life and entire cities. Frenzies triggered **madness** by a high fever that overheated the **brain**. "The marrow-eating sickness" is **consumption**, which dried up and heated the body's humors until the patient remained only a husk or shell. Surfeits were self-imposed excesses in food, drink, **sleep**, love, exercise, or other externals that provoked a distemper or humoral imbalance in the body and thus portended sickness. Imposthumes were **ulcers** or sores that swelled up with liquid and could be dangerous to heal. Grief and despair could cause illness by **perturbation** or emotional disturbance.

(C) Barrough (1583) and Bullein (1579) offer an overview of disorders and remedies respectively. Hoeniger (1992) indexes and identifies specific diseases within Shakespeare's plays. See also **medicine, physic.**

distemper, distemperature, distempered, mistempered (A) Early modern bodies required the constant, balanced mixture or tempering of **humors** for optimal mental and physical health. Not only the whole body but each **organ** and limb of the body had its own **complexion** or humoral temperament. If this temperament were out of balance in any way—if any one of the four humors were present in too great or too small an amount, if any humor were too **hot** (adust) or too **cold**, too "sharp" and biting or too thick and dense, for that particular body, body part, or in general, the body's constitution suffered. Lacking a perfect balance, the body and the emotions became distempered, disordered, **diseased**. The **cure** for distemper was always allopathic: tempering one extreme by the addition or mixing of its opposite.

(B) Pisanio offers Imogen a medicine for "distemper" causing **sea-sickness** or a queasy **stomach** on land (*CYM* 3.4.191). Such ills (which we still call "stomach upsets," in a nod to the early modern connection between **gut** and mind) can come from **surfeit** or too much food and drink. Caithness figures Macbeth's tyrannous reign as a man who has over-eaten and is now suffering from the effects of his indulgence: "He cannot buckle his distemper'd cause /Within the belt of rule" (*MAC* 5.2.15–16). Malvolio is "sick of self-love . . ., and taste[s] /with a distempered appetite," one that makes all other food disgusting (1.5.91). Sometimes distemper is the first stage in what can become, if untreated, a major illness. Henry V argues that "little faults, proceeding on distemper" are like the consequences of overeating, and that if the monarch punishes such gluttony excessively, there will be no due recourse for "capital crimes, chew'd, swallow'd and digested" (2.2.54–7). King John blames Panulph for stirring up the people to an unnecessary war with France:

> This inundation of mistemper'd humor
> Rests by you only to be qualified:
> Then pause not; for the present time's so sick,
> That present **medicine** must be minister'd,
> Or overthrow incurable ensues.
>
> (*JN* 5.1.12–16)

Humor is like a flood or inundation that can only be tempered or qualified by the person who caused it, namely Panulph himself. The people require medicine at once, otherwise the mistemperature will become "overthrow incurable," the complete disarray of order and health in the body politic. (Shakespeare's other use of the word mistempered refers to the tempering of metals in weaponry, rather than to bodily health.)

Usually, however, distemper refers to a moral or emotional upheaval. Helena's teardrop shimmers like a "distemper'd messenger of wet," says the Countess Rousillion, a sign of her distress (1.3.151). More frequently, distempered individuals suffer from an excess of **choler** from anger or jealousy, "hot passion[s] of distempered **blood**" (*TRO* 2.2.169). Master Ford's jealousy is a "distemper" (*WIV* 3.3.216, 3.5.76) so opposed to reason that, says Mistress Page, "any **madness** I ever yet beheld seemed but tameness, civility and patience, to this his distemper he is in now" (4.2.28). Ford's jealousy is again defined by opposites, but treated in the play through homeopathy (encouraging him to greater jealousy by the trick the wives play on Falstaff) rather than allopathy (assuaging his fears and letting him in on the joke, the ultimate **cure** at the end of the play). Leontes' jealousy is more dangerous and leads to seemingly mortal illness; Camillo calls it

> a sickness
> Which puts some of us in distemper, but
> I cannot name the disease; and it is caught
> Of you that yet are well.
>
> (*WT* 1.2.384–7)

Camillo is distempered or out of temper, distressed, by Leontes' unfounded jealousy; he cannot name it, because it is so shameful; and Leontes, ill himself, suspects the healthy relations between Polixenes and Hermione of being sickening adultery.

Hamlet's "distemper" is mysterious to Claudius and to his spies Rosencrantz and Guildenstern, but tentatively diagnosed as grief, love, or ambition (2.2.55, 3.2.337). The sight of the ghost in Gertrude's chamber, however, triggers a distemper that stands his **hair** on end and makes his **eyes** stare, a **malady** that Gertrude calls "the heat and flame of thy distemper," that is a choleric, hot, **dry** imbalance, and bids him calm with "cool patience" (3.4.123–4). Claudius himself is "distemper'd"—by drink, impudently suggests his stepson, or with choler, warns Guildenstern (3.2.301–6). Warwick's advice to the distempered Northumberland resembles Gertrude's to Hamlet: "good advice and little **medicine**" will "cool" the hot, distempered humor of his anger (*2H4* 3.1.41–4).

Stars were known to affect or distemper both health and fortune; such ill-luck might prove **contagious**, like a full-blown disease, as Sebastian observes: "My stars shine darkly over me: the malignancy of my fate might perhaps distemper yours" (*TN* 2.1.3–5). Cardinal Panulph complains bitterly about such superstition when he claims that John's ill-wishers interpret even ordinary changes in the weather as

> no distemper'd day,
> No common wind, no customed event,
> But they will pluck away his natural cause

> And call them meteors, **prodigies** and signs
> . . .
> Plainly denouncing vengeance upon John.
> > (*JN* 3.4.154–60)

Age, likewise, caused what Friar Laurence calls "distemperature," as the elderly became progressively colder, dryer, and more **melancholy**, affecting their **sleep**. Laurence is so concerned at Romeo's early rising that he drops into verse *sententiae.*

> Young son, it argues a distemper'd head
> So soon to bid good morrow to thy bed:
> Care keeps his watch in every old man's eye,
> And where care lodges, sleep will never lie;
> But where unbruised youth with unstuff'd **brain**
> Doth couch his limbs, there golden sleep doth reign:
> Therefore thy earliness doth me assure
> Thou art up-roused by some distemperature.
> > (*ROM* 2.3.33–40)

Care or anxiety keeps old men awake, pushing sleep out of the brain just as it pushes old men from their beds. But just as young men's bodies are hale and strong, and old men's bodies **bruise** easily from the thinness of their wrinkled skins, so their brains have space within for sleep, where the elderly brain is filled with too much **phlegm** and too many thoughts. Thus Romeo must have been awakened by anxiety—or, the Friar adds, he has never gone to bed.

TMP presents a crux: Miranda comments when Prospero becomes aware of the plot to kill him, "Never till this day /Saw I him touched with anger, so distemper'd" (4.1.144–5). She either means that she has never seen him touched with anger before (in which case all anger is by its nature "distempered," unbalanced), or that (if we remove the comma) she has never before seen him in a state of anger so extreme.

(C) Early modern sources use the term distemper to refer to a humoral imbalance in a particular fluid or organ, as in Baley (1588, A2v), who recommends the peppery medicine "*diatrion pipereon*" to warm the body because it does so without "distemper[ing] the blood," for a disease or disorder, as in Barrough (1583, passim), and for the process of tempering or combining medicines, as in Goeurot, who uses it routinely in place of the word "temper," recommending for a cold **liver** one should "Take syxe drammes of [the purge] diafinicon . . . distemper it in .iiii. ounces of the decoccion of the rootes of smalache [pimpernel], percely [parsley], fenell, & drinke it luke warme v. or .vi. houres afore meate" (1550, G8r). Book II of Spenser's *Faerie Queene* (1590) is called "The Book of Temperance," praising the Aristotelian virtue of moderation or temperance and including a sustained allegory of the early modern humoral body (minus the genitals) in the Castle of Alma in Canto 9.

distil, distilled, distillation See also **alchemy, limbeck** (A) Used intransitively, the verb **distil** means to condense or flow or moisten, especially of a fine **vapor** in minute drops, like dew; used transitively, it refers to the process of chemical purification and refinement used even before the advent of **Paracelsian** "chemical" medicine in England to extract herbal ingredients, to refine sugar and to process alcohol. The key to distillation was the separation of parts, of pure from impure, useful from waste, or, in cases where every part of the plant or substance was useful, of root from seed or leaf from flower, so that each could be used for its particular **cure** or function. Just as in the body, **heat** was the primary mechanism for distillation. The substance to be purified was placed in the glass cucurbit (named for its shape, a round body with a long neck, like a crookneck squash), either with water or wine, or, in the case of flowers, alone. On top of the cucurbit the distiller placed the alembic (limbeck) or head, a cap that included a long pipe pointing downwards, sometimes called a **nose**. The nose or pipe rested on or directly above a **receipt** or receiver, which would contain the purified product. In warm climates, liquids could be distilled in the sun, but in England and Germany, chemists heated the cucurbit over a furnace or in a double boiler (some recipes used heating in ashes, some used wood chips and so on). Fluid condensed in the alembic and, as it cooled, liquefied again and dripped into the receiver. Sometimes chemists used the **urinal**, with its wider neck, instead of the cucurbit, especially if they needed to distil a "less tender" liquid, or a thick, **phlegmatic** one, or wanted a speedier delivery (Gesner 1576, D3v), or the Pelican, with two handles and a long neck. Distilled **perfumes** and **medicines** could be stored in small **vials** of glass.

(B) Shakespeare's characters refer to distillation in both its transitive and intransitive senses. Titus imagines his tears as simultaneously the natural rain that drops from clouds upon the soil and as the chemical product of distillation from his **eyes**: "O earth, I will befriend thee more with rain /That shall distil from these two ancient urns /Than youthful April shall with all his showers" (*TIT* 3.1.16–18). *OED* gives the first use of "urn" as a container or bottle for tears in 1753, but Titus clearly imagines his eyes as vials containing therapeutic or at least magical potions, as part of the popular tradition of using human body products as medicine (see **mummy**).

The sestet of Sonnet 5 refers in exquisite detail to the process of distilling flowers to make perfume. In a seasonal comparison, winter chills summer and blights its flowers;

> were not summer's distillation left,
> A liquid prisoner pent in walls of glass,
> Beauty's effect with beauty were bereft,
> Nor it nor no remembrance what it was:
> But flowers distill'd though they with winter meet,
> Leese but their show; their substance still lives sweet.

The "liquid prisoner" is, beautifully, the water or fluid evaporated from summer's flower petals in the alembic and turned into fragrance. Just as distillation can extract the most valuable part of the flower (its scent) even though the blooms' physical appearance is altered, so the beloved will fade with time unless his essence is distilled or extracted (through poetry, or through the generation of offspring). Sonnet 6 refers back in its first three lines to the distillation of summer flowers to sweeten the winter: "Then let not winter's ragged hand deface, /In thee thy summer, ere thou be distill'd: Make sweet some vial."

Sonnet 54 specifies the flowers to be preserved in this way, and clarifies, as it were, that the distillation is the process of writing poetry. Summer's "Sweet roses" do not vanish altogether, because "Of their sweet **deaths** are sweetest odours made: /And so of you, beauteous and lovely youth, /When that shall fade, my verse distills your truth." Parolles tries to convince Helena that Bertram's flight from her will "distil" or purify the "sweets" of consummation, like perfume in a vial that will "o'erflow with joy /And pleasure drown the brim" (*AWW* 2.4.45–7).

The wicked queen in *Cymbeline* takes advantage of the injunction to good housekeepers to **physic** their families, turning the lessons she has had from Doctor Cornelius in perfumery, distillation, and making conserves to an apprenticeship in poisoning. "Hast thou not learn'd me how /To make perfumes? distil? Preserve?" (*CYM* 1.5.12–13), she challenges him, in response to his concern about her request for a strong toxin. Equating the distillation of medicines and poisons with making conserves to eat and perfumes for the closet covers her evil intentions beneath domesticity. King Henry V also links distillation to "good husbandry" such as early rising, and to the separation of useful or pure matter from dross or waste, as in chemistry:

> There is some soul of goodness in things evil,
> Would men observingly distil it out.
> For our bad neighbour makes us early stirrers,
> Which is both healthful and good husbandry.
>
> (*H5* 4.1.4–7)

France makes England wake early in the morning, a practice known to be good for the body and practical for completing tasks. Thus the "evil" of battle has a "soul of goodness" that chemists can carefully heat, vaporize, and condense for **consumption**. A famous crux in *Hamlet* describes (only in the second quarto) those who have seen the Ghost as "distilled /Almost to jelly" (*HAM* 1.2.204–5), almost melted away in fear, turned to a semi-solid state like a fruit conserve. Finally, Falstaff, trapped in the buck-basket, is "stopped in, like a strong distillation, with stinking clothes that fretted in their own grease," stewed as if in a *balneum Mariae* "like a Dutch dish" (*WIV* 3.5.113, 119).

(C) The longest and best-illustrated source is Gesner, translated by Baker (1599). For an illustration of the *balneum Mariae* or *bain-marie*, see Gesner (1599, B5r).

Henry Platt offers recipes for ladies to make perfumes, medicines, and sweets (1602). Simonds (1999) describes the distillation process as part of her analysis of alchemical metaphors and hermaphroditism in Shakespeare; see also Moran (2005), who describes at length the sometimes overlooked or patronized contributions of alchemy to modern chemistry and to the scientific method. Wall interprets Shakespeare's references to "jelly" in the context of early modern candying, distilling, and the production of gelatin (2006). On food and cooking processes in general in early modern England, including how preserves of fruit, vegetables, and purified (distilled) liquids were made, see Fitzpatrick (2007).

distraction see **lunacy, madness**

dizzy, giddy. See also **apoplexy, epilepsy** (A) Many called vertigo or dizziness, when the patient imagined that his head was turning around, or where his surroundings darkened suddenly and swam around him, "the little epilepsy." Like epilepsy, vertigo resulted from either a disturbance in the **brain**, or from **vapors** or **fumes**, "windy **humors**" that came from poorly digested food in the **stomach**, traveled up to the **brain** and there blew about the animal **spirit** in circles, rendering the **patient** dizzy. Often patients had **cold complexions** and lacked the **heat** necessary for the proper digestion of food. Seeing a person, a wheel, or a whirlpool turning might also make one dizzy because the eye-spirit returning to the **eye** and bearing the vision of the revolving object spun around and triggered a corresponding motion in the animal spirit in the brain. Convection currents from sunshine heating the spirits in the brain also spun the humors around and made one dizzy. Unlike in epilepsy, however, patients retained control of their movements, and retained consciousness. Vertigo was potentially serious as a harbinger of apoplexy, however, and needed to be treated with care. Patients should avoid any foods that were too hard for them to digest and that generated "wind" or vapor. Pleasant smells, friction on the temples, **purges**, **clysters** or laxatives, cupping-glasses applied to the back of the head (to cause scarification) and, in serious cases, letting **blood** from the head-vein or from the **arteries** above the ears, on the temples, could relieve attacks. From the 1610s onward references to "vertigo" appear in tracts praising tobacco, which is recommended as a **cure**. Figuratively, "giddy" and "dizzy" heads were easily distractible, shallow in feeling, and untrustworthy.
(B) The triggers for vertigo to which Shakespeare alludes are more familiar from everyday life than from the medical treatises. Characters' heads spin from a choppy sea, from acrophobia, from loud noises, from looking at numbers, from moving at speed, from an incipient **faint** or apoplexy from concussion, from mad love, and from turning themselves around. King Henry IV describes the ship's boy up on the "high and giddy mast" as sleeping better in his elevated roost than does the king (*2H4* 3.1.18). The ship's boy might be expected to suffer from vertigo for two reasons, the turbulent sea and the great height. Edgar uses his imagined vertigo to convince his blinded father that they are climbing a high cliff rather than walking on level ground: "dizzy 'tis, to cast one's eyes so low!" (*LR* 4.6.12). Clarence dreams of the "giddy . . . hatches" of a sinking ship

(*R3* 1.4.17). The "hurricano" or hurricane can "dizzy with . . . clamour," loud noise and turbulence, the ears of both "Neptune" and the sailor (*TRO* 5.2.172–4). Hamlet praises Laertes by claiming that to divide and describe all his virtues would make one's head swim: it "would dozy [dizzy] the arithmetic of memory and yet but yaw neither, in respect of his quick sail" (*HAM* 5.2.114). There are three causes of vertigo in Hamlet's image. First, the lines of numbers confuse the eye; second, the ship yaws or rolls from side-to-side; third, the ship moves quickly.

Dizziness predicts the apoplexy of Henry IV, as does his darkening vision: "my sight fails, and my brain is giddy" (*2H4* 4.4.110), just as King John anticipates fainting at "ill tidings" because of his "giddy" head (4.2.131–2). Henry IV uses giddy figuratively to mean "distractible," advising his son "to busy giddy minds / With foreign quarrels" (*2H4* 4.5.213–14). The Dauphin underestimates Henry V as "a vain, giddy, shallow, humorous youth" (*H5* 2.4.28). The first tetralogy characterizes the common people as a "giddy multitude" that changes its mind so frequently that it both induces vertigo in the beholder and dizzies itself to sickness (*2H6* 2.4.21). The Duke of Gloucester's men "have their giddy brains knock'd out" by thrown rocks; they are giddy from concussion following head-injuries, but also changeable and violent (*1H6* 3.1.83).

Erotic anticipation makes Troilus' head swim: "I am giddy; expectation whirls me round" (*TRO* 3.2.18). Benvolio offers a facetious, allopathic remedy for the giddiness caused by mad love: "Turn giddy, and be holp by backward turning" (*ROM* 1.2.47). *SHR* uses giddiness as an emblem of Katharina's taming. Petruchio renders her "giddy for lack of **sleep**" (4.3.9) but makes her complicit in her taming to such an extent that she defends his strategy in front of her sister and the widow. The widow taunts Petruchio with having wed a shrew because of "giddy" or mad love and of therefore accusing other men of being brow-beaten: "He that is giddy thinks the world turns round." Katharina repeats the sentence bitterly and then launches into her well-known defense of wife-taming (5.2.20, 26).

Cymbeline succumbs to dizziness when he finally realizes that the handsome page-boy Fidele is none but his daughter Imogen, and Posthumus Leonatus to the "staggers" when he realizes that he has cruelly wounded his wife twice: first by planning her murder when he thought she had been unfaithful, and once more when he strikes the "scornful page" Fidele to the ground (*CYM* 4.5).
(C) See Barrough (1583, B2r) for comments about the stomach; Crooke (1615) for a detailed explanation of how the "rowling" of animal spirits in the brain is the main factor in dizziness. Both "C.T." (1615) and Barclay (1614) proffer tobacco as a cure.

dock See also **burdock, burr** Docks are plants distinct from burdock, although Shakespeare sometimes uses the word "dock" for both. Like burdocks, docks are fast-growing weeds, and Shakespeare's Sebastian snidely complains that Prospero's island is planted not with useful crops but with "docks, or mallows"

(*TMP* 2.1.145), just as Burgundy calls them "hateful" plants that drive out helpful fodder such as clover (*H5* 5.2.52). Vicary (1587), however, recommends red dock root to cure a **tetter** or ringworm; *The Good Hous-wife's Treasurie* (1588) recommends yellow dock root for **phlegm** in the **stomach**; and A.T.'s *Rich Store-House or Treasurie* uses it to relieve itching (Tr, 1596).

Doctor She (A) Women of all ranks nursed the **sick** within their households; a good housewife needed to diagnose ailments, to make herbal remedies, and provide primary care for her family. Middle- and lower-class women who attempted to heal those outside their immediate families, however, were the subject of pejorative comment in tracts and treatises by licensed **physicians**, who argued that women lacked the rationality or even the physical strength necessary to effect a **cure**. James VI of Scotland (soon to be James I of England) himself complained about female healers as witches in his *Daemonologie*, and *Newes from Scotland*, published with the king's work, argues that healing or wise-women only cured those whom they had previously bewitched (1597, ed. Harrison 1924). Recent scholarship, however, suggests that women healers of all classes were tolerated and even admired in early modern England to a far greater extent than we previously thought. Traditional histories of medicine have relied upon the printed invectives of licensed physicians, and the records of the Royal **College** itself, but civil records and diaries suggest that not only were women prominent as healers, to a certain extent they were sought out, and successful. Women worked at all levels of the healing professions: as domestic **nurse**-practitioners, and **apothecaries** in their own homes; as **midwives** with regular clients of their own; as **hospital** visitors treating **leprosy**; as apothecaries working alongside their husbands in business; as **plague**-searchers, hired by the council to brave houses of **disease** and diagnose the dead; as wise-women or herbalists in towns, villages, and cities; as specialists in the treatment of ocular and venereal diseases; as unlicensed but popular and effective **empirics** in the City of London. So far from being controversial, the activity of women healers was "business as usual" (Harkness 2008, 59).

(B) Lafew introduces Helena to the King as "Doctor She!" able to "breathe life into a stone" and able to raise King Pippin with the mere touch of her hand (*AWW* 2.1.79, 73). Tellingly, Lafew begins by describing Helen's powers in magical, even erotic terms before he uses the word "doctor" to define her, and then explains the qualities that make him dub her thus: "her sex, her years, profession, /Wisdom and constancy" (2.1.84). Her youth and her femininity belie the serious and sustained study of medicine that she has undertaken.

(C) Anti-woman diatribes include King James's *Daemonologie* (1597) and the appended pamphlet *Newes from Scotland* (Harrison 1924, 1597); Cotta (1617) devotes an entire chapter to the failings of the female practitioner. Pelling and White (2003), and Harkness (2008) have uncovered records showing the popularity and ubiquity of female healers; see also Fissell (2004). Leong (2008) helpfully breaks down the kinds of **medicines** women made at home, and how they prescribed them. Kerwin (2005) suggests that "the word,"—that is, the name "practitioner"—gave offence, rather than "the deed," the practice itself, and both Kerwin and Pettigrew (2007) comment that Helena's triumph represents in the play something peculiar to her as an artist. Stensgaard (1972) suggests that *AWW* evokes both **Galen** and **Paracelsus** in order to cast Helena as one of a class of "honest empirics," well-meaning, often effective, lay-healers associated with neither the Galenic humoralism of the College nor the effrontery (and quackery) of the upstart Paracelsians.

dozy see **dizzy**

dram From the Greek word *drachma*, a **dram** in apothecaries' weight was one-eighth of an ounce. of powder or solid matter or 1 fl. oz. of liquid, or 60 grains. A dram weighed three times as much as a **scruple**. Shakespeare usually uses it in its technical sense, to describe a measure of a **medicine** (most often, a poison) taken orally. **Apothecary** weights were the same as jewelers' troy weights (see **prescription**). For "dram" as a term for a laughably small amount, see discussion under **scruple**. Drams are often used for ill, rather than to heal. The queen in *TNK* lists as means of suicide "cords, knives, drams, precipitance" (1.1.142).

Romeo demands "A dram of poison" from the apothecary (*ROM* 5.1.60). Brabantio believes that Othello has drugged his daughter "with some mixtures powerful o'er the **blood**, /Or with some dram conjured to this effect" (*OTH* 1.3.104–5). *CYM* and *WT* use the dram as a measure of medicine, and, by extension, of female corruption and virtue. Iachimo comments on the market for **mummy** when he impugns Imogen's chastity: "If you buy ladies' flesh at a million a dram, you cannot preserve it from tainting" (1.4.135). Pisanio offers Imogen "a dram of [the queen's medicine to] drive away **distemper**," although he has substituted a sleeping-draught for the deadly poison the queen had requested (see **contagion**; *CYM* 3.4.190). Cloten uses the dram as a troy measure to complain about Posthumus, "From whose so many weights of baseness cannot /A dram of worth be drawn" (*CYM* 3.5.89). The anagnorisis or recognition-scene in 5.5 depends again upon Pisanio, who explains that Imogen was not dead but slept, "By the queen's dram she swallow'd." In *WT*, Camillo refuses to kill Hermione, even with a "lingering dram that should not work /Maliciously like poison" (1.2.320–1). Later, Antigonus, too, refuses to believe that Hermione is adulterous, and argues the contrary, that her flesh is medicinal rather than corrupt: "every dram of women's flesh is false, if she be" (*WT* 2.1.138). Finally, Autolycus' mock-curse imagines the Shepherd's son tortured until he is "three quarters and a dram dead," where the dram measures implausible degrees (4.4.785). Figurative uses include *MV* 4.1.6, when the Duke claims that Shylock lacks "any dram of mercy" and *TIM*, where the people offer "a recompense more fruitful /Than their offence can weigh down by the dram" (5.1.1501).

dropsies, dropsy (A) **Dropsy** swelled up the whole body with superfluous fluids or **moisture** that had not been properly concocted in the **liver**. The liver was responsible for the so-called second concoction, which turned the chyle manufactured in the **stomach** from food into **blood** and **humors** to nourish specific parts of the body. If the liver were imbalanced—too **hot** and moist, too **cold** and moist, too hot and **dry**, or too cold and dry— any one of three or four different dropsies could afflict the patient. In all cases, the **distempered** liver failed to digest the chyle fully, leaving an excess of humors and moisture in the body that settled predominantly in the **belly**. Those who ate too much meat, and whose bodies produced too much salt or watery **phlegm**, were particularly prone to the dropsy. Patients sometimes experienced an inordinate thirst, and yet no matter how much they drank, they were never slaked. **Cures** varied depending on the **complexion** of patients and the kind of dropsy afflicting them, but anything that encouraged the passing of gas would help.

(B) It is tempting to think that Falstaff, whom Hall calls "that swollen parcel of dropsies, that huge bombard of sack" suffers from the kind of dropsy in which the bellies of sufferers swell up like a sounding "bottle" (Batman 1582, L5r) or bag; Falstaff in this figure himself becomes the leathern bottle of liquor that he consumes (*1H4* 2.4.451). The King in *AWW* comments on the hollowness of riches or title without merit: "Where great additions swell's, and virtue none, /It is a dropsied honour" (2.3.127–8). Such prizes puff up the recipient like a joint full of fluid, deforming the body without enhancing its strength. The King may also allude to the greed of such nobles for more recognitions; like dropsied patients demanding water, their thirst is never satisfied. Caliban curses, "the dropsy drown this fool!" (*TMP* 4.1.230), alluding again to the fluid that over-whelmed sufferers, sometimes as a result of intemperate eating or drinking.

(C) Johannes de Mediolano's *Regimen Sanitatis* identifies three kinds of dropsy, including the **colic**, and suggests that dropsical moisture rising to the head causes vertigo or **dizziness**; each of these are disorders of too much cold, and each causes inordinate thirst (1528 and 1541). Batman identifies four different dropsies, each settling in the stomach (1582).

drug, drugs See also **compound, death, medicine, physic** Shakespeare's age saw the development of the word's meaning from an ingredient in cooking, medicine, or any kind of work, to a substance specifically used for healing **disease** or in order to create some sort of physiological effect upon the body (*OED*, drug, sb. 1). In all instances but one, Shakespeare's drugs are dangerous where medicines may be healthful. The **apothecary's** "drugs are quick," says Romeo (5.3.120), but they are "mortal drugs," that he ought not to be selling. Lucianus, whom Hamlet has recast as "nephew to the King," enters with "drugs fit" to perform a murder (3.2.254). Doctor Cornelius rightly suspects Cymbe-line's queen of preparing poisons, and resolves not to trust her with "A drug of such damned nature" (*CYM* 1.5.36), a phrase that Imogen echoes when she fears that "drug-damn'd Italy" has confounded her husband (3.4.15). The Queen gloats that Pisanio has one of her drugs (3.5.57), and when Imogen drinks it she finds that it is not "precious and cordial" but "Murderous" to her, since she awakes beside what she believes to be the corpse of her husband (4.2.38, 326–7). Cleopatra equates "knife, drug, serpents" as all means of suicide (*ANT* 4.15.25). Macbeth wishes he were a "**purgative** drug" to void Scotland of the English (*MAC* 5.4.55). Brabantio worries that Othello has cast a spell upon his daughter with "drugs or minerals" in order to make her love him (1.2.73), and sonnet 118 concludes, "Drugs poison him that so fell sick of you" (line 14); the poet's **love-sickness** is past **cure**. In this context, it is unsurprising that the Abbess promises that she will revive Antipholus' reason with what she carefully describes as "*wholesome* . . . drugs" (*ERR* 1.5.104; emphasis mine), and perhaps equally unsurprising that Adriana should be suspicious of her motives.

dry, dryness See also **cold, complexion, heat, humor, moisture** Dryness or aridity was one of the four qualities that contributed toward the humoral temperament or complexion of human beings, animals, plants, minerals, and bodily fluids. **Choler** was hot and dry, while **melancholy** was cold and dry. The "choleric" Antipholus of Syracuse his servant with a "dry basting" (dry because no moisture is involved, only the heat of his anger, *ERR* 2.2.63). Hotspur is "dry with rage" at the sight of a **perfumed** courtier who approaches him on the battlefield (*1H4* 1.3.31). Although young persons might be choleric, dryness was usually an affliction of age, causing **cramps** like the "dry convulsions" with which Prospero racks Caliban and his co-conspirators (*TMP* 4.1.259). **Pox** might dry out one's bones and joints, causing **sciatica** or hip-gout, "the dryness of . . . bones" that Octavius wishes upon the epicurean Antony (*ANT* 1.4.27). Certain **organs**, such as the **eye** or the **brain**, required plenty of moisture to function. Excessive heat or emotion might dry out the brain and leave it fuming, unable to apply reason to the information it received from the sense, as Hamlet fears (*HAM* 4.5.155) and excessive weeping might dry out the humors in the eye and crack the **eye-string** or optic nerve. Extreme emotion might consume **blood** as well as tears, since humors and fluids were fungible and could convert from one state to another. "[D]ry sorrow drinks our blood," mourns Romeo (*ROM* 3.5.59). Lear curses Goneril with sterility by wishing for heat to "dry up in her the organs of increase" (which were nourished on cold, moist **phlegm** and warm, moist blood, *LR* 1.4.279).

dug See also **breast**, **nurse**, **pap** (A) The **dug** in Shakespeare is specifically the lactating breast of a woman or female animal.
(B) Juliet's **Nurse** fondly reminisces about the infant's weaning:

> For I had then laid **wormwood** to my dug,
> . . .
> When it did taste the wormwood on the **nipple**
> Of my dug and felt it bitter, pretty fool,
> To see it tetchy and fall out with the dug!
> (*ROM* 1.3.26–32)

The passage tells us a little about early modern nursing habits; Juliet was weaned at or close to three years old, and evidently fed on demand. Weaning was nurse-led, rather than child-led, and typically for an infant of her class, Juliet's feeding was outsourced to a countrywoman rather than attended to by her own mother.

Suffolk in *2H6* contrasts the contentment of a nursing infant, even a dying one, with the desperation of a hungry baby:

> Here could I breathe my soul into the air,
> As mild and gentle as the cradle-babe
> Dying with mother's dug between its lips:
> Where, from thy sight, I should be raging mad,
> And cry out for thee to close up mine eyes,
> To have thee with thy lips to stop my mouth.
>
> (3.2.391–6)

Ironically, he delivers the speech to Queen Margaret, characterized throughout the first tetralogy as anti-maternal and unfeminine. For Hamlet, nursing manners, the behavior expected from a nursing infant, are a figure for discipline, "comply[ing] with the dug, before . . . suck[ing]" (5.2.187). Mother's milk transmitted moral influences as well as nutrition, hence the Duke of York's charge against his wife: "Shall thy old dugs once more a traitor rear?" (*R2* 5.3.90), and, in *R3*, the Duchess of York's disclaiming of Richard's villainy even while acknowledging him as her own: "He is my son; yea, and therein my shame; /Yet from my dugs he drew not this deceit" (2.2.29–30). Lactating animal breasts include the "cow's dugs" kissed by Touchstone because Jane Smile had touched them (*AYL* 2.4.50), and the "milch doe, whose swelling dugs do ache," to whom the affectionate Venus is compared (*VEN* 875).

(C) Thomas Elyot's Latin dictionary (1538, N1r) gives the Latin *mamma* as "dugge or pappe." Huloet's French dictionary (1572, P1r) distinguishes between "Dugge, or a teate . . . *mamelle*," "Dugge or pappe head . . . *le petit bout de la mamelle*" and finally, "Dugge or womans breast, whiche is also applied to beasts . . . *mamelle, tetin.*"

ear (A) The ear was the instrument of hearing, and was **cold** and **dry** in its temper or **complexion**. The outer ear protruded from the head so that faint sounds could be amplified by it, and so that objects would not fall into the ear canal. The inner ear contained labyrinths, little windows, a tympanum or sounding membrane, and three small bones, the stirrup, anvil, and hammer. Some writers described a little "teat" that took in the sound and carried it to the "common wits" in the **brain**. Early modern **surgeons** reconciled the new anatomical discoveries of Vesalius and others with ancient philosophy. Plato had posited the existence of a special, rarefied air within the ear (comparable to the glassy **humor** in the **eye**) that was filled with the precious animal **spirit** refined in the brain. When sounds struck the eardrum (carried by external air), the eardrum vibrated and passed the sounds on to this spirituous internal air, which in turn transmitted noises to the brain for comprehension and response. Most philosophers had argued that vision was the supreme sense. But some argued that because sounds corresponded directly with the enspirited air and the animal spirits in the **brain**, hearing was the highest sense, rather than sight. Music could therefore ravish the soul directly, since the sound had direct access to the spirits in the brain, and spirit was the medium between body and soul. The inner air could, however, be consumed by excessively loud sounds and also with age, explaining the **deafness** of the elderly and those who, like blacksmiths in forges, worked in noisy places.
(B) *HAM* has more about ears, and the interaction between ear and eye, than any other Shakespearean play, from the ear of old Hamlet into which Claudius introduces the poison that curdles his **blood** (1.5.63), to the "whole ear of Denmark" (1.5.36), Ophelia's "too credent ear" to Hamlet's suit (1.3.30), the "ears of the groundlings" pleased by the players (3.2.10), and the "mildewed ear" that is Claudius (3.4.64). *Hamlet* is also unusual in featuring the ear as a literal

organ rather than, as is usual, as a metonym for hearing and comprehension. *COR* separates "ears" and "voices" to represent the multiple audiences that Martius must please, the "kindest ears" of the plebeians (2.2.52), the "Volscians' ears" (4.5.58), the "common ears" (5.6.4). He "stop[s] his ears" against Rome (5.3.5) but cannot resist the voice of his mother. *ROM* describes ears as the openings to anger and love. "Bit[ing]" and "drum[ming]" the ear triggers dissension, and Tybalt and Mercutio "pluck" their weapons out "by the ears" (1.4.86, 2.4.77, 3.1.81). Fair-skinned Juliet decorates the dark night "Like a rich jewel in an Ethiop's ear" (1.5.46). Romeo is "run through the ear with a love-song" (2.1.15). Octavius "has no ears" for Antony's request (*ANT* 3.12.20). Tamora is convinced she can persuade the "aged ear" of Titus (*TIT* 4.4.99).

Hermia alludes to the common belief that blindness (whether congenital or temporary from darkness or **illness**) made the sense of hearing more acute:

> Dark night, that from the eye his function takes,
> The ear more quick of apprehension makes;
> Wherein it doth impair the seeing sense,
> It pays the hearing double recompense.
> Thou art not by mine eye, Lysander, found;
> Mine ear, I thank it, brought me to thy sound.
> (*MND* 3.2.177–82)

Pneuma or eye-spirit could not travel in the dark, but hearing depended upon ordinary air in the atmosphere and the rarefied spirituous air within the human air, which never left it, and so hearing could make up sight's deficiencies in the dark. King John laments the necessity for any kind of spirit or medium for sight and hearing, wishing that Hubert could

> . . . see [him] without eyes,
> Hear [him] without thine ears, and make reply
> Without a **tongue**, using conceit alone,
> Without eyes, ears and harmful sound of words.
> (*JN* 3.3.48–51)

John wants Hubert to understand his wish to murder Arthur without his having to express it, to have immediate access to his conceit or fantasy. "Look with thine ears," demands Lear in the synesthesia of **madness** (*LR* 4.6.151). Rosaline harshly demands that Berowne should attempt to make the terminally ill patients in a **hospital** laugh at his jokes for a year before she will consent to marry him, arguing that wit depends upon the response of the listener, not the intention of the speaker:

> A jest's prosperity lies in the ear
> Of him that hears it, never in the tongue

> Of him that makes it: then, if **sickly** ears,
> Deaf'd with the clamours of their own dear groans,
> Will hear your idle scorns, continue then.
> *(LLL* 5.2.863)

Loud noises were known to cause deafness, and the groans of the sufferers in the hospital ring loudly enough to weaken the hearing. If such will listen amiably and be amused by Berowne's witticisms, Rosaline will forgive him his gibes.

(C) Vicary's description idiosyncratically describes "seven pairs of nerves" ending with a bundle resembling a wine-press (1587, D3r); see also Bacon (1626) for theories of hearing. B. R. Smith (1999) summarizes ancient and early modern theories of hearing. Fineman (1986) offers both theoretical and historical arguments for the early modern ear as the site of delay and deferral, especially erotic. Anderson (1991) contrasts the imagery of eye and ear in *HAM* as figures for the workings of theater. Berry (1997) investigates the puns on ear, **hair**, heir, and air in *HAM*. Robson (2001) connects the dramatic and nondramatic verse through the imagined conversation of speaker and listener in both in what he calls a kind of synesthesia. Pollard (2005) argues for the importance of the ear as an aperture for both poison and the words of players in *HAM*; Folkerth (2002) discusses both the early modern "soundscape" in broadly ecological terms and the "public ear" in *ANT*, "ears" of corn and repletion or receptivity in *COR*, and listening and surveillance in *MM* and *OTH*. Both Folkerth and B.R. Smith argue that hearing superseded vision as the superior early modern sense because the ear had direct access to the most refined spirit in the body, in the brain.

earwax Another **excrement** or waste product of the body, "eare-waxe is nothing else but the superfluitie of the chollericke **humor**, which is purged there by those pipes [from the **brain**]" (La Primaudye 1594, H8r). Hence Thersites memorably characterizes the irascible Greek hero Agamemnon as "an honest fellow enough and one that loves quails; but he has not so much brain as Earwax" (*TRO* 5.1.51–3). Quails were a hot food, perhaps explaining Agamemnon's irritability: Bullein (1595, K4r) counsels against their **consumption** because they "ingender agues and the **falling sickness**," Vaughan (1612, D4r) recommends quails to counteract **melancholy**, and Culpeper (1652, E6v) includes quail in his list of "creatures that are lustful and fruitful."

ecstasy see also **Bedlam, crazed, frenzy, lunacy, madness** (A) The first meaning of **ecstasy** (from the neo-Latin *extasis*, to be beside oneself) associates it with a trance-like state caused by religious exaltation or imagination. Later uses apply this out-of-body experience to the dissociation of feverish delirium or bouts of insanity, and colloquial use of the adjective "ecstatic" imagines a person ravished with joy. Common to all senses of the word is the idea of trembling or rapture, absence of mind, and a paroxysm or intense moment of feeling, or transient state of madness.

(B) Shakespeare's ecstatics are beside themselves with puzzlement, grief, love, and guilt; sometimes they seem like madmen to those around them, and once Shakespeare appears to use the word in its modern sense of "overwhelmed with delight." Much of the farcical humor of *ERR* depends upon the confusion of the Antipholuses being mistaken for insanity. The courtesan remarks that Antipholus of Ephesus "trembles in his ecstasy" (4.4.51; see discussion under **madness**). Characters in *HAM* accuse one another of ecstasy in its different senses, unable to distinguish incurable madness from the temporary aberrations of love-sickness or grief. Polonius believes the prince to suffer in "the very ecstasy of love," a love-melancholy that has rendered him temporarily **insane** (2.1.29). Ophelia agrees with the diagnosis of ecstasy or madness, but not the disease's etiology in love-melancholy, nor that it can be **cured**. He is "blasted with ecstasy," like a flower blighted by frost, incurably ill (3.1.160). Hamlet accuses his mother of a madness that has confused her perceptions to such an extent that "sense to ecstasy was . . . thrall'd," her understanding has been imprisoned or captured by the overwhelming pleasure of sensation, specifically sexual desire (in its own way, it is another diagnosis of love-melancholy; 3.4.74). Gertrude turns the imputation of madness back to Hamlet when he sees his father's ghost, but she does not: "This the very coinage of your **brain**: /This bodiless creation ecstasy /Is very cunning in" (3.4.138). She believes that his brain, overheated with anger, has produced **fumes** that have overwhelmed its rational spirit, making his **eyes** and understanding unable to see what is there and instead to see hallucinations, "bodiless creation[s]" crafted by the brain. Hamlet retorts:

> Ecstasy?
> My **pulse**, as yours, doth temperately keep time,
> And makes as healthful music: it is not madness
> That I have utter'd: bring me to the test,
> And I the matter will re-word; which madness
> Would gambol from.

> (3.4.139–44)

He offers her physiological proof to counter her medical explanation. If he were overheated, he would run a **fever**, and his pulse would beat quickly, like that of a madman in a frenzy or delirium. But his pulse runs evenly, and, moreover, he will prove able to repeat what he has said in slightly different ways ("re-word," meaning both to say again and to say in different form), where the ravings of an ecstatic would by their very nature prove ephemeral and unrepeatable. Iago calls Othello's trance or fit "your ecstasy," using it as the excuse to send Cassio away (*OTH* 4.1.79). Macbeth has likewise suffered fits of abstraction, fearing that the dagger he sees leading him to Duncan is a frenzied hallucination, a "dagger of the mind," a brooding upon madness to which he returns in 3.2 as he regrets his unquiet mind:

> better be with the dead,
> Whom we, to gain our peace, have sent to peace,

115

> Than on the torture of the mind to lie
> In restless ecstasy.

> (*MAC* 3.2.22)

He suffers either from a guilty conscience or because he fears for the safety and continuance of his crown, knowing that Banquo's descendants, not his, will rule. A few lines earlier he has commented on "life's fitful fever"; the dead **sleep** well, and coolly, while the living are driven to delirium and frenzy. Ross mourns that in Scotland, "violent sorrow seems /A modern ecstasy": so hardened have the people become to sudden **death** and tyranny that to grieve appropriately for a loved one looks to others like a fit of madness and abstraction (4.3.170). The three "men of sin" in *TMP* are so dazed with remorse that Prospero sends Ariel to make sure that they do not hurt themselves in "this ecstasy" (3.3.108).

The "ecstasies" of Titus Andronicus are both feigned and genuine. Marcus attends Titus "in his ecstasy," his overwhelming sorrow and unhinging grief. But when Saturninus complains about Titus' vengeful arrows, "his feigned ecstasies /Shall be no shelter to these outrages" (*TIT* 4.4.21–2), he only partly guesses Titus' true state of mind. Insane or not, Titus' plan to revenge himself upon Saturninus, Tamora, Aaron, and the Goths will succeed by tricking them into believing him more deluded and vulnerable than he is.

Benedick ought to have guessed that Leonato, Hero, and the others were gulling him, from the excessive love-melancholy they attribute to Beatrice in his hearing: "the ecstasy hath so much overborne her that my daughter is sometime afeared she will do a desperate outrage to herself: it is very true" (*ADO* 2.3.151). Beatrice is reportedly suicidal, driven mad by unrequited love for Benedick, but can be cured by a return of his love, the standard cure for **love-sickness**. Portia, in contrast, fears she will be driven mad by too much delight or "ecstasy":

> O love,
> Be moderate; allay thy ecstasy,
> In measure rein thy joy; scant this excess.
> I feel too much thy blessing: make it less,
> For fear I **surfeit**.

> (*TN* 3.2.111)

A surfeit of love, like a surfeit of food, could make one sick, and Portia fears she will **faint** or swoon from the rapid expansion of her **heart** as vital **spirit** rushes into it with love and delight. Shakespeare's Venus, too, finds herself in a "trembling ecstasy" of futile desire for Adonis (895), almost fainting with desire, and the maid of *LC* recounts her own tale of unsuccessful love in "suffering ecstasy" (69) that her elderly listener cannot soothe.

(C) Geninges' hagiography uses the phrase "extasy of joy" for a religious exaltation in which the recipient "shake[s] and tremble[s]" as if with a **palsy** (1614, F1v–F2r). Lyly (1580, X3v) distinguishes between an "Extacie, or . . . a Lunacie" of rage, suggesting that what both states have in common is a paroxysmic emotion. Crystal (2003) glosses Shakespeare's uses of the word to conclude that it most usually means madness.

element See also **complexion** (A) The four classical elements, fire, air, earth, and water, formed the basis for all earthly substances, including the human body. Elements coexisted with bodily **humors** and shared some of the same qualities (one early modern writer calls humors "the elements of the body"). Each element comprised two qualities. Fire was **hot** and **dry**; Air, **moist** and hot; Earth, dry and **cold**; Water, cold and moist. Each of these qualities existed in different degrees or levels within a substance, from the first to the fourth degree. Empedocles is generally attributed with specifying the four elements and their qualities, and early moderns learned about them from summaries and translations such as Polydore Virgil's. Instead of the four mixed elements of classical cosmology or the four humors of classical **medicine**, **Paracelsus** claimed that each of the four elements consisted of one quality only (fire, hot; earth, dry; air, moist; water, cold) and only three "substantives" or fundamental principles in nature: **salt**, or solidity; **sulphur**, or fire; and mercury or liquidity. Some followed Aristotle in believing in a fifth element, the invisible spirit of aether or **quintessence**, of which heavenly bodies were made (Paracelsus also called the "astral body" or metaphysical human body the fifth element).
(B) "Elements /so mixed" in the human body created persons with even temperaments or complexions (*JC* 5.5). Shakespeare uses the elements to aggrandize or elevate the subjects and characters of tragedy; the plays that most frequently allude to the elements, *OTH* and *ANT*, also share imagery of the stars, moon, and the cosmos, as if these stories are world-shaking or epic in their scope. Antony's reference to the crocodile's elements is jocular (2.7.45), but Octavius bids "the elements be kind" to Octavia on her journey (3.2.40). Cleopatra's eulogy on Antony includes praise for his capacity for pleasure: "his delights /Were dolphin-like; they show'd his back above /The element they lived in," turning what Octavius dismisses as mere lasciviousness into a cosmic joy (5.2.88–90). Most famously, Cleopatra commits suicide with the comment, "I am fire and air; my other elements /I give to baser life" (5.2.289–90). Fire and air as elements are under normal circumstances invisible in the human body; the lightest of the elements, they could rise most easily to heaven. Earth and water, the elements she leaves behind, were notoriously the "dull elements of earth and water" (*H5* 3.7.21), the heavier and slower parts of matter. As in *ANT*, *OTH* begins with element used in a casual sense and develops it to encompass heaven, earth, and hell. Cassio hopes Othello will have "defense against the elements" on "a dangerous sea," using the term to mean "weather," in the way we still do today (2.1.45). Iago characterizes the three lads of Cyprus whom he has made intoxicated as "the very elements of this warlike isle," where elements are the epitomes or representatives of the Cypriots (2.3.57). In the same scene, he describes Desdemona "as fruitful /As the free elements," generous as the uncontained fire, earth, air, and water in their natural states (2.3.341–2); compare Prospero's manumission of Ariel, "to the elements /Be free," *TMP* 5.1.318–19). Finally, Iago

calls upon the stars and the "elements that clip us round about" in his pact with Othello to murder Desdemona (*OTH* 3.3.464), enlisting terrestrial and celestial phenomena in his scheme.

Sonnet 44 wishes the poet were made of pure thought, which could travel instantaneously across the world to his love; "of earth and water wrought," however, he must wait patiently with "heavy tears, badges of either's woe." Earth, the cold, dry, heavy element associated with melancholy or sorrow, and water, the cold, moist, and heavy element associated with patience, manufacture the tears he sheds at his loss. Sonnet 45 identifies "slight air" with "thought," and "purging fire" with "desire." Both thought and desire, fire and air, the "quicker elements," remain with the poet's beloved; the poet is left with "two alone" of the four elements, earth and water, and so is rendered heavy, "oppressed with **melancholy**" until he hears good news. His respite is, however, only temporary; both thoughts and wishes, fire and air, leave him post-haste to his sorrow again.

(C) For early modern summaries of the classical four elements, see Polydore Vergil (1546); Bullein (1558); and esp. Moore (1564). The English Paracelsians Hester (1596) and Bostocke (1585) describe the Paracelsian cosmos. See also **alchemy**.

empirics See also **alchemist, apothecary, herb-woman, mountebank, midwife, Paracelsus, physician, surgeon** (A) Lay or vernacular healers, not members of the Royal **College** of Physicians or the Guild of Barber-Surgeons, so-called because they **cured** from observation and experience, rather than through the practice of the **Galenic, Hippocratic** or Paracelsian theories taught in the medical schools.

(B) Empirics were often women, explaining the reluctance of the sick King in *All's Well* to "prostitute [his] past-cure **malady** /To empirics," to entrust his care to the unlicensed Helena (2.1.121–2). The term "prostitute" links the empiric to the mountebank, who practiced for profit upon gullible patients.

(C) Herring (1604) accuses empirics of spreading false hopes about magical cures for the plague such as the wearing of amulets, or the new Paracelsian medicine. Cotta (1617) argues that all empirics (in which category he includes apothecaries, mountebanks, surgeons, and women healers) are unreliable, but that women in particular are dangerous because they lack the ability to reason. Of secondary materials, Pelling and White (2003) are indispensable, pointing out, contrary to G. Clark (1966) and an earlier generation of historians, the porousness of the supposed boundary between empirics and licensed healers, and the effectiveness and renown of many sixteenth-century empirics. P. Smith (2004) discusses the accusations of "empiricism" made against craftsmen and early scientists. All women healers were classified as empirics, even licensed midwives, as Fissell discusses in *Vernacular Bodies* (2004). Fissell's special edition of the *Bulletin of the History of Medicine* (2008) on "Women, Health and Healing in Early Modern Europe" includes a useful introduction by her and, in particular, an essay by Harkness on female empirics and the range of vernacular healing practices they espoused (2008). Paracelsians and alchemists were also invariably and pejoratively called empirics. Debus' *The English Paracelsians* (1968) offers brief accounts of the few well-known adherents of Paracelsian medicine in sixteenth- and early-seventeenth-century England. Kassell (2007) offers a scholarly yet readable account of the astrologer, alchemist, play-goer, and medical practitioner Simon Forman, who treated patients both as an empiric and (eventually) as a licensed physician.

empiricutic See also **empiric** Pertaining to an empiric or lay-healer, this word appears to be a Shakespearean coinage. Menenius expresses his delight at Coriolanus' early victory by claiming that the letter announcing the news is so revitalizing to him that a prescription from **Galen**, the father of medicine, himself would be "empiricutic" quackery in comparison, "no better than a horse-drench" or **medicine** administered by a farrier to an animal (*COR* 2.1.117).

epilepsy, epileptic (A) Epilepsy convulsed the entire body at periodic intervals in a fit that included the loss of feeling in the body (numbness) and perception in the **brain**. It appeared when the **spirits** that transmitted nutrition and energy through the body could not flow freely in the brain, either because of too much thick **phlegm** (the **cold, moist humor** that enabled defecation and nourished the brain but that in excess led to lethargy) or from a sharp attack of **choler** (the **hot, dry** humor that energized the body and nourished the gallbladder but in excess led to anger) blocking the way; from noxious humors from improperly concocted or digested food in the **stomach**; and, rarely, from a cold, creeping draught beginning in one of the extremities and proceeding up to the brain. Sometimes **melancholy** (the cold, dry humor that nourished the **spleen** and thickened the **blood** but in excess caused fear, sorrow, and malice), when retained in the brain rather than naturally **purged**, impeded the flow of spirit too, provoking an attack. Before an episode sufferers experienced headaches, memory loss, sadness, and bad dreams; during an attack they immediately fell to the ground (hence the name, **falling sickness**), some cried out or grunted, some bit their **tongues**, some trembled, and others jerked spasmodically, and a few foamed at the mouth. Physicians could trigger (and thus diagnose) an epileptic fit by asking the patient to smell a strong odor such as bitumen or goats' horn, or to taste or smell goats' **liver**. (Classical texts thought goats especially susceptible to epilepsy, because of the accounts of augurers.) The foaming, writhing, and numbness distinguished epilepsy, sometimes called the "little **apoplexy**," from **dizziness** or vertigo and from apoplexy proper. Moreover, epilepsy afflicted the young more than the old, unlike apoplexy, in which the reverse was true. Epilepsy often resolved itself naturally in children before they reached adulthood, but those contracting it in young adulthood experienced it for the remainder of their lives. Others, however, classified epilepsy as a disorder of later old age, like apoplexy. **Cures** included a hot and dry **diet**, with no pulses, fish, old wine, and with minimal meat except the flesh of a hare, although Barrough recommends that the patient abstain from "all flesh" except that of mountain birds, hares from all pulses, fish, and old wine. Anything that generated dryness or heat was helpful, such as

119

breathing hot, dry air; consuming capers and weak beer; rubbing the head and other members to create friction (as, indeed, Shakespeare's Cassio suggests in *OTH* 4.1); and observing rigid sleep hygiene, but foods or activities that were too hot, such as garlic, onions, mustard, or sexual intercourse, worsened symptoms. Chronic sufferers endured a strong purge; blood let from a **vein** in the hamstring muscle or the ring finger; and their heads heated with warming pans, morning and night, for up to forty days. During a fit the physician was to straighten out the limbs of convulsing patients, place a wedge between their teeth, and tickle their throats with a medicated feather to stimulate **vomiting**. If the disorder came from melancholy, however, the healer should follow the appropriate cures for that imbalance and use cupping-glasses or the **surgeon's box** to scarify the neck and shoulders.

Despite the sophisticated distinctions among epilepsy, vertigo or dizziness, apoplexy, *hysterica passio*, and other sorts of fits noted by **physicians** (from **Galen** and Soranus onwards through to sixteenth-century writers such as Barrough), a pre-Hippocratic belief that spirits possessed those who suffered from these disorders persisted through the Middle Ages and, to a lesser extent, in Shakespeare's time. In 1602 the Lord Chief Justice called in physicians from the Royal College to testify on whether fourteen-year-old Mary Glover, who had had fits, had been bewitched by Elizabeth Jackson or whether she suffered from a natural hysteria; later the same year, Samuel Harsnett consulted physicians (at the Bishop of London's request) to find out whether Jesuit priests were tricking naïve rural folk into believing they were possessed by demons and needed the services to exorcise them.

(B) There are three possible epilepsy sufferers in Shakespeare: Julius Caesar, Othello, and Macbeth. Each of these is diagnosed for on- and off-stage audiences by third parties (Casca, Brutus, and Cassius; Iago; and Lady Macbeth) and each would-be clinician has an ulterior motive. "Shakespeare takes great care that the descriptions of Caesar's epileptic fits and other illnesses do not lessen our sense of his greatness," notes Hoeniger (1992, 203), but the plays clearly show that Shakespeare was also aware of the ancient prejudice against those who suffered fits. Casca, full of masculine contempt for a "sick girl" such as the infirm Caesar, describes Caesar in a fit triggered by an **ague**:

> when the fit was on him, I did mark
> How he did shake: 'tis true, this god did shake;
> His coward lips did from their colour fly,
> And that same **eye** whose bend doth awe the world
> Did lose his lustre: I did hear him groan.
>
> (*JC* 1.2.120–4)

Casca willfully misinterprets the standard symptoms of an epileptic fit (trembling, pallor, groaning, rolling eyes) as the signs of "coward[ice]." Thus Caesar's lips are not pale because, under the influence of his **disease**, blood has rushed to his **heart** to succor him in his **swoon** and bring him back to consciousness, but because, like pusillanimous soldiers, they flee their "colour[s]" or flags; similarly, his body shudders not in rigors but in fear, an irony compounded by Casca's bitter phrase "this god" and his repetition of "shake" to emphasize Caesar's regular, convulsive tremors. Brutus' motives when he characterizes Caesar's **malady** as the "falling sickness" later may be purer, but Cassius, like Casca, reads the ailment metaphorically: "No, Caesar hath it not; but you and I, /And honest Casca, we have the falling sickness" (255–6). Caesar rises to success even as Casca, Brutus, and Cassius fall into obscurity; calling Casca "honest" authorizes the latter's malicious account of Caesar's suffering.

Iago explains Othello's "trance" as "an epilepsy" (*OTH* 4.1.50) and even offers a history for the disease, claiming that Othello had a "fit" the previous day. As many commentators have noted, there is no evidence for this (unless we take his headache as evidence of a migrainous aura preceding the attack), and Iago appears to be bolstering outdated associations among epilepsy, **madness**, and hysteria, confirmed by his anticipation of Othello's "savage madness" if disturbed before the fit outlives its course (55). Moss reads the conversation between Cassio and Iago over Othello's unconscious body as a conflict between Galenic and **Paracelsian** understandings of disease: Cassio suggests a standard Galenic therapy for epilepsy (rubbing Othello's temples to generate heat, imagining a disorder generated from within), but Iago figures himself as an external, disease-causing agent, who has administered a Paracelsian **medicine** from without in order to trigger a paroxysm of jealousy and, indirectly, a fit (Moss 2004).

Macbeth's fit is even more dubious. Lady Macbeth explains away Macbeth's horror at the sight of Banquo's ghost by claiming that her husband has a history of "fit[s]" "from his youth," a history that suggests epilepsy. Macbeth's symptoms, however, belie the diagnosis both to the on-stage audience (the diners) and to us: he gazes upon vacant space and, although moved by "passion," as his wife insists, he retains the powers of controlled speech and movement, both of which were lost in epileptic fits (*MAC* 3.4.53–6). Finally, Kent angrily denounces Oswald's "epileptic visage," equating his repeated, sarcastic "smile[s]" with the involuntary, tooth-baring grimace of *grand mal* (*LR* 2.2.81–2).

(C) Landi explains epilepsy as the retention of phlegm (1566, K3v). Barrough (1583, C4r–v) has a chapter on "Epilepsia, or the Falling Sickness" in which he identifies the characteristic sign of the disorder as "foming at the mouth" (1583, C4r). Jorden (1603) irritably testifies that Mary Glover suffered from the natural hysteria of a teenage girl, not from witchcraft, and Harsnett's account of his own investigation (1603) blames "Egregious Popish Impostures," in his famous title, for the confusion between spirit possession and disease. Temkin's invaluable account provides a history of attitudes towards epilepsy and epileptics from the Greek world to the mid-twentieth-century (1945). Hoeniger briefly describes the involvement of the Royal **College** in the trial of Mary Glover for witchcraft in 1692 (1992, 200–2) and Moss sensitively argues that *OTH* employs witchcraft and hysterical epilepsy to dramatize debates between the radical Paracelsian practice becoming associated with Protestantism and the traditional Galenism of the Royal College that was linked to royal Anglicanism (1997). On epilepsy and

apoplexy, see *Regimen* (Mediolano 1528, Xr); Lowe (1597, D3v). On **diet**, see
Lemnius (1576, V1v); Barrough (1583, C4r). On goats and epilepsy, see Temkin,
and Moss (2004, 160). Both Moss and Dimmock adduce the intriguing and
well-known early modern association of Mahomet with epilepsy, Moss suggesting
that Othello's epilepsy reinforces his cultural and religious otherness (Dimmock
2005, 204; Moss 1997). Noble (2004) reads Desdemona's corpse as pure Paracelsian **mummy**, the handkerchief akin to the blood-soaked plasters recommended
in seventeenth-century cures for epilepsy, and Desdemona herself a sacrificial
virgin.

erection Shakespeare twice uses the word erection to refer to a man's penis in a
state of sexual arousal. Timon of Athens alludes to the impotence that accompa-
nies advanced syphilis (see **pox**), which "quell[s]/The source of all erection" (*TIM*
4.3.164), and Mistress Quickly innocently malaprops of the merry wives of Windsor, "they mistook their erection," meaning their direction or address. "So did I
mine," retorts Falstaff, "to build upon a foolish woman's promise" (*WIV* 3.5.40–2).

eryngo, eringoes Prepared as a sweetmeat, the root of sea-holly was called
eryngo and considered to be an aphrodisiac. Falstaff calls for the sky to "snow
eringoes" (*WIV* 5.5.20) as he awaits his rendezvous with the merry wives. Hall
(H7r, 1613) lists "Eringo's" and "Potatoes" foods used to inflame lust in women;
Burton (2R4r, 1621) includes it among the "lasciuious meats [that] must be
forsaken" by those suffering from love-melancholy. See also Williams' dictionary of Shakespeare's bawdy (1994); Fitzpatrick's guide to comestibles in
Shakespeare (2011).

eunuch (A) Many ancient civilizations in regions such as Sumeria, Ancient
Greece, Egypt, India, and China, had employed as slaves eunuchs, boys castrated
by the removal of their testicles before puberty. Such slaves attended royal families; guarded queens and the *zenana* or women-only chambers; officiated at temples; and performed other activities that required a high degree of loyalty without
passion or danger (castration was thought to remove both aggression and ambition). Many also sang, since castration before puberty sometimes allowed them
to keep their boyish treble voices (though this was by no means guaranteed).
The word could be also used figuratively, to refer to a man who retained male
genitals but could not sire a child, or to one who deliberately refused sexual
intercourse for religious reasons. Body-servants and courtier-eunuchs had traditionally ranked low on the social scale, although singing *castrati* had by the eighteenth century become celebrities. In Shakespeare's time, two cultures were
known to employ eunuchs: *castrati* had by 1600 replaced male falsetto singers in
the Sistine Chapel, and the Ottoman Empire used eunuchs and mutes (servants
chosen for their congenital or acquired mutism so that they could not discuss
what they saw with others) to guard the women's chambers or *seraglio*.
(B) Shakespeare shows us eunuchs in two of their established roles: singers,
and servants in royal households. The plays also use the term to refer to men

who are low in status because they cannot father children. Most references allude to singers. Viola establishes herself in Orsino's court as an "eunuch" because she "can sing" (1.2.56–7), that is, she is one of the *castrati* who were known all over Europe but, at least officially, banned from English services. The captain responds that he will serve as her "mute," meaning that he will not reveal her secret, alluding to the practice attributed to the Ottomans of cutting out the **tongues** of servants in the *seraglio* to prevent them from discussing the queens' beauties with outsiders. Theseus refuses to hear "The battle with the Centaurs, to be sung /By an Athenian eunuch to the harp," out of consideration for his relation Hercules, he says (*MND* 5.1.44–5). Cloten tries futilely to woo Imogen with music, "the voice of **unpaved** [stoneless, that is, without testicles] eunuch" (*CYM* 2.3.30). Martius complains that returning to ask the tribunes' favor would turn his martial voice "into a pipe /Small as an eunuch" (*COR* 3.2.113–14).

Jack Cade delights in an ancient English prejudice impugning the masculinity of the French when he argues that Lord Say has compromised English self-rule: "I tell you that that Lord Say hath **gelded** the commonwealth, and made it an eunuch: and more than that, he can speak French" (*2H6* 4.2.153–5). Chiron turns rape into a perverted measure of manhood when he determines to assault Lavinia: if she holds out against him, "I would I were an eunuch," he adds (*TIT* 2.3.128). Lafew, shocked by the lords' refusal to marry Helena, thinks that they might as well be *castrati*: "An they were sons of mine, I'd have them whipped; or I would send them to the Turk, to make eunuchs of" (*AWW* 2.3.86–8). The association of ancient Egypt with women-only quarters and eunuchs gives us Shakespeare's character Mardian, who sings, though not for Cleopatra, who "takes no pleasure /In aught an eunuch has" (*ANT* 1.5.10) and later complains that Mardian is as weak as her women: "As well a woman with an eunuch play'd /As with a woman" (2.5.5–6). Enobarbus tries to warn Cleopatra of the political damage she is inflicting upon Antony, who is said in Rome to be unmanned to such an extent that "that Photinus an eunuch and your maids /Manage this war" (*ANT* 3.7.14–15). Mardian's histrionic skills rival Cleopatra's; so "piteously" does the "saucy eunuch" tell Antony of his lover's supposed **death** that Antony himself attempts suicide (4.14.25).

(C) Taylor (2000) discusses the history of eunuchs and castration at length. Elam (1996) discusses Shakespeare's classical sources. Orgel (1996) discusses *TN*'s pun on Viola's assumed name, Cesario, as one who is cut or castrated.

evil (A) "The Evil" or "The King's Evil," also called "struma" and sometimes "scrofula," swelled up the necks and throats of afflicted persons, often with **skin** lesions or broken sores on the skin. Some **patients** suffered lesions in the armpit and in the **breast**; they were often **phlegmatic** persons, who lacked activity or who were congenitally lacking in warm **blood**. The condition was incurable by **physicians** and **surgeons**, although sufferers might get relief from the sacred touch of an anointed monarch. Queen Elizabeth I and King James I both touched for the evil. A physician examined the patients to make sure that they were not suffering from **pox** or other disorders distinct from the king's evil, and also to see whether any of the sores were so offensive to look at that the patient should cover them with **linen** before the queen touched them (since most monarchs touched the sores directly with their hand). Prayers were conducted and the sick were led to the sovereign. While the chaplain read a passage from St. Mark's Gospel, the sick knelt in front of the monarch, who pressed their sores. The patients were then led away and brought back to the ruler while the chaplain began to read from the Gospel of John. The second time, the sovereign threaded a string through a golden coin (an "angel"), with a hole bored in it, and hung it about the neck of each sick person, earnestly bidding patients not to sell it or give it away, since the amulet would protect them from a recurrence of the **disease**.

(B) *MAC* offers us a description, in the mouth of Malcolm, of the ceremony, and the patients trooping up to the monarch for their second visit and the heavenly "angel" coin to protect them:

> 'Tis call'd the evil:
> A most miraculous work in this good king;
> . . .
>
> How he solicits heaven,
> Himself best knows: but strangely-visited people,
> All swoln and **ulcerous**, pitiful to the **eye**,
> The mere despair of surgery, he **cures**,
> Hanging a golden stamp about their necks,
> Put on with holy prayers: and 'tis spoken,
> To the succeeding royalty he leaves
> The healing benediction.
>
> (*MAC* 4.3.46–56)

In *MAC*, the ritual of touching for the evil is attributed to Edward the Confessor, but it is more likely to have come to England from France in the twelfth century (Hoeniger 1992, 277). Given the initial reluctance (or professed reluctance) of King James to touch for the evil as Queen Elizabeth had done, this scene may compliment the monarch on his salvific abilities. Within the play, the attribution of miraculous and saintly powers to King Edward absolves Malcolm of any putative charge of treachery in his flight from Scotland to another monarch, since Edward is so clearly a divine messenger rather than a competitor for the Scottish throne.

(C) The well-known surgeon William Clowes blames a phlegmatic **complexion** (1602, B2r) and offers recipes for ointments, but concludes that the King or Queen is the best physician for this disorder which is so difficult to cure. Hoeniger's detailed chapter (1992) compares the description of the ritual in *MAC* to the practice of touching for the evil by both Elizabeth and by James. William Tooker's Latin paean to the ceremony, *Charisma* (1597), documents Elizabeth's willingness not merely to touch the open sores of the people but also to massage them with her bare hands; Crawfurd (1911, 74) translates portions of the text into English. Tooker's text triggered something of a chauvinistic battle; he asserted that only the English monarchs could heal the evil in this way, to which the French royal physician André Du Laurens retorted furiously that, on the contrary, no English ruler after Edward the Confessor had had the gift, but only the French (Crawfurd 1911, 78–9). Willis (1992) comments on James's initial reluctance to participate in what he might have thought was a Popish ritual and attributes to James the view that the cure was anti-miraculous, "the product of the power of the human imagination responding to a ruse" (151). Fusch (2008), however, argues that James's seeming hesitation was carefully crafted, staged in order to "perform visible miracles while insisting that nothing miraculous was occurring" (Fusch 2008).

excrement (A) Excrements were the body's natural way of purging, the products of excess **humors**. They included ordure or feces, **urine**, **sweat**, tears, **vapors**, and **hair** and **nails**.
(B) Shakespeare uses "excrement" to refer to hair in most instances. Antipholus of Syracuse wonders why Time makes old men bald when hair is "so plentiful an excrement" (*ERR* 2.2.78). Hamlet's hair stands on end when he sees the Ghost, "like life in excrements," as if it had a life of its own (*HAM* 3.4.121). Armado may feel compelled to explain that when he plays with "my excrement" he means "with my mustachio" (*LLL* 5.1.104). Bassanio complains that the addition of a beard makes even the cowardliest youth seem valiant because they wear "valour's excrement" (*MV* 3.2.87; see discussion under **hair**). Autolycus, astonished to find he has done someone a good turn "by chance," pockets up his "pedlar's excrement," presumably his pack (*WT* 4.4.714).
Typically, Timon of Athens equates excrement with its common meaning, dung, when he argues with the bandits that all the forces of nature are thieves, too: "the earth's a thief, /That feeds and breeds by a composture stolen /From general excrement" (4.3.440–2). The earth is a thief because it steals the waste products of humans and animals, especially manure, to make compost, that it then uses to grow plants.
(C) Elyot's *Dictionary* (1538, N3v col. 1) defines excrement as ordure or dung. Langton (1547) specifies the origins of individual bodily secretions or excrements such as spittle and mucus and distinguishes between humors such as phlegm and excrements such as mucus: "The excrement which falleth fro[m] [th]e **brain** into [th]e mouth can not properly be called flewme [**phlegm**] but rather muck, or snivel" (C7r). Lemnius (1576, E7v) derives black hair from a "fuliginous and gross excrement of the third concoction" (see also **hair**). The jokes about mustaches or facial hair resembling another kind of excrement might have been widespread; consider the response of the Welsh courtier Nucome ("New-come") to the merchant's daughter Nan Venter (venter="seller") when she asks why he has grown a moustache, in Sharpham's play for the Children of the King's Revels, *Cupid's Whirligig*: "before when we were poore countrie fellowes, wee suffered our beardes careleslie to growe downeward, and

then they growe into our mouths in spite of our teeth, now you know haire is but excrement, & for mine owne part, I had rather haue my excrement in my **nose**, then in my teeth" (1607, D1v–D2r).

eye, eyne See also **apple, blind, eye-strings** (A) The **eye** served two purposes: it was both the **organ** of sight and the window that displayed a person's soul and emotions to others; it allowed in light and spirits from the outside world and sent out spirits in its turn. Aristotle, Avicenna, and others had argued that objects were illuminated by daylight, which bounced off the object and then into the human eye. Thus the eye merely received impressions—through the rays emitted from objects—of the outside world. Plato, **Galen**, and the influential Neoplatonic medieval philosopher Ficino, however, suggested that the eye itself sent out light or **spirit** (which Galen calls *pneuma*) into the air. Eye-spirit flowed from the **brain** along the eye-strings or optic nerves to the eyeball, where it mingled with the three specialized **humors** of the eye, the vitreous (glassy), the albugineous (albuminous, like egg-white), and the crystalline. When the flow of "spiritus visibilis" or visible spirit hit something outside the eye, it flowed into the light emitted by that object and then returned back to the eye of the beholder. The optic nerve was divided in two to serve each eye, but united when it entered the brain, so that viewers did not see double. Vision thus required three things: eye-beams needed access to the air; viewers needed to have enough eye-spirit within the eye itself; and eye-spirit needed to mingle with the air before it returned.

God placed the eyes at the top of the head, as befitted the organs of the highest sense, and because they served as "Watches" or guards and as beacons. Eyes displayed emotions or passions to outside observers, but to a physician they could also indicate disorders of the **heart**, brain, and **liver**, as well as the state of the animal spirits. For example, those with very pure, but scant, spirit were nearsighted; those with impure, but abundant, spirit, saw a great distance, but not sharply. In the elderly, the jelly-like crystalline humor, thickened and dried with age, failed to catch or send out enough light, a problem remedied by spectacles that replaced the glittering crystal. Too much light, however, dispersed the eye-spirit, which is why bright, polished objects or sunshine could **blind** the viewer when they reflected light back to the eye. Tears came from either the eye itself or from the whole body; their origin determined how harmful they might be and whether they needed any treatment. Too much weeping was a known cause of blindness, because it dried out the crystalline humor and could crack the eye-strings.

Ailments that afflict eyes in Shakespeare include temporary blindness or clouding of vision from the **pearl** or **pin and web**, from weeping, from brilliant objects, from darkness, or from wearing a blindfold; permanent blindness from maiming; the putrid discharge from **raw eyes**; and **sand-** or **gravel-blindness**. Love also enters the mind through the eye; eyes send out rays like darts that enter the eyes of another; these rays of love then travel to the liver, then the heart, and finally the brain (see **liver-vein**). The best therapy for **inflammations**

126

and pain was usually bleeding, from behind the ear, or dry-cupping on the neck (see **surgeon's box**). General **purges**, rather than particular ones, relieved the humors in the head, and **medicine** to be chewed, or to be inserted rectally through a **clyster**, was the best method of administration. Where there was no discharge or **flux**, surgeons might apply ointments or collyriums into the eye with a dove's feather. Egg-white—perhaps because of its similarity to the albugineous humor—was standard treatment both as a dressing after cataract surgery and as a collyrium to treat inflamed eyes, sometimes mixed with woman's **milk**. Should surgery or sewing become necessary, as in the operation for cataract, a golden needle worked better than a silver, because of its greater purity.

There is some evidence that women practitioners or **empirics** were known and trusted (at least by the general public, if not by physicians) to treat eye disorders; Banister's *Breviary* (1622) singles out women's errors in particular in his overview, complaining that the former sometimes "Licke the eyes with their **Tongue**" or infuse goose- or hen's-dung into inflamed eyes rather than curing them by purging or bloodletting.

(B) Although Aristotle's theory of vision, which held that the eye passively accepted rays of light sent out by objects in the world, rather than emitting beams itself, dominated early modern thinking about vision by Shakespeare's time, Shakespeare prefers the interactive model of eye-spirit, especially to discuss the mutuality of love. Benedick "with an eye of love requite[s]" or gives back "the eye of favor" with which Beatrice regards him (*ADO* 5.4.22–4). Leonato points out that the lovers in turn received these adoring eyes from Hero, Leonato, Claudio, and the Prince. Lovers "changed eyes" (*TMP* 1.2.442), exchanged images of each other in the other one's eyes, and the sonnets discuss the paradoxical function of the eye as both a watchman or guard of the body and the dangerous aperture that lets in love. Sonnet 61 comments on the paradox: "It is my love that keeps mine eye awake /Mine own true love that doth my rest defeat, /To play the watchman ever for thy sake" (61.10–12). The eye's alarm keeps him alert instead of allowing him to **sleep**, as he guards his loved one. In Sonnet 148, his eyes see only with "Love," not with "true sight." Both "watching," lying awake at night, and "tears" cloud the lover's vision, in order that he shall not see the faults of his lover: "O cunning Love! with tears thou keep'st me blind, /Lest eyes well-seeing thy foul faults should find" (148.1–2, 10, 13–14). Shakespeare is also fond of the concept of the "mind's eye" (*HAM* 1.1.112). Sonnets 113 and 114 engage optical theory in order to criticize it:

> Since I left you, mine eye is in my mind;
> And that which governs me to go about
> Doth part his function and is partly blind,
> Seems seeing, but effectually is out;
> For it no form delivers to the heart
> Of bird of flower, or shape, which it doth latch:
> Of his quick objects hath the mind no part,
> Nor his own vision holds what it doth catch:

> For if it see the rudest or gentlest sight,
> The most sweet favour or **deformed'st** creature,
> The mountain or the sea, the day or night,
> The crow or dove, it shapes them to your feature:
> Incapable of more, replete with you,
> My most true mind thus makes mine eye untrue. (113)

The poet's eyes send out eye-spirit as they are supposed, but instead of returning to the heart and the mind a true impression of everything that they see— a mixture of beams emitted by the object seen and by the eye that is seeing—his eyes return only a vision of his beloved to his mind. Sonnet 114 develops the metaphor, in which the poet's eye "make[s] of **monsters** and things **indigest** /... cherubins," imposing a beautiful form upon inchoate patterns, "Creating every bad a perfect best, /As fast as objects to his beams assemble?" (114.5–8). The eye engages in both sonnets actively with the objects seen, and its beams or eye-spirit "shapes" vision as maternal impression (what **pregnant** women saw) was thought to influence the appearance of a gestating child (hence the metaphors of monstrous, deformed, or indigested birth).

Sonnet 24 figures the eye whose shaping force makes it a "painter" on the canvas of the heart, a "shop" with "windows glazed" with the glassy humor of the beloved's eyes; even "the sun /Delights to peep" through his lover's eyes at the image of the poet's lover painted on the former's heart (24.4, 7–8, 11–12). Sonnets 46 and 47 imagine a war between eye and heart over which has the true image of the beloved. In Sonnet 46, the eye agrees to take custody of the lover's appearance, the heart, of his "inward part" or mind; in Sonnet 47, eye and heart are guests at a banquet where they companiably share the main dish, the sight of the beloved. When the lover is not visible to the eye, the eye may refresh itself by looking at the image "painted" on the heart, and when the heart is over-whelmed by love it may sustain itself by visiting the eye to obtain a glance at the lover (47.6).

MND literalizes the conceit that love enters in at the eye, through the device of the **potion** Puck **distils** from the purple flower, **love-in-idleness**, and squeezes into the eyes of the lovers and of Titania to induce infatuation. Throughout the play, love is literally and figuratively caught or transmitted through the eyes. Hermia wishes her despotic father "looked . . . with [her] eyes" (1.1.56). To Helena, Hermia's "eyes are lode-stars," magnetic in their attraction for Demetrius (1.1.183). "**Sickness** is catching," observes Helena, who wishes that she could likewise "catch" Hermia's appearance, "my eye your eye" (1.1.188). Cupid is "painted blind" because, paradoxically, "love looks not with the eyes, but with the mind"; although Demetrius has fallen in love with "Hermia's eyne" (1.1.234, 242). Helena again comments on Hermia's "attractive eyes" so "bright" in contrast to her own (2.2.91). "What wicked and dissembling glass of mine /Made me compare with Hermia's sphery eyne?" she asks, continuing the figure of magnetic attraction that designates Hermia's eyes two of the Ptolemaic spheres and the young men satellite planets compelled to follow her (2.2.98–9). The love-juice transforms Helena's "celestial . . . eyne" into the classical spheres, however, as the enchanted Lysander abandons Hermia. The "Dark night . . . from the eye his function takes, [and] The ear more quick of apprehension makes" (3.2.177–8), observes Hermia, though in this case it is the fairy magic, not the night, that has obfuscated the lovers' vision. Oberon's pity for the deluded Titania is awoken by "tears" standing not in her eyes but as the dew on the flowers with which she has crowned the ass-headed Bottom:

> that same dew, which sometime on the buds
> Was wont to swell like round and orient pearls,
> Stood now within the pretty flowerets' eyes
> Like tears that did their own disgrace bewail.
>
> (4.1.53–6)

Astonished at the events of the night, Hermia comments: "Methinks I see these things with parted eye, /When every thing seems double," a reference to the eye-string or optic nerve, which divided in two as it left the brain, so that each eye could benefit from the necessary eye-spirit, but which was united inside the brain, so that each eye's returning spirit could coalesce into one vision (4.1.189–90). If the eye-strings did not join correctly in the brain, or were inflamed in some way, the parted eye gave one double vision.

Theseus famously connects the poet's eyesight to his imagination:

> The poet's eye, in fine **frenzy** rolling,
> Doth glance from heaven to earth, from earth to heaven;
> And as imagination bodies forth
> The forms of things unknown, the poet's pen
> Turns them to shapes and gives to airy nothing
> A local habitation and a name.
>
> (5.1.12–17)

Vision works through the influence of invisible eye-spirit in the "airy nothing" of the atmosphere, and through the bodiless spirits that carry the impressions of the eye to the heart and the brain, just as imagination can assemble hitherto-unknown circumstances and creatures, and as a writing implement can make a physical mark upon a paper that is material and positioned in time and space. Other plays that foreground vision through the word eye include *LLL*, in which women's eyes again both send out "eye-beams" (4.3.27) that illuminate love and receive loving rays in return; *HAM*, in which "the mind's eye" (1.1.112, 1.2.185) dominates sensory perception; *CYM*, which opposes "eye or ear" (1.3.9), and of course *LR* and *JN*, which feature blindings or attempted blindings (see discussion under **blind**). Lear sardonically counsels Gloucester to get himself "glass eyes," in what may be the earliest reference to such prostheses, or may instead refer to the eye-glasses or spectacles used by cataract patients (the Worshipful Company of Spectacle-Makers was founded in 1629, but individual craftsmen had been putting together lenses to be worn or carried on the face since the Middle Ages). Spectacles with a fixed bridge were invented in the late sixteenth century; Jaques associates weak eyes with old age, the "lean and slipper'd pantaloon, /With spectacles on nose" (*AYL* 2.7.158–9), but Benedick diagnoses Claudio with the near-sight of love; he himself "can see yet without spectacles," and finds Beatrice far more beautiful than Hero (*ADO* 1.1.189).

(C) Vicary (1587, D3r–4r) describes the **anatomy** of the eye in detail "sufficient for a chirurgion"; he is less interested in theories of spirit, referring readers to **Galen** on the optic nerve and Lanfranco on the "panicles" or membranes. For Vicary, the ancient debates about whether the eye is active or passive are moot, since the eye's function is clearly two-fold: "these senewes [the optic nerves or eye-strings] bée hollowe as a réede, for two causes: The first is, that the visible spirite might passe freely to the Eyes: The seconde is, that the forme of visible thinges might freely be presented to the common wittes." **Hippocrates** (1610) and Baley (1616) give accounts of the operation for cataract, and Banister's translation of Guillemeau (1622) describes "One hundred and thirteen **diseases** of the eyes, and eye-liddes" (short title). The Shakespearean bibliography on eyes, vision, and the theater is substantial, although much of it discusses eyes figuratively, rather than as physiological organs. S. Clark (2007) provides the definitive account of early modern vision, and includes an excellent chapter on *Macbeth*. Lobanov-Rostovsky discusses the debate among theorists as to whether the eye emitted or received rays (1997). Mazzio (2009) sensitively analyzes the role of air in early modern sensory perception, including vision. Fineman (1986) uses the eye as a figure for Shakespeare's "I," a new subjectivity that he argues comes into being in the 1609 sonnet sequence. Scott (1988) uses the eye as a metonymy for self-knowledge in *JC*. Schwartz (1990) relates the sonnets to *MND* through the mechanisms and sequencing of sensory perception, intellectual knowledge, and bodily action in Shakespeare's works. Aronson's Jungian analysis (1995) interprets Shakespeare's healers (such as Helena in *AWW* or the doctors in *MAC*) as Jungian archetypes and blindness and eyesight as metaphors for universal human evil. O'Connell (2000); Anderson (1991) contrasts eye and ear as organs of perception in *HAM*. Sloan (2002) coins the term "eyeconography" to describe Iago's gendered sign-system in *OTH*. Freeman (2004) employs cognitive theory to awaken the dead metaphors in *OTH* that connect comprehension to sight. Hatchuel (2005) interprets cinematic versions of *MAC* through images of sight and spectacle in the play. Newman (1991) discusses scopophilia in *OTH*; Bosman (1999) calls *H8* by its original name, "All is true," in order to argue for the relationship between truth and seeing in the play, and B. R. Smith (2008) investigates the color green as not just a response to visual stimuli but as an enworlded or phenomenological state of early modern being.

eyebrow (A) The eyebrow protected the **eyes** from dust and dirt, while their **hair** dissipated **sweat** and other **humors** from the head. They also beautified the face by adding symmetry and form. Bushy eyebrows indicated an envious disposition, high brows a hard **heart**, faint brows, cowardice, and slender ones, gentleness.

(B) Thus the eyebrow stands as a synecdoche for beauty when Jaques' imagines the youthful lover singing "a woeful ballad /Made to his mistress' eyebrow" (*AYL* 2.7.149), and Rosalind/Ganymede lambastes the haughty Phoebe for her pride in her "inky brows" (3.5.46) since brown hair and **skin** were considered less attractive than pink-and-white fairness. Mamillius precociously summarizes the standards of early modern beauty:

> [Y]et black brows, they say,
> Become some women best, so that there be not
> Too much hair there, but in a semicircle
> Or a half-moon made with a pen.
>
> (*WT* 2.1.8–11)

(C) Mamillius' makeover instructions contradict those of Bulwer, who maintains that plucking and threading the brows is acceptable but that painting them is not (1653, O2v). Vicary warns **surgeons** that they should cut "according to the length of the bodie," that is, vertically, because the muscle runs all the way from one ear to the other, and a horizontal incision can result in "the Browe to hang ouer the Eye without remedie . . . the more pitie" (1587, D2v). Crooke includes a chapter in Book 10 of *Microcosmographia* on the **eyelids** and eyebrows (1615, A22[1]v–A224r).

eyelid (A) The eyelids covered the **eyes** to defend them from dust and to enable them to rest; the eyelashes directed *pneuma* or eye-spirit into the eye in order to make objects visible.
(B) Eyelids in Shakespeare demonstrate the ability to **sleep** soundly, with a peaceful mind. Deep and refreshing sleep is like magic; Mortimer's Welsh wife can charm him to sleep by singing, and "on your eyelids crown the god of sleep," boasts Glendower (*1H4* 3.1.214). Henry IV loses this ability with anxiety about his kingdom. He calls for sleep to "weigh [his] eyelids down /And steep [his] senses in forgetfulness" (3.1.7). The speaker in Sonnet 27 similarly mourns the thoughts that wander and "keep my drooping eyelids open wide," and, in Sonnet 61, the image of his beloved, or his own love that "play[s] the watchman" calling out the hour and keeping him awake. In *MND* eyelids serve as a metonymy for sleeping eyes hoodwinked by Puck and treated with the juice of **love-in-idleness** or heartsease in order to inspire love (2.2.81). Sebastian's wakefulness in *TMP*, however, indicates his immunity from Prospero's benign magic; his eyelids do not "sink" and he is "not disposed to sleep" (2.1.201–2).

Eyelids remain lowered permanently in **death**. When Hamlet insists he will fight Laertes "Until my eyelids will no longer wag" (5.1.267), he means that he will remain resolute as long as he is alive. Thaisa's resurrection is heralded when her fluttering "eyelids . . . Begin to part their fringes of bright gold" (3.2.98–9). Eyelids can also be used in those who are awake, to indicate pity (when one "wipe[s] a tear," as in *AYL* 2.7.116); courtly affectation (when one "turn[s] up [one's] eyelids" in *LLL* 3.1.13); greed (when Stephano, Trinculo, and Caliban follow Ariel in pursuit of "trash," with "advanced . . . eyelids" or eyes wide, *TMP* 4.1.177); surprise or skepticism (when Claudio claims he will never love again, since "on [his] eyelids shall conjecture hang" *ADO* 4.1.106); or feigned respect (when Richard II is by Bolingbroke's account cozened by the crowds who "hung their eyelids down" in a parody of reverence but were actually just asleep, *1H4* 3.2.81).

(C) Vicary compares the eyelids to covers under which one takes rest (1587, D2v), but Crooke calls the eyelids "leaf-dores" or "leaf-gates" in his continuing metaphor of the body as a fortress (1615, Book 10, A222r). Crooke identifies their substance as "gristle" and their skin as the thinnest in the whole body.

eye-string See also **eye, heart-string** The optic **nerve**, colloquially called first by playwright Ben Jonson the eye-string or (more commonly) the **sinew** of the eye, was known to be crucial for vision (*OED*, eyestring, sb.). Since it was considered a sinew, it was thought susceptible to damage or overstrain from prolonged peering or straining to see faraway objects (much as a muscle or sinew might be strained from lifting excessive weight or moving awkwardly). Imogen mourns her husband's absence by wishing she could have watched him travel until she "broke [her] eye-strings . . . crack'd them" by looking (*CYM* 1.3.17). Banister (1622); Batman (1582); Vicary (1587); and Crooke (1615) each contain chapters upon the **anatomy** of the eye, but employ the terms "optic nerve" or "sinew of the eye" rather than the coinage "eye-string."

faint See also **swoon** (A) While it is mostly Shakespeare's women who swoon, both Shakespeare's men and women might faint. One swooned because the body used up vital and rational spirit more quickly than the **heart** and **brain** could manufacture them, because the heart constricted under the duress of negative emotions such as fear, sorrow, or anxiety, or because spirit rushed to sustain the heart too quickly, depriving the brain of the rational spirit needed to remain conscious and to move, speak, and act voluntarily. One might faint from loss of vital spirit in the heart from cowardice, treason, grief, or remorse, but one might also lose rational and vital spirit from physical weakness after long travel; hard work; loss of **blood** in battle, or starvation. Women might also faint in **pregnancy**, since so much blood was diverted to the uterus to nourish the fetus. In Shakespeare there is often a pun on the faintness of color (of the face or of the blood-producing organs the heart and **liver**) and the fainting patient.

(B) The first tetralogy presents a weak king in Henry VI, whose army "is grown weak and faint" (*1H6* 1.1.158), whose nobles offer "fainting words" (*1H6* 2.5.95), and whose lords "faint" at the thought of defending his title (*3H6* 1.1.129). The "faint-hearted and degenerate king" lacks vital spirit in his heart and blood in his liver (*3H6* 1.1.183). In contrast, the Duke of York, and the warlike Clifford, "faint" only from "much effuse of blood" (*3H6* 1.4.48; 2.6.28). Oxford speaks rousingly of his mother to Queen Margaret, who retains her "high . . . courage" even when "warriors faint!" (5.4.50–1). Lady Anne, in contrast, "faint[s] and shrink[s]" with "heavy nothing" (*R2* 2.2.32). Her body trembles or shrinks with fear just as her heart constricts. The Ghost of Buckingham wishes a comparable fate upon Richard: "Fainting, despair; despairing, yield thy breath!" (*R3* 5.3.172). *TIM* 3.1.54–5 asks, "Has friendship such a faint and milky heart, /It turns in less than two nights?" The heart of a false friend is not red with blood but pale and milky with cowardice and treachery, or even curdled like sour **milk**. In *CYM*, both

Cloten and Iachimo "faint" upon discovery of their villainy (4.2.63, 5.5.149). Iachimo explains the physiology behind his trembling as he "faint[s]" to remember Imogen, "For whom [his] heart drops blood, and [his] false spirits /Quail to remember" (5.5.148–9). His remorse constricts his heart and uses up his vital spirit. His rational spirit, which falsely led him to betray her, becomes weak as he realizes his wickedness. Sonnet 80 imagines the spirits of the poet overcome for a different reason. "O, how I faint when I of you do write, /Knowing a better spirit doth use your name" (80.1.2) begins the poet-speaker. Even the poet's strongest spirits or talents seem inadequate in comparison to those of the rival poet; the sonnet-writer uses up his store of vital spirit in order to write. Queens faint at the thought of being replaced in their lovers' affections. Anne claims fear "faints" her at Katharine's fall (*H8* 2.3.103). Cleopatra claims to "faint" at the news of Octavia's marriage to Antony (*ANT* 2.5.110). Portia "grow[s] faint" with fear at her husband's plot (*JC* 2.4.43).

Non-emotional causes for faints in Shakespeare include hunger, blood-loss, fever, violent exercise, and pregnancy. In contrast to Ganymede's swoon from loving fear, Celia "faints for succor" or "faint[s] almost to **death**" in Arden (*AYL* 2.4.75, 66), and Orlando "faint[s]" from loss of blood after "The lioness . . . tor[e] some flesh away . . . And cried, in fainting, upon Rosalind" (*AYL* 4.3.148–9). Hermia is "faint with wandering in the wood" (*MND* 2.2.35). Hotspur, Mercutio, Martius Coriolanus, Cassio, and the Sergeant in Macbeth faint from blood-loss. Hotspur is rude to the king's messenger because he was "Breathless and faint" from his **wounds** (*1H4* 1.3.32). Northumberland knows Morton's news is bad when he sees him "so faint, so spiritless" (*2H4* 1.1.70). Mercutio asks Benvolio to "help [him] into some house /Or I shall faint" (*ROM* 3.1.105–6). Martius' faint is indicated only by his words, "I am weary" and Cominius' response (1.9.91). We are twice told that Cassio faints from his wounds (*OTH* 5.1.84), and the Sergeant tells us, "I am faint, my gashes cry for help" (*MAC* 1.2.42). Lear "faints" as he approaches death (5.3.312), and the "fainting hands" of Martius and his brother portend their doom in *TIT* 2.3.133. Burned by **fever**, King John exclaims, "Weakness possesseth me, and I am faint" (5.3.17). Troilus insists upon war with a metaphor comparing war to a foot-race: "Paris should ne'er retract what he hath done, /Nor faint in the pursuit" (*TRO* 2.2.141–2). Running might induce fainting by consuming the body's blood and **heat** too quickly, leaving none left for the brain and heart to generate spirits. Finally, the mother of both Antipholuses is separated from Aegeon as she is "fainting under /The pleasing punishment that women bear," almost collapsing under the burden of pregnancy that is both a joy and a pain to her (*ERR* 1.1.45–6).

(C) Crooke (1615) discusses the flow of blood toward the heart during "passions of the mind," which can provoke fainting fits, and also the greater susceptibility of women to fainting and swooning because of the correspondence between the womb and other parts of the body, including the heart (Book 7, Vv6r; Book 4, Zr). Both Wright's *Passions of the Mind* (1604) and Lemnius' *Touchstone of Complexions* (1576) deal with the sensitive relationships among emotions, embodiment, and physiology. Rowe, Floyd-Wilson, and Paster's edited collection *Reading the*

Early Modern Passions (2004) offers useful readings of individual plays and guides to further reading; see also bibliography under **perturbation**.

falling sickness, Any one of several disorders causing a temporary loss of motor control and/or consciousness, including **apoplexy, dizziness, epilepsy** and **palsy**; see **epilepsy**

femiter see **fumiter**

fennel One of the herbs in Ophelia's posy (*HAM* 4.5.180), associated with **heat** and considered very good for the "yard, or secret part of man," that is, the penis, either when added to a **bath** or made into an ointment (Dodoens 1595, W8v–X1v). Falstaff explains the Prince's attachment to Poins to Doll Tearsheet by saying that both Prince Hal and Poins engage in active, masculine, youthful activities such as swearing, playing quoits, drinking hard, and eating "conger and fennel" (*2H4* 2.4.245). See, however, Fitzpatrick (2007, 31), who argues that conger means cucumber, not the conger eel, and that Falstaff is arguing that the young men eat cooling foods that remove, rather than augment, their manhood.

fever See also **ague, frenzy, quotidian, tertian** (A) The adage "Starve a fever, feed a **cold**," dates to the sixteenth century, if not before (some claimed it to be **Hippocratic**) and is in keeping with received wisdom about the causes of each ailment. Fevers came from an excess of **heat** in the body, and so the physician needed to reduce the body's temperature by prescribing cooling medicines, such as **lettuce** and sorrel, and by reducing the food that the body took in and could not concoct or digest sufficiently (wine was particularly dangerous because of its heating powers). At root, the heat from fevers derived from corrupted or "adust" **humors** within the body, either because the person had too much **blood** altogether in the body, too much of one particular humor for the body (plethora), or too much of a particular quality, such as heat, chill, **dryness**, **moisture**, astringency, heaviness, and so on in a humor (cacochymia). The **physician** needed to temper or moderate the patient's blood to a reasonable amount or quality once more. Phlebotomy or bloodletting by a surgeon was the most reliable way of reducing plethora or cacochymia, but those who were too weak to be let blood (such as children, **pregnant** women, or the elderly) needed to be **purged** by emetics or laxatives. One might diagnose a fever by the body's elevated temperature and quick, hard **pulse**; patients might also **sweat**, or suffer chills. Serious fevers might cause **ecstasy** or frenzy (delirious **madness**). A "burning fever" was a specific type of ailment (called a "double tertian") that derived from choler or yellow bile "adust" or corrupted. Unlike a quotidian, which spiked once a day, or a tertian, which spiked on days one and three, or a quartan, which spiked on days one and four, or a **hectic**, which consumed a patient from within over a long period, a "burning fever" did not remit during the day or from day to day. Several accounts comment on the difficulty of compelling **patients** with high fevers to remain still in order to be bled, or to prevent them from consuming food and drink (which only nourished the **disease** and weakened the body's defenses, according to humoral theories of temperature regulation). Poor patients might need to be bound with ropes, but the wealthy might have servants to restrain them for their own good (see discussion under **frenzy**). (B) Sonnet 147 elaborates a love intemperate:

> My love is as a fever, longing still
> For that which longer nurseth the disease,
> Feeding on that which doth preserve the **ill**,
> The uncertain **sickly** appetite to please.
> My reason, the physician to my love,
> Angry that his **prescriptions** are not kept,
> Hath left me, and I desperate now approve
> Desire is **death**, which **physic** did except.
> Past **cure** I am, now reason is past care,
> And frantic-mad with evermore unrest;
> My thoughts and my discourse as madmen's are,
> At random from the truth vainly express'd;
> For I have sworn thee fair and thought thee bright,
> Who art as black as hell, as dark as night.

Like a feverish patient who demands (for example) warm bedclothes and food rather than the starvation **diet** and cooling **medicines** that his physician recommends, the poet demands the continuing presence or sight of his beloved. The physician, reason, has abandoned him, and so he can no longer distinguish between what he desires and the death that it will bring to him. The fever is incurable because it has affected his reason, like a frenzy (making him frenetic or "frantic-mad"), so that his words and thoughts wander like a **lunatic**'s, "At random from the truth vainly express'd," believing the opposite of what is true. The sonneteer is **crazed** by fever, too, in Sonnet 119, in which his "**eyes** out of their spheres [have] been fitted /In the **distraction** of this madding fever!" (119.7–8). His **eyes** stare and roll in his delirium, a symptom noted in descriptions of frenzy. Cymbeline's queen suffers "A fever with the absence of her son, /A madness, of which her life's in danger" (*CYM* 4.3.2); Ariel, at Prospero's behest, induces "a fever of the mad" in the refugees from the sinking ship (*TMP* 1.2.209).

Patients might endure fits or rigors until the fever broke, especially at night, which interfered with **sleep**. "After life's fitful fever he sleeps well," comments Macbeth on the murdered Duncan (3.2.23). The Abbess blames Adriana's "railing" for Antipholus' sleeplessness and what they have misdiagnosed as a fevered frenzy. "Thereof the raging fire of fever bred; /And what's a fever but a fit of madness?" asks the Abbess confidently (*ERR* 5.1.75–6). In their madness, feverish patients might attempt to escape the servants restraining them. Northumberland leaves his sick-bed

> as the wretch, whose fever-weaken'd joints,
> Like strengthless hinges, buckle under life,

136

Impatient of his fit, breaks like a fire
Out of his keeper's arms.

(*2H4* 1.1.140–3)

Fever deprived the body of strength as the **heart** used up its vital spirit in generating excess heat, hence Nestor's phrase, "the fever whereof all our power is sick" (*TRO* 1.3.139). The **consumption** of blood in the heart might also blanch the face in what Ulysses calls "an envious fever /Of pale and bloodless emulation" (1.3.133–4). Other patients seized and trembled during fits of fever or **ague**. Antony sends Thidias out to be whipped so badly that he hopes "The white hand of a lady [will] fever [him]," and he will "Shake . . . to look on 't" (*ANT* 3.13.138–9). Caesar "shake[s]" both in his **epileptic** fit and in the "fever . . . in Spain," according to Cassius (*JC* 1.2.121, 119). The Archbishop of York diagnoses the country with civil war that is a "burning fever" brought on by too much food and idleness (*2H4* 4.1.56). Henry V argues that the monarch's "fiery fever" of flattering sycophants cannot be extinguished by "ceremony" (*H5* 4.1.253). King John prefigures the "tyrant fever" from which he will die (5.3.14) by describing the French attempt for peace as "calm words folded up in smoke" instead of the "bullets wrapped in fire /To make a shaking fever" that they had previously proffered (2.1.227–9).

"**Infectious** fevers" such as **plague** (*TIM* 4.1.22) might prove fatal when they finally broke or "dissolved." Vincentio predicts such an outcome in *MM*: "there is so great a fever on goodness, that the dissolution of it must cure it," and indeed the solution to Claudio's purported beheading is the death of the prisoner Ragozine from a "cruel fever" and the absence of the supposed friar—really Vincentio in disguise—because of a "strange fever" (3.2.222, 4.3.70, 5.1.152). Timon also describes the physiological action of wine on the body: "Go suck the subtle blood o' the grape, /Till the high fever seethe your blood to froth" (see **heat**; *TIM* 4.3.430). Wine inspired the body with joy and delight, expanding the heart and increasing the production of blood and vital spirit (which enabled life and heat).

(C) For the recommendation to "sterue for hunger three dayes" with a fever, see Guy de Chauliac's *Questionary* (Chauliac 1542, D3v). The *Precepts of Plutarch* offer a response to hungry and fevered children (and impatient adults) that one can only assume was singularly ineffective: "if any (like children) thynke it harde to forbeare meate till the feuer come [break] whiche he mistrusteth will come in deede, it shalbe conuenient for hym to drynke water" (Plutarch 1543, e2v). Bullein (1579, Br) recommends purslane and sorrel for a "burning feuer."

fistula (A) A fistula is a long, hollow, ulcerated passageway in the body, usually caused by **disease**, childbirth, or extensive time on horseback; in the Renaissance the disorder is thought to be caused by sexual promiscuity or syphilis. Modern **surgeons** also use the term to refer to artificial canals created in the body during sex-change operations. Fistulae often connect the body's internal **organs** or passageways like a canal or pipeline. The word itself means "pipe" or cistern, and in its ecclesiastical sense denominates the tube through which the Pope (in earlier eras, all communicants) receives sacred wine.

(B) Shakespeare refers only once to the fistula, the mysterious ailment from which the King of France suffers in *All's Well That Ends Well*:

> Bertram: What is it, my good lord, the king languishes of?
> Lafew: A fistula, my lord.
> Bertram: I heard not of it before.
> Lafew: I would it were not notorious.
>
> (*AWW* 1.1.32–6)

The dialogue surrounding the **illness's** naming suggests that there is something secret about this **wound**, either because of its severity or because of its presumed location "most commonly in a man's fundament" or anus, as Andrew Boorde writes. While Shakespeare's Boccaccian source specifies that the King suffers from a wound in the bosom, in *AWW* both the location of the wound and the means of curing remain mysterious. The many sexual innuendos surrounding the King's ailment and Helena's **cure**, seem to support the implication that the wound is a sexual or genital one—a *fistula in ano*. Helena, "**Doctor She**," claims to have cured the fistula by her father's **prescriptions**, that is to say, by working as a **physician** offering **medicines** to be taken internally rather than as a surgeon operating on the wound. But in Shakespeare's time, a *fistula in ano* or anal fistula could only be healed by surgical means. Legally, Helena, a woman, could belong neither to the Royal **College** of Physicians nor to the Guild of Barber-Surgeons. The cure, like the bed-trick itself, belongs to the world of fairy- or folk-tale.

(C) Medieval surgeon John Arderne (1910) first outlined in England the surgical method for the cure of the fistula. This was a procedure that involved cutting through the fistular passage so that it became part of the rectum itself. Arderne recounts a cautionary tale of a woman physician whose patient, suffering from fistula in the fingers, had to have them amputated because she tried to heal him "oonly with drink of Antioch" instead of essaying a surgical cure (44). Arcaeus, translated by Read (1588), repeats Arderne's method.

Hoeniger (1992) argues that Shakespeare is playing a trick on the audience by implying that the King is suffering from the incurable and embarrassing *fistula in ano* when in fact he is experiencing the minor *fistula in mano* (nail-bed infection or whitlow), which Helena can easily cure. Lecercle's sophisticated Lacanian reading takes the fistula as a metaphor for transgression or unauthorized connections between things that ought not to be connected (1985). Masten (1997) characterizes the fistula as a sexual wound and Helena's cure as a displaced homoerotic encounter; Skwire (2000) and Iyengar (2003) independently suggest that Helena cures the fistula not through miraculous means but as a practicing surgeon. Adelman (1989) also comments on the sexual innuendo surrounding the King's wound and Helena's remedies and helpfully characterizes both Helena's cure of the fistula and her eventual **pregnancy** as ways of ensuring that Helena both employs her sexuality and simultaneously remains pure. In this sense, Helena's cure parallels the bed-trick: an off-stage, sexualized encounter with a more powerful man in order to obtain, first, the ceremony, and second, the consummation, of marriage.

flax See also **linen** (A) Both flax- or linseed and linen cloth (spun from flax plants) were frequently used in medicine, the former as a **poultice** or **plaster** and the latter to make bandages or **tents** (probes) to insert into healing **wounds**. **Flax** was **hot** and **dry** and so was useful in dissolving thick **phlegm** or **humors** corrupted by **cold,** such as tumors or **ulcers** that were swollen. Flax-seed or linseed **decocted** (boiled in water) made a plaster that relieved pain and **cold imposthumes**. Pounded and made into a **clyster** to be inserted rectally, it helped aching **stomachs** and **wombs**. Mixed with honey to make an "electuary," or licking medicine, it cleansed the **lungs** and so could alleviate **consumptions** and **hectic fevers** that wasted the body. Water in which flax had been boiled was particularly valuable in making drops for **eye** disorders, since it brightened and cleared the sight. Similarly, authorities recommended that **patients** recovering from eye-surgery wear bandages made from flax and egg-white.
(B) One of the servants who witnesses the horrific blinding of Gloucester recommends a plaster of "flax and **whites of eggs** / To apply to his bleeding face" (3.7.106–7), a compassionate intervention present in the quarto of *LR* but not in the folio (see also discussion under **eye** and **blind**). Peter Brook famously cut these lines from his influential production of *Lear* at the National Theatre in 1962 and placed the blinding of Gloucester right before the interval, leaving the helpless and bleeding old man to wander off-stage alone, or on some nights aided by aghast theater-goers.
(C) For the uses of linseed, see Dodoens (1595, F7r–8r); for the use of a flax or linen plaster with egg-white after cataract surgery, see **Hippocrates** (1610, I2r) and Baley (1616, E3r). Charles Marowitz's "Lear Log" (1963) recounts Brook's rehearsal process, including the decisions about the blinding of Gloucester. Bergeron (1972) finds a possible source for this treatment in the casebook of John Hall, Shakespeare's son-in-law. Urkowitz (1980) discusses the different versions of *LR* at length, including the servants' help.

flux (A) Flux, meaning flow, could refer to **blood**, pus, or any liquid of the body, but most often referred to "flux of the **belly**" or flux of the **womb**, that is, loose stools, either from dysentery or another cause, or a vaginal discharge, respectively. Flux of the belly resulted from too much **heat** in the **stomach**, which turned food into liquid instead of concocting it correctly, and so the **cure** required cooling medicines such as sorrel, **wormwood**, rose oil, and **plantain** juice, although healers had known the beneficial effects of opiates such as **poppy** on the symptoms of dysentery from the earliest days. Such cures might be administered internally through a **clyster**, externally via a **poultice** on the belly, or consumed by mouth. Women's menstrual flux, however, was usually healthy and needed no treatment, while some kinds of anal flux, for example, from hemorrhoids, might be treated by letting blood from elsewhere in the body to draw away the **humors** (see **blood**).

(B) When the awestruck shepherd Corin comments that courtiers' hands smell sweetly of **civet**, Touchstone rudely retorts that this fragrance comes from "the very uncleanly flux of a cat" (*AYL* 3.2.68), a deliberately inaccurate way of describing the anal secretions of the civet cat used in **perfume**. The associations of flux with diarrhea evoke disgust, especially since Corin has been explaining that shepherds, unlike courtiers, do not kiss hands upon greeting each other, because their ewes' fleeces are greasy. Touchstone argues that the cat's civet is filthier than the sheep's lanolin because of its anal origins.

(C) On flux as the result of superfluous heat, see Vicary (1587, K2r); for cures, see Goerot (1550, I6r–K2r).

folly see **madness, natural**

frantic see **frenzy**

frenzy See also **Bedlam, crazed, lunacy, madness** (A) Frenzy was madness or insanity associated either with a high **fever**, which inflamed or overheated the **brain** or the meninges (membranes) surrounding it, or with noxious **vapors** or **fumes** rising up from poorly digested (unconcocted, in the language of the day) food in the **stomach**. There were three kinds of frenzy, which in some ways corresponded to the three internal senses of the brain (imagination, reason, and memory). In the first kind, **patients**' common sense remained intact, but drew erroneous conclusions; in the second, patients imagined strange things; and in the third, both imagination and reason, and even memory, were disordered. The **inflammation** of the brain and meninges came from an excess of two particular **humors, blood** or **choler**. If the choler were burnt or "adust," the danger was more severe. Frenetic (frantic) patients ran a constant fever, could not **sleep** (or walked in their sleep), pulling imaginary specks of dust from their bedclothes. If the frenzy stemmed from choler, patients might rage so furiously that they had to be bound (if poverty-stricken) or held by servants (if wealthy). Raving frenzy was rarely curable, but the physician should attempt to provide a temperate atmosphere, without too much stimulation. The patient's friends should speak gently to him or chide him (though without inducing anger or sorrow), and he should eat digestible food such as **barley-broth**, gruel, and cooling foods. The most immediately helpful remedy, however, was to let blood from the cephalic **vein** in the upper arm, which immediately cooled the frenzy, or from the vein in the middle of the forehead. Patients too weak to be bled might be cupped on the neck instead, to draw down the dangerous humors that were damaging the brain (see **surgeon's box**). Binding the extremities might also prevent humors from traveling to the brain. Sometimes patients required nightshade or **poppy** to help them sleep, but cooling the fever quickly ran the risk of converting it to a lethargy, or deadly **cold**, a sleep from which they would not wake. The convalescent should avoid alcohol, idleness, unusual or old food, and especially the **heat** of the sun.

(B) Venus includes "frenzies wood" in the list of human **diseases** that she marshals to try to convince the reluctant Adonis to become her lover (*VEN* 740).

Shakespearean characters run frantic or frenetic from extremes of emotions such as lust, grief, and rage, rather than from fever. Several, however, are misdiagnosed as frenzied or delirious when they are merely confused by circumstances, especially in the comedies. Doctor Pinch misdiagnoses Antipholus of Ephesus' indignation as the outrage of delirium. "Yielding to him humors well his frenzy," Pinch confirms, and follows standard practice in treating poor patients when he recommends that the officers bind Dromio, too: "Go bind this man, for he is frantic too" (*ERR* 4.4.81, 113). Malvolio is sent to a darkened chamber to nurse what Maria and Sir Toby and Fabian have told Olivia is his "frenzy." Olivia apologizes for having forgotten him during "a most extracting frenzy of [her] own," her confusion over Cesario and Sebastian (*TN* 5.1.281). Falstaff alludes to the archaic belief that frenzied patients were demonically possessed when he describes Ford as possessed with a "jealous . . . devil of frenzy" (*WIV* 5.1.19). Rosalind alludes to the dream-like state of delirium when she defends herself against her uncle, protesting that she knows her own innocence "If that I do not dream or be not frantic" (*AYL* 1.3.49). The lover, like the "lunatic," is "frantic" or deluded enough to think his mistress beautiful even when she is not, opines Theseus, just as "the poet's **eye**, in fine frenzy rolling" shapes the imagination (*MND* 5.1.12). Holofernes similarly defines "frantic" as "lunatic" or **insane**, and Katharina thinks that Petruchio's rapid changes are sure signs of the choleric frenzy of a "frantic fool" (*SHR* 3.2.12).

These situations are usually comic to audiences, but misdiagnoses of frenzy prove fatal in *TIT*. Young Lucius is frightened of his aunt Lavinia's urgent queries, thinking she suffers from "frenzy," and Saturninus mortally misinterprets Titus' plans for revenge as the ravings of "frenzy," twice calling the old man a "frantic wretch" (4.1.17, 4.4.12, 5.3.64). Belarius identifies the etiology or progression of "one bad thing to worse," arguing that Cloten must have pursued them with company, since "not frenzy, not /Absolute madness could so far have raved /To bring him here alone" (*CYM* 4.2.134–6). Pisanio describes Cloten "in a frenzy" of lust to rape Imogen (5.5.282). Cassandra predicts a similar progression on Hector's impending **death**, "distraction, frenzy, and amazement, /Like witless antics" *TRO* 5.3.85–6). Troilus reminds us of the speed at which the delirious patient moves from one idea to the next, "like a wicked conscience . . . /That mouldeth goblins swift as frenzy's thoughts" (5.10.28–9). The history plays imagine a Britain frenzied with civil war, and monarchs maddened by grief. Talbot is "frantic" with warlike rage (*1H6* 3.3.5), as are Queen Margaret (*R3* 1.3.246) and the Duchess of York (2.4.64). The lady Constance dies "in a frenzy" of sorrow at her son's death (*JN* 4.2.122), and "Sorrow and grief of **heart** /Makes [King Richard II] speak fondly, like a frantic man" (*R2* 3.3.185).

(C) Bartolomeus Anglicus (Batman 1582) and Barrough (1583) discuss frenzy at length; the former distinguishes between "phrensie" and "madness" and accounts frenzy a sign of "deep displeasure from God" as well as an inflammation of the brain (Q4v). Healy discusses frenzy as political disorder in the history plays (2004).

fume (A) Although in Renaissance English the words fume and **perfume** could be used interchangeably, in Shakespeare fume always has a technical meaning, namely the **vapors** of corrupted **humors** rising in the body to provoke an intemperate or confused emotional response, often anger. Although the four cardinal or major humors (body fluids) were liquid, and although they each had varying **complexion**s or humoral characteristics, they could nonetheless each produce fumes or waste products that the body dispersed through **sweat**, **hair**, **nails**, gas, and other **excrements**. If such fumes remained in the body, they could cause ill-health or emotional distress. Medically, a fume was also a method of **drug** delivery, particularly in the **quicksilver** or mercury cure for **pox**; see **tub-fast** for details.

(B) Upon seeing Cloten's corpse, Imogen dismisses her life with Guiderius and Arviragus as "a bolt of nothing, shot at nothing, /Which the brain makes of fumes" (*CYM* 4.2.300–1), a fantasy based on something insubstantial. Ironically, her life with the boys proves to be real and her belief that Cloten's body is her husband's, the fantasy or fume. Eleanor, Duchess of Gloucester, is so "tickled" with anger at Queen Margaret's broils that "her fume needs no spurs" (*2H6* 1.3.150), an image that recalls smoke or a fragrance tickling the **nostrils** and provoking a sneeze. Katharina is likewise reportedly furious at the difficulty of learning to find the frets or markings on the lute, breaking the instrument over her master's head with the punning words "Frets? . . . I'll fume with them" (*SHR* 2.1.152). "Love is a smoke raised with the fume of sighs," rhapsodizes Romeo, using the common analogy comparing the **heart** to a hearth or fireplace in which air combusts to create the vital **spirit** and pure **blood** that are the food for love, and that the sighs or groans of a true lover consume (*ROM* 1.1.190). Prospero compares the process of his magic fading away to the dawn breaking, as the three men of sin find "their rising senses / Begin to chase the ignorant fumes that mantle /Their clearer reason" (*TMP* 5.1.66–8). Prospero imagines the **brain** overcome with fumes or vapors that, like smoke, obfuscate the ventricle or chamber of the brain that is responsible for reason, just as Lady Macbeth imagines the fumes of wine overpowering Duncan's guards (see **limbeck**).

(C) Many of the popular **physic** books in English provide instructions for preparing fumes and recommendations on when to inhale them. Pope John XXI's *Treasury of Helthe* includes fumes of frankincense and laudanum, and burned leather (roe- or kid-) against **rheums** (1553). Gesner (1559) explains the upward movement of fumes or vapors to the brain as he explains the process of **distillation**.

fumiter, fumitory, fumitor So-called because its acrid smoke or **fume** was inhaled as a treatment, fumiter could help a quartan **ague** and the **measles** and smallpox in children, through inducing sweating and **urination**. It was also used to **cure** the **leprosy**, **scab**, and **dropsy**, to cleanse the **liver** and **spleen**, and to mitigate *hysterica passio*. Medicinal fumitory could be easily confused with the poisonous plant **wormwood**, and Shakespeare's references play up the plant's "rank" potential to confuse, making it a fitting figure for usurpation and loss of self in *Henry V* (5.2.45; see discussion under **kecksies**) and *King Lear* (4.4.3; see discussion under **burdock**). On its use as a diuretic and in inducing **sweat**, see Ascham (D1v, 1561), while Gerard (1633, 4Y3r) praises its use in children, as does Lemnius (1587, I4v). Copland lists other uses (1552, K2r).

G

Galen See also **complexion**, **humor** (A) The founder of the popular theory of complexion or temperament, Galen was born in Pergamum (Anatolia, present-day Turkey) in September CE 129. Pergamum was a center of medical knowledge in the ancient world and home of a large shrine to **Aesculapius**, the god of healing. Trained by his father in Greek, geometry, arithmetic, logic, and astronomy, Galen was raised to become a Stoic and a philosopher. After a vivid dream at the age of sixteen in which Aesculapius himself appeared to him, however, Galen took up **medicine**, which he practiced and about which he wrote for more than fifty years. He trained in Pergamum, in Smyrna, Corinth, and Alexandria before returning to Pergamum after completing his studies in **anatomy**. While in practice at Pergamum he undertook surgical operations, and a series of experiments on the nervous system, on breathing, and the gastro-intestinal tract. The high priest of the Aesculepian temple made him **physician** to the gladiators, giving Galen the opportunity to study the healing of **wounds** and to develop further his understanding of anatomy. In his thirties, he traveled to Rome, where he wrote more books and was fêted in the upper ranks of Roman society, then back to Pergamum, perhaps to escape the controversies he had generated among the Roman physicians by his reportedly rough manners and by his support for therapeutic bloodletting, which countered the received wisdom of the then-popular sect of the Erasistrateans. Upon his return to Rome, the emperor Marcus Aurelius appointed him personal physician to his son Commodus. Commodus' disastrous reign had some unfortunate consequences for Galen (including the loss of more than half his library in a fire), but he continued to write "almost one work a year" (Garcia-Ballester 2002, 46). He may have traveled between Pergamum and Rome several more times during his lifetime, but he probably died in Rome. His surviving works form a significant portion of surviving Greek literature, and he was famous both in his own day (in Rome, in Asia Minor, and in Greece) and for centuries afterwards for the humoral theory that took his name, and his many textbooks.

Although Vesalian dissection overthrew Galenic anatomy by the second half of the sixteenth century, Renaissance physicians took from Galen theories of temperament or *crasis* (see **complexion** and **humor**); his emphasis on bloodletting and on curing by opposites (allopathy); and an understanding of the six "non-natural" causes of **disease** and health (eating, sleeping, exercise, repletion, air, and affections or strong emotions; the so-called naturals included the body's natural temperament, bodily humors themselves, and the body parts). Galen also transmitted to the early moderns his anatomical development of the Platonic tripartite soul. Under this model, the vegetative soul, housed in the **liver**, was responsible for growth, excretion, and nutrition; the vital or sensible soul, housed in the **heart**, for the diffusion of the **blood** around the body, for movement, and sense-data; and the ration soul, housed in the **brain**, for reason and apprehension.

(B) Galen beats out his later rival, **Paracelsus**, in Shakespeare handily, perhaps attesting to the overwhelming persistence of humoral theory even after the advent of so-called chemical medicine in the late sixteenth century. Usually, Galen is a byword for medical expertise and efficacy. The Host in *WIV* uses his name as a term of endearment to hearten Dr. **Caius** in his duel with Sir Hugh Evans, and Evans later denigrates Caius' skill by accusing him of not having read Galen, in effect suggesting that he is an unqualified **empiric** (2.3.29; 3.1.66). Protestant Huguenot refugees had landed on England's shores to escape the massacres in France, and many of them were physicians with an interest in the new Paracelsian medicine, so Evans' accusation might seem appropriate. In *COR*, Menenius delights in the news of Coriolanus's return by saying it makes Galen's **cures** seem like those of an amateur (**empiricutic**) in comparison, a telling hyperbole because of the **College**'s opposition to empirical and Paracelsian medicine in favor of a highly theoretical Galenism (2.1.117). **Doctor She**, or Helena, cures the King of France even though all the best physicians, learned in the opposing techniques of both "Galen and Paracelsus" (allopathic and homeopathic, respectively) have failed (*AWW* 2.3.11). Falstaff claims to have read Galen for himself, diagnosing King Henry IV's **apoplexy** from "much grief, from study and **perturbation** of the brain: I have read the cause of his effects in Galen: it is a kind of **deafness**" (*2H4* 1.2.116–18). Perhaps the fat knight in this instance is telling the truth; Galenic explanations for apoplexy did indeed proceed from too much study or sorrow, or from watching (lying awake) at night, which thickened the **cold phlegm** in the brain, and its most notable symptoms were the paralysis of the body and senses, including the hearing.

(C) Theories of complexion appear everywhere in the period, from Johannes de Mediolano's *Regimen* of Salerno (1528) and Boorde's *Breviary* (1542) to Lowe's *Whole Course of Chirurgery* (1597 and 1634) or Burton's summary in *The Anatomy of Melancholy* (1621). Gale translated books three to six of *On the Therapeutic Method* (1586). Further reading on Galen himself includes Temkin's *Galenism* (1973); *The Cambridge Companion to Galen*, which includes a useful essay by Nutton on his transmission in early modern England (see also Nutton's monograph on John Caius and Galen's manuscripts, 1987); Mattern's narratological reading of his case-histories (2008); and Garcia-Ballester (2002). Keller (2006) attributes a renewed Galenism of the late sixteenth century more to the vernacular popularization of anatomy in Helkiah Crooke's *Microcosmographia* (1615) than to the Latin translations of Caius and Linacre (on Linacre's achievements, including his involvement in the founding of the Royal College of Physicians, see Pelling and Webster 1977 and Clark 1966). MacLean (1980) suggests that Galen's writing provided the early modern period with a proto-feminist medicine, since he argued that women were not, *pace* Aristotle, imperfect men but "inverted" ones; Laqueur (1990) argues for the dominance of Galenic homology, the so-called one-sex model, over the **Hippocratic** belief in woman's fundamental difference from man and over Aristotle's belief in female incompletion. Keller (2006) argues that any two-sex taxonomy in early modern Galenism (as evidenced in Crooke) examines the body of woman only to deny women's bodies the coherent psychological and topographical space afforded to men's bodies and consciousness.

gall See also **choler** (A) The bitterest substance in the whole body, gall or choler or yellow bile was **hot** and **dry** and helped the body digest food and void waste products. Associated with the **planet** Mars, it nourished the gallbladder or "chest of gall," which was like a purse in the middle of the **liver**. The gallbladder had three vents, one through which it sucked choler from the liver, so that the **blood** would not become too hot and dry; the second to send **choler** to the **stomach** to aid with digestion; and the third to send bile to the **gut** or lower intestine to help with defecation. Emotional benefits of a balanced amount of gall included military prowess or courage, just anger, and determination. A gall on the body is a sore or **ulcer** from rubbing, perhaps derived from association with the bitter burning thought to come from the astringent humor of choler or bile, and to gall another creature is to inflict on it a hurt, either literally through chafing (as with a saddle on a "galled jade," *HAM* 3.2.242) or figuratively (through annoying behavior or words).
(B) Usually Shakespeare employs the word to evoke bitterness, and puns freely between its meaning as a bodily fluid or as a sore on the body. Biron tells the disguised Princess, "Thou grievest my gall," when she thwarts his attempts at wit and wooing, and she retorts, "Gall! Bitter!" (*LLL* 5.2.237). Romeo's oxymoron, "A choking gall and a preserving sweet," contrasts the vile asperity of gall with the sugar used to conserve fruit (1.1.194). Tybalt picks up the same metaphor when he notices the Montague boys gatecrashing the ball:

> Patience perforce with wilful choler meeting
> Makes my flesh tremble in their different greeting.
> I will withdraw: but this intrusion shall
> Now seeming sweet convert to bitter gall.
> (*ROM* 1.5.89–92)

146

The gentle emotion of patience wars with anger or choler in Tybalt's body, making him tremble at the conflict. For the time being, patience wins, but within his body, his sweetness (associated with pure blood and the good cheer of a **sanguine** temperament) will turn into the bilious bitterness associated with anger and revenge. See also *OTH* 1.3.216, "to sugar, or to gall," or Priam's observation that Paris enjoys "the honey still, but these the gall"; he keeps Helen, while his brothers fight the battle (*TRO* 2.2.144).

Suffolk curses his enemies with poisonous drink that tastes worse than "Gall, worse than gall" (*2H6* 3.2.322). Hamlet complains that he lacks the gall "To make oppression bitter" (2.2.557–8) and to force him to revenge (see **pigeon-liver'd**). Falstaff jokes that he is younger than the Lord Chief Justice and bears a liver hot from youth and drinking rather than "the bitterness of [old men's] galls" (*2H4* 1.2.176). Later in the same scene he turns one part of speech into another, when he uses the word gall as a verb to describe the actions of old age upon an elderly man and "lechery" upon a young: "the **gout** galls the one, and the **pox** pinches the other" (*2H4* 1.2.230). Lear similarly complains that Goneril is "a pestilent gall to me," both a sore spot and a source of bitterness; later in the same scene he rues his treatment of Cordelia for the "small fault" that "drew from **heart** all love, /And added to the gall," that replaced the sweet blood in the heart and the loving image of Cordelia set there with bitter choler (1.4.114; 269–70). Reignier in *1H6* puns on the relationship between injuries that gall and the **humor** of gall or choler itself in his comments on mad-brained Salisbury: "he may well in fretting spend his gall," that is, in his anxiety over battle, Salisbury may use up the store of choler that otherwise he would expend in fighting (1.2.16).

Sometimes gall appears to evoke malice or revenge (cf. **spleen**) rather than justifiable anger. Thersites is, in Nestor's memorable phrase, "A slave whose gall coins slanders like a mint" (*TRO* 1.3.193). Buckingham insists that he acts not from "the flow of gall . . . but /From sincere motions," from the action of pure or **spirited** blood on his heart rather than the movement of bile to excrete waste matter (*H8* 1.1.152–3). In *H5*, gall refers to the **bladder** that contains choler, not to the fluid itself. Grey disingenuously tells King Henry that during his "sweet" reign, "those that were your father's enemies /Have steep'd their galls in honey" (2.2.29–30); similarly, the "gall of goat" in the witches' brew may be either goatish bile or bladder (*MAC* 4.1.27). Emilia insists that women, too, have the right to commit adultery if their husbands so do: "we have galls, and though we have some grace, /Yet have we some revenge" (*OTH* 4.3.92–3).

Galled **eyes** sting from weeping; Hamlet expresses his outrage at Gertrude's hasty wedding while her "galled eyes" were still red from weeping for the **death** of his father (*HAM* 1.2.155). Upon parting from his wife Imogen, Posthumus urges her to write, and swears, "with mine eyes I'll drink the words you send, /Though ink be made of gall" (*CYM* 1.1.100–1). Sir Toby urges Sir Andrew to use "gall enough in [his] ink" in writing his challenge to Cesario (3.2.49).

Hotspur, himself ruled by gall throughout the play, vows to "gall and pinch" Bolingbroke (*1H4* 1.3.229), and Laertes testifies to the virulence of the poison on his foil: "if I gall him slightly, / It may be death" (*HAM* 4.7.147–8).

Best known, however, must be Lady Macbeth's famous plea to the spirits to "take [her] milk for gall" (*MAC* 1.5.48) to replace **breast milk**, considered one of the purest and sweetest fluids in the human body, the best nourishment, and a **medicine** for all manner of ills, with the bitter liquid responsible for anger, malice, and excretion.

(C) Vicary (1587, G3v) describes the gallbladder and the function of gall or choler in the human body. Lady Macbeth's speech has received much critical attention. Some interesting medical interpretations include Levin (2002), who sensitively reads Lady Macbeth's speech in the context of early modern interest in demonology and spirit familiars, and Swain (2004), who investigates the ways in which Lady Macbeth's blood and milk both engage with and diverge from the "one-sex" model of gender.

gangrened Shakespeare's unique reference to gangrene, the scourge of soldiers, sailors, and other active men, appears, unsurprisingly, in *Coriolanus*, when Menenius compares the eponymous hero of Rome to a foot, now gangrened and useless to the body (3.1.305). Gangrene did indeed render limbs useless at this period; unless the patient was strong, healthy, and lucky, the best treatment was amputation of the **infected** limb. Amputation was, however, a last resort; first, the **surgeon** would attempt to draw away the **blood** thought to cause the **inflammation** by bleeding and scarifying the **wound** repeatedly, and by **purging** and **dieting** the patient. He might also wash the wound with **salt** water before applying a **plaster** of beanflower and **barley**, with rosewater, myrrh and other aromatics, and keep the wound as warm as possible. In an extreme case he might add **ratsbane** to the scarified wound, removing the **scab** with honey, butter, and egg-yolk.

geld, gelded See also **eunuch, glib, splay, unseminar'd** (A) To remove the testicles of a male animal or the ovaries of a female; to castrate; to compel to chastity. To geld properly describes removal of the testicles in a male (orchiectomy), and to splay or to spay, removal of the ovaries in a female (oophorectomy), but Shakespeare sometimes uses them interchangeably.

(B) Gelding is often political. Jack Cade complains that "Lord Say hath gelded the commonwealth, and made it an eunuch" (*2H6* 4.2.165) by negotiating with the French, and Ferdinand complains to have "Aquitaine so gelded" by the payment of tribute (*LLL* 2.1.148). Lord Ross warns that Bolingbroke will not much longer brook being "gelded of his patrimony" (*R2* 2.1.237). For low-lifes, the alternative to rape is castration; like Chiron in *TIT* (see **eunuch**), Boult determines to assault an unwilling girl or to "be gelded like a spaniel" (*PER* 4.6.124). For the slightly less seedy Pompey, the only way to enforce chastity and to close down the brothels would be for the Duke to "geld and splay all the youth of the city" (*MM* 2.1.230). Antigonus offers to castrate his three daughters before puberty if Hermione proves false: "I'll geld 'em all; fourteen they shall not see, /To bring false generations" (*WT* 2.1.147), and Autolycus compares his techniques of cutting the string on a money-bag to a **surgeon's** severing the seminal vesicle during an orchiectomy: " 'twas nothing to geld a codpiece of a purse" (*WT* 4.4.610).

(C) Accounts of the operation are common in veterinary manuals but rarely described in this period in the English surgical manuals; as Taylor (2000, 56) points out, the operation parodied in Middleton and Webster's *Anything for a Quiet Life* (1621) is the removal of the penis and entire genital apparatus, not just the stones or testicles (that is, not orchiectomy, the recognized operation on man and animal since at least the seventh century). Taylor suggests, probably correctly, that in a predominantly agricultural society, such an operation would already have been familiar.

glib See **geld** Shakespeare's use of the word **glib** is ambiguous enough that annotators cannot decide whether Antigonus offers to castrate himself, should Hermione prove false, or whether a word is missing and he is merely adding detail to his previous offer to geld his daughters, by suggesting he will perform the operation himself. "I had rather glib my selfe, than they /Should not produce faire issue" (*WT* 2.1.149), he says: if Hermione is unchaste, then so are all women, including his young daughters, and it would have been better that they had never been born and that he sires no more fair children, or that he render them infertile by castrating them so that they cannot produce offspring.

Goose of Winchester Pandarus worries in his epilogue lest "some **galled** goose of Winchester should hiss" (*TRO* 5.10.54). "Goose of Winchester" can mean both one of the prostitutes who worked in Southwark, under the nominal jurisdiction of the Bishop of Winchester and also, as Harris (2004, 209) points out, to a bubo in the **groin** or genitals, which was called a "goose," that is, the chancre or initial symptom of syphilis or **pox**. Here, however, Pandarus identifies those audience members who dare to hiss him as **diseased** themselves, and promises to go seek a **cure** in the **tub**.

gore See also **blood** (A) Blood, especially when thick and clotted, dark red, or present in quantities vast enough to bathe or drown in, especially in war and murder.

(B) Shakespeare typically uses the term to intensify a reference to blood, in either the context of military valor or of poetic (occasionally parodic) hyperbole. Tybalt's corpse appears "all bedaub'd in blood, /All in gore-blood," reports Juliet's **nurse** (*ROM* 3.2.55–6). *MND* mocks the mechanicals' old-fashioned and clumsy verse when Thisbe, mourning over Pyramus' corpse, asks the Fates to "lay their hands in gore" (5.1.339).

Hamlet finds the player's speech about "the rugged Pyrrhus" moving, but Shakespeare marks its language as archaic through its hyperbolic diction. Pyrrhus is as if steeped in blood, "Smear'd" from "head to foot":

> Now is he total gules; horridly trick'd
> With blood of fathers, mothers, daughters, sons,
> Baked and impasted with the parching streets,
> That lend a tyrannous and damned light
> To their lord's murder: roasted in wrath and fire,
> And thus o'er-sized with coagulate gore,
> With **eyes** like **carbuncles**, the hellish Pyrrhus
> Old grandsire Priam seeks.
>
> (*HAM* 2.2.457–64)

Colored heraldic red ("gules") with blood, Pyrrhus is as if decorated ("trick'd") in a way to make the **hair** stand on end ("horridly"). The blood is crusted on him, hardened by the sun like the pastry around a meat-pie ("impasted"), a casing that makes him "o'er-sized." The gore is "coagulate," clotted in lumps or layers, and even his eyes are blood-shot and staring, like rubies ("carbuncles").

Henry V also imagines blood as an ornament, and hardening gore solidifying the bond between soldiers as red wax congeals and seals a letter. The **deaths** of York and Suffolk present the former "insteeped" in "gore" and the latter "kiss[ing] the gashes /That bloodily did spawn upon his face"; "with blood he seal'd /A testament of noble-ending love" (4.6.13–277). Alcibiades similarly calls the blood shed in war "valiant gore" (*TIM* 3.5.83). Montjoy pleads with Henry V for the corpses of the French on the grounds that promiscuous mixing of bloods and classes on the field is "killing them twice":

> many of our princes—woe the while!—
> Lie drown'd and soak'd in mercenary blood;
> So do our vulgar drench their peasant limbs
> In blood of princes; and their wounded steeds
> Fret fetlock deep in gore.
>
> (*H5* 4.7.75–9)

Drowning, soaking, and drenching compare gore to the "deep" water of a flood through which warhorses wade unwillingly. Joan of Arc similarly compares blood to water and contrasts blood to gore when she maintains that "one drop" of native blood is more valuable than "streams of foreign gore" (*1H6* 3.3.55), and Macbeth, in a speech that borders dangerously on the parodic, describes Duncan's alleged murderers as "Steep'd in the colors of their trade, their daggers /Unmannerly breech'd with gore" (*MAC* 2.3.115–16); as many have commented, it is unclear whether his wife truly **faints** in horror at his description or feigns a **swoon** to stop his exaggerated speech.

(C) On Shakespeare's goriness and "blood-baths," see Kirschbaum (1949).

gout (A) Notoriously painful and hard to **cure**, gout primarily afflicted wealthy, old men with agonizing pains in the joints of the feet and ankles. **Paracelsus** argued that the **disease** came from **gravel** or stony deposits in the joints; more orthodox, **Galenic** physicians explained gout as a humoral imbalance in the elderly, who were naturally **cold** and **dry** and whose thick, heavy, **melancholy humors** settled in the joints of the feet. Middle-aged men who ate food that was too rich, drank too much sack (sherry wine), and took too little exercise, suffered from gout because the excessive food they consumed produced **vapors** that descended to the feet and made them **ache**. Travelers in **hot** or cold weather, or those who had wet their feet, might acquire gout as a response to the environment. Finally, men with an excess of **choler** or **gall** suffered from gout because the choler corroded their joints from within; they sometimes ached so badly that they imagined dogs were gnawing their bones. Women and **eunuchs** tended to be immune from the gout, because women naturally cleansed themselves through menstrual **blood** and so did not build up an excess of melancholy in the feet, and eunuchs because they abstained from sexual intercourse, which weakened the joints. Gouty men needed to avoid wine altogether and to moderate their **diet**, labor, or idleness, depending on which was the proximate cause of their disease. Other cases required laxatives administered orally or by **clyster**, followed by bloodletting from the basilic vein on the side of the painful joints. **Poultices** of rose oil and white wine could also help draw up the heavy humors from the joints. Since only God could cure the gout, however, the best course was prophylaxis, notably by moderating one's diet (consuming fish, vegetables, and eschewing dairy products, sweets, and wine); avoiding fens and marshy places with cold, **moist** air; taking only short naps, upright in chairs rather than prone on a bed; exercising the upper body with weights; enjoying sexual relations with caution; purging the lower body with laxatives regularly; and soaking the feet in warm **baths** with astringent **medicines** to soften the joints. (B) Falstaff cannot decide whether his big toe throbs with gout or **pox** (see discussion under **pox**; *2H4* 1.2.243). He also characterizes gout as a disease of old men, just as pox is a disease of the young (see **gall**). Shakespeare characterizes the gout not only as a rich man's disease but also one that is incurable except by **death**, which is preferable to its pangs. Rosalind argues that Time "ambles" comfortably with "a rich man that hath not the gout," because he can enjoy his wealth without "pain" (*AYL* 3.2.320). Posthumus argues that, even imprisoned, he is better off "Than one that's **sick** o'the gout; since he had rather /Groan so in perpetuity than be cured /By the sure **physician**, death" (*CYM* 5.4.5–7). Duke Vincentio, in his guise as the Friar, urges Claudio to "Be absolute for death" in part because of the afflictions of old age such as "the gout, sapego, and the **rheum**" (*MM* 3.1.31).
(C) Holland (1633) summarizes the reasons old men succumb to the gout and some remedies; he is careful, however, to distance himself from the Paracelsians who identify mineral deposits as the cause for gouty pain.

gravel This word appears only once in its medical sense, in Thersites' magnificent catalogue of ills in *Troilus and Cressida* (5.1.19); "loads of gravel i'th' back" are **kidney** stones. Then as now, "gravel i'th' back" caused extreme pain in the kidneys or lower back and upon urination, until the patient passed the stone naturally. We rarely allow stones to reach this point, but early modern patients frequently **vomited** from the pain and found themselves unable to void **urine** altogether, or passed gravel in their urine, with difficulty. Stones built up in the kidneys when crude or raw **humors** became dried out or parched by excessive **heat** around the kidneys. Strong men might be let **blood** from the **vein** in the hamstring, but if the stones came from an immoderate **diet** and too much of a particular humor, the sufferer needed a strong **purge**, preferably with a **clyster**. Fomentations of bran were helpful, and lowering the patient into a **bath** of warm water; or one could use cupping-glasses on the upper thigh (see **surgeon's box**). The **Hippocratic** oath includes an injunction to **physicians** never to cut for the stone but to leave it to experts, a reflection of the difficulty and danger of performing such an operation. Even a **surgeon** as experienced as Paré (1634) calls cutting "the extreme remedy," although he does include instructions on inserting a catheter to draw urine from men and women.

gravel-blind, high-gravel blind see **sand-blind**

green-sickness See also **love-sick** (A) What medical treatises called love-sickness, pale face, white **fever**, or (in women) chlorosis, afflicted both sexes, though to different degrees in different historical eras. During the middle ages, young aristocratic men suffered from love-sickness, a feverish, wasting disorder cured only by marriage to the woman they adored. Love-sick swains sighed, blanched, burned, ate little, forswore exercise, and took relief only in music, sonnets, and the presence of the loved one. They turned pale because their sighs and groans used up sustaining **blood** from the **heart**, they ran fevers because they generated more **heat**, from their love, than their bodies could contain, and they became thin because what little food they consumed was burnt up in their love-sick warmth. Fortunately, noble parents could save their sons by arranging their marriages to their beloveds. From the fifteenth century onward, however, love-sickness became commonly called green-sickness, and affected predominantly young women. **Hippocratic** texts, and, later, early modern physicians, had described the delirium, **frenzy**, palpitations, green or yellowish skin and pica suffered by young girls of marriageable age who were not yet sexually active. Such girls were stifled by the menstrual blood retained in their unopened **wombs**; the **cure** was sexual intercourse, as soon as possible, and "opening **medicines**" (emmenagogues), such as **rue**, to release the corrupted blood. Nubile virgins might also suffer from retained **seed** because they did not have the opportunity to ejaculate it (both men and women ejaculated seed during sexual congress; both needed to climax in order for conception to occur; see **sex**).

Some, however, blamed autoeroticism, and a seed ejaculated by women themselves, for green-sickness. A girl might experience warmth and tingling in her genitals, fantasize about sexual intercourse, and release her seed by herself, but since her womb had not yet been opened by penetrative sexual intercourse with a man, she could not expel this seed from her body. This seed therefore remained in the stones (ovaries) or the womb, putrefied or corrupted, and sent noxious **fumes** or **vapors** to the rest of the body, including the **brain**.

(B) Shakespeare's girls are often accused of green-sickness when their fathers, or those with power over them, want to control their sexual desires and activity, by forcing them to marry or copulate against their will, or with partners of their fathers', not their own, choosing. Capulet diagnoses his daughter as a "green-sickness carrion" (*ROM* 3.5.156), a "tallow-face" (3.5.157) whose dislike for Paris is pathological; the cure is immediate marriage, just as Culpeper and other medical men recommend. "Tallow" and "green" comment on her perceived unhealthy pallor, and "carrion" compares her putrefying blood and seed to rotting, dead flesh. Polonius calls Ophelia a "green girl" when he wishes to dismiss her love-affair with Hamlet as a passing fancy (1.3.101). The Bawd who attempts to "cry up" (*PER* 4.2.93–4) Marina's beauty in the marketplace curses, "A **pox** upon her green-sickness!" (4.6.13) when Marina's chastity freezes the ardor of her best clients, and avers that only by contracting the "pox" through sexual intercourse can Marina "be rid on't" (4.6.15). Her outrage reflects the popular belief that sexual intercourse with a virgin could both cure the French pox or syphilis in the male lover and green-sickness in the girl herself. An exception to green-sick girls who are victims is Viola's imagined sister, who suffers from "a green and yellow **melancholy**," a love-sickness that makes her pale as a statue, "Smiling at grief" (2.4.113, 115). Changing genders to Cesario allows Viola, paradoxically, to cure her own love-sickness by marrying the man she loves.

Shakespearean characters impute green-sickness to men in order to impugn their masculinity. Falstaff identifies the drinking of strong sack (sherry) with manhood because of its ability to heat the blood (see **blood**):

> There's never none of these demure boys come to any proof; for thin drink doth so over-cool their blood, and making many fish-meals, that they fall into a kind of male green-sickness; and then when they marry, they get wenches: they are generally fools and cowards; which some of us should be too, but for **inflammation**. (*2H4* 4.3.90–6)

Thin drink or small beer cools their blood, as do "fish-meals" (as opposed to red meats, which would heat it). Their blood flees their extremities, including their faces, making them look green and pale; it also leaves their **livers**, removing their courage (see **lily-liver'd**). Too cool a man could not provide enough heat to complete the fetus, and would sire an imperfect, incomplete girl-child, while simultaneously becoming more feminine himself. Enobarbus similarly associates male green-sickness with weakly cowardice when he reports that the hungover Lepidus "is troubled /With the green sickness (*ANT* 3.2.5–6).

Shakespeare inverts the association of green-sickness with women, and the coercive use of sexuality as a cure, to comic effect in *VEN*. While Venus is "sick-thoughted," and "love-sick," requiring a specific love-object as therapy,

Adonis is the one whose face is pale or "leaden," "green," like an unripe plum, and who is forced into sexual activity undesired by him (*VEN* 5, 175, 34, 527).

(C) Lange (1554) blames too-thick or too abundant menstrual blood in virgins, and Varandaeus (1615) associates chlorosis with nobly born girls. Culpeper (1655) comments that lay-people call love-sickness green-sickness. Paré worries that suffering virgins will worsen their condition by attempting to expel their own seed (1634). Fleissner (1961) argues that Falstaff dies of a metaphoric green-sickness stemming from a broken heart. Starobinski (1981) identifies the disorder's Hippocratic roots. Neely (2004) argues that love-sickness in Shakespeare has no definite object-choice or even gender direction in *TNK*, and especially in *AYL* and *TN*. On *TNK*, see also Bonelli (1993). On *HAM* see Roberts (1995). On Adonis as green-sick virgin, see Iyengar (2005), although Starks (2007) argues that Venus evokes our compassion for her love-sickness. Dawson (2008) suggests that, while the Jailer's daughter in *TNK* and Ophelia in *HAM* are driven mad by love-sickness, Viola in *TN* offers a model of female love-sickness that is joyfully liberating.

groin The groin or the twist joined the thigh-bones to the genitals but also **purged** or cleansed fluids into the **liver**; what Vicary calls the "curnelly flesh in the piping or bowing of the Thyes," the hard flesh in the crease, we might now call lymph nodes (1587, H4r). In Shakespeare's unique reference it appears to have a sexual or bawdy overtone, as Mistress Quickly worries that Pistol "hurt [Falstaff] i'the groin" with "a shrewd thrust at [his] **belly**" so that he will be unable to enjoy the company of Doll Tearsheet (*2H4* 2.4.210–11).

gum, gums (A) Gums are the soft tissues in the mouth, in which the **teeth** are rooted; the thick, yellowish, sticky secretion from the **eyes** of the elderly or those with eye-**infections**; and so-called gum Arabic, the sap of the acacia tree, used to treat the discharge from a sexually transmitted infection such as gonorrhea, to reduce menstrual flow and, most frequently, to temper or soften **medicines** into which it was mixed.

(B) Lady Macbeth refers to the "boneless gums" of the infant she imagines throwing to its **death** (see discussion under **teeth**, *MAC* 1.7.57). Hamlet mocks Polonius by characterizing old men as half-blind, "their eyes purging thick amber and plum-tree gum" (*HAM* 2.2.199). The Poet compares poetry to "a gum, which oozes /From whence 'tis nourished," like the sap of the acacia tree (*TIM* 1.1.21). Othello compares his tears to the "**medicinable** gum" of "Arabian trees," (*OTH* 5.2.351) an allusion that turns his body into an exotic ingredient for medicine and that suggests his suicide will be therapeutic and perhaps bind together the **wounds** he has inflicted on the state.

(C) See Gerard: "the gum doth binde and somewhat coole: it also hath ioyned vnto it and emplaistick or dawbing qualitie, by which it dulleth or alaieth the sharpnes of the medicines, wherewith it is mixed" (1597, 4E5v).

gut (A) The guts conveyed the waste matter left over from the first concoction or digestion away from the **stomach**, and cleansed the whole body of its superfluous

humors. There were six portions of the guts, which began at the lower mouth of the **stomach**, and ended at the rectum or "fundament." By extension, gut or guts refer to the flesh surrounding the intestine, such as a (usually large) **belly**, or sometimes to the lower abdomen or **bowel**. So-called catgut (usually some animal's intestine, but rarely feline) was used to string instruments such as **viols** or lutes.

(B) Falstaff's "fat-guts" (*1H4* 2.2.31) are held in by his enormous belly, and often mocked by Hal, who argues that "there is no room for faith, truth, nor honesty in [Falstaff's] bosom . . . it is all filled up with guts and midriff," to such an extent that he will attempt to cheat the hostess rather than pay his bill (*1H4* 3.3.154–5). Falstaff comes in for particular mockery for his cowardly behavior at Gadshill and his bragging account of it afterwards. Hal lambastes him for a "stuffed cloak-bag of guts," a traveling-case of innards, a "clay-brained guts," a fat man with dirt for **brains**, because he "carried [his] guts away as nimbly, with as quick dexterity, and roared for mercy" (2.4.452, 227, 258). Mistress Page echoes Hal's insult to Falstaff when she imagines that "his guts are made of puddings," part of the imagery of the play that compares the fat knight to a deer or other animal to be consumed—in this case, equating the intestines inside his body to a black-pudding or blood-sausage (*WIV* 2.1.31). Even the slender Pistol comes in for associated mockery, when Nym threatens to "prick [Pistol's] guts a little" with his rapier (*H5* 2.1.58). Thersites complains that Ajax "wears his wit in his belly and his guts in his head" (*TRO* 2.1.73).

Hamlet vividly clarifies the transformation from living body to murdered corpse when he tells Gertrude that he will conceal Polonius' body and "lug the guts into the neighbour room" (3.4.212). The "wretched, rash, intruding fool" (3.4.31) is now merely meat that has been butchered. Later, Hamlet claims he is not threatening Claudius but merely "show[ing him] how a king may go a progress through the guts of a beggar," a proverbial figure for **death** as the equalizer among rich and poor but one that Hamlet, typically, explores in visceral detail through allusion to digestion (4.3.31).

(C) Vicary (1587, G1v) describes the function and appearance of the guts; Fitzpatrick (2007, p. 90) comments on the preparation and consumption of blood- or black-puddings.

guts-griping In cases of **jaundice**, in which the passage of **choler** was obstructed and returned to the **liver**, the **guts** did not receive the **gall** they required in order to help the body to defecate. If the small intestine were affected, **patients** were tormented by intolerable **cramps**, and their guts became wrung, convoluted like the strings of a harp. If the upper part of the intestine were affected, patients **vomited** food; if patients were extremely "costive" or constipated, and the stool **dry** and hard, patients vomited stool itself. Thersites maliciously includes "guts griping" in his list of "**plagues** of the South" (*TRO* 5.1.18). Pistol similarly curses Falstaff, long associated with guts, "Let vultures gripe thy guts!" and plans to reveal him to Ford (*WIV* 1.3.85). Lemnius (1576, Kr) vividly describes the foul vomiting of patients suffering from the griping pain of **bowel** obstructions.

hair (A) Hair in the Renaissance is an **excrement** or bodily secretion, the projection of **vapors** or **fumes**, coming out of the body like plumes of smoke. Its color might indicate the humoral personality or **complexion** of a person: a red-haired person was **sanguine**, a blonde-haired one **phlegmatic**, a black-haired, **melancholic**. Hair turned grey with age as the body lost **heat**. Head-hair protected the **brain** from the **elements** and added to the beauty and symmetry of the human body. Medically, it permitted vapors from the brain to pass out healthfully.

Men grew hair on their faces (moustaches and beards) at puberty, when their production of **seed** became very great. A beard demonstrated a man's fertility, since it grew from the superfluous seminal **humor** or seed. Hence beards appeared on a man's chin, nearer to his stones, or testicles. Women who were exceptionally hot and who produced an excess of seed (or whose seed was relatively hot and strong in comparison to the majority of women) might also grow beards, but such were rare.

Baldness might on the one hand indicate mental activity or intelligence so great that its heat burned off the hair as it was generated. On the other, old men over the course of years became bald because their humors burnt up and became "fuliginous" or sooty (powdery and black). In others, baldness was a symptom of **diseases** such as secondary syphilis or French **pox**; **leprosy**; or **fever**. Scar tissue from old **wounds** might also cause baldness, or it might be iatrogenic or doctor-caused, from depilatory **salves** used because of their therapeutic heat and **dryness**. A physician could detect which humor was responsible for baldness by matching the color of any **ulcer** or sore at the root of falling hair: red for **blood**, yellow for choler, white for phlegm, and black for melancholy. Baldness was almost impossible to **cure**. **Physicians** might chafe the scalp and apply **decoctions** of vine- and oak-leaf, burnt doves' dung, woodbine, **quicksilver**, or various liniments.

156

(B) Hair in Shakespeare can mark **sex** and age (in both men and women); **race**; rank; the presence of venereal disease; female beauty or ugliness; emotional upheaval, even to the point of insanity; smallness or insignificance on the one hand or of plenitude on the other; and the distinction between animal and human, or natural and human-made. Perhaps the association of hair with seminal humors led to the folk-belief that a horse-hair ("courser's hair"), laid in water, would generate life spontaneously (*ANT* 1.2.193). The early history plays and *Macbeth* pun implicitly on the roots of the words "horror/horrid/horrible" (from Latin *horreo*, "I bristle" or "my hair stands on end"). In the first tetralogy, hair bristles with horror: at the sight of murder or a murdered corpse (*2H6* 3.2.171, 174, 3.3.15); at Margaret's curses (*R3* 1.3.303); from night-mares (*R3* 1.4.53). And in *MAC*, the "horrid image" of murder "doth unfix [Macbeth's] hair" (1.3.135) even as he contemplates the act. Tearing one's hair, as does Constance in *JN* (3.4.45), or appearing with it disheveled, as Ophelia does in the stage directions of the first quarto of *Hamlet*, indicates an unhinging grief. Burgundy laments France's scattered state by comparing the body politic to prisoners who appear with "wildly overgrown" hair (*H5* 5.2.43). Brutus' hair, too, stands on end when he sees Caesar's ghost (*JC* 4.3.280). Elsewhere in the second tetralogy facial hair or its lack indicates male sexual maturity, as Falstaff swears that he will drive off Prince Hal or "never wear hair on [his] face" again (*1H4* 2.4.139), the chorus in *H5* maintains that even the young man with but "one appearing hair" on his chin will be drawn to fight for Harry (3.Pr.23). At the other extreme, the "coal-black hair" of Warwick signifies his youth and vigor (*3H6* 5.1.54). Nerissa jokes that "the clerk will ne'er wear hair on's face that had [the ring]" (*MV* 5.1.158). Bassanio complains that external signs of masculinity such as the beard do not indicate inner signs of manhood such as blood and strength:

> How many cowards, whose **hearts** are all as false
> As stairs of sand, wear yet upon their chins
> The beards of Hercules and frowning Mars;
> Who, inward search'd, have **livers** white as **milk**;
> And these assume but valour's excrement
> To render them redoubted!
>
> (*MV* 3.2.302)

A beard evokes the mythological heroes Hercules and Mars, and yet those who bear them might nonetheless be weak as sand and, lacking the hot blood that inspires martial courage, have "livers white as milk" (see discussion under **liver**).

A single hair on the head measures smallness and care throughout the plays (*H8* 3.2.259). Prince Arthur echoes the Geneva Bible's "all the heares of your head are nombred" (Matt. 10: 36) and the parable requiring a fault-finder to find first the "mote" or speck in his own **eye** before criticizing another when he pleads with the man commanded to **blind** him to feel "a wandering hair" or "mote" in his own eye so that he will realize the "horrible" commission he has

hair

been given (*JN* 4.1.92). John himself evokes the classical story of the sword of Damocles, reportedly suspended from a single hair above the hero's bed, to describe his heart anchored like a ship by only one string or "one little hair" (*JN* 5.7.54), and Benedick characterizes Beatrice's extreme fierceness by claiming he would rather fetch a hair from the Great Ham's beard than encounter her (*ADO* 2.1.268). Most telling is the "estimation of a hair" that Portia, as Balthasar, requires from Shylock, should he insist upon his pound of flesh (*MV* 4.1.331), or the "not so much perdition as an hair" that Prospero promises Miranda shall befall the shipwrecked mariners (*TMP* 1.2.30), like the "hair-breadth scapes" experienced by Othello (1.3.136).

1H4 puns on heir/hair throughout, and also uses the hair as a unit of measurement (itself a comment on the play's themes of the weighing and comparison of *heirs*). Hotspur uses the hair as a measure of smallness to challenge the king "to the ninth part of an hair" (3.1.138); the Hostess brags that "the tithe of a hair was never lost in my house before," to which Falstaff retorts that "Bardolph . . . lost many a hair" (with an implicit suggestion of venereal disease, 3.3.60). The Earl of Worcester has two of the best examples: "the quality and hair of our attempt /Brooks no division" (4.1.61) crystallizes the play's concerns with the relations between father and son, between Hotspur and Hal, and with the quality of the heir, while his epithet, "hair-brain'd [also spelled **hare-brain'd**] Hotspur" collapses the latter's rashness into the **madness** of lusty hares in March, the overflow of choleric humors, and Hotspur's having heirs on the brain (5.2.19). *2H4* begins with Falstaff's intended put-down of the prince, "not a hair amiss" (1.2.24), turning into instead a figure for Falstaff's own obsolescence. The Lord Chief Justice chides him for his lack of "gravity," given the "white hair" on his chin, and Falstaff himself alludes to his white hair when he complains of the **ills** of aging, including the **gout** and the **pox**. The "silver" hair of "Old Salisbury" (*2H6* 5.1.162), and Falstaff's "white" beard (*2H4* 1.2.181) demonstrate their age, if not their wisdom. Baldness can also indicate old age, as in *ERR* 2.2.70, or treatment for venereal disease, as in *TMP* 4.1.237 (since secondary syphilis could include alopecia and skin lesions as symptoms). Edgar's "elf-knots" or dreadlocked hair indicates his madness and poverty, as opposed to the hair "curl'd" by a "serving-man" (2.3.10; 3.4.86).

Hair, especially "perfect yellow" (*TGV* 4.4.189) evokes female beauty: Lucetta cautions Julia that she must cut off her hair to masquerade as a boy (*TGV* 2.7.44) and in the same play, Speed and Launce joke that a woman with "more hair than wit" has "more faults than hairs, and more wealth than faults" (3.1.354, 364). This association can make a woman's hair a love-token, as in the bracelets that lovers exchange (*MND* 1.1.33). Black or "amber" hair can be a sign of ugliness in women, as in the extended debate on female beauty in *LLL* (4.3.255) or Rosalind's stern exhortation to the deluded Phoebe (*AYL* 3.5.46). Cleopatra poignantly exhorts her messengers not to "leave out /The color of [Octavia's] hair" (*ANT* 2.5.114), and even returns to the question at 3.3.32. Red hair was the "dissembling color" (*AYL* 3.4.7), because traditionally it was thought that Judas Iscariot, Christ's traitorous disciple, had red hair. Venus's "disheveled hair"

158

(*VEN* 147) indicates her youthfulness and arousal; in Lucrece, the "golden threads" that make her beautiful make her seem "wanton" even though it is a "wanton modesty," wanton in the sense that it fails to protect her from Tarquin's ravishing stride (*LUC* 400). Paradoxically, however, to be married "in one's hair," that is, with one's hair dressed but hanging loose, denoted one's virginity; Anne Bullen's appearance at her wedding to King Henry "in her hair richly adorned with pearl" demonstrates to all onlookers that the king has not made her his mistress before marriage (*H8* 4.1, s.d., "The Order of the Coronation").

(C) On the origins and significance of beards, see esp. the beautifully illustrated Hill (1571, Chapter 33, M1v–6v [many signature- and page-errors]); see also Prynne's later exposition against long hair in men (1628). On "Shakespeare's Hair," and the cultural history of relics or artifacts, see Harris (2001). Fisher (2001) argues that the "genital focus" of critics has obscured the importance of hair, particularly facial hair, as a sexual marker in early modern portraits and writing. On Tudor beards, see also Doyle (1981).

hare-brain'd See also **brain**, **hair** Hare-brained properly means "with the brains of a hare," or small intelligence, with uncontrolled impulsiveness. Thus "hare-brain'd Hotspur, govern'd by a **spleen**" demonstrates his immaturity (*1H4* 5.2.19). The spleen might be responsible for both **melancholy** and for **choler**, for malice or for anger. Given the characterization of Hotspur elsewhere in the play, and his emblematic name, he is probably acting out of wrath rather than out of spite.

hare-lip See also **deformed, mole**, **monster** (A) The term "hare-lip", meaning a cleft lip or cleft palate, entered the English language in the sixteenth century, presumably by analogy to a hare's broad, flaring, top lip. A child with cleft lip is born with a fissure in its top lip; in cases of cleft palate, this fissure extends to the palate. This condition prevents infants from successfully nursing and sometimes from feeding at all. Early modern women who saw hares suddenly in pregnancy, or who suddenly craved hares' meat, might give birth to such children, although they could protect themselves and their offspring from such encounters by wearing a smock with the lower part of the seam left unsewn, or cloven.

The prognosis for cleft lip was good, but for cleft palate, unpromising. **Surgeons** could manufacture a prosthetic palate from sponge or some other soft substance, to allow the child to swallow food, but such children usually perished after two or three months, because it was difficult to keep the artificial palate in place long enough for the child to suck or eat. Hare-lips, on the other hand, were eminently operable. Today and in Shakespeare's time, surgeons operated as soon as possible in order to fuse the lip and palate and allow the child to eat. Present-day surgeons like to operate on a cleft lip before the infant is three months old; sixteenth-century surgeons had to wait until the child was at least old enough to tolerate surgery without anesthesia and to avoid unpicking the surgeon's stitches. Very young children reportedly struggled so much that they sometimes broke the surgeons' needles. After cutting off or debriding the top layer of **skin** on either side of the cleft, the surgeon would stitch the two sides of the cleft together, and finally apply a **balm** or emollient ointment.

(B) Both Shakespeare's references to this birth defect allude to the belief that fairies or spirits from the devil bewitched the **pregnant** mother and maimed her child. When Edgar feigns **madness** in his guise as a **Bedlam** beggar he claims to be pursued by the "foul fiend Flibbertigibbet" who causes the eye disorder **web and pin**, **squints**, and the hare-lip (*LR* 3.4.115–18); Oberon and his company bless the newlyweds against such misfortune as "**mole**, hare-lip, nor scar" or other "mark prodigious" (*MND* 5.1.411–12).

(C) The word is rare enough that Edward Phillips includes it in his dictionary of "hard" words (1658); Shakespeare seems to have been one of its earlier adopters. Lupton describes its supernatural causes and **cure** (1579, E1v, M2r). Guillemeau describes the cure of fistula as being "like" the cure of the hare-lip (1612, 2D3r–v), and Paré (1634) describes the cure of hare-lip as one of the primary duties of the surgeon.

heart See also **blood, brain, eye, liver, lung, heart-string** (A) The heart vied with the brain for the title of ruler of the body; a common analogy held the heart in the middle of the body as a feudal King sat enthroned in the middle of his court, of which the brain was a chief member (an alternate model had the brain as the King to which the general, the heart, was subservient). All other members of the body served the heart just as the king's subjects served him, and the heart sustained them just as the feudal lord or king provided for his vassals. Shaped like a pineapple, the heart gave blood, life, breath, and **heat** to the body, expanding and contracting with the **pulse** according to whether it was attracting nutritive blood or sending spirituous blood to the brain and expelling waste. Each ventricle of the heart had two valves. When the heart expanded, the right ventricle valve to the *vena cava* opened, letting in blood. The left ventricle valve from the pulmonary **artery** or lung **vein** then opened to let in blood and air from the lungs. The right ventricle refined blood, a mixture of all four **humors**, into pure blood, before the left refined it still further into "spirituous blood." When the heart contracted, the other two valves opened and expelled the blood from the right ventricle and the spirituous blood to the arteries. Strong emotions or **perturbations** might also affect the heart. Joy, delight, generosity, and bravery expanded the heart so that it could consume more nutritive blood (containing natural **spirit**), and generate more pure blood (containing vital spirit). Fear, sorrow, hatred, and pusillanimity shrunk the heart and reduced its supply of vital spirit. Sighs, words, and expressions of emotions consumed the heart's supply of vital blood, and yet it was necessary to express emotion lest the heart become **o'ercharged** or overfull of blood and break or crack its heart-strings.

(B) Hearts in Shakespeare provide blood, warmth, and spirit, variously associated with the emotions of love, anger, remorse, and sorrow. The history plays evoke the "heart-blood" of the body politic dismembered by civil war. The "heart-blood" can be the figurative or literal sons of the monarch, such as the "heart-blood warmed" traitors who deny their king (*R2* 3.2.131), the "heart-blood of the House of Lancaster" (*2H6* 2.2.66) or the "dearest heart-blood" that is Prince Edward to Margaret and Rutland to the Duke of York (*3H6* 1.1.223). Henry VI's "lukewarm . . . heart" indicates his cowardice and weakness (*3H6* 1.2.34). Richard of York vows to avenge his father with "furnace-burning heart" (*3H6* 2.1.80). Although some authorities granted the **eye** and the **liver** the power to generate lust or erotic desire, and the heart and the brain to involve the rational soul and love, Shakespeare grants both heart and liver the ability to engender sexual love. Sonnet 154 presents Cupid with a "heart-inflaming brand" (2); Armado expresses his "heart-burning" love for Jacquenetta (*LLL* 1.1.277); Mistress Quickly urges the fairies to pinch Falstaff because his heart burns with lust:

> Lust is but a bloody fire,
> Kindled with unchaste desire,
> Fed in heart, whose flames aspire
> As thoughts do blow them, higher and higher.
> (*WIV* 5.5.95–8)

Quickly's image conforms to standard early modern anatomical imagery in figuring the heart as a bellows that generates heat through the action of air from the lungs. It differs, however, in the meaning of the fire that Falstaff's heart sparks. His heart does not refine or purify blood for the brain to turn into animal spirit (which would involve the rational soul or uniquely human part of him in true love, not lust). Instead, the addition of air merely fans the flames of his vital spirit or erotic energy, so that lust generates more lust. Joy made a heart "light" by warming it so that the heavy humors of **melancholy** could be purged in the **spleen**, leaving the rest of the body happy. King Henry V complains, "having neither the voice nor the heart of flattery about me, I cannot so conjure up the spirit of love in [Katharine of France]"; here he puns on the vital spirit engendered by love and the ghost or spirit of love as an apparition magicked into existence by enchanters (*H5* 5.2.287–8). A "**cold** heart" was literally so, shrunken and contracted with small-minded emotions or the approach of **death**. Katharine warns King Henry that "Cold hearts freeze /Allegiance in them" at his new wars in France (*H8* 1.2.61). In contrast, Wolsey describes the hearts of princes enlarging in righteous rage: "The hearts of princes kiss obedience /So much they love it; but to stubborn spirits /They swell, and grow as terrible as storms" (*H8* 3.1.162).

Heart, brain, and liver are each "sovereign thrones" in Shakespeare (*TN* 1.1.36). Agamemnon's necessity to the Greeks makes him all parts of the body and the eternal soul that animates it, "nerve and bone of Greece, /Heart of our numbers, soul and only spirit" (*TRO* 1.3.56). When Hamlet vows to love the man who is not "passion's slave" and wear him in his "heart's core, yea in my heart of heart" (*HAM* 3.2.73), the phrase "heart's core" seems a tautology (since "core" means "heart"), but Hamlet alludes to the heart's expansion and contraction under perturbation. A man who is not passion's slave retains a core or kernel within his heart that is immune to strong emotion and so can retain his personality and integrity at all times.

(C) Vicary (1587, F2v) compares the heart to both a King and a pineapple. Slights' monograph on the Shakespearean heart argues in part for a heart at war with the organs of the senses (eye, **tongue**, **ear**) that provide the only external outlets for its emotions (2008). See also Robson (2001), who discusses the engagement of ear, eye, and heart in love in *VEN*; Schoenfeldt (1999), who comments upon the degree of control one could exert upon the heart and its perturbations; Maus (1995), who paradoxically identifies theatricality with the emergence of privacy and the internal in the period.

heart-string The **heart** in **Galen** grew or shrank under the experience of strong emotion; it was covered with strong bands or muscles that likewise expanded and contracted with the heart. In Shakespeare, these bands or cords become "heart-strings" or "bands" or "threads" that can "crack" under stress or emotional upheaval. Shakespeare seems to imagine that one heart-string in particular is "The master-cord on[one]'s heart!" (*H8* 3.2.106), and signals the utmost a heart can expand in love: "from heart-string /I love the lovely bully!" avows Pistol (*H5* 4.1.47). Claudius' "heart with strings of steel" (*HAM* 3.3.70.) has been hardened by villainy (see discussion under **sinew**). Extreme love or grief can pull or break the heart-strings, compelling Antony to abandon his troops after Cleopatra flees the battle: "My heart was to thy rudder tied by th'strings" (*ANT* 3.11.57), and triggering Lear's death ("His grief grew puissant and the strings of life /Began to crack" (5.3.217–18)). Proteus in *The Two Gentlemen of Verona* is "so false that he grieves my very /heart-strings," mourns Julia (4.2.62). A passage in *King John* (5.7.52–6) gives us the sense that the heart enlarges to such an extent with strong emotion that only the strings can hold it together:

> The tackle of my heart is crack'd and burn'd,
> And all the shrouds wherewith my life should sail
> Are turned to one thread, one little **hair**:
> My heart hath one poor string to stay it by,
> Which holds but till thy news be uttered.

This rich metaphor turns the heart into a vessel tossed upon a sea of **humors**, one that is now burning like a ship on fire. The excessive **heat** of emotion has burned the "tackle" and the "shrouds" that hold the rigging upright. The sails are held in place by only one string, and will fall once King John, the speaker, hears the "news" (Faulconbridge's tidings that the Dauphin of France is on the march).

heat, hot See also **cold, dry, moist** (A) Heat was the fundamental quality of all life, basic to all bodily functions. Heat differentiated men from women, one **complexion** from another, youth from age, and southerners from northerners (thus Italians were hot-blooded and vengeful, while Danes were cold and dull). Too much heat, however, whether from climatic conditions or from food, or from warming emotions such as love or anger, could trigger the overproduction of **choler** or **blood** in the body, or dry out ("make adust") the **humors** into gases or **vapors**, or thick, coagulated dregs.

(B) Heat could also trigger hallucinations, such as Macbeth's "dagger of the mind, a false creation /Proceeding from the heat-oppressed **brain**" (*MAC* 2.1.39), the result of **fumes** obscuring his reason and overheating the ventricle of fantasy in the **brain**; or **agues** and **fevers**. In such cases, the body needed to be cooled down. When Gertrude fears that Hamlet is **insane**, she urges him, "Upon the heat and flame of thy **distemper** /Sprinkle cool patience" (*HAM* 3.4.136). In a burn or inflamed **wound**, however, "hot" medicines or herbs would draw out pus, an analogy that Proteus employs to explain his newfound love for Sylvia over Julia "Even as one heat another heat expels" (*TGV* 2.4.193). "Youth and heat of blood" went together (*2H4* 5.2.18), explaining the propensity of the young to fall in love, to love ardently, to fight valiantly but at a moment's notice, and to be quick-tempered. Leontes finds the conversation between Hermione and Polixenes "too hot!" (*WT* 1.2.108) or evocative of sexual desire, just as Othello finds Desdemona's palm too warm and moist (*OTH* 3.4.36; moisture or humidity was another quality of youth and vigor). Hermione and Desdemona are too hot to be chaste women, who were cool and temperate. Katharina, hotter still, choleric in complexion or temperament, is put on a cooling **diet** by Petruchio (deprived of food, **sleep**, and a fire, all of which made the body hotter).

(C) **Galen**, translated by Culpeper (1652), offers the standard account of the importance of heat to human life, as does Hippocrates (1983). Laqueur (1990) argues that early modern understandings of sex-difference as a "one-sex" continuum rather than as binary categories base their assertions about gender on Galen's belief that women were colder than men, both from conception and from the blood that they lost during menstruation; King (2007), however, argues that Laqueur ignores the Hippocratic belief that women were in fact constitutionally hot, and bled monthly to cool their over-heated bodies.

hebona Usually glossed as henbane or **yew**, both of which are toxic. Shakespeare uses the word to refer to the mortal poison that kills Hamlet Senior by coursing through his veins as fast as **quicksilver** and curdling his **blood** into "droppings" or small clots like congealed **milk**, presumably because of its extreme **cold** (1.5.62). Piny (1601, Book 25, chapter 4) lists henbane along with quicksilver as one of the poisons that curdle or **dry** up the blood, although most sources call white henbane wholesome or beneficial, especially in curing **wounds** and **ulcers**: see Lanfranco (1565); Ruscelli (1569); Banister (1575); Bullein (1579). Bartolomeus Anglicus (Batman 1582) and Topsell (1607) comment on the venomousness of yew.

hebenon see **hebona**

hectic A hectic **fever**, unlike a **quotidian**, **tertian**, or quartan, raged continually, never abating (in this sense it differs from a present-day medical "hectic fever," which intermits and returns every day). Unlike other sorts of fevers, the hectic originated not from corrupted **phlegm** (as in a quotidian) nor from corrupted **melancholy** (as in a quartan) nor from corrupted **choler** (as in a tertian), but from the solid and fleshy parts of the body. It heated the body from within like a hot vessel, Barrough says (1583, P1v), melting away **humors**, flesh, and even bones in a kind of **consumption**, leaving sufferers flushed and wasting. In Shakespeare's single usage, Claudius says of Hamlet, "Like the hectic in my **blood** he rages," he burns Claudius like an unremitting fever that sears him from the inside out (*HAM* 4.3.66). A medically minded listener would know, however, that the hectic (unlike other fevers) had been considered incurable since **Galen**'s time. If Hamlet is indeed "like the hectic," England cannot relieve Claudius, and the state of Denmark will melt away like the "too solid flesh" (*HAM* 1.2.129) that Hamlet himself imagines disappearing.

Hem! see **cough**

hemlock A known poison, hemlock was used in **medicine** as a **poultice** to reduce or suspend sexual development or desire, to dry up breast **milk**, and, dissolved in wine, to treat **epilepsy**. Hemlock is one of the "idle weeds" that grow in decayed France in *Henry V* (5.2.45) and that are braided in Lear's mad crown (*LR* 4.4.4). Its root appears in the witches' brew in *Macbeth* with a double aptness, as poison for the witches but medicine for Macbeth, since Lady Macbeth claims during the banquet scene that her husband has suffered from fits, presumably epileptic, "from youth" (*MAC* 4.1.25; 3.4.53). On its coldness, see Culpeper (1652, Lr); on its general use, see Langham (1597, Ur); for a description, see Gerard (1633, 4v1r–2v).

herb-grace, herb of grace See also **marjoram** and **rue** Ophelia comments that one may call rue "herb-grace o' Sundays," (4.5.182), and the gardener in *R2* sets a bank of "rue, sour herb of grace" in memory of Queen Anne (3.4.105). Herb of grace is sweet, not sour, however, in *AWW*, in which the clown compares Helen to the "sweet" herb of grace in a mixed salad (4.5.15–17). In Shakespeare's usage, then, a herb of grace is one associated with the divine, either through remorse leading to redemption or, as in Helena's case, to her miraculous **cure** of the king (Laroche 2009, 1).

herb-woman Wise woman or **empiric**, often associated with witchcraft or evildoing, in particular, with the prescription of emmenagogues, **medicines** to induce menstruation or **abortion**. Lord Lysimachus, unable to believe that Marina is truly chaste, equates the procuress of a brothel with "your herb-woman; she that sets seeds and roots of shame and iniquity" (*PER* 4.6.85–6), that is the bawd who makes sure that her girls do not get into trouble, by growing plants that will terminate a pregnancy. Newman (1979) argues that Ophelia's flowers are herbal abortifacients. Pearce discusses Shakespeare's herbal knowledge (2006), and Levin (1996) maintains that Shakespeare's women in particular serve as sources for this kind of knowledge. Laroche (2010) compiles a detailed account of domestic herbals and discusses the "medical authority" of women in the early modern household.

Hibocrates (A) Hibocrates is a comic mispronunciation of **Hippocrates**, still revered today for the large body of work attributed to him and for the oath or protestation of medical ethics that he reportedly insisted all his students recite. There are few verifiable facts about the author to whose name these works are attached: born in Cos, around 460 BCE, Hippocrates was admired even in his lifetime for his skill as both teacher and doctor, and for his theory that illnesses came from an unbalanced **diet** that, insufficiently digested, created **disease**-causing **vapors**. He died in Thessaly in about 375 BCE. Soranus' unreliable fifth-century biography of Hippocrates was probably the source of the legends surrounding him thereafter and that circulated in Shakespeare's time, for example in Lowe (1597). These emphasized Hippocrates' high ethics, his dislike of pomp and show, his humility, his generosity, and other altruistic traits. **Galen** claimed Hippocrates as the source of his own theories, but the Hippocratic corpus is less abstract and more empirical than what became Galenic medicine. In Shakespeare's time, Hippocrates and Galen were both spoken of as the fathers of medicine and given credit for the **humoral** theory that dominated diagnosis, treatment, and **cure**.
(B) Sir Hugh Evans maligns the comic French physician Dr. Caius by accusing him of having read nothing in either Galen or "Hibocrates" (*WIV* 3.1.65; see also **Caius**). Sixteenth-century England saw an influx of French Huguenot refugees (Protestants persecuted by French Catholics who fled to England for relief), many of whom were doctors with an interest in the new therapies of **Paracelsus**. The Royal **College** opposed the Paracelsian tendency on the Continent and called adherents of the new so-called chemical medicine quacks or **mountebanks**, insisting that its licensees should follow a highly complex and theoretical humoralism and claiming Hippocrates as the intellectual ancestor of Galen. Sir Hugh is therefore accusing Caius of practicing as an **empiric** or unqualified **physician**.
(C) Peter Lowe's hagiography of Hippocrates (1597) emphasizes his moral fiber, reprints a version of the oath, and the famous *Prognostication* or diagnostics, going through each body part or function in turn. King (2007) argues that historians of medicine have underestimated the reliance of early modern physicians upon the Hippocratic corpus with regard to theories of gender and sexual difference.

high-gravel-blind see **sand-blind**

hip-gout see **sciatica**

Hippocrates see **Hibocrates**

hor-dock see **burdock**

horse-leech See also **leech** Horse-leeches are now considered a different species from medicinal leeches, bloodsucking aquatic worms, but early moderns used the same term for both. They were used in cases where the **surgeon's box** or cupping was impossible, such as on the **gums**, sexual **organs**, lips, hands, or on open **wounds**, in cases where the **patient** was too frightened to endure boxing or cupping, or where venom needed to be extracted from a bite or sting. Pistol orders his companions to France "like horse-leeches . . . to suck!" (*H5* 2.3.55–6), that is, to plunder rather than to fight. On the appropriate use of horse-leeches, see Guillemeau (1597, Fol. 32); for a description, see Bartolomeus Anglicus (Batman 1582, chapter 93).

hospital, 'spital, 'spital-house See also **Bedlam, leprosy** (A) Hospitals or 'spitals originated in priories or monasteries, as part of religious orders' duty to tend the **sick**, succor the poor, and aid travelers. Their religious purpose was integral, and inmates, whether lay or clergy, followed the rhythms of the monastery. In the late medieval period, hospitals gradually began to specialize in treating the sick, rather than in taking in wanderers or helping the poor. They were often named after saints particularly associated with **disease**, such as St. Leonard (reputed for curing diseases in cattle and aiding the labors of **pregnant** women), St. Mary Magdalene (patroness of **apothecaries** because of the gift of myrrh or fragrant ointment she bore to Christ), or St. Lazarus (patron saint of lepers). Because of their association with religious houses, hospitals suffered after the Reformation. Cut off from church support, they were forced instead to rely upon stingy stipends from the current monarch. By the reign of Elizabeth, however, they had recovered somewhat and were considered an important part of early modern town life, independent of religious institutions.

(B) The words hospital and 'spital or 'spital-house are usually employed interchangeably in the period, although Shakespeare associates the hospital with festering or incurable disease, implicitly **leprosy**, and the 'spital with lower-class characters and with venereal disease, or **pox**. The only use of the term "hospital" in Shakespeare comes from *LLL* (5.2.871), as part of its surprising, non-comic ending. Chastised by the Queen for his levity and commanded to wait a year before their marriage, Berowne is charged to "jest a twelvemonth in an hospital" and make the poor souls in **agony** smile (see discussion under **agony**). Pistol, however, clearly connects the new disease of syphilis and the ancient disease of leprosy when he asks for Doll Tearsheet: "To the 'spital go /And from the powdering-tub of infamy /Fetch forth the lazar kite of Cressid's kind" (*H5* 2.1.74–6). Doll is in the throes of **quicksilver** treatment for syphilis (see **tub**), but her skin scales like that of a lazar or leper. Later in the same play, Pistol mourns, "my Nell is dead i' the 'spital /Of **malady of France**" (5.1.81–2); the treatment came too late for Mistress Quickly, who died either of syphilis or **pox** or from the harsh treatment used to **cure** it. Timon, too, imagines that the 'spital-house treats venereal disease. Gold, he argues, can make, "the **wappen'd** widow wed again; /She, whom the 'spital-house and **ulcerous** sores /Would cast the gorge at" (4.3.39–41). The widow is so riddled with syphilis that even the 'spital-house would refuse to take her in and treat her; even the physicians would **vomit** ("cast the gorge") at her.

(C) John Howe's fascinating 1582 manuscript about the founding of the three Royal Hospitals of Christ, Bridewell and St. Thomas the Apostle is reproduced in Morgan (1904). *Orders and Ordinances* (1652) recounts the duties of hospital staff, including its healers. On the history of English hospitals, see Orme and Webster (1995).

hot see **heat**

humor See also individual entries on **blood, choler, complexion, melancholy, phlegmatic** (A) Early modern English employs the word humor both in its medical meanings of body fluid, personality- or body-type, and in its vaguer sense of mood, whim, or state of mind. From ancient times until the nineteenth century, humoralism dominated the practice of medicine in the West. Based on **Galen's** theory of *crasis* or temperaments (also called "complexion"), humoral theory held that four fluids or cardinal humors—blood; choler or **gall** or yellow bile; phlegm; and melancholy or black bile—were held in balance in the human body. All bodily secretions and excretions (**sweat, breast milk, urine**, pus, saliva) were refined or vaporized versions of these four humors. Each of these fluids was fungible and could change into another, under the right circumstances (such as the application of **heat**; the weather; physical activity; passionate feeling; sleeplessness; and many other subtle environmental or behavioral stimuli). Moreover, each bodily part or organ ("member," in the language of the time) had its own complexion or humoral temperament. If the body as a whole, or any part of it, suffered from an imbalance in any particular humor, it became **distempered** and fell prey to **disease**. Humor additionally denotes fluids devoted to particular functions in the human body, such as the vitreous humor in the **eye**, or the seminal humor in the "stones" (testicles or ovaries, from which both men and women released **seed** during orgasm).

Humors, conceits, and whims of behavior were also temporary freaks of action that might not appear to have any causal relationship to the bodily humors at all; Jonson's humor plays (particularly *Every Man in His Humor*) establish the word as a shorthand for a character-type (and for types that do not necessarily correspond to the four complexions of early modern medicine, nor to the stock characters of *commedia dell'arte*). From Jonson (in at least one of whose "humors" comedies Shakespeare is known to have performed) Shakespeare developed his own, modified "sense of humor"—comedy based upon characters who act according to a particular obsession or tic even against their own interests and in defiance of all common sense, not for tragic or epic cause, but for the most trivial of reasons—a kind of comedy that descends through Jane Austen (Elizabeth Bennet in *Pride and Prejudice* observes, "Follies and nonsense, whims and inconsistencies, do divert me, I own, and I laugh at them whenever I can"; Austen 2003, 400) to present-day television sitcoms. (B) Shakespeare thus employs the word "humor" in both its technical sense, meaning a fluid in the air or of the body, and its colloquial sense, to mean a mood or a fancy. *OED* does not indicate "humor" to have been used in the sense of "amusement" until later in the seventeenth century, but Shakespeare's Benedick in *ADO* and Nym (in the *Henriad* and in *WIV*) do seem to connect "wit" or laughter with "humor" in our modern sense. Friar Laurence describes the action of his medicine on Juliet as "a **cold** and drowsy humor" in her **veins** (*ROM* 4.1.96) and Portia urges Brutus to stay indoors rather than "suck up the humors" of the "dank" morning air (*JC* 2.1.262), but Ganymede boasts of having driven his previous "suitor from his mad humor of love to a living humor of **madness**" (*AYL* 3.2.418), and York comments that Henry Lancaster's piety renders him a weak king, because his "church-like humors fits not for a crown" (*2H6* 1.1.247). *ADO* employs humor to mean physiological complexion, mood, whim, **sickness**, and wit. Beatrice thanks her "cold blood, I am of your humor for that: I had rather hear my dog bark at a crow than a man swear he loves me" (1.1.131). Don John tells Conrade that he is honest to a fault and can neither feign pleasure at others' good fortune nor flatter them when they wish it: "I cannot hidewhat I am: I must . . . laugh when I am merry and claw no man in his humor" (1.3.13–18). Don Pedro tells Hero "how to humor [her] cousin," how to trick Beatrice out of a mindset stubbornly determined against Benedick into one receptive to love of him (2.1.380). So quickly does the trick work that Benedick resolves that mere wit or "quips and sentences and these paper bullets of the **brain**" cannot deter him "from the career of his humor" (2.3.241–2). Leonato mocks Benedick's **tooth-ache** as caused by a **"humor or a worm,"** meaning both a diagnosis of distemper in the tooth (or **infection** by a worm within it), and sighing from **love-sickness** (3.2.27). Benedick in turn accuses Claudio of engaging in maliciously feminine slander against Hero through his "gossip-like humor" (5.1.186). After the resolution, Benedick still bears the brunt of his friends' jokes, but maintains his resolve to ignore the paper bullets: "a **college** of wit-crackers cannot flout me out of my humor," he adds, where there is perhaps an allusion to the learned College of **physicians**, which could not **cure** this humor of love (5.4.101).

Humor can denote the specific cardinal humors of melancholy, choler, and blood. Sonnet 91 alludes to the four complexions or humoral temperaments, arguing that "every humor hath his adjunct pleasure, /Wherein it finds a joy above the rest," a medicalized version of the argument that true lovers are ideally suited to each other and to no-one else (91.5–6). The "melancholy humor" or black bile (*LLL* 1.1.233) overshadows *ROM* from the very first scene, in which Montague comments, "Black and portentous must this humor prove" (1.1.141). Don Armado, the affected melancholic of *LLL*, informs on Costard (who has been caught dallying with Jacquenetta) to Ferdinand (who has prohibited all erotic relations). "Besieged with sable-coloured melancholy," Armado decides that his "black-oppressing humor" can be healed by "the most wholesome **physic** of thy health-giving air," by taking a walk so that the dark clouds of melancholy can disperse (1.1.232–4). The "choleric" mood of Cassius is a "testy humor," complains Brutus (*JC* 4.3.46), elsewhere a "rash humor" (*JC* 4.3.120). Lady Percy's character analysis of her son Hotspur perhaps points to a change in English attitudes toward the choleric humor:

> In **diet**, in affections of delight,
> In military rules, humors of blood,

He was the mark and glass, copy and book,
That fashion'd others.

(*2H4* 2.3.29–32)

The *Henriad* does not present the brave, impulsive, angry Hotspur as a "copy" or model for young manhood, or at least, only very early in *1H4*. It is the arguably **sanguine** Hal, not Hotspur, who becomes the type of English masculinity, in peace and in war, nourished by such sanguine foods as small beer and capons and low-born but English companions. Hal warns us very early on of his intentions to temper Falstaff's phlegmatic cowardice with sunny sanguinity:

I know you all, and will awhile uphold
The unyoked humor of your idleness:
Yet herein will I imitate the sun,
Who doth permit the base **contagious** clouds
To smother up his beauty from the world,
That, when he please again to be himself,
Being wanted, he may be more wonder'd at,
By breaking through the foul and ugly mists
Of **vapours** that did seem to **strangle** him.

(*1H4* 1.2.195–203)

The madcap prince "redeem[s] time" by banishing his old "contagio[us]" colleagues, whose poorly concocted or digested nourishment threatens to suffocate or strangle the prince, the royal sun, with disease-ridden **fumes** or clouds. Hal's ruthless banishment of Falstaff in *2H4* thus indeed "run[s] bad humors on the knight," as Nym suggests (*H5* 2.1.121). Nym comforts his companions with fatalism: "The king is a good king: but it must be as it may; he passes some humors and careers" (*H5* 2.1.125–6). The king himself has his whims and inconsistencies. Nym has the same humoral phrase in both *2H4* and *H5*, as he complains sarcastically, "These be good humors, indeed!" (*2H4* 2.4.163; *H5* 3.2.26).

WIV presents Falstaff and his followers flowing with humors predictable in their effects on personality but not in their outcomes on situations. Nym is particularly apt to characterize Falstaff's vagaries and plots as humors (1.1.166, 1.3.22, 1.3.77; and so on), a motif in keeping with the allopathic cure by opposites that the play performs (cooling the hot or lusty Falstaff in the Thames and turning him from hunter into prey). The "conceited" humor of the drunken Bardolph secures him a job as a tapster (1.3.22); Nym wonders whether Falstaff's seduction-plot is a "humor" that "will . . . pass" (1.3.51); both Falstaff's followers refuse to carry his love-letter to Mistress Page: "I will run no base humor: here, take the humor-letter," indignantly retorts Nym (1.3.77–8); Falstaff himself swears to "learn the humor of the age" and to banish his old followers (perhaps in emulation of his own master, *WIV* 1.3.83).

Chatillon characterizes the English soldiers as the dregs of the body politic, "unsettled humors of the land," monstrous chimeras, half-human and half-beast: "Rash, inconsiderate, fiery voluntaries, /With ladies' faces and fierce dragons' **spleens**" (*JN* 2.1.66–8). These noble soldiers ("voluntaries," not mercenaries) are young enough to have smooth, unbearded "ladies' faces" but are also full of youthful choler or "spleen," eager to fight, and therefore unpredictable. Mercutio uses "humors!" as a shorthand for "Romeo! . . . madman! passion! Lover!" (*ROM* 2.1.7). Richard III famously gloats as he wins the hand of Anne over her dead husband's corpse, "Was ever woman in this humor woo'd? /Was ever woman in this humor won?" where humor refers to the absurd and horrific circumstances of the proposal, to the vagaries of womankind, to his own malicious wit, and perhaps to his own **deformity** (*R3* 1.2.227–8). Ultimately, human humors or freaks of behavior cannot be reduced to bodily humors; when asked why he wants Antonio's pound of flesh, and told that his evocation of the law is insufficient, Shylock adds: "But, say, it is my humor: is it answer'd?" (*MV* 4.1.43). "This is no answer, thou unfeeling man," retorts Bassanio, but humors testify to an excess of embodied feeling, not to anaesthesia. All are answered; humors are unanswerable.

(C) Jonson's comedies *Every Man in His Humor* (1598, published 1601) and *Every Man Out of His Humor* (1599, published 1600) provide ample evidence that although humoral theory was widely accepted, lay-people nonetheless mocked it for its simultaneous complexity and reductiveness. For an overview of the theory as understood in early modern England, see Bodin (1566; trans. 1966); also Elyot (1539); Levinus Lemnius (1576); Wright (1604); *Regimen Sanitatis Salernii* (1528). Floyd-Wilson (2003 and 2007) helpfully coins the term "geo-humoralism" to describe the subtle negotiations among inherited complexion or humoral temperament, environmental stimuli such as temperature, humidity, latitude, diet, and exercise, and emotional triggers such as love or anger; see esp. her chapter on *Othello* and her treatment of nationalism in early modern interpretations of humoral theory. Campbell (1962) offers character-criticism inflected by humoral theory and identifies Shakespeare's tragic heroes according to their complexions or humoral temperaments. Knoepflmacher (1963) analyzes the *Henry IV* plays, and Draper (1964) the tragedies; Schoenfeldt (1999) investigates the relations among the inside of the body, the outside of the body, and spirituality in early modern literature. Paster, Rowe and Floyd-Wilson (2004) continue to historicize emotions in the early modern body as a symbiotic flow between passionate or intellectual trigger and humoral, physiological response. Hobgood (2006) argues that the early modern audience participates, in humoral terms, in the shame of Malvolio in *TN*. Melchiori's edition of *2H4* reads the play as a humors comedy (2007).

hymen, maidenhead, virgin-knot (A) The membrane or **skin** covering the neck of the **womb**, thought to bleed at a woman's first penetration during sexual intercourse and thus to indicate virginity if left intact. Medical authorities, however, recognized that not every woman had a hymen, not every woman's hymen remained intact until sexual intercourse, and that not every hymen bled. Social historians have found no evidence, however, for the legendary practice of hanging out a married couple's wedding sheets to see whether they were blood-stained (supposedly, the absence of **blood** would indicate the woman's prior sexual experience, and shame her new husband). The persistence of the legend, however, attests to the cultural wish to make visible that which is secret or hidden, and immaterial: virginity itself.

(B) Shakespeare uses the term "hymen" not in its medical sense, however, but to refer to the institution of marriage (*TIM* 4.3.413) or to the presiding deity of marriage, as in *AYL* 5.4, in which the god Hymen comes down from heaven to marry Orlando and Rosalind. The usual term in Shakespeare for both the membrane and the virginal state that it connotes is "maidenhead". "By my troth and maidenhead, /I would not be a queen," says Anne Bullen disingenuously (*H8* 2.3.23), but holding on to her maidenhead, refusing Henry's advances, is what ultimately makes her a queen. *ROM* puns on "the heads of the maidens . . . or their maidenheads" (1.1.24–6) and employs the term in a number of different registers. The Nurse bawdily swears "by my maidenhead at twelve year old" (1.3.2), implying that she lost her virginity while still a child herself. Juliet, distraught at the **death** of her cousin, determines, "death, not Romeo, take my maidenhead!" (3.2.137). *PER* connects "the loss of maidenhead" and the ensuing blood to the matter from which "a babe is moulded" (pr. 10–11); the babe described, Marina, has her own maidenhead threatened first by the Bawd's advertisement to all brothel customers in the market (*PER* 4.2.60) and then by the angry Boult himself (4.6.127). Marina herself describes her maidenhead as a virgin-knot that she will rather kill herself than "untie" (*PER* 4.2.147). In *TMP*, Prospero describes Miranda's virginity as a "virgin-knot" that Ferdinand must not break before marriage (4.1.15). The word "knot" may allude to the traditional term for marriage, "wedding-knot," with implications that daughters are knotted or bound to their fathers until marriage.

(C) Guillemeau (1612), Raynalde (1565), and Rivière discuss the membrane or hymen, as does Crooke (1615). Balizet (2007) weighs the evidence for and against the custom of hanging out bloodied sheets after a wedding-night. See also Bellamy, "Waiting for Hymen" (1997); Jankowski, *Pure Resistance: Queer Virginity* (2003); Loughlin (1997).

hyssop Although not native to England, **hot, dry hyssop** was cultivated in herb gardens and, commonly mixed or boiled with figs and honey, used as an expectorant, laxative, antiseptic mouthwash, and liniment (Dodoens 1595, R8r–v). Its most common use was in **lung** disorders, although in early modern England it was often mistakenly identified with the Biblical plant called hyssop that was used in purification rituals and to treat **leprosy** and itching **skin**. It worked by breaking down **cold, moist humors** such as **phlegm**. Iago contrasts hyssop to thyme (another hot, dry herb) when he dismisses both love and virtue as subsidiary to will (1.3.322). See discussion under **nettle**.

hysterica passio See also **madness, womb** (A) *Hysterica passio* or suffocation of the mother (also known simply as "the mother") was an uterine disorder in which **vapors** from unused or extra menstrual **blood** which had become corrupted traveled up to the head and throat, causing a choking or smothering feeling, or in which the womb itself moved around the body or wandered (the so-called wandering womb). Female **seed** might also be to blame, as in the disorder of **green-sickness** (to which the mother was related). Suffocation might be only one of many symptoms, since the womb was porous and mobile. Sufferers might tremble, or become insensible, or mute, or struggle so violently that observers thought the **patient** possessed by the devil (though Jorden and Harsnett, both published in 1603, are at pains to debunk this hypothesis). Victims' bodies might contort in **agony**, and they might be possessed of preternatural strength. They might shriek, or pass gas, or **vomit**, or become incontinent of **urine**. Sometimes not only sense-perception but reason and memory were affected, and women could not remember that they had had fits at all. Fits of insensibility resembled **apoplexy**, and for this reason it was best to wait at least three days before burying a woman known to suffer from the mother, in case she was not dead but lying in a fit. Women were congenitally prone to the mother, but could control the rate at which they produced blood and seed by restricting themselves to lean meats in their **diets** and by avoiding sweet-tasting or -smelling things. Observers should hold a woman who was in the throes of a fit tightly, upright, applying foul-smelling items to her **nostrils** and holding down her **belly** and throat. Placebos were often effective, and jokes or songs, to cheer up women in whom too much **melancholy** had triggered the mother.
(B) It is peculiar, to say the least, that King Lear diagnoses himself with an ailment attributed since Hippocratic times only to women. And yet, seeing his servant in the stocks, himself ignored by both his daughters, he cries, "O, how this mother swells up toward my **heart**! / *Hysterica passio*, down, thou climbing sorrow, /Thy **element**'s below!" (*LR* 2.4.56–8). He certainly experiences similar symptoms: the palpations that thrill his heart, and the sensation of choking in his chest and throat. Peterson (2006) and Hoeniger (1992) argue that Shakespeare cannot be mistaken; he chooses to have Lear attribute a specifically female complaint to himself, perhaps to demonstrate that he is already deluded, perhaps as an indication of the extent to which he is feminized by his daughters' betrayal.
(C) Scholars have long identified Shakespeare's source as Samuel Harsnett (1603), who was at pains to argue that **ecstasies**, fits, **frenzies**, the mother, and so on resulted not from supernatural causes but from physiological illness, and that Jesuits who claimed to be casting out demons were merely engaging in "Egregious Impostures," the title of his book. Edward Jorden likewise urges medical and laymen not to be taken in, reminding physicians that both Avicenna and **Hippocrates** had noted the **disease** and its natural origins (B2v, 1603). Peterson notes that Shakespeare's known source, Harsnett (1603), reports a case of the mother in a male, but only ironically; it is clear that the source (Mainy) is mistaken, since Mainy himself acknowledges that a physician later diagnosed

him with "vertigo" instead. But perhaps Jorden's most sensitive observation is that political or social powerlessness might be the leading cause for hysteria: "For seeing we are not maisters of our owne affections, wee are like battered Citties without walles, or shippes tossed in the Sea, exposed to all maner of assaults and daungers, euen to the over-throw of our owne bodies" (G2v).

illness Evil inclination. Lady Macbeth characterizes her husband as ambitious, "but without /The illness should attend it" (*MAC* 1.5.20), power-hungry, but unwilling to commit the evil acts necessary to grasp the throne. Ill appears ubiquitously in Shakespeare, but again, usually meaning evil or unlucky, rather than "in poor health," although Aemilia makes the connection clear: "Unquiet meals make ill digestions" (*ERR* 5.1.74), commotion or bustle makes one digest food poorly or improperly ("ill"), which in turn leads to **sickness** (illness). In the few instances where ill clearly intends sickness, there is often a pun on ill-fortune, ill-will, or ill intention. The ailing John of Gaunt puns on his own sickness and the misgovernment he sees in his nephew Richard II: "Now He that made me knows I see thee ill; /Ill in myself to see, and in thee seeing ill" (*R2* 2.1.93–4). Illness may portend **death**. Falstaff's boy tells Quickly, "Faith, he's very ill," as the fat knight lies on his deathbed (*H5* 2.1.85). "I am much ill," concludes Henry IV (*2H4* 4.4.111). Imogen is "ill" but claims she is "not very **sick**" (*CYM* 4.2.11, 13).

imposthume See also **bladder, canker, carbuncle, ulcer, wound** (A) An abscess or ulcer that festers from within, swelling up with pus inside the body without necessarily showing any external sign of **disease**. Imposthumes could develop from **pox, plague**, erysipelas, improperly concocted **choler**, anthrax, carbuncles, knobs, the king's **evil**, and cankers. They were treated by both surgical and medical means, depending on the cause of the ailment and the skills of the healer treating it.
(B) The word appears only in the second quarto of *Hamlet*, the quarto of *Troilus and Cressida*, and *VEN*. Hamlet compares Fortinbras' eagerness to go to war over trifles to "the imposthume of much wealth and peace, /That inward breaks, and shows no cause without /Why the man dies" (4.4.27–9). Too much prosperity paradoxically leads to combat, and to the eventual demise of the state. Hamlet

174

may also be referring to the disease eroding Denmark secretly, under cover of Claudius' "wealth and peace," since he goes on to compare his own occasion for revenge with Fortinbras'. Thersites (*TRO* 5.1.21) calls down "**bladders** full of imposthume" upon Patroclus (and upon the war in general) as part of his catalog of medical curses. The word bladder refers not to the anatomical bladder but to the body of an ulcer, swollen with fluid just as the bladder is filled with **urine**. Venus includes "impostumes" as part of her litany of the "**maladies**" to which human beauty may succumb (*VEN* 743).

(C) Vigo (1543) devotes the second book of his treatise to "Apostemes" and includes two chapters upon bladders. Guillemeau (1597) includes a beautiful illustration of the instruments used to open "Apostemations," and his "Fourth Treatise" discusses them at length. Lowe (1634), however, includes imposthumes under "tumors," distinguishing between those caused by "fluxion," the flow of **humors** to a part of the body where they ought not to be, or "congestion," unnatural fluid caused by improperly concocted food (F2r).

incision See also **blood** (A) The deliberate cut of the **surgeon's** knife or lancet in order to let blood to **cure** a **disease** or **distemper** in the body, to remove diseased tissue, to cut for "the stone" or "strangury"; or to sever a **web** in the **eye** or a ligament making a child **tongue-tied**. Only surgeons were allowed to make incisions, because of the strong medieval prohibition against **physicians** shedding blood. Moreover, it was crucial that only surgeons learned in **anatomy** make incisions to let blood or to operate, and that such surgeons were motivated by good will rather than greed or spite, since unskillful or malicious phlebotomists might inadvertently kill their **patients** by incising too deeply, by drawing too much blood, or by cutting into an **artery** rather than a **vein**. Spring was the best time for letting blood, depending on which constellation was paramount in the sky and on the sign of the zodiac that governed the part of the body that was to be bled (for example, the neck could not be bled if the moon were in **Taurus**, which ruled that part). The **complexion** or humoral personality of the patient also dictated the best time of day or year to bleed him. A patient preparing to be bled might first undergo a **purge**, or be **dieted** on **dry** bread for three or four days in order to minimize **choler** or bile in the **stomach**. Sometimes surgeons recommended hot **baths**, to soften the **skin**. A surgeon preparing to bleed a patient required a fine, sharp lancet or penknife, clean bandages for the **wound**, and a basin to catch the blood. Incisions ought to be made in the direction of the **sinews** or **nerves**. If a surgeon were planning to use dry- or wet-cupping, or to scarify the wound, he required the **surgeon's box** and perhaps candles or a flame. After bleeding, surgeons anointed the incisions with rose-water or the **salve** known as "**Galen**'s wax" (beeswax, almond or rose oil, and borate).

(B) Shakespeare's references imagine incision for bloodletting rather than for any other cause. Morocco alludes to the common heliotropic theory explaining variations in skin-color (see **race**): the belief that the sun's tanning rays darkened skin and that therefore Northerners were pallid and Equatorial residents **tawny**. He attempts to dispel Portia's prejudice against his dark skin by observing that both he and "the fairest creature" living near the North pole have blood that is the same color: "let us make incision for your love /To prove whose blood is reddest, his or mine" (*MV* 2.1.6–7). In volunteering to undergo phlebotomy— usually a cause for fear—he also asserts his manliness and bravery. When Dumaine compares his beloved to a **fever** in his blood, Berowne returns that, in that case, he could be cured by phlebotomy: "incision /Would let her out in saucers" (*LLL* 4.3.95–6). Touchstone mocks the unsophisticated, "raw" Corin by recommend- ing "God make incision in thee!" Corin is full of uncooked or undigested **humors** and needs phlebotomy to draw off the excess and refine him into a courtier (*AYL* 3.2.72). Richard II reflects common fears about phlebotomy when he urges for peace between Mowbray and Bolingbroke. "Let's purge this **choler** without letting blood," he comments, and explains, "Deep malice makes too deep incision" (*R2* 1.1.155), a surgeon with a grudge might murder his charge under the guise of therapy. Pistol compares fighting to the bloodletting of the surgeon, calling belligerently, "Shall we have incision?" (*2H4* 2.4.196).

(C) Gyer (1592) offers detailed instructions on bloodletting and on how to incise.

indigested Used only of Richard of Gloucester; unformed, inchoate, insuffi- ciently developed in the **womb**, like food that has not been concocted and that issues poisonous **vapors** that cause **sickness** to those around it. Clifford calls Richard a "foul indigested lump" (*2H6* 5.1.157) and Henry VI himself repeats the charge almost verbatim: "indigested and **deformed** lump" (*3H6* 5.6.51). Both accusers twit Richard with his deformity, which they connect with his pre- maturity and also to his wickedness.

infect, infected, infection, infectious See also **contagion, Paracelsus, plague, pox** (A) Theories of infection in early modern medicine were undergoing a transi- tion. The *miasma* theory held that infectious **diseases** were transmitted through foul air or water, and **Galenic** humoral medicine, that disorders stemmed from internal imbalances of the bodily **humors**. Under a strictly Galenic model, suffer- ers could contract even ailments such as plague only if their own bodies were overabundant or deficient in a particular humor. The environment might cause infection by encouraging the body to overproduce a particular humor in response to the unbalanced atmosphere in which it found itself. Thus **cold**, foggy mists might stimulate the body to produce more **choler** to counteract the weather; the choler then overheated the body, or became corrupted, and thus triggered a **tertian ague** (chills, bodyache, and **fever** spiking every thirty-six hours). Or the cold air might encourage a body already abundant in **phlegm** to produce more in sympathy with it, and to contract a **quotidian** or daily fever. One might simi- larly catch infections through repletion or too much food, through poor **sleep** habits, through ingesting poison, or through emotional distress or **perturbation**. Galenic **physicians** might starve those suffering from infections causing a fever (such as plague), in order to reduce the excess **heat** that caused such diseases. Nonetheless both popular and medical literature appeared to recognize that disease could be transmitted from person to person or through physical contact, although it was also believed that bed **linens**, shared utensils, and so on could be a source of infection. In many instances, surgeons writing about communicable diseases such as smallpox or the French pox (syphilis) seem to anticipate theories of microbial transmission, although spiritual healers insisted that, for example, the French pox or the plague could only be acquired by those who had already succumbed to lust or sin in their hearts.

With the advent of Paracelsian theories of disease, something approaching modern germ-theory entered early modern culture. Paracelsus distinguished between the qualities of a disease and the disease itself. Paracelsian diagnostics required the physician to use his senses to identify the particular illness that caused various symptoms in the patient and then to uncover a specific remedy for the underlying ailment. Diseases originated outside the body, from "seeds" scattered when man fell from grace. The world as God originally created it was unified and virtuous, filled with "perfect" seeds of herbs, plants, minerals, and all human and animal parts, but when mankind listened to the devil, God cursed the world with "impure seeds" that "did cleaue fast to them, and doe couer them as a garment: and **death** was ioyned to life" (Bostocke 1585, B4v). Thus everything in the world is mixed good and bad, with impurities present in that which seems pure and wholesome nourishment present in that which seems corrupt. The physician must become a chemist or **alchemist** in order to isolate the pure seeds within the three substantive or fundamental building blocks of the world (**salt, sulphur,** and **mercury**) and to treat the disease caused by the impure "spirituall Seedes of all maner deseases" within the body and the world (E1r). Once the pure and impure seeds unite, the body returns to integrity and to health. Thus an **ague** is properly not a disease of heat, as in conventional Galenic medicine, but the disease of sulphur, or saltpeter kindled, and must be treated with sulphur.

In practice, civic authorities controlled the spread of diseases known to be highly infectious (such as bubonic plague) by techniques we would recognize today, such as the isolation of sick individuals and households and an emphasis on hygiene and removing waste. The employment of women as plague-searchers, who went from house to house looking for and removing the bodies of plague victims, also suggests that lay-people believed in person-to-person transmission or animal-to-human transmission via an external agent that could be acquired from without, whatever their physicians or clergy might say.

(B) Both Old Gobbo and Quickly confuse the word "infection," meaning "disease," with the word "affection," meaning "liking." Gobbo describes "a great infection . . . to serve" (*MV* 2.2.121) and Quickly comments that Mistress Page's "husband has a marvelous infection to the little page" (*WIV* 2.2.109).

Infection in Shakespeare sometimes originates outside one's own body, but then capitalizes upon one's proprietary weaknesses, as in humoral medicine, a process described in Sonnet 111. Infections conquer sufferers' bodies just as the "dyer's hand" becomes colored by the dye in which it works or just as public life "brand[s]" the speaker with an external mark that alters or "subdue[s]" his

177

nature. The patient drinks "potions of eisel 'gainst my strong infection," medicines of extreme bitterness or astringency, such as vinegar, "to correct correction," to counter the imbalance acquired from his surroundings (111.5–7, 10–12). Sometimes infection is clearly associated with what we would now call an infectious disease, that is, one transmitted by an external agent or germ, even if such a germ works through earth, water, or air as a medium, like "a **pestilence** / That does infect the land" (*1H4* 5.1.54–5). With tragic consequences, Friar Laurence's letter cannot be delivered because of plague, "so fearful were they of infection" (*ROM* 5.2.16), in what is typical of the late-sixteenth-century triumph of practical measures such as quarantine over the medical theory that held plague to proceed, like all other diseases, from internal humoral disorder rather than from an external seed or germ of disease. Timon similarly describes plague as an "infection" (*TIM* 5.1.221) that afflicts persons with "potent and infectious fevers" (*TIM* 4.1.22). Moral qualities, too, are contagious, transmitted through touch: "I'll beat thee, but I should infect my hands," cries Timon to Apemantus, who has tried to convince him that any **leprosy** is in his mind (4.3.364). Infections undetectable from the outside of the body can be the deadliest. Hamlet urges Gertrude to chastity by comparing temporary abstinence to a bandage that "will but skin and film the **ulcerous** place, /Whilst rank corruption, mining all within, /Infects unseen" (*HAM* 3.4.147–9).

At other times infection comes from unhealthy climates, as when Caliban curses Prospero with "all the infections that the sun sucks up /From bogs, fens, flats" (*TMP* 2.2.1) or in Leontes' benediction, "Blessed Gods /Purge all infection from the air whilst you /Do climate here" (*WT* 5.1.169). Lear cries, "Infect [my daughter's] beauty, /You fen-suck'd fogs" (*LR* 2.4.166), and Timon calls upon the "blessed breeding sun [to] draw from the earth /Rotten humidity; below thy sister's orb /Infect the air" (*TIM* 4.3.1–3). Often the foul smell of bad air indicates its infectious qualities. Benedick jokes of Beatrice, "if her breath were as terrible as her terminations, there were no living near her; she would infect to the north star" (*ADO* 2.1.150). Infection turns fairest things foul through the mechanism of olfaction: "if that flower with base infection meet, /The basest weed outbraves his dignity . . . Lilies that fester smell far worse than weeds" (*SON* 94.11).

Political intrigue is an infection that spreads from person to person and can be controlled only by quarantine. John of Gaunt praises England's isolation as a defense against physical illnesses and political disorders: "infection and the hand of war" (*R2* 2.1.44). Prince Edward worries that a traitor "might infect another / And make him of like spirit to himself" (*3H6* 5.4.46–7). Brutus worries that Martius' insubordination will spread to others: "Pursue him to his house, and pluck him thence: /Lest his infection, being of catching nature, /Spread further" (*COR* 3.1.307–9). Oswald warns Edgar against supporting Gloucester, a "publish'd traitor," "Lest that the infection of his fortune" corrupt him, too (*LR* 4.6.233). Other instances of political or moral infection appear in *2H6* 3.2.287: "He shall not breathe infection in this air" and "the infection of the time" (*JN* 5.2.20). Lady Anne calls King Richard III an "infection of a man" (*R3* 1.2.78). Corrupt companions provide the infectious matter in Sonnet 67, in which the speaker asks, "wherefore with infection should he live?" (1). Claudius similarly says that Hamlet "wants not buzzers to infect his **ear** /With pestilent speeches of his father's death" (*HAM* 4.5.90–1), and Nestor that "many are infect" (*TRO* 1.3.187).

Perturbation or strong emotion of any kind might trigger infection. Love itself is an infection for Benvolio, who urges Romeo to **cure** his infatuation with Rosaline by finding another love, in perhaps a nod to Paracelsian homeopathy (*ROM* 1.2.50). The sea-storm conjured up by Prospero and Ariel is so terrifying that the latter confirms no-one was "so firm, so constant, that this coil /Would not infect his reason?" (*TMP* 1.2.208). Hal swears that the sight of his **apoplexied** father did not "infect [his] **blood** with joy" at the acquisition of the crown but with sorrow at his supposed demise (*2H4* 4.5.169). In two comic cases of trickery, infection is both a "device" to introduce an idea from without and a response to wants or desires that the character already possesses. Thus it is not clear whether love, or the trick played by his friends, is "the infection" acquired by Benedick in *ADO* (2.3.121); similarly, when Malvolio's "very genius [takes] the infection of the device" of the forged letter, the letter is the vector of infection, but Maria's counsel to Toby to "pursue him now, lest the device take air and taint" suggests that the letter is more like rotten food or water than an external disease-germ (*TN* 3.4.129).

Poison can introduce infection through an aperture in the body, such as the **eyes**, ears, **nose**, or mouth. Lady Anne chides Richard, "Never hung poison on a fouler toad. /Out of my sight! thou dost infect my eyes" (*R3* 1.2.147–8). Pisanio in Cymbeline compares Posthumus' jealousy to an infection induced by poison inserted in the ear:

> what a strange infection
> Is fall'n into thy ear? What false Italian,
> As poisonous-**tongued** as handed, hath prevail'd
> On thy too ready hearing?
>
> (*CYM* 3.2.3–6)

Jealousy can be an infection that, introduced from outside through the ear (via Iachimo's suggestive speech, in Cymbeline) or the eye (via Leontes' suspicious gaze in *WT*) overwhelms the whole body through "the infection of [the] **brains**" (*WT* 1.2.145). Camillo, bewildered, asks, "Who does infect her?" (*WT* 1.2.306). Later Polixenes develops Leontes' infective metaphor. If Leontes' suspicions are true, he says, "my best blood turn /To an infected jelly . . . worse than the great'st infection /That e'er was heard or read" (*WT* 1.2.418). "Jelly" evokes the action of poison in the blood, curding it and making it too thick to flow—a humoral model of infection. But "the great'st infection /That e'er was heard or read" alludes to notorious epidemics such as the sweat, plague, or pox, that spread quickly and devastatingly across entire continents. Words, too, bear and transmit disease through nose and mouth. To call Antonio "brother" would "infect [Prospero's] mouth" with the sound of the word (*TMP* 5.1.131). The "false gallop of verses" may "infect" lovers (*AYL* 3.2.114). "[Y]our conversation would infect my brain" complains Menenius to the plebeians' tribunes (*COR* 2.1.94). The Surveyor tells King Henry VIII that Buckingham's ambition "every day . . . would infect his speech" (*H8* 1.2.133). The frightened messenger justifies his reluctance to tell Mark Antony about the wars in Rome with the saw, "The nature of bad news infects the teller" (*ANT* 1.2.95).

Two botanical references suggest different mechanisms for humoral infections. "Usurping ivy, brier, or idle moss / . . . all for want of pruning, with intrusion / Infect [the] sap" by mechanically stifling a tree's access to nourishment and air (*ERR* 2.2.180). But "knots, by the conflux of meeting sap, / Infects the sound pine" (*TRO* 1.3.8), by directing fluid to the wrong parts of the tree-trunk (like humors pooling in the wrong parts of the human body).

(C) Goeurot (1550) discusses the most common infections in children. The *Plague Orders* (1578) require the quarantining of plague sufferers and recommend other measures such as sending away animals, removing rubbish, and so on. Kellwaye (1593) offers traditional herbal prescriptions for remedies against the plague. Dekker and Lodge (1603) offer vivid, eye-witness accounts of London in a plague year. The English Paracelsian Bostocke outlines the minority view (at least among English physicians) that infection proceeded from outside the body from external disease-germs, rather than from humoral imbalance (1585). Pagel (1958) suggests that rudimentary germ-theories existed even prior to the sixteenth century. Healy (2001) argues that Shakespeare deliberately debunks then-contemporary theories of syphilis and contagion in *MM* and *PER*; for example, Paracelsian germ-theory would hold that Marina cannot help but be contaminated or infected by her union with the poxy Lord Lysimachus, belying her status as magical virgin within a Galenic mythos. Qualtiere and Slights (2003) read *TIM* as a satire in which the protagonist imagines a sustained campaign of syphilitic infection, arguing that the play disavows older theories that blamed the patient's own moral turpitude, or the wrath of God, for sexually transmitted infections. Harris (2004) juxtaposes the implied transmission of syphilis in *ERR* with the language of mercantilism and trade and the perceived dangers of foreign contact; the language of contagion in *MV* with fears of Jewry; and the conflict between humoral and infective early modern models of disease alongside controversies about the nature of woman and whether her value is internal and unchanging or external and contextual. Hunter (2004) reads the Friar's mistakes in *ROM* as the failures of a healer who understands neither Galenic nor Paracelsian medical models of infection and disease and who fails to diagnose the pervasive melancholy of the lovers.

inflammation In its medical sense, inflammation characterized a **wound** or sore part of the body that became red, swollen, **hot** to the touch, and very tender. Typically, Shakespeare's Falstaff appropriates the word to describe what he claims to be the beneficial effects of alcohol, in particular, of sack or sherry wine. Many men would be "fools and cowards," he argues, "but for inflammation" (*2H4* 4.3.96). Thus while standard therapies would try to reduce or control inflammation, Falstaff would encourage it, just as he encourages young men to drink strong liquor and to eat red meat when the **physicians** prescribe thin beer and fish.

insane Shakespeare employs this word as a transferred epithet, the only example of this usage in *OED*. Banquo asks Macbeth whether they have truly seen supernatural phenomena or whether they are merely experiencing hallucinations after eating "the insane root /That takes the reason prisoner" (*MAC* 1.3.85). The "insane root" is probably **hemlock**, known as a poison and hallucinogen but also as a therapy for **epilepsy**.

insanie Editors routinely follow the Theobald/Warburton emendation of "infamie" to "insanie" in the following speech by the pedantic schoolmaster Holofernes in *LLL* as he complains about Don Armado's pronunciation of English words: "it insinuateth me of insanie: *anne intelligis, domine?* to make frantic, lunatic" (5.1.25–6). "Infamy" makes no sense in this context, where "insanie" exists in sixteenth-century English as a rare synonym for **madness** (*OED*, *insanie*). Hibbard, however, argues that the text should be emended to the Latin *insanire*, to madden, as befits Holofernes' frequent and affected dropping into Latin and the grammar of the sentence (Hibbard 2002, 81).

jakes, close-stool, stool (A) Jakes is an Elizabethan word for a toilet, also called the privy closet (meaning the secret or private place) or close-stool. The close-stool looked like a chair with arms and beneath, a box with a lid, which was sometimes cushioned but more usually made of wood. It might be kept in a small closet or chamber, or concealed behind a screen or curtains. Noble users cleansed themselves with paper, though the poorer sort employed wool, rags, or water. Privies were often noisome, even in fine households, although the air was freshened with herbs. Sir John Harington, Queen Elizabeth's godson, is usually credited with inventing the first flush toilet in 1596, but flush toilets were not generally used until the nineteenth century. Harington understood little or nothing of the principles of hygiene or sanitation, however; his main concern is minimizing odor.

(B) In Shakespeare, the jakes or close-stool evokes most obviously disgust and abasement, and arguably **purgation** or cleansing. There may be puns on the name of Jacques in *AYL* (the words are homonyms in Elizabethan Anglicized French) and of Ajax ("a jakes") in *TRO*, the former as a **melancholic** who purges through tears, the latter as the receptacle of Thersites' filthy wit and emblem of all that is corrupt about the camp as he walks up and down the field "asking for himself," that is, Ajax is asking for a jakes or close-stool (3.3.245). Costard jokes in *LLL* that Alexander the Great "holds his poll-axe sitting on a close-stool," a lavatorial, rather than a royal, throne, and that he will be replaced by Ajax (through a pun on his name, "a jakes") in the parade of the Nine Worthies of ancient history (5.2.577–8). In *King Lear,* an irate Kent threatens to "daub the wall of a jakes" with the insolent Oswald (2.2.67).

(C) The best, and wittiest, early modern source is Harington (1596), unless one turns to Rabelais' discursus on methods of wiping in *Gargantua and Pantagruel* (chapter 13, book 1). For the history of toilets, see Wright (1960), or Horan's popular *The Porcelain God* (1996). Scott-Warren (2001) explores in detail the complex political intrigues surrounding Harington's *Metamorphosis of Ajax* in chapter two, "Privy Politics" (56–80). Paster (2001) comments upon the mingling of the erotic and the excremental in Harington's text and perhaps in early modern culture at large; on the scatological puns on Jacques and Ajax, see P. J. Smith (1996).

jaundice, jaundies (A) There were three types of jaundice, a **disease** of excessive **choler**: yellow, green, and black, named for the **humors** associated with them (yellow choler; green and yellow choler mixed with putrefied **phlegm**; and yellow choler mixed with burnt, black **melancholy** and corrupted **blood**). Patients with the yellow jaundice turned golden or saffron yellow all over their bodies. Sufferers of all three types experienced a **heat** on the right side of the body, a bitter taste in the mouth, headaches, tinnitus, and bodily secretions and excretions (such as **sweat** and **urine**) colored yellow, green, or black, according to the kind of choler that was blocked in the body. Both physiological and emotional stimuli could trigger jaundice. If one of the ducts or "ports" of the gallbladder was blocked and therefore unable to consume or evacuate all the choler, the gallbladder sent the unused choler back to the **liver**, which dispersed it throughout the blood. Other causes included raging **imposthumes** or burning **fevers**, each of which heated the blood and encouraged the overproduction of choler. Foul air or food, or snake-venom, also encouraged more bile in the body than it could comfortably process. Too much study, or prolonged sorrow, could induce the yellow melancholy in particular.

It was important to diagnose the correct kind of jaundice the patient suffered, so that the **physician** could correct the abundance of whichever humor was ultimately responsible for the blocked choler. Phlebotomy, especially in the region of the liver (from the hepatic or basilic **vein**), was always helpful, since it encouraged the body to void its excess humors in the place that was suffering the most from corruption. **Diet**, however, was the best **cure**; some authorities maintained that high living or a princely diet was responsible for yellow jaundice, since rich foods encouraged heat (and thus the overproduction of choler). Such patients were prescribed a diet of cooling foods such as **lettuce** or sorrel. If the disease were associated with **guts-griping** or constipation, the physician prescribed "opening medicines" or laxatives to encourage choler to flow and fulfil its function in enabling excretion.

(B) Both Shakespeare's specific references to jaundice connect it to melancholy, what physicians call the "black jaundice," rather than to choler. Antonio complains of an unspecified sadness or melancholy in the *Merchant of Venice,* and Gratiano tries to jolly him out of it:

183

> Let me play the fool:
> With mirth and laughter let old wrinkles come,
> And let my liver rather heat with wine
> Than my **heart** cool with mortifying groans.
> Why should a man, whose blood is warm within,
> Sit like his grandsire cut in alabaster?
> **Sleep** when he wakes and creep into the jaundice
> By being peevish?
>
> (*MV* 1.1.79–6)

As the body aged, it grew cooler and dryer, creating wrinkles in the skin, or what Shakespeare's Thersites calls "the rivelled fee-simple" (*TRO* Q1 5.1.22); Gratiano suggests that he would rather his face wrinkled with laughter than with old age, and that he would rather counteract his cooling age with an excess of wine (which would heat his blood) than use up the warm blood of his young heart by sighing and groaning, both of which consumed the animal spirit necessary for vigor and life. Gratiano appears to believe that untreated melancholy (manifested as "peevish[ness]," pallor, **cold, dryness**, and stillness, like an alabaster statue) could cool the blood enough to cause jaundice. Agamemnon asks, "What grief hath set these jaundies on your **cheeks**?" (*TRO* 1.3.2), clearly connecting yellow pallor with sorrow or care. Thus the "green and yellow melancholy" of Viola's imagined sister might be a kind of jaundice, the result of prolonged sorrow and stillness (*TN* 2.4.113). Beatrice may also be diagnosing Don Pedro with jaundice when she jokes of his "jealous **complexion**" which is "civil as an orange," that is, as yellow as a Seville orange (*ADO* 2.1.295–6).

(C) Primary sources with chapters on jaundice include Lanfranco (1565); Lemnius (1576); and Batman (1582). On Don Pedro's yellow skin, see Madelaine (1982).

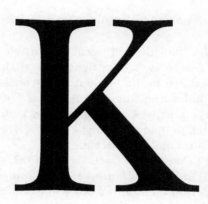

kecksies A kecksie, kecks, kex or kix is the dried-out, hollow stalk of a weedy plant, usually cow-parsley (wild chervil) or **hemlock**. The Duke of Burgundy in *Henry V* compares the state of France to a garden overgrown with weeds, "**darnel**, hemlock and rank **fumitory** . . . hateful **docks**, rough thistles, kecksies, burs," instead of the useful "**cowslip, burnet** and green clover" that should flourish there (5.2.45–53). Unlike the helpful herbs, hemlock is poisonous rather than medicinal, and cow-parsley, although edible, is frequently confused with it.

kibe See also **blain** (A) The word kibe refers to chilblains (perniosis), the swollen growths that appear on the hands and feet of persons exposed to **cold** in a humid climate for a long time.
(B) Shakespeare's allusions, all figurative, evoke a constant, low-level itch or pain, the result of chafing anxiety. Lear's Fool suggests that "if a man's **brains** were in's heels, were't not in danger of kibes?" (*LR* 1.5.8–9); Antonio dismisses the nagging of his conscience with the comment that "if 'twere a kibe, / 'Twould put me to my slipper" (*TMP* 2.1.276–7); Pistol imagines kibes ensuing as the result of argument (*WIV* 1.3.32). Hamlet imagines the irritant an obsequious peasant flattering a courtier, dogging his heels so closely that "he **galls** his kibe" (5.1.141).
(C) Lowe (1634) blames tight shoes or dirty heels as well as the cold for chilblains, treating blains or kibes with an embrocation of **salt** water, a **plaster** of cyclamen root, or even an exfoliant of mastic and incense (T1v).

kidney See also **reins** (A) The kidneys or reins cleansed the **blood** of excess water, drawing water up from the **liver**, where blood was made, and then sending it to the **bladder** for excretion. Covered with fat so thick and **cold** that it could almost be considered an **organ** in its own right, the kidneys also retained **heat**, gave blood its red color, and helped to engender **seed** (and its associated lust) in both men and women.

(B) Hal calls Falstaff a "fat-kidneyed rascal," a corpulent deer (2.2.5). Falstaff himself is one of the first to use kidney figuratively to describe temperament or **complexion**. Immersed first in the hot and smelly buck-basket and then in the frigid Thames as he hides from the jealous Master Ford, Falstaff describes his experience as a kind of horrific **Galenic** allopathy, a curing by opposites that is particularly detrimental to "a man of [his] kidney" (*WIV* 3.5.115), that is, a man already fat, lustful, gluttonous, and sweating.

(C) On the function of the kidneys, see Vicary (1587, G3v); Batman (1582, *De Proprietatibus Rerum*). On Falstaff's fatness and the aptness of his dunking in the Thames, see Jonathan Hall's, Laroque's essays in Knowles (1998). On his grease, the best is still John Dover Wilson (Wilson 1979, p. 29).

lavender Perdita famously refuses to set slips of gillyflowers, to grow flowers by grafting, claiming that such techniques are artificial. Her preferred blossoms are "Hot lavender, mints, savoury, **marjoram** . . . [and] marigold" (*WT* 4.4.104–6). Lavender was indeed **hot** and **dry**, and, when boiled in wine, was a diuretic, an emmenagogue, and an abortifacient. It was also widely used, however, for milder purposes, to comfort a headache, to enhance **brain** power, to prevent the **falling sickness**, as an antidote to poison, and, scattered on floor-rushes, to protect against **disease**. See Dodoens (1595, W6r–7v); Gerard (1597, 2g2r–3v).

lazar see **leprosy**

leech A leech is either the bloodsucking water-worm used in Shakespeare's day for the routine bleeding of **patients** or the healer who employs them. Leeches were employed in cases where cupping or boxing (scarification) was impossible, such as on the **gums**, sexual **organs**, lips, hands, or on open **wounds**, or in cases where the patient was too frightened to endure the **surgeon's box** or where venom needed to be extracted from a bite or sting. Shakespeare refers to the water-worm as the "**horse-leech**" (horse-leeches are now considered a different species from ordinary leeches, but early moderns used the same term for both) and to the physician as a "leech." Pistol orders his companions to France "like horse-leeches . . . to suck!" (*H5* 2.3.55–6), that is, to plunder rather than to fight—and Timon of Athens' bitter epitaph inspires Alcibiades to begin a healing process in which Timon's friends will "Prescribe to other as each other's leech" (5.4.84). Calling a physician a "leech" appears to have none of the pejorative associations of the present day. Guillemeau (*Chirurgerye,* 1597) has a chapter on horse-leeches.

legs forward See also **childbed, midwife** (A) Breech presentation of a fetus, feet-first. Such a birth was thought to portend not only a difficult delivery but also **deformities** in the infant, as did other variants considered unnatural, such as being unusually large or toothed at birth. Midwifery manuals include instructions on how to turn fetuses in the **womb** and on how to deliver babies feet-first, by using a speculum or by cutting the perineum with a knife if necessary (presumably in violation of the prohibition against **midwives** using instruments).

(B) Richard III demonstrates both these ominous prognostications: not only is he "born with **teeth**," he appears "legs forward," to "make haste," he suggests (*3H6* 5.6.71–5). The known difficulty in safely delivering breech babies without harming either mother or child might factor into both Richard's own deformity (which has been cited as both a cause and as a consequence of his breech presentation) and his mother's references to the pain he has caused and continues to cause her.

(C) Raynalde's *Birth of Mankynde* (1565 and multiple editions), Guillemeau (1612) and Rüff (1637) all include instructions for delivering a breech baby, and illustrations of various breech presentations. Bicks (2003) offers an overview of breech presentation in midwifery texts and a close reading of Richard's breech birth in the play, arguing for his presentation as part of the general monstrosity or prodigiousness associated with the character.

leprosy, lazar (A) What we now call Hansen's disease has been known since Biblical times. But the term "leprosy" has a confusing history, based on mistranslations and retranslations. Leprosy, the disease known as *tzaraath* in the Hebrew Bible, was translated into Greek as *lepra*. *Lepra* referred in Greek, however, to any peeling or scaling **skin** disorder; Greek had a specific word, *elephantiasis*, for Hansen's disease. But when Greek medical texts were translated into Arabic, the translators found that there was already a "disease of elephants" (what we now call "elephantiasis") and so generated a new word to refer to what the Greeks had called elephantiasis (that is, Hansen's disease), which when retranslated into Greek became the inaccurate *lepra* rather than the specific *elephantiasis*. Medieval physicians probably identified Hansen's disease accurately, although they mistakenly believed it to be highly contagious and isolated **patients** for fear of its transmission. Again, **contagion** in this instance referred to the sin that triggered the disorder; one contracted leprosy not from an external germ or agent but from an internal imbalance or a moral failing, usually corrupted **melancholy** from too much anger, envy, or greed. The Hebrew Bible, especially Leviticus, supported the characterization of leprosy as an "unclean" disease whose sufferers required shunning (the so-called leprosy stigma). So successful was the medieval policy of isolation and quarantine in 'spital-houses that some believe leprosy had been eradicated from England by the early modern period altogether. The term lazar derives from Lazarus, "leper" in Latin and the name of the patron saint of lepers; it was thought that in the Biblical parable of the poor man and who enters heaven while the rich man in hell (Dives) cannot obtain a drop of water to cool his burning **tongue**, Lazarus (the poor man) was a leper. Thus some

hospitals treated lepers as holy sufferers, chosen by God to bear the sins of the world.

Early modern doctors and lay-people, however, confused leprosy with the new disease of syphilis, probably because both caused **skin** lesions, and mistakenly attributed leprosy to sexual contact or immorality. Thus when Shakespeare refers to the hospital, 'spital, or 'spital-house, he probably does not refer to the leprosaria or lazar-houses of ancient and medieval times but to the houses of healing associated with certain cities and institutions in early modern England.

(B) Shakespeare refers to leprosy and lepers in terms of the physical, visible marks upon their bodies, rather than as sources of contagion. Queen Margaret alludes to leprosy stigma when she asks, "What, dost thou turn away and hide thy face? /I am no loathsome leper; look on me" (*2H6* 3.2.74–5). Her husband knows her guilt, however, and even if she does not carry the physical disease, she is a moral leper whom he shuns. Scarus equates leprosy and bubonic **plague** when he compares Cleopatra to the "token'd **pestilence**," a disease with distinguishing marks, "where **death** is sure"; he wishes "leprosy o'ertake" her for her flight from Actium (*ANT* 3.10.10–1). Most references, however, appear in *TIM*; Grigsby suggests that leprosy takes on some of its Biblical connotations in this play, which equates the leper with the false witness. Timon attributes skin ailments to leprosy, wishing pruritus and boils upon the Athenians: "Itches, **blains**, /Sow all the Athenian bosoms; and their crop /Be general leprosy" (4.1.29–30). He alludes to the leper's pallor in the phrase "hoar leprosy" (4.3.36), and Apemantus aptly retorts, "There is no leprosy but what thou speak'st" (4.3.362).

The Ghost in *Hamlet* evokes the disgust and stigma connoted by leprosy, as the poison poured in his ear curdles his **blood** and makes his skin peel with "a most instant **tetter** bark'd about, /Most lazar-like, with vile and loathsome crust" (1.5.71–2), like the bark peeling off a tree in tatters (tatter and tetter are the same word in early modern English) or the scaling skin of a leper or lazar. Canterbury worries lest the church lose its monies, including the bequests intended for "relief of lazars and weak age, /Of indigent **faint** souls past corporal toil, /A hundred almshouses right well supplied" (*H5* 1.1.15–16); the leprosaria from such bequests founded the modern hospital. Falstaff memorably compares his recruits to "slaves as ragged as Lazarus in the painted cloth" (and one text adds, "where the glutton's dogs licked his sores," a vivid image of abjection and of Falstaff's moral cannibalism), the picture of Lazarus on a painting or "staining" of cloth to decorate a room (*1H4* 4.2.25). Pistol calls Doll Tearsheet "the lazar kite of Cressid's kind" (*H5* 2.1.76), meaning that she suffers from venereal disease, as Cressida was supposed to have done, and plunders, like a kite or bird of prey, to obtain victims to infect in her turn. Shakespeare's *Troilus and Cressida* does not accuse Cressida directly of leprosy, but Thersites curses Patroclus, "if she that lays thee out says thou art a fair corse, I'll be sworn and sworn upon't she never shrouded any but lazars" (2.3.33); Patroclus is attractive only to one who is used to burying the corpses of lepers. Thersites later comments that none of the so-called heroes are worth emulating, but that Menelaus is the worst of them all: "I care not to be the **louse** of a lazar, so I were not Menelaus" (5.1.65).

189

The louse is a low parasite, and the leper the lowest in the social hierarchy, but Menelaus is basest of all.

(C) Bullein (1558) illustrates the early modern use of the term leprosy to refer to any sort of skin condition, even among **physicians**. Brody (1974) is the standard text on the literary history of leprosy. Hoeniger (1992) argues that, since leprosy had been eradicated from England by Shakespeare's time, his references are purely figurative. Grigsby (2004) summarizes the problems in translating *lepra* and argues that while medieval physicians correctly identified Hansen's disease, early moderns mistakenly attributed the skin lesions of syphilis to leprosy, conflating the two illnesses.

lethargy, lethargies The loss of torpor of movement in some part or all of the body, often as the result of **cold humors** in old age; see **apoplexy**

lettuce Cold and **moist**, lettuce was a cooling **medicine** and an anaphrodisiac. Iago contrasts it to **nettles** in *Othello* 1.3.322, imagining the body as a garden and human volition as the gardener than can choose to plant nettles and engage in lust or to "sow lettuce" and to refrain. On the cold and moist nature of lettuce, see Ascham (1561, D6v–7r); Dodoens (1595, 2V1v–3r). Dodoens adds, "Letuce seede being often vsed to be eaten a long space, drieth vp the naturall **seede**, and putteth away the desire to Lecherie" (2V2v).

lice see **louse**

lily-liver'd See also **pigeon-liver'd** Lacking **blood** in the **liver** and thus courage; cowardly, pusillanimous. Courage, lust, and other strong passions were housed in the liver because there they could consume more nutrition brought to them from the **stomach** (the liver refined chyle, the product of digested food, into blood and **humors** that sustained the **organs** of the body). A pale liver meant that one lacked blood, and blood was necessary as the vehicle for valor, love, loyalty, and other noble emotions. Cowards might lack blood in the liver from birth, or blood might flee the liver in response to threats. Kent thoroughly enjoys castigating the idle and vain Oswald as "A knave; a rascal; an eater of broken meats; a base, proud, shallow, beggarly, three-suited, hundred-pound, filthy, worsted-stocking knave; a lily-livered, action-taking knave, a whoreson, glass-gazing, super-serviceable finical rogue" (*LR* 2.2.15–19). Other signs of fear comprised trembling limbs, a pale face, and a quavering voice, which Macbeth anatomizes in his servant:

> Go prick thy face, and over-red thy fear,
> Thou lily-liver'd boy. What soldiers, patch?
> **Death** of thy soul! those **linen cheeks** of thine
> Are counsellors to fear. What soldiers, whey-face?
>   (5.3.14–17)

Fear has made the boy's blood rush from his face and his liver to his **heart**, to sustain him with vital, life-giving **spirit**. Pricking his face will make it bleed and look red again. His face is pale as linen cloth or the whey left after cheese-making; "whey-face" also alludes to the **milk** and curds consumed by those of a **phlegmatic**, cowardly, slothful **complexion** or humoral personality (as opposed to the beef or mutton eaten by **choleric** soldiers or **sanguine** lords).

limbeck See also **distil** (A) Distilling vessels used to refine ingredients for **medicines**, conserves, and **perfumes** included the cucurbit (used for heating liquid, and named for its cucumber- or squash-like shape); the head or alembic, sometimes contracted to limbeck (the top of the still or distilling device, including a long pipe or nose pointing downwards), and the receiver or **receipt**, which collected the condensed and purified liquid from the nose.

(B) Sonnet 119 imagines that the lyric speaker, ill with a "madding **fever**," has consumed "**potions** . . . drunk of Siren tears, / Distill'd from limbecks foul as hell within" (119.1–2, 10, 12). Paradoxically, this vile medicine, which itself causes "evil," has remedied his love, making it "fairer than at first, far greater" than before, having purified his love just as medicines are purified in a still. His lover's tears are those of the Sirens, the winged songstresses of Greek myth who lured sailors to their **deaths** and whose tears, when purified in this way, evoke the virgins' tears or body products allegedly present in the popular **Paracelsian** remedy of **mummy** or prepared human flesh.

Lady Macbeth imagines that the guards to Duncan's chamber, when drugged with wine, "shall be so stupefied / That memory, the warder of the brain / Shall be a **fume**, and the receipt of reason / A limbeck only" (*MAC* 1.7.65–7). Lady Macbeth imagines a **brain** partitioned in three: fantasy, memory, and reason. Early modern authorities vary on the question of whether the three chambers are located next to each other or front to back. Shakespeare's model for the brain here, though, locates its chambers upstairs and downstairs like a three-story house, with memory on the ground floor, fantasy on the second, and reason on the first. Memory, personified, is the warden or keeper of knowledge within the brain. Under the influence of "wine and wassail," memory is **heated** (like liquid in a cucurbit) by the warming effect of wine into fumes or steam that ought to condense into the receipt or receiver of reason; that is, scattered memories ought to coalesce or become refined in the receipt into reasonable conclusions (for example, a memory of Macbeth entering the chamber the night of Duncan's death might after being distilled by reason turn into the conclusion that Macbeth was responsible for the murder). Lady Macbeth's wassail, however, will so confuse the guards that what ought to be the receptacle for their memories—their reason—will instead become the alembic, the top of the still, so that their memories remain as vague impressions rather than as matter for rational conclusions.

(C) Gesner (1576) is the most useful source for illustrations of an early modern still, and clearly labels its constituent parts; see also the expanded version of his works, translated by George Baker (1599). In Sonnet 119, Vendler sees an allusion to the application of **poultices** to injuries, to correspond to the potions to be consumed for internal ills in the lines "Applying fears to hopes and hopes to fears" (Sonnet 119, 502–6). Schanzer (1957) suggests that in *Macbeth* "the receipt of reason" is both the container for reason but also the receiver of the still that receives the purified product of the brain's processes, that is pure reason. Limbeck, he suggests, is used in its more common Renaissance sense of cucurbit or retort, the vessel in which the liquids are heated, rather than in its technical sense of the top or head of the still (1957, 224).

lime-kills i'th' palm see **lime-kilns i'th' palm**

lime-kilns i'th' palm This obscure and figurative description in Thersites' long catalog of the "**diseases** of the South" could allude to the painful chalk deposits found in the hands in chronic **gout**, or, more likely, to the excruciating, burning itch of palmar psoriasis (*TRO* Q1 5.1.18–21). Most editors prefer the explanation of psoriasis, but see McGeoch (2007), who surveys a range of medical views, including those suggesting the possibility of gouty deposits. For a contemporary reference, see Robert Armin, *Two Maids of More-Clacke*, "a hand whose palme dus itch with fire" (1609, E4v).

linen See also **flax** Both **sick** and healthy prized **linen** cloth, woven from thread spun from the linseed or flax plant, for its cleanliness, using it for clothing (especially "shifts" or underclothes), bedsheets, handkerchiefs, and bandages or **tents** (probes for **wounds**). Clean linen (clean shifts and clean sheets) helped prevent the **diseases** transmitted by foul odors; moreover, clean sheets might be free from bedbugs or **lice**. Cerimon calls for linen as well as for fire and fragrance when he revives Thaisa (*PER* 3.2), planning to offer her the clean, warm, comfortable surroundings where she ought to have given birth, rather than the "terrible **childbed**" she endured at sea (3.1.56). **Midwives** might have carried their own clean linens with them when they visited parturient mothers (Harkness 2008).

lisp, lisping See also **tongue-tied, stammer** Although Hill (1571, Sr) identifies as "lispers" those who cannot pronounce the letters L and R because they are tongue-tied, in Shakespeare lisping denotes affectation and insincerity rather than any physiological deficit. Ganymede bids farewell to Jaques, who affects the modish, foreign fashion of **melancholy**, with the mock-benediction, "look you lisp and wear strange suits" (*AYL* 4.1.34); Berowne scoffs at Boyet, the perfect courtier, who can "carve, and a' can lisp" (*LLL* 5.2.323); Hamlet bitterly compares Ophelia to all women, who put on false faces and voices and walks: "you jig, you amble, and you lisp" (*HAM* 3.1.144). Mercutio curses, "The pox of such antic, lisping, affecting fantasticoes; these new tuners of accents!" (*ROM* 2.4.28). The fashion for lisping is both antiquated or quaint ("antic") and new-fangled, with no precedent in custom or habit (a "fantastico"). Poins accuses Bardolph of flattering or "lisping" to Falstaff (*2H4* 2.4.266), and Falstaff himself opposes his rough wooing to the "lisping hawthorn-buds" of men who might flatter Mistress Ford (*WIV* 3.3.71).

liver See also **lily-liver'd, liver-vein** (A) Shaped a little like the moon, the liver manufactured nutritive **blood** from chyle, the product of digested food in the **stomach**, in a process known as the second concoction (the first concoction was the transformation of food into chyle in the stomach; the third was the refinement of nutritive blood into pure blood through the addition of spirit in the **heart**). Nutritive blood included the four cardinal **humors**—blood, **choler**, **melancholy**, and phlegm, which nourished the **liver** and heart, the gallbladder, the **spleen**, and **lungs** and **brain** respectively—and some additional watery humors that nourished the **kidneys** and veins. The veins surrounded the liver like fingers on a hand, or the roots of a tree within the earth. The liver distributed the four humors around the body through two large veins, the portal **vein** or liver-vein (which also produced phlegm, in some sources) and the concave vein that distributed the humors to their respective seats for nourishment and further refinement. If the body lacked **heat**, the blood remained thin, pale, and insufficiently concocted, or **phlegmatic**. Thus the liver also played an important role in emotions that required a good store of blood, such as courage and love, especially erotic love. In the early modern tripartite soul, the liver manufactured natural spirit (which was responsible for growth and basic body processes) and housed the vegetative soul. Paradoxically, cowardly men—and those Crooke calls "ravenous gourmandizers," with huge appetites (1615, M6r)—had larger livers than the brave and the temperate, because the weak-hearted needed to make up with natural spirit the vital spirit that they lacked, and because the greedy supplied the **organ** with so much provender.

(B) In Shakespeare the liver is the seat of love (sometimes of lust), courage, wrath, and **disease**. As Ganymede, Rosalind offers to "wash [Orlando's] liver as clean as a sound sheep's heart, that there shall not be one spot of love in't" (*AYL* 3.2.422). The Friar plans Hero's false **death** to trick Claudio into grieving, plotting: "Then shall he mourn, /If ever love had interest in his liver" (*ADO* 4.1.231). Ferdinand, however, distinguishes between the "white **cold** virgin snow upon [his] heart," his true love for Miranda that will wait until marriage, and "the ardour of [his] liver," the strong urge for consummation (*TMP* 4.1.55–6). Orsino cannot wait to command in Olivia "liver, brain and heart, those sovereign thrones" of the early modern tripartite soul (*TN* 1.1.36). Cymbeline similarly classifies the three souls of Britain as "liver, heart and brain" (*CYM* 5.5.14). Fabian comments on the success of Maria's plot to gull Malvolio, "this wins him, liver and all" (2.5.95).

Falstaff's famous paean to sherry outlines the role of the liver and its blood (helped, he characteristically claims, by alcohol) in generating courage:

> The second property of your excellent sherris is, the warming of the blood;
> which, before cold and settled, left the liver white and pale, which is the badge
> of pusillanimity and cowardice; but the sherris warms it and makes it course

from the inwards to the parts extreme: it illumineth the face, which as a beacon gives warning to all the rest of this little kingdom, man, to arm; and then the vital commoners and inland petty spirits muster me all to their captain, the heart, who, great and puffed up with this retinue, doth any deed of courage; and this valour comes of sherris. (*2H4* 4.3.103–13)

A cowardly man's liver is white and pale because he constitutionally lacks blood altogether, or because he does not consume enough food to generate blood, or because his liver does not "concoct" or "cook" the blood sufficiently for it (this is the case that Falstaff is imagining). Insufficiently concocted blood was pale, thin, and cool rather than red, sustaining, and warm. Sherry warms the blood so that it can travel from the body's innards (the liver) to the extremities such as the **nose**, causing the red face of the drinker. Then, in Falstaffian physiology, the warmer, better-concocted blood travels to the heart, which refines it further into vital spirit. The heart is enlarged or "puffed up" with its extra blood supply and also by the **perturbation** or strong emotions caused by drinking. Both Charmian in *ANT* and Gratiano in *MV* enjoy "heat[ing the] liver with" drinking (*ANT* 1.2.24; *MV* 1.1.81).

"Hot livers" (*1H4* 2.4.323) were signs of youth, hence Falstaff's claim to the Lord Chief Justice that he is young and the Justice is old: "You do measure the heat of our livers with the bitterness of our **galls**" (*2H4* 1.2.175). Anger could heat the liver, as well as drinking; conversely, "reason and respect /Make livers pale and lustihood deject," argues Troilus (*TRO* 2.2.49–50). Pistol warns (and warms) Falstaff: "My knight, I will inflame thy noble liver /And make thee rage" (*2H4* 5.5.31–2). Falstaff's liver is "burning hot" for the merry wives (*WIV* 2.1.117).

A healthy liver was dark, but solid-colored. "Spotted livers" indicated serious disease (*TRO* 5.3.18). The "dirt-rotten livers" in Thersites' curse might be spotted or streaked, or the blood they produced might contain the thick, cloudy sediment of the melancholy humor (*TRO* Q1 5.1.20). When Leontes is adamant that he will not believe Hermione's innocence, he vows to punish her "were [his] wife's liver /Infected as her life" (*WT* 1.2.304–5). He imagines her liver, the seat of love or of lust, stained irrevocably by adultery. The witches in *MAC* include "liver of blaspheming Jew" in their hell-broth (4.1.26).
(C) Brunschwig (1525, B5v) describes the function of the liver; Vicary (1587, G2v) describes its appearance in more detail, and Crooke, still more. Crooke calls it "the seat of concupiscence" (1615, M5r).

liver-vein (A) The large liver-vein or basilic vein was believed to travel from the **liver** to the **heart** via the right arm, bringing to it nutrition in the form of **blood** that had been through the second concoction or cooking process in the liver. Some of this blood would be used as nutrition, and some would be further refined into spirituous blood, the union between body and soul, and sent to the **lungs** and the rest of the body in the **arteries**.
(B) Shakespeare's whimsical usage clarifies the physiological mechanism of love. Biron jokingly comments on love: "This is the liver-vein, which makes flesh a deity,

/A green goose a goddess: pure, pure idolatry" (*LLL* 4.3.72–3). It was well-known that the liver was responsible for strong passions, including concupiscence, the "flesh." The liver then involved the heart, and finally the **brain**, in tempering feelings of lust with idealism or altruism and then with reason. In Biron's summary, love stops at the heart, turning an ordinary woman, however young or "green," a "deity."

(C) Johannes de Mediolano's *Regimen* (1528, F3r–4r) describes the travels of the liver-vein and retells a famous story that Galen discovered its path in a dream. Gyer (1592, N1r–v) recommends incising the liver-vein only in the spring. Neely's work on love-sickness and love in Shakespeare considers the physiology of the liver-vein (2004).

long purples, dead men's fingers Variously called dogs' balls, fools' ballocks, hares' ballocks, priest's pintell (penis) and goats' cullions, this dwarf orchis was **hot** and **moist** and therefore an excellent **cure** for **consumption** or **hectic fevers** that burned or consumed a body from within. The fresh plant was an aphrodisiac, but the withered root repressed lust. Gertrude describes Ophelia sinking into her watery grave with flowers including "long purples, /that liberal shepherds give a grosser name, /But our **cold** maids do dead men's fingers call" (*HAM* 4.7.169–71). For description and names, see Dodoens (1595, R3r).

louse, lousy, lice, nit (A) One of several different types of body-parasite of the genus *phthiraptera* that feed on the **blood** of mammals, including human beings. All three types of pediculosis—infestation with head lice, body lice, and pubic lice—afflicted early modern people. Head lice lay eggs at the base of **hair**, close to the scalp, and are transmitted mostly from head-to-head contact within the family rather than through **linens**, but body lice then and now have evolved to lay eggs in clothing and could spread typhus and other illnesses. Pubic or "crab" lice are unique to humans and can live anywhere on the body but are most usually transmitted through sexual contact. In Shakespeare's time, however, the transmission of the parasite was unknown, although it was clear that the homeless, the poverty-stricken, the overcrowded, and children suffered disproportionately from infestation. Lice were thought to develop from corrupted **humors** in the **blood** and to escape through small holes or pores in the **skin**. If the patient had been cursed by God, as in the **plagues** of Egypt, lice-infestation was incurable, but if the infestation was natural, sufferers ought to abstain from foods that would breed **phlegm** and particularly from figs and dates, and to wash their bodies twice a day in **salt** water and a mixture of lye and **wormwood**. Mustard-**plasters** and **quicksilver** dissolved in grease or oil was also effective.

(B) Shakespeare refers to both crab lice and head lice in the verses of Lear's Fool on the heath:

> The **cod-piece** that will house
> Before the head has any,

> The head and he shall louse;
> So beggars marry many.

(3.2.27–30)

A lecherous man who marries before he has a dwelling-place will end up home-less and liable to **infection** with lice from one of his sexual partners in both his pubic- and his head-hair; he will end up breeding "many" lice along with many impoverished offspring. Poverty and pediculosis (presumably because of over-crowding and filth) went together, so that King Henry VIII curses his lords for making Cranmer wait like a "lousy footboy" outside the door, as if they would be infected by his presence because they might catch lice from him (*H8* 5.2.174). Sir Hugh's Welsh accent confuses the luces (freshwater fish or pike) on a coat-of-arms with louses in his comment that a "dozen white louses become an old coat well" (*WIV* 1.1.19). Critics have long taken the pun (on "lousy" and "Lucy" and on "luce" and "louse") as an allusion to the coat-of-arms of the Lucy family of Charle-cote in Warwickshire. Thersites takes the louse as a figure for the utmost baseness when he claims that he would prefer to be a parasite on the body of a leper, "a louse on a **lazar**," rather than to be the cuckolded Menelaus (*TRO* 5.1.65).

At close confines in an army camp, soldiers suffered notoriously from head lice and also crab lice from contact with prostitutes or camp-followers. Parolles calls Captain Dumain of the Duke of Florence's army "lousy" (*AWW* 4.3.194) and Fluellen variously castigates his fellow-soldiers as "arrant, rascally, beggarly, lousy knave[s]" (*H5* 4.8.34) or Pistol as a "lousy, pragging [bragging] knave," and (twice) "scurvy, lousy knave" (*H5* 5.1.6, 18, 22). Sir Hugh Evans may be calling the jealous Ford a "lousy knave" in anger at his being called out on what proves a wild-goose chase, since the wives have hidden the would-be philan-derer Falstaff in the buck-basket with their dirty linens (*WIV* 3.3.242). Nits or nymphs are notoriously tiny, and tenacious. Both Shakespeare's references to nits allude to their smallness. Petruchio insults the tailor by comparing him to both a "nit" and another parasitic insect, a "flea" (*SHR* 4.3.109), and Costard insults the tiny Moth by praising his wit but also calling him a "pathetical nit" (*LLL* 4.1.148).

(C) Parents of school-age children may know to their cost the increasing resist-ance of head lice to insecticides, and the popularity of olive oil for their eradication, a remedy that dates at least as early as the *Treasure of Pore Men* (1526, M2v), which recommends pounding olive oil with Rhenish wine and the unidentified "Aruement" (arrowmint?) and applying it to the body (the alter-native is smearing the body with grease from an ungelded pig, mixed with **brimstone** and **quicksilver** in Rhenish wine and arrowmint). Elyot suggests in *The Castel of Helthe* (1539) that eating dried figs breeds lice, since the dessicated fruit is by **complexion** so **hot** and **dry** (L4v). Goeurot includes pediculosis among his *Diseases of Children*, describes the origins of lice in the blood, and expresses sympathy for those who seem to be almost "eaten to **death**" by the insects (1550, Bb2r–3v).

love-in-idleness Also called pansies, from the French *pensées* or "thoughts"; hearts-ease; knapweed; call-me-to-you; three-monks-in-a-hood; and (today), *viola tricolor*, **love-in-idleness** was **cold** and helped to generate **moisture**, especially to cure cases of **ague** or **fever** in children. Shakespeare's Oberon identifies the little tripartite flower, "before milk-white, now purple with love's wound" as a sure way to instill love if the juice is squeezed into the **eye** (*MND* 2.1.167). There is no precedent for Shakespeare's invention except perhaps Gerard's prescription that the **distilled** water of the herb, drunk for ten days day and nights, will ease the pains of the French **disease** (syphilis or **pox**) and can even cure it if the patient is made to **sweat** (Gerard 1597, 2Y1r). Shakespeare may also have known the colloquial name "call me to you" for pansies or heartsease or maybe a folk or magical use for the flower in love-**potions**. Dodoens (1586, M3v–M4r) also identifies pansies with heartsease and love-in-idleness, and asserts its usefulness in treating **vomiting** children.

love-sick See also **green-sick, melancholy** Love-sickness could mean either green-sickness, the pallor, **fever**, lethargy, and wasting associated with unsatisfied love, or the more serious condition of love-melancholy. Enobarbus' famous speech about Cleopatra in her barge describes the purple sails as "so **perfumed** that /The winds were love-sick with them" (2.2.193–4), imagining the breeze as the sighs thought to consume the **heart** of a lover, since fragrance particularly stimulated desire. Marcus imagines Dido hearkening to Aeneas intently, "love-sick" and therefore **blind** to the larger questions of national duty that would call her lover away (*TIT* 5.3.82).

Lucina (A) The Roman goddess of childbirth, Lucina could aid or hinder parturition as she chose, by crossing her fingers, arms, or legs to prevent the child's entry into the world, or by loosening them to release it. Bribed by a jealous Juno to kill Alcmena during the birth of Hercules, Jove's son, Lucina crossed her fingers to prevent the birth until she was tricked into leaping up from her place, opening her arms and allowing the babe to be born (Lucina turned the unfortunate trickster into a weasel). Lucina is doubled with Diana, goddess of virginity and, in some accounts, with Juno, goddess of marriage; Proserpina, goddess of spring; and Hecate, goddess of witchcraft.
(B) Lucina retains her vengeful character in Shakespeare, refusing to aid the labors of Posthumus' mother (*CYM* 5.4.43) or Thaisa (*PER* 3.1.10), both of whom die or are thought to die in **childbed**. Posthumus is "ripp'd" or born via postmortem caesarean section (*CYM* 5.4.45; see **untimely ripp'd**), and Marina parted from her mother, who is laid in a caulked casket and set to sea as a corpse. Pericles calls alternately for Lychorida, the **midwife**, and Lucina, the goddess, but neither human nor divine aid can resuscitate Thaisa. The only Shakespeare birth Lucina blesses is that of Antiochus' incestuous daughter (*PER* 1.1.8).
(C) The story of Alcmena appears in Ovid's *Metamorphoses*, Book 9 (1567, Q3r–v). On Lucina's doubling with Diana, Juno, Hecate, and Proserpina see

Linche's chapter on Diana (1599, G4v–I2r), and Roberts' detailed discussion of the "Triple Hecate" in *MAC* and *MND* (1992, 137–40). Bicks (2003) argues for a recuperation of Lucina via her doubling with Diana and her adoption as patron of midwives, performed through Thaisa's long stay at Ephesus.

lunacy, lunatic See also **Bedlam, crazed, madness** (A) Lunatics suffered periodic bouts of madness interspersed with regular bouts of sanity, although most sources use the word as a synonym for insanity of all kinds, including **frenzy** or feverish madness. Lunatics' **brains** traveled to the top of the skull as the moon waxed, and descended as it waned, which prevented their reason from controlling their emotions or bodily urges. The **cure** required cooling the brain so that the frenzy could subside, hence the persistent belief that mad persons needed to be confined in cool, dark places, even when healers did not believe that sufferers were possessed by evil spirits.

(B) Theseus argues that "The lunatic, the lover, and the poet /Are of imagination all compact" (*MND* 5.1.7–8). The brain of each one is overheated from passion, which overwhelms their reason, "shaping fantasies" that re-make the external world into objects with a personal significance and context to their emotional lives. The madman "sees more devils than vast hell can hold," driven **insane** by fear (a known cause of madness). Even the rational will imagine, anticipating pleasure, that someone approaching is a "bringer of that joy," and at night-time, if we are afraid, we might suppose "a bush . . . a bear" (5.1.9, 20, 22). At different points in the play the lovers fear that they are "mad," but the term lunatic is particularly apt for a play in which the moon features as a character on stage (the need for whom the mechanicals discuss at great length in 3.1.51–8 and who is the subject of mockery from the nobles in 5.1.238–61); the celestial clock whose aspects will mark the time until Theseus' and Hippolyta's wedding (1.1.3–9), the speed of a fairy's wing-beats (2.1.7), the distance from Lysander's former love and his displeasure with Hermia after Puck's mischievous magic (3.2.53); the harbinger of **rheumatic diseases** (2.1.103); and the oracle of virginity for the chaste nuns with whom Aegeus threatens to imprison Hermia (1.1.73) and the vestal who escapes Cupid's dart thanks to its rays (2.1.162).

SHR reminds us that the Americanism that calls both the insane and the angry "mad" derives from early modern usage, presenting both Katharina and Petruchio as furious, violent, and each at odds with those around them. Katharina is "stark mad or wonderful forward" (1.1.69), Petruchio's servant calls him "mad" even before he begins his campaign to tame Katharina (1.2.18), and they find themselves "mad . . . [and] madly mated" by their match (3.2.244). Katharina deems Petruchio a "mad-brain'd rudesby" (3.2.10), a "mad-cap ruffian and a swearing Jack" (2.1.288), and Petruchio vows to "curb her mad and headstrong **humor**" (4.1.209). By the end of the play, however, nobody calls them mad any longer. Instead, they turn the accusation into an in-joke. Katharina has called Petruchio "one half lunatic" (2.1.287), and the control of sun and moon proves crucial to his strategy for taming Katharina when he insists that she call the sun, the moon, and vice versa, before he will stir a step further to her father's house (4.5.2–20). It is following this conversation that Petruchio and Katharina begin to joke about their own madness and to try to madden others instead of suffering the imputation of insanity themselves. Petruchio challenges Kate to greet old Vincentio as a young maid, a challenge she willingly takes up and that threatens to "make the man mad, to make a woman out of him" (4.5.35), and that elicits the mocking, "How now Kate! I hope you are not mad!" from Petruchio (4.5.42). Katharina's "Pardon, I pray thee, my mad mistaking" (4.5.49) may be played either as her joyful participation in a game that she and Petruchio have invented together, or the passive acceptance of a victim of Stockholm syndrome, brainwashed by her captor (as in Detmer 1997). Either way, the person called "mad" at the end of the play is neither the shrew nor the ruffian but Vincentio, Lucentio's father, the same old man whom Katharina has greeted as a flowering virgin and who is now called "lunatic" (5.1.72), a "mad ass" by the Pedant impersonating him and a "mad knave" by his son's servant, who threatens to send him to jail (5.1.84, 92).

Rosalind's words in *AYL* allude to a cruel cure for madness, but the therapy she offers is notably humane: "Love is merely a madness, and, I tell you, deserves as well a dark house and a whip as madmen do: and the reason why they are not so punished and cured is, that the lunacy is so ordinary that the whippers are in love too. Yet I profess curing it by counsel" (3.2.400–2). The "dark house and a whip" would be used to whip out the demon love possessing the infatuated Orlando. Love is like lunacy because it waxes, like the moon, to a crisis; this lunacy is "ordinary" because everyone sees the moon (falls in love). In *WIV*, the changing freaks and inconsistencies of Ford in his jealousy lead Falstaff to deem him a "lunatic knave" (3.5.103) and Evans to comment, "this is lunatics!" (4.1.124). Quickly thinks she is protecting William from obscenity, misunderstanding the genitive case in Latin for a smutty comment about "Jenny's case" or vagina. Evans retorts, "'oman, art thou lunatics?" his accent and usage error compounding the joke (4.1.69).

In *TIT*, Tamora plans to trick Titus, telling her sons, "This closing with him fits his lunacy. /Whate'er I forge to feed his brain-sick fits, /Do you uphold and maintain in your speeches" (5.2.70–2), a celestial reference that reminds us of Titus' arrows, intended for the heavens, "a mile beyond the moon" (4.3.66). The arrows to the moon, and his invitation to Tamora to dinner, signify Titus' "lunacy" to Tamora, but his carefully plotted plan for revenge to Titus himself. It is notable that Claudius describes Hamlet both as "a mad young man" (4.1.19) and "mad" (5.1.272), but also as suffering from a "turbulent and dangerous lunacy" (3.1.4). Polonius thinks he's found "the very cause of Hamlet's lunacy" (2.2.49), but Claudius is more suspicious, seeing in his nephew's actions a challenge to the state: "The terms of our estate may not endure /Hazard so dangerous as doth hourly grow /Out of his lunacies" (Folio only, 3.3.7). The quarto reads "out of his brows," but the Folio reading "lunacies" characterizes Hamlet's state of mind as changeable, unpredictable except that it will wax hour by hour. Claudius and Polonius present two versions of the critical argument about the authenticity and ferocity of Hamlet's madness. Polonius (and the audience) treat Hamlet as a kind of wise fool—"though this be madness, there is method in't" (2.2.205)—and his distraction as benign, until he kills Polonius "in madness" (4.1.34). *LR* associates lunacy with the wandering or fleeting nature of the moon; Edgar describes the "lunatic bans" or wild curses of the wandering Bedlam beggar (2.3.19), a state to which Lear himself is reduced as he wanders the heath, cursing his daughters. Regan dismisses her father as the "lunatic king" as she interrogates Gloucester as to his whereabouts (3.7.46). Queen Margaret's propensity for witchy cursing perhaps earns her the title of "lunatic" from Dorset in *R3* (1.3.253), and King Richard II calls John of Gaunt "a lunatic lean-witted fool" (*R2* 2.1.115) because of his ability to "chas[e] the royal **blood** /With fury from his native residence," to appall him with his advice as the moon's rays shine whitely on the ground.

(C) Ruscelli (1558) attributes lunacy in children to a "worme with twoo heads" that infests their **hearts** and thus triggers excessive **perturbation** or emotional upset, a known cause of distraction or madness. Vicary, however, attributes to Aristotle the suggestion that the brain moves within the skull according to the motions of the moon:

> the brayne hath this propertie, that it moueth and followeth the mouing of the Moone: for in the waxing of the Moone the Brayne followeth vpwardes, and in the wane of the Moone the brayne discendeth downwardes, and vanisheth in substaunce of vertue: for then the Brayne shrinketh togeather in it selfe, and is not so fully obedient to the spirit of feeling. And this is proued in menne that be lunatike or madde, and also in men that be epulentike or hauing the **falling sicknesse**. (1577, D5v)

Batman (1582, N1r) concurs. Bullein (1579, D1r) recommends "penicialle" (which seems, from context, to be a lichen or fungus) to counteract "the Fransy, or Lunatyke sycknes." Schaar (1970) surveys and enumerates Shakespeare's usage of the words "lunatic" and "lunacy."

lungs (A) Lungs produced voice and breath. Naturally **cold** and **dry** in their constitution, they were rendered **moist** in the body by the watery **phlegm, rheum**, and other sorts of mucus that they received from the **brain**. They were spongy and absorbent in texture, and so required thin or refined **blood** for their sustenance. The right lung had three lobes, the left, two (though Crooke and others say that each lung has only two lobes, and the lobes of the right are merely larger). Healthy lungs were yellowish, with a few black streaks; blackened lungs indicated chronic and usually fatal **disease**. The lungs were nourished by three kinds of fluid: **veins** brought nutritive blood from the **liver** (processed from the chyle or digested food in the **stomach**); the **artery** from the **heart** (now called the pulmonary artery; called by **Galen** the arterial vein) brought blood bearing vital spirit from the heart; and the "venous artery" returned a tiny bit of blood (together with purified air) to the left side of the heart. The purpose of the lungs was likewise tripartite. They drew in cold air from the atmosphere in order to cool the **heart**, which might otherwise overheat from the effort of purifying the blood and enspiriting it with vital **spirit** or life-force. The heart required clean air to do its job, and the lungs also helped to filter air before it came to the heart for this purpose. Finally, the lungs removed from the heart **fumes** or **vapors** left over from the refining process, and expelled these through the mouth and **nose** in the breath. Diseases of the lungs included **pleurisy**, wheezing, **coughing**, and pneumonia.

(B) The lungs in Shakespeare produce breath, speech, curses, benedictions, laughter, and **infection**. Thersites includes "whissing [wheezing] lungs" in his catalog of "diseases of the South" (*TRO* Q1 5.1.21) and, in the same play, Ajax urges a trumpeter to blow so hard that he will "crack [his] lungs" (4.5.7). "Speak from thy lungs military," the host urges Falstaff (*WIV* 4.5.17). Martius' "lungs / [will] Coin words" as the **measles** generate pustules or **tetters** (*COR* 3.1.77–8). "Thou but offend'st thy lungs to speak so loud," remonstrates Shylock (*MV* 4.1.140), since his mind is unchanged, and great effort would use up nutrition and moisture from the lungs and vital spirit coming from the heart. King Henry IV finds his "lungs . . . wasted" in illness "so /That strength of speech is utterly denied [him]" (*2H4* 4.5.216–17). Pistol is fond of employing body parts in curses and blessings, and the lungs are no exception. "Let vultures vile seize on his lungs!" he cries (*2H4* 5.3.139), but bids farewell to Falstaff kindly, "God bless your lungs, good knight" (5.5.9). In *H5* he curses again, "thy hateful lungs!" (2.1.49).

Hamlet praises the players' clown as one who "shall make those laugh whose lungs are tickled o' the sere," that is, even those who are cold and dried out with age will enjoy the expansion of the heart (and increased vital spirit) associated with mirth (2.2.323). Menenius makes the **belly** in his fable express amusement "With a kind of smile /which ne'er came from the lungs" (*COR* 1.1.107–8). Two melancholics laugh at the sight of clowns but blame their lungs, rather than their **spleens**, for their merriment. When Jaques encounters Touchstone, his "lungs began to crow like Chanticleer" (*AYL* 2.7.30), and Armado's "heaving . . . lungs provokes [him] to ridiculous smiling" (*LLL* 3.1.76). Physiologically, **melancholy** men might express an immoderate mirth or sarcastic glee, especially if their melancholy was "non-natural" or the result not of innate melancholy but of another **humor** that had become burned or "adust." Mocking laughter came from the lungs and not from the heart. Iachimo tries to convince Imogen that her husband does not value her by describing him as a "jolly Briton [who] laughs from's free lungs" (*CYM* 1.6.68) at the notion of remaining faithful to one woman, and Gonzalo, unable to share the mirth of the sardonic Antonio, pretends to admire the "sensible and nimble lungs that . . . use to laugh at nothing" (*TMP* 2.1.174).

"Infected lungs" (*PER* 4.6.169; see also **belch**) breathed out putrid air that could contaminate anyone exposed to it by inducing a corresponding humoral imbalance that could, in turn, trigger a disease. Ironically, disorders might make the breath smell sweet or fruity; when Adrian comments that the air of Prospero's island "breathes . . . most sweetly," Sebastian wryly retorts, "As if it had lungs and rotten ones" (*TMP* 2.1.48).

(C) On the **anatomy** and workings of the lungs, see Vicary (1587, F4r); Crooke (1615).

M

madness See also **Bedlam, crazed, ecstasy, frenzy,** *hysterica passio,* **love-sick, lunacy, melancholy, natural** (A) The early modern period saw what one scholar has called "a Renaissance of madness" (Neely 2004, 1) in its attempts to treat, control, or relieve symptoms that an earlier era might have concluded were manifestations of demonic possession. The term "madness" itself connoted multiple syndromes. "Naturals" or natural fools (as distinct from licensed fools or zanies, who were paid to joke at the expense of their superiors, to sing, and to entertain the court or noble household in motley) were dull and slow-witted, whether because they had been born with insufficient spirit in the **brain** to process information about the world surrounding them (the "rational soul" was weak within them, perhaps because of faults in the **seed** of either parent), or **perturbation** had consumed the animal spirits in the brain, or an attack of brain-fever, a head-injury, or other impairment had blasted their wits in infancy or adulthood. Melancholy might, if left untreated, render the **patient** lethargic and passive, or suicidal, or violently active with unreasonable and irrepressible laughter. Fits of shaking or delirium or distraction in which sufferers spoke nonsense and attempted to harm themselves might accompany a high **fever**; **epilepsy** might make the body shake and become incontinent. Strong emotions such as anger or grief (as well as fever) might lead to frenzy, including assaults on oneself or other persons, or to an ecstasy or paroxysm of feeling in which the sufferer might seem to be taken out of this world. *Hysterica passio* or "the mother" might make mature and young women **faint** or choke or scream, because of **fumes** or **vapors** rising from the **womb**, and **green-sickness** in young women or love-sickness in men might make them disdain their daily activities and become faint and pale. Lunatics suffered periodic bouts of insanity according to the moon's phases. Women and young people were particularly susceptible to madness, especially after the loss of a family member or friend or the breakdown of a marriage. At the same time,

202

although **physicians** such as Edward Jorden testified to the medical, rather than devilish, origins of fits, texts such as Reginald Scot's *Discovery of Witchcraft* (1584) or King James's own *Daemonologie* (1597, ed. Harrison 1924) averred the existence not only of witches but also of their ability to madden others by bewitching them, and to the existence of demonic possession (hence the accepted treatment of confining sufferers to a dark place and whipping them, to frighten away the demon inside).

(B) The plays most concerned with madness in all its senses are, chronologically, *ERR*, *SHR*, *TN*, *HAM*, *LR*, and *TNK*, and it seems as though the imputation of madness takes on a greater poignancy in each of them, from high farce in *ERR* to high tragedy in *LR*. *ERR* finds Antipholus of Syracuse and Antipholus of Ephesus, and their servants the Dromios, mistaken for each other and for madmen when they do not recognize their spouses, parents, and servants. The play stages several of the debates surrounding the diagnosis and treatment of madness, by presenting several different explanations for the confusion of both sets of twins. If the Ephesians are all sorcerers and witches, as Antipholus of Syracuse fears, then the seeming madness of Adriana and Dromio of Ephesus, and his own increasing confusion, can only be explained by demonic possession. Even his twin, native to Ephesus, starts to wonder whether magic is involved, chiding the would-be exorcist Pinch: "Peace, doting wizard, Peace! I am not mad" (4.4.58). But if Antipholus and Dromio of Syracuse are suffering from a feverish delirium, they should be restrained for their own protection, since they are overheated with raging **choler** in "a most outrageous fit of madness" (5.1.139; see also discussion under **frenzy**); Dromio of Ephesus thinks his master (for whom he has mistaken Antipholus of Syracuse) to be, "stark mad," "horn-mad," like a raging bull (2.1.59, 58). Aemilia believes Antipholus of Syracuse (whom she, too, appears to have mistaken for Antipholus of Ephesus) to have been driven **insane** by Adriana's "jealous fits": "To be disturb'd, would mad or man or beast" (5.1.84). She prescribes her own "wholesome **syrups**" and the calm of the abbey to restore his peace of mind.

SHR presents two lovers repeatedly called "mad" by outsiders; some critics argue that they find a kind of sanity or safe haven with each other, while others argue that Petruchio browbeats Katharina into catatonic passivity, a different kind of mental collapse (see discussion under **lunacy**). Rosalind's comment that "love is merely a madness" is amply illustrated in the romantic comedies such as *MND* (see discussion under **lunacy**) or *TN*, which accuses nearly every character of "midsummer madness" (3.4.56) or folly: Olivia is a fool, mad with excessive and self-indulgent grief for her brother (1.5.58); Feste is an "allowed fool," a jester (1.5.94), or a "barren rascal . . . put down . . . with an ordinary fool" (1.5.85), and later, with deep irony, a "good fool" to the imprisoned Malvolio (4.2.105, 109); Aguecheek sadly confides, "Many do call me fool" (2.5.81); Malvolio himself is Olivia's "good fool" when she exposes both his folly and the cruelty of his treatment at the plotters' hands (5.1.369). Malvolio uses the word "mad" early on, accusing Sir Toby and Sir Andrew, "My masters, are you mad?" (2.3.86) and giving Maria the idea of making him "mad indeed" (3.4.133). Feste already bears a grudge against Malvolio for mixing up the two senses of "fool": Feste is a jester, a licensed fool, not the natural or simpleton for whom Malvolio takes him. Olivia is convinced "he's mad" (3.4.136) because of the yellow cross-garters Malvolio wears in obedience to what he thinks are her instructions and, more importantly, from his excessive smiling, a known symptom of frenzy or non-natural melancholy. When Sir Thopas the curate comes to visit "Malvolio the lunatic" (4.2.22), Malvolio pleads (in vain, since his interlocutor is none other than his old enemy Feste, in disguise), "Good Sir Topas, do not think I am mad" (4.2.29). Feste maliciously repeats back to Malvolio his protestations of sanity at the end of the play: " 'By the lord, Fool, I am not mad' " (5.1.374).

In the history plays, women run mad from grief and men from rage or drinking. Constance runs mad with sorrow for the loss of Prince Arthur, and yet insists that hers is the only sane response to an insane tragedy:

> I am not mad: this **hair** I tear is mine;
> My name is Constance; I was Geoffrey's wife;
> Young Arthur is my son, and he is lost:
> I am not mad: I would to heaven I were!
> For then, 'tis like I should forget myself:
> O, if I could, what grief should I forget!
> Preach some philosophy to make me mad,
> And thou shalt be canonized, cardinal;
> For being not mad but sensible of grief,
> My reasonable part produces reason
> How I may be deliver'd of these woes,
> And teaches me to kill or hang myself:
> If I were mad, I should forget my son,
> Or madly think a babe of clouts were he:
> I am not mad; too well, too well I feel
> The different plague of each calamity.
>
> (*JN* 3.4.45–59)

She tears her hair in the response to sudden bereavement typical of women distracted from their wits by grief. Yet step by step she proves her rationality: first, she can describe her name and origins, and the cause of her sorrow, unlike a madwoman. Second, she is self-aware, unlike a natural fool or a lunatic. Nor is she frenzied, insensible to pain. If she is mad, she suffers a melancholy so intense that it "teaches [her] to hang or kill [her]self," a suicidal impulse born, she says, of reason. Again, she reminds us that she is not frenzied or out of her senses: she can recall the past and make sense of the present, knowing what objects in the world are (so that a rag doll or "babe of clouts" cannot replace her son). In Renaissance terms, we could argue that she is indeed mad, however, because only two of the three chambers of the brain—imagination, reason, and memory, which governed comprehension of the future, present, and past respectively, are functional: she can remember the past in all its detail, so her faculty of memory is intact; she is obsessively and painfully aware of the present, and can make sense of her perceptions, so her faculty of reason is intact; but she cannot conceive of a future without her son, so she has lost the ability to imagine a future world. Other "mad mothers . . . howl" in *H5* at the loss of their children (3.3.39). Volumnia is reportedly "mad" at the loss of Martius from Rome (*COR* 4.2.9). Notably, Queen Margaret is an exception to her **sex**, attempting instead to make the Duke of York "mad" with grief by mocking him with a napkin dipped in his young son's **blood** (*3H6* 1.4.89–90). In *1H4* Hotspur and Hal represent different types of masculine madness or folly, the "mad fellow Percy" seething from choler or rage (*1H4* 2.4.335), the "mad wag" Hal overheated and impulsive, playing the fool with drink, taverns, and women (4.2.50). Even Justice Shallow joins in the act, boasting about the "mad days" of his youth (3.2.33).

The plays of mixed genre we call problem plays illustrate further the difficulties of distinguishing true from feigned madness, and ways that the powerful may oppress the weak under the guise of therapy. Lucio complains about the Duke's "mad fantastical trick" (*MM* 3.2.92) of leaving the dukedom to Angelo, who perhaps hopes to keep his authority if, as he suggests, the Duke's "reason is tainted" and "His actions show much like to madness" (4.4.4). Angelo imputes insanity to Isabella in order to clear himself of her charge of illicit sex; the Duke pretends to believe him—even telling Isabella when she avers that she is not "touched by madness" (5.1.51) and becomes agitated, "that's somewhat madly spoken" (5.1.89)–but then uses Isabella's own rational speech himself to make the case against Angelo:

> If she be mad,—as I believe no other,—
> Her madness hath the oddest frame of sense,
> Such a dependency of thing on thing,
> As e'er I heard in madness.
>
> (5.1.60–63)

He adds that her speech, if she is mad, reflects poorly on the sane: "Many that are not mad /Have, sure, more lack of reason" (5.1.67). In *AWW*, even though we sympathize with Helena's love for Bertram, the King's comment that Bertram is "mad in folly" (5.3.3) to refuse her, and Parolles' description that Bertram was "mad for [Diana]" (5.3.26), continue this pattern of monarchical control. *TRO* combines the comic view of love as madness or folly with the tragedy of delusion and powerlessness. Troilus dismisses the predictions of his "mad sister" Cassandra, urging the Trojans to take courage; they need not give up just "because Cassandra's mad" (*TRO* 2.2.98, 122). He himself is "mad in Cressid's love" (1.1.51), resistant in his "mad idolatry" to Hector's advice that "value dwells not in particular will" (2.2.56, 53). Madness here is the collision between the value that the world places upon an object, or a woman's love, and that of the "particular will" that desires it. Thersites cynically comments that Achilles and Patroclus are more likely to "run mad" from their own stupidity or intemperance than to suffer the loss of blood in battle: "With too much blood and too little brain, these two may run mad; but, if with too much brain and too little **blood** they do, I'll be a curer of madmen" (5.1.49–50). Indeed, Troilus' madness makes him a better

205

warrior, one who battles with "mad and fantastic execution" (5.5.38), like a character in a story.

HAM thematizes the difficulty of distinguishing between feigned and genuine madness, and the question of what we define as madness in the first place, in the person of its hero, whose "antic disposition" may be partly "mad in craft" (3.4.188) but whose melancholy seems deeply felt (see also discussions under **ecstasy**, **lunacy**, and **melancholy**). Ophelia is "distract" from grief and loss, "a document in madness, thoughts and remembrance fitted," according to her brother (4.5.78). *LR* again contrasts the licensed fool (Lear's fool), the loving or doting fool (Cordelia), the choleric man driven mad with rage (Lear himself), and, in Edgar's guiding his blinded father up an imaginary peak to attempt suicide, a tragic reworking of Malvolio's plight (Malvolio is blinded by the darkness, Gloucester by the loss of his eyesight; Feste disguises his voice and his accent, as does Edgar, and both select for their performances persons different in rank from their own; both Feste and Edgar claim to be offering a cruel but therapeutic strategy to correct a perceived imbalance in a social superior). Kent diagnoses his monarch at the very beginning of the play, when Lear banishes his favorite daughter: "Be Kent unmannerly, when Lear is mad" (1.1.146). As Lear comes to greater self-knowledge, he comments heart-breakingly on his own perilous state of mind, "Let me be not mad, not mad, sweet heaven!" (1.5.46), begs his daughters, "I prithee . . . do not make me mad" (*LR* 2.4.218) and exclaims, "O Fool, I shall go mad!" (2.4.286). Edgar re-enacts as Tom of Bedlam the poverty and madness of the ageing monarch, additionally exposing more questions about the causes and cures of madness: if Lear's grief and age make him mad, then why does not Gloucester lose his reason? Gloucester even comments, "Better I were distract" (4.6.281). If poverty unhinges Lear, then why not Edgar, as poor Tom?

Paulina in *WT* calls Leontes "mad" with jealousy and then suggests that if he knew the consequences of his rash actions, he would "run . . . stark mad" indeed (2.3.72, 3.2.183). Prospero "mad[s]" the mariners in the shipwreck that he has devised (1.2.209), Caliban with "adders that hiss [him] into madness" (2.2.14) and then the three men of sin in Ariel's diatribe (3.3.58); this therapeutic "madness" allows Alonso to experience remorse and beg for "pardon" (5.1.116), Caliban to become "wise hereafter" (rather than a fool), "and seek for grace" (5.1.296) and Ferdinand and Miranda to marry, but it is unclear that it has any lasting effect upon Antonio and Sebastian. *CYM* associates madness with sexual desire. The irascible Cymbeline accuses his daughter of a dangerous and inappropriate passion for the lower-born Posthumus that has made her "mad" (1.1.147), and Iachimo tries to convince Imogen that Posthumus is no longer faithful to her by claiming that Posthumus must be deluded if he does not value her: "What, are men mad? Hath nature given them **eyes** /To see . . . /and can we not /Partition make /'Twixt fair and foul?" (1.6.32–8). The exchange between Cloten and Imogen as he tries vainly to woo her contrasts folly and madness:

> Cloten: To leave you in your madness, 'twere my sin;
> I will not.

> Imogen: Fools are not mad folks.
> Cloten: Do you call me fool?
> Imogen: As I am mad, I do.
> If you'll be patient, I'll no more be mad;
> That cures us both.
>
>   (2.3.99–104)

Cloten again accuses Imogen of inappropriate lust, "madness," to which she replies that she is not mad, but foolish—foolish to love against her father's will, and foolish to bandy words with such as Cloten. When Cloten responds indignantly, however, she agrees that if she is mad, he is a fool for thinking so. If he can listen to her "patient[ly]" (with the pun on patient, or sufferer of illness, however, she can cure him by telling him downrightly that she cannot love him— indeed, she "hate[s]" him) (2.3.110). *TNK* exposes the susceptibility of lower-ranking women as well as the high-born to love-melancholy when the Jailer's Daughter "run[s] mad" for Palamon (4.2.12). The play highlights her vulnerability to exploitation when the countrymen cry, "A madwoman! We are made, lads!" (3.5.76) and plan to exhibit "the dainty mad woman" (3.5.72) in their morris dance for profit. Shakespeare's Venus becomes "mad" with love-sickness at the sight of Adonis' dimples (249), with fear at the thought that Adonis is hurt (904), and ultimately curses all lovers with a love that hitherto shall be associated with madness: "[Love] shall be raging-mad and silly-mild, / Make the young old, the old become a child" (1151–2). Sonnet 140 describes just such a maddening love, pleading with the beloved to show kindness to the poet, even if only to humor him,

> As testy **sick** men, when their **deaths** be near,
> No news but health from their physicians know;
> For if I should despair, I should grow mad,
> And in my madness might speak ill of thee:
> Now this ill-wresting world is grown so bad,
> Mad slanderers by mad **ears** believed be,
> That I may not be so, nor thou belied,
> Bear thine eyes straight, though thy proud **heart** go wide.

Just as the physician attempts to make the last hours of a dying man peaceful by telling them (falsely) that they will recover, so he urges his love to give him hope. The absence of hope would breed despair, and despair would breed madness, and madness might make him malicious, and the world is now so corrupt that even "mad slanderers" such as the poet might prove convincing to "mad ears" of listeners.

(C) Barrough (1583) distinguishes among frenzy, mania, and madness, associating frenzy with a fever, and mania with too much blood flowing to the brain and causing immoderate laughter or, if mixed with choler, violent agitation. Jorden (1603) argued that the young woman Mary Glover suffered not from bewitchment but from physiological disorder in the body, namely "the suffocation of the mother" or *hysterica passio*. Harsnett (1603) likewise argues that only the gullible would trust an exorcist or Jesuit priest to treat madness, rather than relying on a physician to distinguish between natural and unnatural disorders of the mind and body. Nonetheless, in 1634 we find in Paré's treatise "On Monsters and Prodigies" (in the English translation of his *Complete Works*) a conviction that demonic possession does exist and can indeed cause mental and physical illness:

> it may appeare that devills sometimes entring into the body, doe somewhiles torment it by divers and uncouth waies; other whiles they doe not enter in, but either agitate the good humours of the body, or draw the ill into the principall parts, or with them obstruct the veins or other passages, or change the structure of the instruments, from which causes innumerable **diseases** proceed: of these, Divells are the authors, and wretched and forlorne persons the ministers: and the reason of these things is beyond the search of nature. (pp. 991–2, 4O4r–v)

Adams' *Mystical Bedlam* (1615) describes and catalogs the "world of mad-men" in order to diagnose "spiritual madness" in unbelievers and unholy persons. What Jaques Ferrand dubs *Erotomania* (1640) combines elements of medieval love-sickness with the humoral logic of green-sickness, as he argues that erotomania is a disease of both body and mind. Both Bright (1586) and Burton (1621) distinguish between the "natural" melancholy of the melancholy temperament and the "unnatural" melancholy that is pathological, urging sufferers to seek treatment quickly for the latter lest it turn to madness. Garzoni (1600) distinguishes, tongue-in-cheek, among "frantic" fools who run fevers, "solitarie" or melancholy fools who suffer from an abundance of melancholy, "idle and careless" fools who act against their own best interests, drunken fools, "**harebrained**" fools, "ecstatic" fools, "gross" fools, "shallow-pated" fools, "giddie-headed" fools, "natural[s]," "vicious" fools, "vain-glorious fools," "amorous" fools, "desperate" fools, and many others.

Useful secondary sources abound. Foucault's germinal *Madness and Civilization* (2001) argues that insanity itself is culturally constructed, often in order to control political, social, and sexual rebels and literally to hide them out of sight by incarceration. MacDonald's *Mystical Bedlam* tabulates and analyzes the cases of seventeenth-century physician and parson Richard Napier ("one of the last Renaissance magi," MacDonald 1981, 16), celebrated for his treatment of the insane; MacDonald's exhaustive tables offer a sociological snapshot of Napier's patients and their reasons for consulting him. Shenk (1978) reads madness in *HAM* and *LR* as the conflicts among vice, passions, and "habit." Schleiner (1991) historicizes the medicalization of melancholy and madness in early modernity, using Hamlet and Timon as case-histories to track the movement from the melancholy "genius" who can divine the truth (a descendant of the "holy fool") to the madman. Salkeld's Foucaultian interpretation considers Shakespearean madness in the context of early modern political institutions such as the monarch, and reprints Barrough's 1583 chapters on frenzy and madness (1993, 66–7). Daalder (1997) usefully distinguishes among folly (congenital stupidity), illusion (deception by others) and delusion (distorted perceptions of reality) in *TN*, but also argues that madness in Shakespeare in general has "no physical cause" (106). Thiher's deeply pondered contribution agrees that Shakespeare subscribes to no one single theory of madness (despite what he identifies as the persistence of **Galenism**), but identifies his "mad discourse" as part of a larger exploration of hermeneutic or interpretive uncertainty surrounding language (1999, 73–100). On individual plays, see Neely's essential *Distracted Subjects* (2004), which distinguishes among early modern madnesses in Shakespeare and historicizes them with particular reference to gender, including discussions of "distraction" in *HAM, MAC,* and *LR*; love-sickness in *TNK, TN,* and *AYL*; frenzy and imprisonment in *ERR, WIV,* and *TN*. Hamlet's madness and melancholy has historically received overwhelming attention, from Ernest Jones's Freudian account (1949) to John Dover Wilson's classic text, *What Happens in Hamlet* (1936, repr. 1951), which argues that Ophelia's genuine madness contrasts to Hamlet's feigned insanity. Showalter's germinal essay (1985) considers artists' representations of Ophelia's madness; see also Chapman (2007); Chakravarti (2008). On Lear's madness, see also Muir (1960); Bennett (1962); Jackson (2005). Most considerations of Malvolio's madness discuss early modern instances of exorcism and demonic possession, such as Van Dijkhuizen (2007) or Kallendorf (2003), who also investigates tragedy as "the absence or failure of exorcism" in *LR* and *HAM*.

maidenhead see **hymen**

malady An ailment, disorder; see **disease**

malady of France The so-called French **disease**, or syphilis; see **pox**

mallicholy see **melancholy**

mandragora, mandrake (A) Mandragora or mandrake was the subject of many legends, mostly inspired by its hallucinogenic properties and its supposed resemblance to a human shape. These myths held that mandrake grew under a gallows from **seed** that fell from a felon's body; that mandrake emitted a shriek deadly to the human **ear** and must therefore be harvested by dogs, who would then shriek instead; and that women who carried around a mandrake root would become fertile. **Physicians** scoffed at the legends, which nonetheless must have persisted in lay-wisdom, since the published herbals repeatedly decry them as "olde wiues'" tales (Gerard 1597, S4v). The dreadful chill of mandragora root made it extremely soporific, especially when taken in a **clyster**, or drunk in wine, as **Galen** had recommended, to relieve pain. With **poppy**, it was used to make *Trifera,* the strongest sleeping-draught available to early modern physicians.

209

(B) Shakespeare distinguishes between mandragora, used as a soporific medicine, and the unearthly, ill-omened shriek of the uprooted mandrake plant that uncannily resembles human beings. Cleopatra calls, "Give me to drink mandragora, /That I might **sleep** out this great gap of time /My Antony is away" (*ANT* 1.5.4–6). Iago gloats that "Not poppy, nor mandragora" will help Othello sleep now that he believes Desdemona unchaste (*OTH* 3.3.330).

Falstaff calls his page a man in miniature, a "whoreson mandrake . . . fitter to be worn in my cap than to wait at my heels" (*2H4* 1.2.14); he later describes Justice Shallow in his youth as "lecherous as a monkey, and the whores called him mandrake" (3.2.315). Suffolk tells Queen Margaret that there is no point in cursing, unless curses could kill, "as doth the mandrake's groan" (*2H6* 3.2.310). Juliet fears she will awaken early and, hearing the spirits of her ancestors, run mad, "what with loathsome smells, /And shrieks like mandrakes' torn out of the earth" (*ROM* 4.3.46–7).

(C) Turner (1562, N4r) disavows the legends of mandrake's origins from male seed; Dodoens (1595, 2K4v–5v) warns that the sleep it causes can be deadly, and Gerard (1597) attempts to dismiss the tales about its uprooting.

mandrake see **mandragora**

mare see **sleep**

marjoram **Hot** and **dry**, the natural sweetener marjoram was very good for treating the **dropsy**, and for "those who cannot urinate except with drops and difficulty" (Dodoens 1595, S5r), that is, who were suffering from what we might now diagnose as prostate trouble. Perhaps this use explains why Perdita offers it to "men of middle age," but since (like many of the other flowers in her bouquet) it is also an emmenagogue or early abortifacient, it leads Polixenes to impugn her chastity (*WT* 4.4.108). Elsewhere in Shakespeare it is a byword for sweetness, as in *AWW* 4.5.16; Edgar's password to Lear, "Sweet marjoram" (*LR* 4.6.93); and in Sonnet 99, in which the buds of marjoram become the beloved's **hair**.

marrow Either the fatty, innermost part of the bone, or the spinal cord, understood to be made of the same substance as the **brain**. Shakespeare usually uses the word figuratively to mean vital essence or vigor, often erotic. Parolles argues that soldiers who stay at home with their sweethearts are "spending [their] manly marrow" on love instead of war (*AWW* 2.3.281), and Venus coos to Adonis, "My flesh is plump, my marrow burning" (*VEN* 142). Richard of Gloucester connects Edward's virility to his "marrow, bones and all" (*3H6* 3.2.125), and Timon wishes sexually transmitted **infections** upon the "minds and marrows of our youth" (*TIM* 4.1.26). Alcibiades, however, uses marrow to mean strength, describing "crouching marrow in the bearer strong" (*TIM* 5.4.9) and Hamlet worries that the sottish drunkenness of the Danes takes from them "the pith and marrow" of their achievements (*HAM* 1.4.22).

measles (A) The term measles has been used for the common **infectious disease** *roseola epidemica* since the middle ages, although the **illness** was often confused with smallpox. In fact, they were for the early moderns the same disease, except that measles stemmed from an **inflammation** or overheating of the **blood** and smallpox from the inflammation of **blood** and **choler** combined. Symptoms included itchy, **dry skin** or **leprosy**, headache, shivering, red spots on the face and body or pustules erupting all over the body, red **eyes**, dry mouth, hoarseness and **fainting**. Since infants and children were particularly prone to measles, it was clear that the most likely cause was corrupt maternal **humors** in the **womb**, remaining dormant in the child's **veins** until it reached a certain age and then erupting to the surface of the skin. Or such infants might have been conceived during a menstrual period, since such rarely escaped the measles or **leprosy**. Children could also catch measles or smallpox from a wet-**nurse** who maintained a poor **diet**, or from following an unhealthy diet themselves, such as eating meat and fish at the same meal. Finally, it could be transmitted through **contagion**, the direct contact of one person with another, like the **pestilence**. The best remedy was to allow nature to take its own course, but if the child suffered extreme pain, before the wheals appeared, one could bathe it in hollyhock, dill, camomile, and **fennel**: if the wheals were pustulous, one could sponge the child with fennel, **wormwood**, and sage. If the eyes watered copiously, rose-water and fennel could soothe them.

(B) Martius imagines the plebeians as measles disfiguring the body politic with **tetters** or pockmarks:

> As for my country I have shed my blood,
> Not fearing outward force, so shall my **lungs**
> Coin words till their decay against those measles,
> Which we disdain should tetter us, yet sought
> The very way to catch them.
>
> (*COR* 3.1.76–80)

Just as Martius has shed his blood freely in battle, so he will spend his spirituous blood and air in speech advocating against plebeian representation, since allowing the lower ranks political access would be tantamount to seeking out those suffering from measles and contracting the infection oneself. Martius' metaphor may also allude to the measles' association with childhood ills, bringing out his paternalistic contempt for the plebeians.

(C) Goeurot (1550) notes that it is a disease to which children are particularly susceptible. Barrough (1583) attempts to dispel the prevailing wisdom that only children are affected.

medicine, medicinal See also **med'cine potable, physic, tincture** (A) Both the practice of medicine and the medicaments used to treat **disease** and illness.
(B) Shakespeare most frequently employs the word to mean a medicament to be taken to counteract a **sickness**, either by mouth as a **potion**, or as a topical

application to the **skin**. Figuratively, Shakespearean medicines may be "moral" (*ADO* 1.3.12) or spiritual, though such treatments are often ineffectual. Don John refuses "moral medicine" for his ill-temper, arguing that the "mortifying" **wound** under which he suffers cannot be talked away but requires action (revenge against his brother) for a "remedy." Leonato likewise complains about the inadequacy of "preceptial medicine to rage," because his sorrow cannot be calmed by words of consolation alone (*ADO* 5.1.24).

MAC sustains medical metaphors throughout the play, especially those of purgation and evacuation. Malcolm urges Macduff to "make medicines of our great revenge" (4.3.214), and Caithness imagines Macduff himself to be "the medicine of the sickly weal" that will purge the country of Macbeth (5.2.27, see discussion under **purge**). *LR* opposes good and bad daughters schematically and also as revivifying or destructive medicines. "[R]estoration hang /Thy medicine on my lips" (4.7.26), prays Cordelia as she kisses her father out of his distracted stupor, and she does manage, if only briefly, to return Lear almost to his "perfect mind." But Goneril employs physic to mortal use, commenting as her sister cries, "Sick!" "If not, I'll ne'er trust medicine" (5.3.96). Both *OTH* and *AWW* personify human agents or catalysts as medicines. Such a strong potion is Iago that "Not **poppy**, nor **mandragora** . . . Shall ever medicine [Othello] to . . . **sleep**" again, because there is no antidote (3.3.332). Iago mocks, "Work on, my medicine," over the prostrate Othello, as if his accusations of adultery have counteracted the "medicines bought of **mountebanks**" with which Brabantio imagines Othello to have convinced Desdemona of his love (4.1.45, 1.3.61). In a different register, Falstaff comments that Hal must have given him love-philtres to keep him by his side: "If the rascal hath not given me medicines to make me love him, I'll be hanged; it could not be else: I have drunk medicines" (*1H4* 2.2.18, 20). Lafew describes Helena as a "medicine /That's able to breathe life into a stone," to bring things back to life almost like the elixir or philosopher's stone (*AWW* 2.1.72–3), an allusion picked up in the King's irritated comment about the ring he gave to Helena:

> Plutus himself,
> That knows the tinct and multiplying medicine,
> Hath not in nature's mystery more science
> Than I have in this ring.
> (5.3.101–4; see discussion under **tinct**)

Helena is, however, not merely medicine herself, nor just the vector to provide a medicine for the King, but also in need of medicine or therapy for her **love-sickness** for Bertram, an series of associations that she makes early on to the Countess: "My lord your son made me to think of this; /. . . Paris and the medicine and the king" (1.3.233).

Isabella tells the self-righteous Angelo that "authority, though it err like others, /Hath yet a kind of medicine in itself, /That skins the vice o' the top" (*MM* 2.2.135). If he himself has committed or imagined a sin, his position protects him from investigating or **tenting** any such moral wound deeply, even though it permits him to "skin" or cover his vice. Her brother responds to the disguised Vincentio's injunction that he should prepare his soul for imminent **death** with the plea, "the miserable have no other medicine /But only hope," the hope of present, rather than after-life (3.1.2).

The late plays contrast the healthful use of medicine (both as a literal medication and as a figure for a person who transforms the plot for good) with medicine's deployment for evil. Cerimon in *PER* presents a learned and virtuous healer, in contrast to the "**herb-woman**'s iniquity" (see discussion under **physic**). Both Paulina and Camillo function as medicinal catalysts to heal affliction in royal families. Paulina comes "with words as medicinal as true" to Leontes, the news of Perdita's birth (2.3.37), although he ignores her counsel. Florizel calls Camillo "the medicine of our house" when he comes up with the plan to flee to Sicilia (*WT* 4.4.587). Cornelius in *CYM* tries to prescribe only wholesome preparations, but Cymbeline's wicked queen learns from him to **distil** not just **perfumes** and healing therapies but poisons, ultimately dying from her own machinations. Cymbeline himself calls her a thwarted "doctor": "By medicine life may be prolong'd, yet death /Will seize the doctor too" (*CYM* 5.5.29). Cymbeline utters what is perhaps a fitting gloss on these tragicomedies: "Great griefs . . . medicine the less" (4.2.243), or deaths from the first half of the play (such as Cloten's, or the Queen's, or Posthumus' attempt on Imogen's life) do not prevent the play from concluding as a comedy. Hippolyta in *TNK* falls to her knees to plead to Theseus the suit of the three weeping queens, arguing:

> Did I not by th'abstaining of my joy,
> Which breeds a deeper longing, cure their **surfeit**
> That craves a present medicine, I should pluck
> All ladies' scandal on me.
>
> (1.1.189–92)

It is her duty as a woman to give up her own present happiness, and by doing so she will both increase her own, delayed, gratification, and help to treat their overdose or surfeit of grief through treatment by opposites, healing their sorrow with the pleasure that she has willingly given up.

(C) Barrough's *Methode of Physicke* (1583) describes the theory and practice of medicine, as does Bullein's *Bulwarke* (1579). Bright (1615) declares *The Sufficiency of English Medicines*, but Monardes (1580) recommends new plants and minerals from the Americas. Lux (2002) comments on **Paracelsian** medicine in *OTH*. Bevington (1996) comments on the inadequacy of medicine for Lady Macbeth's madness. Overviews of medicine and healers in Shakespeare include Hoeniger (1992) and Pettigrew (2007).

medicinable Therapeutic, healing. Othello's tears flow as quickly as "medicinable **gum**" (5.2.351), although it is too late for his tears to revive Desdemona. Don John has refused "moral medicine" or talk as therapy, but demands an allopathic treatment consisting in action that will be opposite to his brother's intents: "Any bar, any cross, any impediment will be medicinable to me: I am sick in displeasure to him, and whatsoever comes athwart his affection ranges evenly with mine" (*ADO* 2.2.5). Ulysses praises the "medicinable **eye**" of the sun as that which orders and ranges the rest of the heavenly bodies (see discussion under **planet**, *TRO* 1.3.91). He believes "derision medicinable," or healthy scorn, will **cure** Achilles of his excessive pride, another cure-by-opposites (3.3.44). Unaware that Posthumus has vowed her **death**, Imogen hopes that his letter contains good news about his health but also his sorrow at being parted from her, since "such griefs are med'cinable; . . . For [they do] **physic** love" (*CYM* 3.2.33). Separation from a lover can strengthen love by **dieting** it or by restricting its freedom.

med'cine potable See also **alchemy** (A) Med'cine potable or *aurum potabile* (literally, drinkable medicine; drinkable gold) was supposedly a pure essence of gold (perhaps colloidal gold or a solution of gold in a solvent of some kind), used as a remedy for mortal ailments since medieval times. It was popularly confused with the "elixir" or **tincture** of the alchemist, the so-called philosopher's stone sought as a catalyst to convert lead, other metals, stones, earth, and so on into gold.
(B) Prince Hal contrasts the gold of the crown to potable gold in his defence to the mortally ill King Henry IV. He claims that he was not trying on the crown in anticipation of his father's **death**, but chastising it for the anxiety it has brought:

> I spake unto this crown as having sense,
> And thus upbraided it: "The care on thee depending
> Hath fed upon the body of my father;
> Therefore, thou best of gold art worst of gold:
> Other, less fine in carat, is more precious,
> Preserving life in med'cine potable;
> But thou, most fine, most honour'd: most renown'd,
> Hast eat thy bearer up."
>
> (*2H4* 4.5.157–64)

As a metonym for kingship, the crown is the best of gold, the highest in rank, divinely sanctioned; as a metonym for death (through the order of succession), it is the worst, especially in comparison to the life-giving force of potable gold. "Less fine in carat" seems confusing—after all, *aurum potabile* was allegedly the refined or purified essence of gold—but, as the Quarto spelling shows, there is a pun on *carat*, the purity of gold, and *charact*, character, meaning both "personality" and "graven impression," picking up the play's concern with the prince's moral fiber and its sustained imagery of coining. The credibility of Hal's defence here is quite another question, especially since we, the audience, have heard him say no such thing.

Other references in Shakespeare elide medicinal, drinkable gold with the elixir or tincture of the alchemists, such as the "great medicine" that has "gilded"

Mark Antony's breathless messenger (*ANT* 1.5.36–7), making his face red from exertion but also, Cleopatra insists, ennobling him. Caliban similarly asks how the red-faced drunkards Stephano and Trinculo came to be "gilded" with "grand liquor" (*TMP* 5.1.280), in a possible reference to the alchemical "liquor of gold" mentioned in Hester's remedies and elsewhere (A3r; Warburton, quoted in *Variorum*; E. Hall, 1980).

The King in *AWW* irritably questions Bertram about the ring he gave to Helena:

> Plutus himself,
> That knows the **tinct** and multiplying medicine,
> Hath not in nature's mystery more science
> Than I have in this ring
>
> (5.3.101–4)

Plutus, the god of wealth, can presumably generate as much gold as he wants from his existing stores through the magic of the elixir or philosopher's stone, but the King's ring can simultaneously create wealth (by enriching Helena), as does the grand elixir, and restore her to life, as does potable gold.
(C) Ruscelli (1558) has a recipe for potable gold (B2v–4r), as does Hester's collection of Paracelsian remedies (1596; from its description either a suspension of colloidal gold or gold dissolved in pure alcohol, A5v). Bostocke (1585) insists that the universal Paracelsian tincture is *not* literally gold, despite the human lust for lucre, but "a temperate medicine . . . brought to such puritie that it worketh in mans bodie as the vertue and power of the Starres worke in . . . nature"(C1r); **Paracelsus**, he avers, wrote mysteriously in order to hide his secrets from all but the "Godly" (C2r).

melancholy See also **complexion, love-sickness, madness, spleen** (A) One of the four fundamental **humors** of the body, melancholy or black bile was **cold, dry,** thick, dark, sour, and earthy. Its name means "black **choler**," and an excess of it was thought to cause excessive sorrow or lethargy (giving us its modern sense). It nourished the spleen, thickened the **blood**, and slowed the progression of food through the alimentary tract, ensuring that the body could properly concoct or digest food. Since melancholy was the heaviest humor, its excesses were most dangerous to the human body. Those suffering from the disorder were fearful and sad, for no apparent reason. Authorities disagreed on the bodily origin of an excess of black bile, but concurred that, untreated, an excess of melancholy could produce various physical ailments, depending on the **organs** affected: black **jaundice**, the quartan **ague, leprosy, scurvy, canker** or cancer, and, in the mind, madness or folly. Men suffered from this **disease** more than women, but women's expression of grief was far more violent. While men might suffer from melancholy in the spleen, women retained excessive melancholy in their **wombs** (see *hysterica passio*). Causes included ill-affected planets (notably **Saturn** and the moon), melancholy parents, dark or excessively rosy complexions, small heads, long illness, love of solitude, too much studying, too little work, and too much contemplation. Melancholy was at its worst in the autumn of the year and in old age, or, under special circumstances, during middle age. None were thought to be immune to it but fools and stoics. The sixteenth and seventeenth centuries moved away from blaming melancholy upon external causes (such as witchcraft, demonic possession, guilt) to seeking a natural or physiological, internal cause. Spiritual healers recommended that sufferers turn to the Christian god for salvation; true faith would allow practitioners to diagnose and treat a condition of natural melancholy without confusing it with spiritual or moral turpitude. Moral philosophers recommended that melancholics cultivate calm and avoid **perturbation** or the rapid flood of humors to the **heart** under the duress of strong emotion, since the heart could rule the passions instead of (as in a case of melancholia, wrath or other strong emotion) being ruled by the passions.

The symptoms of melancholy on the personality were so various and manifold that almost any mental affliction or characteristic could be attributed to it, from love to grief to mockery. The late sixteenth century saw a fashion for affecting melancholy as a species of wit, since study could trigger the ailment and there was a Continental tradition of respecting learned and melancholic men. Some authorities therefore distinguished between natural and unnatural melancholy: the former was endogenous, an excess of the melancholy humor in the body from birth, the latter environmental, formed from an excess of any other humor in the body burned or "adust." The former might remain benign, controlled by more physical and less intellectual exercise; **moist** and heating foods such as freshwater fish and most herbs (but no wine, since it was drying); pleasant conversation; fragrances; and cheerful music. Non-natural melancholy was extremely dangerous, however, and needed to be treated through both non-natural means such as **diet** and exercise and medically by **purging** or letting blood from the so-called head-vein (cephalic vein). Untreated, it could overwhelm the chamber of reason within the **brain** and cause madness.

(B) Several of Shakespeare's characters display well-known symptoms of melancholy—especially of love-sickness—even if the word is not used of them or used only rarely (perhaps Shakespeare's most famous melancholic, Hamlet, is only explicitly diagnosed with melancholy twice). Romeo displays many of the symptoms of love-sickness or love-melancholy when we first encounter him pining for Rosaline: sighing, lethargy, insomnia, obsessive thoughts about an unattainable beloved, isolation from one's same-sex friends, and carelessness of one's own appearance or well-being. Polonius diagnoses Hamlet as a sufferer (although Claudius remains dubious, and Hamlet himself claims his "antic disposition" is merely "put on"). Ophelia's description of Hamlet as he comes to her chamber is a textbook description of love-melancholy:

> Lord Hamlet, with his doublet all unbraced;
> No hat upon his head; his stockings foul'd,
> Ungarter'd, and down-gyved to his ancle;

> Pale as his shirt; his knees knocking each other;
> And with a look so piteous in purport
> As if he had been loosed out of hell
> To speak of horrors,—he comes before me.
>
> (*HAM* 2.1.275–81)

Hamlet's subsequent behavior suggests melancholy of another order and from another cause, however. Hamlet himself equates his "weakness and . . . melancholy" (2.2.601) as possible reasons for a devil to take the "pleasing shape" (2.2.600) of his dead father and trick him into sin; half-way to suicide, he is already on the way to damnation, and he wonders whether the devil has decided to take advantage of his sorrow. Claudius characterizes Hamlet's melancholy as neither love-melancholy, nor melancholy-madness, but as the treacherous melancholy of the political rebel:

> Love! his affections do not that way tend;
> Nor what he spake, though it lack'd form a little,
> Was not like madness. There's something in his soul,
> O'er which his melancholy sits on brood;
> And I do doubt the hatch and the disclose
> Will be some danger.
>
> (3.1.162–7)

Claudius acknowledges that Hamlet is moved by "affections," or strong passions, but identifies the impetus as not love but something more sinister; similarly, he dismisses Hamlet's words, although broken in "form," as "not like madness." Hamlet's soul is instead incubating a clutch of eggs, mothered by a careful melancholy and that will prove venomous like those of a snake or a dragon.

"In sooth I know not why I am so sad," complains Antonio in *MV* (1.1.1); not knowing why you are sad but experiencing it anyway was a symptom of melancholy in the Renaissance and of what we call depression even now. Viola/Cesario narrates an imagined case-history for her "father['s] . . . daughter" who loved "with a green and yellow melancholy," her blood consumed by fruitless love and her skin pale with the **green-sickness** of unrequited love (*TN* 2.4.113). Orsino demands music to soothe his love-sickness at the beginning of the play (*TN* 1.1.1) but is only affecting melancholy, like Olivia; both are "addicted to a melancholy" because it seems fashionable, rather than from genuine love or grief respectively (*TN* 2.5.202). The Jailer's Daughter runs mad from "thick and profound melancholy," a "melancholy humor that **infects** her" because her love for Palamon is unrequited (*TNK* 4.3.49, 5.2.38). Her blood has been made heavy, slow-flowing, by undissolved humors that the spleen has failed to consume and that therefore prevent vital **spirit** from reaching her heart and brain and enlivening her mind.

Both Jaques in *AYL* and Armado in *LLL* are called melancholics by other characters, and accused of affectation. "The melancholy Jaques" weeps at the sight of a wounded deer (AYL 2.1.26, 41) and "sucks melancholy out of a song" like a weasel (notorious for its spleen; 2.5.13). "Monsieur melancholy" (3.2.294) suffers from "a melancholy of [his] own" (4.1.15):

> Neither the scholar's melancholy, which is emulation, nor the musician's, which is fantastical, nor the courtier's, which is proud, nor the soldier's, which is ambitious, nor the lawyer's, which is politic, nor the lady's, which is nice, nor the lover's, which is all these: but it is a melancholy of mine own, **compounded** of many **simples**, extracted from many objects, and indeed the sundry contemplation of my travels, in which my often rumination wraps me in a most humorous sadness. (*AYL* 4.1.10–20)

The scholar is melancholy because he wishes to emulate others in his learning, but is doomed to frustration; the musician is melancholy because he plays music to soothe the sufferings of others and suffers imaginatively with them; the lawyer affects melancholy to convince his clients that he cares about their cases; the lady is fussily miserable when her things are not arranged according to her desires; the lover's melancholy combines aspects of all the others. Jaques, however, is unique, in his estimation; he is melancholy because he is thinking about his own melancholy, in "contemplation . . . [and] rumination."

Armado is one of the witty, fashionable melancholics from southern Europe who has taken refuge in a more cheerful, more Northern (and therefore more **sanguine**) clime. "[B]esieged with sable-coloured melancholy, I did commend the black-oppressing humor to the most wholesome **physic** of thy health-giving air," he writes to Ferdinand (*LLL* 1.1.232–4), alluding to the heavy and dark qualities of the melancholy humor in the body. Berowne's word "mallicholy" is an alternate spelling for "melancholy"; he claims that love for Rosaline has tamed his mocking wit, "taught [him] to rhyme and be mallicholy" (*LLL* 4.3.13). Aaron is another Southerner oppressed with "cloudy melancholy" (*TIT* 2.3.33), one in whom the humor of Saturn (*TIT* 2.3.31) engenders malice. Don John in *ADO* is another whose sallow "melancholy" **complexion** compels him to hurt others (2.1.5, 12). Melancholy is both "dull" in itself and causes dullness or lethargy (*ERR* 1.2.20, 5.1.79, *PER* 1.2.2). Melancholy "baked" and thickened the blood, making it "heavy-thick" along with the spirits that otherwise would make the heart "light" or merry (*JN* 3.3.42). Missing Valentine, Silvia is "lumpish, heavy, melancholy" (*TGV* 3.2.62). Blood containing too much melancholy tasted "sour" (*R2* 5.6.20) rather than sweet.

Hosts and hostesses seem aware that melancholy was peculiarly apt to afflict the young and in love, especially those who were nobly born. The Host in *TGV* diagnoses Julia with what he calls an "allycholly" (4.2.27), and Quickly claims to observe Anne Page's "allicholy" of love for young Fenton (1.4.154).

(C) Bright offers us a definition that distinguishes between melancholy as a humor and as a disorder: "the melancholie passion is a doting of reason through vaine feare procured by fault of the melancholie humor" (1586, A1r). He calls the laughter of melancholics "fained laughter." Burton's compendious *Anatomy of Melancholy* (1621) surveys the state of knowledge about almost everything that came to Burton's mind and is in itself, he claims in "Democritus to the Reader," a **cure** for his own melancholy. The great literary physician William Osler comments on Burton, "No book was ever so belied by its title as the *Anatomy of Melancholy*. . . . Except Shakespeare, no writer has realized more keenly that all thoughts, all passions, all delights, and whatever stirs this mortal frame, minister to the one great moving impulse of humanity . . . love" (Osler 1916, 3). Burton devotes two volumes to love-melancholy but attributes almost every kind of symptom to some version of melancholy; his prescription for the melancholic is constant activity, including study and writing. This remedy (which evidently worked for him) varies from Bright, Du Laurens, and others who recommended quietness for the suffering melancholic, less intellectual stimulation rather than more. *Problemes of Aristotle* (1595) characterizes "the melancholy" as "the worst of all complexions" (F8v) because it is cold and dry, like **death**, and comes from "the dregges of the bloud." Babb (1951) offers what was for many years the standard account of what he terms "the Elizabethan malady," including a useful overview of the early modern tripartite soul, but has in recent years been modified to take account of melancholy's medieval and classical roots, as in Heffernan (1995) and Siraisi (1990); the gendering of early modern melancholy, in Lyons (1971) and Paster (2004b); and its association with race and skin-color, in Floyd-Wilson (2003). Trevor (2004) identifies Hamlet's sadness with the fashionable and increasingly respected scholar's melancholy, and Parker (2003) connects Hamlet's melancholy to the play's engagement with racialized blackness. Neely's *Distracted Subjects* (2004) considers melancholy in the context of early modern (Shakespearean) madness of different kinds, and reads the Jailer's Daughter in *TNK* alongside the creation of specifically female melancholies in the late sixteenth and early seventeenth centuries. One cannot, of course, equate modern "depression" with early modern melancholy—each has different origins, priorities, effects, and remedies—but Bright's description of the obsessive thoughts, sadness, and loquacity of "non-natural melancholy" laid alongside, say, David Foster Wallace's short story "The Depressed Person" (1998) makes for illuminating reading.

mercury see **quicksilver**

mettle is both temperament (personality)—often one of bravery or pluck, as in present-day usage—and a pun on the earthy metals found within the ground, since the human body itself (and all its **humors, complexions, organs,** and members) was constituted of the four **elements** of fire, air, earth, and water. In Shakespeare, mettle connotes both a specific, home-grown valor nourished chthonically in the veins of the earth (as in *1H4* and *H5*) and the capacity for being molded, like metal (as in *JC*). Hal is "a lad of mettle"; brave "boy[s] /Lend mettle to us all" (*1H4* 2.4.12; 5.4.23–4) and the English in *H5* demonstrate "the mettle of their pasture" (3.1.27). Casca, on the other hand, has become a "blunt" weapon in mid-life where he was "quick mettle when he went to school" (*JC* 1.2.296); he is clumsy and slow to take new ideas. Brutus somewhat mysteriously asks his co-conspirators not to "stain . . . the insuppressive mettle of our spirits" (2.1.134); most editors gloss Shakespeare's neologism "insuppressive" as "unstoppable," so that Brutus is forging steel that cannot be broken or melted (alternatively, the mettle/metal cannot be molded or hardened with alloy). *TN* figures mettle as the tender or soft quality determining **sex** or gender. Cesario attempts to escape the duel with Sir Andrew by claiming his "mettle" will not allow it (3.4.272) and, as Viola, is praised by Orsino for overcoming "the mettle of [her] sex" (5.1.322). See Floyd-Wilson, "English Mettle" (2004).

midwife See also **childbed** (A) Midwives delivered babies, often helped by other women as birth attendants. They were responsible for assuring a child's legitimacy or determining its paternity, since they could see the birth itself (men were traditionally not permitted into the chamber when a mother was giving birth), delivering the infant whole, deciding the **sex** of the child, and in some cases, "shaping" the fetus by swaddling its head or body, or by cutting the "**navel**-string" (umbilical cord) of a girl-child short so that she would not have a "long **tongue**," that is talk incessantly or profanely. In the sixteenth century, male **physicians** were not permitted to assist at births (although in the case of posthumous Caesarean sections, a male **surgeon** or barber might be called in; see **untimely ripp'd**). Midwives might also test for virginity (since, unlike the male physician, they were allowed to touch and investigate the **hymen**), and baptize infants (although Protestant divines objected strenuously to this practice). King (2007, 21) even suggests that some midwives, especially those in the provinces and away from the control of the **College** of physicians, the Guild of barber-surgeons, or the Grocers' Company (later the Worshipful company of **Apothecaries**) might have used knives or the "crotchet" to extract fetuses; prescribed and administered **medicines**; and even mixed their own powders. Many midwives also served as **empirics**, sick-nurses, or **plague**-searchers; women appear to have practiced the healing arts in early modern England in many different ways. Midwives were unique among women healers, however, in that they could be licensed if they were chosen by the Bishop of London or the Archbishop of Canterbury. Although such a license was ecclesiastical, rather than civil, women who were granted one appear to have been saved the more rigorous prosecutions of the College of Physicians. To earn a license, a midwife had to be examined by the bishop and to provide up to half-a-dozen clients as witness to her expertise or to provide written statements. Some of the witnesses were wives of physicians or surgeons, others were midwives themselves, and still others were high- or middle-ranking women who had employed the midwife at their own lyings-in. Many midwives appear to have earned a comfortable income, and to have owned the equipment that they brought to childbeds (such as bolsters, birthing stools, and fine **linen**).

Despite their relatively high status among women healers, however, popular and medical literature by men often associated midwives with witches and "gossips," old women who told tales and spread rumors. The role of the midwife in witnessing legitimacy made her suspect in the eyes of some, since she could choose to cover up a woman's illicit affair or even conceal a birth from the public. And since only women were allowed in the birthing chamber, conspiracy theories about what the women were doing—or at the very least, the belief that women were laughing drunkenly and riotously about their menfolk—proliferated.

(B) Figurative midwives ease the transition from one world to the next. Queen Mab is the "fairies' midwife" who delivers dreams to the fertile **brains** of young girls, according to Mercutio (*ROM* 1.4.54), a reminder to us that both the **womb** and the brain were nourished by **phlegm** or mucus, soft and impressionable. Upon hearing the news of Northumberland's defection to Bolingbroke, the Queen of Richard II begins an extended metaphor of parturition in which the messenger becomes the attendant upon a monstrous birth:

> So, Green, thou art the midwife to my woe,
> And Bolingbroke my sorrow's dismal heir:
> Now hath my soul brought forth her **prodigy**,
> And I, a gasping new-deliver'd mother,
> Have woe to woe, sorrow to sorrow join'd.
>
> (2.2.62–6)

The pain of treason mimics the pangs of labor. Bolingbroke is either the wonder or monstrous "prodigy" that the Queen has borne and whose birth leaves her grieving at his **deformity** rather than rejoicing at the cessation of travail, or he is the inheritor of the "sorrow" that she has gestated in her womb at the thought of his treason, a sorrow that compounds or multiplies itself once it is realized in the act of rebellion rather than existing in imagination only.

Pericles frames his prayers to the goddess of childbirth, **Lucina**, to ease Thaisa's birth pangs with calls for the actual midwife, Lychorida:

> Lychorida! Lucina, O
> Divinest patroness, and midwife gentle
> To those that cry by night, convey thy deity
> Aboard our dancing boat; make swift the pangs
> Of my queen's travails! Now, Lychorida!
>
> (*PER* 3.1.11–12)

The "dancing boat" painfully literalizes the pun on travel/travail; both sailing from one place to another, and giving birth, involve dangerous, hard work.

Shakespeare's few midwife-characters assist at births and determine or conceal legitimacy. The unnamed midwife in *TA* is impaled on Aaron's knife "like a pig prepared to the spit" because only she and the **nurse** can testify to the dark-skinned baby born to Tamora by Aaron. Aaron adds: "Send the midwife presently to me. /The midwife and the nurse well made away /Then let the ladies tattle what they please" (4.2.166–8). Both midwife and nurse were central to the gossiping activity that gave husbands and other men so much anxiety over a childbed (as Bicks points out, the very word "gossip" moves via the midwife

221

from its origins as the "god-sib" responsible for the spiritual welfare of a friend's child to being the chatty female friend who attends on a woman at a birth, 2003, 27). Dick mocks Jack Cade's mother as "a midwife," a reference meant to cast doubt upon his insistence that she was "a Plantagenet" (*2H6* 4.2.43), since midwives had the power to confirm (or to conceal) a child's parentage. Toby Belch repeats the stereotype of the drunken, gadding midwife by comparing the effectiveness of the trick played on Malvolio to "*aqua vitae* with a midwife" (*TN* 2.5.196). Paulina, whom Leontes castigates as a "mankind witch," serves as at least figurative midwife to the falsely accused Hermione, bringing the baby Perdita to Leontes to witness her legitimacy. Leontes calls her "Lady Margery, your midwife there" to her husband Antigonus because of her role in insisting that what he calls "this bastard" is his own (2.3.160), and because of her refusal to be silent. Autolycus characterizes a midwife as "Mistress Tale-Porter" and says that her presence, along with "five or six honest wives," means that there is no need for him to "carry lies abroad," since they will spread the gossip for him (*WT* 4.4.269). Midwives also documented ominous or monstrous births. "The midwife wonder'd and the women cried, / 'O, Jesus bless us, he is born with **teeth**!'" at the birth of Richard III (*3H6* 5.6.74–5). Richard's birth becomes additionally outrageous since even the midwife, experienced in many kinds of delivery and deformity, "wonder[s]" at his dentition.

(C) Primary sources range from *The Birth of Mankynde, or the Woman's Book* (Raynalde 1565), to Guillemeau's *Childbirth: Or the Happy Delivery of Women* (1612) to Jane Sharp's *Midwives Book* (1671) and Elizabeth Cellier's defense of an imagined college of midwives (1688). There is an enormous secondary literature on midwifery. Marland's edited collection (1993) includes several useful essays, including Evenden (9–26; for greater detail, see her book, *The Midwives of Seventeenth-Century London*, Cambridge University Press, 2000) on seventeenth-century midwives and the patients of all ranks who chose to employ them; Harley on the greater liberty that regional midwives enjoyed to work free from the control of the Royal College (1993); and King (2007, 115–30) on the literary and medical models of the notorious "Popish midwife" Elizabeth Cellier. Eccles (1982) offers an overview of the apprenticeships that trained midwives and argues for their exclusion from public life; later accounts, such as those of Pelling and White (2003), or Evenden (1993), observe that the College wielded much less power over midwives and other "irregular practitioners" than it might have wished; Evenden offers evidence that wealthy women in fact preferred the expertise of trusted and reputable London midwives over the untried skills of the so-called men-midwives or *accoucheurs*. A. Wilson (1995) offers both an account of the rise of man-midwifery in the late seventeenth and early eighteenth centuries and an argument for a greater presence of male medical midwives in the sixteenth and seventeenth centuries than scholars have hitherto acknowledged, including a chapter on the forceps, reputedly the technological innovation of the famous Chamberlen family of *accoucheurs*. King (2007) argues controversially for the existence of a sixteenth-century medical science of gynecology—the study of women as a separate medical field—not just obstetrics, the study of childbirth, as the center of her contention that the one-sex model that Laqueur (1990), Schiebinger (1991), and others suggest dominated early modern thinking about gender ignores the two-sex model centered around the Hippocratic texts and women's reputed plethora or excess of **moisture**, rather than the limited **Galenic** texts that emphasize homology or sameness. Harkness (2008) has collected additional, invaluable information on early modern midwifery "practices" in early modern London and the licensing procedure. On Shakespeare's midwife-figures, see Bicks (2003), who offers readings of *Pericles* in the light of debates about the Anglican practice of "churching" women after childbirth; the midwife's power to confer sex and legitimacy upon an infant in *Titus Andronicus* and *Winter's Tale*, and obstetric technologies and deformity in *Richard III*.

milk See also **breast, dug, nurse, pap, sex** (A) Milk in Shakespeare refers to what was known as woman's milk, mother's milk or breast milk, or to animal milk consumed by humans. Mother's milk was best for a baby because, physiologically, it was nothing but the same **blood**, "whitened," on which the infant had been nourished *in utero* and was thus absolutely appropriate for the child's own **complexion** or humoral temperament. If a mother nursed her own child, she would not usually do so straight after birth, but would wait at least eight days for her milk to come in, in some reported instances using puppies or cupping-glasses to draw down the milk to the breasts. The milk of a mother or a wet-nurse could also transmit moral qualities (or **disease**) to a suckling infant, along with nourishment. Cows' milk and dairy products engendered **phlegm** and were therefore recommended to cool **choleric** or hot-tempered persons and contra-indicated for those with excessively **cold** or cowardly dispositions. Animal milk was not recommended for infants, but was acknowledged to be necessary when neither mother nor wet-nurse were available to nurse a child, usually because of financial or health constraints (thus Aaron imagines his newborn son "suck[ing] the goat" after his rescue from a murderous mother, *TIT* 4.2.178).
(B) In Shakespeare, mother's milk marks femininity and its associated qualities: mercy, gentleness, vulnerability, peaceableness or cowardice, and also infancy. Such qualities were imbibed by the infant from the mother or from the wet-nurse, which made the quality of a mother's milk fundamental to infant development and even the course of life of an adult. In *MAC* it indicates not only femininity but fundamental humanity or fellow-feeling. Lady Macbeth asks the invisible spirit of evil to "unsex" her and "Come to [her] woman's breasts /And take [her] milk for **gall**" (see **sex**; *MAC* 1.5.48) when she wants to replace her compassion with "direful cruelty." She worries that Macbeth himself is "too full o' the milk o' human kindness /To catch the nearest way," too sympathetic and too full of shared humanity to murder Duncan (*MAC* 1.5.17). She herself knows "how tender 'tis /To love the babe that milks" her (*MAC* 1.7.55), and uses her determination to murder such a child as a model to her husband. Malcolm attempts to convince Macduff that he is not fit to rule because he, too, lacks this basic humanity and would pour the "sweet milk of human concord into hell" if he were king (*MAC* 4.3.98). Lavinia believes the malice of Demetrius and

Chiron must have come to them from their vindictive mother: "The milk thou suck'dst from her did turn to marble; /Even at thy teat thou hadst thy tyranny" (*TIT* 2.3.144). Martius similarly suckled tyranny; there is "no more mercy in him than there is milk in a male tiger" (*COR* 5.4.28). The Shepherd curses Joan of Arc, "I would the milk /Thy mother gave thee when thou suck'dst her breast, /Had been a little **ratsbane** for thy sake!" (*1H6* 5.4.27), comparing her to the vermin exterminated by this common poison. Malvolio connotes Cesario's apparent youthfulness with the comment: "One would think his mother's milk were scarce out of him" (*TN* 1.5.161). Parolles "weeps like a wench that had shed her milk" (*AWW* 4.3.108), perhaps a reference to what we might now call the "baby blues" or weepiness experienced by many women a few days postpartum or perhaps merely to a milkmaid who has dropped a pail full of cows' milk and fears the farmer's wrath.

Animal and human milk was a byword for sweetness, as in the flirtation between the Princess and the Lords, which joins "honey, and milk, and sugar" (*LLL* 5.2.231), or the characterization of "adversity" as the "sweet milk [of] philosophy" (*ROM* 3.3.55). Both cows' milk and breast milk connote pallor in Shakespeare, as a sign of fairness in women (or in the objects of erotic desire, such as Adonis; *VEN* 902), and cowardice in men. Marina's fingers are "white as milk" (*PER* 4.ch. 22), a comparison that was evidently a cliché, since Thisbe/Flute calls to the "sisters three . . . with hands as pale as milk" in the farcical "Pyramus and Thisbe" (*MND* 5.1.338). Goneril calls Albany a "milk-liver'd man" (*LR* 4.2.50; see also **lily-livered**). Instead of a **liver** red with valiant blood, she says, her husband's liver is pale and phlegmatic, as if nourished on milk, a "milksop" (*R3* 5.3.325), one of the men with "livers white as milk" (*MV* 3.2.86).

(C) Fildes (1988) discusses the qualities attributed to human milk and the supposed dangerous **contagion** that could occur if parents hired an inappropriate wet-nurse. Wall (2002) argues that the whiteness of milk becomes a metonymy for the whiteness of the milkmaid, who becomes in turn an emblem of a new English nationalism in the late sixteenth and early seventeenth centuries. On the transformation of milk into gall in the breasts of Lady Macbeth, see Swain (2004). Fitzpatrick (2007) discusses the nutritional and medicinal effects of both human and animal milk in early modern England.

milk-liver'd see **lily-liver'd, pigeon-liver'd**

milk-pap see **pap**

mistempered see **distemper**

moist, moisture One of the four qualities essential to all things (the others were **heat**, chill, and aridity), humidity or moisture characterized both **blood** and **phlegm**, though the former was warm and the latter, **cold**. Moisture indicated a strong or even **sanguine** temperament, which accompanied youth and vigor. The **brain, womb**, and **veins** thrived on the cold moisture of phlegm, and the **heart**

and **liver** required the hot humidity of blood. Shakespeare's characters, however, associate moisture with female sexual irregularity. Othello takes Desdemona's "moist" palm as a sign of her adultery (3.4.36, 39), and Venus praises her own "smooth moist hand" to Adonis (*VEN* 143). Venus finds Adonis' breath "heavenly moisture" (*VEN* 64, 542), discovering a potential for erotic love within the boy that he himself denies. "The **infected** moisture of [a lover's] **eye**" signifies not love but falsehood (*LC* 323).

mole See also **hare-lip, monster** (A) Moles, birthmarks, supernumerary digits, and other genetic variations on an infant's body could be demonstrations of awe-inspiring divine power or manifestations of God's punishment to the wicked. In early modern medical language a mole is also the product of a failed pregnancy. In both cases (birthmark and molar pregnancy), the mole appears because the shapeless matter that the fetus took from its mother, the basic stuff of which it was made, did not properly take up the perfect form of its father but remained misshapen or incomplete, with patches or gaps rather than a complete container of **skin**. Such stains might also proceed from impurities in the mother's menstrual **blood** or **breast milk**, used to nourish the child before and after birth respectively. There is some evidence, however, that during the sixteenth century the medieval view of moles as omens or curses from God coexisted with a newer belief that such marks, depending on their location on the body, might be divine messages or blessings. A mole on the neck predicted future wealth, and a man with a mole on his brow would marry a virtuous woman, for example. Skin-tags (fleshy protuberances) were usually removed at birth, by tying a thread around them to cut off the blood supply. Some surgeons may have removed strawberry-marks (strawberry-naevi) in this manner, too.

(B) Oberon blesses Theseus and Hippolyta with children free from "mole, hare-lip, nor scar, /Nor mark prodigious" (*MND* 5.1.411–12), in a reflection of such marks' association with witchcraft or omens of future ill. Constance shares this belief, praising her son Arthur because he is free from birthmarks, all of which she classifies as harbingers of future doom (*JN* 3.1.43–50):

> If thou, that bid'st me be content, wert grim,
> Ugly and slanderous to thy mother's womb,
> Full of unpleasing blots and sightless stains,
> Lame, foolish, crooked, swart, prodigious,
> Patch'd with foul moles and eye-offending marks,
> I would not care, I then would be content,
> For then I should not love thee, no, nor thou
> Become thy great birth nor deserve a crown.

Constance's words could almost serve as a commentary on Shakespeare's antihero Richard III, in whom birth-defects do indeed serve as indices of future corruption and unfitness to be king. The term "Patch'd" recalls the belief that birthmarks and **deformities** indicated a baby who was incomplete or **abortive** at the time of birth, and thus suffered from telling gaps or absences in its matter, the stuff of which it was made and which came from its mother's body. The mole demonstrated that the fetus had not taken on the proper form that its father would have imposed upon the raw matter, had conception proceeded correctly. Hamlet calls birthmarks such as these "vicious mole[s] in nature" (1.4.24), explaining their presence as the "o'ergrowth of some **complexion**" (27); this tiny stain or imperfection, he argues, corrupts the entire skin or form of the man just as a grain of yeast leavens an entire loaf or a single vice corrupts a virtuous personality, or just as a molar pregnancy grows undetected in the **womb**.

Variegated moles, spotted or red, seem in Shakespeare to be less ominous than these solid marks or stains, with one notable exception. From classical times on, the mole served as a common literary device for a recognition-scene, and Shakespeare uses it as a "voucher" for authentic identity several times. Viola convinces Sebastian that she is his long-lost twin by adducing the evidence of their father's "mole upon [his] brow" (*TN* 5.1.242), a proof, in popular belief, that he had married a virtuous woman. Dromio of Syracuse appears to share his twin's birthmark, the "mole on [his] neck" that leads the latter's lover to misidentify Dromio of Syracuse as Dromio of Ephesus (*ERR* 3.2.143). Such a mole on the neck might popularly prognosticate future wealth. In *Cymbeline*, Guiderius' "sanguine star" (presumably a strawberry-mark) on the neck likewise confirms his identity to Cymbeline, who calls it a "mark of wonder" (5.5.364–5), a portent of heaven's blessing rather than the stamp of hell. But Iachimo's testimony about the "cinque-spotted" (*CYM* 2.2.38) mole on Imogen's breast (see discussion under **breast**) convinces Posthumus he is a cuckold. Confirming Posthumus' belief might be the common wisdom, adduced by Hill, that a mole on the left breast of a woman (or the right breast of a man) indicated a person "undoubtedly wicked" (Hill 1571, 2H4v).

(C) See Hill's prognostication (1571, esp. 2H3r–2H4v); Paré's famous "Of Monsters and Prodigies," which appears as Book 25 of Thomas Johnson's 1634 translation of his *Complete Works*. Crooke (1615) defines the mole as a moon-calf and suggests that, unlike a true pregnancy, moles are generated parthenogenetically in a woman's womb. Guillemeau (1612) distinguishes between types of molar pregnancy (see **abortive**). Drake-Brockman (1973) argues that both Hamlet's "old mole" and his "vicious mole" refer to a figurative molar pregnancy or abortive birth gestating through the length of the play. Ginsberg (1996) argues that the "mole" in *Hamlet* is the non-natural **melancholy** adust or scholar's melancholy from which the prince suffers and that it genders melancholy as a female vice. Hunt (2002) suggests that both Guiderius' and Imogen's moles take the form of a pentangle or five-pointed star, insignium of royalty from as far back as *Sir Gawain and the Green Knight*.

monster See also **prodigy** (A) A monster was usually a baby born with some sort of **deformity** or unusual variation, while a prodigy was a creature not recognizable as human, despite being born to a human mother. Monsters were born as signs of

God's glory and power, or as divine punishments for human sin and folly. Notably, twins, even if sound and healthy, were monsters or marvels. Material causes for monstrosity were manifold. If the copulating couple ejaculated more **seed** than was necessary to generate one child, that extra seed turned into more limbs and body parts, such as supernumerary digits, without being sufficient to generate another child. If too little seed appeared at conception, then the child was born missing an arm, a leg, or even a head. The power of imagination was notorious for creating monsters, such as the **hairy** girl born to a woman who beheld a picture of John the Baptist wearing a camel's skin, at the time she conceived, or the classical tale of Chariclea, born white to black parents because her mother looked upon a picture of Andromeda during coitus. A **womb** that was too narrow and that lacked sufficient space for a child to grow could cause a **palsied** infant, while a **pregnant belly** constrained by having other organs poorly placed close by, by sitting cross-legged, by wearing restrictive clothing, or by plying the needle to excess and sitting still for too long, could cause a hunch-back or crooked limb. Other causes of monstrosity included: the mother's unsatisfied cravings during pregnancy; her sudden shock, fright, or accident; the mingling of human and animal seed (through intercourse with a beast) or of human and devil's seed (through intercourse with a succubus or incubus); and, lastly, the workings of the devil.

(B) Shakespeare's best-known monster is probably Caliban, called "half a fish and half a monster" (*TMP* 3.2.39) by the drunken Stephano and Trinculo who find him sheltering under the former's gabardine. Caliban is "a most delicate monster" (*TMP* 2.2.90), "a very weak monster!" (145), "a poor credulous monster" (146), "a most perfidious and drunken monster" (151), "a most ridiculous monster" (165), "a howling monster; a drunken monster" (188). Their intention to show or de*mon*strate him for money returns to the root of the word, the Latin *monstrare*, to show, a sense that Antony uses when he imagines Cleopatra hoisted up in front of the Romans, "monster-like" (*ANT* 4.12.36) when Caesar marches her in triumph. Figurative monsters include the "green-ey'd monster" of jealousy (*OTH* 3.3.166), which is engendered in Iago's **brain** like a deformed child in the womb and delivered via a "monstrous birth" (*OTH* 1.3.404); the "monster of ingratitudes" (*TRO* 3.3.147); "that monster custom" (*HAM* 3.4.161); "monstrous villainy" (*TIT* 4.4.151).

(C) Paré's crucial chapter, "On Monsters and Prodigies," appears as book twenty-five of the 1634 translation of his complete works and offers a taxonomy of unusual births and what they might portend. The secondary bibliography on this topic is extensive. Daston and Park (1998) survey the territory in early modern Europe, particularly England and France. Iyengar (2005) charts the transmission of the Chariclea story in early modern England alongside discussions of "maternal impression." Burnett interprets Shakespearean monsters as political or social allegories (2002); Burns (2006) reads Richard III as monster, while Johnson (1995) examines the resonance of "monsters" in Shakespeare as gures for both female depravity and loci for antitheatrical anxieties.

mother see *hysterica passio*

mountebank (A) Named after the high bank or bench on which he displayed his wares, the meretricious mountebank pushes unnecessary **drugs** upon unsuspecting customers. Since the word's etymology is Italian, mountebanks were often called Italian or, particularly, Venetian. **College physicians** blamed all **empirics**, and many **Paracelsians**, as mountebanks or showy, secretive "chymists" who poisoned **patients** with their new, under-theorized and little-studied **cures**. According to these "cony-catching" pamphlets or rogue literature, mountebanks set up their benches and appealed in particular to the women in their audiences, flirting if necessary. Their "prittle-prattle" took a specific form: first, they boasted of the miraculous cures they had effected in the past. Second, they offered the ladies seemingly precious stones or jewels (which were in reality of little value). If it seemed possible that someone might discover his ignorance, the mountebank took out an old pamphlet, and read from it in Latin that he understood as little as his audience did. They allegedly sweetened poisonous **medicines** with so much sugar that patients took it thankfully, in preference to the healing but painful **purgative** draughts that true physicians prescribed.

(B) Shakespeare's references emphasize the mountebank's skill as a theatrical performer—in particular as a magician or sleight-of-hand artist—and his possible connection with supernatural or devilish forces. Antipholus of Syracuse compares him to "jugglers," "sorcerers," "witches" "cheaters," and other supernatural or simply deceitful tricksters (*ERR* 1.2.98–101). His twin of Ephesus complains of having been beset by another mountebank, the skeletal Pinch, a "juggler," "fortune-teller" and "conjuror" whose scrawny appearance predicts that of the **apothecary** in *ROM* (*ERR* 5.1.240). When Coriolanus agrees grudgingly to display his **wounds** in the market-place, he compares himself to a showy mountebank who will magic away the **hearts** of the populace (3.2.132). Laertes buys the "unction" that will poison Hamlet's wound from a "mountebank" (4.7.141); it, like the "spells and medicines bought of mountebanks" that Brabantio fears Othello has used to attract Desdemona (1.3.61), is magical in its effectiveness, killing with a mere "scratch."

(C) Oberndorf's treatise (1602), translated by "a fellow of the Royal College of Physicians" entertainingly berates empirics and mountebanks as thieves, pickpockets, and foreign agents who "earne their liuings, by killing of men" (B2r). On the connection between stage-plays and mountebank shows, see Lehnhof (2007).

mummy (A) Human flesh could be made into mummy, an ingredient for **medicine**, by embalming a dead body and mixing it into various recipes. Traditional pharmacology used bodies decayed from natural causes, but Paracelsian mummy preferably came from the bodies of hanged felons, because **Paracelsus** believed their life-force was still intact, since they had not suffered from **disease**, had died in the air, and thus their vigor could be transferred to the **patient**. Paracelsians also argued that the fittest remedy to treat the human body was the body itself, prescribing secretions and excretions such as human **milk**, human **blood**, and bone **marrow**, or embalmed body parts, such as muscles and

brain tissue. Although Renaissance patients may have been less disgusted by this practice than present-day ones, the references in Shakespeare associate mummy with both the feminine (since virgins' flesh was thought to be particularly useful) and with fear, witchcraft, and decay.

(B) Othello attempts to scare Desdemona into finding his love-token by claiming it was "dyed in mummy, /. . . conserved of maidens' **hearts**" (3.4.74–5), "[W]itches' mummy" forms part of the weird sisters' brew in *Macbeth* (4.1.23), along with the various body parts (fingers, **livers**, etc.) that go into the cauldron. Falstaff fears that, carried ignominiously out of Mistress' Ford house in a washing-basket and doused in the Thames, he will blow up into a "mountain of mummy" (*WIV* 3.5.18), a metaphor that corresponds to the play's figuring of the fat knight as meat and particularly as venison in his disguise as Herne the Hunter. The King of Antioch's daughter in *PER* is "no viper" and "yet . . . feed[s] /On mother's flesh that did [her] breed" (1.1.65) a riddling confession of incest that parallels it to cannibalism (she is later called an "eater of her mother's flesh," line 1.1.130) and may continue the play's contrast of benign **physic** (in the person of Cerimon) and dangerous medicine (the Queen whom Cornelius has unwittingly trained to **distil** poisons).

(C) Croll (1609, trans. 1670) offers recipes for manufacturing mummy. Guibert (1639) describes the process of embalming a corpse. Sugg (2006) looks at the variety of early modern responses to medicinal cannibalism and Dannenfeldt (1985) at its associations with Egypt and with embalming. Noble (2003) quotes several recipes and identifies the two "pasties" that Titus Andronicus makes of Demetrius' and Chiron's flesh and feeds to their mother Tamora as medicinal cannibalism to **cure** a **sickened** body politic; Noble (2004) sensitively investigates Desdemona herself as a sacrificial virgin whose flesh is the mummy or "medicine" to cure Othello's jealousy. Moss (2004) argues for a specifically Paracelsian use of medicinal cannibalism, especially in *OTH*, that is distinct from earlier ancient or **Hippocratic** strategies of cacophagy (the ingestion of "dirty" objects).

nail (A) Like the **hair**, nails were an **excrement** or superfluous **humor**, made of smoke or **fume** from the **heat** of humors cooked in the body. Softer than bone but harder than flesh, they were **cold** and **dry**, and allowed persons to grasp objects more easily, and to scratch itches. In emergencies, they could also serve as tools.

(B) Shakespeare's nails function as erotic aids, weapons, ingredients for spells, and desperate tools to dig one's way out of prison. In *H5* 3.4.16–58, Katherine of France repeats "hand, fingers, nails" over and over again in her English lesson with her maid Alice, culminating in the obscene "coun" for gown. Antony imagines Octavia scratching Cleopatra's face "With her prepared nails" (*ANT* 4.12.39), and Hermia, irritated beyond measure by being called "little," retorts to the tall Helena, "I am not yet so low /But that my nails can reach unto thine **eyes**" (*MND* 3.2.297–8). Queen Elizabeth accuses Richard III of murdering his nephews and wishes her "nails were anchor'd in [his] eyes" (*R3* 4.4.232). The Duke of Gloucester gives Lear's daughters the idea to **blind** him by imagining that they will maim their father, rescuing his King "Because [he] would not see [their] cruel nails /Pluck out his poor old eyes" (*LR* 3.7.56–7). Lear himself has imagined blinding himself with his nails rather than weep with rage (*LR* 1.4.307). Antipholus of Syracuse threatens to pluck out Adriana's eyes with his nails (*ERR* 4.4.104–5). Caliban's "long nails" mark his proximity to the animal kingdom (*TMP* 2.2.168). Nail-parings were known to help witches curse the innocent: "Some devils ask but the parings of one's nail," observes Dromio of Syracuse (*ERR* 4.3.71). Talbot breaks free from the officers holding him and, he says, "with my nails digg'd stones out of the ground" to hurl at them (*1H6* 1.4.45). Richard II wishes for superhuman strength and, in its absence, imagines a miracle, "how these vain weak nails /May tear a passage through the flinty ribs /Of this hard world, my ragged prison walls" (*R2* 5.5.19–21).

230

(C) Vicary (1587 C2v) describes the origins and purpose of the nails.

natural See also **madness** (A) A natural was a "natural fool," a person born with a low intellect who was congenitally unable to learn, as opposed to the allowed or licensed fool or jester (the zany, to use a term that some believe Shakespeare to have coined) who pretended to folly for the entertainment of his master or mistress. Sometimes a natural might also have a kind of natural wit that could see the truth; this figure was the wise fool or "fool sage," who could expose the true folly of those around him.

(B) Mercutio compares the effects of love on Romeo to the absence of motor and impulse control in a "driveling . . . great natural, that runs lolling up and down to hide his bauble in a hole" (*ROM* 2.4.92). The bauble properly belonged to the artificial fool or zany, who bore a stick with a figure carved on the top, but Mercutio deliberately confuses the plaything or doll of the natural with the ceremonial stick borne by the jester. Trinculo wonders of Caliban, "That a **monster** should be such a natural!" (*TMP* 3.2.33). Celia and Rosalind joke with Touchstone that he is a natural fool, not a licensed fool, and that it is appropriate for Touchstone to outwit them, for "Nature's natural [to be] the cutter-off of Nature's wit" (1.2.49). Punning on the "stone" in his name, Celia calls him the "natural for our whetstone," the appropriate tool on which to sharpen their wit (1.2.54). Lear contrasts his own state with that of his allowed fool; Lear is the "natural fool of fortune," his companion the licensed fool of fate (*LR* 4.6.191).

(C) Brant's 1509 *Shyppe of Fooles* takes for its central metaphor the Christian allegory of humankind as idiots sailing in a rudderless and unpiloted boat to damnation; he calls all his readers "natural fools" for their thoughtless insouciance about sin. Garzoni (1600) and Adams (1615) catalog the different kinds of fools and madmen, including naturals. *A Nest of Ninnies*, by Robert Armin, one of Shakespeare's fools, tells irresistibly the story of Jack Oates, an artificial fool who behaves like a natural in that he cannot please his master (1608). Bate (2000) examines the influence of Sir Thomas More's *Praise of Folly* in *LR*. Kaiser (1963) reads Falstaff as wise fool.

navel Shakespeare's only reference to the navel seems to allude to the **midwife**'s duty of tying the navel-string or umbilical cord of a newborn. Martius argues that the plebeians do not deserve corn because of their cowardice: "being pressed to the war, /Even when the navel of the state was touched /They would not thread the gates" (*COR* 3.1.122–4). When the enemy threatened the very center of the commonwealth, the people refused to pass through the gates to fight. The metaphor imagines the state as a newborn baby (in the common analogy of the "body politic") in danger of **disease** creeping from the navel. The plebeians are either the midwife who should tie off the umbilical cord that is sustaining the enemy, or the thread itself that must be cut in order to save the realm; the gates of Rome are the narrow **eye** of the needle through which the enemy must pass.

neeze sneeze; to expel mucus from the **nose** in response to tickling, irritation, laughter, or a **cold**. Puck imagines the choir laughing so hard that they splutter or **neeze** when he makes an old lady topple off her stool by pretending to be a withered apple in her drink and then bobbing up suddenly to hit her on the chin (*MND* 2.1.56).

Neopolitan bone-ache see **bone-ache, pox**

nettle The two kinds of **nettle**, stinging nettle and dead nettle, shared many of the same qualities. **Hot** and **dry**, stinging nettle dissolved thick, congealed **phlegm** and other **cold** or corrupted **humors** in the body, helping to clear the **lungs** in cases of **pleurisy**, **cough** (especially in children), and shortness of breath. If taken with wine, it encouraged bodily, sensual pleasure; laying the leaves on the body with oils and wax could **cure** the **spleen** (low **spirits**). Pounded nettles alone provoked or stopped a nosebleed, while nettles pounded with myrrh provoked menstruation if drunk or inserted as a pessary. Dead nettle or "archangel" cured wens and **imposthumes** (sores and **ulcers**) if mashed with **salt** and laid on the sore spot. Iago opposes hot, dry, lust-inducing nettle to cool, **moist**, chastening **lettuce** when he imagines the body as a garden and the will as the gardener planting the seeds of appropriate or inappropriate desires (1.3.322). Hotspur compares the sting of a nettle to a burning ant-bite when he complains he is "nettled and stung by pismires [ants]" (*1H4* 1.3.240) at the very name of Bolingbroke. For the uses of nettle, including its efficacy as an aphrodisiac, see Dodoens (1595, K7r–8v).

night-mare see **sleep**

nipple See also **dug, milk-pap, pap, breast** Shakespeare associates the nipple, the teat of the breast in female mammals, with the enforced weaning of a child. Juliet's **nurse** remembers applying the bitter herb **wormwood** to the "nipple of [her] dug" to wean the toddler from the breast (1.3.30–1; discussion under **dug),** but Lady Macbeth imagines weaning as a spectacular act of murder:

> I have given suck, and know
> How tender 'tis to love the babe that **milks** me:
> I would, while it was smiling in my face,
> Have pluck'd my nipple from his boneless **gums**,
> And dash'd the **brains** out, had I so sworn as you
> Have done to this.
>
> (*MAC* 1.7.54–9)

The image is horrific in part because of its evocation of infantile softness (through the play on "tender," and the coinage "boneless") coupled with the hard consonants of the finite verbs "pluck'd" and "dash'd," both of which suggest the killing of an animal, as does the gruesome plural "brains," which vividly realizes the consequences of smashing a baby's head to the floor. "Boneless" also emphasizes that this infant, unlike the young Juliet, has no **teeth** and is presumably entirely dependent on his mother for succor. The detail of the "babe that milks" suggests close observation of nursing mother-infant pairs, as babies often massage or "milk" their mothers' breasts with their hands while feeding in order to control the flow of milk. On wormwood for weaning, see Charron 1608, V7r.

nit see **louse**

nose, nostril See also **fume, perfume** (A) The nose and nostrils first protected the primary **organs** of smell and second, purged **phlegm** or mucus from the **brain**. The nose directed air and smell up the nostrils, which in turn supported the nose and helped the muscles to smell. Nostrils that were too narrow indicated a mean spirit or a contracted **heart**, while nostrils that were too wide or that flared could demonstrate indignation or strong emotion. The organs of smell proper were two hidden **nerves** at the base of the brain, and the nose and nostrils were the pathways that led to them. Scholars and anatomists debated, however, whether smells had a physical component, such as particles, smoke, or **vapor**, or whether they consisted of a kind of **spirit** or immaterial essence that was borne on the air and taken through the nose to the brain, as Aristotle had suggested. Most seem to agree, however, that smells reached the brain directly and affected the spirits within it. Foul-smelling air was thus both the medium that transmitted **infection** and the infection itself, when it reached the brain.

Noses might also display vice. A red nose was a sure sign of drunkenness, since alcohol made the heart expansive and increased its production of vital spirit (through the medium of pure **blood**). This extra spirit could travel to the extremities, reddening them. Untreated secondary syphilis (see **pox**) could result in a nose whose bridge had collapsed (like other cartilage in the body). Finally, a "sharp" nose in a dying person indicated that **death** was imminent. The so-called **Hippocratic** face or face of death included a sharp or pointed nose, sunken **eyes** and **cheeks**, an **ashy** face, **dry skin**, and slack lips.

(B) Shakespeare's references to the nostrils employ them as paths for scent and indicators of passion. "Crooked smokes climb to [the] nostrils /From . . . blest altars" as if the fragrance of burning incense is an entity separate from the air it perfumes (*CYM* 5.5.447–8). Falstaff's complaint of "the rankest **compound** of villainous smell that ever offended nostril" similarly imagines the air carrying some sort of compound or material vehicle for odor, in this case the stench of dirty laundry (*WIV* 3.5.93). Cerimon and Polixenes imagine fragrance assaulting the nostril as a blow. "A delicate odor" described by the Gentleman is as gentle a one "As ever hit my nostril," interrupts Cerimon (*PER* 3.2.62), admiring the subtle fragrance of the **balms** laid in the chest with Thaisa. Polixenes denies the charge of adultery by comparing his own "fresh . . . reputation" to "A savour that may strike the dullest nostril," a usage of the word "savor" that persists in present-day English only in the term "unsavory" to mean offensive or disgusting (*WT* 1.2.421). The nose might serve as the route for the "great'st infection /That e'er was heard or read" (*WT* 1.2.423–4) through such an unwholesome stench.

Noses are, of course, ubiquitous in Shakespeare. *WT* and *OTH* employ diction and metaphors of olfaction to evoke a husband's visceral disgust at the idea of his wife's adultery. "Meeting noses" is one of Leontes' metonyms for illicit sex, and the smudge on Mamillius' nose draws Leontes' attention to the child and makes him question his paternity. "Hast smutch'd thy nose? /They say it is a copy out of mine," he comments, and indeed Paulina alludes to the infant Perdita's "nose" as evidence of her legitimate paternity, too (*WT* 1.2.121–2, 2.3.100). Convinced that Antigonus is wrong to swear Hermione innocent, Leontes rages: "You smell this business with a sense as **cold** /As is a dead man's nose" (2.1.151–2). Adultery has a stink that only he can perceive. Autolycus sells "Masks for faces and for noses" (4.4.221), presumably to cover up the collapsed nasal cartilage from advanced syphilis (see **copper nose** and **pox**). Othello famously "smell[s] . . . villainy" and curses, "Noses, ears, and lips!" "Heaven stops the nose" at Desdemona's adultery, and of course Iago has begun the whole plot by insisting that "The Moor will be tenderly led by the nose /As asses are" (5.2.191, 4.1.42, 4.2.77, 1.3.401–2).

Other notable noses include Bardolph's red nose, Falstaff's sharp nose, and Troilus's imagined copper nose. Bardolph's nose is so red from drinking that when the delirious Falstaff sees a flea settle upon it, he imagines it to be "a black soul burning in hell" (*H5* 2.3.41–2). Fluellen describes it "like a coal of fire, sometimes plue and sometimes red" (*H5* 3.6.104–5). Falstaff's nose in death, as described by Mistress Quickly, comes from a textbook *facies Hippocratica* or Hippocratic face: his nose was "sharp as a pen" (*H5* 2.3.16; see **death**).

(C) Vicary (1587, D3v) and Crooke (1615, p. 620) describe the nose and summarize classical accounts of smell and the nose's position on the face. Dugan (2005) describes and analyzes the workings of olfaction in Shakespeare. Harris (2007) imagines the reek of **blood** on stage in *MAC*. Vinge's investigation of the five senses in literature includes the association of smell with the erotic in sixteenth- and seventeenth-century love poetry (1975). Mazzio considers the ontological, physiological, and metaphysical functions of air and the senses (2009). Fleissner (1983) argues that the sharpness of the dying Falstaff's nose is one of the six signs of Hippocratic face.

nose-herb see **pomander**

nostril see **nose**

nurse, nursery, nursing See also **milk** (A) Wet-nurses were employed to nourish wealthy infants with **breast** milk; dry-nurses or nurse-maids were employed to care for babies and young children; **sick**-nurses were employed to tend **patients** at home. Noble women rarely nursed their own babies, usually employing wet-nurses either in their own households, or, more usually, sending infants away to live with a host family until weaning. Since both mothers and nurses transmitted qualities to infants, wet-nurses needed careful scrutiny. Some wet-nurses might transmit **pox** or other disorders not only to the infants they nursed but also, in an often-repeated anecdote, to the entire family. Moral qualities, too, came from breast milk and were highly **contagious**. Children sent away to the country to be nursed might be starved, poisoned, or maltreated by the host family, being fed fruit rather than milk, or bread dipped in wine. At the opposite extreme, children might refuse to leave a nurse to whom they had become profoundly attached.

For these reasons, there was a movement among medical and religious authorities in the early seventeenth century to urge mothers of all classes to feed their own babies. Husbands, however, were notoriously dismissive of a lady's responsibility to nurse her own child, and some ladies were too weak or sickly to produce good milk for their babies. In such cases, the hiring of a nurse was necessary. Nursing mothers, and wet-nurses, needed to follow a **diet** of easily digestible foods such as new eggs, broth, jelly, and white meats, so that they could easily concoct **blood** into milk, avoiding all strong flavors and raw fruit, and drinking wine only sparingly. Good milk was white, sweet, and had no odor; it neither curdled nor ran like water, but flowed slowly. The ideal wet-nurse needed to be of good birth; fully grown but not too old (say, between twenty-five and thirty-five years old); not a red-head (chestnut **hair** and brown **skin** was best); well-behaved and temperate in her activities and the food she consumed (not being a drunkard, for example); and wise enough to care for an infant without placing him in danger. Her honesty was paramount, since some nurses fed their charges water or poured water on the baby's bed to mislead parents into thinking the child was well hydrated. The nurse ought ideally to have few or no other responsibilities apart from the nursing infant, since he should be fed on demand, "as often as he crieth" (Guillemeau 1612, 2N1v). Although medical authorities recommended weaning a child after he was two years old and had all his **teeth**, Shakespeare's Juliet may be more typical of actual practice in nursing for three years.

(B) Nurses in Shakespeare tend young children and, in one instance, the sick. Juliet's Nurse is the best-known of his nurse-characters, her lines about Juliet's weaning vividly evocative and topical (see discussion under **dug**). She has evidently continued to serve in the Capulet household long after Juliet's weaning, as, presumably, has Lychorida in *PER* (called Thaisa's nurse but serving as maid and **midwife** in Thaisa's shipboard **childbed**). Mistress Quickly serves as Dr. Caius's "nurse, his sick-nurse, or his cook, or his laundry, his washer, and his wringer," a statement that emphasizes Caius's dependence upon Quickly in all practical matters and that implies his childishness (*WIV* 1.2.3). Lear's statement that he had hoped to rest in Cordelia's "kind nursery" may similarly infantilize the ageing king (*LR* 1.1.124), as does Edgar's careful "nursing" of his blinded father (*LR* 5.3.182). Caius Martius Coriolanus' enemies charge him and his supporters with immaturity by comparing them to sucklings. Brutus imagines the "prattling nurse" keen to see Martius' wounds, and Aufidius blames Martius for his submission: "at his nurse's tears /He whined and roar'd away [our] victory" (*COR* 2.1.206, 5.6.96).

Volumnia has sternly told her son, "The country [is] our dear nurse," a senti-ment paralleled in the history plays, in which the mother country nurses or succors its peoples (*COR* 5.3.110). Richard II's refusal to act as a good "child" to his mother or to the kingdom contrasts to Bolingbroke's filial regrets upon leaving England:

> England's ground, farewell; sweet soil, adieu;
> My mother, and my nurse, that bears me yet!
> Where'er I wander, boast of this I can,
> Though banish'd, yet a trueborn Englishman.
> (*R2* 1.3.306–9)

Richard II has complained that he is "too old to fawn upon a nurse" (1.3.170) but his cousin proudly figures himself as the youngest of newborns—a child that is still in the process of being born, a child that is continuously born to his mother England. Gaunt's famous speech picks up Bolingbroke's equation of fertility and sustenance in "this England, /This nurse, this teeming **womb** of royal kings" (*R2* 2.1.51). The Duchess of York, however, thinks that Bolingbroke's nurse, England or not, has been remiss: "And if I were thy nurse, thy **tongue** to teach, /'Pardon' should be the first word of thy speech," she complains, urging him to make peace (5.3.113). Peace is the "dear nurse of arts, plenties, and joyful births," claims Burgundy (*H5* 5.2.35), but the English history plays more often nurse or foster grief or war. The young Duke of York in *R3* learns from Gloucester's "nurse" about his uncanny dentition at birth and his slow growth in childhood (2.4.32–3), gossip that leads his mother to retort, perhaps in anxiety for his precocity, "Pitchers have ears" (2.4.37). Later, the Duchess of York in *R3* calls herself both "the mother of . . . moans" and "sorrow's nurse," the mother of the murdering Richard and the person who will "pamper . . . with lamentations" the excessive grief of the weeping queens (2.2.87–8). Queen Elizabeth calls the Tower a "rude ragged nurse" for her "tender babes," her "tender princes," repeat-ing the word "tender" again to emphasize the roughness of the rocks and the delicacy of the children (*R3* 4.1.101, 98, 102).

Since a good nurse, dry- or wet-, was responsible for instilling discipline, teaching language, and other nursery tasks, "the baby beat[ing] the nurse" (*MM* 1.3.30) or the "testy babe scratch[ing] the nurse" (*TGV* 1.2.58) signaled the reversal of natural order. Lucio argues that the Duke himself participates in this topsy-turvy world when he scurrilously claims that Duke Vincentio himself has paid for the "nursing [of] a thousand" bastard infants at wet-nurses (3.2.118); even Escalus points out the paradox when he pities Claudio with the words, "pardon is the nurse of second woe" (*MM* 2.1.284).

A cluster of references associate nursing with **sleep** and rest. Cleopatra's asp "sucks the nurse asleep" (*ANT* 5.2.310), sending the queen to the great equalizer, **death** and decay, "dung, /The beggar's nurse, and Caesar's" (5.2.8). "The foster-nurse of nature is repose," argues Lear, who cannot rest for grief (*LR* 4.4.12). The erotic and the infantile are salaciously mixed in Tamora's relationships to her husband Saturninus and lover Aaron in *TIT*. Tamora proclaims, "If Saturnine advance the Queen of Goths, /She will a handmaid be to his desires, /A loving nurse, a mother to his youth" (1.1.331–2). Emphasizing both her submission ("handmaid") and her authority ("mother"), her sexuality ("desires") and her tenderness ("loving nurse"), Tamora recreates herself as the fount of every one of Saturninus' physical needs, from nutrition to service. Later Tamora uses the same figure to address her lover Aaron in the woods as she urges him to rest:

> We may, each wreathed in the other's arms,
> Our pastimes done, possess a golden slumber;
> Whiles hounds and horns and sweet melodious birds
> Be unto us as is a nurse's song
> Of lullaby to bring her babe asleep.
>
> (2.3.25–9)

Here Tamora imagines sibling incest rather than mother-son relations, comparing herself and Aaron to babies fostered together and rocked to sleep by the same nurse. The play clarifies for us that both a nurse and a midwife attend Tamora's childbed and that Aaron kills them both in order to save his newborn son (4.2). Aaron wishes only his own, tough qualities to enter his baby and therefore imagines rearing him without access to a mother or to a nurse:

> I'll make you feed on berries and on roots,
> And feed on curds and whey, and suck the goat,
> And cabin in a cave, and bring you up
> To be a warrior, and command a camp.
>
> (4.2.177–80)

With a goat for foster-nurse, curds and whey for pap, and a crowded cave for a cradle, the infant will become hardy and robust rather than tender, he hopes.

Shakespeare's late plays address many then-current anxieties about wet-nursing and its consequences, especially the fear that a wicked wet-nurse could deliberately injure a child. Like Juliet's nurse, Thaisa's nurse Lychorida in *PER* has remained in the household of the young one for whom she cared. She serves as midwife to Thaisa at sea, as many wet- and dry-nurses may have done in early modern London, taking on apprenticeships with experienced midwives after they had weaned their most recent charges. Pericles plans to leave the infant Marina with Dionyza for "careful nursing" (3.1.80) and Dionyza tells Marina, "Have you a nurse of me" (4.1.24), but she proves an evil foster-nurse. Marina does not imbibe evil qualities from her bad nurse, but Dionyza does prefer her own daughter to her foster-nurseling, planning Marina's murder with the justification that "nurses are not the Fates"; nurses can foster life, she argues, but not preserve it (4.3.14). If an infant or a child is fated to die, a nurse cannot intervene. (In a different register, Jack Cade's claim to the throne in

2H6 avers that he is the son of a royal child "stolen away" while "being put to nurse"; 4.2.142.) Leontes in *WT* cruelly claims to be "glad that Hermione did not nurse" Mamillius (2.1.56), because she has already contributed too much blood to him (and presumably her milk would nourish him with more of her supposedly corrupt qualities). Immune to Paulina's and Antigonus' claims on behalf of the infant Perdita, Leontes decrees that "chance may nurse or end" her (*WT* 2.3.183). Charged with exposing the child, Antigonus mourns that "kites and ravens [will] be [her] nurses," creatures that will consume the child rather than offer her nourishment (2.3.187). *CYM*, in contrast features a good wet-nurse, the ideal Euriphile, so like a mother to the princes Belarius has kidnapped that Cymbeline's sons believe themselves to be Belarius' and Euriphile's own children (3.3.104, 5.5.340). Their sister Imogen, as the page Fidele, bears herself "so nurse-like," so gently, to her master Caius Lucius that the last favor he pleads from Cymbeline is her freedom (*CYM* 5.5.88). *H8* includes allegorical wet-nurses, good and bad. Rome is at first the "nurse of judgement," but proves lacking (2.2.93); by the end of the play, "truth shall nurse" Elizabeth, in the institution of the reformed English church (5.4.28).

The comedies joke about wet-nurses and the transmission of qualities good and bad through breast milk. Dogberry and Verges, Shakespeare's excruciatingly slow-witted constables, urge the Watchman to "call to the nurse and bid her still" a crying child, only to be asked what the Watchman should do if the nurse herself is asleep and will not hear (3.3.66–7). Rather than confront the nurse, returns Dogberry, he should retreat and allow the child to wake the nurse by itself. Rosalind jokes that any woman who cannot make her faults into her husband's is so dull that she should "never nurse her child herself, for she will breed it like a fool" (*AYL* 4.1.175). Finally, Adriana in *ERR* observes that it is a wife's duty to "attend [her] husband, be his nurse, /Diet his sickness" (5.1.98), reflecting the responsibility of women of all ranks to **physic** their own families and tend them in illness.

(C) Guillemeau's *Childbirth* (1612) includes an addendum, *The Nursing of Children*, which "exhort[s] ladies, to nurse their children by themselves," and recounts a case in which an infant contracted syphilis from a wet-nurse and then transmitted the **disease** to its parents when they shared a bed (1612, 2I2r, 2Kr). Invaluable for this topic is Valerie Fildes' detailed account of infant feeding throughout the world, which includes recipes for "pap," the mixture of flour or breadcrumbs and water that might constitute an early modern infant's first solid food (1986), and her history of wet-nursing, especially her chapters on the Renaissance and the seventeenth century (1988, 68–100). Kahn (1983) and Hardy (1990) consider the loquacity of Juliet's nurse. Paster (1993) discusses early modern breastfeeding and metaphors of nursing infants, especially in *HAM*, at length in two chapters of *The Body Embarrassed*. Rackin suggests that Lady Macbeth's nursing her own baby modifies the suggestion in Holinshed's *Chronicles* that feeding their own children showed that Picts and Scottishwomen were hardier and more barbaric than the civilized English, and demonstrates her maternal zeal, thus participating in the play's project of "the domestication of women"

(1999, 26). Wall (2002) describes the ways that an emergent English nationalism associates the whiteness of milk with the skin of the milkmaid in seventeenth-century England. Pelling and White (2003) include sick-nurses, along with **plague-searchers**, among the "Irregular Practitioners" whose lives and occupations they document and analyze in *Medical Conflicts*. Weil (2005) considers the mutual reliance of master and servant in early modern culture and the parallel dependencies of wife/servant, daughter/servant and other familial categories.

O

o'ercharged, o'erfraught (A) Overfilled, overburdened, both by external burdens (such as too much food in the **stomach**) but also from emotional triggers. For the early moderns, strong emotion (affection) was not only physiological but also literally fluid, as **humors** rushed toward the **heart**, **eyes**, or **brain**: under the influence of anger, **choler** poured from the gallbladder; in sorrow, **melancholy** from the **spleen**; in joy, **blood** from the heart; in **lethargy**, **phlegm** from the **lungs**. Particular body parts could thus become flooded or o'ercharged by humors under strong affections. Such strong feelings needed purging from the body, but usually **purges**, evacuations, or bloodletting were not necessary: natural outlets such as tears, **sweat**, **urine**, **belching**, and (Shakespeare insists) words could vent feelings healthily and prevent **death**, **swooning**, or cracked heart- and **eye-strings** from an overfilled heart.

(B) Shakespeare's gentleman-**physician**, Cerimon, uses a medical metaphor to reassure the sailors drawing up Thaisa's heavy coffin from the ocean: "If the sea's stomach be o'ercharged with gold, / 'Tis a good constraint of fortune it belches upon us" (*PER* 3.2.54–5). Just as a **surfeit** of food in the stomach is eventually eased by the passing of gas, so the sea gives up this box, to the sailors' benefit. Henry VI imagines his own heart and eyes breaking under the pressure of too much sorrow, too many tears, at the sight of a son who has unknowingly killed his father in the civil war that rages around him (*3H6* 2.5.78). He imagines himself going **blind** via two bodily processes: first by weeping excessively (which would **dry** out the humors in the eye itself, hardening it and making it difficult for the spirit of sight or *pneuma* to enter it) and second by filling his eyeballs with tears to such an extent that the eye-string or optic nerve cracks, making the eye useless. After Paulina accuses Leontes of killing his wife by his cruel accusations of infidelity, he defends himself by claiming "Her heart is but o'ercharged," that too much emotion has overwhelmed her, and that "remedies for life" or resuscitating agents will restore her (*WT* 3.2.150–3). Sonnet 23 compares the lover, his heart o'ercharged with too much affection, to the actor who does not know his part and is overburdened with fear or the wild animal overfilled with rage. Writing, suggests the poet, provides both an outlet for the burdened heart and an entry point for love into the "hear[ing] . . . eye" of the reader. Malcolm urges Macduff, aghast at the murder of "all [his] pretty chickens and their dam /At one fell swoop" (*MAC* 4.3.218–19), to voice his grief, lest it "Whispers the o'er-fraught heart and bids it break" (4.3.210).

(C) Wright (1604) describes the workings of the passions upon the early modern mind and heart. Paster, Floyd-Wilson and Rowe, eds. (2004) historicize emotion on the early modern stage. Kennedy distinguishes between male anger and female grief (2000).

organ See also *hysterica passio* (A) The organ is both the bodily part itself that performs a physiological function and the mechanism by which that function is performed. Two opposing traditions about organ-functions prevailed in early modern England. The Aristotelian view held that the **heart** was the "throne" or chief seat of affections or passions, but the **Galenic** attributed angry or irascible passions to the heart and erotic or concupiscible emotions to the **liver**. In addition, early modern English physicians also associate specific organs with specific **humors** and passions, such as the **spleen** with **melancholy** or the gallbladder with **choler.**

Unlike modern organs, which are understood as body parts fixed in their functions and locations, early modern organs can migrate to different parts of the body under certain circumstances, and a particular organ's function might become diffused among other parts of the body. Thus the **womb** or **mother** might threaten to suffocate a **patient** by rising into her throat under the duress of strong emotion. Shakespeare's characterization of Lear's madness as *hysterica passio* or hysteria appears, however, to be unique and figurative; hysteria is from ancient times understood as a **disease** affecting women, not men.

(B) Shakespeare uses the term "organ" to refer to internal bodily parts and processes; vehicles for sense-data to enter the body; external body parts or appearances; as a surrogate for sex-difference and, in *Hamlet*, puns on the senses of organ as "musical instrument," "body part," and "mechanism." Internal processes include the "organs of increase" or reproductive organs, in Lear's rank curse of sterility against his daughter Goneril (*LR* 1.4.279); Shylock's assertion of the common humanity of Christian and Jew based on their shared embodiment of "hands, organs, dimensions, senses, affections, passions" (3.1.59); Mark Antony's joking description of the crocodile as a creature that "moves with its own organs" (*ANT* 2.7.44); or Sir Hugh Evans' description of the sleeping, pious maid whose "organs of fantasy" (the second chamber of her **brain**) will provide her with pleasant dreams while heedless sinners are "pinch[ed]" by the fairies (*WIV* 5.5.51). Henry V imagines "the organs" almost as independent entities, **"quicken'd"** or enlivened by emotion "though defunct and dead before"; like snakes sloughing off their dead skins, body parts under the experience of strong feeling will "Break up their drowsy grave and newly move" (*H5* 4.1.21–3). External organs include the **eyes** and **ears** (*TRO* 5.2.123), or outward features, such as "every lovely organ of [Hero's] life" (*ADO* 4.1.226).

The voice-box as sound-organ illustrates both the extent to which Shakespeare's women can impersonate men and the limits of that transformation. The King agrees to let Helena try to **cure** him because it is possible that "in [her] some blessed spirit doth speak /His powerful sound within an organ weak" (*AWW* 2.1.175–6). This formulation imagines masculine power or voice working through Helena's feminine body just as air is forced through an organ-pipe or, metaphysically, the soul can speak through the mechanism (organ) of the material body. The gendering of the voice-box is more apparent in *Twelfth Night*, in which Orsino praises Viola/Cesario's "rubious lip" and other features, including her high-pitched voice: "thy small pipe /Is as the maiden's organ, shrill and sound, /And all is semblative a woman's part" (*TN* 1.4.32–5). Here the "maiden's organ" implicitly evokes the "woman's part" of both drama (the female roles played by boy-actors on stage) and the body parts unique to women; the comparison thus illustrates both the fundamental sameness of men and women (the so-called one-sex model) and their essential differences, evoked also by Viola's transgendered name, Cesario, one who has been "cut" or castrated in order to sing.

Hamlet imagines the faculty or organ of speech diffusing through a crowded room to voice his father's betrayal, "For murder, though it have no **tongue**, will speak /With most miraculous organ" (*HAM* 2.2.593–4). The play will become the organ (mechanism) to "catch the conscience of the king" (2.2.605) by serving as the organ of speech for the victim and as a sounding organ to broadcast the crime as if in church. Similarly, the recorder is a "little organ" containing "much music," yet Rosencrantz and Guildenstern "cannot . . . make it speak," any more than they can compel Hamlet to confide in them (*HAM* 3.2.368–9). Laertes wishes to be the organ or means of Hamlet's destruction (4.7.70), picking up the sustained metaphor of a diseased body politic in the play.

(C) Paster (2004a) helpfully adduces the "Body-Without-Organs" of theorists Deleuze and Guattari as a way of thinking of early modern organ-systems and their mobility. See also Hillman and Mazzio (1997) for individual analyses of particular parts, and Hoeniger (1992) for accounts of organ-systems and physiological processes. Jeffrey Knapp (1993) and Claire McEachern (1994) puzzle out Henry V's image as the resurrection of the Christian body and the reunified body politic respectively. On the voice-box or pipe as woman's organ, see esp. Orgel (1996); Elam (1996).

palsy (A) Palsy or paralysis afflicted one half of the body, the right or the left, at a time. Occasionally only one limb was affected, or one half of the face. Palsy came from thick and sluggish **humor**s building up in the body and preventing the animal **spirits** from traveling to the limbs and **heart**, or even the **brain** (if the brain were affected, the disorder was properly an **apoplexy**). **Cold** weather or, paradoxically, **inflammation**, might also induce palsy, or binding with a tight cord, or an injury to the backbone (especially the **marrow**) or the brain. The elderly suffered from palsy more than the youthful, because of their greater cold, just as they were more likely to suffer apoplexy or **lethargies** for the same reason. Palsy following an apoplexy was sometimes called paraplegia, though paraplegia affected sensation, and in palsy, both sensation and movement were lost. The ability to move voluntarily came from the brain, transmitted through the animal spirits refined there, and so any disorder that prevented the flow of these spirits resulted in paralysis. Since less spirit was required for sensation than for movement, it was impossible for a limb to remain mobile but insensate, although conversely it was perfectly plausible for limbs to experience **heat**, cold, and even pain, but to remain unable to move. In such cases the prognosis was good; motion might well return to the limb as the animal spirits recovered. If, however, the limb changed color, or shrunk, recovery was extremely unlikely, because not only the animal spirits (the vehicle for the rational soul that controlled voluntary sensation and response) but also the vital spirits (the vehicle for the sensitive soul that controlled heat and motion) and the natural spirits (the vehicle for the vegetative soul that controlled growth) were affected.

Any **cure** required the body and especially the afflicted limbs to be warmed and dried so that its humors could flow freely once more. The patient should be placed in a warm, **dry** room and kept fasting for about three days before beginning to eat a little **barley-broth**, eggs, partridges, pine-nuts, or almonds, avoiding fish, fruit and other cold and **moist** foods. Phlebotomy should be used carefully, in case it cooled the body too much; dry-cupping on the back of the head or the neck was preferable to wet-cupping or scarification (see **surgeon's box**). Wrapping the affected parts in **linen** or a fox-skin to warm them, or visiting hot springs or **baths** might also be helpful. Palsy or paralytic fomentations might include oil or **balm** of earthworms (since they were hot in **complexion**), placed on the nape of the neck along with the oils of camomile, dill, spikenard, lily, nutmeg, and St. John's wort.

(B) The Lord Say claims to "quiver" with "the palsy, and not fear" (*2H6* 4.7.93), to be brave despite his advancing years. The irascible Duke of York bewails the "palsy" that has paralyzed his arm and prevents him from thrashing his nephew Bolingbroke for daring treason (*R2* 2.3.104). In *1H6* Mortimer suffers from a palsy that has left him with "pithless arms, like a withered vine" (2.5.11), and in *R3* Gloucester claims Edward's wife has blasted his arm like a withered shrub, and induced his paralysis through witchcraft (3.4.68–9); the play emphasizes the sheer impudence of his claim through the many references to his **deformity** at birth. In *TRO*, Patroclus imitates Nestor "with a palsy" to signify his age, presumably mocking his trembling gait and shaky hands. Thersites later includes "cold palsies" in his catalog of ailments (*TRO* 1.3.174, 5.1.20). Vincentio, disguised as the Friar, attempts to convince the doomed Claudio to "Be absolute for **death**" by listing the **illnesses** and ailments to which the elderly look forward, including "palsied eld" (*MM* 3.1.36).

The first senator in *COR* dismisses the pleas of Menenius to Martius in Aufidius' camp as "the palsied intercession of a decayed dotant" (5.2.44) Menenius "dotes" with age and also upon Martius, who is like a son to him. His pleas are "palsied" not only because of his advancing years but because he makes them tremulously and tentatively.

(C) Barrough explains the mechanisms underlying palsy and recommends the oil of earthworms, applied topically to the skin, to treat it (Barrough 1583, C3r). Bullein explains that earthworms' heat makes them especially useful in closing **wounds** and treating ailments of chill and old age such as **gout** (1579, Fo. 84v).

pap, milk-pap See also **breast** The **pap** is both the milk-producing mammary gland in women and the pectoral muscle in men; Vicary argues that in men, the paps defend the inner **organs**, especially the **heart**, from hurt and insulate the body from cold, while in women they produce **milk**. Shakespeare alludes to this protective function in men except when he qualifies the term as "milk-pap," in *TIM* 4.3.116. In all three Shakespearean instances the word "pap" connotes **humor** or contempt. As Pyramus, Bottom in *MND* directs his suicidal sword to "that left pap, /Where heart doth hop" (5.1.298), and Biron in *LLL* (4.3.24) jokes that Cupid has shot Ferdinand right under the "left pap." Timon, however, derisively argues that even the young breasts of a virgin, showing through her clothing, ought not to excite Alcibiades' pity (*TIM* 4.3.116).

244

Paracelsus See also **alchemy, contagion, distil, element, infection** (A) The icono-clastic Philip Theophrastus Bombast von Hohenheim (1493–1541) reportedly called himself Paracelsus because he believed himself "greater than Celsus," the first-century Roman medical writer who advocated basic hygiene and documented the advanced state of ancient medicine during his time. Born to a poor family in Germany, Paracelsus spent his youth rejecting the traditional training of medical schools in favor of chemical investigations. Paracelsus challenged the old **Galenic**, humoral, allopathic treatments, and the ancient theory of the elements, in favor of "chemical" or mineral remedies prescribed according to **alchemical**, astrological, religious, and Platonic homeopathy, or "natural magic." Moreover, instead of prescribing herbal medicines to correct perceived imbalances in the body's **humors**, he recommended distilling herbs or refining chemical remedies, often metal **salts**, to treat specific **diseases**. **Illness** proceeded not from an excess or deficit of humors, but from the "seeds" of external disease, seeds left behind as relics of the fight between Lucifer and the angels. Diseases such as **epilepsy**, goiter, or **madness** resulted not from present-day demonic possession but from these leftover spiritual seeds, and could be cured by mate-rial, chemical means—better living through chemistry. In 1530 Paracelsus wrote an acclaimed account of syphilis and a therapy that involved the carefully gradu-ated administration of mercury treatments; he followed this in 1536 with a book about the treatment of **wounds** that restored his reputation worldwide.

English doctors in Shakespeare's time were probably more familiar with popular Paracelsian therapies, such as the use of **quicksilver** for the **pox**, than with Paracelsian theories, although Bostocke's Paracelsian apology, the first in English, appeared in 1585. What Debus (1965) and others call "The Elizabethan Settlement" between the established Galenic **College** of **Physicians** in England and the new science of European Paracelsians seems to have taken the form of prescribing the new **drugs**, especially popular treatments such as mercury for the great pox, without ascribing to the new theories.

(B) Paracelsus appears by name only once in Shakespeare, evoked by a gloating Lafew to commemorate Helena's successful **cure** of the King: "relinquished by the artists . . . both of Galen and Paracelsus" (*AWW* 2.3.11). Given out as "incur-able" (2.3.14), the King nonetheless now appears able to lead Helena in a sprightly dance. Nonetheless, Paracelsian elements are present in Shakespeare, especially in the later canon. *OTH* and *TIT* employ a figurative (in the former) and a literal (in the latter) medicinal cannibalism (see **mummy**); *PER* similarly presents Cerimon as a chemical healer who seeks the secret virtues in minerals (see **physic**). *TMP*'s Prospero, "rapt in secret studies," may resemble a Paracel-sian magus (1.2.77). *ERR* integrates new understandings of germ-theory and Paracelsian magical healing with the transmission of syphilis or sexually transmit-ted infections (see **pox**).

(C) Paracelsus' own works were translated into Latin and circulated in England during the sixteenth and seventeenth centuries, but they are difficult for even an accomplished Latinist because of his neologisms, verbosity, and abstruse-ness. Easier to understand are Bostocke (1585), or John Hester's collection of

Paracelsian cures (1596). Bostocke (1585) compares "ethnicke" or heathen (Galenic) and "chymicall" or chemical (Paracelsian) **medicine**, justifying the latter on overtly Christian grounds. While Aristotle and Galen were "heathens," Paracelsus reads in "Gods booke" of nature; while Galenists cure the material body, Paracelsians cure the spiritual one; while the Greeks wrote for ancient, pagan bodies, Paracelsus writes for present-day Christians, whose bodies are now different; while Galenists offer the same remedy for all ailments, Paracelsians know that each disease has its own remedy and each organ needs to be treated with specifics for that location; while Galenists employ impure, earthly medicines, Paracelsians refine everything by fire down to its fundamental "substantives" of salt, **sulphur** and mercury, and thus find out the secret "filthinesse" in sugar and the curative powers of arsenic or **ratsbane**. "[H]umors are dead thinges without life or power of life" (D8r), writes Bostocke, and only the three substantives, plus the astral body, create life and health. Furthermore, a physician should work from

> visible and palpable experience, so that the true proofe and tryal shal appeare to his **eyes** & touched with his hands. . . . For the[n] shall he know, not by his owne braines, nor by reading, or by reporte, or hearsay of others, but by experience, by dissolution of Nature, and by examining and search of the causes, beginnings and foundations of the properties and virtues of thinges, which he shall finde out not to be attributed to colde or heate, but to the properties of the three substantives of each thing and his Arcanum. (D5r)

Bostocke's summary beautifully demonstrates both Paracelsus' contribution to what would become the scientific revolution (experimental or empirical investigation of physical, material phenomena, and chemotherapy rather than treatment "by reporte, or hearsay,") and the, to us, peculiar, simultaneous belief in the metaphysical "Arcanum" or astral body to be cured.

Pagel's classic work (1982) introduces fundamental Paracelsian principles; Debus's two-volume *Chemical Philosophy* goes into more detail (1977), and his *English Paracelsians* (1965) examines the dissemination of Paracelsian knowledge in Britain. Ball's engaging biography of Paracelsus (2006) retells many of the stories about Paracelsus' life. Hoeniger (1992) insists that what seem like Paracelsian references in the Shakespearean corpus are merely reiterations of traditional Galenic remedies, and that what seem like understandings of infectious disease are but restatements of **Hippocratic** *miasma*. But Murray (1967) finds *Macbeth* suffused with the language of Paracelsian alchemy, and, more convincingly, Hunt (1988, 1989) argues for the presence of Paracelsian homeopathy throughout Shakespeare, especially in the tragedies. Bentley (1986) reads Helena's cure of the king as Paracelsian "natural magic." Harris's influential study helpfully connects the language of contagion in the plays to new, Paracelsian understandings of infectious disease (2004). Harris, Healy (2001), and others argue independently that there was indeed a rudimentary understanding of germ-theory in the period, brought about in part by the epistemological upheaval presented by syphilis, the **sweating** sickness, and other clearly contagious epidemic diseases. Moreover, they suggest, earlier critics have overstated the controversy between Galenists and Paracelsians in early modern England; despite the disapproval of the Royal College, most successful practitioners, such as Shakespeare's son-in-law John Hall (himself possibly an **empiric**), seem to have employed both Galenic, herbal treatment and the newer, chemical remedies of Paracelsus, preferring practical solutions to polemical outbursts. Finally, Moss (2004) and Noble (2003, 2004) argue for the use of Paracelsian mummy or body-products in Shakespearean plays.

parmaceti More commonly called spermaceti, parmaceti was a white wax found in the head of the sperm whale, used, because of its purity, as a base for **medicines**, cosmetics, and candles. Hotspur reports snapping at a courtier who recommends "parmaceti for an inward bruise" (*1H4* 1.3.58), presumably because he resents the associations of the fragrant oil with courtliness and vanity, and does not believe that the perfumed courtier has any personal experience with the **wounds** of battle. The courtier might have been reading Newton, who recommends that spermaceti be compounded with herbs and fried with sheep-fat in order to **salve** a bruise (1580, M4r). (The elderly, women, and children were particularly prone to bruising, because of their relatively thin and porous **skins**.) Gesner incorporates spermaceti along with human **blood** in an "elixir of life" or "**quintessence**" to be used in extremity, perhaps because of the belief that spermaceti was in fact the sperm of the whale and thus contained a principle of life (see Gesner 1559, D3r–D4r). Guillemeau recommends that **pregnant** women apply an ointment of spermaceti on their **breasts** and **belly** to prevent stretch-marks (1612, D3r, D4r).

parti-ey'd A textual crux. Edgar greets his blinded father Gloucester with the words "My father, parti-ey'd?" in the corrected first quarto of *LR* (1608), but with the words "poorly led" in the uncorrected first quarto (1608) and second quarto (1619). Editors emend variously; until the late twentieth century, commentators seem to have preferred "poorly led," with its emphasis on rank, but the Riverside (Evans 1997), Cambridge (Halio 1996), and Penguin (Orgel 1999) retain "parti-ey'd," and suggest that Gloucester's **eyes** are multi-colored because of bleeding bandages. Watt (1997) suggests that the text should read "gory-eyed."

patient (A) A person undergoing treatment under the care of a healer; a sufferer, one who waits with patience for a **disease** to be cured.
(B) The Lord Chief Justice offers to become Falstaff's "**physician**," and Falstaff responds: "I am as poor as Job, my lord, but not so patient: your lordship may minister the **potion** of imprisonment to me in respect of poverty; but how should I be your patient to follow your prescriptions, the wise may make some **dram of** a **scruple**, or indeed a scruple itself" (*2H4* 1.2.127–31). "Dram" and "scruple" are measurements of liquid used by **apothecaries** and physicians in **compounding** and prescribing **drugs**. If the Justice is the physician and Falstaff the patient, then Falstaff's medicine is the "potion of imprisonment," to remedy his poverty. Falstaff puns on "patient" as an adjective, long-suffering, to argue that he is not,

however, the Justice's patient, because of his rank. Imogen, too, puns on patience, sickness, and suffering, telling Cloten, "If you'll be patient, I'll no more be mad; /That cures us both" (*CYM* 2.3.103–4; see discussion under **madness**). Conrade intrigues Don John in his plan to slander Hero by offering "If not a present remedy, at least a patient sufferance" (*ADO* 1.3.8).

Physicians had a proprietary relationship with their patients, who were responsible for choosing sound healers. John of Gaunt blames Richard II for his choices: "too careless patient as thou art, /[thou] Commit'st thy anointed body to the **cure** /Of those physicians that first **wounded** thee" (2.1.97–9). Desperate for a cure, or to hang on to his kingdom, Richard returns to the flatterers who misguided him in the first place, just as a **sick** man returns to a comforting but ineffectual quack. Doctor **Caius** offers to reward Quickly with the services of "de good guest, de earl, de knight, de lords, de gentlemen, my patients" in return for speaking well of him to Anne Page (*WIV* 2.3.93). There is a hierarchy: the physician wields power over the patient, regardless of the latter's rank. Pericles is Marina's "kingly patient" (*PER* 5.1.71). The King of France trusts Helena enough to declare himself "Thy resolved patient" (*AWW* 2.1.204) and after the cure, makes sure that she displays herself publicly in court as his physician and he as her patient: "Sit, my preserver, by thy patient's side" (2.3.47). Apothecaries, too, had practices and patients, even though they were not supposed to have patients of their own. Dromio of Ephesus asks Aegeon, "You are not Pinch's patient, are you, sir?" (*ERR* 5.1.295). Macbeth asks the doctor, "How does your patient?" after the sleepwalking scene (5.3.37). Some ailments, however, are beyond a doctor's proprietary care and require an effort from the sufferer, such as the "mind diseased" about which Macbeth consults the doctor on his own account: "Therein the patient /Must minister to himself," advises the physician (*MAC* 5.3.45). When Ajax curses, "I'll let his humor's **blood**," Agamemnon retorts, "He will be the physician that should be the patient" (*TRO* 2.3.213–14).

Of course, patients could choose to ignore medical advice. The lyric voice in Sonnet 111 is "a willing patient" who drinks up his foul-tasting eisel or vinegar, but Chamberlain jokes to Surrey about Henry VIII's marriage to Anne Bullen, "he brings his **physic** /After his patient's **death**: the king already /Hath married the fair lady": what the physician calls illness, the patient calls love (H8 3.2.40–2).
(C) Kerwin (2005) explores the cultures and institutions that produce both healers and patients in early modern England; Pettigrew's chapters focus more narrowly upon Shakespeare's plays and the healer-characters within them (2007). Both, however, are concerned with the healer rather than with the experience of being a patient. Pelling and White (2003) vividly evoke multiple historical contexts for healing in early modern England, including a perhaps surprising degree of sophistication among patients choosing among various practitioners. Porter (2003) devotes an entire collection to "lay" perceptions of healing, but moves from the ancient world to the seventeenth century without pausing in Shakespeare's time. Much recent critical work engages with the status of the woman-patient in early modern culture. Sawday (1996) analyzes Mary Carey's 1657 mourning-poem "Upon [th]e sight of my abortive birth" in the context of early

modern women's fears of childbirth; Howard (2003) reads the diary and letters of Alice Thornton in the service of a similar analysis, and Fissell's special issue of the *Bulletin of the History of Medicine* on "Women, Health and Healing" (2008) includes several essays on women as patients. Joan Lane's *The Making of the English Patient* (2000), guides readers to primary socio-historical sources (such as diaries, or letters) from 1700–1900 that directly address the experience of being a patient.

pearl See also **web and pin, eye** (A) Medically, the pearl or web in the eye was a cataract that rendered the **patient** unable to distinguish anything but light and darkness. Cataracts afflicted the eye when the **humors** of the eye became too thick, a consequence of old age. The **cure** was "couching" or needling, using a needle to break up or displace the cloudy lens.
(B) Julia responds to Proteus' "Black men are pearls in beauteous ladies' eyes" by punning on the double meaning of pearl as both a jewel of great price and a film that obfuscates the vision: "such pearls as put out ladies' eyes" (*TGV* 5.2.12–13). Lucius in *TIT* uses a version of the same proverb to mock Aaron the Moor, "the pearl that pleased [the] empress' eye," again punning on pearl as both jewel and cataract or eye-disorder to call Aaron a "**wall-eyed** slave" (*TIT* 5.1.42, 44).
(C) On the term "pearl" for web or cataract, see, for example, A.T., *A Rich storehouse* (1596).

perfume See also **fume** (A) Fragrant, sweet-smelling perfumes protected persons against **infections** transmitted by foul air or noxious smells, especially during times of **plague**. Some recommended carrying a **pomander** or a scented handkerchief when walking outside; all urged cleanliness within the home to scour away odors, and the frequent changing of floor-rushes. Since foul-smelling or damp air could transmit infection by inducing the body to produce corrupted bodily **humors**, pleasant or sweet-smelling air conferred protection by inducing joy or delight, which enlarged the **heart** and increased the production of vital **spirit** or pure **blood**, allowing the body to maintain a temperate **complexion** or humoral temperament even in inclement or unpleasant conditions. The **womb** was known to be especially sensitive to scent, and **midwives** were advised to keep pleasant fragrances such as musk away from a laboring woman lest the sweet smell draw the womb upwards and thus delay childbirth (see **childbed**). Conversely, unpleasant odors such as burnt feathers could also speed up labor and revive women suffering from *hysterica passio*, or the "suffocation of the mother"—in which the womb, or properly, **vapors** from the womb, traveled up to the throat and **brain** and triggered paroxyms in a susceptible woman—because the womb and its corrupted vapors would return to its usual position in the lower part of the body as it attempted to escape the noxious smell. A fume was also a specific early modern therapy, often associated with mercury treatment, although Shakespeare does not appear to use the word in this sense (see **tub-fast** for details).
(B) Shakespeare refers to perfumes as aphrodisiacs, mnemonics, cleansing agents, agents of prayer, and poisons or therapies. Perfumes often originate with

burning, smoke, or fire, as they might in a therapy, in a Catholic church service, or on stage. "Three April perfumes in three hot Junes burned" describes the means of dispensing the fragrance (through burning) and the ability of smell to trigger and consolidate memory (Sonnet 104.1; see also **distil** for discussion of Sonnet 54). Lucius sends prayers to heaven with "the sacrificing fire, /Whose smoke, like incense, doth perfume the sky" (*TIT* 1.1.144–5). Iachimo notices tapers in Imogen's chamber but concludes " 'Tis her breathing that /Perfumes the chamber thus" (*CYM* 2.2.18–19). Lucentio rhapsodizes that Bianca's breath "perfume[s] the air" (*SHR* 1.1.175), "sacred and sweet," like the odor of a church. Gremio "perfume[s]" the tokens he sends to her, calling her "sweeter than perfume itself" (1.2.151–2). But the sonnet-mistress of 130 rejoices in "breath that . . . reeks" rather than "perfume" (130.7–8). Laertes refers to the evanescence and intangibility of scent when he describes Hamlet's affection for Ophelia as "the perfume and suppliance of a minute" (*HAM* 1.3.9). "Their perfume lost, take them again," remarks Ophelia as she returns Hamlet's gifts (*HAM* 3.1.98), fragranced like the "excellent perfume" of the gloves the Count gives Hero (*ADO* 3.4.63). Cleopatra's "strange invisible perfume" enchants Antony and makes the very winds "**love-sick**"; it is "strange" because there is no visible, smoky origin for the fragrance (*ANT* 2.2.212, 194).

Henry IV lies uneasily even in one of "the perfumed chambers of the great" (*2H4* 3.1.12), fragranced to protect him against **disease**. The sleepwalking Lady Macbeth alludes to the use of exotic, fragrant ingredients such as ambergris, musk, or Turkish rose-water in cosmetics and what Autolycus calls "Perfume[s] for a lady's chamber" (*WT* 4.4.223) when she moans, "All the perfumes of Arabia will not sweeten this little hand" (*MAC* 5.1.51). Scent might signify a courtier or wealthy man in "gilt and . . . perfume" (*TIM* 4.3.302), but also could cover up the stench of infection, as Apemantus imagines, the "diseased perfumes" (4.3.207) of prostitutes stinking from sexually transmitted infections (such as the "perfumed" Bianca in *OTH* 4.1.146, according to Cassio). Antonio complains that Prospero's island is "perfumed by a fen" (*TMP* 2.1.49), breathing out noxious air and infection. Cymbeline's queen connects "mak[ing] perfumes" to her skills in toxicology and **medicine**, as do many early modern recipe books. Mistress Quickly presumably malaprops again when she describes Canary wine that "perfumes the blood"; she probably means "perfuses" or "pervades" (*2H4* 2.4.27).

(C) John Caius recommends purifying the air against the **sweating** sickness by infusing the air "with swete odoures of roses, swet perfumes of the same, rose-mary leaues, baies, and white sanders cutte, a fewe cloues steped in rose water and vinegre rosate" (1552, C8r, fol. 24r); the *Plague Orders* of 1578 also recommend fragrance to protect against infection. Dugan writes extensively about olfaction, scent, and perfumers in early modern England, connecting fragrance to rank in *COR* and to the erotic in *ANT* and *TN* (2011). Forthcoming work by Dugan explores the gure of the perfumer onstage.

perturbation (A) Strong passions or perturbations unsettled the **humors** and could, if unrestrained, induce **illness** in the person who experienced them.

Positive emotions such as joy made the **heart** dilate or expand; negative ones such as sorrow made the heart constrict or tighten. Perturbations and passions did not merely exacerbate illness or **disease**; they could serve as the underlying causes. Pleasure and delight might briefly cloud one's judgment, but on the whole were good for the health, encouraging the development of pure **blood** and pure spirit in the heart so that the concoction or digestion of food in the **stomach**, of chyle in the **liver**, of **phlegm** in the **brain** and of other humors to their relevant organs became more efficient and effective. Too much joy, however, enlarged the heart and the supply of blood too greatly and would burn the blood, making it **choleric**, and weakening the heart itself. Such weakness explained the sudden **deaths** of persons from fits of laughter, and the dejection that sometimes followed excessive mirth. Fear and sorrow, which contracted the heart, were much more dangerous even than too much pleasure. Sluggish, melancholic blood slowed the movement of spirit from the heart to other **organs** of the body, and impaired the digestion or concoction of spirits that went on in the heart when the body was healthy; the blood thus retained in the heart thickened into still more **melancholy**, which cooled and dried the whole body.

(B) Shakespeare often associates perturbation with **sleep** interrupted by care or ghosts, or night-mare. Falstaff diagnoses King Henry IV's **apoplexy** as coming from too much "study and perturbation of the brain" (*2H4* 1.2.116). Seized with regret for his usurpation of the throne, "shaken [and] . . . wan with care" at the threats to his throne, and fearful of his son's future on that throne, Henry IV succumbs to melancholy (a known cause for **apoplexy**) that thickens his blood and cools his body to such an extent that his son believes him to be dead. Hal therefore addresses the crown as a "polished perturbation" (4.5.23) that prevents his father from easy rest. The doctor diagnoses Lady Macbeth's sleepwalking as "a great perturbation in nature" (*MAC* 5.1.9), because "her **eyes** are open, but their sense is shut"; the animal spirits that would normally be refined into the "eye-spirit" or *pneuma* that enabled sight and recognition in the early modern **eye** are trapped in the brain, even though the vital spirits from the heart (which enabled involuntary motions and sensation, and **heat**) were evidently still flowing to her body. For an early modern **physician**, the sight is indeed horrific: in sleep, the healthy body retracted its animal (soul-enlivening) spirit back into the brain, so a sleepwalker is a wandering body without its soul. Ghosts perhaps horrify viewers for similar reasons. Lady Anne's ghost "fills [her murdering husband's] sleep with perturbations" and night-mare (*R3* 5.3.161), and Old Hamlet's Ghost is a "perturbed spirit" (*HAM* 1.5.182). "[H]orror and perturbation follow" Beatrice, cries Benedick facetiously; the sight of her makes his **hair** stand on end as if he has seen a ghost (*ADO* 2.1.260). Imogen's description of "the perturb'd court" is then a much stronger statement about turmoil than it might sound; she asks Pisanio why he has gone to so much trouble to cover her absence, which the court is discussing, if he plans not to kill her as directed (*CYM* 3.4.105).

(C) Wright (1604) recounts in detail the effects of feelings such as anger, grief, shame and love upon the body, and Lemnius (1576) discusses individual **complexion** or humoral personality both as a type that remains constant through life and as a delicate balance that can be **distempered** by perturbed emotions. Secondary material includes the invaluable collection *Reading the Early Modern Passions* (Paster, Rowe, and Floyd-Wilson 2004), which considers the roles of sense-perception (B. Smith), the animal-human divide (Paster 2004b), and ecology (Floyd-Wilson 2004) in emotion; Schoenfeldt (1999), who locates the locus of early modern self-control or temperance in a willed and individualistic bodily constraint rather than in statist strictures; Kennedy (2000), who discusses the gendering of wrath; Marshall (2001), who argues for the forcible yet pleasurable separation of mind and body, thought and emotion, for an early modern viewer of Shakespeare's plays; Paster (2004a, *Humoring the Body*), who discusses emotional and urinary incontinence in *MV*, among others; Vaught (2008), who interprets the emotionalism of Richard II and the "stoicism" of Bolingbroke in light of changing attitudes toward the chivalric and about emotional expressiveness in men; and Baumbach (2008), whose semiotic analysis of Shakespearean physiognomy includes the analysis of **skin**-color, voice, and headdresses such as veils.

pestilence See also **plague** (A) Like plague or **pox**, pestilence can refer to any **disease** that spreads quickly among people and that afflicts large numbers of sufferers at a time, such as typhus **fever**, commonly spread by **lice** in Shakespeare's England, which produced a red rash upon the trunk that rapidly spread over the whole body. Usually, however, pestilence refers to the bubonic plague. (B) Shakespeare often uses the term as an expletive. Volumnia curses, "[T]he red pestilence strike all trades in Rome" (*COR* 4.1.13). Cressida wishes "A pestilence on" her interfering uncle (*TRO* 4.2.21). The gravedigger, remembering Yorick, exclaims, "A pestilence on him for a mad rogue!" (*HAM* 5.1.179). Cleopatra curses the ill-fated messenger who tells her of Antony's marriage to Octavia, "The most **infectious** pestilence upon thee!" (*ANT* 2.5.61). Scarus compares the state of Antony's army to an infected body on which buboes or plaguesores, sometimes called "God's tokens" (Lodge 1603, B2v), appear, "like the token'd pestilence, /Where **death** is sure" (*ANT* 3.10.9). Typically, pestilence in Shakespeare appears to be associated both with bad air or water, in traditional **Galenic** terms (Olivia, for example, is like a fragrance that "**purged** the air of pestilence," *TN* 1.1.19), and with the new measures against diseases transmissible from person-to-person taken in Europe and England during the sixteenth century. John of Gaunt warns Bolingbroke to flee the king as if "Devouring pestilence hangs in our air /And thou art flying to a fresher clime" (*R2* 1.3.284). The King himself employs providential explanations for the pestilence: "God omnipotent, /Is mustering in his clouds on our behalf /Armies of pestilence" (*R2* 3.3.87); with the rain will fall down **contagious** disease or mist, in vengeance for rebellion. Political discord is likewise "a pestilence /That does infect the land" in *H8* (5.1.45). Iago compares his plan to accuse Desdemona falsely of adultery both to poison and to contagious disease, vowing "I'll pour this pestilence into [Othello's] **ear**," part of a system opposing the evidence of **eye** and ear throughout the play (*OTH* 2.3.356).

At least three references seem specifically to allude to plague. Beatrice compares the friendship between Claudio and Benedick to the relationship between plague-**patient** and the disease: "he will hang upon him like a disease: he is sooner caught than the pestilence, and the taker runs presently mad" (*ADO* 1.1.87), an account of the progression of bubonic plague to nerve damage and insanity. *TGV* compares love to an infection that compels one "to walk alone, like one that had the pestilence" (*TGV* 2.1.22), alluding to the distinguishing marks on the clothing of sufferers or the white rod they had to carry under the plague orders of 1578. Finally, the pestilence (plague) determines the outcome of *ROM*. Friar John explains why Friar Laurence's letter explaining the crucial, desperate plan to feign Juliet's death never reached Romeo:

> Going to find a bare-foot brother out
> One of our order, to associate me,
> Here in this city visiting the **sick**,
> And finding him, the **searchers** of the town,
> Suspecting that we both were in a house
> Where the infectious pestilence did reign,
> Seal'd up the doors, and would not let us forth.
> (*ROM* 5.2.5–11)

The 1578 plague orders clearly outline such a course of action; while clergy were bound to continue visiting the sick, especially the poor, searchers who discovered visitors to plague-stricken houses were bound to restrict the movement not only of the inhabitants of the house but also of those who had visited it.
(C) See Queen Elizabeth, *Plague Orders* (*Plague Orders* 1578); Kellwaye (1593); Lodge (1603); Dekker (1603). Bullein's *Dialogue against the Fever Pestilence* (1564) offers a chilling story in which the dying patient is abandoned by his **apothecary**, doctor, wife, and servant; only the pastor remains, who offers him a prayer to help him die. Secondary sources include Healy (2003); Grigsby (2004); on plague-searchers, see Pelling and White (2003). Cox (2008) reads MM as a "pestilence play," full of references to the plague that ravaged London during its composition.

phlegm see **phlegmatic**

phlegmatic See also **complexion** Shakespeare has little interest in phlegmatic characters, fat, sleepy, lazy, dull, peace-loving, and white-skinned. Phlegm was manufactured in the **kidneys**, **bladder**, or **veins**, according to different sources, and nourished both the **brain** and the **womb** (the one generated ideas, the other engendered children). Women, who were naturally colder and moister than men, tended toward the phlegmatic, especially in **cold**, damp, Northern climes (see **sex**). The only reference in the canon to the watery **humor** of phlegm comes in a malapropism from Mistress Quickly in *Merry Wives of Windsor* (1.4.75). Caught by her master Dr. Caius with the messenger Simple in her closet, she pleads, "Be not so phlegmatic," when she wants him to be less **choleric**, less irritable.

physic

See Elyot (1539); **Galen**, trans. Culpeper (1652). On phlegm as nourishment for the brain and womb, see Crane (2001); Floyd-Wilson (2003) argues that both **sanguine** and phlegmatic temperaments became idealized as characteristically English (for men and women, respectively) in a nationalistic appropriation of humoral theory that devalued "Southern" **choler** and **melancholy**.

physic (A) Physic in the early modern period means any therapy used to control **disease**, with the implication that such therapy will provide a corrective to the disease or ailment from which the **patient** is suffering. Physic can mean both the study of the human body and the **medicine** used to treat it; this is its sense when used in the word **physician**. Unlike the **surgeon**, the physician prescribes medicines, **potions**, **pills**, boluses, **plasters**, **poultices**, **fumes** and so on to **cure** disease. Only men could join the Royal **College** of Physicians, founded in 1518, but many women practiced as vernacular healers or **empirics**. The physician cannot, however, **compound** these medicines himself, but requires the services of a trusted **apothecary**. Recipes (the abbreviation for which, *Rx*, gives us our abbreviation for a medical **prescription** even up to the present day), appear in collections called pharmacopoeia.
(B) Shakespeare uses the term physic in both a literal and a figurative sense, most frequently in plays that feature medicine and healing as a motif. Caius in *WIV* is a "doctor of physic" (3.1.4). Although only men could join the Royal College, in both *All's Well* and *Pericles* the youth, beauty, and, most importantly, virginity of Helena and Marina respectively function as "physic" to correct disorders associated with sexuality (the King's **fistula** in *AWW*; the sexually transmitted **infections** of *PER*). In *Pericles*, physic first appears with reference to the incestuous daughter of Antiochus, and sets up the combination of magic, healing, likeness and parenthood that structures the entire play:

> I am no viper, yet I feed
> On mother's flesh which did me breed.
> I sought a husband, in which labour
> I found that kindness in a father:
> He's father, son, and husband mild;
> I mother, wife, and yet his child.
> How they may be, and yet in two,
> As you will live, resolve it you.
> Sharp physic is the last: but, O you powers
> That give heaven countless **eyes** to view men's acts,
> Why cloud they not their sights perpetually,
> If this be true, which makes me pale to read it?
> (1.1.65–76)

The beginning of the speech alludes to two rare but increasingly popular seventeenth-century pharmaceuticals, snake venom and mummified human flesh (**mummy** or *mummia*). Antiochus and his daughter have taken the therapeutic

254

principle of homeopathy—like calling to like—to excess, searching for and finding a husband in a father, that is, committing incest. At the turn of the seventeenth century, **Galenic** allopathy (treatment by opposites) conflicted with **Paracelsian** homeopathy (treatment by likeness). The practice of medicinal cannibalism derived both from cacophagy, the Hippocratic practice of ingestion of disgusting or dirty objects, and from the Paracelsian use of mummy. Pericles compares Helicanus, his adviser, to a physician who practices Paracelsian medicine (presumably with a frightening pharmacopoeia): "Thou speak'st like a physician, Helicanus, That minister'st a potion unto me, That thou wouldst tremble to receive thyself" (1.2.67–9).

And Cerimon, Shakespeare's master healer, enjoys almost supernatural Paracelsian powers:

> 'Tis known, I ever
> Have studied physic, through which secret art,
> By turning o'er authorities, I have,
> Together with my practise, made familiar
> To me and to my aid the blest infusions
> That dwell in vegetives, in metals, stones;
> And I can speak of the disturbances
> That nature works, and of her cures.
>
> (*PER* 3.2.26–33)

He practices with some success: "hundreds call themselves /Your creatures, who by you have been restored" (3.2.45–6). In the brothel, Marina herself becomes the physic or medicine to cure the sinful urges of the would-be customers:

> though most ungentle fortune
> Have placed me in this sty, where, since I came,
> Diseases have been sold dearer than physic,
> O, that the gods
> Would set me free from this unhallow'd place . . . !
>
> (4.6.96–100)

This equation of Marina's virtue with her healing power, and with her rank, becomes more explicit when she awakens her ailing father from his grief-stricken trance; Lord Lysimachus is so impressed by her "sacred physic" that he woos her for himself. In contrast, Leontes imagines no cure for lewdness: "Physic for't there is none . . . /No barricado for a belly" (*WT* 1.2.200).

H8 equates King Henry's marriage to Anne with his **death**, his counselors' dissuasions "physic" brought too late, "after [the] patient's death" (3.2.40). The ailing Katharine employs the same metaphor to describe Henry's wishes for her recovery: "That gentle physic, given in time, had cured me; /But now I am past an comforts here, but prayers" (4.2.122). Gardiner compares the new religion of Cranmer to a "**contagious sickness**," insisting that his peers send Cranmer to tower, or else, "Farewell all physic," the change in the commonwealth's state and practices will be irremediable (5.2.62). Others who imagine political change as physic include Menenius, who imagines the commonwealth to suffer in a fit from which only the medicine that is Martius can save it (*COR* 3.2.33); Macbeth, who "Throw[s] physic to the dogs" (*MAC* 5.3.47) because the Doctor cannot prescribe a **purge** to Scotland to void the English; and Lear, who tells ceremony or pomp to "take physic" to cure its **surfeit** (3.4.33).

Some characters comment on the dangers of physic; in some instances the remedy is only marginally better than the disease. A political option may be distasteful as a foul medicine. "In poison there is physic," argues Northumberland (*2H4* 1.1.37). Martius, full of contempt, recommends that rather than give plebeians representation, the senators should

> jump a body with a dangerous physic
> That's sure of death without it, at once pluck out
> The multitudinous **tongue**; let them not lick
> The sweet which is their poison.
>
> (*COR* 3.1.154)

He refers to a linctus (a medicine to be licked with the tongue), either a lozenge-like sweet or a thick **syrup**, often highly sugared to make it palatable. The nobly-born Romans are the civilized physicians who know what is best for the body politic and will not permit it to surfeit on the sweets of proposed democracy that would be fatal to it. The King in *AWW* turnst his fear of potions into power, calling Helena a "sweet practiser" whose "physic" may nonetheless kill them both (it "ministers [her] own death if [he] die[s]," 2.1.185). Arviragus includes medicine in his song as one of the institutions of civilized life and education that will eventually come to naugh, such as monarchy, the universities, and the medical schools: "The sceptre, learning, physic, must /All follow this, and come to dust" (*CYM* 4.2.268).

Ironically, Romeo requires only the "holy physic" of marriage from Friar Laurence, not the deadly poison that the Friar provides (*ROM* 2.3.52). Hamlet's equation of prayer with physic is deeply ironic, too, given Claudius' later admission that he cannot pray at all. Hamlet refuses to kill Claudius "while he is praying" but concludes that the holy "physic but prolongs thy sickly days" (*HAM* 3.3.96). Aaron, characteristically, jokes about physic that poisons the patient. Having killed the **midwife** who has witnessed the birth of his illegitimate child, he claims to have cured her ailment, namely loquacity, mocking, "Ye see I have given her physic" (*TIT* 4.2.162).

(C) Barrough's "Preface to the Reader" in his *Methode of Physicke* offers a lengthy justification of the art and science of medicine (and of his daring to publish a book in the vernacular tongue of English, which lay-folk might read) upon the following grounds:

> God created the world full of healthful and wholesome plants, animals
> and minerals to serve humankind, and humankind **brains** to discover their

medicinal virtues and tongues to teach others and thereby to proclaim God's glory; Biblical and classical kings such as Solomon or Mithridates explored physic in order to help their peoples; **Hippocrates** and Galen cemented not only their own renown but that of their societies through their medical endeavors; the body is a microcosm of the larger world, and therefore it is the pious duty of both patient and physician to keep it in good working order; finally, it is only through the workings of experience added to the theoretical learning from Galen and others that the physician may continue to prosper and heal sufferers. (1583, *iiii recto-*vii verso)

Other attempts to popularize medicine for a lay-audience include A.T.'s advice from a "homish apothecary" (1596); the *Pharmacopoeia* of 1618; Bullein's *Bulwarke of Medicine* (1579). Kerwin (2005) argues convincingly that we cannot talk about a single culture of medicine or physic during the early modern period and that instead competing beliefs and systems operate among the different practitioners, such as apothecaries, surgeons, **mountebanks**, virtuosi, physicians, wise-women, and so on. Pollard (2005) and Pettigrew (2007) address the presence of medicines and of medical practitioners on the Shakespearean stage respectively.

physical (A) Medicinal, like **physic**; healing to the body.
(B) Martius disowns Lartius' praise of his martial prowess by claiming that for him, the loss of **blood** in battle is more like a therapeutic phlebotomy or bloodletting than a perilous chance: "The blood I drop is rather physical /Than dangerous to me" (*COR* 1.5.18–19). War revitalizes and rejuvenates him. Another Roman for whom bloodletting is therapeutic, Portia, suspects Brutus of hiding "some **sick** offence" in his mind when he leaves the house early on a **cold**, dank morning into "the vile **contagion** of the night": "Is Brutus sick? and is it physical /To walk unbraced and suck up the **humors** /Of the dank morning?" (*JC* 2.1.261–3).
Portia's phrase "suck up the humors" clarifies the concept of **contagion** as a mirror; the only reason for walking around with inadequate protection against the weather would be if Brutus were already unbalanced, **hot** and **dry** with **choler**, and the cold, **moist** morning functioned as **medicine** to correct his **distemper**.
(C) Marshall (1996) comments on Martius' hardened body and its **wounds**, and Poole (2002) on contagion as violence in *JC*.

physician See also **college, surgeon** (A) Physicians were rare in early modern England; few patients had access to them, in part because of the extensive classical education they needed to undertake before they could be licensed by the College of Physicians. The College had been founded in 1518 by Thomas Linacre, physician to Henry VIII. It licensed physicians by examining them in front of their peers and ensuring that they were well-versed in **Galenic humoral** theory. Most licensed physicians attended grammar schools in their youths (where they would learn Latin) and then went to Cambridge or Oxford for degrees in divinity. Medical faculties in England were limited. Many physicians therefore traveled to Europe, to the famous medical schools at Montpellier,

Paris, or Basle, before returning again to the university for examination and qualifying as bachelor or doctor of medicine. In London and the south-east, the College monitored and licensed physicians, but in the provinces, physicians could seek licenses from their own bishops and practice beyond the college's regulation. Noble **patients** could make a doctor's living or reputation; it was better still to become the physician who served in a royal or noble household.

The ecclesiastical Council of Tours in 1163 had ruled that no churchman might shed **blood**, which led to a wide professional separation between the physicians and the surgeons. The medical faculty in Paris, moreover, forbade its students and graduates to work with their hands at all, limiting their prescriptions to strictly internal remedies. Nonetheless, several in Tudor London practiced both medicine and surgery. John **Caius**, master of Caius College in Cambridge, had roomed with Vesalius, the famous anatomist, himself, and introduced dissection to England (although he had to undertake his operations in the hall of the Company of Barber-Surgeons, since the College of Physicians objected so strongly). Anatomical knowledge gradually became more acceptable—even required—knowledge for a physician; in 1615 the King's own physician, Helkiah Crooke, became the first physician to publish a work of **anatomy**, his *Microcosmographia*. The medical schools in Paris, Oxford, and Cambridge taught strictly Galenic, humoral theory, although in the late sixteenth century **Paracelsian** ideas began to influence a few iconoclasts. The College stated its disapproval of the new methods and therapies, but some of them (such as the **tub-fast** or **mercury** treatment for syphilis) quickly became widely used, and new chemical refining processes for medicaments were disseminated to **apothecaries**.

(B) Several of the plays oppose an **empiric** or unlicensed physician to a licensed healer. *AWW* contrasts the learned physicians of the College who do not succeed with Helena, the empiric woman healer or **Doctor She** who does. *WIV* opposes "soul-curer and body-curer," the **urinals**, astrology and other traditional therapeutic tools employed by Dr. Caius (who is a parody of his famous namesake) to the spiritual healing offered by the churchman Sir Hugh (2.3.54, 3.1.61, 3.4.97). *CYM* places "Doctor" Cornelius alongside the poisoner, Cymbeline's queen, whom he unwittingly trains as his apprentice in the arts of **distillation**. In *PER*, Cerimon, another doctor, this time of noble blood, seems to represent the helpful pharmacopoeia of the learned Paracelsian physician in opposition to the medicinal cannibalism practiced by Antiochus and his daughter, or the figurative toxin offered to Pericles by Helicanus, moral physician and counselor (*PER* 1.2.67).

Such ambiguities explain the warning in *TIM*, "trust not the physician; his antidotes are poison" (4.3.431–2), or John of Gaunt's admonishment to Richard II not to "Commi[t] thy anointed body to the **cure** /Of those physicians that first wounded thee" (2.1.98–9). Physicians famously hate delivering bad news. Cornelius reports the Queen's **death** to Cymbeline with the words, "Who worse than a physician /Would this report become?" (*CYM* 5.5.28). The "fearful physicians" in *R3* and *1H4* fear not only for the lives of Edward and Northumberland respectively but for their reputations as well (*R3* 1.1.137 and *1H4* 4.1.24).

Sonnet 140 describes physicians who conceal the truth from "testy **sick** men, when their deaths be near" and offer "No news but health from their physicians" (*SON* 140.7–8). Kent offers a scenario for what might happen to an unsuccessful physician, advising Lear to "kill the physician, and the fee bestow upon thy foul **disease**" (*LR* 1.1.163–4).

Honest physicians told the truth, however, just as, Sempronius says, Timon's "friends, like physicians, /Thrive, give him over: must I take the cure upon me?" (3.3.11–2). A true friend, like a true physician, is honest even with words that seem poisonous. Paulina serves as "physician" to a Leontes diseased with jealous suspicion (*WT* 2.3.54), and the Lord Chief Justice will serve as Falstaff's "physician" and tell him to amend his way of life (*2H4* 1.2.125). Richard II imagines himself as a righteous physician when he recommends that Bolingbroke and Mowbray "purge [their] **choler** without letting blood" (*R2* 1.1.153–4). Dr. Butts, "the king's physician" suspects Cranmer of malice, ministering to the King's body politic as well as his body mortal (*H8* 5.2.10–11).

In incurable illness, however, only "death is our physician" (*OTH* 1.3.310), "the sure physician, death" (*CYM* 5.4.7). The recommendation that physicians should not treat themselves dates to antiquity, and is repeated by Agamemnon on the subject of the **brawny** but slow-witted Ajax, who "will be the physician that should be the patient" (*TRO* 2.3.213).

(C) Ironically, our best descriptions of the true or honest physician come from Oberndorf's diatribe against the **mountebank** or false physician (1602). Such a man ought to remain honest, pious, humble, and scholarly, since medicine is the highest human art or skill, he writes. Cooke (1679) translates and prints selected case-histories from the diary of John Hall, Shakespeare's physician son-in-law. Physician R. R. Simpson (1959) tabulates references to medicine and medical concepts within Shakespeare's plays and outlines the life of John Hall in order to investigate the general sentiment that Shakespeare's references to doctors increased after his daughter married one. Clark (1966) details the history of the founding of the Royal College, including the work of the physician Thomas Linacre. Joseph's biography of John Hall (1964) contextualizes the physician as "Shakespeare's Son-in-Law." Bergeron (1972) finds the casebook of John Hall, Shakespeare's son-in-law, to be a direct source for the bandage of **flax and whites of eggs** used by the servant on the blinded Gloucester's **eyes** in *LR*. Pelling and White (2003) identify celebrated and lay-practioners and their clientele in London. Hoeniger (1992) offers the definitive account of Shakespeare's relationship to Galenic medicine and a useful summary of the three professional groups that comprised the healing profession. Hardin (2002) investigates the late-appearing physician onstage as a miraculous healer with roots in folkloric drama. V. A. Jones (1977) treats John Hall as a model physician, praising in particular his use of antiscorbutics. Lane (1996) reprints and edits Hall's casebook, and includes medical commentary by a physician. Silvette surveys popular therapies and their representation on the early modern stage, with chapters on uroscopy, bloodletting, herbal and chemical medicines, magical and folk-healing, and a discussion of theatrical references to famous physicians such as **Paracelsus** or Galen. He concludes that Shakespeare's medical references stem from "observation and felicity of expression" rather than any "technical knowledge of the healing art," reserving his medical plaudits for Webster's "technical grasp of surgical matters" (1967, 244). Traister (2004) argues on the evidence of the successful healers in *PER* and *AWW* that Shakespeare's attitude toward physicians changed after his daughter Susanna's marriage to John Hall in 1604. Kerwin (2005) argues for the embedding of antitheatricalism in the way that physicians sought to codify themselves and their work, suggesting that the early seventeenth century recuperated performance and the public presentation of medicine through the new scientific or empirical displays of knowledge. Pettigrew (2007) argues that physicians in Shakespeare's plays (especially the doctors in *MAC* and *LR*) are constrained by their relationships to those who outrank them from attempting fully effective or honest cures and that the scandal attached to Queen Elizabeth's physician Dr. Lopez (accused of poisoning the queen with a **syrup**, tortured and finally executed in 1594) testifies to the perceived centrality of physicians (with their proximity to poisons) to political plots. On the supposed battle between Paracelsians and Galenists, see Debus (1965), who notes that most physicians ignored the controversy and mixed various methods and medicaments according to what they found effective.

pia mater (A) Literally the "gentle mother," the innermost and thinnest membrane or meninx around the **brain** and spinal cord, *pia mater* nourished the brain tenderly with **spirit** from the **heart** and nutrition from the **liver**, and divided the brain into ventricles or compartments for its separate functions. It was distinguished from the *dura mater*, or "hard mother", the thick membrane that protected both the *pia mater* and the brain itself from knocks or injuries from the skull.
(B) By extension, Shakespeare uses the phrase to mean the brain itself, or natural intelligence. Feste jokes that Sir Toby Belch has a "most weak *pia mater*" or limited intelligence (*TN* 1.5.115), and Thersites that Ajax's "*pia mater* is not worth the ninth part of a sparrow" (*TRO* 2.1.71–2). In *LLL* 4.2.68–70, on the other hand, Holofernes appears to use *pia mater* in a more technical sense when he modestly disavows the "foolish extravagant spirit" that allows him to compose verse extempore: "these are begot in the ventricle of memory, nourished in the **womb** of *pia mater*, and delivered upon the mellowing of occasion." The early modern brain held three chambers or ventricles. The foremost one contained the five "outward" or "common wits" (what we now call the five senses), and the imagination or fantasy. The central ventricle or compartment contained reason or thoughtfulness, and at the rear was the library of memory. Holofernes imagines that his creative powers search in his memory for appropriate subjects or words or figures, polish them into a gem of wit, and then that he utters them when the middle ventricle, his reason, tells him that the "occasion" is appropriate. Most editions of the play alter the printed copy, which reads "primater," on the grounds that the word is a printer's error for *pia mater*, rather than Holofernes' coinage for the primary or first ventricle of the brain.

(C) Vicary calls the *pia mater* the "meeke mother" and explains its function (1587, C4r–v). Both Hoeniger (1992, 151) and Crane (2001, *passim*) discuss the delicate covers of the brain and its nerves.

pigeon-liver'd See also **lily-liver'd, milk-liver'd, white-liver'd** When Hamlet complains that he is "pigeon-liver'd, and lack[s] **gall**" (*HAM* 2.2.577), he refers to the belief that the gallbladder was the seat of **choler** or anger and that the **liver** was thought to transform chyle (made from digested food) into **blood**. The timid bird was thought to lack gall or choler altogether, and a liver lacking blood would necessarily be pale and pigeon-colored, its owner pusillanimous. See Browne (1646, O3r); Hoeniger (176, 1992).

pills See also **drug, medicine, physic, potion** (A) A concentrated amount of a therapeutic substance, macerated and rolled into a ball and sometimes combined with oil, vinegar or some other ingredient in order to make it hold its shape, to be swallowed whole.
(B) Proteus teases the **love-sick** Valentine, "When I was **sick**, you gave me bitter pills, /And I must minister the like to you"; just as Valentine had mocked Proteus for his love for Julia, so he will now chide Valentine for his love for Sylvia (*TGV* 2.4), a true **Galenic** prescription of bitter or harsh medicine to counteract the sweetness of love. After his involuntary ducking in the Thames, the chilled Falstaff complains, "my belly's as **cold** as if I had swallowed snowballs for pills to cool the **reins**," a reminder that pills were larger than the capsules or tablets we consume today.
(C) The bitterness of pills was proverbial; preacher William Loe tells readers in his preface that beauty is a "bitter pill lapt in sugar" (1614, B2v). **Physicians** might try to conceal the harsh taste of a herb with sugar or honey. Bullein's *Bulwarke* (1579, I2r) describes the manufacture of pills made with vinegar: "if the sayd rootes be fyrst steeped in strong [V]ineger and beaten in a morter, and small round pilles made of them, putting them into the mouth, they wil . . . ease the **tooth ache**."

pin and web see **web and pin**

piss see **urine**

plague See also **bubukle, contagion, infection, pestilence** (A) Plague can mean generally any troublesome or epidemic **disease**, but most frequently alludes to *Yersinia pestis*, or bubonic plague, now known to have been transmitted to humans from fleas borne on rats. The Great Plague (now usually called the "Black **Death**," after a nineteenth-century treatise) ravaged Europe between 1347–51, killing one half to one quarter of the population. Sixteenth- and seventeenth-century outbreaks were less devastating, but still serious enough that during Shakespeare's lifetime, the plague epidemics in London in 1593 and 1603 closed down the theaters and public gathering places by royal order, to prevent contagion. Plague manifested in sixteenth-century London as a **fever**, followed by the development of buboes, black spots that rapidly became swollen and purple, especially in the areas of the **groin**, neck, and armpit. The patient's **pulse** was **faint** and thready, his **urine** malodorous; death was likely within a week, although some folk died even before they developed the characteristic "tokens" or buboes of plague (we might now diagnose such sufferers with septicaemic plague, transmitted directly to the **blood** by a flea-bite, known to be 100 percent fatal).

Plague victims mainly had their own sinfulness and God's justifiable wrath to blame, but many learned **physicians** thought that the 1603 epidemic had been caused by the conjunction of **Saturn** and Jupiter in the constellation of Sagittarius. Other causes included bad air (a sudden change in temperature or humidity; **fumes** from dead bodies or battles, fogs, and fens); a **diet** that caused repletion or excessive fullness; poverty (since the poor were overcrowded in their houses, and overworked, the argument went, they were congenitally prone to spread infection); animals, especially pigs, dogs, cats, and weasels ("suffer no dogges to come running into your houses," warned the Royal College, 1636, A6v); and eclipses of the sun and moon. Rats and mice fleeing houses *en masse*, abandoning their young, often heralded an imminent epidemic. Prophylaxis was one's best hope, but patients who succumbed might be purged and then bled, depending upon their **humoral** constitutions. The best prevention was to avoid the company of the infected, and ideally, to leave the city, although some felt that this course was un-Christian (wives and children might be sent away, but citizens ought to remain, lest civilization itself collapse).

Until the sixteenth century, English authorities had not quarantined sufferers, but in 1578, Queen Elizabeth and her Privy Council issued a set of orders commanding every parish council to appoint the persons who would become known as "plague-searchers," to investigate the causes of death in all corpses and to report back to the churchwardens. The Worshipful Company of Parish Clerks kept registries of burials and employed these searchers, usually women, to go into houses and diagnose and quarantine the sick or even entire houses. The searchers reported back to the clerks who then kept records of the causes of death and, in particular, how many had died from plague. The searchers were to earn a salary during times of plague so that they did not need to consort among healthy people, since they were routinely exposed to the plague. If the searchers found plague in a house, they had the authority to seal up the house and its inhabitants for up to six weeks. Those who had to leave their sick-houses to tend to animals were required to wear clothing with a special mark or to carry a white rod as a warning to others; those who lived in densely populated areas were to be guarded by watchmen to make sure no-one left the house. Sick-houses were to be marked with a cross (white, or, by 1603, red) or other mark; sometimes the words "Lord have mercy upon us" were written beneath the sign on the door. The plague orders also enjoined churchwardens to employ persons to deliver food to the infected poor quarantined in their houses; these compassionate visitors were also to quarantine themselves, or wear a mark on their upper garments and to carry a white rod when in public. Victims who succumbed to the disease were to be buried in a separate area of the churchyard, after sunset but still during daylight; their clothing was to be burned, and their families recompensed for the loss of their goods, to encourage compliance.

Moreover, the presses were to print lists of the dead and of advice from the physicians on how to protect oneself from the plague. Controversially, the orders prohibited churchmen and lay-preachers from preaching sermons against quarantine or for claiming that none would die except at the hour appointed by God and that therefore such protective measures were vain and worldly. The plague orders threaten such preachers with imprisonment, but make clear that "for Christian charity" no persons were to be left unaided for want of means or fear of infection.

The College of Physicians recommended, in addition to the quarantine measures imposed by the plague orders, the use of "spiritual **medicines**," especially humility. Some physical remedies might nonetheless prove helpful. Sage, **rue**, elder-leaves, red bramble and **wormwood**, pounded together, strained and put into white wine and vinegar with a quarter-ounce of ginger, might protect someone who took a spoonful of the mixture every day, for up to a year. **Perfumes** such as frankincense, juniper, dried rosemary, and bay-leaves purged infection from noisome air when burned on a charcoal fire; cut onions placed on the floor of an infected house might draw contagion from the air in a house, and could then be buried deep in the ground. It was also important to wash clothes frequently and to dry them in the sun or over a charcoal burner. A prophylactic diet included sorrel in vinegar (sorrel and lily root could also be made into a plaster); drinking small ale, and **milk** in which garlic had been steeped; and chewing **angelica** root or cinnamon. If one succumbed despite these measures, adding a **compound** of betony-water and scabious-water, along with treacle, to the sage-and-rue mixture might expel the poison, together with the topical application of elder-leaves, red bramble, and mustard-seeds upon the bubo. A hot loaf placed on the sore ripened it marvelously, but it was important to bury the loaf deep within the ground, since a stray dog consuming the loaf could subsequently infect very many. In the last stage, palliative measures included laying rags steeped in **breast milk** and *aqua vitae* on patients' foreheads to help induce **sleep**, and offering fevered sufferers buttermilk to drink. But the physicians' recommendations begin and conclude with spiritual exhortations, testifying to their acknowledged powerlessness in the epidemic.

(B) Shakespeare's characters employ plague as an expletive; as an exaggerated term meaning "to trouble" or "to hurt"; as a synonym for any kind of disease that causes marks upon the skin; as the vengeance of Providence or some higher power, sometimes marked by celestial catastrophes such as planetary conjunctions; in various figurative ways, such as "the monarch's flattery" (Sonnet 114) or, more commonly, **love-sickness**; and sometimes to refer to bubonic plague. Falstaff curses, "a plague upon" Bardolph, Peto and Poins (*1H4* 2.2.20); "A plague of all cowards" upon Hal when he thinks mistakenly that the latter has failed to appear at Gadshill (2.4.114); "what a plague call you him?" he asks with regard to Owen Glendower (2.4.339). Hotspur curses "a plague upon" whatever name, term, or map he happens to have forgotten (*1H4* 1.3.243; 3.1.5). Monarchs and nobles frequently compare war to a plague, presumably because of the high mortality of both. Clarence, regretting his treachery to his brother, threatens to attack Warwick like a persistent disease if the latter continues with his plans: "I will meet thee, if thou stir abroad—/To plague thee for thy foul misleading me" (*3H6* 5.1.96–7). "We will plague thee with incessant wars," York warns Reignier (*1H6* 5.4.154). Queen Margaret compares Gloucester to an epidemic scourge: "Thou wast born to be a plague to men" (*3H6* 5.5.28).

Occasionally, however, plagues are sent by the heavens rather than engineered by men. Volumnia curses the tribunes with "the hoarded plague o' the gods," their stored-up ills (*COR* 4.2.11) and tries to threaten her son into compliance, warning him that "the gods will plague [him]" before she sinks to her knees (5.3.166). Silvia believes that "heaven and fortune still rewards with plagues" inopportune or forced marriages (*TGV* 4.3.31). Ulysses observes that "plagues and . . . portents," heavenly phenomena, appear together when "degree" or rank is overthrown (*TRO* 1.3.96). Sonnet 14 lists "good or evil luck /. . . plagues . . . dearths, or seasons' quality" (14.4) among the items that some kinds of "astronomy"— though not the poet's—can predict. Claudius figures himself and Gertrude as two **planets** whose conjunction, though inevitable, could prefigure either

> My virtue or my plague, be it either which:
> She's so conjunctive to my life and soul,
> That, as the star moves not but in his sphere,
> I could not but by her.
>
> (*HAM* 4.7.13–16)

The Ptolemaic spheres were solid, crystalline balls nested inside one another and bearing the stars, planets, moon, and sun. Claudius and Gertrude are in this figure not merely planets whose spheres happen to correspond at a particular time; Claudius is transfixed by Gertrude as a planet in its sphere, and she is fundamental to his existence.

LLL and *AWW* both figure love as "a plague /That Cupid will impose for . . . neglect /Of his almighty dreadful little might" (*LLL* 3.1.201–3). Cupid seems small and helpless, yet he is mighty and dreadful, awe-inspiring. Biron compares his love-struck friends to plague victims and Cupid to the plague-searchers:

> Write, "Lord have mercy on us" on those three;
> They are infected; in their **hearts** it lies;
> They have the plague, and caught it of your **eyes**;
> These lords are visited; you are not free,
> For the Lord's tokens on you do I see.
>
> (5.2.419–23)

Cupid, the searcher, writes the warning upon the three lords that they have caught the plague of love from ladies' eyes. Having been "visited" by the searcher, Cupid, they are no longer at liberty to wander freely, since they have the marks of love/plague upon their bodies and must remain in quarantine or prison. "God's tokens" or "the Lord's tokens" were common terms for the buboes of plague (see, for example, Lodge 1603, B2v). Helena in *AWW* imagines both love and plague as fatal:

> The ambition in my love thus plagues itself:
> The hind that would be mated by the lion
> Must die for love. 'Twas pretty, though [a] plague,
> To see him every hour.
>
> (1.1.90–3)

"Ambition" is presumably her dangerous aspiration to a lover of higher rank than a "poor physician's daughter (2.3.123)." She is the hind or doe, passive, herbivorous prey of the royal lion that will mate and then eat her. The incongruous juxtaposition of "pretty" and "plague" testifies to the disease's ubiquity in early modern life and its passing into "dead" metaphor. Venus imagines Adonis' breath to be so sweet and healthful that "the plague is banish'd by [his] breath" (510), a reference to the supposed ability of fragrant herbs and perfumes to drive out sickness.

Plays notably concerned with plague include *ROM*, whose plot is arguably concluded by it and that literalizes the curse that Mercutio utters thrice, "a plague on both your houses" (*ROM* 1.3.91, 99, 106); *1H4*, in which Falstaff frequently employs the term as an expletive; *TIM*, in which both plague and syphilis function as figures for deceit and corruption; *TRO*, in which, as in *TIM*, plague and venereal disease are connected as punishments for hypocrisy and sexual licentiousness; and *LR*, in which the king appears to conflate **pox** and plague in his famous curse against Goneril:

> But yet thou art my flesh, my blood, my daughter;
> Or rather a disease that's in my flesh,
> Which I must needs call mine: thou art a boil,
> A plague-sore, an embossed **carbuncle**,
> In my corrupted blood.
>
> (2.4.241–5)

Goneril is the bubo, the plague-sore, part of his body and yet erupting outside it with infection or disease. The plague is both intrinsic to him ("my flesh") and something apart, that penetrates from without, "a disease that's in my flesh." Some readers find in Lear's plague-references allusions to inherited sexually transmitted infections such as syphilis, which Lear could have transmitted to his daughters (as Henry VIII was rumored to have transmitted to his). A figurative notion of inherited plague runs through Constance's angry tirade against Elinor in *JN*:

> I have but this to say,
> That he is not only plagued for her sin,

> But God hath made her sin and her the plague
> On this removed issue, plague for her
> And with her plague; her sin his injury,
> Her injury the beadle to her sin,
> All punish'd in the person of this child,
> And all for her; a plague upon her!
>
> (2.1.183–90)

Constance imagines Elinor suffering from pox, a punishment from sexual sin that is passed on to the next generation (her son) and the next (her grandson, Constance's son Arthur). Her sin becomes Arthur's injury (figuratively, her disease; in the play, literally her sin in denying Arthur's right to the throne). His injury is her injury because of their blood-relationship; she is punishing herself. Her injury becomes the "beadle" or warden who drags the pox-ridden sinner off to the **'spital-house** (as Doll Tearsheet is carried away by the Beadle in *2H4* 5.4). Arthur is the innocent scapegoat of the sins of his elders, a role he sustains throughout his imprisonment and attempted blinding.

(C) Primary records include the so-called plague orders of 1578; Kellwaye's prescriptions (1593); the recommendations of the College of Physicians from 1604 (Royal College, *The King's Medicines for the Plague*, pub. 1636); Dekker's diatribe against those who fled the city (1603); Lodge's account of plague's symptoms (1603). Slack (1985) is the foremost historian of plague in early modern London; Greenberg (2004) argues convincingly that the first public health document printed in London is a bill reporting the numbers of persons sick from plague. Wallis (2006) discusses the controversies over whether doctors, magistrates, and other professionals ought to leave the city or stay to help. On the dating of the plague orders, see McKeithen (n.d.). On Shakespeare and Shakespeare's London, see Barroll (1991), who examines the impact of plague epidemics upon Shakespeare's writing process in the Stuart plays; Healy (2003), who examines the tension between emergent germ-theory and Galenic humoral theory; Grigsby (2004), who argues that the lower mortality rate (in comparison to the "Black Death" of the Middle Ages) from plague in the sixteenth century allowed the authorities to focus upon person-to-person and human-animal transmission for the first time; and Totaro (2005), who reads *TIM* as an allegory of the ineffectiveness of gold or wealth in plague-time.

planet, star (A) Early modern doctors, like their medieval predecessors, believed that the heavens influenced human health and well-being. The heavens began exercising their influence even before birth, forming the child in the **womb** and continuing to affect the preponderance and balance of **humors** within the body. Unusual celestial activity heralded outbreaks of **pestilence** (usually **plague** or smallpox). The moon altered the workings of the mind (by moving the **brain** upwards toward the top of the skull when it waxed, and down toward the base of the skull as it waned) and could cause what we still call **lunacy**. Different planets ruled different **complexions** or humoral temperaments, with the **sanguine**

temperament ruled by Jupiter, the **melancholic** by **Saturn**, the **phlegmatic** by the Moon or by Venus, and the **choleric** by Mars. Moreover, different constellations governed corresponding parts of the body: Aries ruled the head, Taurus the neck, Scorpio the genitals, Pisces the feet, and so on. **Blood** could only be let at certain times of the year, and that time of day varied according to the zodiacal sign of the patient to be bled. Astrological medicine did have its critics, but these mostly complained about the inaccuracy of ephemerides or natal charts and the impossibility of ascertaining which specific heavenly body had triggered the particular ailment the patient presented. Skeptics might offer naturalistic explanations for plague's following a comet (such as the theory that the comet dried out and heated the earth to excess), but did not usually question that such a connection existed.

Later occultists practiced Paracelsian astronomy, which was slightly different in its intents if not in its tables. Astronomy (knowledge of the macrocosm), virtue (the moral character of the healer and the power or strength of the purest form of a substance), **alchemy** (the chemical refinement of pure substances from nature), and natural philosophy (experimental investigation of **cures**) provided the foundation for all Paracelsian cures. Astronomy enabled the physician to find not only the signature that corresponded to a particular **disease** (and hence to its cure) but also to treat *arcana* or astral bodies (see **alchemy**, **Paracelsus**).

(B) Shakespeare's planets control human impulses and render people susceptible to diseases of both mind and body. The strongest statement about the influence of the planets on human health comes from Shakespeare's Ulysses, who always has an ulterior motive:

> The heavens themselves, the planets and this centre
> Observe degree, priority and place,
> Insisture, course, proportion, season, form,
> Office and custom, in all line of order;
> And therefore is the glorious planet Sol
> In noble eminence enthroned and sphered
> Amidst the other; whose **medicinable eye**
> Corrects the **ill** aspects of planets evil,
> And posts, like the commandment of a king,
> Sans cheque to good and bad: but when the planets
> In evil mixture to disorder wander,
> What plagues and what portents! what mutiny!
> What raging of the sea! shaking of earth!
> Commotion in the winds!
>
> (1.3.85–99)

Ulysses argues that once we remove rank or "degree" as a fundamental organizing principle for society, all morality and institutions break down, just as the earth and its people suffer when the sun can no longer gaze with "medicinable eye" to counteract the "evil mixture" of disordered or **distempered** planets. The sun's gaze functions as a healthful antidote to the perilous **compound** put together by the other heavenly bodies, which can lead to plague and other illnesses, heralded by enskied "portents" such as eclipses (as in *LR* or *MAC*) or comets.

Marcellus associates the influence of the planets with occult magic when he praises Christmas Eve for its power against any "planets, . . . fairy . . . [or] witch" that may "strike" (*HAM* 1.1.162). Caius Martius earned his laurels—and his sobriquet—when he "struck /Corioli like a planet" (*COR* 2.2.114). Exeter in *1H6* 1.1.23 blames the "planets of mishap" for King Henry's **death**, and Bedford's prayer to the dead Henry V is interrupted in a most untimely way by a messenger:

> Henry the Fifth, thy ghost I invoke:
> Prosper this realm, keep it from civil broils,
> Combat with adverse planets in the heavens!
> A far more glorious star thy soul will make
> Than Julius Caesar or bright—
>
> (*1H6* 52–6)

Henry's ghost, however, proves ineffective against the deadly **wounds** that the body politic will sustain during his son's reign. In *2H6*, Queen Margaret claims that the "lovely face" of Henry VI has ruled her like a "wandering planet" but now cannot change the course of other bodies (4.4.16). Henry VI is not the royal sun (or son) that can control lesser satellites and wield influence over them (it is instructive to contrast him with Prince Henry in the second tetralogy, who explicitly imagines himself as the "sun" hiding behind "base **contagious** clouds" that he can chase away whenever he wishes) but a planet that moves, like the moon (also associated with weakness and changeability). Cleopatra emphasizes her readiness for death by insisting, "the fleeting moon /no planet is of mine" (*ANT* 5.2.240–1). Jealous Leontes blames a "bawdy planet" for what he thinks is his wife's infidelity, a corruption from birth for which there can be "no **physic**" (*WT* 1.2.201, 200). Hermione believes instead that it is now that "some ill planet reigns" and that the cureless **sickness** Leontes has identifies lies in himself rather than in her (2.1.105). Titania blames the moon's **raw** humors for creating sickness in human beings (see discussion under **rheumatic**).

There is evidence that astrological medicine, like uroscopy, encountered some skepticism in the late sixteenth century. Some of the plays mock characters who appear to believe that their fates—or their health—are determined by the stars. Sir Toby compels Sir Andrew to "cut a caper" and demonstrate his "back-trick" by arguing (disingenuously) that **Taurus** rules "legs and thighs" (see discussion under **Taurus**; *TN* 1.3.121, 123, 140). Helena first suggests that her love for Bertram is as hopeless as if she were to love "a bright particular star" (*AWW* 1.1.86) but then later takes courage and avers, "Our remedies oft in ourselves do lie, /Which we ascribe to heaven" (1.1.216). Edmund insists he would have been the same kind of person whether he had been born under the sign of Capricorn or the goat, notorious for lewdness

(Moulton 1561, D7v), or under "the maidenliest star in the firmament," that is, Virgo, the virgin, and takes advantage of his father's gullibility to trick him into suspecting Edgar (*LR* 1.2.132). Edgar himself is surprised to hear his half-brother profess a belief in astrology, asking him, "Do you busy yourself with that?" (1.2.142). On the other hand, Kent, Lear's honest follower, blames "the stars" for his former master's fall (4.3.32), and the Prologue to *ROM* presents the lovers as "star-crossed" (Pr. 6; perhaps another instance where plague intervenes in the plot, since epidemics routinely followed unusual or alarming celestial phenomena).

(C) Moulton's popular *Mirror of Helthe* (1561, C4r–E1v) gives astrological signs for the days of the week, seasons, and months of the year, and hours of the day, and offers a kind of zodiacal guide to health, going through each sign and detailing its characteristics and incipient maladies. Brasbridge (1578) argues that outbreaks of plague have little or nothing to do with the stars, and Stubbes (1583) includes astrology as one of the "abuses" of six-teenth-century England that he anatomizes. Parson-physician Timothy Bright warns us that the efficacy of **medicines** depends upon the patient's age and constitution but also upon the "time of the yeare" (1615, B2r). Chapman (1979) is essential reading and lists the almanacs and astrological manuals published in the early modern period in English, discusses the "considerable degree of skepticism . . . although qualified" in the period, and notes that astrological theory, charts, and so on appear in dedicated treatises rather than in medical books of the era (279, 283). Briggs (1962) considers astro-logical medicine in light of folk therapies and belief in magic rather than as part of a learned tradition. Both Siraisi (1990) and Hoeniger (1992) explain the origins of astrological medicine in Arabic and classical sources; Siraisi is especially helpful on the transmission and dissemination of astrology in West-ern Europe. See also Siraisi's essay in Newman and Grafton (2001) on the medical astrologer Girolamo Cardolano, and the other essays in Newman and Grafton's volume; Kassell's biography of famed London astrologer, medical man, and playgoer Simon Forman (2007); and Marion Gibson's forthcoming "Shakespeare's Demonology."

plantain (A) Neither the tropical, fruit-bearing tree, not the broad, spreading Mediterranean shade-tree, but a low-growing English herb with flat, wide leaves like the sole of the foot (hence its name), plantain was thought to be good for salving **bruises**, stanching bleeding, and for driving out **infections** from **ulcers** or dog-bites.

(B) Shakespeare's two references allude to both the plantain's salvific and antidotal properties:

> Benvolio: Tut, man, one fire burns out another's burning,
> One pain is lessen'd by another's anguish;
> Turn **giddy**, and be holp by backward turning;
> One desperate grief **cures** with another's languish:

> Take thou some new infection to thy **eye**,
> And the rank poison of the old will die.

Romeo:	Your plantain-leaf is excellent for that.
Benvolio:	For what, I pray thee?
Romeo:	For your broken shin.

(ROM 1.2.45–3)

Benvolio may recommend a **Paracelsian** homeopathy to cure Romeo's love for Rosaline: one fire will burn out another, turning around will cure dizziness, and one infectious agent will drive away any existing toxins. Or he may imagine "backwards turning" to be a **Galenic** remedy to cure a vertigo induced by forward motion. Romeo's response is obscure. Benvolio asks, "Are you **mad**?", but Romeo may mean that, while Benvolio has enough medical knowledge to dress a minor scrape, he cannot minister to a **heart**-rending disorder such as Romeo's love. Alternatively, there may be a piece of stage business here, with an irritable Romeo attempting to kick Benvolio in the shin or trip him up; or Romeo might be suggesting that a new infection is as inadequate to minister to his disorder as a plantain-leaf dressing would be for a fractured bone (though this is not the usual meaning of "broken shin").

In *LLL*, 3.1.70, Shakespeare engages in bilingual punning as Costard demands for his own broken shin "no l'envoy, no l'envoy; no **salve**, sir, but a plantain!" Don Armado cannot believe that Costard has confused the l'envoy, the motto or, as Armado says, "epilogue," with the Latin greeting "salve" and then in turn with the healing salve that comes from a plantain. Initially Armado is amused, even to the "heaving of [his] **lungs**" with "enforc[ed] laughter" from the **spleen** (evidently his **melancholy** is the kind that provokes merriment, or "melancholy adust"). Eventually, however, even Armado tires of the punning, calling for "no more of this matter." Poor Costard, who never did get his plantain, observes: "Till there be more matter in the shin," that is, they will talk no more of it until his **wound** becomes infected and produces pus or matter.

(C) On plantain as a salve for wounds, see Gerard (1597, Y1v–Y6r); on its use against rabies, see Dodoens (1595, N2r–N6r).

plaster See also **cataplasm, poultice** (A) A dressing applied to a **wound**, sore, or **ulcer** to soothe it, keep it clean, and close it. Plasters could be made of almost any herb, grain or other **medicine** and then made to adhere to the wound. Some plasters were intended to draw out poison from the wound.

(B) Martius curses, "Boils and **plagues** /Plaster you o'er" as part of his vehement litany of the **contagions** or **diseases** of the south (*COR* 1.4.31–2), calling for boils and boil-causing plagues to cover his enemies thickly as a dressing. The good old lord Gonzago chides Antonio and Sebastian with augmenting, rather than relieving, Alonso's grief: "you rub the sore, /When you should bring the plaster" (*TMP* 2.1.139–40).

A longer passage in *JN* evokes the plaster's utility in bringing infected matter out of a wound. Salisbury tells Lewis upon the conclusion of peace:

> I am not glad that such a sore of time
> Should seek a plaster by contemn'd revolt,
> And heal the inveterate canker of one wound
> By making many.

> (*JN* 5.2.12–15)

Historical wrongs had created a sore or ulcer that required a plaster or bandage to help it heal and draw out the **canker** or hidden poison within, but in this case the prescription of war cured the single wound but made many more.
(C) Every surgeon had his favorite prescriptions for plasters: for a typical description and recipes, see Lowe (1634, 444–7).

pleurisy see **plurisy**

plurisy (A) Plurisy or pleurisy was an often deadly **inflammation** or **imposthume** either between two ribs or above the diaphragm, on one side of the body. The symptoms of pleurisy had been known since **Hippocrates** and **Galen**: sufferers experienced a sharp pricking or stabbing pain when they talked, breathed, or **coughed**; ran a high **fever**; were short of breath; coughed frequently, and often had a headache; and their **pulses** beat intemperately, without a regular rhythm or strength. The characteristic pricking pain came from the hot impostume or **ulcer** pressing on the ribs or diaphragm. Putrefying **blood** or other **humors** that were stuck between the **heart** and **lungs** produced a fever that endangered the heart itself, since the heart could no longer manufacture the spirituous, pure blood necessary for all bodily functions and to preserve life itself. **Patients** suffered shortness of breath because their windpipes, throats, and **nostrils** were filled with thick, "filthy" or corrupt humors that prevented the air from getting through; they coughed because the lungs themselves were painful, narrowed, or even blocked. Since the flow of **spirit** was blocked, and the blood could not diffuse nourishment to the rest of the body, the pulse beat irregularly, increasing in speed and force as the patient grew sicker.

Bloodletting was the surest **cure** for pleurisy, since it emptied out any corrupted humors quickly, and cooled down the **heat** of a fever (other therapies included hot fomentations, and wet- or dry-cupping with the **surgeon's box**). It was important to know the temperament of the patient and to diagnose the correct form of pleurisy (from the color of the **urine** and the spittle) so that blood could be let from the correct **vein**. Patients needed to avoid **perturbation** or strong emotions such as fear, anger, or anxiety, because they either drew too much blood to the heart from the **liver** (in the case of fear) or sent too much blood away from the heart to the liver (in the case of anger). If the body did not naturally **purge** itself after phlebotomy, physicians needed to administer a **clyster** to encourage defecation.

(B) Shakespeare refers twice to pleurisy, once in *Hamlet* and once in *TNK*. Claudius urges Laertes to avenge his father quickly, arguing that delays from "goodness, growing to a plurisy, /Dies in his own too much . . . then this 'should' is like a spendthrift sigh, /That hurts by easing" (*HAM* 4.7.117–23). If Laertes hearkens to his qualms, they will prevent him from taking action until the action itself will cause more pain, just as in the pleurisy sighing or breathing, although required by the body for "easing," uses up or spends the blood and "hurts" even as it brings air into the lungs. In *TNK*, Arcite prays to Mars for Emilia's love, invoking him as the deity "that heal'st with blood /The earth when it is sick and cur'st the world /O' the pleurisy of people" (5.1.64–6). Furness and several early commentators (including Coleridge) thought that Shakespeare must be using pleurisy to mean "plethora" or too much blood (1905), but it seems more likely that he was aware of bloodletting as the standard therapy for pleurisy (in both *HAM* and *TNK*) and of the typical pain experienced on breathing (in *HAM*; see Jenkins' Arden edition, 1982). The god of war purges the world of the superfluous populace through the **deaths** of soldiers in battle just as the physician purges the pleuritic body of corrupt humors through bloodletting.

(C) Bullein (1562) offers a detailed regimen against the pleurisy, including a recipe for the relatively unusual **medicine** delivery device of a lollipop or "lohoch" made of acacia, white sugar-candy, maidenhair **syrup**, white **poppy**, and licorice: "mingle all together, and put them in a close potte, or a glasse, then make cleane a Liqueris sticke, and put into it the same stick and licke of it often tymes" (D8r). The treatise is also notable for its compassion for the poor and Bullein's insistence that he writes in order to deliver the impoverished from the unlicensed practitioners who kill them with misguided care.

pomander, nose-herbs See also **cloves**, **fume**, **perfume** (A) Since bad air and foul smells carried **disease** and **infection**, walkers protected themselves, especially while traveling, by inhaling the aroma from a pomander, a box or bag of fragrant nose-herbs (plants grown for their aroma and medicinal value, such as oranges, roses, myrtle, aloes, cloves, nutmeg, and cinnamon) to be carried in the hand. Later, the term was applied to the gold or silver ball used to contain the herbs, and, in the twentieth century, to an orange or lemon stuck with cloves and used as a decoration or as *pot pourri*.

(B) Disguised as a pedlar, Autolycus includes pomanders in his pack (*WT* 4.4.598), perhaps hoping to hawk them to unsuspecting country folk as tokens of courtly sophistication. Lafew irritably corrects the Clown in *AWW*: "They are not herbs, you knave; they are nose-herbs" (4.5.19). A courtier would know the difference between plants prized for culinary use (and grown for economic and practical reasons) and those for fragrance (cultivated for luxurious sophistication).

(C) Early modern instructions for making pomanders abound; see, for example, Goeurot (1550, P2v); Ruscelli (1558, P1r–v); Lodge (1603, C3v–C4v).

poppy (A) Known since classical times for its soothing effect, wild poppy flower in a **compound** was considered **cold** in the fourth degree and used in early modern **medicine** to digest **choler**, to promote **sleep**, calm St. Anthony's fire (shingles), and to lighten heavy menstrual periods. Cultivated white poppies were used for a variety of ailments, but were particularly helpful when juiced and made into opium suppositories for dysentery or belly **flux**; as **simples** to treat mastitis in **nursing** women, to relieve pain and to induce sleep; and compounded to treat **consumption**. Opium, made from black poppies, was considered dangerously soporific, and the strongest sleeping-draught prescribed was *Trifera*, a compound of black poppy and **mandragora**.

(B) Iago seems to refer to the compound of *Trifera* when he gleefully comments of the newly jealous Othello,

> Not poppy, nor mandragora,
> Nor all the drowsy **syrups** of the world,
> Shall ever medicine thee to that sweet sleep
> Which thou owedst yesterday.
>
> (*OTH* 3.3.330–3)

Opium was also used to treat the **falling sickness** or **epilepsy**, from which Iago later claims Othello suffers. Iago lists the ingredients of the physical world in order to imply that Othello's pain is supernatural in origin and can have no earthly **cure**. He may also be mocking Othello with the phrase "syrups of the world," suggesting that although Othello's origins, like many of the ingredients for new medicines, are exotic, his travels and his rareness cannot save him from Iago's machinations.

(C) Ascham (F7v–8r, 1561) suggests a **plaster** made of **breast milk**, white poppy seed, and egg-white, applied to the temples to induce sleep. Bullein (1579) refers throughout to the uses of the different kinds of poppy (see esp. E1v–E2r for general use; 3D4v for suppositories; 3Ar for its use to treat epilepsy; 3E4v–3E5r for poppy with mandragora). On medicine in *Othello*, see Lux (2002); Moss (2004); Neely (2004); Paster (2004a).

potato Probably the sweet potato, thought to incite lust if consumed. Thersites imagines the "devil Luxury, with [a] fat rump and potato-finger" (*TRO* 5.2.55–6) salaciously watching the amorous Troilus and Cressida, and Falstaff, too, exploits this connotation when, awaiting what he thinks will be an erotic tryst with Mistresses Ford and Page, he calls, "Let the sky rain potatoes!" (*WIV* 5.5.19). Hall (H7r, 1613) lists potatoes along with **eringoes** as "dishes of lusts devising"; Holinshed (P5r, col. 1, 1587) calls it a "venerous root"; see also Fitzpatrick (81–104, 2007) on the confusion among yams, sweet potato, and white potato in the period.

'pothecary see **apothecary**

potion (A) Therapeutic **compound** in liquid form to be taken orally, often of doubtful, dangerous, or **purgative** effect.

273

(B) Shakespeare's potions are often poisons, causing or imitating **death**. Friar Laurence confesses to drugging Juliet with a "sleeping potion" (*ROM* 5.3.244) that does indeed prove mortal, though through indirect means rather than by poisoning her at once. Camillo contrasts "rash potion[s]" that kill at once to "lingering **dram**[s]" that mimic **sleep**, commenting that he could provide the latter except that he is convinced of Hermione's innocence (*WT* 1.2.319, 320). Hamlet forces Claudius to consume the poison intended for himself with the words, "Drink off this potion" (*HAM* 5.2.320). Prince Hal compares Douglas's martial wrath to a "poisonous potion" (*1H4* 5.4.56) against the health of his declining father. Pericles accuses Helicanus of "speaking like a **physician**" in offering him words of counsel that are a "potion . . . that" he would "trembl[e] to receive" himself (*PER* 1.2.68). The sonnet-speaker of 119 drinks "potions . . . of Siren tears / **Distill'd** from **limbecks** foul as hell within" (*SON* 119.1–2) love-medicines that seem attractive and yet whose disgusting origins derive from the sulphurous **heat** of damnation.

Many of Shakespeare's potions are **purges**, so violent in their action that the takers fear their effects. The Host in WIV jokes about the readiness of physicians to administer such purges when he praises "his doctor" Caius for giving him "the potions and the motions" (*WIV* 3.1.102) the laxatives that induce defecation. Men who "drink potions" (*2H4* 1.1.197) are "divided" like rebellious soldiers, comments Morton: they act as if against their will, because the action is so unpleasant. Sonnet 111 offers to consume "potions of eisel" (*SON* 111.10–12) or vinegar, renowned for its bitterness, in order to "correct correction" if his friend wishes it. Similarly, with the **love-in-idleness** upon his **eyes**, Hermia appears as a "hated potion" (*MND* 3.2.264) to Lysander rather than the wholesome food she was to him before.

(C) Ruscelli (1558) routinely refers to "potion or drinke" (B1v, B2r). The idea of the "bitter potion" that works a **cure** appears frequently in sermons as a figure for remorsefulness; Joseph Hall (1609) refers to the "bitter potion of vinegar and **gall**" offered to Christ in his sermon on Good Friday and accuses sinners of making Christ drink such a preparation anew when they fail to worship him (E2v). Willet (1611) comments upon St. Paul's skill in the epistle to the Romans in compelling his audience to listen to his chiding words by beginning with praise, "like as Physitions do anoin[t]e the lippes of the cup, which containeth the bitter potion, with honie" (2P5r).

poultice See also **cataplasm, plaster** An application either emollient or irritating, depending upon the ailment it was used to treat, usually made with warm or hot water and some herb or grain, put on a painful or **fevered** body part to relieve symptoms and then covered with muslin or soft cloth. Note that, unlike the plaster, which is similar, the poultice is usually applied to closed **skin**, not to an open **wound**. Shakespeare's figurative use is one of the earliest in written English. Juliet's Nurse, teasing her by withholding her good news, jokes of her charge's impatience, "Is this the poultice for my **aching** bones?" (*ROM* 2.5.63), one of several references in the play that emphasize the Nurse's age relative to the youth of both Lady Capulet and Juliet herself. Recipes for poultices abound in the medical literature of the period: see, for example, those in the diary of

John Hall, Shakespeare's son-in-law (1679) although John Hall usually prefers the term plaster, even for an application to unbroken skin.

powdering-tub see **tub-fast**

pox See also **infection, plague, bone-ache, nose, tub-fast** (A) Pox in the period can refer either to any infection causing pock-marks or scarring, such as small-pox, or to sexually transmitted infections such as gonorrhea and the infection usually transmitted through sexual contact or *in utero* now known as syphilis but called in the Renaissance the great, French, or Spanish pox. (The name syphilis was coined in 1530 by the Italian physician Girolamo Frascatoro in his long poem, *Syphilis, sive Morbus Gallicus*, but does not appear in English until 1718.) Syphilis began with single or multiple chancres or sores upon the genitals, which if untreated progressed to joint pain, **fever**, a rash (hence the name pox), and baldness. After a latency period, the final stage (now called tertiary syphilis) could include the collapse of bodily cartilage, including the bridge of the nose; impotence; blindness; numbness or paralysis; insanity, and ultimately **death**.

Sexually transmitted infections challenged the **humoral** belief that illness marked an internal imbalance, both because they were so clearly the result of person-to-person transmission, and also because they were considered unknown in Europe until an epidemic among German troops in Naples in 1494. Folklore held that the **disease** came from the New World, brought back by Christopher Columbus, and that it ravaged Europe in the trail of mercenaries and the prostitutes or camp-followers who accompanied them. (The disease's origins are still mysterious; current evidence suggests that the disease was in fact known in the premodern Mediterranean, but was misidentified as **leprosy** in Europe.) Each country blamed its neighbor for the **sickness**. Thus syphilis was called the French disease in Italy, but the Italian disease in France, and the Neapolitan, Spanish, or French disease ("**malady of France**," in Shakespeare, *H5* 5.1.82) in England.

Although **physicians** and lay-people knew the great pox had an infective component, they identified the sharing of **linens**, cups, and bathwater, as well as sexual contact, for the disease. The victim also endured a fair amount of opprobrium, since the pox punished sin, whether pride, blasphemy, or (after Frascatoro's poem) sexual intercourse. Women were especially at fault in transmitting the pox, since it could be generated spontaneously from semen from different men in a single **womb**, and through the **milk** of an infected **nurse**. Consequently, religious writers began a campaign in the seventeenth century to encourage well-to-do mothers to breastfeed their own children rather than relying on wet-nurses. But the single most important factor in contracting the pox was **heat**. The hotter one's constitution, the more likely one was both to acquire and to transmit it, because a hot **complexion** burned or made "adust" black and yellow **choler** (**melancholy** and choleric **humors**) and **phlegm**, any of which alone or together burned and dried the **skin**, filling it with **scabs**. Sometimes the **blood** itself became burnt or adust and, having dried, turned into swollen, knobby joints and corrupted the **liver**. Treatment for the French pox included the

tub-fast or **powdering-tub**, the application of mercury (see **quicksilver**), and the resin of the guaiacum tree, or *lignum vitae* (wood of life) taken as a medicine, or the bark ground up into chips and made into a **decoction** or tea.

(B) Pox in Shakespeare is most frequently an expletive, sometimes with a sexual connotation (as in Prince Hal's mocking question, "What a pox have I to do with my hostess of the tavern?" [*1H4* 1.2.46], which implies that having "to do with" the hostess sexually would have infected him with the pox), and sometimes not (as in Sebastian's tirade, "A pox o' your throat, you bawling, blasphemous, incharitable dog!" [*TMP* 1.1.29–30]). Other examples of the first, sexually allusive epithets include Bertram's grumpy asides in *AWW* (4.3); Lucio's untimely unmasking of the Duke, whom he calls "bald-pated" as he declares "a pox to you!" (*MM* 5.1.374); Mercutio's opprobrium toward "fashion-mongers", "The pox of such antic, **lisping**, affecting fantasticoes; these new tuners of accents!", a diatribe that ends with an apostrophe to "their bones," implying that they will suffer from the joint pain of tertiary syphilis (*ROM* 2.4.28). Falstaff jokes, of this tendency to take pox as an expletive, "A pox of this **gout**! or, a gout of this pox! For the one or the other plays the rogue with my great toe" (*2H4* 1.2.243–4) Falstaff would be a prime candidate for both gout and pox, associated as he is with high living and sexual incontinence. We see Mistress Quickly dragged off by the beadles to the **'spital** for the mercury-cure in *2H4*, and in *H5* Pistol mourns for his "Nell . . . dead i'th'spital of a **malady of France**" (5.1.82).

Qualtiere (2003) points out that the following speech in *TIM* is almost an exact catalog of the progress of syphilis, as Timon urges the prostitutes to take their revenge upon mankind:

> **Consumptions** sow
> In hollow bones of man; strike their sharp shins,
> And mar men's spurring. Crack the lawyer's voice,
> That he may never more false title plead,
> Nor sound his quillets shrilly: hoar the flamen,
> That scolds against the quality of flesh,
> And not believes himself: down with the nose,
> Down with it flat; take the bridge quite away
> Of him that, his particular to foresee,
> Smells from the general weal: make curl'd-pate
> ruffians bald;
> And let the unscarr'd braggarts of the war
> Derive some pain from you: plague all;
> That your activity may defeat and quell
> The source of all **erection**.
>
> (4.3.165–79)

"It is all here—high fevers, falling **hair**, **ulcerated** lesions on the vulva, collapsed nasal cartilage, erectile dysfunction—the complete catalogue of disgusting syphilitic symptoms" (Qualtiere 2003, 18).

Pox clearly refers to the smallpox, rather than the so-called great pox, in *Love's Labor's Lost*, as part of the exchange of insults between Rosaline and Katherine. When Princess and Katherine mock Rosaline for her complexion dark as "ink," "like a text . . . in a copybook," she responds that, if her face is like black print, Katherine's pockmarked one is like a book with red letters: "O that your face were not so full of Os!" to which Katherine retorts, "A pox of that jest!" in either a crestfallen allusion to her encounter with the disfiguring disease, or a light-hearted brushing-off of Rosaline's barb (5.2.41–6).

(C) Primary sources in addition to Frascatoro include Clowes (1579), who claims to have cured more than 1,000 patients with quicksilver within the space of five years in St. Bartholomew's hospital, and who identifies a rotten liver as the ultimate cause of the disease; Hutten (1533) on the usefulness of Guaiacum; and of course multiple accounts of the mercury-cure (see **tub-fast**). Useful secondary sources include Fabricius' now-standard account of *Syphilis in Shakespeare's England* (1994); Healy (2001); and Harris (2004) on emergent Paracelsian understandings of infectious disease; Grigsby (2004); and historian Kevin Siena, who writes about the sufferings of the poor in particular (2004). Physician John Ross speculates that Shakespeare himself suffered from the disease, as do Fabricius and others (2005).

pregnant See also **brain**, **womb** (A) With the potential to give birth to ideas, off-spring, wealth, argument, attention; full of ideas; ready to learn or to hear or conceive new ideas.

(B) Shakespeare never uses the term "pregnant" to describe a gestating woman: instead, pregnancy in Shakespeare indicates the gestation of possibilities. "How pregnant sometimes his replies are!" exclaims Polonius of Hamlet's antic witticisms, which seem full of a certain logic (*HAM* 2.2.209). Courtiers "crook the pregnant hinges of the knee," their joints too apt to kneel for the possibility of preferment (*HAM* 3.2.61). Pompey anticipates dissension between Octavius and Antony, but hopes for the "pregnant" or potential peace between them (*ANT* 2.1.45). Edmund tricks his father into believing Edgar's guilt by encouraging him to think of an eldest son's incentives to have a father killed, those "pregnant and potential spirits" such as inheritance (*LR* 2.1.76). But Edgar is "pregnant" only "to good pity" (4.6.223), not to covetousness. "The Grecians are most prompt and pregnant" to battle (*TRO* 4.4.88).

In other instances, pregnant almost takes on the status of a transferred epithet, since female characters who might be fertile or pregnant are instead—for various reasons—kept barren. Disguise as Cesario hides Viola's "pregnant enemy" or the devil, since it leads her into falsehood (*TN* 2.2.28). Cesario hopes that Olivia's "**ear**" will be "pregnant" to his proxy wooing (3.1.89). Imogen misidentifies Cloten's headless corpse as her husband's and calls it "pregnant, pregnant" (*CYM* 4.2.325). Iago convinces Roderigo that Desdemona's chastity is "pregnant and unforced"—that is, full of possibility and with no rules restraining it, and therefore hopeful to his suit (*OTH* 2.1.236). Dionyza hires "The pregnant instrument of wrath" to kill Marina, the murder gestating unseen in her mind prescription

(*PER* 4.ch.44). The Third Gentleman who describes the recognitions at the end of *WT* wonders at the confluence of coincidence, as if "truth were pregnant by circumstance," a reminder of Hermione's pregnancy at the beginning of the play and Leontes' haling her from her **childbed** (5.2.30). Finally, another play in which a pregnant woman's body triggers a criminal suit describes not the woman but the man trying her as "pregnant." Vincentio describes Angelo as suitable for office because he is "pregnant" in the nature of the people; he has been gestating his dissatisfaction with Vincentio's leniency for years (*MM* 1.1.11). Angelo himself imagines a thief tempted by riches, or any sinner, unsympathetically: " 'Tis very pregnant, /The jewel that we find"—temptations are everywhere (2.1.23).

(C) Crane (1998) argues that both men and women may be "pregnant" in Shakespeare, cognitively receptive to new ideas in a characteristically embodied way. Thoughts and babies were each conceived in organs nourished by **phlegm** and enlivened by spirit or semen.

prescription See also **apothecary** (A) Instructions for manufacturing and consuming a **medicine** recommended by a **physician** to a **patient**. The patient took the prescription to an apothecary, who **compounded** the **drugs** and sold them to him or her. Prescriptions (also known as **receipts** and abbreviated "Rx" for the Latin *recipere*, to take), were written in Latin, so that physicians and apothecaries all over Europe could read them; for similar reasons, they employed the apothecaries' system of weights and measures, in which a "grain" (0.65g) was the same as a "troy" grain (in the jewelers' system of weighing precious metals) and the same as in what would later be called the "avoirdupois" system (1 pound in the avoirdupois system equals 0.45359237 kg or 1.22 apothecary pounds). A **scruple** was twenty grains, and a **dram** was three scruples.

(B) Helena claims to have inherited from her father, the eminent physician Gerard de Narbon, "some prescriptions /Of rare and proved effects" (*AWW* 1.3.221–2). Menenius finds the news of Martius' victory more invigorating than "the most sovereign prescription in **Galen**" (*COR* 2.1.116). Falstaff refuses to follow the "prescriptions" of the Lord Chief Justice (*2H4* 1.2.129), but Buckingham grudgingly concedes to Norfolk, "I'll go along /By your prescription" against an excess of **choler** (anger) or **gall** (*H8* 1.1.150–1). Rodrigo offers to incontinently drown himself at Desdemona's lack of interest, only to be dissuaded by Iago, although he still insists: "It is silliness to live when to live is torment; and then have we a prescription to die when **death** is our physician" (*OTH* 1.3.308–9). In Sonnet 147, "reason" provides "prescriptions" to love (see discussion under **fever**). Warwick uses the term figuratively to counter Oxford's championing of Henry VI's claim to the throne. Henry's track record (having "lost /All that which Henry Fifth had gotten") makes his reign "a silly time /To make prescription for a kingdom's worth" (*3H6* 3.3.93–4).

(C) Wecker recommends a "dietarie prescription" in his "book of **ulcers**" (1585, V2r). The term "prescription" (as opposed to, say, "receipt") appears more frequently in the "chemical" or **Paracelsian** tracts, such as Du Chesne (1590,

N1r), perhaps leading to Cotta's exhortations against "rash prescription[s]" in favor of "prudent" ones (1612, C1r, B4r).

prodigy See also **monster** In routine use, any strange phenomenon, such as an eclipse, or a comet; also used to mean an unusual birth, as in the title of surgeon Ambroise Paré's book, translated as part of the English edition of his *Workes*, "Of Monsters and Prodigies" (1634). Queen Margaret calls Richard of Gloucester the "valiant **crook-back** prodigy," an omen of ill (*3H6* 1.4.75). Richard II's Queen compares her grief to a prodigy or **deformed** child born in "woe" (*R2* 2.2.64; see discussion under **midwife**).

prunes, stewed See also **Abhorson**, **abortive** Stewed prunes were associated with brothels, perhaps because they were provided as a snack on the tables within and possibly placed in the windows as a sign to passers-by. Known as a laxative from ancient times, they were also thought to help with throat ailments, to prevent **humors** from descending too low in the body, to **cure** rashes in children, and other ills. *MM* features a "dish" of stewed prunes in the window of the house called upon by Mistress Elbow (2.1.92–100). Shakespeare also associates stewed prunes with Falstaff at his most gluttonous and lustful. "There's no more faith in thee than in a stewed prune," he complains about the Hostess (*1H4* 3.3.112–13), and he himself is described as living upon "mouldy stewed prunes and dried cakes" (*2H4* 2.4.147), for which he jokingly offers "three veneys," or thrusts with a fencing foil, in *WIV* 1.1.285. Gerard (6K2v–4v, 1633) describes the plant and the fruits' consumption by children, and Elyot their laxative effect (C6v–C7r, 1539). Ascham (N1r, 1561) recommends prunes for **tertian agues**, against **choler**, against **jaundice**, and to stimulate the appetite. DiGangi (1993) suggests that they were a known abortifacient in the period, presumably because of their laxative effect.

P's see **urine**

puking See also **vomit** Jaques describes the newborn baby "mewling and puking in the **nurse**'s arms" (*AYL* 2.7.144), wailing and "spitting-up" or vomiting small amounts of curdled **breast milk**. Goeurot and others invariably blame the quality of the nurse's milk for the "sickenesses of tender babes" who are unable fully to concoct or digest it (N1v, 1550). Paster (1993, 218) speculates that nobly born babies, sent away to nurse and denied their mother's colostrum (thought to be unhealthy) right after birth, were more likely to suffer from gastric pain or infant reflux, that is, to "puke."

pulse See also **heart** (A) Pulse is an early modern synonym for **artery**, although Shakespeare does not use it in this sense. **Physicians** could use the pulse in the wrist to identify a person's **complexion** or **humoral** personality as well as to diagnose illness. The health of the heart and the throbbing of the pulse were closely associated. The pulse beat in the arteries according to the expansion and contraction of the heart, which grew larger when it needed to attract useful matter from the **blood**; remained clasped shut when it needed to consume the blood it had attracted; and contracted when it needed to send out what was left over (called "superfluities" or **excrements**, sometimes in liquid form and sometimes as **fumes** or **vapors** sent to the **lungs** to be expelled via the breath). The heart also dilated and contracted according to various **perturbations** or emotions: joy opened up and expanded the heart, increasing the supply of **heat** and vital spirit to the whole body, including the **brain**, while fear and sorrow and shock shrunk the heart, depriving life-force from the face (making it pale), the brain (causing **swooning** or **faintness**), and the extremities. **Fever**, excitement, and passionate love (including **madness** induced by **love-sickness**) made the pulse throb quickly and hard; fear and horror made it thready and weak; and **death** stopped the pulse altogether.

(B) Shakespeare's characters use the pulse to diagnose ailments or to prove their own physical and mental health. Hamlet uses the steady beat of his pulse to convince Gertrude that he is neither mad nor feverish: "My pulse, as yours, doth temperately keep time, /And makes as healthful music" (*HAM* 3.4.140–1). Troilus connects the quick pulse of fever and the rapid heartbeat of love as he awaits Cressida: "My heart beats thicker than a feverous pulse" (*TRO* 3.2.36). When the Courtesan diagnoses Antipholus of Syracuse with an "**ecstasy**" of madness, **apothecary** Pinch attempts to verify the symptom ("Give me your hand and let me feel your pulse" *ERR* 4.4.52), only to have Antipholus threaten to box his ears instead. That **anatomy** or skull-face, Pinch, "with no face," Antipholus relates later, "feeling my pulse /. . . Cries out I was possessed" (5.1.244–5). The Countess grabs Helena's wrist in order to diagnose her love-sickness. "Daughter and mother /. . . strive upon [her] pulse," she notes (*AWW* 1.3.168–9), and concludes that the war between Helena's filial love for the countess and her urge not to be designated Bertram's "sister" indicate: "You love my son" (*AWW* 1.3.173). Friar Lawrence clearly connects the existence of the "pulse of life" (*JN* 4.2.92) to vital force. The **potion** he gives Juliet will remove her vital heat, shrinking the heart so that "no pulse /shall keep his native progress, but surcease" (*ROM* 4.1.96–7). Conversely, the presence of a pulse proves to fathers who believe themselves bereaved that their children are alive again, and no ghosts: "Have you a working pulse?" Pericles poignantly demands of Marina (5.1.153), and Alonso wonders to Ferdinand, "thy pulse /Beats as of flesh and blood" (*TMP* 5.1.113–4). Airy sprites such as Ariel lack human blood and pulsation, hence Ariel's use of the pulse as a measure of human time: "I drink the air before me, and return /Or ere your pulse twice beat" (5.1.102–3).

(C) Elyot (1539) outlines the diagnostics, and the basic schema is repeated in later manuals. The pulse beat strongly and regularly in a **sanguine** temperament; slowly and faintly in a **phlegmatic**; strongly and quickly in a **choleric**; and faint and fluttering in a **melancholic**.

pulsidge Mistress Quickly, full of medical malapropisms, calls Doll Tearsheet's quick **pulse** her "pulsidge" and praises its **temperality** (another nonce-word, for "temperance") and Doll's flushed face when a truly temperate pulse would beat evenly, not "extraordinarily" and a temperate woman's face would blush red and white rather than remaining "rose"-red from drinking (*2H4* 2.4.23).

purgation, purge See also **blood, clyster-pipe, humor, potion, puking, sweat, vomit** (A) A purge or evacuation corrected a body either of plethora—too much blood in the body, often caused by repletion or over-fullness from eating or scant exercise—or of cacochymia, too much of one particular humor in the body (often also caused by **diet**, exercise, weather, the wind, and **complexion** or humoral personality). Such imbalances could cause **disease** and discomfort in the body, and purgation was the body's first line of therapy in any disease. The body purged itself naturally, through for example the menstrual **flux** in women, which corrected the plethora or overload of healthy blood that women needed to maintain in order to nourish a fetus. Sufferers of a head-cold naturally purged the **brain** of excess **phlegm** through nasal mucus. Overeaters vomited or voided by siege (seat, that is, by diarrhea) their excess. Sometimes, however, natural purging did not suffice to correct the humoral imbalance in the body. In such cases, **patients** experienced particular diseases in body parts, such as the **pin and web** in the **eye**, or full-body symptoms such as **quotidians** or **scurvy**, and healers would be required to purge or evacuate patients through non-natural means. Shakespeare's line in Sonnet 118 is perhaps the best summary (*SON* 118.4): "We sicken to shun **sickness** when we purge." Non-natural purges included remedies that functioned as laxatives; diuretics; emetics; sudorifics; expectorants; suppurants; caustics, and the procedure of phlebotomy (in other words, medicines that made patients defecate, **urinate**, vomit, **sweat**, **cough** and **neeze**, or sneeze, fester, **scar**, and through a procedure that drew from them blood). Physicians could administer purgative medicines orally as **pills**, boluses, drinks, **syrups**, **decoctions** or teas; rectally as clysters or pessaries; superficially as **plasters**, **poultices**, or **cataplasms**; internally as ointments or unctions. Most commonly, however, purge refers to an emetic, taken by mouth, or to a laxative, also taken orally. It can also refer to a whole course of diet and clean living, or "regimen," as in the title of several popular books on health and medicine.

(B) In several places Shakespeare deploys purging as a figure for clearing one's name or relieving one's feelings by words, as if speaking is compulsive and spasmodic, like vomiting. *2H6* imagines a crime that may be purged with words (3.1.135). Prince Hal begs to extenuate himself and to purge the crimes of which he is accused through his urgent flow of words (*1H4* 3.2.20). Aufidius accuses Martius of wishing to "purge herself [the city] with words" (*COR* 5.6.8); this play contrasts the laudable bloodshed of war with the ignoble and involuntary purging of logorrhea. King Henry VIII offers Cranmer the chance to purge himself of the crimes imputed to him (*H8* 5.1.102). Friar Laurence "stand[s], both to impeach and purge" himself, to blame and to clear himself of murdering the lovers (*ROM* 5.3.226).

Elsewhere, purges remove people, objects, or humors that are either unwanted or unnecessary, or in the wrong place. Titania offers to "purge [Bottom of his] mortal grossness" and to leave him an "airy spirit" (*MND* 3.1.160–1). *2H4* includes the Archbishop of York's lengthy metaphor comparing the state of the kingdom to a diseased body with a "burning **fever**" (see discussion under **tertian**) that needs the "obstructions" in the veins to be purged by bloodletting (that is, by removing the lords who are preventing his access to the king, (4.1.56–66). Henry IV himself chides Hal with wanting to "purge [neighboring regions] of their scum," and to invite all lazy wretches in the kingdom to the court after the king's **death** (*2H4* 4.5.123). Gloucester and Henry VI vie for the role of physician. Henry VI blames "black despair" for crime and calls on God to purge the **melancholy** that he imagines has caused it. Gloucester, however, appropriates a tenet of **Galenic** medicine—that opposites cure each other through contraries—by prescribing the death of King Henry VI as a **cure** to "purge [Edward's] fear" (*3H6* 5.6.88). Richard II wishes to "purge this **choler** without letting blood" (see **blood** for discussion, *R2* 1.1.153). The French in *H5* long to purge their country of the English, their "hilding foe" (see discussion under **vapor**; 4.2.29). Mark Antony attempts to reconcile Cleopatra to his leaving Egypt by comparing the civil broils in Rome to a diseased body attempting to cure itself: "quietness, grown sick of rest, would purge /By any desperate change" (1.3.53–4). A hard-working fisherman wishes he could "purge the land" of the rich misers or "drones" who "rob the bee of her honey," a reference that alludes to honey's laxative effects (*PER* 2.1.46–7). Both Macbeth's enemies and Macbeth himself employ the figure of the purge to discuss Scotland's governance. Caithness, resolved to join the English, tells Menteith, "Meet we the medicine of the sickly weal, /And with him pour we in our country's purge /Each drop of us" (5.2.27–9). Malcolm is the medicine that will heal the commonwealth (with perhaps a pun on *wheal* or injury). The other lords are the drops of liquid that form the purge itself. "Sickly" suggests an emetic, but in the following scene Macbeth argues that the country needs a laxative for purgation. He wishes the doctor could perform uroscopy ("cast /The water") on Scotland, "find her disease /And purge it to a sound and pristine health"; the **drugs** he recommends for this sickened body politic are "**rhubarb** and **cyme** [senna]," known, strong laxatives (5.3.51–2, 55). Sometimes characters imagine themselves undergoing literal purges: Falstaff speaks, tongue-in-cheek, of wanting to purge, and "leave sack, and live cleanly as a nobleman should do" (*1H4* 5.4.164–5).

The air and the words carried by it purges guilt melancholy, and tyranny in *WT*. Paulina uses "words as **medicinal** as true . . . /. . . to purge [Leontes] of that humor /That presses him from **sleep**" because of his guilt at banishing the chaste Hermione (*WT* 2.3.37–9). Autolycus describes the King's change of air as purgative: "he is gone aboard a new ship to purge melancholy and air himself" (*WT* 4.4.763). The fresh air on the new ship may purge melancholy by exposing the king to freshness and cheer to encourage his body to produce less melancholy and more **sanguine** humor. Finally, Leontes himself blesses the young lovers Florizel and Perdita with pure air and a healthy clime: "The blessed gods /Purge all infection from our air whilst you /Do climate here!" (5.1.168–70).

(C) Most of the vernacular medical manuals include justifications and instructions for purging the body through laxatives (purgation by siege), emetics (purgation by vomit), phlebotomy (bleeding), and other means. *The Treasure of Pore Men* (1526) tells readers how to purge the head and **wounds**. Guy de Chauliac (Chauliac 1542) explains the efficacy of purging with phlebotomy (bloodletting), ventousing (dry-cupping; see **surgeon's box**), or **leeches**. Bullein (1558) offers purges for each of the various humors that may be in excess in the body. His verses aver that only humans cannot vomit up their excess as animals do, making people dangerously apt to "repletion" or over-fullness and testifying to the necessity of artificial or medical purging for the stomach and other organs:

> Beastes and foules, of nature rauenous,
> . . .
> Consum[e] by glottonie, many a creature,
> Yet eche of theim, according to their nature[,]
> Can purge their Cruditie, with casting venomous[:]
> Man through replecion, is in daunger parelous.
> (Bullein 1558, A5v)

Ruscelli (1569, C2v and *passim*) includes many recipes to purge the "matrix" or **womb**. Paster (1993) identifies the role of purging, bleeding, and other means of letting out the body's fluids in constituting gendered subjectivity in early modern England. Saunders (2004) analyzes Iago's "excremental" language in *OTH*. Several critics discuss what has become known as "Shakespeare's purge of Jonson," after early modern journalist Thomas Nashe's obscure reference, and suggest that this "purge" is Shakespeare's *TRO* or another play; see Bednarz (2001).

qualm See also **stomach-qualmed** Trembling, **faintness**, nausea, from fear or foreboding (as in present-day usage), or love. The Duke of Gloucester is struck by a "qualm . . . at the **heart**" that "dim[s his] **eyes**" when he reads the letter announcing the marriage of Henry VI to Margaret (*2H6* 1.1.54–5). Physiologically, he quails when **blood** rushes to his heart suddenly (removing blood from his **brain** and thus precious eye-spirit from his eyes, depriving him of vision) in order to encourage him at these ominous tidings. When Katharine boasts of her conquest of Longaville, "Trow you what he called me?" the Princess retorts, "Qualm, perhaps . . . go, **sickness** as thou art" (*LLL* 5.2.279–80), mocking the symptoms of love that mimic the nausea of food-poisoning or **sea-sickness**. Margaret similarly equates **stomach**-sickness and love-sickness when she mischievously recommends *carduus benedictus* to Beatrice, "the only thing for a qualm" (*ADO* 3.4.75).

quat A pimple or pustule. When Iago gloats that he has rubbed that "young quat [Roderigo] almost to the sense" (*OTH* 5.1.11), he compares the young man to a "whitehead" whose "head" has been chafed nearly to the point of removal.

quick, quickens, quickening See also **pregnant** (A) A quick child is alive and kicking in the **womb**, while a quick woman has conceived and is nurturing an infant *in utero*. Quickening is the term used to describe the moment at which the soul entered the fetus in the womb (thought to coincide with the mother's first sensation of its kicks).
(B) "Quick bright things come to confusion" in *MND* (1.1.149) in Lysander's analogy to lightning. Lightning, like quickening, is sudden, brilliant, and mysterious. When Angelo realizes that Vincentio, urged by Isabella and Mariana

284

on bended knee, will pardon him, there appears "a quick'ning in his **eye**" (*MM* 5.1.405) to mark his return to life, a particularly apt image given the play's focus on fecundity and conception. A reference in *TIM* (4.3.184) forms part of a sustained metaphor about birth:

> Common mother, thou,
> Whose womb unmeasurable, and infinite **breast**,
> Teems, and feeds all; whose self-same **mettle**,
> Whereof thy proud child, arrogant man, is puff'd,
> Engenders the black toad and adder blue,
> The gilded newt and eyeless venom'd worm,
> With all the abhorred births below crisp heaven
> Whereon Hyperion's quickening fire doth shine;
> Yield him, who all thy human sons doth hate,
> From forth thy plenteous bosom, one poor root!
> Ensear thy fertile and conceptious womb,
> Let it no more bring out ingrateful man!
>
> (4.3.177–88)

Fire commonly figures in Shakespeare that which quickens or brings to life, either through the sun's **heat** or through the bodily heat of conception. Like "the fire that quickens Nilus slime" (*ANT* 1.3.69), the sun generates all sorts of creatures from mud, including the poisonous snakes and creepy-crawlies that Timon compares favorably to "ingrateful man." Like a human mother, the earth provides the mettle or matter, the **raw** material, of conception, and, like a human father, the sun forms and enlivens the offspring. In Aristotelian terms, heat was essential for conception, but Timon calls for the sun to overheat or parch the earth so that human conceptions can no longer take place, because all human births are "abhorred" (with a pun on the homonym "whored"), the products of venal sexuality.

Bertram in *AWW* attempts to woo Diana by alluding to the "quick fire" (4.4.5) in her eye, again as part of a pattern of metaphors of conception throughout the play. Diana puzzles the King by referring to Helena's supposed **death** but actual pregnancy: "Dead though she be, she feels her young one kick: /So there's my riddle: one that's dead is quick" (5.3.301–3). Both Helena and her fetus are alive or quick, revived and vivified by the bed-trick. Jacquenetta in *LLL* is similarly "quick" with "the child [that] brags [leaps] in her belly already" (5.2.676). *LLL* presents another child as quick, this time in his wits: Moth (whose name can mean "mote," or speck, that is, a small object) is "quick" as an eel in his responses to Armado, who is sluggish with **melancholy** (1.2.29).

To touch or **tent** to the quick is to probe a **wound** until a living **nerve** shudders with pain. Claudius calls Hamlet's return the "quick o'the **ulcer**," the sharpest pang (4.7.123). At least pain proves that life exists; Hamlet contrasts the earth's life-giving qualities with the deathly embrace of the grave when he chides the grave-digger, "'tis for the dead, not the quick," "a quick lie" detected by the grave-digger and a phrase echoed again by Laertes as he leaps in his sister's grave and bids the onlookers cover with dust "the quick and the dead" (*HAM* 5.1.126, 128, 251). Not to be outdone, Hamlet joins in to be "buried quick" with an Ophelia who may herself have been quick with life (5.1.279).

(C) Bicks (2006) comments upon the early modern connection between fetal kicking and quickening, while Crane (2001) documents the common language used of the "quick" or lively **brain**, since both brains and wombs share a fertility to conceive.

quicksilver See also **tub-fast** (A) Quicksilver is mercury in its liquid state, also used to prepare cinnabar or mercury sulphide, which sublimed when heated and was used in the tub-fast or **powdering-tub** (also called the sweating tub). Mercury formed one of the three fundamental **Paracelsian** principles (the other two being **salt** and sulphur, or **brimstone**) and a controversial **cure** for the French **pox** and other sexually transmitted **infections**. Although ancient Arabic **physicians** had recommended mercury-cures for sexually transmitted **infections**, **Galen** himself had not used it, and many early modern physicians preferred to treat their **patients** with guaiac wood or *lignum vitae*. Authorities even disagreed on whether quicksilver was **cold** or **hot**. Quicksilver was known to be a poison; it ulcerated the **gums**, head, and **skin** of the body during the treatment for venereal **disease**. Early modern healers were unclear *why* quicksilver worked, but they were certain that it *did* (presumably it killed the bacillus that caused syphilis, even when applied topically in the lesions). Moreover, untreated pox was so serious that even desperate cures were preferable to none.

(B) The Ghost of Old Hamlet alludes to quicksilver's swiftness and mortal venom when he compares the effect of the juice of **hebona** inserted in his ear to the introduction of quicksilver into the body:

> swift as quicksilver it courses through
> The natural gates and alleys of the body,
> And with a sudden vigour doth posset
> And curd, like eager droppings into **milk**,
> The thin and wholesome **blood**: so did it mine;
> And a most instant **tetter** bark'd about,
> Most **lazar**-like, with vile and loathsome crust,
> All my smooth body.

(1.5.66–73)

The "gates and alleys of the body" figure the king's body as the body politic, invaded by something alien to it in an ambush. The scale on his body resembles the **scabs** and scaling resulting from the mercury treatment, like the peeling bark of a tree, or milk curdled by lemon juice or sudden heating, or the pustules of **measles** (tetter), or the scabs of syphilis or pox, which were often confused with the "vile and loathsome crust" of **leprosy**. Old Hamlet emphasizes the speed of the attack, "swift," "sudden," and "instant" in its execution. Similarly, Falstaff complains about the celerity of Hal and Poins' escape: "the rogue fled from me /Like quicksilver" (*2H4* 2.4.229).

(C) Paracelsus had argued that quicksilver was hot and **moist**, as evidenced by its natural flow, where other metals required fire to melt, but royal **surgeon** George Baker advocates for its use in part by asserting its coolness, in an appendix to Clowes (1596, Ffv). Clowes, Paré and other renowned surgeons swore by the efficacy of quicksilver, and pointed out that despite what Baker calls "that cruel qualitie," it was easily as effective as other equally "cruel" medicines then in use, such as **poppy**, **mandragora**, or henbane and that, like "bread and meat," it was wholesome in small amounts but dangerous in vast ones; it was all about the handling (Clowes 1596, Ffr; see also X4v). Ironically, Paracelsus himself wrote *against* the indiscriminate use of quicksilver in curing syphilis; he called such treatments "horse cures" and complained about the Fuggers of Augsburg who held the monopoly on guaiac imports from the New World and profited from such useless treatments (Pagel 1982). The Paracelsian John Hester disseminated Paracelsus' writings about the mercury-cure for syphilis in English and warned surgeons against heating the mercury too greatly. Hester returns to Paracelsian theory in arguing that the mercury needed to be purified first and then to be heated only enough to make it "attractive" or to draw out the disease of mercury (the pox) from the body, not to produce the **fumes** that proved poisonous to so many (Paracelsus 1590, B1v–B3r; see also Du Chesne, 1591).

quintessence (A) Quintessence is both an ancient **alchemical** term for the heavenly matter supposedly concealed in even all earthly things, and a **Paracelsian** term for the **distilled** essence or **tincture** of some substance, usually used therapeutically. Sometimes it refers to *aqua vitae*, the distilled alcohol used medicinally to revive the **faint**, clean **wounds**, and dissolve **medicines**. Philosophically, quintessence comes to mean the purest form of a thing, or a pattern for all others, the sense in which Shakespeare uses it in *AYL* (3.2.139).

(B) Orlando's overblown paean to Rosalind claims that her name itself teaches readers to understand her as the repository for the most perfect "faces, **eyes** and **hearts**" of the world, the Platonic perfection of femininity. Hamlet famously calls the human being a "quintessence of dust" (2.2.308), alluding to the Genesis creation story that derives man from the earth. For **melancholic** Hamlet, the quintessence is not spiritual but earthly matter.

(C) Gesner offers instructions for drawing out the quintessence or refined form of anything by dissolving it in the quintessence of wine (that is to say, in *aqua vitae*) and then parching it in the sun or heating it over a fire (1559, D1v–D3r, pp. 99–101), and for purifying the quintessence of alcohol, water, or dew (1576 E2r–E3r, pp. 26–8). On the metaphor of dust throughout *Hamlet*, see Reno (1961).

quotidian See also **ague, tertian** (A) A quotidian was a **fever** (elevated body temperature) that spiked once a day, usually in the evening, accompanied by chills, shivering, and **aches** and pains. A temperature sufficiently high might provoke a fit or paroxysm once a day. Patients ran such fevers in order to burn off too much of a particular **humor** (plethora), especially **phlegm**, or to expel corrupted phlegm from the body. Once the fever broke, the patient **sweated** copiously and produced phlegm or other secretions as a sign that the body had used up its excess nourishment and was ready to balance itself once more. Women, the elderly, and fat children were most susceptible to quotidians, because they were either innately **cold** and **moist**, or, in the case of children, although naturally **hot**, their passages were stopped up and they were unable properly to concoct the food that they consumed. Early **cures** included **plantains** and **fennel**, and ferns were helpful in cooling the fever and preventing fits, as was fly agaric (which we know today as a toxic hallucinogen). If oral medicines did not stop the fits, a **purge** of the whole body through emetics such as cassia might be necessary to expel the excess phlegm, after which the physician could apply **plasters** of **nettles**, morels and cobwebs under the arms. If the paroxysm persisted, patients might take **breast milk** from a woman nursing a male child, pieces of wall-wort dried in wine, or hares' **liver**, or asses' **blood** mixed with wine. Paré, however, preferred to make his patients vomit not only with agaric but also with treacle dissolved in *aqua vitae* (1634, Bbr).

(B) As Ganymede, Rosalind diagnoses Orlando's versifying as the "quotidian of love," an unremitting **love-sickness** manifesting as the daily fever to produce verses (3.2.365). Orlando agrees that he is indeed "love-shaked," trembling and pale as if from feverish rigors (3.2.367). Mistress Quickly diagnoses Falstaff with a typical malapropism, the nonexistent "burning quotidian tertian" (*H5* 2.1.119). A tertian **ague** included a fever that spiked every other day (every three days, counting inclusively), so Falstaff could not suffer from both a quotidian and a tertian at the same time. Quickly may also be confused by the existence of "quartan" agues, illnesses in which a fever spiked once every four days (again, counting inclusively, that is, every seventy-two hours). Or she may be mistaking the so-called "double tertian," which spiked every day, with the quotidian.

(C) Pope John XII (trans. Lloyd 1553, S1r–S2v) includes a chapter on quotidian fevers; see also Lanfranco (1565, B3r), and Barrough's book on fevers in his *Methode of Physicke* (1583). Paré (1634, Bbr) warns against confusing the "double tertian" with the quotidian; although the patient runs a fever every day in both, the former spikes at noon, the other in the evening. Jarcho (1987) argues that Falstaff could indeed have both a quotidian and a tertian at once.

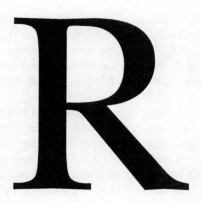

race See also **complexion** (A) Early modern race (here understood to mean perceived bodily differences between groups of persons associated with a particular part of the world) connoted geographical origin, **skin** color, **humoral** complexion, behavior, morality, and many other social as well as medical categories. Heliotropic theories considered the sun (through its tanning rays) to be the sole or chief author of both dark and light skin, and skin-tone the most noticeable mark of differences among the peoples of the world. The sun drew **blood** to the surface of the skin, darkening it with sun-burn and making it **tawny** or tanned. The sun also dried and parched the skin, as it did to the skins of those who tanned leather for a living. The tightly curled **hair** of Africans was likewise thought to derive from the action of the sun's rays in heating the body and making the humor into **fumes** or **vapors**. Climate-theory extended the sun-burn theory to take account of environmental features in addition to the sun, and also integrates humoral theory, connecting dark skin with **melancholy** or black bile, brown or "yellow" skin with **choler** or yellow bile, and fair, blushing skin with blood, the **sanguine** humor, and each with its associated temperament. Sailors who circumnavigated the globe, however, noted that the Inuit at the North Pole bore brown skins despite the sun's absence for six months of the year. Other explanations for variations in physical features and skin color therefore circulated: blackness was the supposed curse of God against Cham, Noah's son, for illicit sexual activity in the Ark; skin might have been darkened or lightened by the exotic cosmetics used by foreigners, and heads and bodily attributes altered by the extravagant swaddling of **midwives.** Such proto-Lamarckian theories of race were perfectly consistent with a humoral **Galenism** in which influence or **contagion** induced corresponding changes in the body, so that merely being in the presence of a particular complexion could trigger an imitative change in an observer. Race, moreover, was overwhelmingly a social or moral category, so that it was possible for black "Ethiops" to be "washed white" by the love of Christ, and for the "black" bride in the Biblical Song of Songs to represent the purified and reformed Anglican church. There are also occasional forays into polygenesis, the belief that black and white peoples descended from two separate origins (rather than both being children of the first man reported in the Bible, Adam), or even from animals.

Sometimes theories of racial difference overlap to provide a justification for emerging economic ventures such as chattel slavery. In the second half of the seventeenth century, New World landowners might combine the Biblical verse that appeared to curse Noah's son Cham with perpetual slavery, a legend that God's curse blackened Cham's skin, and the cult of the "Black Magus" (the belief that one of the three wise men or kings who visited the infant Christ with gifts was a black-skinned African king descended from one of Noah's sons) in order to argue that black Africans were divinely ordained for enslavement. In Shakespeare's time, however, such assumptions are not routine. More typical is **physician** Thomas Browne's statement that black and white skin each represent normal human variation; that human beings share a common ancestor regardless of skin-tone; and that "if we seriously consult the definitions of beauty, and exactly perpend what wise men determine thereof, we shall not apprehend a curse, or any **deformity** [in blackness]" (1646, Vol. 3, p. 245).

(B) Race in Shakespeare is most commonly understood as lineage, the inheritance of qualities and features from parent to child through relationships and heredity, as Hendricks has suggested (1996), through its origins from Latin *radix* or "root." Thus *R3* describes "the happy race of kings" (5.3.151), a family group united by its blood-line or blood-purity; Suffolk accuses Warwick of not belonging to the "Nevils['] noble race" (*2H6* 3.2.215); the ghosts of the murdered princes curse their Uncle Richard with barrenness but bless his opponent Richmond with "a happy race of kings" (*R3* 5.3.152). Marina's pupils are all "of noble race," drawn to her instinctively by her modesty and skill (*PER* 5. Ch. 9). A "race . . . of colts" runs in *Merchant of Venice* (5.1.72, with the pun on "contest" and "tribe"), and Timon detests "the whole race of mankind" (*TIM* 4.1.40), references that appear to ground a particular group as a species. Thus when Prospero suggests that Caliban comes from a "vild race"—he is savage in both his ancestry from Sycorax and in his behavior to Miranda and Prospero (*TMP* 1.2.58)—his vileness or wildness marks both his similarity to the other humans on the island and his radically (or rootedly) different origins. The Roman plays foreground race and skin color as measures of legitimacy in, for example, Antony's complaint that he has forborne "the getting of a lawful race" in his union with Cleopatra (*ANT* 3.13.107) and in the anxiety over the tawny child of Aaron the Moor and the Gothic queen Tamora. Cleopatra asserts her refusal of the Roman color by describing the union of herself and Antony as one that begets indeed a different race—not a debased branch of humanity, however, but "a race of heaven," "parts" or attributes with their roots or origins in Platonic ideals of perfection and that thus generated a love (and offspring) pure and complete in themselves (*ANT* 1.3.37). A more unusual use of the word in Shakespeare is Angelo's giving his "sensual race the rein" (*MM* 2.4.160). Angelo's "race" is his inner nature, his root, that which grows inside him.

Shakespeare literalizes the metaphor hidden in "race" (as "root") in *WT*'s debate on art versus nature. Perdita has refused to grow gillyflowers, because they are cultivated through grafting, through cloning or parthenogenesis rather than through sexual reproduction. Polixenes, amused, retorts

> You see, sweet maid, we marry
> A gentler scion to the wildest stock,
> And make conceive a bark of baser kind
> By bud of nobler race: this is an art
> Which does mend nature, change it rather, but
> The art itself is nature.
>
> (*WT* 4.4.92–7)

Polixenes argues that such grafting is not parthenogenetic but sexual and therefore natural; the "bud" is male, and noble at its root ("race"), and the bark is "baser," and female, impregnated or "ma[d]e [to] conceive" by it. "Bark" connotes "ship" or vessel as well as the outer layer of a shrub or tree, and "mend" means not only "amend" or improve but also alludes to the mechanical process of grafting or tying plants together or of repairing a bark or wooden vessel. Polixenes' metaphor implicitly compares the country girl Perdita, thought by him to be base-born, to the inferior bark, and Florizel to the nobler bud, but she rejects his analogy outright, proclaiming:

> I'll not put
> The dibble in earth to set one slip of them;
> No more than were I painted I would wish
> This youth should say 'twere well and only therefore
> Desire to breed by me.
>
> (*WT* 4.4.99–103)

The dibble is a tool used to plant seeds or seedlings in the ground so they can form roots or races, but Perdita would rather e*radic*ate such blooms, prevent them from rooting, since the union of plants would take place at the level of the bark or stem (the graft) rather than at the root. In other words, Florizel will not elevate her by their union—she is already noble enough to wed him as a peer—and "race[s]" engendered by such grafting are as contingent or false as those skin colors created by face-paint.

(C) Sailor George Best (1598, E2v) expresses his belief that climatological conditions cannot cause blackness, since all shades of skin are found in all sorts of climate-bands. Browne offers a famous argument that black skin demonstrates the mystery and power of God (1646, 245). Fryer (1984) gives a history of black persons in Britain and accounts of early encounters, to a certain extent countering the view of Hunter (1967) and Jordan (1968) that Shakespeare's black characters were based on legend, myth, and folklore rather than upon an actual black presence. Dabydeen, ed. (1985) and D'Amico (1991) look specifically at black or Moorish characters in English literature. Loomba (1989) investigates the interplay among sexuality, race, and gender, in Shakespearean and Jacobean drama, while each of the essays in Hendricks and Parker's edited collection (1994) treats race as an epistemological category to be considered not in isolation but along with other social categories such as rank, gender, nationality, religion, and so on. Kim F. Hall (1995) historicizes the development of whiteness alongside the black presence in early modern literature and culture, especially in writing by and about women. Little (2000) considers the trope of contamination or pollution in cross-race unions in early modern drama, especially in *ANT*. MacDonald (2002) argues that early modern women deployed race and racialized diction for political expediency, authority, and erotic power. Royster reads the "white-lim'd" **cheeks** of Demetrius and Chiron in *TA* as indicators of their Gothic barbarism (2000); Floyd-Wilson discusses what she calls early modern geohumoralism (the cluster of beliefs about climate, **diet**, temperament, and bodily humors) at length and its relation to complexion, nationalism, and skin color in *OTH* (2003); Iyengar (2005) discusses the process of blanching, blushing, and blackened women's faces in *ADO* and the supposed race of Cleopatra in classical sources, early modern stage-plays and *ANT*; Bovilsky (2008) usefully unpacks the associations of Italy with moral and physiological blackness.

ratsbane The mineral poison arsenic, used to kill rats, mice, and other vermin. It appears in Shakespeare as part of genuine curses in two instances, and a feigned one in the other. Falstaff, furious at being denied credit, curses "I had as lief they would put ratsbane in my mouth as offer to stop it with security" (*2HIV* 1.2.42–3), and the French wish that Joan La Pucelle had consumed "ratsbane" instead of mother's **milk** (*1H6* 5.4.27). In his disguise as "Poor Tom," Edgar blames the "foul fiend" who "set ratsbane by his porridge" (*LR* 3.4.55).

raw eyes Eyes swollen, red, and sore from **inflammation** because of unconcocted or raw **humors** that might exude from them as liquid; part of Thersites' list of "rotten **diseases** of the South" (*TRO* Q1 5.1.20).

receipt See also **prescription** A recipe, for food or for **medicine**; a prescription for a medicine; the retort or receiver in **distillation**. Helena puns on the learning she has *received* from her father as also prescriptions: "his good receipt" (*AWW* 1.3.244), or the "Many receipts" she reports she received on his death-bed (2.1.105). Whether or not Helena received these prescriptions or recipes is debatable; the precious "triple **eye**" she stores up may refer to her virginity or miraculous healing powers rather than to a prescription for a particular **medicine**. Gadshill boasts "we have the receipt of fern-seed, we walk invisible" (*1H4* 2.1.87), the first reference to "fern-seed" in *OED* and usually glossed as a magical belief that fern-seed, invisible itself, made those who came into contact with it invisible too. Macbeth imagines reason as the receipt or receiver of memory (see discussion under **limbeck**, *MAC* 1.7.66).

reins See also **kidney** Falstaff complains after his impromptu dip in the Thames that he is as chilly as if he had taken "snowballs as **pills** to cool the reins" (*WIV* 3.5.23) or kidneys, ice to serve as an anaphrodisiac medicament to counteract the **hot** lustfulness of his temperament and to cool his immediate ardor.

rheum, rheumatic See also **catarrh, neeze** (A) The thin, watery, **salty** discharge rheum (also sometimes called a catarrh or a **distillation**) flowed from the head to the **nose**, mouth, or **eyes** of a sufferer from **cold**, old age, or from the otherwise healthy and strong peoples of Belgium and the Low Countries, because of the cold, damp climate that engendered too much **phlegm** in the body. Healthy persons might also suffer from rheums if they consumed too much cold, **moist** food (such as dairy products) or took too little exercise (since activity heated the body and thinned the thick, cold, clammy phlegm into warmer, dryer **blood** or **choler**). The loss of **heat** associated with old age likewise could produce too much rheum in the body, which the body would **purge** from the orifices of the head. Moist, northerly climes, and foggy or cloudy weather might be called rheumatic by association, and the moon was known to draw liquids to the head, causing a cold rheum in susceptible persons (winter was also a season that provoked rheums). The best treatment for a cold rheum was allopathy, or treatment by opposites: consuming a hot, **dry** medicine such as vinegar, breathing in warm, dry air, and drinking purified alcohol or *aqua vitae* (since alcohol warmed the blood). After the first day, the **physician** might provoke sneezing by inserting betony or laurel leaves into the **nostrils**, and encourage the patient to gargle with honey, warm water, and black pepper. By the turn of the seventeenth century, some recommended the inhalation of the new **drug** tobacco to ease the flow of watery rheum from the nose and throat. In cases where a rheum was hot, rather than cold, however, standard **prescriptions** for heating medicaments would only worsen the situation. A mistreated rheum that descended to the **stomach** affected the process of digestion or "concoction," causing foul-smelling breath or **vapors** to ascend to the throat; in the throat, it caused hoarseness; in the nose, polyps or a perceived noxious odor; in the eyes, **pin and web**; in the head, vertigo or **dizziness**, and **epilepsy**. Hot rheums therefore required treatment with medicines that would dissolve the thick **humor** without overheating the stomach, such as white **poppy** or pomegranate or cucumber.
(B) Shakespeare associates the salty fluids of the body—tears, saliva, and nasal mucus—with the rheums that come, according to early modern geohumoralism, from the cold, from the sharp Northern wind, from the moon, from fog, and from old age. Shakespeare's manly warriors and their advocates insist that their eyes do not weep but are instead "troubled with a rheum," as Enobarbus maintains of Mark Antony at the **death** of Brutus (*ANT* 3.2.57). Othello claims to be

troubled with a "salt and sorry rheum" for which he requires Desdemona's fateful handkerchief (*OTH* 3.4.51); he is generating an excuse to borrow her handkerchief (and to test Iago's assertion that she has given it away), but he may also have tears in his eyes from grief and anger at the thought that Desdemona is unchaste. Aufidius contrasts the "cheap" "drops of women's rheum," the tears of Volumnia, with the "blood and labor" of the fighting men whom, he avers, Martius has betrayed by returning to Rome (*COR* 5.6.45, 46). Rheums, tears, and blood were all manufactured in the body and could change into one another under the appropriate circumstances (a theory of interchangeability critics call "fungible fluids"). Aufidius is therefore accusing Martius of effeminacy, of cooling his hot masculine, military blood into womanish, cool, phlegmatic or rheumatic tears through a kind of **contagion** from his proximity to his mother. Aumerle tells King Richard that no tears were shed on the former's behalf; bystanders felt only "the north-east wind /Which then blew bitterly against our faces, /Awaked the sleeping rheum, and so by chance /Did grace our hollow parting with a tear" (*R2* 1.4.8). Even Pandarus, certainly no warrior, disdains to confess to tears, claiming instead "a rheum in [his] eyes too" (*TRO* 5.3.104). Shakespeare indicates both the extent of Hecuba's grief and the old-fashioned diction of the first Player when he uses the already-archaic term "bisson [blinding] rheum," the tears that dazzle the queen's eyes (*HAM* 2.2.506).

Tears could **blind** a sorrowing person by drying out the humors in the eye and making the **eye-strings** crack. *JN* features the rheum of tears as a sign of human sympathy, associated particularly with the boy Arthur and with the organ of the eye when Hubert makes as if to blind him with hot irons at King John's command. Constance realizes that Salisbury is telling the truth about her son's disinheritance by Lewis' marriage to Blanche from Salisbury's expressive visage, full of tears: "Why holds thine eye that lamentable rheum?" she asks (*JN* 3.1.22). Hubert's sympathy for Arthur, his "foolish rheum /Turn[s] dispiteous torture out of door" and makes it impossible for him to blind the boy as John has asked him (4.1.33). Arthur escapes, only to plunge to his **death** from the battlements, his fate unknown to Hubert. Salisbury, however, cannot trust Hubert's honesty, nor his tears, adjuring Bigot and the Bastard, "Trust not those cunning waters of his eyes, /For villainy is not without such rheum" (4.3.108). Hubert's tears are genuine, however, unlike those of the imaginary widow whose sorrowful weeping lasts only "an hour in clamor and a quarter in rheum," more in noise than in feeling, according to Benedick (*ADO* 5.2.83).

Rheum can in expressions of disgust refer to saliva and mucus. The King of France urges his troops to rid the country of King Henry V by an onslaught as fast and fierce as the thawing of snow in the Alps and as malicious as a man spitting upon his social inferior: "Rush on his host, as doth the melted snow / Upon the valleys, whose low vassal seat /The Alps doth spit and void his rheum upon" (*H5* 3.5.52). Shylock gloats at Antonio's request to him by reminding the latter of the times when he kicked and spat upon "the Jew": "You, that did void your rheum upon my beard /And foot me as you spurn a stranger cur" (*MV* 1.3.117). The large lady whose body Dromio of Syracuse describes as like a globe suffers from a prominent chin, like the "chalky cliffs" of Dover although her **skin** is dark, not light, and a "salt rheum" running from her nose as the Channel runs between England and France (*ERR* 3.2.128).

Mistress Quickly, confused about her humors, calls Falstaff and Doll Tearsheet rheumatic when she probably means choleric, or **quick** to anger, since she compares them to hot, dry "toasts," and choler was constitutionally hot and dry in **complexion** (*2H4* 2.4.57). She confuses the word with **lunatic** in *H5*, when she describes the dying Falstaff as "rheumatic, and talk[ing] about the Whore of Babylon" (2.3.38). Titania describes the discord between herself and Oberon as a cosmic catastrophe that upsets the seasons and orders of nature, causing the sun and moon to rise at the wrong times. And when "the moon, the governess of floods, /Pale in her anger, washes all the air," the human consequences of excessive moonlight are "rheumatic **diseases**" (*MND* 2.1.105). Only the young and hot-blooded can withstand the climatic forces that induce too much phlegm or raw humor, as Master Page asserts to Sir Hugh: "youthful still! In your doublet and hose this **raw** rheumatic day!" (*WIV* 3.1.47). Vincentio likewise characterizes "the **gout**, **sapego**, and the rheum" to the doomed Claudio as the disorders of old age that he will escape by remaining "absolute for death" as a young man (*MM* 3.1.31). The disguised Polixenes likewise interrogates Florizel about his secrecy about his love affair with the supposed shepherdess Perdita: "Is [your father] not stupid /With age and altering rheums?" (*WT* 4.4.399).

(C) Lemnius comments on the tendency of the cold and moist constitution (such as the Netherlander's) to suffer from a rheum even when otherwise vigorous, in his chapter on phlegmatic temperaments (1576, O6r). Gesner recommends vinegar, *aqua vitae*, and tansy water to dissolve and melt a rheum (1576). The greatly expanded edition of Elyot's *Castell of Helthe* includes a detailed description of the transformation of phlegm into rheum, the circumstances that can aggravate and alleviate it, and remedies. Elyot cites his personal experience with physicians who wrongly prescribed heating therapies for his hot rheum, and how he was cured only when he "did throw away [his] quilted cap, . . . and onely did lye in [a] thinne coyfe [head-dress], . . . both winter and summer, and ware a light bonet of veluet onely" (1595, Q4r). The *Defense of Tabacco* recommends smoking tobacco to **cure** "rheumaticke **fluxes**" (1602, B2r).

rhubarb (A) Rhubarb, especially taken with senna, purged **phlegm** and **choler** downwards, that is, it was a strong laxative. It was useful in treating **jaundice**, **stomach**-aches, the bloody **flux**, shortness of breath, and against venomous beasts.

(B) Filled with contempt for the Doctor's suggestion that only a spiritual, not a physical, healer can "minister to a mind **diseased**," Macbeth dismisses all **physic** unless a doctor could "cast /The water of my land," diagnose the **illness** from its **urine,** and then administer a strong **purge** or evacuation to remove the disorder and return it to "sound and pristine health" (5.3.50–2). In particular, Macbeth demands bitterly, "What rhubarb, **cyme** [senna], or what purgative **drug** /Would scour these English hence?" (5.3.55–6). If any laxative could compel Scotland to void the English as the body passes waste products, that would be a **medicine** worth taking.

(C) For rhubarb's value to purge choler and phlegm downwards, see Gerard (1597, V6r–7v); Dodoens (1595, 2B5v–6v).

ripp'd see **untimely ripp'd**

rue See also **herb-grace** (A) The **hot** and **dry** herb rue was frequently used as a **purgative** and an astringent agent against excessive **phlegm**. Its name herb-grace or herb of grace comes from the pun on its name, rue or ruth, meaning mingled compassion and regret, keys to divine forgiveness. At the same time, its use as an abortifacient went back as far as Pliny.
(B) The gardener sets a bank of "rue" or "herb of grace" in memory of Richard II's sorrowful queen, in the space where she "let fall a tear" (*R2* 3.4.105–6). Rue both commemorates her tears and, medicinally, dries them. Perdita tellingly offers rue to the "reverend sirs" Polixenes and Camillo, as if to remind them of their past losses and to anticipate their rueful exile of Florizel (*WT* 4.4.73–4). Shakespeare's Ophelia distributes rue to the court (*HAM* 4.5.181) but specifically allies it with herself and with Gertrude, suggesting that they both regret or rue the loss of Hamlet's love. Ophelia's herbs may also hint at a pregnancy accidentally or deliberately aborted; she scatters her flowers in a literal defloration, while singing about pregnancy and, to borrow Hamlet's phrase, "country matters."
(C) Gerard (1597, 3X7v–10v) identifies rue as an emmenagogue and an antidote to poison or **plague**; Dodoens (1595, W3v–5v) recommends it to expel a dead fetus from the **womb**, to bring on menses, and to dry up **breast milk**. Turner (1562, X3v) adds a **Galenic** recommendation for its use as an anaphrodisiac. Riddle (1992, 49) sensitively reads the rue in *Richard II* as a figure for **abortive** kingship; Bruun (1993) and Newman (1979) argue that Ophelia's herbs are abortifacients and that Ophelia herself may be **pregnant**.

ruptures (A) Hernias, caused by long labor pangs in women or by unaccustomed, prolonged exercise in men, which encouraged one or other of the abdominal membranes to break and the **organ** behind it to protrude painfully. Ruptures needed surgical repair, with a ligature or tie to hold the offending organ in place until the abdominal wall could heal.
(B) Ruptures are part of Thersites' long list of "rotten **diseases** of the South" (*TRO* 5.1.18). Duke Vincentio urges Isabella to the bed-trick so that she can make up the quarrel between Angelo and his abandoned love Mariana: "It is a rupture that you may easily heal, and the **cure** of it not only saves your brother, but keeps you from dishonor in doing it" (*MM* 3.1.235–7). Many editions gloss rupture as "legal breach," but the Duke sustains his medical metaphor through the words "heal," and "cure" deliberately; the break between Angelo and his betrothed will require an artificial ligature to hold it together until they can grow together more naturally.
(C) Crooke includes both an explanation of and instructions for corrective surgery for the rupture (1615, H4r).

salt See also **tub-fast** One of the three "substantives" or fundamental principles (the others being sulphur or **brimstone**, and mercury or **quicksilver**) that **Paracelsus** argued formed the basis of everything in nature, rather than the four **humors** of **choler**, **melancholy**, **blood**, and **phlegm**, or the four classical **elements** of fire, earth, air and water. Under a Paracelsian model, **disease** proceeded not from imbalances in the bodily humors (as in the classical model derived from **Galen**) but from "seeds" or germs outside the body that affected particular organs or processes when salt, or the principle of solidity acted upon it (Pagel 1984). Salt could both cause disease (through the workings of a disease-bearing seed upon a body part) and **cure** it (as the new Paracelsian iatrochemists refined metal salts to employ as **medicines**). Shakespeare appears to associate salt only indirectly with Paracelsian medicine, however, via the mercury cure for syphilis (sometimes called the **powdering-tub** because the tubs in which patients sat were more commonly used to salt or preserve meat). "Salt Cleopatra" (ANT 2.1.21) is in Caesar's view a concubine aged prematurely by her treatments for venereal disease, while Timon urges prostitutes to **infect** their clients with **pox** during their "salt hours" (*TIM* 4.3.86).

salve See also **balsam, plantain, wound** (A) Any unction or ointment applied to a wound to heal it. **Surgeons** applied salves, since they were responsible for the outside of the body and for wound-care (while **physicians** aided the inside of the body, and could prescribe **potions** or **clysters** to be taken internally). Popular salves for wounds included "Galen's wax" (beeswax, almond and rose oil, and borax), balsam, **plasters** of barley, and what Vicary calls the five herbs that no surgeon should do without: "Mouse-ear [hawkweed], Pimpernel, Avence [wood Avens or Herb Bennet], Valerian, and Gentian" (1651, H3v). These might be emollient, but other salves burned and chafed—a good sign that they were drawing out corrupt **humors** or fluids.

(B) Costard calls for a plantain leaf and salve to bandage up his broken shin (*LLL* 3.1.72–80). Hal asks his father to "salve /The . . . wounds of [his] intemperance" and forgive him his riots with the Eastcheap crew (*1H4* 3.2.155). "Speak[ing] fair" may prove a "salve" for Martius' emotional wounds, suggests Menenius (*COR* 3.2.70). Warwick urges his king to provide "a salve for any sore that may betide," part of the motif, common in the history plays, of a body politic wounded by civil war (*3H6* 4.6.88). To Venus, Adonis' perspiring palm is "earth's sovereign salve, to do a goddess good" and heal her wounded **heart** (*VEN* 28). The daylight makes Lucrece lament at that which ought to make her happy, the morning benighted by her rape: "to see the salve doth make the wound **ache** more" (*LUC* 1116). Sonnet 34 expresses a similar sentiment: "no man well of such a salve can speak / That heals the wound and **cures** not the disgrace" (6–7). "Myself corrupting, salving thy amiss," complains the sonnet-speaker; he acts as a soothing emollient to a wound or ill that corrupts or infects the injury instead of curing it (35.7). Instead of offering each other "The humble salve, which wounded bosom fits," the lovers of Sonnet 120 offer each other only blackmail and injury (120.12).

(C) Vicary's *Surgion's Directorie* (1651) includes salves for "green" or fresh wounds, old wounds, new healing wounds, and so on. A.T. (1596, H3r) recommends crushed snail shells for a boil. The 1630s saw a pamphlet-war over the mysterious, magical "weapon-salve," with which one anointed the weapon that had injured the patient, rather than the wound. Through "sympathy," the salve (often made of **mummy** and other magical ingredients) healed the wound the weapon had originally inflicted (Foster 1631; Fludd 1631; Sennert 1637).

sand-blind See also **blind, eye** (A) Early modern English medical texts refer to sand- or **gravel-blindness** as either weakened or darkened vision (purblindness), or near- or short-sightedness (myopia). Johnson's Dictionary (1755) defines it as vision obscured by specks of "sand" or dust, but this is probably a later understanding of the word.

(B) Old Gobbo fails to recognize his son Launcelot because he is "more than sand-blind, high-gravel-blind" (*MV* 2.2.36). "High-gravel-blind" is Shakespeare's neologism and Launcelot's intensifier for the degree of his father's deficiency. *OED* suggests that the term "stone-blind" enters English after Shakespeare's coinage, as a development of "gravel."

(C) For sand-blindness as purblindness, see Elyot (1538, "Lippio . . . to be sand blynde"); for sand-blindness as near-sight, see Huloet (1572, "court veue, to be sandblind").

sanguine Shakespeare employs the word sanguine as an adjective to describe objects or bodies colored blood-red, or filled with **blood**. Guiderius' birthmark is a "sanguine star" (*CYM* 5.5.364); Basset compares his master's "blushing **cheeks**" to "sanguine . . . leaves," in a continuation of the gardening and plant metaphors sustained throughout the first tetralogy (*1H6* 4.1.92); Aaron mocks Demetrius and Chiron as "white-lim'd walls" and "sanguine, shallow-hearted boys," white-skinned and savage Goths with cheeks red as if painted like "ale-house" signs, "shallow" because their blood and emotions are visible on the surface of their **skins** and because their color fades where Aaron's own dark skin remains constant (*TIT* 2.4.97). Hal calls Falstaff a "sanguine coward," presumably because he is red-faced from drink, but also perhaps commenting on the irony of Falstaff's pusilla-nimity despite his redness, since cowardice was thought to result from a lack of blood in the **liver**. Falstaff's blood has presumably all rushed to his face, **heated** with wine, and thus left both **heart** and liver lacking in bravery (*1H4* 2.4.242).

sapego, suppeago Dry, itchy, scabbed **skin** was a symptom of the serpigo, any spreading, scaling skin disorder that spread or crept like a *serp*ent (hence its name). Duke Vincentio associates the sapego with **gout** and **rheum**, ailments of old age, in his exordium to Claudio to "Be absolute for **death**" (*MM* 3.1.31). Thersites curses the Trojan war with the "dry suppeago," among other ills, in *Troilus and Cressida* (2.3.74). Lanfranco (1565) blames "burned **humores**" (e.3r–v), and Bartolomeus Anglicus (Batman 1582), who explains its name, agrees that it comes from too much **choler** or perhaps **melancholy** (112–13). Harris (2004) argues that serpigo is associated with the **scabs** of syphilitic **pox** and illustrates the confusion between early **Galenic** theories of humoral excess and emergent **Paracelsian** theories of **contagion** (87–8).

Saturn See also **melancholy, planet** In astrological **medicine**, "heavy Saturn" (*SON* 98) ruled melancholy, **cold, dryness**, blackness, jealousy, taciturnity and, positively, pensiveness and wisdom. In the body, Saturn controlled the **spleen**, and, according to the theory of antipathies, it **cured** the adverse effects of lust. When Leonatus wants to evoke the shocking extent of Imogen's chastity, he claims that even "old Saturn" would be, paradoxically, aroused by her shamefast-ness (*CYM* 2.5.12), and Hal exclaims in surprise to see Doll Tearsheet in Falstaff's arms, an emblem of "Saturn and Venus . . . in conjunction" (*2H4* 2.4.263). Those ruled by Saturn had a yellowish or dark **complexion**, such as Don John, the color of a "civil [Seville] . . . orange" (*ADO* 2.1.294) and Borachio, "born under Saturn" (1.3.11), or Aaron in *TA*, "dominat[ed]" by "cloudy melancholy" and a "deadly-standing **eye**" (2.3.31–3).

scab See also **cicatrice, skin** Both the itchy scales of scabies, eczema, ringworm, or syphilis, and the thick crust formed over a **wound** while the skin heals beneath, often leaving a scar behind and itching as it heals. In Shakespeare, the word "scab" is usually an insult applied to a person perceived to belong to a lower rank than the speaker. Martius comments on the pruritus of injuries as they heal (and the propensity of patients to scratch or pick their scabs) when he accuses the plebeians of "rubbing the poor itch of [their] opinion, /[to] Make [them]selves scabs" (*COR* 1.1.166). Borachio finds Conrade "at [his] elbow" and claims to notice his presence by an itch so insistent that he "thought there would be a scab follow" (*ADO* 3.3.100). Sir Toby exclaims "Out, scab!" upon hearing Malvolio's fantasy of scolding him for his drunkenness (*TN* 2.5.74). Falstaff's page **Wart** is, paradoxically, a "good scab" (*2H4* 3.2), presumably because, despite his lowliness, he will aid healing. When Ajax roars that his fingers "itch" to beat Thersites, the latter retorts, "I would thou didst itch from head to foot and I had the scratching of thee; I would make thee the loathsomest scab in Greece" (*TRO* 2.1.29). Thersites may imply a curse of venereal **disease** with the term "loathsome," and there may be a pun on Greece/grease, since itchy skin could be soothed with pig-fat or olive oil. John Clarke (1602) calls syphilis the "scab of Venus" (A4r). Fioravanti includes an entire chapter on "all sorts of scabs" (1580, C2v).

scar see **cicatrice, skin**

sciatica, hip-gout (A) By Shakespeare's time the terms hip-gout and sciatica were beginning to be used interchangeably, although the origin of what we now call sciatica in nervous **inflammation** would not be identified until Cotugno's treatise in 1775. Hip-gout came from thickened **humors** stuck in the hip, that were unable to pass downwards out of the body. The elderly, because they were **cold** and **dry**, were particularly susceptible, and those suffering from venereal **disease**.
(B) When the gentleman questions Mistress Overdone, the brothel-keeper, "Which of your hips has the most profound sciatica?" he assumes that her **aches** and pains result from secondary syphilis or **pox** (*MM* 1.2.59). Timon's reference to "cold sciatica" (4.1.23) perhaps alludes to the association of the disorder with old age and lameness, and Thersites includes "sciaticas" in his catalog of "diseases of the South," that is, sexually transmitted infections (*TRO* Q1 5.1.21).
(C) Vicary (1587) outlines the humoral cause of sciatica or hip-gout and requires **clysters**, **vomits**, **purges**, and unctions, in order to drain the neighboring tissues so that the excess humor would flow into them and ease the pressure on the joint.

scruple See also **dram, prescription** 1/24 oz. in **apothecaries**' weight (twenty grains); a third of a dram. Shakespeare usually uses the term to mean moral misgivings (our present-day sense), such as Hamlet worrying that his misgivings about killing his uncle are a mere "craven scruple" (*HAM* 4.4.40), but sometimes it refers to a tiny measure, or both senses are present at once. Malvolio has not the slightest doubt that Olivia loves him, "no dram of a scruple, no scruple of a scruple" (*TN* 3.4.79). Lafew warns Parolles that not only has the latter deserved his punishment, "every dram of it; . . . [he] will not bate [him] a scruple" (*AWW* 2.3.222). Portia's threat to Shylock to cut no more than a pound, not "the division of the twentieth part /Of one poor scruple" is impossible, since the twentieth part of a scruple was a "grain," the smallest unit of measurement in use (*MV* 4.1.329–30). Shakespeare also imagines women's flesh measured as the **medicine mummy**, in drams and scruples: Diomedes bitterly complains of Helen, "for every scruple /Of her contaminated carrion weight, /A Trojan hath been slain" (*TRO* 4.1.71–3), with an additional pun on "troy weight," the measurement jewelers used to weigh precious metals.

scurvy (A) Scurvy, now known to be vitamin C deficiency, was common in Renaissance England. Coming out of what geologists now call the "little Ice Age,"

Northern Europe suffered from long, bitter winters, when fruit and vegetables were scarce. The **disease** especially prevailed among sailors, who lacked fresh food on long sea-voyages. **Humoral** theory explained scurvy as a blockage in the **spleen** that prevented **melancholy** (or, in some accounts, **phlegm**) from mixing with the rest of the **blood**, forcing it to come out as spots in the legs or sores in the **gum**. Left untreated, scurvy resulted in leg **ulcers**, **tooth** loss, peeling **skin** and internal bleeding. The popular **cure** for scurvy was the consumption of raw scurvy-grass (also called spoon-wort), or watercress, which presumably reintroduced the missing vitamin to the **diet**, but, unfortunately, in the hands of the **physicians**, scurvy-grass was **compounded** and cooked until the vitamin (which is both water-soluble and destroyed by **heat**) was almost certainly lost. Shakespeare's son-in-law, John Hall, built up his practice in part on his reputation for skillfully healing scurvy.

(B) Shakespeare's frequent use of scurvy as an insult indicates both how prevalent the disease was and how far it would progress before diagnosis and treatment. Parolles calls Lafew a "scurvy, old, filthy, scurvy lord," clearly for once at a loss for words (2.3.236). "Filthy" often connotes scaling or scabbed skin. Lafew himself complains of "curtsies" that are "scurvy" (5.3.324). See also "scurvy companion" (*2H4* 2.4.123), "scurvy young boy" (272), "scurvy, lousy knave" (*H5* 5.1.18, 22), "scurvy fellow" (*MM* 5.1.136), and so on. Lear refers to the bleeding of the conjunctiva seen in scurvy when he urges the **blinded** Gloucester, "Get thee glass **eyes**; /And like a scurvy politician, seem /To see the things thou dost not" (*LR* 4.6.170–2). *TMP* associates the disease with sailors and ships. Stephano sings a "scurvy tune" or sea-shanty (2.2.44, 55); Caliban is a "scurvy **monster**" (2.2.155) and calls Stephano (as he thinks) a "scurvy patch" (3.2.63). Emilia may make a similar connection when she wishes that the "scurvy" knave who has gulled Othello may be "lash[ed] . . . naked through the world /Even from the east to the west" (4.2.140–4), like the slaves captured on Ottoman galley-ships.

(C) *A Treatise of the Scorby*, printed as part of Guillemeau's *Worthy Treatise of the Eyes* (1587), translates Johann Weyer's *Medicarum Observationum Rararum Liber* (1567). It defines the disease, outlines its progression, blames diet (especially the "Northern" and sea-farers' consumption of "rotten swine's flesh and sea-biscuit," 7v), climate, and melancholy for its onset, and recommends "green" grasses such as watercress, wintercress and scurvy-grass, as long as they are not too aggressively compounded (11v–12r). Notably, it commends lay female practitioners, both humble and noble, for their success in treating this disease. Gerard (1597) identifies scurvy-grass with Pliny's herb "Britannica" and notes that scurvy is especially common among "fishermen and Freshwater Soldiers" who eat dirty "bisket bread" (sea-biscuit, X3r).

searchers see **pestilence, plague**

sea-sick Nausea and **vomiting** at sea; motion **sickness** from choppy waters, common to land-lubbers and sailors alike. Sea-sickness made one pale and weak, and could also make one light-headed and apt to pass out. Berowne, disguised as a Muscovite, anticipates Rosaline's harsh words at their discovery. "Help, hold his brows! He'll **swoon**! Why look you pale? Sea-sick, I think, coming from Muscovy," she diagnoses, offering the standard therapy of chafing and **heat** to the forehead to prevent a **faint** (*LLL* 5.2.392–3). Romeo imagines **death** as a welcome ship-wreck for a body that is already "a sea-sick weary bark" (*ROM* 5.3.118). Perdita "began to be sea-sick, and himself little better," according to Autolycus, on board the prince's ship for Bohemia (it is unclear whether "himself" refers to the shepherd or to Florizel) (*WT* 5.2.119). Johannes de Mediolano (1607) asserts that sea-sickness is common on choppy seas, and recommends sage-water taken prophylactically before traveling.

seed See also **sex** (A) Seed was seminal **humor**, the re ned product of spirit, produced within the gonads and contributing to the generation of offspring. While Aristotle had held that only men produced seed and that women served merely as incubators, Renaissance **Galenism** held that both men and women could ejaculate seed and that, moreover, sexual climax was necessary in both sexes during coitus in order for seed to be released and for conception to take place (see **sex**). Seed was so-called because in it originated the forms of all parts of the body, present as Platonic ideas and fastened in the seed through the vehicle of spirit.
(B) By extension and by figure in Shakespeare, seeds are the descendants of an individual, and people are plants that may be planted, grafted, uprooted, cultivated, and propagated. Macbeth rues his "unlineal sceptre," the childless-ness that ensures that only "the seed of Banquo" (*MAC* 3.1.69) will become kings. The "seeds of time" (*MAC* 1.3.58) about which Banquo asks the witches in the same play are thus his own offspring that will "grow" while Macbeth's will fail. Even the King of France fears the "heroicall seed" (*H5* 2.4.59) of Edward the Black Prince (*H5*), of which King Henry is a valiant "stock" or stem. Prospero calls Caliban "Hag-seed" (*TMP* 1.2.365) with the implication that he is the child or seed of the witch Sycorax but also a potential source for future disruption and dangerous magic, especially given his unsuccessful attempt to rape Miranda and "people . . . the isle /With little Calibans" (*TMP* 1.2.351). Hector's bootless plea for peace among Greek and Trojan is based upon their common ancestry, since Diomedes is "A cousin-german to great Priam's seed" (*TRO* 4.5.121).
(C) Crooke (1615, pp. 282–9, 2B3v–2B7r) addresses at length the questions of whether the body's **organs** are made of seed and the relationship of seed to conception. Seed itself, he writes, is "a moyst; spumous and white body, com-pounded of a permixtion of **blood** and spirits, laboured and boyled by the Testicles, and falling onely from them in the time of generation, or from the adiacent parts." The question of whether women produce seed he dismisses with the argument that, since ["t]here is nothing more certayne then that woemen in their accompanying with men doe loose somewhat from whence comes their pleasure and delight. That therefore which is auoyded is either bloud, or a thinne and serous humor, or perfect and laboured seed" (2B3v). He is uncertain, however, whether women need to experience orgasm in order to

ejaculate their seed and conceive a child (2B5v), in contrast to earlier authorities such as Avicenna who had deemed it necessary, and to Paré (1634, p. 889), who recommends talk and tickling to titillate a reluctant wife to climax. Laqueur (1990) discusses the controversy over female seed at length; Paster (1993); Park (1997); and King (2007) all challenge his argument for a dominant "one-sex" model.

senna see **cyme**

serpigo see **sapego**

sex, unsex (A) In the early modern period there existed several, perhaps contradictory, ways of considering sexual difference. On the one hand, the "one-sex" model regarded men and women as points along a continuum of sexual difference rather than as polar opposites. Aristotelian **medicine** regarded women as imperfect, infertile men, because of their perceived **cold** and **moisture** fitted only for the incubation of the embryo, not for its generation; indeed, women were thought to be incapable of producing semen or **seed** because of their lack of **heat**. Instead, Aristotle argued, women contributed only the "matter" to generation, and their primary function was to nourish the embryo. His definition of sexual difference enshrined this distinction: a man engendered life in another, a woman nourished another's seed in herself. Renaissance scholars often evoked two Latin puns here: *mater*, meaning mother, and a false etymology of the Latin word *mulier* for woman, thought to derive from the phrase *mollis aer*, soft air, connoting women's contribution of formless or soft *matter* to the embryo and men's attribution of firm form. Heat also accounted for men's greater hirsutism and perceived roughness or hardness, since men were further concocted than women.

Renaissance **Galenism** extended Aristotle's theories by supposing women to be not incomplete or infertile but "inverted" men, who possessed the same sex organs as men but, because of their relative coldness, retained those organs inside the body, rather than outside. Emphasizing homology or sameness, Galenic **anatomy** held that the testes in the man corresponded to the ovaries in the woman (the same term, stone, was used for both), the prepuce to the vulva, the penis to the cervix, and so on. Both men and women were thought capable of generation, however, contributing seed to conception by ejaculating it at sexual climax (leading to the widespread early modern belief that a woman's orgasm was necessary for conception to occur, and to instructions in obstetric texts on how to arouse women to sufficient heat to achieve orgasm). Male children were conceived on the hotter, right-hand side of the **womb**, females on the colder, left-hand side.

At the same time, gender could and sometimes did change over the course of a human lifetime. Although women were associated with chill, moistness, softness, and matter, and men with warmth, **dryness**, hardness, and form, a man with too much sexual interest in women could become "effeminate," woman-like, through prolonged association with them, and a woman who demonstrated too much desire for men, a woman who generated too much heat, could become a virago or mannish woman. Although women were innately colder than men, their "non-natural" Galenic habits (eating, **sleep**, exercise, the air they breathed, satiety, and their affections or strong emotions) exacerbated their pathological difference from men through custom as well as inherited humoral **complexion**.

On the other hand, midwifery manuals, vernacular healers, and some prominent **physicians** insisted on the distinctness of the sexes, leading to a proto-feminist Galenism calling women not imperfect or inverted but "perfect in their own sex." Such physicians argued that women's **breasts**, unlike men's, were designed as glands producing nutritive material, not (as Aristotle had argued) as vehicles primarily for evacuating noxious **humors**, and, moreover, that the clitoris (recently "rediscovered"), although called the woman's yard, did not resemble the man's yard or penis in either form or function. It seems that the one-sex or single gender model coexisted in the period alongside more familiar (to us) beliefs in binary, determinable, biological sex. Moreover, hierarchical distinctions between men and women were clearly of paramount importance in law, religion, and social life.

(B) In every instance of the word in Shakespeare's plays, "sex" belongs to women; sexual difference becomes important at moments when women threaten, through their words or through their behavior, to break down the social barriers between what men and women are supposed to do. York castigates the "she-wolf of France," Margaret of Anjou, as she taunts him with a napkin steeped in the **blood** of his youngest son, in terms that accuse her of being "ill-beseeming in [her] sex /To triumph, like an Amazonian trull" or masculine woman over him (*3H6* 1.4.113–14). "Amazonian trull" combines two sexual insults. The Amazons were a legendary tribe of warrior women in South America who were thought to wage war on men, banishing all men from their kingdom except once a year, when they lured men into sexual congress to impregnate them. They were thought to expose their boy-children and to rear only their girls, and a false (but prevalent) Renaissance etymology for their name, Amazon, derived it from *A-mazos*, without a breast, from the belief that they amputated one breast in order to make it easier for themselves to shoot a bow and arrow. The word "trull" means a prostitute, a trollop. Just as the Amazons, implies York, willfully deprive themselves of their maternal breast in order to become better fighters, and kill their young, so Margaret contradicts the natural love women ought to feel for children in murdering the young Duke of Rutland. Women, he argues,

> are soft, mild, pitiful and flexible;
> Thou stern, obdurate, flinty, rough, remorseless.
> . . .
> These tears are my sweet Rutland's obsequies:
> And every drop cries vengeance for his **death**.
> (*3H6* 1.4.141–8)

The evocation of tears (elsewhere in Shakespeare called "womanish" as in *JN* 4.1.36, *ROM* 3.3.110, *H8* 2.1.38, or more fitting to "the gentle sex", *LUC* 1237) at the end of his speech allies York with what true femininity would experience and revalues it, since it is his weeping, he avers, that makes him human, rather than the wild beast or **monster** that is Margaret. Shakespeare's women often present themselves as exceptions to their sex, as if anticipating expected complaints about a proposed course of action. Hermione claims that she is "not prone to weeping, as our sex /commonly are," but argues that her dry **eyes** aver her "burning" and righteous rage (*WT* 2.1.108–9). Joan La Pucelle "exceed[s her] sex" in preparing for trial by "combat"; she offers herself as a "warlike mate" rather than an espoused one (*1H6* 1.2.89–92). Sexual difference appears as morality when women are calumnied, both by men (such as Benedick, "a professed tyrant to [the female] sex" [*ADO* 1.1.169]) and by women cross-dressed (such as Rosalind in her guise as Ganymede) (*AYL* 3.2.350) or betraying a lover such as Cressida, who blames her "poor . . . sex" for her "turpitude" in being led by her "eye" rather than her "**heart**" (5.2.108–12).

Sometimes sexual activity determines sexual difference. Angelo uses Juliet's illegitimate **pregnancy** ("the testimony of your own sex") as evidence that although sex before marriage is wrong, Juliet's fall proves not its wrongness but the inherent weakness of Isabella's "own sex" (women) to have sex (intercourse). "We are made to be no stronger /Than faults may shake our frames," he argues; in other words, overcoming woman's inherent flaw—sexual temptation, in Juliet's case, or vulnerability to sexual coercion, in Isabella's—would mean that one was no longer a woman. "External warrants"—outward appearances or secondary sexual characteristics—demonstrate Isabella's ostensible sex, he gloats, but being a woman means putting on the "destined livery" of sexual servitude so that external appearance, hidden bodily features, moral behavior and erotic action coincide (2.4.131–8). Troilus defends "the general sex" of women by arguing that one sexually unfaithful Cressida does not make a "rule" by which to measure all women; we should "rather think this not Cressid" (5.2.132–3). Either Cressida is false, and so are all women, or (since women such as "mothers" are true) a sexually licentious Cressida cannot be a woman. Equally, the absence of heteroerotic relations may change a woman's sex. Posthumus' treatment of Imogen leads her to say that she would change [her] sex to be companion with [her disguised brothers], /Since Leonatus' false" (*CYM* 3.6.87–8). Miranda becomes aware of both sexual difference and erotic desire when she sees Ferdinand and suddenly tells him that she knows none of her sex, nor men, neither (*TMP* 3.1.49). Helena chides Demetrius for expecting masculine behavior from her: "Your wrongs do set a scandal on my sex: /We cannot fight for love, as men may do; /We should be wooed and were not made to woo" (*MND* 2.1.240–2).

Later, Helena pleads for sexual solidarity as she imagines Hermia to "join with men in scorning her poor friend," an offence that will lead her whole "sex, as well as [she to] chide" (3.2.216–18). Celia, horrified at Rosalind's misogyny when dressed as Ganymede, complains, "you have simply misused our sex in your love-prate" and threatens a physical disclosure: "we must have your doublet and hose plucked over your head, and show the world what the bird hath done to her own nest" (*AYL* 4.1.201–4). Orsino re-sexes the unsexed Viola, who as the cross-dressed Cesario acts "against the **mettle** of your sex, / So far beneath your soft and tender breeding," by making her her "master's mistress" (5.1.322–6). The common pun on metal/mettle evokes female malleability and the "soft and tender" nature of women, as well as the "breeding" of tender affections within Viola/Cesario and her gentle birth. Helena transcends "her sex, her years, profession" in treating the King of France (*AWW* 2.1.83), but only surrounded by prolonged sexual innuendo and, paradoxically, a magical virginity (see **fistula**). The performance of gender resounds to greatest metatheatrical effect in Cleopatra's fears about being "boy[ed] . . . i'the' posture of a whore" by ribald actors, a fear that has been stoked by Antony's fantasy of her demonstrated as "the greatest spot /Of all thy sex" (*ANT* 5.2.220–1, 4.12.35–6). Throughout the play she challenges such reductions of her femininity to biological sex, deploying femaleness only to trick Octavius and Dolabella by claiming "frailties" that "before /Have often shamed our sex" (5.2.124).

Portia implicitly argues against the belief that women cannot keep secrets by claiming she is "stronger than [her] sex," adducing as evidence the **wound** in the thigh that she has inflicted upon herself. Portia wishes to transcend her pathological, periodically bleeding body in favor of the impermeable, military masculine body of Cato or Brutus (*JC* 2.1.296). Lady Macbeth wishes to transform or "unsex" her body, too, but her call to the "spirits /That tend on mortal thought" demands a kind of super-virility, a superfluity of hot, dry humor untempered by the benign or **sanguine** influence of **milk** or blood (*MAC* 1.5.40–1). She pleads for her breasts to become instead gallbladders (seats of **choler**, or yellow bile). **Gall**, considered one of the bitterest substances known, broke down the viands or foodstuffs consumed by humans. Breast milk, in contrast, encouraged growth rather than breakdown, its taste "sweet" rather than bitter. The "thick" or gross blood that Lady Macbeth demands also characterizes the **spleen**, associated with black bile or **melancholy**. Blood, the sanguine humor, acts in humoral theory as a kind of messenger to the rest of the body, bearing necessary nutriments to its internal organs and extremities. Under strong emotion, however, blood abandoned its natural course and either returned to the heart to sustain it and enlarge it (in joy or hope), or shrunk into a contracted heart (in fear or sorrow or malice). Here Lady Macbeth pleads for the coagulated gall and spleen in her lower body to remain thick and inaccessible, undiluted by the blood that would bring with it cheer, optimism, and good health.

(C) As Adelman (1999) and Schleiner (2000) have noted, Crooke's *Microcosmographia* (1615) provides both the fullest early modern account of the one-sex model and its strongest English refutation. The *Problems of Aristotle* (1595) addresses the controversy, as does Raynalde's obstetric manual, *The Birth of Mankynde* (1565). Maclean's extensive survey (1980), still fresh and useful, discusses the differences between men and women as understood in legal, medical, and moral treatises. Laqueur (1990) provides the most accessible account of the "one-sex" model, arguing that it predominated in early modern Europe until the eighteenth century. Schleiner (2000) more strongly makes the case for a "feminist" two-sex model in the early seventeenth century, while Park (1997) and Paster (1993) argue against Laqueur and comment upon the specific ways in which female bodies are sexed in early modern medical writing and other forms of literature. Swain (2004) reads the "unsexing" of Lady Macbeth alongside early modern debates about scholasticism and medicine. King (2007) specifically counters Laqueur and Schiebinger (1991), suggesting that they have underrepresented the early modern transmission of the **Hippocratic** belief in women as a distinct sex, and argues for the emergence of a new science of gynecology, the study of **diseases** pertaining specifically to women, in the late sixteenth century as a response to a crisis in masculinity triggered by the rule of female monarchs in England, Scotland, and France.

sexual, sexuality see **sex**

sickness, sick See also **infection, green-sick, love-sick, plague, sea-sick, vomit** (A) **Illness, disease, distemper**; sometimes with an association of nausea, and figuratively evoking moral or political corruption; sometimes used to describe epidemics such as plague; the condition of being in such a state. Early modern sickness developed from humoral imbalance rather than from an external germ or agent. Bad air, water, or food; inclement or unseasonal weather, or behavior inappropriate to one's **complexion** or humoral personality could induce sickness in someone by encouraging the body to produce an abundance or deficit of one of the four cardinal corporeal **humors** of **choler, melancholy, phlegm**, or **blood**. Others "caught" sickness from the influence of persons who were themselves sick and exuded **vapor** or **fumes** that triggered the overproduction of humors in others as their bodies tried to compensate for the damaging breath. **Patients** only became sick, however, because of their own humoral susceptibility; emotions altered the complexion of the body and could indirectly cause disease. Even sicknesses known to be highly **contagious**, such as **pox**, could only be transmitted to persons with constitutional weaknesses that permitted it (such as bodies **heated** by lust), although the effectiveness of quarantine and hygiene measures against plague in the late sixteenth century had encouraged some to wonder about an external disease-causing microbial agent rather than humoral imbalance as the cause for the disease.
(B) Shakespearean emotions such as love, grief, and rue sicken both body and mind if untreated. Love in *MND* is highly contagious ("[S]ickness is catching" 1.1.186) and Lysander's phrase "war, **death** and sickness" (1.1.142), equates sickness with large-scale epidemics of **pestilence** or plague that fell dozens or hundreds and that, arguably, have an external cause. Demetrius is at first "sick" with hate for Helena (2.1.212) but explains his renewed love for Helena as his recovery from a "sickness" that took away his appetite; in health, he "long[s] for"

her, his "natural taste" (4.1.173–4). Characters who are "sick" with fear include Constance (*JN* 3.1.12) and Henry VI, whose feelings of nausea stem from "hope and fear" (*1H6* 5.5.86).

The word often has moral or political connotations, such as the "inward sickness" conveniently afflicting Hotspur's father that "maim[s]" their campaign (*1H4* 4.1.31, 42). Quarantine can be convenient. Imogen recommends her maid "feign a sickness" so that she may go home and see her father while Imogen and Pisanio escape the court (*CYM* 3.2.74). It is telling that Lepidus asserts his loyalty by claiming, "Not sickness should detain me" (*ANT* 2.2.170). Laertes' grief is a "sickness in [his] **heart**" (*HAM* 4.7.55). Beaufort's remorse takes the form of a "grievous sickness" in which Duke Humphrey's ghost whispers in his ear (*2H6* 3.2.370). Treason is a "contagious sickness" (*H8* 5.2.61). Treason even cures the sickness of Ligarius in JC: "I here discard my sickness! Soul of Rome! /. . . /Thou, like an exorcist, hast conjured up /My mortified spirit" (2.1.321–4), he crows, claiming that Brutus has given his weakened vital **spirit**, the source of life in the body, new energy through his plan.

The elderly were prone to sickness because they were **colder** and **dryer** than young persons, prey to "sickness, age and impotence" (*HAM* 2.2.66), "sickness and . . . **crazy** age" (*1H6* 3.2.89). The King in *AWW* is the subject for "debate" between "nature and sickness" (1.2.74–5) until Helena bids "sickness freely die" instead of the King (2.1.168). The **apoplexy** of King Henry IV is referred to as his sickness (*2H4* 3.1.106); the King mistakenly dubs it Hal's "friend sickness," thinking that his son is impatient for his demise (4.5.81). Sedentary life also weakened the body by cooling it, and the impoverished were notoriously plague-struck. Say identifies his occupation as unhealthy because it keeps him stationary and exposes him to the poor: "Long sitting to determine poor men's causes /Hath made me full of sickness and diseases" (*2H6* 4.7.88–9). Although sickness was humoral in origin, some, like plague, might be outrun by fleeing the infected area. The Surveyor imagines that the Duke of Buckingham's "sickness /Pursued him still" (*H8* 4.2.24). Henry V determines to retreat to Calais because of the onset of winter and "sickness growing /Upon our soldiers" (*H5* 3.3.55–6); his army's delay does indeed render them "with sickness much enfeebled" (3.6.145). Shakespearean wives succumb to sickness, real or feigned, regularly, usually from poisoning, but sometimes from mental illness: Regan (*LR* 5.3.105), Derby's wife (*R3* 1.3.29), the Lady Anne (*R3* 4.2.57), Portia in *JC*, whose "sickness" is "distract[ion]" or **madness** (4.3.152), and Lady Macbeth, although she is "Not so sick /As she is troubled with thick coming fancies, that keep her from her rest" (*MAC* 5.3.37–8).

(C) Culpeper's popular seventeenth-century translation of and commentary on **Galen** offers the following definition of an "unhealthful" or sick body:

> A Body is simply unhealthful which is born mutilated by Nature, as wanting some Members, or some Operations or sences, that is not perfect in respect of

those Seven Natural things before mentioned, as that cannot See, Hear, or Smel, or is a Fool, &c.

According to time a Body is unhealthful that is at present sick in Body, or distemper'd in mind, or his Body broken or bruised in any part of it, whether internal or external, that hath an accidental distemper in any of the seven Natural things. (1652, C5r)

Later chapters outline the "signs of a sick body," namely if a body part is hurt in itself, or if it produces **excrements** (pus, **sweat**, **blood**, swelling, and so on) that seem against nature (H3r). Moulton's frequently reprinted *Mirror or Glass of Helthe* (1561) offers an extended astrological guide to sickness, especially focusing on the pestilence. Bullein's *Government of Health* (1595), like many **dietaries** or regimens, concentrates upon the need for effectively regulating what one consumes, how one constructs a daily routine, how one maintains temperance in emotions and action, and so on. Hester's collection of **Paracelsian** aphorisms and therapies argues that sickness is caused not by distemper or humoral imbalance but from "seeds" in the outside world, and that cures could be effected not by herbal **simples** or **purges** but by chemical **medicines** such as metal **salts**. (1596). Siraisi (1990), Hoeniger (1992), and Paster (1993) offer the most useful introduction to humoral notions of sickness, concentrating respectively upon existing medieval practices (such as uroscopy and astrology), upon Shakespeare's figurative use of medical treatments and humoral language, and upon the gendering of therapy and humoralism. Healy (2001) argues that both syphilis and Paracelsianism challenged humoral explanations of disease in the late sixteenth and early seventeenth centuries, and Harris (2004) explores contagious diseases as figures for emergent capitalism and suggests a **Paracelsian** aspect to Shakespeare's syphilitics.

simple (A) A single-source, herbal remedy, a **drug** made from only one ingredient. **Physicians** and wise-women were permitted to prescribe their own simples, but technically required the services of an **apothecary** to dispense **compounded** medicaments.

(B) Lafew may be punning on simple (elementary) and simple (**medicine**) when he describes Helena's "simple touch, . . . powerful to araise King Pepin" (*AWW* 2.1.75); the play comments frequently on Helena as a "simple maid," in contrast to both the sophisticated "girls of Italy" against whom Bertram is warned and against the elaborate but ineffectual remedies prescribed by the "congregated **college**" (2.3.66, 2.1.19, 2.1.117).

The **mountebank**'s poison that anoints Laertes' foil is proof against antidotes "Collected from all simples that have virtue /Under the moon," immune to all but magical responses, perhaps (*HAM* 4.7.144–5). Cordelia, however, calls the "simples operative, whose power /Will close the **eye** of anguish" for her **sleepless** father "blest secrets," heavenly remedies (*LR* 4.4.14–15). *WIV* builds up to a practical joke about the name of the messenger, Peter Simple: Quickly forces him to hide in Dr. **Caius**'s closet lest the doctor becomes jealous, but Dr. Caius threatens to open the hiding place: "dere is some simples in my closet, dat I vill not for the varld I shall leave behind" (1.4.63). Romeo spots the desperate apothecary in *ROM* 5.1.39–40, "In tatter'd weeds, with overwhelming brows, / Culling of simples," in both ragged clothing (weeds) and wild plants (weeds), gathering the raw materials for his compounds. Sonnet 125 dispraises "compound sweet" over "simple savour," preferring wholesome but single flavor "not mix'd with seconds . . . me for thee" over mingled or sophisticated tastes (*SON* 125.7).

(C) Bullein's Humfrey comments that "the almightye God hath couered the whole face of the earth wyth many precious simples" (1558, R6v). The aptly named Gardiner (1611) recommends to his readers the herbals of Gerard (1597) and Doedoens (1595). The dedicatory epistle to Gardiner's book puns on both his name and the unaffected, honest, "simple" nature of his book:

> Reioyce, O *Britaine,* that thou hast brought-forth
> A Gardiner of such admired skill.
> Thou showest the vertue, the effect and worth,
> Of this rare Simple, the good vse and ill.
> Then vse it well, for *Gardiners* good sake:
> And from his Garden a choise flower take.
>
> (1611, A4v)

Bright, however, cautions readers against equating simples with medicines in his *Sufficiencie of English Medicines*: "no more is *Lettis* [**lettuce**], *Poppie, Rhewbarb* [**rhubarb**] . . . a medicine, then an Oake a Table or Ship, or a quarrie of stones, an house . . . no nature which alwaies keepeth constant in the own kind can therefore either bee a medicine, or properly beare the name thereof: which I wish to be noted, least it be thought the simples, and such other naturall things were medicines, because commonly they carry the names of them" (1615, B2r).

sinew (A) Early modern sinews were either flexible, sensitive fibers that ran from the **brain** or the spinal cord and carried sensation and the impulse to move throughout the body (i.e. **nerves**) or strong, tough cords that attached muscle to bone (i.e. tendons). Shakespeare also uses the word to refer to catgut, the animal-derived fibers used to string instruments such as lutes.

(B) It is sometimes difficult to see whether Shakespeare uses sinew to mean "nerve" in its archaic sense—the agent of sensation—or to mean "tendon," its meaning for us, something that strengthens the muscles and holds the body upright almost like a scaffolding. When Aufidius vows that his "sinews shall be stretch'd" in vengeance against Martius, he may mean that he will strain his nerves, or that he will stretch his muscles (and tendons; *COR* 5.6.44). Exeter's description of the body's decay, "bones and flesh and sinews fall[ing] away"

(*1H6* 3.1.192), is similarly ambiguous. The treacherous Scroop appeals to his monarch by evoking "steeled sinews," which may mean either (in the figure still popular today) "nerves of steel," a mind immune to fear, or muscles hardened for action (*H5* 2.2.36).

In other instances, Shakespeare clearly associates sinews with muscular vigor, "lusty sinews" (*JC* 1.2.108), especially in the context of war. Talbot's list of his bodily attributes, "sinews, arms and strength" seems to allude to muscular prowess rather than to sensation, and thus to mean "tendon" rather than "nerve" (*1H6* 2.3.63). Warwick laments that his injuries have "robb'd [his] strong-knit sinews of their strength" (*3H6* 2.3.4), but the king-maker remains strong enough to plan to "sinow both these lands together" (2.6.91), where the sinew is a figure for a strong and flexible cord, like a tendon. King Henry V figures his lords and armies as "the noble sinews of our power" (1.2.223) and urges his foot soldiers "once more unto the breach" with "stiffen[ed] sinews" (*H5* 3.1.7). Thersites often mocks the soldiers for their **brawn** or mindless strength without intelligence, suggesting that "a great deal of your wit, too, lies in your sinews" (*TRO* 2.1.99). Paris equates "the edge of steel," or weaponry, with the "force of Greekish sinews" (*TRO* 3.1.152–3). Hector's catalog of Ajax's body, half-Greek and half-Trojan, and hence his own "cousin-german" lists "the sinews of this leg" along with blood and the hand, the one spilled by the action of the other in war (*TRO* 4.5.126). Ferdinand vows rather to "crack [his] sinews" than to allow Miranda to help him in his hard labor (*TMP* 3.1.26).

Sinews hold the body upright and bind muscle and bone together, sometimes in political alliance with another body politic. Owen Glendower is "a rated sinew," a noted support or staff, for Hotspur and his allies (*1H4* 4.4.17). Lewis urges Salisbury to "knit your sinews to the strength of mine" in amity (*JN* 5.2.63). Achilles is "The sinow and the forehand" of the Greek army (*TRO* 1.3.143), but Hector is Troy's "**heart** . . . sinews, and . . . bone" (5.8.12). Ulysses complains that, with the overthrow of "degree" or rank, Greece becomes so weak that Troy can thrive in the war despite its military inadequacy. The loss of rank is a **sickness**, and " 'tis this **fever** that keeps Troy on foot, / Not her own sinews" (*TRO* 1.3.135–6). A distraught Hamlet urges his "sinows, grow not instant old, / But bear me stiffly up" (*HAM* 1.5.94), to retain the vigor necessary for him to pursue his revenge upon Claudius. Claudius himself uses the term, unusually, to refer to his "heart with strings of steel," to the strong cords that bound the heart and threatened to break under the duress of extreme emotion (3.3.70). Claudius wishes for his **heart-strings**, toughened by his age and his crime to such an extent that his heart, bound tightly, cannot expand with remorse and sorrow, to become soft and flexible as "sinews of the newborn babe," malleable and soft enough for virtue and regret to force their way into his heart (*HAM* 3.3.71). Hector urges Troilus not to fight because of the latter's youth for similar reasons: "Let grow thy sinews till their knots be strong" (*TRO* 5.3.33). Sinews hardened but also "shorten[ed]" with advancing years, resulting in "aged **cramps**" (*TMP* 4.1.259–60). Figuratively, the sinew can be the financial support that sustained Mariana until she lost "the portion and sinew of her fortune" and Angelo abandoned her (*MM* 3.1.221), or the backbone or mainstay of a story, "the sinews of our plot," as Fabian suggests about the gulling of Malvolio (*TN* 2.5.75).

In Greek mythology, Typhon cut the sinews from Zeus, hid them, and left him helpless in a cave; Zeus escaped when Apollo convinced Typhon to give Apollo the sinews to string his instrument. Shakespeare may allude to this story when Thersites mocks that Achilles will have no more music (life, sound) in him after fighting Hector, unless "the fiddler Apollo get his sinews to make catlings on" (*TRO* 3.3.304). "Orpheus' lute was strung with poets' sinews," Proteus reminds us (*TGV* 3.2.77).

(C) Vicary (1587, Cr) anatomizes the sinew and defines it as a nerve. Texts that appear to define the sinew as a tendon are harder to find; see *OED* 1, which quotes Boorde's *Breviary* (1547).

sinow, sinows see **sinew**

skin (A) Human skin in the early modern period serves as an index of **race**, gender, sexuality and other social categories. Woven out of threads, **nerves**, **veins**, and **arteries** like a kind of cloth, skin defended the body and distinguished fundamental qualities of the world, such as **heat** from **cold** or **moisture** from **dryness**. Unlike the **eye** or **ear**, skin uniquely needed no other medium (such as air) in order to gather information; it was itself both the interface and the analyst with and of its surroundings. The outer- or "scarf-skin" collected sense-data about the world, and the "skin proper" weighed those sensations, deciding how important they were and how much attention the **brain** needed to pay to them. The dual status of skin as both inside and outside, porous and impermeable, explains its value in early modern diagnostics; like the eyes, skin served as a window into the inner body or state of health of the **patient**.

(B) Shakespeare distinguishes between the human skin and the animal hide, but human skin can be used to *hide* an unworthy personality trait on the one hand or to infuse the qualities of a particular animal into the wearer of its hide on the other. "What shall he have that killed the deer? His leather skin and horns to wear," sing the forest nobles in *As You Like It*, turning a hunting trophy into the comic costume of cuckoldry (4.2.11). The most famous example of this kind of magical usage comes from *2H6* and *3H6*, in which Margaret first warns that Richard of Gloucester is no "sucking lamb" or "gentle dove," as Henry believes, but a "ravenous wolf" clad in a lamb's skin (3.1.71, 4.2.79), and is, later in the sequence, called a "tiger's **heart** wrapt in a woman's hide" by the grieving Duke of York (*3H6* 1.3.147). *MAC*'s overblown description of the murdered Duncan's "silver skin laced with his golden **blood**" (2.3.112) turns the corpse into a jerkin or rich garment (picking up the imagery of clothing that fills the play). The image reverses the natural from the early modern skin-coat, which is in this instance inside out; instead of the skin holding in the liquid blood as a jerkin covers the body, Duncan's congealed blood "laces" or keeps entire his fragmented skin. Tender, smooth, and white skins indicate nobility, youth, femininity, or all three, as in Othello's mortal paean to Desdemona's "whiter skin . . . than snow," "smooth" as the "monumental alablaster" of her own imagined tomb effigy (5.2.4–5). But the rude mechanicals of *MND* are "the shallowest thick-skin[s] of that barren sort" (3.2.13) and the Host calls Simple in *WIV* an ignorant "thick-skin" (4.5.2). Skin keeps **disease** out but can also cover up the "**ulcerous** place," as in *HAM* (3.4.147), until, as in *MM*, "authority," like "medicine," can "skin the vice o'th'top"(2.2.136).

Hamlet asks, "Is not parchment made from sheepskins?" and Horatio replies, "Ay . . . and of calf-skins too" (*HAM* 5.1.114–15), but human skin is also a canvas or parchment, figuratively in some instances (including at the end of *JN*) but literally in others. Adriana's great speech to the "wrong" Antipholus in *ERR* (2.2.110–46) imagines (correctly, as it turns out) that her husband has been split in two, "estranged from [him]self" by his seeming estrangement from her. Adriana imagines her Antipholus' fury, were she to commit adultery as she thinks he has done, "as he would tear the stain'd skin off my harlot-brow / And from my false hand cut the wedding-ring / And break it with a deep-divorcing vow" (2.2.136–8).

In her **frenzy** she evokes tortures inflicted on some felons but not, as far as we know, upon harlots; "rogues and sturdy beggars" could be literally branded or stained on the forehead (hence Dogberry's comment that Verges is "honest as the skin between his brows" [*ADO* 3.5.12]), and thieves and slanderers could have hands and fingers amputated, but not fornicators or adulterers.

Dromio of Ephesus wishes that his "skin were parchment, and the blows you gave were ink," so that Antipholus of Syracuse's "own handwriting would tell you what I think" (3.1.13–14). **Scars** can be "character'd on . . . skin" (*2H6* 3.1.300); character is writing but also reputation (cf. *COR*, in which scars mark the writing of battle, or the scarred soldier Scarus in *ANT*, who boasts that the **wound** he had that was like a T is now like an H [4.7.7–8]). And Aaron turns dead men's skins into epistles from the underworld:

> Oft have I digg'd up dead men from their graves,
> And set them upright at their dear friends' doors,
> Even when their sorrows almost were forgot;
> And on their skins, as on the bark of trees,
> Have with my knife carved in Roman letters,
> "Let not your sorrow die, though I am dead."
> (*TIT* 5.1.135–40)

The "Roman letters" are interesting, and remind us of the shift from "Gothic" (called "Gothian" or "Gothical" in Shakespeare's time) or black-letter to Roman print. Both punitive scarification and tomb carving necessarily used the Roman characters rather than Gothic or Italic (Edward VI's statutes specify that rogues be marked "with a great Romane R"; [March 1648]). Jack Cade comments on the legal status of animal- and human-skin when, agreeing that the rebels should "Kill all the lawyers!" he wonders: "Is not this a lamentable thing, that of the skin of an innocent lamb should be made parchment? that parchment, being scribbled o'er, should undo a man?" (*2H6* 4.2.79–82). It can "undo" you because your skin could be literally "undone" with punishments for treason (such as drawing and quartering), just as the lamb's skin is "undone" and made into parchment.

Cade's comment is one of only two instances in which Shakespeare uses the word "scribbled"; the other is in King John's death-speech, in which the poisoned monarch complains,

> There is so hot a summer in my bosom,
> That all my **bowels** crumble up to dust:
> I am a scribbled form, drawn with a pen
> Upon a parchment, and against this fire
> Do I shrink up.
>
> (*JN* 5.7.30–4)

Shakespeare keeps the language of **heat** and dryness from John's historical **fever** after poisoning, but changes the source's central image from inscription or carving on a stone to handwriting. Shakespeare's John becomes himself the "scribbled form," his skin the "parchment" ready to be consumed by the fire of fever.

(C) Vicary attributes perception and temperance to the skin (1587, C2v); both Vicary and Brunschwig (1525) describe skin as woven cloth. On "the Renaissance skin envelope," see E. D. Harvey (2003); Hillman (2007) describes the tension between skin that defends the body from external threats and yet must converse with that external world. On the misapprehension that harlots were branded, see Henning (2000).

sleep, mare, night-mare (A) Along with air, **diet**, exercise, **excretion**, and **perturbation** or emotion, sleep formed one of **Galen's** six "non-natural" causes of **disease** (as opposed to the "natural" causes of **distemper** such as **complexion** or humoral personality, or the "contra-natural" pathologies of disease). A moderate amount of sleep, taken at the correct time and in a room and bed filled with clean, fragrant air and at a comfortable temperature, was essential for good health, in particular for allowing the **brain** to process the day's activities and to replenish the animal **spirit** that permitted rational thought. Until children were about two years old, they were allowed to sleep at will. Between ages three and four, it was advisable to restrict a child's sleep if it were excessive, since too much sleep could make children (and adults) dull-witted. During sleep, the body continued to produce vital spirit (so that it continued to breathe, to roll over, to have a **pulse**, and so on) but the animal spirit (including the eye-spirit that was responsible for vision) retreated back into the brain, making sleep, in the common comparison, the picture of **death** or "death's counterfeit" (*MAC* 2.3.76). **Melancholy** was a common cause of sleepwalking and of night-mares. The melancholy **humor**, improperly concocted (processed) by the **spleen**, sent dark

vapors or **fumes** to the brain and affected the chamber or ventricle of fantasy. But the rational part of the brain was asleep and unable to bring in the impressions of the senses to mitigate the wild ravings of the imagination by demonstrating that the room was actually dark, there were no **monsters** or visions there, and so on. The sensation of suffocation or **strangulation** that many felt during a night-mare resulted from the thick melancholic fumes traveling up to the brain from the lower body.

(B) Edgar, disguised as Poor Tom, blames the "foul fiend" for the "night-mare" (*LR* 3.4.121), and Mistress Quickly swears to Falstaff that she "will ride [him] o' nights like the mare" (*1H4* 2.1.77) unless he finally pays her what he owes. Central to Petruchio's strategy of taming Katharina is depriving her of sleep (*SHR* 4.3.9, 13). Love may also "chase sleep from [one's] enthralled **eyes**" (*TGV* 2.4.234), although the Lords in *LLL* vow "to sleep but three hours a night" and to abjure love in order to discipline their bodies and minds (1.1.42, 46). *A Midsummer Night's Dream* mixes sleep, dream, and waking. Titania and the lovers are enchanted while they sleep and wander through the woods "half sleep, half waking" (*MND* 4.1.147); Bottom "sleep[s] . . . on pressed flowers," a phrase deeply ironic given that the pressed juice of **love-in-idleness** has bewitched the fairy in whose arms he rests (*MND* 3.1.159). Minus enchanted petals, however, bed-sharing is difficult. As "Rosalind," Ganymede claims he will keep Orlando awake by talking, particularly when he is "inclin'd to sleep" (*AYL* 4.1.156). The history plays present kings sleepless both from their own moral failings and through no faults of their own. Sleep may be "golden" (*1H4* 2.3.41), but the "golden rigol" can divorce a monarch from his rest (*2H4* 4.5.35). Prince Hal believes his father to be in an **apoplectic** sleep from which he will never wake (4.5.35). Richard III is tortured by dreams and "**perturbations**" of those whom he has murdered, while Richmond is rewarded by pleasant dreams and restful sleep (*R3* 5.3.161, 164).

Sleep disorders plague jealous Leontes and the criminal Macbeths. A "humor / . . . presses [Leontes] from sleep" (*WT* 2.3.39), and he famously imagines Hermione's life lived "at the level of [his] dreams" (3.2.80). Macbeth eulogizes

> the innocent sleep,
> Sleep that knits up the ravell'd sleave of care
> The death of each day's life, sore labour's **bath**,
> **Balm** of hurt minds, great nature's second course,
> Chief nourisher in life's feast.
>
> (2.2.33–6)

Infants slept notoriously well, free from sin and care, in what *R2* calls "the sweet infant breath of gentle sleep" (*R2* 1.3.133). Macbeth has lost both innocence and sleep, and thus his mind unravels as he lives through what seems an unending day. Neither of the Macbeths have the opportunity to replenish their spirits in sleep, "the season of all natures" (*MAC* 3.4.140), the rest that allows the body to season or temper or moderate its humors. Sleepwalking was thus "a great perturbation in nature," as the Doctor tells Macbeth (5.1.9). The Doctor claims to have known those who "have walk'd in their sleep who have died holily in their beds" (5.1.60), but both on- and off-stage audience doubt this resolution for Lady Macbeth, who is trapped within her own memories of the murder and fantasies of the past and future without access to reason or to the present (ironically, the very fate she has wished upon the guards; see **limbeck**).

(C) Lavater (1572, F4v–G1r) discusses sleepwalkers who are mistaken for ghosts. Burton (1621) discusses both sleepwalking and fearful dreams in his section on "**cure** of head melancholy" (356–7, 476–7). Lowe's second treatise, fourth chapter (1634, E2v–E3v) discusses sleep at length, as does a chapter in Lemnius (1576). Bright (1586, I2r) analyzes the sensation of choking experienced by so many during the night-mare. Guillemeau propounds a theory of childhood sleep in *The Nursing of Children* (1612). Most secondary material concentrates on *MAC*, *HAM*, *LR* and the late plays. Although her focus is less medical than ontological, Lewin is useful (2002, 2003, 2005), especially on the dream-world of *WT* and the body of the sleepwalker or watching insomniac in *MAC* as a **physical** correlate for the contest between fate or witches and individual human will. For diagnoses (including the hypothesis that Falstaff suffers from sleep apnea) see Fogan (1989); Furman et al. (1997).

sound see **swoon**

spear-grass Spear-grass, or spear-wort (*ranunculus flammula*), was so **hot** and **dry** that it would burn and blister the body. Crafty rogues reportedly pounded it and placed it on their legs and arms to create **ulcers** that would evoke pity (and cash) from observers; others put it to their **noses** to provoke bleeding, a practice that Bardolph recalls: "[we used to] tickle our noses with speargrass to make them bleed, and to beslubber our garments with it and swear it was the **blood** of true men" (*1H4* 2.4.309). Gerard (1597) identifies it with spear-wort (3E7v), as does Doedens (1595, 2I6r–v), but the plant has also been identified as needle-grass, foxtail, or even yarrow and horsetail, both of which were colloquially called "nosebleed" (Brotherston 1902).

'spital see **hospital**

splay see **geld**

spleen (A) The **spleen** received the black bile or **melancholy humor** from the **liver**; it simultaneously drew on this melancholy for nourishment, and purified nutritive **blood** so that it would not be made too thick from the black melancholy. Although the melancholy temperament, **cold** and **dry**, was also called "the spleen," many writers associated the spleen with **choler** and anger, perhaps because the word bile could mean either yellow bile (choler) or black bile (melancholy). In addition, too much of the melancholy swelling the spleen might result in a humoral imbalance whereby the **patient** experienced unpredictable mood swings, moving from laughter to tears to anger to love in the space of a few minutes. Moreover, a working spleen consumed the dark, melancholic humor from the liver and left only light humors or laughter behind, so that the spleen, like its associated humor of melancholy, could be used to explain almost any state of malice, anger, or joy.

(B) Shakespeare associates the spleen with malice, the vengeance of warriors, choler and rashness, and laughter, both bitter and heartfelt. Lear wishes a "child of spleen" to torment Goneril (*LR* 1.4.282), and Rosalind characterizes Cupid as one such infant, "conceived of spleen and born of **madness**" to torture poor lovers (*AYL* 4.1.212). Katherine of Aragon warns the surveyor to "charge not in your spleen a noble person" (*H8* 1.2.174), convinced that the king and his minions proceed against her out of spite. Wolsey denies the charge—"I have no spleen against you," he declares—but Katharine retorts, "Your **heart** /Is crammed with arrogancy, spleen and pride" (2.4.89, 110). Richard III is both malicious and valiant; what the Duchess of York calls his "damned spleen" (*R3* 2.4.64) or hellish vengeance is to him "the spleen of fiery dragons," the brave force of England's protector (*R3* 5.3.350).

"[T]he unruly spleen /Of Tybalt **deaf** to peace" participates in the blood-feud of *ROM* (3.1.157). In the first tetralogy, Talbot praises his son's "youthful spleen and warlike rage" (*1H6* 4.6.13) and the "heated spleen" of soldiers (*3H6* 2.1.124). Several choleric characters are also splenetic. The "testy" Cassius can process all the thick, melancholic humors of his companions and provoke them to laughter (see discussion under **choler**, *JC* 4.3.47). Hotspur's wife complains that "A weasel hath not such a deal of spleen /As you are toss'd with"; he is more irascible than the animal noted for its peevishness (*1H4* 2.3.78–9). The King worries that "Base inclination and the start of spleen" will make people fight against him and side with Hotspur (*1H4* 3.2.125), but the latter's rash courage proves his downfall: "**hare-brain'd** Hotspur, governed by a spleen" leads his troops to their downfall (5.2.19). The choleric Martius is both angry and vindictive against his "cankered country" and "will fight . . . with the spleen" of the devil (*COR* 4.5.91); Alicibiades pairs "my spleen and fury" (*TIM* 3.5.112).

JN associates the "hasty spleen" (4.3.97) with rash judgment, and actions impulsive to the point of stupidity. Soldiers combine immaturity and unthinking violence, "ladies' faces and fierce dragons' spleens" and travel with "swifter spleen than powder can enforce," faster than a bullet from a gun (2.1.68, 448). The Bastard himself is "scalded with . . . violent motion, /And spleen of speed to see your majesty!" (5.7.49–50). Speed might also explain Lysander's comparison of the "brief . . . lightning" to "a spleen [that] unfolds both heaven and earth," a sudden attack of illuminating anger (*MND* 1.1.145–6). When Iago urges Othello to patience, he accuses him of being "all in all in spleen /And nothing of a man" (*OTH* 4.1.88–9), and when Katharina wishes to characterize Petruchio as unpredictable, unreliable, and inconsistent, she calls him "a mad-brain'd rudesby full of spleen" (*SHR* 3.2.10).

LLL twice connects the spleen to merriment. Moth "enforce[s] laughter" in Armado, a "silly thought" provokes the latter's "spleen" (3.1.76). Boyet's "spleen" produces a "zealous laughter" at what is "ridiculous" (5.2.117). In *TN*, the gulling of

Malvolio offers participants "the spleen" to "laugh [themselves] into stitches" (3.2.68–9). More sardonic is the celestial laughter Isabella imagines the angels enjoy from human "spleens" to "themselves laugh mortal" (*MM* 2.2.122–3), or Ulysses' hilarity in his response to war: "I shall split all /In pleasure of my spleen" (*TRO* 1.3.178). Troilus himself, typically, takes the spleen—and war—more seriously. The Trojans cannot subdue their "heaving spleens," he argues, having seen "Such things as might offend the weakest spleen /To fight for and maintain!" (2.2.196, 128).

(C) Vicary (1587, G3v) describes the function of the spleen, and Bright connects its working to laughter (1586). Burton (1621) does not seem to follow Bright's distinction between laughter from the spleen (false) and from the diaphragm (genuine), as Hoeniger observes (1992).

squint see **web and pin**

staggers see **dizzy**

stale see **urine**

stammer See also **tongue-tied** A humoral **flux** of the **belly** could cause the **tongue** to turn downwards and the speaker to stutter or stammer as **moist phlegm** thickened the **tongue**. Ganymede urges Celia to tell her the name of the man who is writing love poems to Rosalind and leaving them in the forest, even haltingly, rather than remaining silent: "I would thou couldst stammer, that thou mightst pour this concealed man out of thy mouth, as wine comes out of a narrow-mouthed bottle, either too much at once, or none at all" (*AYL* 3.2.199–201). Those who stammered refrained from strong wine, because they were so soon rendered drunk because of the moist **humors** in their heads; moreover, the **vapors** of alcohol swelled up the tongue so that their speech was further impaired. Octavius, who unlike Antony has no head for hard liquor, complains when in his cups, "My own tongue /spleets what it speaks" (*ANT* 2.7.123–4). See Hill (1571, R8v–S1r).

star see **planet**

stigmatical Ill-shaped or **deformed**, marked by God's curse as if with a brand or stigma. (*OED* stigma sb. 1); G. Harvey (1597, E1r), "stigmaticall, that is burnt with an hot iron." A furious Adriana calls the man whom she thinks to be her husband from Ephesus (but who is, unknown to all, his twin from Syracuse) "stigmatical in making, worse in mind" (*ERR* 4.2.22), born with an ugly form.

stomach (A) The stomach converted food and drink into "chyle" during the process known as the "first concoction" (the second concoction converted chyle into **blood** and the other **humors** in the **liver**, and the third converted blood into **spirit** in the **heart**, or into animal spirit in the **brain**). If the stomach failed to digest food properly, the whole body itself became **sick**. The most common analogies for the stomach were that it served as a store-house for the body, supplying provisions for all the **organs**, and that it was a cook, converting food into matter fit for each organ. The stomach looked like a cucumber or other gourd, long, narrower at the bottom than at the top, with a cork-like block at the end like a bottle. Its capacity was about two pitchers of water. It refined gross or thick meats and food at the top and passed them down into the intestine, then converted them into chyle to send to the liver. Finally the waste matter that the body did not need went to the **guts** for defecation. Figuratively, the stomach could stand for will or determination or appetite, for anger, or for a stubborn desire for something inappropriate; it can also mean courage (compare our term "guts") or stoicism.

(B) The most common Shakespearean usage of stomach is to denote appetite or hunger, especially one that **surfeits** or eats too much. Lady Percy mourns her husband's loss of "stomach, pleasure, and . . . **sleep**" as he plans his battle (*1H4* 2.3.41). Benedick "is a very valiant trencherman; he hath an excellent stomach," mocks Beatrice (*ADO* 1.1.52). Men are "all stomachs, and we all but food," remarks Emilia (*OTH* 3.4.104). Titus urges Tamora to eat his gruesome anthropophagous feast: "Fill your stomachs; please you eat of it" (*TIT* 5.3.29). Mysteriously, "Virginity . . . dies with feeding his own stomach," opines Parolles (*AWW* 1.1.143): in remaining isolated, in attending selfishly only to her own interests, the virgin leaves no copy to the world when she dies.

SHR is exemplary in its use of the word stomach in several different senses. Tranio uses the word as a synonym for pleasure, telling his master to study only as his "stomach serves" him (1.1.38). Gremio cannot believe that Petruchio has the "stomach" or strength of body to woo the "wild-cat" Katharina (1.2.194). Petruchio urges Kate to eat the meat that he will shortly take away from her, professing care: "I know you have a stomach" (4.1.158); she does not hear the pun, but the audience might realize that Petruchio is commenting on her stubbornness and hunger for power as well as upon her appetite for food. Lucentio wants literally to "close [the] stomachs up" of his guests at the wedding banquet (5.2.9). Finally, Katharina tells all wives, "Vail your stomachs," control your impulses and anger, because it is their duty to be subservient (5.2.176). *SHR* contrasts the angry stomachs of women for power with the hungry stomachs of men for food, but *H5* parallels the body's stomach or appetite for food (and the nausea that can afflict it) to the stomach for battle that Henry V raises in his troops. The prologue to Act 2 of *H5* reassures his audience that he'll "not offend one stomach with our play"—their motion will be imaginary, rather than tossed on turbulent seas or jolted on horseback (2.pr.40). Falstaff's boy feels queasy for a different reason. The "villainy" of Bardolph, Nym, and Poins "goes against [his] weak stomach, and therefore [he] must cast it up," figuratively **vomit** it out by leaving them (3.2.53). The Constable contrasts "stomachs to eat and none to fight," the two senses of the word (3.7.154). The "Crispian's Day" speech specifically sends away those who have "no stomach to this fight" (4.3.35). The infant Miranda "raised in [Prospero] /An undergoing stomach" to support his ill-fortune, but Stephano's stomach is "not constant"—he is **sea-sick** after the wreck (1.2.156–7, 2.2.114).

(C) Vicary (1587, G1v) describes the anatomy, function, and health of the stomach. Boorde's *Dietary* and the *Regimen of Health* provide relevant **dietary** information. Schoenfeldt (1999) and Maus (1995) discuss in different ways the relations between the inside and the outside of the early modern body. Fitzpatrick (2007) describes food and digestion.

stomach-qualmed See also **sea-sick** Queasy, nauseated. Pisanio offers Imogen a **dram** of medicine to help her if she is "**sick** at sea also, or stomach-qualmed on land" (*CYM* 3.4.190).

strangle, strangled (A) The word strangled can refer in Shakespeare to **death** from any kind of asphyxiation, whether deliberate or accidental, including drowning, choking, hanging, smothering, suffocation, intra-uterine oxygen deprivation, and so on. Physiologically, strangulation was thought to prevent the passage of **humors** to and from the **brain**, and to prevent the **blood**'s **spirits** from transferring nutrition around the body.
(B) Shakespeare uses the word to mean legal execution by hanging, in *2H6*, 2.3.8, when King Henry condemns Southwell, Hume, and the conjuror Boling-broke to be "strangled on the gallows." In *1H4*, Falstaff jokes "I hope I shall as soon be strangled with a halter as another" (2.4.498), an ominous prefiguring of the execution of Bardolph in *Henry V*.
In *2H6*, Warwick uses forensic evidence to determine that Gloucester has been murdered, specifically, that he has been strangled:

> But see, his face is black and full of blood,
> His **eye**-balls further out than when he lived,
> Staring full ghastly like a strangled man;
> His **hair** uprear'd, his **nostrils** stretched with struggling;
> His hands abroad display'd, as one that grasp'd
> And tugg'd for life and was by strength subdued:
> Look, on the sheets his hair you see, is sticking;
> His well-proportion'd beard made rough and rugged.
>
> (3.2.168–75)

Gloucester's face is cyanotic, his eyes protruding, his hair and beard disheveled, and his nostrils flared as if fighting for breath. The word appears as a synonym for murder again in *Othello* 4.1.207, as Iago urges the Moor to murder Desdemona "not . . . with poison" but to "strangle her in her bed, even the bed she hath contaminated," advice that Othello follows. In *Macbeth* the witches include in their brew "finger of birth-strangled babe," a reference to the common crime of infanticide (4.1.30). *Richard III* contains a similar reference when the Duchess of York wishes that she had killed Richard before or at his birth "By strangling [him] in her accursed **womb**" (4.4.138). In *King John* (4.3.127–9), the Bastard warns Hubert that if he has murdered young Arthur, the heir to the throne, the remorse should drive him to suicide: "the smallest thread /That ever spider twisted from her womb /Will serve to strangle" him. Holofernes in *Love's Labour's Lost* twice characterizes the strength of the infant Hercules through his ability to "strangle serpents in his *manus*" (bare hands; 5.1.135 and 5.2.591).

In *Romeo and Juliet,* Juliet worries that she will run out of air in the tomb "and die strangled ere my Romeo comes" (4.3.35). This sense of suffocation or silencing becomes the word's usual figurative meaning in Shakespeare's work. Just as the sun, hidden by dark clouds that "strangle" him, appears in greater glory when the clouds disperse, so, argues Prince Hal in *1 Henry IV*, the Prince will shine more splendidly when he throws off his base companions and (1.2.203) reveals his true nature and intentions (1.2.203). In *Twelfth Night* (5.1.146–7), Olivia argues that it is the "baseness of [Cesario's] fear /That makes thee strangle thy propriety," that is, to refuse her proposal. Florizel urges Perdita to "strangle such thoughts" as his betrayal of her at his father's behest in *The Winter's Tale* (4.4.47). King Henry VIII comments of the chastened Cranmer, "He has strangled /His language in his tears" (5.1.156). The word's use in Sonnet 89, "I will acquaintance strangle and look strange" picks up the language of criminality in the sonnet ("fault," "offence," "defence," "disgrace") and plays on the similarity between "strangle" and to make "strange" or estrange (89–8).

(C) Barrough (1583) frequently uses the word "strangle" to describe the rising of foul vapors from raw or undigested humors in the body.

strings see **heart-strings**

sulphur see **brimstone**

suppeago see **sapego**

surfeit (A) A surfeit was an excess of something, usually food or drink, and especially sweets and alcohol. Too much of one particular food led the body to reject it with disgust, since the **humoral** body strove for balance and proportion. Sometimes, however, the body's natural repugnance for the food that had caused the surfeit or overdose set in too late to prevent illness, which arose in consequence of humoral imbalance or **distemper** from eating or drinking the surfeit. The **cure** for an illness caused by surfeit was **dieting** or fasting: moderating one's intake of food and drink and making sure to consume foods that were appropriate for one's **complexion** or humoral personality. More severe cases of surfeit called for purging by **vomit** (by taking emetics) or **purgation** by siege (by taking laxatives orally, or a **clyster** rectally). Children and the weak-willed were most likely to surfeit, because they lacked self-control, especially around sweets. Other populations at risk included the wealthy, especially monarchs, because of the wide range of rich foods readily available for their consumption; King John was known to have died of a surfeit of peaches, and King Henry I of a surfeit of lampreys. Occasionally, however, impoverished or starving persons could surfeit when they finally obtained enough food, from inordinate hunger, and thoughts of their deprived past.

(B) Too much love might provoke a surfeit; Orsino, languishing for love of
Olivia, demands the same music over and over again to feed his love, "that,
surfeiting, /the appetite might **sicken** and so die" (*TN* 1.1.2–3). Later, Orsino
argues that he *cannot* surfeit on Olivia's love, because he is a man. Women's love,
he suggests, is inferior to men's on physiological grounds:

> There is no woman's sides
> Can bide the beating of so strong a passion
> As love doth give my **heart**; no woman's heart
> So big, to hold so much; they lack retention.
> Alas, their love may be call'd appetite,
> No motion of the **liver**, but the palate,
> That suffer surfeit, cloyment and revolt;
> But mine is all as hungry as the sea,
> And can digest as much.
>
> (2.4.93–101)

Women are inferior on two grounds: first, their hearts are not as strong as men's,
and so will crack or break under strong emotion, and second, their loving feelings do not travel along the **liver-vein** to the heart and then to the **brain**, as men's
do; women's love remains an action of the sensible soul or vital **spirit** (which
conferred involuntary movement and apprehension through the bodily senses)
rather than of the rational soul or animal spirit (which conferred reason and
bound the soul to the body). Orsino's digestive metaphor adds a third, implied,
physiological insufficiency in women. Food was digested at least three times in
the humoral body. Nutrition became chyle in the **stomach**, a mixture of the four
humors. Chyle traveled to the liver, where it became **blood** (which was also made
up of the four humors, in appropriate proportions). From the liver, the humors
traveled to the organs they sustained; blood went to the heart, which refined it
still further, with the help of the **lungs**, into spirituous or pure blood, the vehicle
of the vital spirit. Pure blood and **phlegm** might also travel to the brain to become
in turn the animal spirit that was the vehicle of the rational soul. Just as men
could eat and digest larger amounts of food (by virtue of their **hotter** and **dryer**
constitutions) than women, so they could process larger amounts of the pure
blood that nourished passionate love, where a woman's heart might break and
her body compel her to refuse any more love in order to cure itself of surfeit.

Portia seems to believe a version of Orsino's argument; when Bassanio picks
the correct casket, she pleads,

> O love,
> Be moderate; allay thy **ecstasy**,
> In measure rein thy joy; scant this excess.
> I feel too much thy blessing: make it less,
> For fear I surfeit.
>
> (*MV* 3.2.110–4)

But Lysander, enchanted by **love-in-idleness**, believes that men, too may surfeit on love, rejecting his former lover Hermia just "as a surfeit of the sweetest things /The deepest loathing to the stomach brings" (*MND* 2.2.137–8). The cure for any surfeit was dieting; "surfeit is the father of much fast," as Claudio in *MM* puts it, in this case, separation from the once-beloved (1.2.126).

Hal banishes Falstaff, "surfeit-swelled . . . old, and . . . profane," his **belly** distended with too much victualling just as his mind is distempered by his idle life (*2H4* 5.5.50). Indeed, as Nerissa tells her mistress, "they are as sick that surfeit with too much as they that starve with nothing" (*MV* 1.2.6). Queen Margaret curses, "by surfeit die your king" (*R3* 1.3.196). Richard II, according to Gaunt, suffers "the sick hour that his surfeit made" (*R2* 2.2.84), the consequences of his own excessive love for pomp and authority and flatterers. "The younger of our nature, /That surfeit on their ease, will day by day /Come here for **physic**" (*AWW* 3.1.17–19). Apemantus dismisses Timon's misanthropy as the willful self-indulgence of the rich, and bids him learn from the poor what hardship really is: "will the **cold** brook, /Candied with ice, caudle thy morning taste, /To cure thy o'er-night's surfeit?" (*TIM* 4.3.225–7). Cold water and air are interesting changes for a rich man; ice is like "candy," spring water like a "caudle" or posset (**milk** and spices, mixed with ale or wine) to cure a hangover from the night before. The most gruesome vengeance against an overeating monarch comes to Tamora, whom Titus vows to "surfeit on" the flesh of her own sons (*TIT* 5.2.193).

COR questions what constitutes a surfeit: for the starving plebeians, "What authority surfeits /on" would enable bare sufficiency for them (1.1.16–17). For Volumnia, "eleven" sons perishing "nobly" on the battlefield would be barely sufficient to fill her hunger for "good report," but civilian life itself presents the dangers of "voluptuous . . . surfeit" (*COR* 1.3.22–4). For Martius, the **wounds** of war can themselves provide "surfeits" to sicken the sufferer (*COR* 4.1.46). Octavius compares Mark Antony to boys who, despite knowing better, cannot stop eating, part of a series of images that associate Cleopatra with food:

> If he fill'd
> His vacancy with his voluptuousness,
> Full surfeits, and the **dryness** of his bones,
> Call on him for't: but to confound such time,
> . . .
> 'tis to be chid
> As we rate boys, who, being mature in knowledge,
> Pawn their experience to their present pleasure.
> (*ANT* 1.4.25–32)

If Antony spent only his free time enjoying Cleopatra's caresses and banqueting, complains Octavius, his own body would call him to account with stomach-aches from surfeit and "dry . . . bones" from venereal **disease** (see **sciatica**). But spending his political capital in Egypt instead of attending to his business in Rome makes Antony like a boy who demands instant and constant sensual gratification. Edmund in *LR* consistently denies the workings of a higher power—whether divine or astrological—in human life, dismissing misery as the self-created consequences of our own actions: "[W]hen we are sick in fortune, [it is] often the surfeits of our own behavior" (1.2.119).

Queen Margaret urges Suffolk to leave the country quickly after his banishment, so that she may fully know her grief, rather than anticipating it. While she imagines his absence, she continues to enjoy his presence, "As one that surfeits thinking on a want" (*2H6* 3.2.348). The metaphor is particularly apt for the first tetralogy, in which Yorkists constantly kill Lancastrians while thinking about the Lancastrians who have previously killed Lancastrians, an unhealthy cycle of murderous gluttony and grieving fast. Valentine similarly compares an excess of sorry at banishment to a self-indulgent gluttony of grief: "I have fed upon this woe already, /And now excess of it will make me surfeit" (*TGV* 3.1.221–2).

Sonnet 75 figures the poet's beloved "as food to life" to him, necessary and sustaining. But the poetic speaker cannot find a balanced diet of beloved, alternating between wanting "the world" to see his lover and wanting "to be with [the lover] alone." "Thus do I pine and surfeit day by day," he concludes, either thinking constantly of his lover or trying not to think at all (*SON* 75.7–8, 13).

(C) Bullein admonishes readers to eat and drink temperately: "Through surfet haue manie a one perished, but hee that dieteth himselfe temperately, prolongeth his life" (1595, E1v–E2r). Gascoigne's invective against "fowle" drunkenness urges readers not to indulge in drinking games and asks rhetorically, "geue mee leaue (O *Droonkards*) to aske you this question, if by this curtesy, & friendly entertainement of yours, a friend which is constrayned thus to pledge you, doo chance to surfeyte, & to fal thereby into such distemper, that he dye thereof: what kind of curtesie shall we then accoumpt it?" (1576, C4v). Twyne's *Schoolemaster, or Teacher of Table Philosophy* (1576) pleads for moderation at table in food and drink, including stories of famous, gluttonous monarchs and their ignominy.

surgeon (A) Although officially surgeons and barbers belonged to the same trades-guild, the United Company of Barber-Surgeons, in practice the two occupations only overlapped—or ought only to overlap—in tooth-drawing (see **teeth**). The ideal surgeon was learned, practiced, clever, and well-mannered. Unlike **physicians**, who outranked them socially, surgeons did not train at a university but "on the job." Like members of other trades-guilds (such as the Grocers', the Goldsmiths', the Shoemakers', and so on), surgeons apprenticed for at least seven years with senior colleagues who trained them in **wound**-care, amputation, phlebotomy, and any task that involved using a knife (since physicians were forbidden from working with their hands and especially from shedding **blood**). The act providing for the foundation of the Company of Barber-surgeons in 1540 also allowed the company a set number of dead bodies (convicted felons) for dissection, so that an apprentice surgeon could also learn **anatomy** from a human corpse. After completing an apprenticeship, a surgeon might join the Army or Navy to learn more about the profession, both from experience and from European surgeons whom they might meet on their travels. Others might be appointed as personal surgeons to noble men and women; some of these practitioners, such as Thomas Vicary, the surgeon to Henry VIII; Thomas Gale, surgeon to Queen Elizabeth; George Baker, surgeon to James I; or William Clowes, surgeon to Charles I, wrote or translated important anatomical and medical books and became quite well-known.

The Company of Barber-Surgeons examined and granted licenses to barber-surgeons twice in a surgeon's professional life, first directly after his apprenticeship and then again after he had earned some experience in practice on his own. The Company's difficulties were two-fold: on the one hand, unlicensed, unskilled, and often illiterate barbers, castigated as butchers or tinkers or farriers, practiced freely in the provinces and armed services, despite its attempts to rein them in; on the other, physicians tried to prevent even learned surgeons who had years of experience and could read medical books from treating any of the body's internal complaints. There may, however, have been a movement in Shakespeare's London to integrate the two practices of medicine and surgery, internal and external treatments. The **Paracelsian** surgeon John Banister was successfully licensed by the **College** of Physicians to practice both medicine and surgery, despite his having being trained as a surgeon, perhaps in part because he provided a testimonial from Queen Elizabeth herself. Surgeons tended to be more open to new **cures** and ideas, such as the **mercury** treatment or **tub-fast** for syphilis, since they were less hampered by Galenic theory than the university-trained physicians. Since they wrote more frequently in the vernacular, rather than the erudite Latin of the college physicians, they arguably had more influence upon medical knowledge within the general community (including **empirics**, women healers, **midwives**, and so on) than did physicians.

(B) Shakespeare's characters call for surgeons to treat wounds acquired in battle, duels, feuds, and, once, in sexually transmitted **infections**. The soldier Williams vividly tells the disguised King Henry V about the monarch's responsibility for those deathly injured in war, "some swearing, some crying for a surgeon, some upon their wives left poor behind them, some upon the debts they owe, some upon their children rawly left" (*H5* 4.1.139–41). "Go get him surgeons," demands Duncan for the sergeant whose "gashes cry for help" (*MAC* 1.2.44). "Fetch a surgeon," cries the wounded Mercutio (*ROM* 3.1.94). Othello vows "[him]self to be [Montano's] surgeon" (2.3.254), although he does seem to have a surgeon of his own, whom Gratiano offers to fetch to treat Cassio. "The general's surgeon" would have a higher standard of education and practical knowledge than the surgeons pressed to serve the lower ranks, who might even at the turn of the century be barbers with little or no medical training (*OTH* 5.1.100). Portia requests Shylock to "Have by some surgeon . . . on your charge, /To stop [Antonio's] wounds, lest he do bleed to **death**" (*MV* 4.1.257–8), a moral "charge" as well as a financial one that Shylock refuses because it is not "in the bond." Figuratively, Lear is "cut to the **brains**" with sorrow and asks, "Let me have surgeons," although he is clearly beyond medical help (*LR* 4.6.191–2). Vernon defends his "opinion" to Somerset even if it makes him "bleed"; "Opinion shall be surgeon to my hurt /And keep me on the side where still I am" (*1H6* 2.4.53–5). The knowledge that he has remained loyal will **salve** his injury.

In a different register, the Cobbler in *JC* serves as "a surgeon to old shoes; when they are in great danger, I recover them" (*JC* 1.1.23–4), a comic testament to the perceived skill of the good surgeon to cheat death itself. The noble lovers mock Bottom's dying cry as Pyramus by alluding to this reviving skill: "With the help of a surgeon he might yet recover, and prove an ass" (*MND* 5.1.310–1), and Sir Andrew comically calls for a "surgeon" after his run-in with Sebastian (*TN* 5.1.172). It is fortunate that he is not badly wounded, since "Dick surgeon" turns out to be "drunk"—since eight o'clock in the morning—and unable to attend him (5.1.197). Finally, Lord Lysimachus asks the Bawd how a man may "defy the surgeon," that is, avoid the mercury treatment for **pox** (*PER* 4.6.25–6). He learns the answer very quickly, though from Marina, not the Bawd: abjure the brothel itself.

(C) Vicary lists the duties and ethics of a surgeon, and repeats **Galen**'s observation (still quoted by internists) that surgery is "the last instrument of **medicine**," to be employed only when "**diet**" and "**potion**" have failed (1587 B2r–B3r, B2v). Gale (1586) imagines a conversation among three healers on the nature and principles of surgery, but warns that surgeons cannot cure all **diseases**, only those that are "curable" (A2v). Kerwin credits Vicary's *Englishman's Treasure* (1587) with the responsibility for elevating the status of the surgeon in England (Kerwin 2005, 100–5). Pelling and Webster (1979) Clark (1966); and Hoeniger (1992) discuss Thomas Linacre and the founding of the Royal College of Physicians, together with the historical distinction between the physician and the surgeon. J. Dobson and R. M. Walker's history of the Barbers and Barber-Surgeons of London (1979) includes information about surgeons' fees, examinations, and the training of surgeons in the Navy, together with details about the separation of the Barbers' company from the Surgeons' in 1745. Garber (1980) suggests that the call for a surgeon in Shakespeare always precedes the "departure of the injured man from the stage," reflecting Shakespeare's boredom with "physical ailments of a literal kind" (105, 104). Sawday (1996) connects the increased interest in anatomies and dissection in the period to a new kind of subjectivity or interiority based on the unprecedented visibility of the human body. Kerwin (2005) considers surgery as an art of concealment as much as of revelation (through close readings of the texts of William Clowes, among others), through the increase in cosmetic surgery and the treatment of venereal disease such as the pox and its associated highly visible depredations (decayed nasal cartilege; **scars** and **scabs**; baldness). Pettigrew suggests that the absence of surgeons in Shakespeare's works reflects the lack of a consistent narrative about them in the culture at large, suggesting that, for example, they were considered to be both "healers of wounds . . . and . . . foolish and rash" (2007, 134).

surgeon's box See also **tent** (A) Sometimes called a "cup," a box had a wide mouth, a broad bowl, and thick, blunt edges. It was made of copper, horn, tin, glass, wood, or earthenware, and came in various sizes. **Surgeons** used boxes for cupping **patients** to draw out ill **humors** and to help the body expel **disease**; they were also used to draw out venom in cases of snake- or insect-bite. Some surgeons applied cups directly to the affected area, but others applied them lower down (for example, on the neck to draw down ill humors from the **eye** or mouth). In dry-cupping, surgeons heated the box and then immediately applied it to the **skin**, creating a vacuum. Large boxes had a small hole on one side stopped up with wax, and some practitioners put a small stick, which they lit like a candle, across this opening. Others heated the box itself, or a piece of **plaster** and tow inside the box and covered it with a warm cloth, or placed a coin, heated with a lit piece of tow, directly on the patient's skin. Horn-boxes had a little hole in the bottom and a leather **tongue** inside that stopped it up when the surgeon applied his mouth and sucked, either directly or through a quill or pipe. They were heated in warm water, put on the skin, and then heated once more with a candle. Wet-cupping, or scarification, was used when the surgeon believed that the **blood** itself needed to be drawn: after dry-cupping, the surgeon would cut the skin with a lancet or razor blade and then re-apply the box, just once for the delicate, but two or three times at least for those of greater fortitude. After wiping and drying the cut, the surgeon dressed the **wound** with rose oil, butter, or "**Galen**'s wax" (beeswax, almond and rose oil, and borax).

(B) Shakespeare's Thersites retorts that "The surgeon's box, or the patient's wound" (*TRO* 5.1.11) keeps the "tent" of the war, referring either to the box in which the surgeon contains his implements or to the cup itself. In either case, the war is dominated by the injuries, not the honors, that it inflicts upon the Trojans (see **tent** for further discussion).

(C) For a description of the box and instructions on its use, see Guillemeau (fo. 32–3, 1597), Lowe (pp. 388–91, 1634).

sweat (A) The "sweating **sickness**" was a mysterious **disease**—still unidentified by modern epidemiologists—that ravaged England in particular, hence its European name, "the English sweat." The first documented outbreak occurred in 1485, the first year of Henry VII's reign, and then it reappeared in 1506, 1517, 1528, 1551, and finally in 1578, after which it disappeared completely (the so-called Picardy sweat appeared in France between 1718 and 1861 but was much less virulent and had different symptoms). The **physician** John **Caius** witnessed several of the outbreaks, all of which (except in 1506) had extremely high mortality rates, and wrote an account of the disease in 1552. The sickness began not just with copious sweating all over the body but also **fever**, along with body **aches**, especially in the back (near the **liver**), shoulders, arms, legs, and **stomach**. Sufferers also endured a headache severe enough to feel like "**madness**," and a "passion of the **heart**," perhaps breathlessness or anxiety. **Patients** also experienced an overwhelming desire to **sleep**, and once slumbering, might never awaken from their coma.

Caius avers that the sweat itself did not cause the patient's **death**—in fact, sweat demonstrated the body's fight against the **infection**, just as **flux** or diarrhea might represent the body's natural **purge**, or mucus from the **nose** drain excess

moisture from the **brain**. Strong natures could cast out the poison by sweat, in which case the patient escaped; otherwise, the patient would die. Patients caught the infection from too much **heat**, in turn caused by repletion (too much or unwholesome food), by weather that was too **cold** or too hot, too **dry** or too moist for the time of year (in other words, by the unpredictable English climate), by unfortunate conjuctions of the stars, or by bad air or water. Children and the elderly often survived, the former, paradoxically, because of their innate heat, which meant that they rarely ate more than they could digest and were "alwaies redy to eate" (Caius 1552, C3r), the latter because they were cold and dry. In contrast, "ale drinkers" and "tauern Haunters" proved particularly susceptible, because they were "idle" and could not use up the food and drink that they consumed.

The English could avoid the sweat by eating wholesome food in moderate amounts, keeping canals and dunghills clean, burying the dead promptly, avoiding mists, bogs, and fens and living instead in high, open places, sweeping the house and renewing the floor-rushes, and **perfuming** the air. When traveling it was best to purify the air one breathed by inhaling through a handkerchief impregnated with vinegar and rose-water, or by carrying a **pomander** infused with nutmeg, mace, **cloves**, saffron, and cinnamon. If, however, one succumbed to the disease, one's best protections were to abstain from excessive food, to evacuate one's body with the help of a physician and perhaps with a special **bath**, and to chafe the sick, perspiring invalid to increase the production of sweat and hasten the release of toxins.

(B) Mistress Overdone complains in *MM* that her business is "custom-shrunk" because of "the sweat . . . the gallows and . . . poverty" (1.2.83–4). The sweat has killed her clients by natural means, the gallows has executed them, and poverty has made her prostitutes unaffordable to them. Possibly Falstaff's lasciviousness, as well as his liking for ale and taverns and his dislike for exercise, makes him susceptible to "d[ying] of a sweat" as the epilogue in *2H4* predicts. Some editors take both references to evoke the **tub-fast** or the sweating-cure for syphilis rather than the sweating sickness. If this is the case, then Mistress Overdone's clients have been driven away by her workers' sexually transmitted infections and sent to the **'spital** for the mercury-cure, and Falstaff dies of untreated **pox** or from the drastic **quicksilver** therapy that was the syphilitic's last resort.

(C) We are lucky to have Caius' first-hand account of the epidemics (1552). See also Boorde (1547, D3v–D4r), who comments on the disease's contagiousness and recommends quarantining the sick and also the use of sweet-smelling herbs such as juniper, rosemary, or bay leaves. For the dates of epidemics, see also Holinshed (1577), and Hall (1548). Twentieth- and twenty-first-century clinicians and medical historians have suggested as possible causes of the sweating sickness miliary fever or the Picardy sweat (Tidy 1945); food poisoning via a fungal toxin (Patrick 1965); influenza (Roberts 1965); enteroviruses and resulting dehydration (Hunter 1991); "a virus with a rodent vector" (Thwaites et al., 1997); airborne arbovirus (Dyer 1997), and anthrax (McSweegan 2004).

swoon, swooning, swooned See also **faint** (A) Men and women could faint from inanition, fatigue, blood-loss, and the sight of **blood**, but women swooned from intense emotions or **perturbation**. Such emotions might constrict the **heart**, reducing the supply of vital **spirit** to the rest of the body (making the face and extremities pale), and diminishing the supply of blood to the **brain**. Lacking blood to refine into rational spirit, the brain could no longer control voluntary functions such as consciousness and speech; as the heart remained constricted, the body used up its vital spirit, too, which maintained the body's constant temperature and allowed involuntary sense-perception (hence the chill and insensate body of one who fainted or swooned). Excesses of joy, too, could trigger a swoon. In such cases, the heart expanded with love or delight and the brain was again deprived of the blood it needed for the production of rational spirit (volitional movement and speech), since all the blood in the body was being converted into vital spirit in the heart. In such cases it was important to restore the body's vital **heat**, by chafing the temples, warming the body, offering restorative or warming cordials such as pomegranate-juice or malmsey wine, and perhaps by offering **patients** lavender-water to smell (**lavender** was hot and **dry**, and thus refreshed the brain).

(B) It is usually Shakespeare's women, and men accused of effeminate cowardice, who swoon, unless men swoon from love or **apoplexy** (both of which prevented the movement and production of rational spirit in the brain and thus took away consciousness). Angelo offers a physiological explanation for his sensations upon seeing Isabel:

> Why does my blood thus muster to my heart,
> Making both it unable for itself,
> And dispossessing all my other parts
> Of necessary fitness?
> So play the foolish throngs with one that swounds;
> Come all to help him, and so stop the air
> By which he should revive.
>
> (*MM* 2.4.20–6)

Angelo's heart is so overwhelmed by his attraction to Isabella that the blood rushes to it from his **liver** so quickly and in such amounts that it cannot mix with air and produce the vital spirit to send to the brain and other organs, nor can it maintain its steady beat and consume the nutrition it needs. His heart lacks air, crowded by **humors** just as "one that swounds" is crowded by well-meaning but misguided helpers (a reminder of the Latin root of the word perturbation, *turba* or "throng," as if passions result from crowds of humors thronging the body's **organs** at once). Troilus worries that if he is this excited or "**giddy**" at the mere thought of seeing Cressida, when he sees her in actuality his spirits will be overwhelmed with "thrice repured nectar": pure spirit in the brain, refined from vital spirit in the heart, refined from blood in the liver, refined from chyle in the stomach. The volume of pure spirit will cause:

> **death**, I fear me,
> Swooning destruction, or some joy too fine,
> Too subtle-potent, tuned too sharp in sweetness,
> For the capacity of my ruder powers:
> I fear it much.
>
> (*TRO* 3.2.22–6)

Presumably the fear contracts his heart and counteracts the dilation caused by extreme joy (see **perturbation**). Aaron reports that when he told Tamora of the success of their plot, "she swooned almost at this pleasing tale" (*TIT* 5.1.119), her heart suddenly filled with happy humors, drawing them away from her brain.

Troilus and Angelo imagine they are about to swoon from delight or lust, both of which expanded the heart and generated heat in the body. More usually, persons swooned from excesses of **cold** emotions or ailments. Henry IV describes his apoplexy in the chamber called Jerusalem as a swoon, following the medical authorities that attributed both states to an excess of cold in an elderly body (*2H4* 4.5.233). Enobarbus, blaming himself for "a master-leaver and a fugitive," "swoonds rather" than "**sleeps**" (*ANT* 4.9.26), his heart contracted by grief and remorse. "I swoon almost with fear," cries the anguished Hermia (*MND* 2.2.154). "Swound for what's to come upon thee" threatens Menenius to the guards who will not let him see Martius in Aufidius' camp; they mock him with his own words a few lines later, since they have no "cause . . . to swound" when Martius rejects his old friend (*COR* 5.2.67, 101). The hitherto unassailable Queen Margaret finally "swoun[s]" when her son is murdered before her **eyes** (*3H6* 5.5.45), and Queen Elizabeth cries at the news of her daughter's planned marriage to Richard III: "O, cut my lace in sunder, that my pent heart /May have some scope to beat, or else I swoon /With this dead-killing news!" (4.1.34–6). Her heart perhaps is swelling with rage, rather than constricting with grief, since she demands more space for it to beat; alternatively, it struggles to produce more vital spirit in response to her fear and sorrow. "Who was most marble there changed colour; some swounded, all sorrowed," reports the third gentleman of the reunion of Leontes and Perdita (*WT* 5.3.90–1). Swooning sorrow removed color from the face as blood rushed to sustain the heart and brain.

Phebe contemptuously demands that Silvius "counterfeit to sound" if her eyes really are "wound[ing]" him by their cruel glances (*AYL* 3.5.17). Silvius cannot swoon, nor demonstrate injuries on his body made by her eyes, but he is correct that a bloody injury, followed by a swoon predicts love in this play. "Many do swoon when they do look on blood," says Oliver comfortingly to Ganymede when the latter passes out at the sight of Orlando's bloodstained handkerchief (*AYL* 4.3.158), but Celia adds darkly, "There's more in't." Women, but not usually men, were known to faint at the sight of a wound or of bloodshed. The Bastard

syrup

asserts his masculinity through his ability to hear bad news and to see injury: "Show me the very wound of this ill news: /I am no woman, I'll not swound at it" (*JN* 5.6.21–2). So Rosalind/Ganymede attempts to cover his weakness by claiming to have "counterfeited to swound" (*AYL* 5.2.25). Rosaline impugns the masculinity of Berowne by claiming he is about to faint at his discovery in the masque of the Muscovites: "Hold his brows! He'll sound!" (*LLL* 5.2.392). Chafing the temples was standard therapy to recover a fainting person.

Finally, perhaps the most famous swoon or faint in Shakespeare has no verbal indication as such in the text, only Macduff's and Banquo's brusque, "Look to the lady!" and the lady's own, "Help me hence, ho!" (*MAC* 2.3.118–19). Lady Macbeth faints from genuine horror at the crime she has committed, or from disgust at the sight of blood, or counterfeits swooning to draw attention away from Macbeth's histrionics.

(C) Gesner (1576) recommends several medicines to recover one from a swoon or a faint, including (in George Baker's preface) "Three drops of the Quintessences of Perle" (*3v). There is an old and august debate about Lady Macbeth's faint: see the *Variorum* note, and most recently, Sutherland, who engages with Bradley's debate on the subject (2000).

swound see **swoon**

syrup A thick, sweet, liquid **medicine**, in Shakespeare's usage a tranquilizer. Iago gloats that even the strongest **sleeping**-draught routinely prescribed in Shakespeare's time, the **compound** *Trifera* (see **poppy**), or any other "drowsy syrup" will not allow Othello to rest, tortured as he is by the belief that Desdemona has betrayed him (*OTH* 3.3.331). Aemilia tells Adriana that the man Adriana believes to be her husband, Antipholus of Ephesus (who is really Antipholus of Syracuse) has been driven to **madness** by her jealous ravings, and that she will not release him until she has restored his reason by ministering "wholesome syrups, **drugs** and holy prayers" (*ERR* 5.1.104). See *OED*, syrup sb. 1a. "A.T.'s" *Storehouse for the Diseased* (1596, D4v) offers instructions on preparing syrups for a **cough**: "take Water and Sugar, and boyle them alltogether, till it become a syrop."

Taurus See also **planet** (A) Traditional astrological medicine held that the sign of Taurus, the bull, ruled the throat and neck, and controlled the **cold** and **dry** humoral temperament, or **complexion,** of **melancholy**, along with **Saturn.** A few sources, however, give Taurus as the secondary ruler of the thighs (after Sagittarius), especially in women.

(B) Sir Toby **Belch** convinces Sir Andrew Aguecheek to "cut a caper" for him by suggesting that they are both "born under Taurus." Sir Andrew argues that Taurus rules "sides and **heart**," but Sir Toby retorts, "No, sir, it is legs and thighs" (*TN* 1.3.121, 138–40). Sir Andrew is entirely mistaken—Leo ruled the heart— and usually, the legs were divided among Sagittarius, which ruled the thighs, Capricorn, which ruled the knees, and Pisces, which ruled the feet. Sir Toby may be ignorant of Taurus' properties himself, or perhaps taking advantage of Sir Andrew's astrological ignorance to impugn his masculinity (by implying that, like a woman, Sir Andrew is ruled by Taurus in his legs). Perhaps Sir Andrew is indulging in wishful thinking; Leo ruled "sides and heart," and the valiant, **choleric** disposition, but Taurus was cold and dry, a sign ruling melancholy.

(C) Most sources assign the neck and throat to Taurus, such as Digge (1555, E1v) or Fine (1558, D5r). Roussat, however, assigns as a "secondary part" to Taurus the **belly**, adding: "Whatsoeuer female or woman that is borne in this signe after her bodies disposition shalbe marked in the face legge or thigh" (1562, C5r).

tawny See also **cheek, complexion, race** Tanned by the sun, hence dark-skinned or dark in color. Early modern geohumoralism explained dark **skin** as the consequence of the sun's tanning rays and of the **choleric** or **melancholic** complexions of southern races such as Italians, Spaniards, Egyptians, and Moors. Some sources distinguish among so-called white Moors, tawny Moors and "blackamoors"; Shakespeare uses "Moor" to refer both to characters whom he seems to imagine as "black" Africans (such as Othello or Aaron or the "sable" Prince of Morocco) and "tawny" to describe characters such as Cleopatra, whose "tawny front" draws Antony from Rome (*ANT* 1.1.6). "Tawny" may in Shakespeare serve as a relative term. Lucius overhears the Moor Aaron calling his child by the Goth queen Tamora a "tawny slave, half me and half thy dam" (*TIT* 5.1.27); the child is neither "black" like Aaron nor "pale" like Tamora. Similarly, "tawny Spain" is such in comparison to the Lords of Navarre (*LLL* 1.1.173). Henry V threatens to "discolor" the "tawny ground" of the French with their "red **blood**" (*H5* 3.6.161), a heraldic, military, and **humoral** pun that evokes the grounds of a coat of arms, the battleground, and the sallow skins of the French. Dark-haired Hermia is a "tawny Tartar" in comparison to the pale Helena (*MND* 3.2.263).

teeth See also **tooth-ache, tooth-drawer** (A) Given the era's ignorance about dental hygiene, few people retained their teeth past middle age. Decay and halitosis were ubiquitous. Like **hairs**, teeth were considered an **excrement** or product of waste **humor**, useful for chewing, speech, and beauty, but inevitably prone to decay, **aches**, and loss in old age. Teeth were thought to continue growing throughout one's life (perhaps because they appeared to grow as one's **gums** receded with age). Early moderns, following their translations of Aristotle, explained the appearance of growth by suggesting that, while other bones came from an innate humidity, from the mother's **womb**, teeth came from a "nutritive" humidity, and were continually refreshed by the food one consumed.

The extent of tooth loss in the early modern era is perhaps suggested by the fact that even Vicary, surgeon to Henry VIII and his daughters, believes that the number of teeth in a healthy adult mouth is variable. Home remedies for a "stinking mouth" abound, and recipes for tooth-whitening. Since many of these included honey or sugar, they were unlikely to help the situation. Picking or washing one's teeth was considered a sign of excessive vanity in men; even very white teeth, much desired in court by men and women, were held up to ridicule, although the blackened stumps of country folk were likewise the subject of contempt.

(B) Shakespeare associates the loss of teeth with aging in *ROM*, 1.3.13, when the **Nurse** jokes of her teeth, "I have but four." Old Adam in *AYL* responds to Oliver's contemptuous "old dog," "Most true, I have lost my teeth in your service" (1.1.82–3); Claudio dismisses Leonato and Antonio as "two old men without teeth" (*ADO* 5.1.116), and in perhaps one of the most famous references to ageing in Shakespeare, Jaques describes the seventh and final Age of Man, senility, as "Sans teeth, sans **eyes**, sans taste, sans everything" (*AYL* 2.7.166).

Shakespeare takes the story of Richard III's birth with teeth from his sources, which took his **legs forward** or breech birth and **crookback** likewise to be signs of his preternatural wickedness. In Shakespeare, Richard's teeth signify both his aggression (he will snap like a dog) and his precocity. Typically, Caius Martius Coriolanus dismisses dental hygiene as wanton effeminacy, scoffing: "Bid [others] wash their faces /And keep their teeth clean" (*COR* 2.3.60–1), while characters in *LLL* (5.2.332) and *WT* (4.4.753) connect tooth-picking with excessive courtliness.

Toothlessness in women, in contrast, signifies not only age, but ugliness, as in *TGV*'s grudging, "she hath no teeth . . . to bite" (3.1.340–4) or Sonnet 130's mock-championing of the "reek[ing]" breath of the sonnet-speaker's mistress (130–8). (C) See Aristotle (1595), sigs. B9v–Cv, on teeth and humors, and the function of teeth in animals. Bullein (1595) encourages all to comb **hair** and wash teeth, urging it as a matter of health rather than vanity (D7v).

temperality See also **pulsidge** Mistress Quickly means to praise Doll Tearsheet's **pulse** for its evenness and her protégée for her temperate equilibrium, but instead she coins the nonce-words temperality and pulsidge (for temperance and pulse, respectively). See *2H4* 2.4.23.

tent (A) The use of the tent was already controversial in Shakespeare's time (see **wound**). Some **surgeons** inserted the tent, or probe, into open wounds in order to encourage them to suppurate, believing that pus was a sign of the body healing itself by evacuating ill **humors**. Tents might be made of rolled-up soft lint (shavings from **linen** cloth), sponges, or a **cataplasm** of rose-water and other **medicines**. Tents might also be used in the surgical **cure** of **fistula**. Not only was the tent extremely painful to insert and dress, outcomes were unpredictable, and many **patients** feared **death**. It is unsurprising, therefore, that surgeons who treated wounds successfully (with or without the tent) developed international reputations, and that their books went into multiple editions.
(B) Tenting in Shakespeare is excruciatingly painful, uncertain, and danger-ous. In Coriolanus, the tent is a figure for Roman ingratitude. When an embar-rassed Martius complains that his wounds bleed anew when he hears himself praised, Cominius responds that the alternative would be for them to "fester 'gainst ingratitude, /And tent themselves with death" (*COR* 1.9.30–1), to produce pus instead of **blood** because of a treatment that prevented them from healing. The speech gains an added poignancy when Martius almost **swoons** from blood loss and Cominius sends him to have his wounds "look'd to" (1.9.94). Later in the play Menenius complains that the Senators cannot **cure** the "sore" that they have created in the Roman body politic by banishing Martius. "You cannot tent yourself," he argues (3.1.235); only an experienced and outside healer can probe to the bottom of a deep wound without endan-gering the patient's life.
At the same time, deep probing is the very purpose of a tent, without which no cure can take place. Hector compares the "modest doubt" that he has about the Greeks' intentions to the tool that must investigate the "wound of peace," "the tent that searches /To the bottom of the worst" (*TRO* 2.2.16–17). Peace is fragile, and it is tempting to leave it alone, yet without probing it, the Trojans will not know what secret **infection** lies hidden within. Shakespeare's Thersites puns on two meanings of the word "tent", one medical, one military. When asked "who keeps the tent now?" Thersites retorts, "The **surgeon's box**, or the patient's wound" (*TRO* 5.1.10–1), a sarcastic response that imagines both peace and war as fatal. Similarly, Hamlet proposes to "tent [Claudius] to the **quick**," with the

play, to search deep in his mind as a surgeon probes a wound, watching carefully lest he "blench" or pale as suffering soldiers did when tented (*HAM* 2.2.597).

Some wounds, however, are too deep to be probed, such as "the untented woundings of a father's curse" that Lear hopes will "pierce" Regan (1.4.300), or Imogen's exquisite torture at the imputation of adultery: "I have heard I am a strumpet; and mine **ear** /Therein false struck, can take no greater wound, /Nor tent to bottom that" (*CYM* 3.4.113–15). No probe could reach deep enough to cleanse such a wound, which has penetrated her through and through.

(C) For detailed instructions on inserting a tent, see Bullein (1579, 2C1r–v) who recommends tenting in both natural and surgical wounds, using a probe made of linen moistened with **whites of egg**. See also Clowes (1588).

tertian, burning fever See also **ague**, **fever**, **quotidian** (A) A "pure tertian" was an ague (with rigors, trembling, and recurrent fever) that spiked every third day, counting inclusively, that is, on days one and three of an illness. (A quartan spiked once every seventy-two hours, or on days one and four of an illness, and a quotidian spiked once a day.) A tertian came from corrupted **choler** within the body; the putrid **humor** was carried to the extremities and then burned off through the fever, leaving the body free from the noxious humor and ready to replenish itself. **Patients** should therefore be purged of the choler quickly, first by **potions** such as **wormwood**, administered orally to induce **vomits**; then by **clysters** such as mallows or **mercury**, administered rectally to encourage defecation; then by oral **medicines** such as marshwort or dill, to provoke **urine**, all to cleanse the lower body. On days when the patient's fever intermitted (for example, on day two or day four), the **physician** should trigger **sweating**, perhaps by prescribing for the patient hot **baths** in drinking water (**salt** water could also be used for bathing, but not as effectively). Sometimes, however, the corrupt choler did not disperse around the body, but remained in the veins with the **blood**. In such a case, the patient suffered not from a pure tertian but from a burning fever, or "double tertian," which did not intermit but burned constantly. The severity and tenacity of a burning fever could trigger fever seizures and required the immediate opening of a **vein** near the **heart**, to let blood even until the patient **swooned**. It was important not to cool a burning fever too quickly by applying vinegar or cooling medicines to the **skin**, however, because such tactics merely drove the fever inwards to burn the internal **organs**. Instead, it was better to sprinkle the floor with **cold** water and cooling, fragrant flowers such as roses, water-lilies, and violets, and to restrict company (since human bodies increased the ambient temperature). Both a pure and a double tertian required a **diet** of cooling foods such as **lettuce**, sorrel, spinach, and the occasional fish or white meat, and strict abstention from "sharp" foods that engendered choler, such as mustard, salted or red meat, and wine.

(B) Shakespeare's Venus includes "burning fevers" (739) in her list of ailments that threaten human life, as part of her argument to Adonis to seize the day rather than maintaining his chastity. When Mistress Quickly sorrows for Falstaff, consumed by a "burning quotidian tertian," she may be confusing the words quotidian with quartan, or the so-called double tertian with the quotidian (*H5* 2.1.119). In either case, patients could not suffer from more than one type of ague at a time.

The Archbishop of York offers a lengthy comparison of England to a diseased body with a burning fever:

> we are all diseased,
> And with our surfeiting and wanton hours
> Have brought ourselves into a burning fever,
> And we must bleed for it; of which **disease**
> Our late king, Richard, being infected, died.
> But, my most noble Lord of Westmoreland,
> I take not on me here as a physician,
> Nor do I as an enemy to peace
> Troop in the throngs of military men;
> But rather show awhile like fearful war,
> To diet rank minds **sick** of happiness
> And **purge** the obstructions which begin to stop
> Our very veins of life.
>
> (*2H4* 4.1.54–66)

Too much food, or **surfeit**, was known to overheat the body and induce a fever; Richard II and his lords overindulged in their own interests at the expense of the health of the kingdom. The quickest, and most assured, way to lower a body temperature elevated by a high fever was to let blood from the patient, as did Bolingbroke by deposing Richard (though it is noteworthy that the Archbishop is clear that Richard died from the "disease" rather than from the **cure**). The Archbishop now claims, however, that he is neither "physician" (nor, presumably, **surgeon**, who would bleed the patient), but merely presenting the show of war to act as an allopathic therapy against the complacent minds "sick of happiness," surfeited on peace. He is hoping that the mere sight of his soldiers, like a "diet" or food-cure, will "purge" or evacuate rebellion before the fever returns and the body politic needs to be bled again.

(C) On the different sorts of tertians, see Barrough's table (1583, P2r). In 1885, the neurophysiologist Camillo Golgi first identified tertian and quartan agues with infections resulting from the organisms *Plasmodium malariae* and *Plasmodium vivax* respectively, each of which causes a fever with a different periodicity (Tognotti 2007, abstract). Jarcho (1987) defends Quickly's diagnostics.

tetter Any kind of scaling, spreading, itchy **skin** rash, usually ringworm but also the papules of impetigo, eczema, herpes, **measles**, and so on. The Ghost of Old Hamlet describes the marks that erupt on his body after Claudius' poison takes effect as a "**lazar**-like" "tetter" (*HAM* 1.5.71), comparing the crust to the scales of **leprosy**, but this is relatively unusual. Thersites includes the tetter in his catalog of "diseases of the South" (see **disease** for discussion of *TRO* 5.1.17–24). For its association with ringworm, see Cartwright, who **plasters** it with salad oil and **salt** (1579); Bullein, who treats it with the mountain wildflower *diapensia* in vinegar, and salt again (1579, D5v), and many others.

tinct, tincture (A) In Shakespeare's time, tincture usually meant a color or tint, or a flavor, but it was also starting to have its alchemical sense: the essence of something, extracted chemically, usually for medicinal purposes. The tinct might also refer to the legendary elixir that could transmute base metals into gold (see **med'cine potable, alchemy**). In alchemy, the tincture was the fifth **element** or immaterial **quintessence** that could be infused into material objects. Hence the sense of the word meaning a **physical** "trace" or "stain" or "color" might overlap with its sense as spiritual "signature" (the invisible correspondent in the metaphysical world to any material object in the physical world).
(B) *JC* parallels "tinctures, stains, relics, and cognizance" (2.2.89) and Paulina, believing Hermione dead (or wishing to convince her audience that she is dead) notes no "Tincture or lustre in her lip, her **eye**, /**Heat** outwardly or breath within," neither bodily attributes such as color, heat, or movement, nor spiritual signs of the presence of her soul, such as "luster" or "breath" (*WT* 3.2.205). The "**perfumed** tincture of the roses" (*SON* 54.6) alludes both to color and fragrance, but perhaps also to the spiritual or metaphysical beauty of the poet's beloved, and when Julia mourns the loss of the "lily-tincture of her face," she sorrows as much for her own misery as for her **complexion** (*TGV* 4.4.155). The clearest medical references to tinct or tincture associate it with the elixir or philosopher's stone. The King of France recognizes his own ring, on Diana's finger, and asserts, *contra* Bertram,

> Plutus himself,
> That knows the tinct and multiplying **medicine**,
> Hath not in nature's mystery more science
> Than I have in this ring.
> (*AWW* 5.3.102)

The mythical god of wealth can generate gold from base metals through the science of alchemy, but the King claims that his ring is equally miraculous, since it has transferred itself from Helena to Diana, and that it is as valuable to him as the philosopher's stone. Cleopatra personifies Antony as the elixir, the mere sight of whose "Great medicine hath /With his tinct gilded" the messenger (*ANT* 1.5.37).
(C) Ripley (1591) outlines the principles of alchemy in verse. Roger Bacon, the famous friar, uses the term tinct as a verb to connote the ability to transmute one substance into another: "Whosoeuer therefore can conuert the soule into the

bodie, the bodie into the soule, and therewith mingle the subtile spirites, shall be able to tinct any body" (1597, F3v). Yates (1979) writes at length about the occult (under which category she includes both astrology and alchemy) in early modern England. Kerwin glosses "tinct and multiplying medicine" in the contexts of both alchemy and medical establishments (2005, 229–31).

tisick See also **consumption** A consumption or wasting **disease**, often following from **pleurisy**, tisick (also spelled phthisis, ptisic, and phthisic) resulted from sharp **humors** flowing down from the head into the **lungs** and overheating and consuming the whole body from within. Sufferers coughed **blood**, ran **hectic fevers**, and developed incurable **ulcers** within the lungs and distinctive features of the face and body such as sharp **nostrils**, hollow **eyes**, and shoulders that "stick out like birdes winges" (Barrough 1583, F6r). Although **cures** were difficult, Barrough advises at least an attempt, by keeping **patients** in a temperate, **dry** air; feeding them **milk** (especially woman's milk) but no flesh or wine, both of which were too **hot**; applying **plasters** of lime seed and fenugreek to cleanse the ulcers, and then offering **medicines** of rose conserve to heal them up. Shakespeare uses the term only twice. Pandarus claims to be close to **death** because "A whoreson tisick, a whoreson rascally tisick so troubles me" (*TRO* 5.3.101), and "Master Tisick" (whom Mistress Quickly typically calls "the debuty" for "the deputy") may look cadaverously consumptive.

tongue See also **tongue-tied** (A) The tongue, the principal **organ** of taste, was placed within the mouth so that it was near the **brain** and so that it could serve both taste and speech, and remain protected. It was made of white flesh, but looked red because of the **veins** and **arteries** that suffused it. A thick tongue suggested an overabundance of **phlegm**, and a thin one, of **choler**. A long, red tongue, on the other hand, usually indicated a **sanguine** or well-balanced **complexion**. Tongues white or black were signs of serious illness, especially in the **breast** or **stomach**. Although small, the tongue was important, since it gave voice to the thoughts of the brain. The tongue was notoriously unruly, and so was restrained by the **teeth**. The length of the tongue could be determined by the size of a baby girl's **navel**-string or umbilical cord, hence the injunction to the **midwife** to "cut it short" (loose-tongued or talkative women were thought to be at risk for sexual adventure).
(B) Tongues, ubiquitous in Shakespeare, refer to the ability to speak; language; votes (in *COR*, along with "voice"); wit (in *LLL*), political power (in *R2*), sexual activity (in *SHR*). The citizen who challenges Menenius' fable of the **belly** figures "the tongue [as] trumpeter" (1.1.17), anticipating Martius' struggle for the plebeians' "voices." Ready at first to give Martius their "own voices with [their] own tongues" (2.3.45), the plebeians hear him complain "I cannot bring my tongue to such a pace" (2.3.51), and recognize his contempt for their "su'd -for tongues" (2.3.208). He "despise[s]" the "tongues o'the common mouth" (3.1.22), and cannot permit "a beggar's tongue /[to] Make motion through [his] lips" (3.2.117). *LLL* mocks the Prince's decree that no woman should approach the

court "on pain of losing her tongue" (1.1.124); "the tongues of mocking wenches" (5.2.256) thoroughly overpower the clichés that the Lords use to woo them. The Princess and Rosaline complain about second-hand courtship, phrases taken from "the base sale of chapmen's tongues" (cheap books) or "the motion of a schoolboy's tongue" (cant phrases learned as lessons) (2.1.16, 5.2.403). The play parodies both the language of courtship in the "vain tongue" of Armado (1.1.166), and the Latin tongue in the lesson of 5.1. Rosaline punishes Berowne for his idle, mocking wit—and for the attempt to silence women ("It were a fault to snatch words from my tongue," she says, 5.2.382)—by sending him to visit the "speechless **sick**" and catering to their **ears** rather than his own tongue (5.2.862).

The penalty played for comedy in *LLL* typifies gruesome tragedy in *TIT*. Demetrius and Chiron rape and mutilate Lavinia, cutting her tongue out so that she cannot speak of their crime and amputating her hands so that she cannot emulate the classical Philomel (also deprived of her tongue) by weaving her story in a tapestry. They mock her horrifically: "go tell, and if thy tongue can speak, /Who 'twas that cut thy tongue and ravish'd thee" (2.4.1–2) and bid her call for water to wash her face before adding, "She hath no tongue to call, nor hands to wash" (2.4.7). The elaborate rhetoric of Lavinia's uncle Marcus when he sees her has received much commentary:

> a crimson river of warm **blood**,
> Like to a bubbling fountain stirr'd with wind,
> Doth rise and fall between thy rosed lips,
> Coming and going with thy honey breath.
> But, sure, some Tereus hath deflowered thee,
> And, lest thou shouldst detect him, cut thy tongue.
>
> (*TIT* 2.4.22–7)

Some have suggested that the only way to make Marcus' loquacity sympathetic or even comprehensible on stage is to have him punctuate his flowery language with compassionate actions ministering to his niece, binding her **wounds** and offering first-aid—to mitigate the dissociated, bookish diction with which he describes her plight. From a medical point of view, Shakespeare might have recalled the use of the **simple** (herbal medicine) "Rosed honey" to **cure** a bleeding tongue. Rosed honey was made from good honey, infused with the essence of roses (ideally Turkish). It worked both by its resemblance to the blood from the tongue (pink, sticky, and sweet, as the sanguine **humor** was supposed to be) and by reducing **inflammation**.

(C) Thomas Tomkiss' play *Lingua* (1607) dramatizes the struggle among the senses for supremacy by personifying the tongue itself. Crooke (1615) describes the **anatomy** and function of the tongue. Mazzio's dissertation (1998) explores the cultural meanings of the tongue (especially its associations with feminine loquacity). Ray (1998) connects the loss of agency for the early modern rape victim to the bodily mutilations (amputated hands and tongue) of the raped

Lavinia. The recommendation for "Rosed hony" for a bloody tongue can be found in Hill (1571, K8r, fo. 128). Gesner (1576) uses "Rosed honey" for a sore throat, among other things.

tongue-tied See also **stammer, lisp** (A) Tongue-tied children were born with **tongues** shortened by a ligament underneath. Although such children took longer to learn to speak than others, and tended to speak more quickly than others when they eventually did, their speech was clear except when they were required to pronounce difficult words. They suffered particular difficulty in distinguishing between the letters L or R, and so were sometimes termed "lispers." In newborns, the ligament could be cut with the point of a pair of scissors and the **wound** cleansed by rubbing a finger dipped in **salt** over the area. Operating was unnecessary, however, unless the tongue-tie interfered with the speech, or unless adults developed **ulcers** under the tongue that prevented them from speaking. In that case, the surgeon bound his fingers with fine **linen**, lifted up the tongue, stretched the membrane with a small hook and divided it with a lancet. If the ligament were too short even to stretch, the surgeon needed to cut out all tissue that did not properly belong to the tongue. Post-surgery after-care required **patients** to wash their mouths with water and vinegar, and to raise the tongue to the roof of the mouth so that the ligament did not grow again.
(B) There is no evidence that Shakespeare imagines any of his characters to be literally tongue-tied, but they are often tongue-tied from shyness, modesty, shame, "guiltiness," (*JC* 1.1.62), anger, and other strong emotions. Often the expression of emotion is inhibited by an awareness of rank or gender difference. Yorkists and Lancastrians are "tongue-tied and so loath to speak," and choose red or white roses instead to declare their loyalties (*1H6* 2.4.25). Theseus praises the mechanicals' performance over "saucy and audacious eloquence" because "tongue-tied simplicity /In least speak[s] most, to my capacity" (*MND* 5.1.103–5). Leontes taunts Hermione with his power and her fatigue, which in tandem render her mute: "Tongue-tied, our queen?" (*WT* 1.2.27). Sonnet 66 bitterly complains of "art made tongue-tied by authority" (66.9). Pandarus wishes all girls who are bashfully "tongue-tied" in the presence of their lovers "Bed, chamber, Pandar" (*TRO* 2.3.210–1). The poet-speaker of Sonnet 80 is "tongue-tied, thinking of [his lover's] fame" (80.4). Disingenuous Gloucester takes advantage of the assumption that a tongue-tied person is shy or modest, refusing Buckingham's offer of the crown with a preterition: "If not to answer, you might haply think /Tongue-tied ambition, not replying, yielded /To bear the golden yoke of sovereignty" (*R3* 3.7.144–6). It is a double-bluff: Gloucester refuses to refuse the crown silently, on the grounds that his silence might be construed as agreement or even ambition to take the throne. The speaker of Sonnet 85 is arguably silent from false modesty, too: "My tongue-tied Muse in manners holds her still," it begins (85.1).

Giving voice to strong feeling can, however, protect the **heart** from breaking with an onslaught of emotion (see **o'ercharged**). "Give my tongue-tied sorrows leave to speak," demands Margaret (*3H6* 3.3.22), and the Duchess of York urges her companions, "Be not tongue-tied: go with me. /And in the breath of bitter words let's smother /My damned son" (*R3* 4.4.132–4). Sonnet 140 unusually presents a tongue-tied speaker holding his tongue despite his irritation: "do not press /My tongue-tied patience with too much disdain," it chides (140.1–2).

(C) See Hill (1571, R7v–Sr); Guillemeau (1612, F4r); Haslem (1996). Crooke (1615) claims that tongue-tied persons do not speak intelligibly (p. 626).

tooth-ache See also **teeth, tooth-drawer** (A) All ranks of early modern dentist (**surgeons**, barbers, and itinerant tooth-drawers, in descending order of status) generally agreed that tooth-ache was felt in the root or **nerve**, rather than in the tooth itself, which was nerveless bone. Tooth-ache was thought to proceed either from either **infective** or **humoral** causes, either by tiny worms who infected the root, or by corrupted **phlegm** or excessive **choler** overloading a nerve or **sinew**. Recommendations include washing teeth with abrasive powder, such as mastic, and/or wine to prevent decay. The first remedy for tooth-ache was through **diet**; sufferers were enjoined to abstain from dairy, white meat, and fish, and to rinse the mouth after meals. The second was **purgation**, through bleeding the cephalic **vein** to draw out the **brain** humors thought to cause decay; scarifying the **gums**; dry-cupping (applying a box or cup with **heat** to create a vacuum and draw out the **ill** humors) the shoulder or neck; or administering oral laxatives such as **rhubarb**. The third line of attack involved local applications of vinegar, pomegranates, or various other remedies, although the use of vinegar was becoming controversial by the sixteenth century despite its recommendation by both Avicenna and **Galen**. Rotten teeth might also be cauterized with a hot iron or oil of vitriol.

(B) An exchange in *ADO* implicitly compares Benedick's nagging tooth-ache to unrequited love and explains it as the result of a "humor or a worm" (3.2.27). Posthumus' gaoler in *Cymbeline* ironically comments that the only benefit of a **death** sentence is freedom from tooth-ache (5.4.173). Iago uses the excuse of a "raging tooth" to explain why, he claims, he was awake at night and could hear Cassio's lustful dreams about Desdemona (*OTH* 3.3.414). No-one knows what Autolycus means when he says that clean **linen** drying on a hedge sets his "pugging tooth an edge" (*WT* 4.3.7), although most editors (and *OED*) gloss "pugging" as "thieving," from "pug," to pull up (*OED* adj. 1). We still have the saying "to set one's teeth on edge" to mean "overwhelmed by nervous tension," usually from an unpleasant or scratching noise, a usage that evidently existed in Shakespeare's time, since Hotspur mocks Glendower's ballads with the comment that he

> had rather hear a brazen canstick turn'd,
> Or a **dry** wheel grate on the axle-tree;
> And that would set my teeth nothing an edge,
> Nothing so much as mincing poetry.

> > (*1H4* 3.1.131)

(C) Guillemeau (1597) discusses tooth-drawing in chapter 7, Book 5. On non-surgical remedies, including vinegar and mastic, and on gold fillings, see Vigo (1543, book 5 chapter 6), who comments sympathetically, "as Galene sayth, the payne of the tethe, is the greatest of all paynes that kylleth not [ye] pacient" (2F2v), or Cogan (1636, Gr–v). Vigo urges surgeons to refer patients who need teeth drawing to "experte . . . vagabounde toothdrawers" or barbers rather than to attempt it themselves (2F4r), but Guilleumeau complains bitterly of ignorant barbers who draw too many teeth. For more recipes, see Cogan (1636); Vicary (1587, L3r).

tooth-drawer See also **surgeon, tooth-ache**, **teeth** Although both barbers and surgeons belonged to the same guild, the only area of overlap between the two professions was tooth-drawing. One might also find a wandering tooth-drawer hawking his services at a marketplace or local fair. Tooth-drawers removed tartar (which was thought to originate from rotten **humors** emanating from the **stomach**) by scraping or rubbing the teeth with instruments. Teeth loosened (again, from humors ascending from the stomach or descending from the **brain**) could be held in place with gold wire, and teeth sensitive to **cold** or **heat** were treated with washes made of *aqua vitae,* rosemary, nutmeg, and **clove**. As a last resort in cases of tooth-ache, surgeons or barbers or tooth-drawers filed rotten teeth down and then filled them with gold leaf, or pulled them out altogether. Lost teeth could be replaced with false ones made of ivory or bone. The tooth-drawer was instantly recognizable from his necklace of teeth or the brooch in his cap or his belt bearing an emblem of a tooth. Our evidence for the brooch in the cap is Shakespearean: the lords mock Holofernes' cadaverous face by comparing him to "the carved-bone face on a flask" or on a "brooch . . . worn in the cap of a tooth-drawer" (*LLL* 5.2.615, 618). The saying "to lie like a tooth-drawer" was proverbial, presumably because these unqualified itinerants claimed that they could extract teeth quickly and painlessly at a low cost (Rous 1654, 2O2r). Woodforde (1983, 15–20) describes the procedure of extraction, and the instruments used, in detail.

tremor cordis Trembling or palpitation of the **heart**, making the sufferer breathless or panting, sometimes unable to speak. The jealous Leontes feels as though his heart is dancing, "but not for joy," for horror at the sight of his wife's supposedly adulterous affection toward Polixenes (*WT* 1.2.110). His choppy verse is here medically and emotionally apt. Barrough comments that *tremor cordis* comes from any **distemper** of the body (such as too much **heat** or **cold**) but especially from emotional triggers that reduce the store of vital spirit in the heart, such as "anger, watching [insomnia], lecherie" (1583, Gr).

tub-fast See also **pox, quicksilver** (A) Also called the powdering-tub for the tub's original purpose, to **salt** or powder meat to preserve it, the tub-fast could be used with either guaiacum wood or quicksilver treatments for syphilis. Typically, the tub-fast combined **Galenic** and Paracelsian **elements**. The strict, fasting **diet** acknowledged **humoral** elements in the disorder, but the quicksilver **fume** or unction displayed Paracelsian chemotherapy (although **Paracelsus** himself disdained "horse doses" or heroic **mercury** therapy; see Ball 2006, 33). To receive the fume, the **patient** would sit naked under a canopy, upon a stool with a hole in it, like a **close-stool**. There might be a small hole in the canopy to let air in so that the patient could breathe. Under the stool the **surgeon** placed a dish of hot coals (and the mercury or quicksilver). After the patient had sweated for a couple of hours, the **nurse** put the patient in a warm bed, wrapped in a heated sheet so that he would sweat some more. Other surgeons administered the fume in the bed itself, in a warming-pan or chafing-dish of coal, sometimes between the patient's legs in bed.

(B) Pistol imagines Doll Tearsheet in "the powdering-tub of infamy," the tub used both for salting meat and for treating the **pox** (*H5* 2.1.69–71). The mistress of the brothel in *MM* has similarly "eaten up all her beef, and . . . is herself in the tub" (3.2.55). Timon too associates the "salt" of preserved meat with venereal **disease**, urging the courtesans to "season the slaves /For tubs and baths; bring down rose-**cheeked** youth /To the tub-fast and the diet" (*TIM* 4.3.86–8); the association with powder or salt may also explain Caesar's dismissal of "Salt Cleopatra" (*ANT* 2.1.21). In *CYM*, erotic love necessarily involves disease: "Desire, that tub /both fill'd and running" is always hungry and always pustulent (*CYM* 1.6.48).

(C) For a sample of the **cure** by fume, see Clowes (1579, Aa4v).

U

ulcer, ulcerous See also **evil** (A) **Surgeons** distinguished ulcers from other sorts of open **sore** because they produced a reddish or yellowish liquid, smelled foul, and could be difficult to **cure**. Ulcers formed by external causes, such as chafing or injury, included virulent ulcers, corroding ulcers, filthy ulcers, hollow ulcers, ulcers with holes and **cankered** ulcers; ulcers resulting from an innate tendency within the body included ulcers of intemperance (from too much food or drink), dolorous ulcers (which were painful), swollen ulcers (**imposthumes**), broken ulcers (which were partially healed), overgrown ulcers (which were hidden), hard ulcers (which needed to be sectioned surgically), cankered ulcers (which indicated a serious inner **disease** or tumor growth), hollow ulcers (which, like imposthumes, filled with fluid), and ulcers corrupt at the bone (long-lasting, deep, chronic **wounds**).
(B) It is typical of *TRO* that the protagonist would characterize his love as a disease in "the open ulcer of [his] **heart**" (1.1.53). *HAM* figures both Gertrude's sexual sin and Hamlet's political treason as painful ulcers that suppurate. Gertrude's "ulcerous place," however, is hidden under a "**skin** and film" underneath which "rank corruption, mining all within /**Infects** unseen" (3.4.147–9). Marriage provides the thin skin of sanctity for relations that are secretly disorderly and undermine or corrupt her from within. The repeated use of the word "rank" in the play evokes the stinking odor of putrefying wounds. Claudius urges Laertes to wound Hamlet "to the **quick** o'the ulcer," to the most painful, inward part, the **nerve** that carries vital spirit from the heart (*HAM* 4.7.123).
(C) Banister (1575) discusses and taxonomizes ulcers in particular, in several chapters; see also Lanfranco (1565).

unpaved See also **eunuch**, **geld**, **splay**, **unseminar'd** Lacking testicles or stones; hence, infertile. Cloten tries "the voice of unpaved eunuch" and other sorts of music to seduce Imogen, in vain (*CYM* 2.3.30).

344

unseminar'd Lacking testicles or **seeds**; infertile. Mardian the **eunuch** points out to Cleopatra, however, that just because he lacks male genitalia and the ability to consummate a relationship with sexual intercourse "in deed," he does not lack the ability to enjoy erotic fantasy: "Yet have I fierce affections, and think /What Venus did with Mars" (*ANT* 1.5.17–18). See **eunuch**; also Elam (1996).

untimely ripp'd (A) Removed from the **womb** during what we would now call a posthumous Caesarean section. Such operations might have occurred routinely in early modern Europe in order to baptize the child, and to make sure that the **dead** mother could be buried in consecrated ground (since if she died with an unbaptized child within her body, she might forfeit her own eligibility for Christian burial). Pliny the Elder had recounted the birth of Gaius Julius Caesar (conflated in the early modern period with the emperor Julius Caesar) in this way, and medieval surgical manuals include instructions on holding open the uterus (to allow the fetus to breathe) and the best place for the **incision** (the left side, where the **liver** would not obstruct the **surgeon**'s work). Barbers or surgeons performed nearly all such procedures, with a **midwife** attending; the midwife or women attendants were generally those who informed the surgeon that the fetus was still alive, and who requested the extraction. After verifying that the woman was really dead (by putting cotton threads or feathers to the **nostrils** to detect even the lightest breath), the surgeon or barber made the incision and removed the infant. The midwife and female attendants immediately succored the baby.
(B) Macbeth believes that the witches' riddle, that he may not be killed by one "of woman born," confers upon him immortality, a "charmed life." But Macduff "was from his mother's womb /Untimely ripp'd" (*MAC* 5.8.15–16). The witches were punning on the nature of birth rather than the nature of woman; Macduff was conceived in the ordinary way, of a man and a woman, but "ripp'd" by surgical means into the world after his mother's death rather than being "born" in the usual way. There may be a pun on "borne" or suffered: Macduff's unlucky mother did not endure the pangs of delivery. "Untimely" does not mean "premature," as some gloss it, but "at an inopportune time": after his mother's death, rather than before. Posthumus Leonatus was likewise "ripp'd" from his mother's womb after her death, giving him his name (*CYM* 5.4.45).
(C) See Guillemeau for the term "Caesarian section" and a description of Julius Caesar "rip't out of his Mothers wombe" (1612, A20r). Crooke reports that both mother and child may be saved (1615, 2G4v), but such an optimistic view is quite unusual. Guillemeau reports that some have tried performing the Caesarean section on living women, but, given the 100 percent maternal fatality rate, "yet ought we rather to admire it, than either practize or imitate it" (1612, A22v). See also Bicks (2003, 113n.49); Chamberlain (2005). Park (2008) offers a fascinating account and transcription of four eye-witness accounts of a "postmortem fetal extraction" in Italy in 1545 (although the baby was reported healthy and pink at birth, it died some days later).

urinal, jordan See also **urine** (A) By Shakespeare's time, the urinal (also called a jordan, presumably because of its association with the Biblical river Jordan), or specimen-bottle, had become something of an insignia for the **physician**. A glass flask with a wide base and a narrow neck that was supposed to resemble the **bladder**, a urinal was made of crystal or, more usually, clear glass, and, ideally, had stoppers of leather or paper to prevent contamination of the urine specimen. It was marked on the outside with eleven levels, to help the physician reach his diagnosis.

(B) That the urinal served as an obvious metonymy for the physician in Shakespeare's day is made clear by the several references in *Merry Wives of Windsor*, the only play that mocks a physician—Anne Page's French suitor, Dr. **Caius**—and that contains the greatest number of explicit references to medical practice. Keen to poke fun and stage a fight between the Welsh Sir Hugh Evans and the French Caius, the Host of the Garter praises Caius as a "Castalion-King-Urinal," a "Hector of Greece" (*WIV* 2.3.33). "Castalion" presumably means "Castilian" or Spanish, which Caius understands as "valorous" but which the Host intends as "braggardly." When the fight finally comes to pass, Evans threatens to "knog [Caius'] urinals about his knave's costard" (to knock Caius' chamber-pots on his head) when he finally encounters him (*WIV* 3.1.14).

In *Two Gentlemen of Verona*, Speed uses the urine in a urinal as a figure for the human body: "these follies are within you and shine through you like the water in an urinal, that not an **eye** that sees you but is a physician to comment on your **malady**" (2.1.38–9). As befits his character, Speed brings Valentine's high-flown **love-sickness**, an ailment associated with the head or the higher part of the body, down to the lower body, emphasizing the carnal nature of Valentine's desire.

Finally, the Second Carrier in *1H4* complains about his uncomfortable lodgings, affording us a glimpse of the exigencies of Elizabethan travel: "Why, they will allow us ne'er a jordan, and then we leak in your chimney; and your chamber-lye breeds fleas like a loach" (2.1.19–21); denied a chamber-pot, the lodgers will be forced to void their bladders in the fireplace, where their urine will encourage the fleas.

(C) Both Fletcher (1598) and the anonymous *Seynge of Urines* (1552) provide diagrams of the ideal urinal; Tate's "Tamburlaine's Urine" (2004) includes a brief history of the vessel.

urine, piss, stale See also **urinal** (A) Urine was considered to be one of the products of concoction in the body, that is to say, the "cooking" of **blood** and other **humors** through the body's natural **heat**. Although urine was one of the body's wastes, its regular evacuation was considered a sign of the body's overall health. One of the most important diagnostic techniques in medieval and early modern England had long been uroscopy, or "casting the **patient**'s water." The ancient works of **Hippocrates**, Avicenna, and **Galen**, widely circulated in Latin and English translations in Shakespeare's England, asserted that **physicians** could analyze the quality of a patient's urine in order to determine the presence or absence of **disease** in the human body. Particular kinds of urine were associated with particular **complexions** or humors: the **phlegmatic** man's urine was white, thick, plentiful and raw, the **choleric**'s yellow and thin, the **melancholic**'s white and cloudy or black, and the **sanguine**'s dark red. Since women were **colder** and moister than men, their urine was thought to be more abundant than men's, and since children were less "concocted" than adults, their urine was supposed to be thicker.

Physicians were instructed to collect the first urine of the day, in one stream, and never to mix samples, even from the same patient. The urine was collected in the physician's urinal, or specimen-bottle, and observed three times, immediately after collection, then after it had had time to cool, and finally once more, at the end of the day. The qualities the physician noted were color (sometimes as many as twenty, ranging from white or clear to yellow, orange, red, green, or black); substance (viscosity, temperature, odor, contents, and amount) and perspicuity (transparency). In earlier eras the physician would also taste the urine, but this practice appears to have fallen out of favor among physicians by the end of the sixteenth century. Color and transparency were determined visually, by holding the urinal and its contents up against the light and perhaps also against a black cloth.

The contents of the urine demanded further analysis, and required observing the specimen over a period of several hours. The contents of the urinal were divided into three: the sediment, the swim, and the cloud, which were visible in the base, the middle portion, and the top of the urinal respectively. The sediment included any precipitation, foreign matter, or visible objects excreted; such objects might include webs, bran, specks, mucus, **hair**, or sticks, according to the ailment. The swim comprised the main part of the urine, and, like the sediment, might include mucus, particles, and so on. Finally, the cloud might include froth or spume, and the garland, also called the corona or crown, at the top of the sample. Just as the sediment, swim, and cloud settled in different parts of the urinal, so their contents indicated the health or disease of the corresponding parts of the human body. Thus **gravel** in the sediment might indicate a **kidney** stone; sand in the swim might indicate problems with **veins**; and bubbles in the cloud might indicate headaches or insomnia. Urine was also used to determine virginity or **pregnancy**.

Diseases affecting the flow and production of urine itself included the stone (kidney stones), thought to be caused by phlegm-inducing food such as **milk**, cheese, apples, and turnips, and cured by emetics and **clysters**; the pissing evil, or diabetes, thought to be caused by too much **heat** in the kidneys and treated by bloodletting (phlebotomy) and by the administration of cooling **medicines** such as **lettuce**, sorrel, **rhubarb pills** and violets; and **dropsy**, or water retention, thought to be caused by **bladder** weakness or urine that was too hot, and treated with cooling foods such as cucumber or by an injection of egg white mixed with **breast** milk.

The urine of humans and animals was itself deemed a healthful remedy for certain ailments. Infants' and children's urine was thought particularly effective in curing running sores, treating asthma, and healing bee, wasp, and hornet stings, while a man's urine might **cure** the **gout**.

(B) Urine in Shakespeare's plays is both a mark of the normal, healthy, function-ing of the body, and of vulgarity or baseness; the characters that speak of it, speak home truths. In *Measure for Measure,* Lucio maintains that the cold Angelo, famed for his virtue, is so chaste that his very urine, blood-hot in normal men, is "congealed ice; that I know to be true" (3.2.110–11). In keeping with his dual function, as both a kind of compassionate chorus and a voice of debauchery in the play, Lucio implicitly suggests that the illicit sexual intercourse to which Angelo is so opposed is a bodily need as natural and urgent as urination, and that in controlling his lust and punishing that of others, Angelo proves only his inhumanity. "That I know to be true" generates a laugh at Lucio's and Angelo's expense; neither character, though they both pride themselves on knowing the truth, recognizes the disguised Duke Vincentio or can separate truth from slander.

The porter at the gates to Duncan's castle in *Macbeth* is similarly both vulgar and truthful. He comments that drink provokes three things, "nose-painting [a red **nose**], **sleep**, and urine" (2.3.28). Lechery, he continues, is both provoked and unprovoked by drink, because it stimulates sexual desire but undermines its enactment, making men impotent. Drink is therefore an "equivocator," saying one thing but meaning another, just as (we infer) the witches, Macbeth, and Lady Macbeth in this play equivocate with one another, with Duncan, and with themselves.

Urged to forfeit the pound of Antonio's flesh to which he is entitled and to accept the sum of three thousand ducats instead, Shylock maintains that his position cannot be supported through logic or reason: it is his "humor." Just as some men have irrational hatreds of cats, pigs, or bagpipes, so he claims to hate Antonio with a loathing that is akin to disgust. Bagpipe-haters who "cannot contain their urine" (*MV* 4.1.50) at the sound of the harmless bagpipe are incontinent from hatred, anger, disgust, and fear, all of which comprise Shylock's sentiments toward Antonio.

Lucio, the Porter, and Shylock pride themselves on their bluntness; other characters prefer the euphemism "water." Sir Toby Belch is both teasing and encouraging Sir Andrew Aguecheek in his pursuit of Olivia when he urges him to dance lustily wherever he goes and claims, "I would not so much as make water but in a sink-a-pace" (*TN* 1.3.130). The hyperbole alerts us that the joke is at Aguecheek's expense. Similarly, when the Host in *WIV* calls Caius "Mock-water," the euphemism prevents Caius, whose English is limited, from understanding that the Host is in fact accusing him of cowardice, of being frightened enough to become incontinent, to make water (2.3.57–8). And although it might be out of character for Shakespeare's Timon to use a euphemism of any kind, it is possible that when he offers his erstwhile friends a banquet of empty dishes and "luke-warm water" (*TIM* 3.6.89), the temperature of the water, and his scatological language throughout the play, are meant to make us think about another kind of warm water, especially since he complains of his friends' "reeking villainy" (3.6.93).

Testing urine functions as a diagnostic for the state of the kingdom in two plays, one tragic, the other comic. Macbeth famously berates the medicine and doctors who have been unable to help his sleepwalking wife:

> If thou couldst, doctor, cast
> The water of my land, find her disease,
> And **purge** it to a sound and pristine health,
> I would applaud thee to the very echo,
> That should applaud again. . . .
> What rhubarb, **cyme**, or what purgative **drug**,
> Would scour these English hence? Hear'st thou of them?
>
> (*MAC* 5.3.50–6)

If there were only a purgative that could force the kingdom to void the English invaders just as a healthy body voids urine and stool, then physicians would deserve Macbeth's praise. As we have just learned, however, Lady Macbeth needs a spiritual counselor rather than a medical man; similarly, the kingdom needs not a violent purgation but a spiritual renewal. What is "disease" to Macbeth is cure to Macduff and Malcolm.

Shakespeare's Falstaff asks his Page for the doctor's opinion on his "water," in *2H4*, only to learn: "He said, sir, the water itself was a good healthy water; but, for the party that owed it, he might have more diseases than he knew for" (1.2.3–5). The joke against Falstaff prepares us for the tetralogy's turn against the fat, old man and for the prince's rejection of him—a rejection not only desirable but necessary in order to save the kingdom.

Merry Wives of Windsor continues Falstaff's decline, and contains an unusual sense of a slang term for urine: "piss." Tricked into disguising himself as Herne the Hunter in horns, supposedly to meet and seduce the merry wives of the play's title, Falstaff pleads: "Send me a cool rut-time, Jove, or who can blame me to piss my tallow?" (*WIV* 5.5.14). Stags "piss their tallow" when they use up their fat stores during the mating season and become lean or wasted; according to humoral theory, fluids in the human body were fungible, that is, they could change into one another, and were consumed by heat, so that fat could indeed be converted into urine. Falstaff's image hints at his imminent come-uppance when, still wearing his horns, he becomes not the hunter he envisioned but the hunted stag, pinched by a pack of children and humiliated by the play's heroines. When Shakespeare uses the term "piss" again, it is once more uttered by a character who is turned into a beast, of sorts, by the play in which he appears: Trinculo, tricked by Prospero's real sprites much as Falstaff is by the disguised children, complains that he smells of the pit into which he has fallen, all of a "horse-piss" (*TMP* 4.1.199). Paster (1993) notes that another slang term, this time, "pee," again becomes a vehicle for humor in Malvolio's unwitting pun on Olivia's handwriting and her excretion: "thus makes she her great P's" (*TN* 2.5.88).

"Stale" connotes the disgust we feel for old food, leavings, and urine, a sense that the Host in *WIV* and, more significantly, Octavius in *Antony and Cleopatra* aim to evoke by their use of the term. The Host presses his advantage over Caius again in using the term "stale": Caius takes "bully-stale" as a compliment, but the Host is again comparing him to urine, the "stale" or waste product of the body (*WIV* 2.3.30). Comparing Antony's brilliant military past to his present infatuation for Cleopatra, Caesar reminisces that Antony used to "drink /The stale of horses" during particularly difficult campaigns when water ran in short supply (*ANT* 1.4.61–2). Antony's physical degradation during that campaign contrasts unfavorably in Caesar's **eye** with his current enjoyment of the pleasures of the East—and Cleopatra.

(C) Fletcher (1598); *Seynge* (1552); and Record (1547) are devoted entirely to the subject of uroscopy, but nearly every medical manual discusses the practice. Fletcher, who specifically sets out to collect and condense the works of other urologists, is concerned with the status of the physician, arguing that it is "too base" for a physician to taste urine (A3r), and possibly even to smell it (F7v; he concedes, however, that the odor has an important diagnostic function). Paracelsians mocked the Galenic practice of diagnosing urine, and **Paracelsus**' treatise on urine (1568, *Libellus*), breaks urine down into his three fundamental **elements**, **salt**, **sulphur**, and **mercury**. See also Hart (1625).

Paster's *Body Embarrassed* (1993) is essential reading, especially the witty chapter on early modern attitudes toward urine (23–63). Paster argues that Jonson, Shakespeare, and Middleton take advantage of the cultural taboo on public urination for women (but not for men) in order to humiliate the incontinent or "leaky" woman, who is shamed into secrecy. This shaming affects ladies, as well as lower-class women, she points out in a detailed reading of *Twelfth Night* (23–34): Malvolio's broadcasting of how his mistress Olivia "makes her great P's" emphasizes the bodiliness that Olivia shares with all women, while Malvolio's inadvertent obscenity as he spells out the letters in the note he has found ("her C's, her U's, and her T's") associates sexual and excretory functions. Paster adds that there were perhaps material, historical grounds for the association of incontinence or "leakiness" with women: difficult deliveries and multiple pregnancies could result in disorders such as **fistula** or in weakened bladder and pelvic floor muscles, while the high fertility rate of upper-class women meant that they were invariably either **pregnant**, lactating, or recovering from **childbed**, that is, leaking milk, blood, or urine, or all three.

Tate (2005) maintained a website containing resources on early modern uroscopy, including scans of *Seynge* and Record; the website is no longer available, but Tate's article (2004) reads the nal illness of Marlowe's Tamburlaine in light of early modern uroscopy, summarizing Record at length (143–5).

vapor, vapour (A) A smokeless **fume**, an imperceptible breath, an invisible exhalation, vapor was the product of excess or corrupted **humor** in the body. Humors traveled around the body and nourished the particular **organs** associated with them (such as the **spleen** for **melancholy** or the **heart** for pure **blood**). The body, however, produced more of each humor than it could consume. Such superfluous humors might become ordure, **urine**, or **hair** or other **excrements**, of which vapor was one. Corrupted humors that had not been **purged** naturally as excrement or bodily waste released vapors that if retained, could cause **disease**.

(B) Shakespeare usually uses the term to describe foul weather, usually impending rain (as in *ERR* 1.1.89 or *LLL* 4.3.66–8). Often, however, vaporous weather proves bad for health because the mists or fogs portend disease (because such conditions encouraged overproduction of **phlegm** and consumed the pure blood and **spirits** too quickly for the body to remain in balance). Hence, **cold** and slimy toads (associated with **sickness**) might thrive in "the vapour of a dungeon" (*OTH* 3.3.271), but not human beings, and Timon includes "vapours" in his list of "detested parasites" (3.6.97). Hamlet calls the sky "a foul and pestilent congregation of vapours," connecting dirt or foulness, misty or rainy weather, with the **pestilence** or **plague** that came from cold, damp conditions (2.2.303). External vapors often bore disease through smell, as in Cleopatra's imagined humiliation at Roman hands: "in their thick breaths, /Rank of gross **diet**, shall [we] be enclouded, /And forced to drink their vapour" (5.2.211–13). The stinking breath of "mechanic slaves" who eat pungent and indigestible food shall surround them and force them to inhale the noxious and disease-inducing fumes of partially concocted food.

Prince Hal combines meteorology and **medicine** in his famous "Redeeming time" speech:

> Yet herein will I imitate the sun,
> Who doth permit the base contagious clouds
> To smother up his beauty from the world,
> That, when he please again to be himself,
> Being wanted, he may be more wonder'd at,
> By breaking through the foul and ugly mists
> Of vapours that did seem to strangle him.
>
> > (*1H4* 1.2.197–203)

Just as the sun reveals himself in all his glory to greater effect if the weather has been cloudy hitherto, so Hal will spend time with idle, low companions until he chooses to display his true, hard-working, princely personality. Physiologically, the personified sun (or "son," in a pun that persists through the play) seems to be smothered by a **contagion** or illness associated with proximity to disease-bearing bodies or air or water (the so-called *miasma* theory of disease). This illness or **infection** produces noxious by-products that block the passage of air and thus **strangle** him until he can force his way through. His explanation is geohumoral in that it accepts the connection between prevailing weather conditions outdoors and blockages or ailments in the human bodies that experience such weather.

Gloucester disingenuously figures himself to Buckingham as a sun similarly smothered by "vapour in [his] glory" (3.7.164). Falstaff, in contrast, recommends wine rather than sunshine to **dry** up exhalations or vapors: "A good sherries-sack hath a two-fold operation in it. It ascends me into the **brain**; dries me there all the foolish and dull and curdy vapours which environ it makes it apprehensive, quick, forgetive, full of nimble fiery and delectable shapes, which, delivered o'er to the voice, the **tongue**, which is the birth, becomes excellent wit" (*2H4* 4.3.96–102). We still say that alcohol "goes to one's head"; Falstaff prescribes the fumes of wine to drive out the cold, **moist** phlegm that nourished the brain but that, he suggests, risk corruption or curding unless they are enlivened by **heat** and dryness. The French Constable boasts in *H5* 4.2.23–4 that the English are so weak from hunger that "let us but blow on them, /The vapour of our valour will o'erturn them." They are so bloodless and "starved" that the hot breath of the French, warmed by their food and by their courageous **livers** full of blood, will knock them over just as gales do in a thunderstorm.

(C) On the connection between weather and health (geohumoralism) see Floyd-Wilson (2003, *passim*).

ventricle see *pia mater*

vial (A) A small container for some precious fluid made by **distillation**, usually **medicine** or, in Shakespeare, a sanctified or medicinal body fluid.

(B) Vials in Shakespeare contain concentrated essences of medicine, poison, or body fluids; their small size makes them easy to conceal. Old Hamlet's Ghost tells his son that Claudius approached him "with juice of cursed **hebona** in a vial" (1.5.62), a "**leperous** distilment" that triggers **disease** instantly instead of curing it.

Friar Laurence instructs Juliet, "Take thou this vial, being then in bed, /And this distilled liquor drink thou off" (4.1.93). Juliet is well aware that the medicine might not work at all, or might be a "poison," as she addresses the little bottle, "Come, vial" (4.3.20) The most precious **perfume** distilled by the summer (the beloved) in sonnet 6 is held in a vial (see discussion under **distil**). Cerimon might offer a vial of medicine to revive Thaisa (see discussion under **viol**, below). John of Gaunt's Duchess castigates her husband by reminding him that "Edward's seven sons, whereof thyself art one, /Were as seven vials of his sacred **blood**," one of which is now "crack'd, and all the precious liquor spilt" (*R2* 1.2.12). The royal blood of Edward III becomes a miraculous elixir of life to be inherited from one generation to the next, its spilling in one man a "murder" that has simultaneously "slain" all other descendants. Hermione addresses not a word to her estranged husband at the end of *WT* but exclaims in joy at the sight of Perdita, "You gods, look down, /And from your sacred vials pour your graces /Upon my daughter's head!" (5.3.122).
C) See OED *vial*, sb. 1, and the alternate spelling, *phial*, sb. 1., and Drey (1978) for a history of pharmaceutical containers.

viol It is unclear whether Cerimon calls for a musical instrument (viol) or a medicine-bottle (**vial**) in *PER* 3.2.90 when he resuscitates Thaisa, since both music and medicaments could be used to restore **faint** or ill patients, and both acoustic senses are clearly present; moreover, although musical therapy features throughout the play, Shakespeare's source, Gower's *Confessio Amantis*, describes the **physician** putting a **medicine** into Thaisa's mouth. Hart (2000) acknowledges the double sense of viol/vial before describing the revivifying powers attributed to "rough" or cultic music in the classical and early modern worlds, especially the "riotous clangor of the Phrygian music" (327).

virgin-knot see **hymen**

vomit See also **puking, purge** (A) Vomiting, a kind of purge or evacuation, might be natural or induced by a **physician**. In either case, it helped to purge the body of too much **choler** or yellow bile, something especially necessary for choleric men. Those who did not vomit easily, however, ought not to be compelled but instead to be purged another way, perhaps by siege (laxatives) or phlebotomy (bloodletting). Each of these methods corrected **surfeit**, or an overdose of food or alcohol.
(B) Shakespeare's characters vomit from excess or surfeit, especially of alcohol. Iago insists that the Englishman can outdrink even the Danes and the Germans, not to mention the Dutch: "he gives your Hollander a vomit, ere the next pottle can be filled" (*OTH* 2.3.82–4). The Dutchman will be vomiting from his own excess while the Englishman is calling for the next round. Titus laments, "my **bowels** cannot hide her woes, /But like a drunkard must I vomit them . . . Losers must have leave /To ease their **stomachs** with their bitter **tongues**" (*TIT* 3.1.230–3). Nauseated patients drank the bitter **potion** eisel or vinegar to provoke vomiting; Titus' words are sharp and bitter as an emetic, and curative in the same way. But a complex passage in *Cymbeline* imagines a man vomiting from

an excess of nothing. Iachimo contrasts Imogen's "neat excellence" to the "slut-tery" or slovenliness of other women. Such an opposition, argues Iachimo, "Should make desire vomit emptiness, /Not so allured to feed" (1.6.43–5). A man seeing Imogen would lose all desire for other women, even if he had not yet slaked his lust, like a man who vomits even without having eaten anything at all.

Kingdoms purge themselves of superfluous people through war. Richard III does not fear the French because their soldiers are the excess "scum . . . Whom their o'er-cloyed country vomits forth . . . to assured destruction" (*R3* 5.3.317–19). Like the curds in vomit, the fighting peasants and "lackeys" are waste matter; killing them would purge France of an unhealthy excess.

Fickle kingdoms also gorge themselves on a king and then sicken of him. The Archbishop of York recasts the familiar Biblical proverb (*PRO* 26: 11) of "the dog that returneth to his own vomit" in a particularly graphic manner:

> The commonwealth is sick of their own choice;
> Their over-greedy love hath surfeited:
> An habitation **giddy** and unsure
> Hath he that buildeth on the vulgar **heart**.
> O thou fond many, with what loud applause
> Didst thou beat heaven with blessing Bolingbroke,
> Before he was what thou wouldst have him be!
> And being now trimm'd in thine own desires,
> Thou, beastly feeder, art so full of him,
> That thou provokest thyself to cast him up.
> So, so, thou common dog, didst thou disgorge
> Thy glutton bosom of the royal Richard;
> And now thou wouldst eat thy **dead** vomit up,
> And howl'st to find it.
>
> (*2H4* 1.3.87–100)

The body politic was hungry or greedy for Bolingbroke's rule when he first took the throne but now has had too much of him (surfeited) that it longs again for Richard II, whom it deposed. The Kingdom eats kings and then tries to "cast" them out. But now it seeks to "eat . . . up" the dead Richard, shocked to find that his corpse has decayed past reconstitution, like the line of succession Bolingbroke has destroyed. (C) Elyot's "Of Vomite" Book 3, chapter 4 (1539) establishes what would become the fundamentals of purgation by vomit, describing the process of triggering vomiting in a sufferer through emetics taken orally, but also warning against the dangers of inducing vomits in those who could not regurgitate food easily. Langton's Book 2, chapter 6 (1547) discusses the theory of fullness or repletion and emptiness or vacancy; too full a stomach triggered **humoral** disorder and required purgation. The popularity of emetics and laxatives led many to fear a visit from the physician; Joan Lane speculates that the popularity of Shakespeare's son-in-law, John Hall, as a healer stemmed in part from his relative reluctance to use strong purges on his patients, especially **pregnant** women, and his casebook indicates a preference for purgation by siege (laxatives) rather than by vomit.

wall-eyed (A) Wall-eyes were either different colors or focused in two different directions at the same time, displaying more of the sclerotic or white of the **eye** than in a direct gaze. The term was more commonly used of horses than of human beings, but angry soldiers glared furiously at their foes with wall-eyes in order to intimidate them and also because they could not control their wrath. The white or wall of the eye looked white either because of thin or scant **humors**, while the pupil or black (**apple**) of the eye looked dark either because of the density of the humors within it, or because the crystalline humor in the eye was **cold**, fatty, and thick, like **bones** and **marrow**, where the **hotter** parts were dark or black.
(B) Lucius describes the captured Aaron as a "wall-eyed slave" both because (as in the common early modern stereotype) the whites of his eyes are prominent against his dark **skin** and because they are glaring or outstanding in anger (*TIT* 5.1.44), and Salisbury characterizes the murder of Prince Arthur as "savagery" worse than "ever wall-eyed wrath or staring rage /Presented to the tears of soft remorse" (*JN* 4.3.49–50).
(C) Pliny (1601) diagnoses Augustus Caesar as wall-eyed and red-eyed, "like to some horses" (2F5v), and Crooke explains that wall-eyes are white eyes in his description of the physiology of the eye and its colors (1615, 3M1v).

wappen'd Unknown; probably "worn-out from **sexual** activity." Timon implies that the "wappen'd widow" is riddled with venereal **disease** so "ulcerous" that even the **'spital-house** or treatment center will refuse to have her (*TIM* 4.3.39), but Shakespeare's is the only known usage, according to *OED*.

wart See also **corn** (A) Black warts came from an excess of **melancholy humor** or black bile within the body; white ones, from an excess of **phlegm**. Some kinds went away by themselves, but others required burning away (cauterization; see **corn**) or treatment with caustics. Still others required surgery: first, scarified with a cup or **surgeon's box** containing a sharp goose-quill or iron pipe, and then scooped out by the same. Some practitioners sucked on warts to draw them out and then bit them off with their front **teeth**. Genital warts, however, were tied tightly around with a silk thread until they fell off; the resulting **wound** was treated as any other.

(B) Shakespearean warts mark both cosmic insignificance ("Make [the mountain] Ossa like a wart!" rages Hamlet in Ophelia's grave, *HAM* 5.1.283), and personal value as identification. Unscrupulous Falstaff chooses the "ragged" Wart among the poor souls he presses for battle (*2H4* 3.2.141). Dromio of Syracuse (and presumably his twin Ephesus) has a "great wart on [his] left arm" (*ERR* 3.2.135). Such a wart above Master Fenton's eye is the subject of Anne Page's joy, according to Quickly: "we had an hour's talk of that wart!" (*WIV* 1.4.147, 152). Cressida jokes that many warts have more "white **hair**[s]" than does Troilus' chin (*TRO* 1.2.141).

(C) Wecker (1585) has a chapter dedicated to all sorts of wart, including corns.

web and pin, pin and web See also **pearl** (A) Unlike the pearl or cataract of old age, pin and web—cloudy vision caused by a film over the cornea like a cobweb, caused by thickened **humors** congealing in the **eye**—could afflict **patients** of all ages and could be cured by drops, especially those containing **fennel** or egg-white. Drops could be stored in a tin box after being made up and then inserted into the eye with a piece of **flax** thread, or a clean feather. A web that appeared to indicate an incipient cataract could be cured surgically, by cutting it with a thread or a lancet or by using a hog's bristle to cut the web away around the **apple** (pupil). One could preserve and protect the sight by using the herb "eyebright" (*Euphrasia*) prophylactically, by eating its leaves in salads, or drinking it in tea or wine. Refined sugar was also good for the sight, although one had to watch out for intemperance or repletion, since **fumes** and **purgations** (especially **vomits** and nosebleeds) damaged the eyes.

(B) The jealous Leontes imagines that all eyes but his are "Blind with the pin and web" because they do not see what he imagines to be the adulterous love between his queen and Polixenes (*WT* 1.2.291). Shakespeare revivifies the (to the early moderns) "dead" metaphor of the web for eye-**disease** by including it in the nexus of language about the spider and its prey that Leontes uses to figure his tortured jealousy: "I have drunk, and seen the spider" (*WT* 2.1.45). Edgar in his guise as Poor Tom invokes "the foul fiend Flibbertigibbet" who "gives the web and the pin" and "**squints** the eye" (*LR* 3.4.117–18). The **Bedlam** beggar "squints" or looks askance as he tries to see through the fog that obfuscates his vision both literally (he suffers from untreated eye-disease) and figuratively (he cannot think clearly, his mind befogged by **madness**).

(C) Recipes abound, for example A.T. (1596, R3v); *A Closet for Ladies* recommends goose-grease inserted, unusually, on the head of a pin (1608, G3r); or "houslick" and three grains of vitriol (Hippocrates, 1610, K3r–v). Baley (1602) offers guidelines for prevention; the 1616 edition includes the surgical **cure** (D3v).

wet-nurse see **nurse**

wezand The wezand (also called the weazon or "sharp **artery**") or windpipe removed waste **fumes** or **excrements** from the **lungs**, and drew air into the **lungs**. It was the secondary instrument of the voice, air sounding within it like the air in the pipes of an **organ**. In this analogy, the larynx itself was the primary instrument of voice, air striking its gristle percussively to make speech. Caliban urges Stephano and Trinculo to kill his master while Prospero is asleep, to "cut his wezand with [a] knife" (*TP* 3.2.91). Without his wezand, Prospero would be unable to breathe in air and to produce pure or spirituous **blood**, and vital spirit, in the **heart**. Crooke (1615) devotes Chapter 18, Book VI of his *Microcosmographia* to the "weazon, or wind-pipe."

whites of eggs see **flax** and **eye**

womb See also **blood**, *hysterica passio*, **pregnant**, **sex** (A) Although the term was still occasionally used to refer to the **stomach** or **belly**, womb predominantly denotes the uterus in Shakespeare's English. **Galenic anatomy** held that the womb was an inverted scrotum, since the woman was an inverted man. Both women and men had testicles or "stones" (gonads), touched by the shaft of the yard or penis in men and by the long neck of the womb (which paralleled the man's yard) in women. In women, the vulva or opening to the uterus was naturally elastic in order to allow it to stretch during childbirth. The uterus itself was supposed to resemble the picture of a **heart** in shape and color. The uterus was peculiarly susceptible to disorders because of its multiple functions: it cleansed the female body of plethora or excess **blood** built up to sustain a pregnancy; it collected male **seed**; it provided the matter of which a fetus was made; it nourished a developing pregnancy; and it produced blood that could be sent up to the **breasts** to be further refined into woman's **milk** for the infant after its birth. The womb periodically evacuated blood from all but women of very **hot complexions** or who regularly engaged in vigorous exercise (Barrough singles out "dauncers" as amenorrhic, for example). Stoppage of the courses in such women was natural, since they purged their excess blood through **sweat**, heat, and activity. Fat or sedentary women, on the other hand, needed to **purge** thick, clammy, or gross **humors**, because if they did not bleed from the womb, the humors escaped elsewhere, from the anus or from the **nose**. Menstruation began at about age fourteen (though some women bled from as early as age twelve) until it ceased at about age fifty or fifty-five. Menstrual periods lasted from two to seven days; such bleeding was pain-free. If women suffered pangs, nausea, or excessive pallor, their flow might be too heavy, and the **physician** could reduce it by cupping them under the breasts (see **surgeon's box**) and putting them on **diets** of **dry** foods such as game or wild birds. Pessaries of **plantain**-juice or nightshade might also prove effective.

Menstrual flow was normal and healthy, but other kinds of uterine discharge signaled serious illness. Physicians could identify the humor causing the **flux** or flow from the color of the discharge: a continuous flow of blackened blood suggested blood adust, or burned into **melancholy**; a thick white discharge indicated **phlegm**; a pale yellow one, **choler**, and the bright red of pure blood, a dangerous erosion or a surplus of blood that needed to be let immediately (other humoral excesses could be cured by **medicines** to purge the appropriate humor). Uterine ailments included *hysterica passio* or "the suffocation of the mother," in which **fumes** from the uterus traveled up to the throat and deprived women of their voices and sometimes of sense-perception and movement. Popular literature claimed that women's wombs might "wander," and that the "suffocation of the mother" might occur as a result of the womb literally wandering up to a woman's throat. The medical manuals are sometimes at pains to dismiss this evidently common understanding of **Hippocratic** theory, insisting that uterine vapors, rather than the uterus itself, caused "the mother," and that the uterus was firmly anchored in place with ligaments. Women might also suffer from the **mole** or molar pregnancy, **inflammation**, and windiness (sometimes conflated with the suffocation of the mother), **ulcers**, the narrow neck of the womb (which prevented conception, because seed could not enter the uterus), and uterine prolapse, the "falling-down of the womb," which could happen after a heavy fall, after a difficult delivery, or if a clumsy healer had attempted to extract a dead child from the womb. Older women were more likely to suffer prolapse and for its **cure** to be more challenging than in younger patients. It was important to empty the rectum with a **clyster** (a liquid laxative inserted rectally through a pipe) and the **bladder** with a syringe or catheter. The womb could be carefully reinserted into the body with fine, clean **linen** and wool, and appropriate emollients. Physicians could then bind the patient's legs together and immobilize her with her legs above her hips, for support. If the womb began to corrupt, however, the surgeon should cut it away; women had apparently been known to live without the uterus altogether.

(B) Falstaff, as befits his age, uses the term womb in its old-fashioned sense, to denote his stomach: "my womb, my womb, my womb, undoes me!" (*2H4* 4.3.22). More usually, the womb is the site of female fertility. Queen Margaret blames the Duchess of York for her son's savagery, and "the kennel of her womb" that sustained "a hell-hound" (*R3* 4.4.47–8). Marina is born from her mother's "womb" at sea (*PER* 3.1.34). Quickly haplessly malaprops in front of the beadles dragging her and Doll Tearsheet away: "I pray God the fruit of her womb miscarry!" (*2H4* 5.4.13). Presumably she wishes the opposite, so Doll will be spared whipping. Joan La Pucelle similarly pleads her belly: "Murder not then the fruit within my womb" (*1H6* 5.4.63). *LR* curses, "Into [Goneril's] womb convey sterility," as if barrenness comes from without (a valid humoral reading; hot, parching climatic conditions might indeed "dry up . . . the organs of increase" as he wishes, 1.4.278–9). Timon similarly wishes that the womb of the earth will "dry up" (4.3.193) and dessicate plants, animals, and peoples alike. A pregnant woman bears a "heavy . . . womb," "burthen[ed]" with the weight of her child (*R3* 1.3.230, 4.4.168).

The womb's generative quality parallels it to the **brain**, especially to the ventricle or compartment of fantasy or wish-fulfilment. Cleopatra's maids joke about how many husbands they shall have, and the Soothsayer retorts, "If every one of your wishes had a womb, /And fertile every wish, a million" (*ANT* 1.2.38–9). Sonnet 86 argues that the rival poet's verse has his "ripe thoughts in [his] brain inhearse[d], /Making their tomb the womb wherein they grew?" (86.3–4) Holofernes' witticisms are "begot in the ventricle of memory, nourished in the womb of *pia mater*" (*LLL* 4.2.69). Richard II's queen imagines fortune as a pregnant woman gestating ill-luck, "Some unborn sorrow, ripe in fortune's womb" (*R2* 2.2.10). Sin, too, may gestate over generations (perhaps with the implicit parallel of sexually transmitted infections such as syphilis or **pox**, which could be visited upon one's offspring).

Constance curses against Elinor's "sin-conceiving womb" (*JN* 2.1), in which children are born into original sin from their parents, or the wish of, first the mother and then the wife of Richard III that he had been smothered in his mother's "accursed womb" (*R3* 4.1.53, 4.4.138). Miranda, however, repudiates the notion that the womb (and the mother) are responsible for sin: "Good wombs have borne bad sons" (*TMP* 1.2.120). "Borne" evokes the state of being "born," and imagines the womb as a fruit-bearing tree once more: just as a healthy fruit-tree may bear rotten fruit, so the womb may nourish both good and bad children.

Paulina figures the womb as a gaol and birth as a great deliverance, an inversion of the religious commonplace that took life on earth to be the prison and **death** to be the great liberator (see discussion under **childbed**; *WT* 2.2.57–9). Leonatus' ghostly father imagines his unborn son the subject of "nature's law" when "in the womb" (*CYM* 5.4.37), a prisoner until his sentence is commuted. Aaron summarizes theories of gestation as he urges Demetrius and Chiron to acknowledge his son by their mother Tamora. The babe has been

> sensibly fed
> Of that self-blood that first gave life to you,
> And from that womb where you imprison'd were
> He is enfranchised and come to light:
> Nay, he is your brother by the surer side,
> Although my seal be stamped in his face.
>
> (*TIT* 4.2.122–7)

Their infant brother was nourished on Tamora's blood, which nurtured them, too; his maternity—his "matter," in the popular Latin /English pun on *mater* (mother) and *matter* (material)—is unquestionable, even though the father, Aaron, has conferred his form or shape or "seal" upon the impressionable matter, to produce a dark-skinned child.

Earth is a mother with a "teeming womb" (*R2* 2.1.51); the "womb of earth" (*HAM* 1.1.137) generates plants, animals, soldiers, peoples, and "treasure."

Florizel unusually uses womb as a verb: he will not break faith with Perdita for all the treasure that "the close earth wombs" (*WT* 4.4.490). Titania turns around the image so that a child is the treasure in her friend's "womb, then rich with my young squire" (*MND* 1.2.131). Lucio leeringly develops the metaphor into an epic simile:

> Your brother and his lover have embraced:
> As those that feed grow full, as blossoming time
> That from the seedness the bare fallow brings
> To teeming foison, even so her plenteous womb
> Expresseth his full tilth and husbandry.
>
> (*MM* 1.4.40–4)

The pregnant Juliet resembles the fallow or idle land left untilled by farmers (without the sanction of marriage) but nonetheless fertilized by seeds lingering in the soil (carrying a bastard child) because Claudio tilled or ploughed her (penetrated her, a graphic, erotic comparison that Shakespeare also uses in *ANT*, 2.2.228, and in Sonnet 3) and cultivated the crop (with a pun on husbandry as home economics and the state of being a husband). In *TIT* maternal earth, like Tamora, is a cannibal; the "swallowing womb" of mother earth consumes the murdered Bassanius (2.3.239). For Timon, mother earth is a whore who produces bastard children, "damned earth, /The common whore of mankind" (4.3.42–3). Exeter threatens the "caves and womby vaultages of France" (*H5* 2.4.24).

ROM frequently compares birth to death, sometimes with overtones of the early modern equation of death and sexual orgasm (since the verb "to die" could mean "to climax"). Friar Laurence identifies the fertile womb of earth with the burial plot: "The earth that's nature's mother is her tomb; /What is her burying grave, that is her womb" (2.3.9–10), a metaphor that Romeo echoes as he enters the Capulet vault: "Thou detestable maw, thou womb of death" (5.3.45). Romeo has requested a poison that will take effect as quickly as powder from the "cannon's womb," as part of an extended metaphor that implicitly compares the "discharge" of powder to the ejaculation of seed thought to be necessary from both men and women in order for conception to occur (5.1.65).

(C) Lanfranco coyly refuses to discuss childbirth and women's generative parts at length (1565). Barrough (1583), however, prints several chapters on disorders of the womb, and has a delightful phrase dismissing the popular notion of the "wandering womb": "it runneth not to an other place like a wandring beast but is drawn backe through the extention" (N3v). Primary sources on the female reproductive organs include *The Birth of Mankynde* (multiple editions); Guillemeau (1612); Rüff (1637). On earth as womb, see Wynne-Davies (1991); on the so-called wandering womb, see Bicks (2003), Peterson (Moss 2004); on pleading the belly, see Levin (1999). On "The Rediscovery of the Clitoris," see Park (1997). Crane deftly notes the concordance between the brain and the womb (both were generative and productive; both were nourished by **phlegm**; both required a kind of refined spirit; 2001).

wormwood Legendary for its harsh astringency, the herb wormwood derived its name from its efficacy at driving out worms or parasites from the **gut** and snakes or earwigs from the **ear.** To drive out ear-worms, one had to drop the juice directly into the ear canal, perhaps explaining young Hamlet's disgusted response, "that's wormwood!" to the Player Queen's comment, "None wed the second but who killed the first" (*HAM* 3.2.181): the murder is both bitter, like wormwood, and effected by a means similar to the way wormwood was administered therapeutically. Juliet's nurse applies wormwood to her **nipple** in order to wean the child (*ROM* 1.3.26, 30; discussion under **dug**), a reflection of its bitterness. Rosaline implicitly compares Berowne's wit to worms in his **brain** when she determines that she will "weed out wormwood" from Berowne's idle brain by setting him to joke in a **hospital** for a year before she will wed him (5.2.847). For uses, see Ascham (1561, K3v–4v); Gerard (1597, 3N4v–5v). On its use for weaning, see Charron (1608). Dodoens recommends its prophylactic use against drunkenness (1595, B2v–B3v). Hockey (1965) cites the *Herbal* published by Richard Banckes in 1525 to argue for its efficacy against worms in the **womb** as well as the ear.

wound See also **tent** (A) Two theories of wound management competed in early modern England, **moist** healing and **dry** healing. Moist healing recommended keeping the wound open (sometimes by the insertion of a piece of clean **linen**, or tent, into the wound) and the use of emollient or soothing ointments to **plaster** it before bandaging it and waiting for it to heal from the inside out. Suppuration demonstrated the body's healthy release of its **humors** through thick, white pus, although malodorous pus was known to be a sign of **gangrene**. Dry healing required cleaning the wound with alcohol (wine or *aqua vitae*), long known as an antiseptic agent, and then stitching it if necessary, changing the bandage daily until the **skin** knit together. Some authorities recommend a combination of both approaches, suggesting that the wound should, if swollen, be encouraged to form pus and only be sewn together once the pus dissipated and the wound was clean (presumably, after whatever local infection was causing the issue of pus had healed by itself or formed an abscess that could be lanced).
(B) New wounds might easily open again, either from chafing or from the **scurvy** from which so many suffered; the Lord Chief-Justice refrains from teasing Falstaff because he is "loath to gall a new-healed wound" (*2H4* 1.2.148). Martius would "rather have [his] wounds to heal again / Than hear say how [he] got them" (*COR* 2.2.69–70). Lepidus compares the fighting among the tribunes to the pain of injuries that are healing, urging his companions not to "commit / Murther in healing wounds" (*ANT* 2.2.21–2). Buckingham warns Edward to travel quietly, with only a "little train," lest the "new-heal'd wound of malice should break out" (*R3* 2.2.125). Sonnet 34 complains that "no man well of such a **salve** can speak / That heals the wound and **cures** not the disgrace": his love's smiles after anger soothe the superficial injury to the body but not the deeper injury to his soul (*SON* 34.7–8). Patroclus, perhaps remembering soldiers who tried to escape from battle by injuring themselves, warns Achilles against spite: "Those wounds

heal ill that men do give themselves" (*TRO* 3.3.229). Joan La Pucelle compares the civil wars in France to children wounding the **breasts** of their mother, perhaps like the pelican whose children were rumored to peck her until she bled. She urges Burgundy to look upon "the most unnatural wounds, /Which thou thyself hast given [France's] woeful breast" (*1H6* 3.3.50–1).

Emotions leave no visible wound but nonetheless **scar** those who experience them. Richard II is amazed to see that his face, beaten by sorrow, bears only wrinkles, and "no deeper wounds" (*R2* 4.1.279). Phebe cruelly mocks Silvius by demanding he show her the wounds he says that her **eyes** have made; he responds that they are "wounds invisible" (*AYL* 3.5.30). Sonnet 139 distinguishes between two kinds of invisible love-wound, from the **tongue** or from the eye. The poetic speaker would prefer a wound from the tongue, so that he can still look at his beloved's face. The flower of **love-in-idleness**, however, bears a visible mark, rendered "purple with love's wound" where it was "**milk**-white" before (*MND* 2.1.167).

Healed wounds can also speak eloquently and testify to their murderer, by bleeding afresh in the killer's presence, as the injuries of the murdered Henry VI were supposed to have done: "dead Henry's wounds /Open their congeal'd mouths and bleed afresh" (*R3* 1.2.55–6). The wounds of Caesar's body, "like dumb mouths, do ope their ruby lips" in the presence of his assassins (*JC* 3.1.260). York alludes to a belief that the **blood** exuded from wounds transported the soul, through the medium of vital spirit (spirit formed the bond between soul and body): "My soul flies through these wounds to seek out Thee" (*3H6* 1.4.178).

(C) Vicary (1587, Iv) recommends human body products both to sterilize the wound (washing a new wound in **urine**) and to stanch excessive bleeding (applying the dried blood of a man to a deep wound either before or after stitching it). Such remedies may indicate an early **Paracelsian** homeopathy, using like to cure like, blood to cure blood, or may simply reflect earlier **Galenic** and **Hippocratic** practices of using body products, as Hoeniger (1992) suggests. Gesner (1559) lists the recipes for generating "**quintessence** of mans bloud" but qualifies his description by first saying he cannot "approve" it and second, quoting another authority to suggest that the old texts are speaking "allegorically" when they recommend the quintessence of blood (D3r–D4r). Guillemeau's third treatise (1635) discusses in detail sewing techniques for wounds. The most immediately useful secondary materials are both on the Roman plays, Marshall on *Coriolanus* (1996) and self-mutilation in *JC* (1994), and Kahn's monograph on wounds as Roman, masculine "fetish" in Shakespeare's plays (1997).

Y/Z

yew The yew-tree was associated with **death** because it was known to be so poisonous that even sleeping beneath it could cause death from its killingly **cold complexion**. Gerard and others attempt to dispel this myth several times, but it evidently persisted in popular lore, perhaps because the trees grew in cemeteries (1597, 4G4v). Shakespeare's witches put "slips of yew" in their hellish broth (*MAC* 4.1.27); yew-trees line Juliet's grave-yard, and Balthasar, napping under a yew, dreams of his master's death (*ROM* 5.3.3, 137). Archers bearing bows of "double-fatal yew" bring down Richard II (*R2* 3.2.117). Tamora claims that Lavinia and Bassanius have enticed her to her doom against "the body of a dismal yew" (*TIT* 2.3.107). Orsino self-indulgently begs a song about a lover's "shroud of white, stuck all with yew" (*TN* 2.4.55), fully to enjoy his **love-sickness**.

zany see **natural**

Bibliography

Primary Texts

An Account of the Causes of Some Particular Rebellious Distempers (1547), London.

Adams, T. (1615), *Mystical Bedlam: Or, the World of Mad-Men.* [e-book] London and Ann Arbor, Michigan: UMI/Early English Books Online. Available through University of Georgia Libraries <www.libs.uga.edu>. [Accessed July 31, 2010]

Arcaeus, F. (1588), *A Most Excellent Methode of Curing Woundes.* Trans. J. Read. London.

Archer, J. (1673), *Every Man His Own Doctor.* London.

Arderne, J. (1910), *Treatise of Fistula in Ano.* D'Arcy Power, ed. Early English Texts Society 139. London: Trübner.

Aristotle (1595), *The Problemes of Aristotle.* Edinburgh.

Armin, R. (1608). [e-book] London and Ann Arbor, Michigan: UMI/Early English Books Online. Available through University of Georgia Libraries <www.libs.uga.edu>. [Accessed July 31, 2010]

—. (1609), *Two Maids of More-Clacke.* London.

Ascham, A. (1561), *A Little Herball.* London.

A. T. (1596), *A Rich Store-House, or Treasury for the Diseased.* London.

Bacon, F. (1626), *Apophthegmes New and Old.* London.

Bacon, R. (1597), *The Mirror of Alchemy.* [e-book] London and Ann Arbor, Michigan: UMI/Early English Books Online. Available through University of Georgia Libraries <www.libs.uga.edu>. [Accessed July 31, 2010]

Baley, W. (1588), *A Short Discourse of the Three Kindes of Peppers in Common Vse and Certaine Special Medicines Made of the Same.* [e-book] London and Ann Arbor, Michigan: UMI/Early English Books Online. Available through University of Georgia Libraries <www.libs.uga.edu>. [Accessed July 31, 2010]

—. (1602), *A Briefe Treatise Touching the Preservation of the Eie Sight.* London.

—. (1616), *Two Treatises Concerning the Preseruation of Eie-sight.* [e-book] London and Ann Arbor, Michigan: UMI/Early English Books Online. Available through University of Georgia Libraries <www.libs.uga.edu>. [Accessed July 31, 2010]

Banister, J. (1575), *A Needefull, New, and Necessarie Treatise of Chyrurgerie.* [e-book] London and Ann Arbor, Michigan: UMI/Early English Books Online. Available through University of Georgia Libraries <www.libs.uga.edu>. [Accessed July 31, 2010]. Also Amsterdam: Da Capo, 1971.

365

—, trans. (1622), *A Treatise of One Hundred and Thirteene Diseases of the Eyes, and Eye-liddes.* By Jacques Guillemeau. London.

Barclay, W. (1614), *Nepenthes, or the General Virtue of Tabacco.* London.

Barrough, P. (1583), *Methode of Phisicke.* London.

Batman, S. (1582), *Batman Upon Bartholome.* London.

Best, G. (1598), "Experiences and Reasons of the Sphere," in R. Hakluyt, ed. (1598–1600), *The Principal Navigations, Voyages, Traffiques and Discoveries of the English Nation.* London. Vol. 3, D6v–E3v.

The Birth of Mankynde (1540), [e-book] London and Ann Arbor, Michigan: UMI/ Early English Books Online. Available through University of Georgia Libraries <www.libs.uga.edu>. [Accessed July 31, 2010]

Bodin, J. [Jean Bodin] (1566, trans. 1966], *Method for the Easy Comprehension of History.* Trans. B. Reynolds. New York: Octagon.

Boorde, A. (1542), *The Breuiary of Healthe.* London.

—. (1547–48), *Extracts from "The Breviary of Health," "The First Boke of the Introduction to Knowledge" and "A Compendyous Regyment or A Dyetary of Helth."* F. Furnivall, ed. (1870), *Early English Texts Society* Vol. 10. London: Trübner.

—. (1562), *The Fyrst Boke of the Introduction of Knowledge.* London.

Border, D. (1651), *Polypharmakos kai chymistes, or, The English Unparalell'd Physitian and Chyrurgian.* London.

Bostocke, R. (1585), *The Difference betwene the Auncient Phisicke, First Taught by the Godly Forefathers, Consisting in Vnitie Peace and Concord: and the Latter Phisicke Proceeding from Idolaters, Ethnickes, and Heathen.* [e-book] London and Ann Arbor, Michigan: UMI/Early English Books Online. Available through University of Georgia Libraries <www.libs.uga.edu>. [Accessed July 31, 2010]

Boyle, R. (1686), *A Free Enquiry into the Vulgarly Receiv'd Notion of Nature* [e-book]. London and Ann Arbor, Michigan: UMI/Early English Books Online. Available through University of Georgia Libraries <www.libs.uga.edu>. [Accessed November 20, 2010]

Brant, S. (1509), *The Shyppe of Fooles.* London.

Brasbridge, T. (1578), *The Poore Mans Jewel, That Is to Say, A Treatise of the Pestilence Unto the Which Is Annexed a Declaration of the Vertues of the Hearbs Carduus Benedictus.* London.

Bright, T. (1586), *A Treatise of Melancholy.* London.

—. (1615), *A Treatise, Wherein Is Declared the Sufficiencie of English Medicines.* [e-book] London and Ann Arbor, Michigan: UMI/Early English Books Online. Available through University of Georgia Libraries <www.libs.uga.edu>. [Accessed July 31, 2010]

Browne, T. (1646), *Pseudodoxia epidemica.* G. Keynes, ed. (1928), Vols. 2–3 of *The Complete Works of Sir Thomas Browne.* London: Faber.

Brunschwig, H. (1525), *The. . . . Vertuous Handi Warke of Surgeri.* London.

—. (1561), *A Most Excellent and Perfecte Homish Apothecarye or Homely Physik Booke.* [e-book] Cologne and Ann Arbor, Michigan: UMI/Early English Books Online. Available through University of Georgia Libraries <www.libs.uga.edu>. [Accessed November 20, 2010]

Bullein, W. (1558), *A Newe Booke Entituled the Gouernement of Healthe.* [e-book] London and Ann Arbor, Michigan: UMI/Early English Books Online. Available through University of Georgia Libraries <www.libs.uga.edu>. [Accessed July 31, 2010]

—. (1562), *A Comfortable Regiment, and a Very Wholsome Order against the Moste Perilous Pleurisi.* London.

—. (1562, 1579), *Bulleins Bulwarke of Defence Against All Sickness.* [e-book] London and Ann Arbor, Michigan: UMI/Early English Books Online. Available through University of Georgia Libraries <www.libs.uga.edu>. [Accessed July 31, 2010]

—. (1564), *A Dialogue Against the Fever Pestilence.* London.

—. (1585), *A Briefe and Short Discourse of the Vertue and Operation of Balsame.* [e-book] London and Ann Arbor, Michigan: UMI/Early English Books Online. Available through University of Georgia Libraries <www.libs.uga.edu>. [Accessed July 31, 2010]

—. (1595), *Government of Health.* [e-book] London and Ann Arbor, Michigan: UMI/ Early English Books Online. Available through University of Georgia Libraries <www.libs.uga.edu>. [Accessed July 31, 2010]

Bulwer, J. (1653), *Anthropometamorphosis: Man Transform'd: or, The Artificiall Changling.* London.

Burton, R. (1621), *The Anatomy of Melancholy.* T. Faulkner, N. Kiessling, and R. Blair, eds. (1989–94). Oxford: Clarendon.

Caius, J. (1552), *A Boke, or Counseill against the Disease Commonly Called the Sweate, or Sweatyng Sicknesse.* London.

Cartwright, T. (1579), *An Hospitall for the Diseased.* [e-book] London and Ann Arbor, Michigan: UMI/Early English Books Online. Available through University of Georgia Libraries <www.libs.uga.edu>. [Accessed July 31, 2010]

Cellier, E. (1688), *To Dr.—an Answer to His Queries Concerning the College of Midwives.* London.

Chapman, G. (1598), *The Blinde Begger of Alexandria.* London.

Charron, P. (1608), *Of Wisdome,* trans. S. Lennard. [e-book] London and Ann Arbor, Michigan: UMI/Early English Books Online. Available through University of Georgia Libraries <www.libs.uga.edu>. [Accessed November 20, 2010]

Chauliac, G. de (1542), *The Questyonary of Cyrurgyens with the Formulary of Lytell Guydo in Cyrurgie.* London.

Clarke, J. (1602), *The Trumpet of Apollo.* [e-book] London and Ann Arbor, Michigan: UMI/Early English Books Online. Available through University of Georgia Libraries <www.libs.uga.edu>. [Accessed July 31, 2010]

A Closet for Ladies and Gentlewomen (1608), London.

Clowes, W. (1579), *A Short and Profitable Treatise Touching the Cure of the Disease called (Morbus Gallicus) by Unctions.* London.

—. (1588), *A Prooued Practise for All Young Chirurgians.* London.

—. (1596), *Booke of Observations.* London.

—. (1596), *A Briefe and Necessary Treatise, Touching the Cure of Lues Venerea.* London.

—. (1602), *Right Frutefull and Approved Treatise, for the Artificiall Cure of that Malady called in Latin Struma, and in English, the Evill.* London.

Coeffeteau, N. (1621), *A Table of Humane Passions*. London/Ann Arbor, Michigan: University Microfilms International.

Cogan, T. (1636), *The Haven of Health*. London.

Cook, J., ed. (1679), *Select Observations on English Bodies*. By John Hall. London.

Copland, W. (1552), *A Boke of the Propreties of Herbes Called an Herbal*. London.

Cotta, J. (1612), *A Short Discouerie of the Unobserved Dangers of Severall Sorts of Ignorant and Unconsiderate Practisers of Physicke in England*. [e-book] London and Ann Arbor, Michigan: UMI/Early English Books Online. Available through University of Georgia Libraries <www.libs.uga.edu>. [Accessed November 20, 2010]

—. (1617), *A True Discouery of the Empericke*. London.

Cotugno, D. (1775), *A Treatise on the Nervous Sciatica, or the Nervous Hip-Gout*. London.

Croll, O. (1609, trans. 1670), *Bazilica Chymica*. [e-book] London and Ann Arbor, Michigan: UMI/Early English Books Online. Available through University of Georgia Libraries <www.libs.uga.edu>. [Accessed July 31, 2010]

Crooke, H. (1615), *MIKROKOSMOGRAFIA [Microcosmographia]: A Description of the Body of Man*. London.

Culpeper, N. (1649), *A Physicall Directory, or, A Translation of the London Dispensatory Made by the College of Physicians in London*. Cushing Collection. [e-book] London and Ann Arbor, Michigan: UMI/Early English Books Online. Available through University of Georgia Libraries <www.libs.uga.edu>. [Accessed July 31, 2010.]

—. (1652), *The English Physician*. London.

—. (1655), *The Compleat Practice of Physick*. London.

Davies, J. (1599), *Nosce Teipsum*. London.

Dekker, T. (1603) *The Wonderfull Yeare . . . of the Plague*. London.

Digges, L. (1571), *A Prognostication of Right Good Effect*. [e-book] London and Ann Arbor, Michigan: UMI/Early English Books Online. Available through University of Georgia Libraries <www.libs.uga.edu>. [Accessed July 31, 2010]

Dodoens, R. (1586), *A New Herball*. London.

—. (1595), *A New Herball, or Historie of Plants*. London.

Drouet, P. (1578), *A New Counsell against the Pestilence*. [e-book] London and Ann Arbor, Michigan: UMI/Early English Books Online. Available through University of Georgia Libraries <www.libs.uga.edu>. [Accessed July 31, 2010]

Du Chesne, J. (1590), *The Sclopotarie of Iosephus Quercetanus, Phisition. Or His Booke Containing the Cure of Wounds Receiued by Shot of Gunne*. Trans. J. Hester. [e-book] London and Ann Arbor, Michigan: UMI/Early English Books Online. Available through University of Georgia Libraries <www.libs.uga.edu>. [Accessed July 31, 2010]

—. (1591), *A Breefe Answere . . . by John Hester*. London.

—. (1605), *The Practise of Chymicall, and Hermeticall Physicke, for the Preseruation of Health*. London.

Du Laurens, A. (1599), *A Discourse of the Preservation of the Sight: Of Melancholike Diseases; of Rheumes, and of Old Age*. [e-book] London and Ann Arbor, Michigan: UMI/Early English Books Online. Available through University of Georgia Libraries <www.libs.uga.edu>. [Accessed November 20, 2010]

Elyot, T. (1538), *The Dictionary of Syr Thomas Elyot Knyght.* [e-book] London and Ann Arbor, Michigan: UMI/Early English Books Online. Available through University of Georgia Libraries <www.libs.uga.edu>. [Accessed November 20, 2010]

—. (1539), *The Castel of Helthe.* [N.p.] Rev. ed. (1595), London.

Estienne, C. (1616), *Maison Rustique, or The Countrey Farme.* Rev. ed. London.

Fage, J. (1606), *Speculum Aegrotorum.* [e-book] London and Ann Arbor, Michigan: UMI/Early English Books Online. Available through University of Georgia Libraries <www.libs.uga.edu>. [Accessed July 31, 2010]

Ferrand, J. (1640), *Erotomania.* [e-book] London and Ann Arbor, Michigan: UMI/ Early English Books Online. Available through University of Georgia Libraries <www.libs.uga.edu>. [Accessed July 31, 2010]

Ficino, M. (1989), *Three Books on Life,* trans. C. V. Kaske and J. R. Clark. Binghamton, New York: Center for Medieval and Renaissance Studies/State University at Binghamton.

Fine, O. (1558), *The Rules and Righte Ample Documentes, Touchinge the Vse and Practise of the Common Almanackes, which are Named Ephemeredes.* [e-book] London and Ann Arbor, Michigan: UMI/Early English Books Online. Available through University of Georgia Libraries <www.libs.uga.edu>. [Accessed July 31, 2010]

Fioravanti, L. (1580), *A Short Discours of the Excellent Doctour and Knight, Maister Leonardo Phiorauanti Bolognese vppon chirurgerie.* Trans. J. Hester. [e-book] London and Ann Arbor, Michigan: UMI/Early English Books Online. Available through University of Georgia Libraries <www.libs.uga.edu>. [Accessed July 31, 2010]

Fletcher, J. (1598), *The Differences, Causes, and Judgements of Urine.* Cambridge.

Fludd, R. (1631), *Doctor Fludd's Answer unto M. Foster, or the Squeezing of Parson Fosters Sponge.* [e-book] London and Ann Arbor, Michigan: UMI/Early English Books Online. Available through University of Georgia Libraries <www.libs.uga.edu>. [Accessed July 31, 2010]

—. (1659), *Mosaicall Philosophy.* London.

Foster, W. (1631), *Hoplocrisma-spongus: or, A Sponge to Vvipe Avvay the Weapon-salve.* [e-book] London and Ann Arbor, Michigan: UMI/Early English Books Online. Available through University of Georgia Libraries <www.libs.uga.edu>. [Accessed July 31, 2010]

Foxe, J. (1583), *Acts and Monuments.* London.

Frascatoro, G. (1530), *Syphilis, sive Morbus Gallicus.* Verona.

Gale, T. (1586), *Certain Workes of Chirurgery.* [e-book] London and Ann Arbor, Michigan: UMI/Early English Books Online. Available through University of Georgia Libraries <www.libs.uga.edu>. [Accessed July 31, 2010]

Gardiner, E. (1611), *Phisicall and Approved Medicines, Aswell in Meere Simples, as Compound Obseruations* [e-book] London and Ann Arbor, Michigan: UMI/Early English Books Online. Available through University of Georgia Libraries <www.libs.uga.edu>. [Accessed July 31, 2010]

Garzoni, T. (1600), *The Hospitall for Incurable Fooles.* London.

Gascoigne, G. (1576), *A Delicate Diet, for Daintiemouthde Droonkardes.* [e-book] London and Ann Arbor, Michigan: UMI/Early English Books Online. Available through University of Georgia Libraries <www.libs.uga.edu>. [Accessed July 31, 2010]

Geninges, J. (1614), *The Life and Death of Mr. Edmund Geninges Priest.* [e-book] London and Ann Arbor, Michigan: UMI/Early English Books Online. Available through University of Georgia Libraries <www.libs.uga.edu>. [Accessed July 31, 2010]

Gerard, J. (1597), *The Herball or Generall Historie of Plantes.* Rev. ed. London.

—. (1633), *The Herball or Generall Historie of Plantes.* London.

Gesner, K. (1559), *The Treasure of Euonymus.* [e-book] London and Ann Arbor, Michigan: UMI/Early English Books Online. Available through University of Georgia Libraries <www.libs.uga.edu>. [Accessed July 31, 2010]

—. (1576), *The Newe Jewell of Health.* [e-book] London and Ann Arbor, Michigan: UMI/Early English Books Online. Available through University of Georgia Libraries <www.libs.uga.edu>. [Accessed November 20, 2010]

—. (1599), *The Practise of the New and Old Physicke.* [e-book] London and Ann Arbor, Michigan: UMI/Early English Books Online. Available through University of Georgia Libraries <www.libs.uga.edu>. [Accessed November 20, 2010]

Goeurot, J. (1550), *The Regiment of Life, Whereunto is Added a Treatise of the Pestilence, with the Boke of Children, Newly Corrected and Enlarged by T. Phayre.* London.

The Good Hous-wiues Treasurie. (1588). [e-book] London and Ann Arbor, Michigan: UMI/Early English Books Online. Available through University of Georgia Libraries <www.libs.uga.edu>. [Accessed July 31, 2010]

Gordon, D. (1625), *Pharmaco-Pinax.* [e-book] London and Ann Arbor, Michigan: UMI/Early English Books Online. Available through University of Georgia Libraries <www.libs.uga.edu>. [Accessed July 31, 2010]

Gratarolo, G. (1574), *A Direction for the Health of Magistrates and Studentes.* London.

Guibert, P. (1639), *The Charitable Physitian, with the Charitable Apothecary, Shewing the Manner to Embalme a Dead Corps.* [e-book] London. Gale/Cengage Learning. Available through University of Oxford <http://galenet.galegroup.com>. [Accessed May 14, 2010]

Guillemeau, J. (1587), *A Worthy Treatise of the Eyes . . . Togeather with a Profitable Treatise of the Scorbie.* London.

Guillemeau, J. (1597/8), *The French Chirurgerye.* Dort.

—. (1612), *Childbirth; or, The Happy Deliuerie of Women. To Which is Added, a Treatise of the Diseases of Infants.* London. Repr. Amsterdam: Theatrum Orbis Terrarum; New York: Da Capo Press, 1972.

—. (1622), *A Treatise of One Hundred and Thirteene Diseases of the Eyes, and Eye-liddes.* Trans. J. Banister. London.

—. (1635), *The Happy Delivery of Women.* London.

Gyer, N. (1592), *The English Phlebotomy: or, Method and Way of Healing by Letting of Blood.* London.

Hakewill, G. (1608), *The Vanitie of the Eie.* [e-book] London and Ann Arbor, Michigan: UMI/Early English Books Online. Available through University of Georgia Libraries <www.libs.uga.edu>. [Accessed November 20, 2010]

Hall, E. (1548), [Hall's Chronicle] *The Union of the Two Noble and Illustrate Famelies of Lancastre [and] Yorke.* [e-book] London and Ann Arbor, Michigan: UMI/Early English Books Online. Available through University of Georgia Libraries <www. libs.uga.edu> [Accessed December 6, 2010]

Hall, J. (1609), *The Passion Sermon*. [e-book] London and Ann Arbor, Michigan: UMI/Early English Books Online. Available through University of Georgia Libraries <www.libs.uga.edu>. [Accessed July 31, 2010]

—. (1613–14), *The Discovery of a New World or A Description of the South Indies*. London.

—. (1679), *Select Observations on English Bodies*. London.

Hall, T. (1654), *Comarum Akosmia, or the Lothsomeness of Long Hair*. London.

Harington, J. (1596), *Metamorphosis of Ajax*. London.

Harman, T. (1567), *A Caveat, for Commen Cursetors*. [e-book] London and Ann Arbor, Michigan: UMI/Early English Books Online. Available through University of Georgia Libraries <www.libs.uga.edu>. [Accessed November 20, 2010]

Harsnett, S. (1603), *A Declaration of Egregious Popish Impostures*. [e-book] London and Ann Arbor, Michigan: UMI/Early English Books Online. Available through University of Georgia Libraries <www.libs.uga.edu>. [Accessed July 31, 2010]

Hart, J. (1625), *The Anatomie of Urines*. London.

Harvey, G. (1597), *The Trimming of Thomas Nashe Gentleman*. [e-book] London and Ann Arbor, Michigan: UMI/Early English Books Online. Available through University of Georgia Libraries <www.libs.uga.edu>. [Accessed July 31, 2010]

Harward, S. (1601), *Harwards Phlebotomy: or, A Treatise of Letting of Bloud Fitly Seruing*. London.

Haworth, S. (1680), *Anthropologia*. London.

Herring, F. (1604), *A Modest Defence of the Caueat Giuen to the Wearers of Impoisoned Amulets, as Preseruatiues from the Plague*. London.

Hester, J. (1575), *The True and Perfect Manner to Distil Oyles*. [e-book] London and Ann Arbor, Michigan: UMI/Early English Books Online. Available through University of Georgia Libraries <www.libs.uga.edu>. [Accessed July 31, 2010]

—. (1580), *The First of the Key of Philosophie*. [e-book] London and Ann Arbor, Michigan: UMI/Early English Books Online. Available through University of Georgia Libraries <www.libs.uga.edu>. [Accessed July 31, 2010]

—. (1596), *A Hundred and Fouretene Experiments and Cures of the Famous Physitian Philippus Aureolus Theophrastus Paracelsus*. London.

Hill, T. (1571), *The Contemplation of Mankinde, Contayning a Singuler Discourse of Phisiognomie*. London.

—. (1577), *The Gardener's Labyrinth*. London.

Hippocrates (1610), *The Whole Aphorismes of Great Hippocrates*. London.

—. (1983), "Airs, Waters, Places." In G. Lloyd, ed. *Hippocratic Writings*. Trans. J. Chadwick and W. Mann. 148–69. Harmondsworth: Penguin.

Hoby, M. (1599–1605), *The Diary of Lady Margaret Hoby*. D. Mead, ed. (1930). Boston: Houghton Mifflin.

Holinshed, R. (1577), *The Firste [laste] Volume of the Chronicles of England, Scotlande, and Irelande*. [e-book] London and Ann Arbor, Michigan: UMI/Early English Books Online. Available through University of Georgia Libraries <www.libs.uga.edu> [Accessed December 6, 2010]

—. (1586), *The Third Volume of Chronicles*. London.

—. (1587), *The First and Second Volumes of Chronicles*. London.

Holland, P. (1633), *Gutta Podrica: A Treatise of the Gout*. London.

Huloet, R. (1572), *Huloets Dictionarie.* [e-book] London and Ann Arbor, Michigan: UMI/Early English Books Online. Available through University of Georgia Libraries <www.libs.uga.edu>. [Accessed November 20, 2010]

Hutten, U. von (1533), *De morbo Gallico.* London.

James I. and VI, King of England and Scotland, (1597), *Daemonologie.* G. B. Harrison, ed., (1924), London: Bodley Head.

Johnson, S. (1755), *A Dictionary of the English Language.* London.

Jonson, B. (1600), *The Comicall Satyre of Every Man Out of His Humor.* [e-book] London and Ann Arbor, Michigan: UMI/Early English Books Online. Available through University of Georgia Libraries <www.libs.uga.edu>. [Accessed November 20, 2010]

—. (1601), *Every Man in His Humor.* [e-book] London and Ann Arbor, Michigan: UMI/Early English Books Online. Available through University of Georgia Libraries <www.libs.uga.edu>. [Accessed November 20, 2010]

Jorden, E. (1603), *A Briefe Discourse of a Disease Called The Suffocation of the Mother.* [e-book] London and Ann Arbor, Michigan: UMI/Early English Books Online. Available through University of Georgia Libraries <www.libs.uga.edu>. [Accessed July 31, 2010]

Kellwaye, S. (1593), *A Defensatiue against the Plague.* [e-book] London and Ann Arbor, Michigan: UMI/Early English Books Online. Available through University of Georgia Libraries <www.libs.uga.edu>. [Accessed July 31, 2010]

Landi, O. (1566), *Delectable Demaundes, and Pleasaunt Questions.* [e-book] London and Ann Arbor, Michigan: UMI/Early English Books Online. Available through University of Georgia Libraries <www.libs.uga.edu>. [Accessed November 20, 2010]

Lanfranco of Milan (1565), *Most Excellent and Learned Worke of Chirurgerie.* Translated by J. Hall. London.

Lange, J. (1554), "De Morbo Virgineo." In *Epistolarum Medicinalium* (1605). Hanover. 89–93. Trans. R. H. Major. In *Classic Descriptions of Disease,* 3rd ed. (1945). Springfield, Illinois: Thomas. 487–9.

Langham, W. (1597), *The Garden of Health.* London.

Langton, C. (1545), *Introduction into Phisycke.* London.

—. (1547), *A Very Brefe Treatise, Ordrely Declaring the Pri[n]cipal Partes of Phisick.* [e-book] London and Ann Arbor, Michigan: UMI/Early English Books Online. Available through University of Georgia Libraries <www.libs.uga.edu>. [Accessed July 31, 2010]

La Primaudaye, P. de (1594), *The Second Part of the French Academie.* [e-book] London and Ann Arbor, Michigan: UMI/Early English Books Online. Available through University of Georgia Libraries <www.libs.uga.edu>. [Accessed July 31, 2010]

Lavater, L. (1572), *Of Ghostes and Spirites Walking by Nyght.* [e-book] London and Ann Arbor, Michigan: UMI/Early English Books Online. Available through University of Georgia Libraries <www.libs.uga.edu>. [Accessed November 20, 2010]

Lemnius, L. (1576), *The Touchstone of Complexions.* London.

—. (1587), *An Herbal for the Bible.* London. BL copy. [e-book] London and Ann Arbor, Michigan: UMI/Early English Books Online. Available through University of Georgia Libraries <www.libs.uga.edu>. [Accessed July 31, 2010]

Linche, R. (1599), *The Fountaine of Ancient Fiction*. [e-book] London and Ann Arbor, Michigan: UMI/Early English Books Online.

Lodge, T. (1603), *A Treatise of the Plague*. London.

Loe, W. (1614), *Come and See*. [e-book] London and Ann Arbor, Michigan: UMI/Early English Books Online. Available through University of Georgia Libraries <www.libs.uga.edu>. [Accessed July 31, 2010]

Lowe, P. (1597), *The Whole Course of Chirurgerye*. London.

—. (1634), *A Discourse of the Whole Art of Chirurgery*. London.

Lupton, D. (1632), *London and the Countrey Carbonadoed and Quartred into Seuerall Characters*. [e-book] London and Ann Arbor, Michigan: UMI/Early English Books Online. Available through University of Georgia Libraries <www.libs.uga.edu>. [Accessed November 20, 2010]

Lupton, T. (1579), *A Thousand Notable Things*. London.

Lyly, J. (1580), *Euphues and his England*. [e-book] London and Ann Arbor, Michigan: UMI/Early English Books Online. Available through University of Georgia Libraries <www.libs.uga.edu>. [Accessed July 31, 2010]

Marbecke, R. (1602), *A Defence of Tabacco*. London.

March, J., ed. (1648), *Reports, or, New Cases with Divers Resolutions and Judgements*. London.

Mediolano, J. de (1528, 1541), *Regimen Sanitatis Salerni*. London.

—. (1607), *The Englishmans Docter*. London.

Monardes, N. (1580), *Ioyfull Newes out of the Newfound World*. [e-book] London and Ann Arbor, Michigan: UMI/Early English Books Online. Available through University of Georgia Libraries <www.libs.uga.edu>. [Accessed July 31, 2010]

Moore, P. (1564), *The Hope of Health*. [e-book] London and Ann Arbor, Michigan: UMI/Early English Books Online. Available through University of Georgia Libraries <www.libs.uga.edu>. [Accessed July 31, 2010]

More, Sir T. (1522), "The Last Things," in A. Edwards, K. Gardiner Rodgers and C. Miller, eds. (1997) *Works. Volume 1*. New Haven: Yale University Press, pp. 128–82.

—. (1564), *History of England*. London.

Moulton, T. (1561), *Mirror or Glass of Helthe*. London.

Newton, T. (1580), *Approved Medicines*. London.

Oberndorf, J. (1602), *The Anatomye of the True Physition*. [e-book] London and Ann Arbor, Michigan: UMI/Early English Books Online. Available through University of Georgia Libraries <www.libs.uga.edu>. [Accessed July 31, 2010]

Orders and Ordinances, for the Better Government of the Hospitall of Bartholomew the Lesse. (1652). London.

Ovid (1567), *The. xv. Bookes of P. Ouidius Naso, Entytuled Metamorphosis*. [e-book] London and Ann Arbor, Michigan: UMI/Early English Books Online. Available through University of Georgia Libraries <www.libs.uga.edu>. [Accessed July 31, 2010]

Paracelsus, T. (1568), *Libellus Theophrasti Paracelsi utriusque medicinae doctoris, De urinarum ac pulsuum iudicijs*. Basel.

—. (1590), *An Excellent Treatise Teaching Howe to Cure the French-pockes*. [e-book] London and Ann Arbor, Michigan: UMI/Early English Books Online. Available through University of Georgia Libraries <www.libs.uga.edu>. [Accessed July 31, 2010]

—. (1596), *A Hundred and Fouretene Experiments and Cures of the Famous Physitian Philippus Aureolus Theophrastus Paracelsus*. Trans. J. Hester. London.

Paré, A. (1630), *A Treatise of the Plague*. London.

—. (1634), *The Workes of that Most Famous Chirurgien Ambroise Paré*. [e-book] London and Ann Arbor, Michigan: UMI/Early English Books Online. Available through University of Georgia Libraries <www.libs.uga.edu>. [Accessed July 31, 2010]

Partridge, W. (1591), *The Treasurie of Commodious Conceits*. [e-book] London and Ann Arbor, Michigan: UMI/Early English Books Online.

Pechey, J. (1694), *The Compleat Herbal of Physical Plants*. London.

Pharmacopoeia Londinensis. London, 1618.

Phillips, E. (1658), *The New World of English Words*. London.

Pindar (2007), *The Complete Odes*. Trans. A. Verity and S. Instone. Oxford: Oxford University Press.

[Plague Orders] Queen Elizabeth I (1578), *Orders thought meete by her Maiestie, and her priuie Councell, to be executed throughout the counties of this realme, in such townes, villages, and other places, as are, or may be hereafter infected with the plague*. London.

Platt, H. (1602), *Delightes for Ladies*. London.

Pliny, the Elder (1601), *The Historie of the Vvorld: Commonly Called, The Naturall Historie of C. Plinius Secundus*. Trans. P. Holland. [e-book] London and Ann Arbor, Michigan: UMI/Early English Books Online.

Plutarch (1543), *The Precepts of Plutarch*. Trans. J. Hales. [e-book] London and Ann Arbor, Michigan: UMI/Early English Books Online. Available through University of Georgia Libraries <www.libs.uga.edu>. [Accessed November 26, 2010]

Pope John XXI (1553), *The Treasury of Health*. [e-book] London and Ann Arbor, Michigan: UMI/Early English Books Online. Available through University of Georgia Libraries <www.libs.uga.edu>. [Accessed July 31, 2010]

Prynne, W. (1628), *The Unloveliness of Love-Locks*. London.

Rabelais, F. (2004), *Gargantua and Pantagruel*, trans. Urquhart, T. <Gutenberg.org.>

Raynalde, J. (1565), *The Birth of Mankynde, or the Woman's Booke*. London.

Record, R. (1547), *The Urinal of Physick*. [e-book] London and Ann Arbor, Michigan: UMI/Early English Books Online. Available through University of Georgia Libraries <www.libs.uga.edu>. [Accessed November 20, 2010]

—. (1679), *The Judgement of Urines*. London.

Regimen Sanitatis Salerni (1528), by J. de Mediolano. London.

Ripley, G. (1591), *The Compound of Alchimie*. London.

Rivière, L. (1657), *The Universal Body of Physick*. Trans. W. Carr. London.

Rogers, T. (1576), *The Anatomie of the Minde*. London.

Rous, F. (1654), *Archaelogiae Atticae libri septem*. [e-book] London and Ann Arbor, Michigan: UMI/Early English Books Online. Available through University of Georgia Libraries <www.libs.uga.edu>. [Accessed July 31, 2010]

Roussat, R. (1562), *The Most Excellent, Profitable, and Pleasant Booke of the Famous Doctour and Expert Astrologien Arcandain or Aleandrin*. [e-book] London and Ann Arbor, Michigan: UMI/Early English Books Online. Available through University of Georgia Libraries <www.libs.uga.edu>. [Accessed July 31, 2010]

Royal College of Physicians (1636), *The King's Medicines for the Plague*. London.

Rüff, J. (1637), *The Expert Midwife.* London.

Ruscelli, G. (1558), *The Secretes of the Reuerende Maister Alexis . . . by Wyllyam Warde.* [e-book] London and Ann Arbor, Michigan: UMI/Early English Books Online. Available through University of Georgia Libraries <www.libs.uga.edu>. [Accessed July 31, 2010]

—. (1569), *A Verye Excellent and Profitable Booke Conteining Sixe Hundred Foure Score and Odde Experienced Medicines.* [e-book] London and Ann Arbor, Michigan: UMI/Early English Books Online. Available through University of Georgia Libraries <www.libs.uga.edu>. [Accessed July 31, 2010]

Scot, R. (1584), *A Discoverie of Witchcraft.* [e-book] London and Ann Arbor, Michigan: UMI/Early English Books Online. Available through University of Georgia Libraries <www.libs.uga.edu>. [Accessed November 20, 2010]

Sennert, D. (1637), *The Weapon-salves Maladie.* London.

—. (1658), *Of Agues and Fevers.* London.

Seynge of Urines (1552), London.

Sharp, J. (1671), *The Midwives Book, or the Whole History of Midwifery Discovered.* London.

Sharpham, E. (1607), *Cupid's Whirligig.* [e-book] London and Ann Arbor, Michigan: UMI/Early English Books Online. Available through University of Georgia Libraries <www.libs.uga.edu>. [Accessed July 31, 2010]

Simpson, C., ed. (1951), *Nosce Teipsum: A Critical Edition,* Ph.D., Stanford University.

Soranus, attrib. (1655), *The Aphorisms of Hippocrates, Prince of Physitians.* [e-book] London and Ann Arbor, Michigan: UMI/Early English Books Online. Available through University of Georgia Libraries <www.libs.uga.edu>. [Accessed November 20, 2010]

Stubbes, P. (1583), *The Anatomie of Abuses.* [e-book] London and Ann Arbor, Michigan: UMI/Early English Books Online. Available through University of Georgia Libraries <www.libs.uga.edu>. [Accessed July 31, 2010]

T., A. (1596), *A Rich Store-house or Treasury for the Diseased.* [e-book] London and Ann Arbor, Michigan: UMI/Early English Books Online. Available through University of Georgia Libraries <www.libs.uga.edu>. [Accessed July 31, 2010]

T., C. (1615), *An Advice How to Plant Tobacco in England.* London.

Tomkiss, T. (1607), *Lingua.* London.

Tooker, W. (1597), *Charisma Sive Donum Sanationis.* [e-book] London and Ann Arbor, Michigan: UMI/Early English Books Online. Available through University of Georgia Libraries <www.libs.uga.edu>. [Accessed November 20, 2010]

Topsell, E. (1607), *The Historie of Foure-Footed Beastes.* [e-book] London and Ann Arbor, Michigan: UMI/Early English Books Online. Available through University of Georgia Libraries <www.libs.uga.edu>. [Accessed July 31, 2010]

Treasure of Pore Men (1526). [e-book] London and Ann Arbor, Michigan: UMI/Early English Books Online. Available through University of Georgia Libraries <www.libs.uga.edu>. [Accessed July 31, 2010]

Turner, W. (1551), *A New Herball.* London.

—. (1562), *The Second Part of William Turners Herball.* Cologne.

—. (1587), *The Rare Treasure of English Baths* [*The Bath of Baeth in England*], ed. W. Bremer, in T. Vicary (1587), *The Englishman's Treasure*. [e-book] London and Ann Arbor, Michigan: UMI/Early English Books Online, signatures Or-P5ᵛ. Available through University of Georgia Libraries <www.libs.uga.edu>. [Accessed November 20, 2010]

Two Remarkable and True Histories (1620). [e-book] London and Ann Arbor, Michigan: UMI/Early English Books Online. Available through University of Georgia Libraries <www.libs.uga.edu>. [Accessed July 31, 2010]

Twyne, T. (1576), *The Schoolemaster, or Teacher of Table Philosophy*. London.

Vaenius, E. (1662), *Tractatus Physiologicus de Pulchritudine*. Brussels.

Valerian, J. (1553), *A Treatise . . . Pro Sacerdotum Barbis*. London.

Varandaeus J. (1620), *De Morbis Mulierum*. Geneva.

Vaughan, W. (1612), *Approved Directions for Health, Both Naturall and Artificiall Deriued from the Best Physitians as well Moderne as Auncient*. [e-book] London and Ann Arbor, Michigan: UMI/Early English Books Online. Available through University of Georgia Libraries <www.libs.uga.edu>. [Accessed July 31, 2010]

Vergil, P. (1546), *Abridgeme[n]t of the Notable Worke of Polidore Vergile*. London.

Vesalius, A. (1543), *Complete Illustrations from De Humani Corporis Fabrica*. J. Saunders and C. O'Malley, eds. (1950). Berkeley, California: World Publishing.

Vicary, T. (1577), *A Profitable Treatise of the Anatomie of Mans Bodie*. [e-book] London and Ann Arbor, Michigan: UMI/Early English Books Online. Available through University of Georgia Libraries <www.libs.uga.edu>. [Accessed July 31, 2010]

—. (1587), *The Englisheman's Treasure*. London.

—. (1651), *The Surgion's Directorie*. London.

Vigo, J. (1543, repr. 1968), *The Most Excellent Workes of Chirurgerye*. Amsterdam: Da Capo.

Walkington, Thomas (1607), *The Optick-Glasse of the Humours*. [e-book] London and Ann Arbor, Michigan: UMI/Early English Books Online. Available through University of Georgia Libraries <www.libs.uga.edu>. [Accessed July 31, 2010]

Wecker, J. (1585), *A Compendious Chyrurgery*. Trans. J. Banister. [e-book] London and Ann Arbor, Michigan: UMI/Early English Books Online. Available through University of Georgia Libraries <www.libs.uga.edu>. [Accessed July 31, 2010]

Weyer [Wier], J. (1567), *Medicarum Observationum Rararum Liber*. [e-book] Amsterdam/ Complutense University of Madrid. Online. Google Books. [Accessed December 6, 2010]

The Whole Aphorisms of Great Hippocrates (1610), London.

Willet, A. (1611), *Hexapla*. [e-book] London and Ann Arbor, Michigan: UMI/Early English Books Online. Available through University of Georgia Libraries <www. libs.uga.edu>. [Accessed July 31, 2010]

Woodall, J. (1617), *The Surgeons Mate*. London.

Wright, T. (1604), *The Passions of the Minde in Generall*. London.

Secondary Sources

Ackerman, D. (2005), *An Alchemy of Mind: The Marvel and Mystery of the Brain.* New York: Scribner.

Adams, J. (2000), *Shakespeare's Physic.* London: Royal Society of Medicine Press.

Adelman, J. (1989), "Bed Tricks; On Marriage as the End of Comedy in *All's Well That Ends Well* and *Measure for Measure*," in N. Holland, S. Homan and B. Paris, eds., *Shakespeare's Personality.* Berkeley, California: University of California Press, pp. 151–74.

—. (1999), "Making Defect Perfection: Shakespeare and the One-Sex Model," in Comensoli, V., and Russell, A. eds., *Enacting Gender on the English Renaissance Stage.* Urbana: University of Illinois Press, pp. 23–52.

—. (2008), *Blood Relations: Christian and Jew in The Merchant of Venice.* Chicago: University of Chicago Press.

Aird, C. and R. A. C. McIntosh (1978), "Shakespeare's *Richard III* and the Ellis-Van Creveld Syndrome." *The Practitioner* 220: 656–62.

Allderidge, P. (1979), "Management and Mismanagement at Bedlam, 1547–1633," in C. Webster, ed., *Health, Medicine, and Mortality in the Sixteenth Century.* Cambridge: Cambridge University Press, pp. 141–64.

Anderson, M. (1991), "*Hamlet*: The Dialectic between Eye and Ear," *Renaissance and Reformation* 15: 299–313.

Anderson, T. P. (2006), *Performing Early Modern Trauma from Shakespeare to Milton.* Aldershot, England: Ashgate.

Andrews, J. (1997), *A History of Bethlem Hospital c. 1600–1750.* Ph.D. University of London.

Appleby, A. B. (1979), "Diet in Sixteenth-century England: Sources, Problems, Possibilities," in C. Webster, ed., *Health, Medicine, and Mortality in the Sixteenth Century.* Cambridge: Cambridge University Press, pp. 97–116.

Ariès, Philippe (1994), *Western Attitudes Towards Death from the Middle Ages to the Present.* London: Boyars.

Arikha, N. (2007), *Passions and Tempers: A History of the Humors.* New York: Ecco.

Aronson, A. (1995), *Shakespeare and the Ocular Proof.* New York: Vantage Press.

Austen, J. (2003), *Pride and Prejudice.* V. Jones, ed. London: Penguin.

Babb, L. (1951), *The Elizabethan Malady.* East Lansing, Michigan: Michigan State College Press.

Balizet, A.M. (2007), "Blood on the Early Modern Stage." Ph.D., University of Minnesota.

—. (2005), " 'Let him Pass for a Man': The Myth of Jewish Male Menstruation in *the Merchant of Venice*," in G. Howie and A.Shail, eds., *Menstruation: A Cultural History,* G. Howie and A. Shail. London: Palgrave, pp. 200–212.

Ball, P. (2006), *The Devil's Doctor: Paracelsus and the World of Renaissance Magic and Science.* New York: Farrar, Straus and Giroux.

Barker, F. (1984), *The Tremulous Private Body: Essays on Subjection.* London: Methuen.

Barroll, L. (1991), *Politics, Plague, and Shakespeare's Theater: The Stuart Years.* Ithaca, NY: Cornell University Press.

Bassi, S. and Cimarosti, R., eds. (2006), *Paper Bullets of the Brain: Experiments with Shakespeare.* Series: *Le Bricole* 12. Venice: Cafoscarina.

Bate, J. (2000), "Shakespeare's Foolosophy," in G. Ioppolo, ed., *Shakespeare Performed*. Newark, Delaware: University of Delaware Press, pp. 17–32.

Baumbach, S. (2008), *Shakespeare and the Art of Physiognomy*. Penrith, England: Humanities ebooks.

Beaumont, F. and Fletcher, J. (1905), *The Pilgrim*. A. R. Waller, ed., Vol. 5 of *The Works of Francis Beaumont and John Fletcher*. Cambridge: Cambridge University Press.

Becker, L. M. (2003), *Death and the Early Modern Englishwoman*. Aldershot, England: Ashgate.

Bednarz, J. (2001), *Shakespeare and the Poets' War*. New York: Columbia University Press.

Bellamy, E. (1997), "Waiting for Hymen: Literary History as 'Symptom' in Spenser and Milton." *ELH* 64.2: 391–414.

Belling, C. (2004). "Infectious Rape, Therapeutic Revenge: Bloodletting and the Health of Rome's Body," in Moss, S. et al. eds., *Disease, Diagnosis and Cure on the Early Modern Stage*. Aldershot: Ashgate, pp. 113–32.

Bennett, J. W. (1962), "The Storm Within: The Madness of Lear." *Shakespeare Quarterly* 13: 137–55.

Bentley, J. S. (1986), "Helena's Paracelsian Cure of the King: Magia Naturalis in *All's Well That Ends Well*," *Cauda Pavonis: The Hermetic Text Society Newsletter* 5.1: 1–4.

Bergeron, J. (1972), "*King Lear* and John Hall's Casebook." *Shakespeare Quarterly* 23.2: 206–7.

Berkeley, D. S. (1984), *Blood Will Tell in Shakespeare's Plays*. Lubbock: Texas Tech Press.

Berry, P. (1997), "Hamlet's Ear." *Shakespeare Survey* 50: 57–64.

Bevington, D. (1996), "'More needs she the divine than the physician': The Limitations of Medicine in Shakespeare's Late Plays," in *"Divers toyes mengled": Essays on Medieval and Renaissance Culture in Honor of André Lascombes*, collected by Michel Bitot. Tours: Université François Rabelais, pp. 391–404.

Bicks, C. (2003), *Midwiving Subjects in Shakespeare's England*. Aldershot, England: Ashgate.

—. (2006), "Planned Parenthood: Minding the Quick Woman in *All's Well*." *Modern Philology* 103: 299–331.

Blank, P. (2006), *Shakespeare and the Mismeasure of Renaissance Man*. Ithaca, New York and London: Cornell University Press.

Bonelli, E. (1993), "The Elizabethan Ma(Lady): Lovesickness and the Medicalization of Desire in *The Two Noble Kinsmen*," *Textus* 6: 48–56.

Boseley, S. (2010), "The Trouble with ME," *Guardian* May 13, 2010. <www.guardian.co.uk/society/2010/may/13/me-chronic-fatigue-syndrome> [Accessed: May 15, 2010].

Bosman, A. (1999), "Seeing Tears: Truth and Sense in *All Is True*." *Shakespeare Quarterly* 50: 459–76.

Bovilsky, L. (2008), *Barbarous Play: Race on the English Renaissance Stage*. Minneapolis, Minnesota: University of Minnesota Press.

Bradshaw, G., Bishop, T., and Turner, M., eds. (2004), *The Shakespeare International Yearbook* 4: Shakespeare Studies Today. Bodmin, Cornwall: Ashgate.

Briggs, K. (1962), *Pale Hecate's Team*. London: Routledge.

Brody, S. N. (1974), *The Disease of the Soul: Leprosy in Medieval Literature*. Ithaca, New York: Cornell University Press.

Brotherston, R. P. (1902), "Speargrass." *The Gardener's Chronicle*, number 819, September 6, 1902, p. 169.

Bruun, E. (1993), "'As your daughter may conceive': A Note on the Fair Ophelia." *Hamlet Studies* 15: 93–99.

Burnett, M.T. (2002), *Constructing "Monsters" in Shakespearean Drama and Early Modern Culture*. Basingstoke, England, and New York: Palgrave Macmillan.

Burns, E. (2006), *William Shakespeare: Richard III*. Horndon, United Kingdom: Northcote House/British Council.

Burton, J. L., ed. (2005), *"Six Hundred Miseries": The Seventeenth Century Womb: Book 15 of "The Practice of Physick by Lazare Rivière."* London: Royal College of Obstetricians and Gynaecologists.

Butler, J. (1990), *Gender Trouble*. London and New York: Routledge.

Campbell, L. B. (1962), *Shakespeare's Tragic Heroes: Slaves of Passion*. London: Methuen, 1962.

Carroll, W. (1987), "'The base shall top th'legitimate': The Bedlam Beggar and the Role of Edgar in *King Lear*." *Shakespeare Quarterly* 38: 426–41.

Chakravarti, P. (2008), "'I have no other but a woman's reason': Folly, Femininity, and Sexuality in Renaissance Discourses and Shakespeare's Plays." *Shakespearean International Yearbook* 8: 136–61.

Chamberlain, S. (2005), "Fantasizing Infanticide: Lady Macbeth and the Murdering Mother in Early Modern England." *College Literature* 32.3: 72–91.

Chapman, A. (1979), "Astrological Medicine," in C. Webster, ed., *Health, Medicine and Mortality in the Sixteenth Century*. Cambridge: Cambridge University Press., pp. 275–300.

Chapman, A. A. (2007), "Ophelia's 'old lauds': Madness and Hagiography in *Hamlet*." *Medieval and Renaissance Drama in England* 20: 111–35.

Christakis, N. and Fowler, J. H. (2009), *Connected: The Surprising Power of Our Social Networks and How They Shape Our Lives*. New York: Little, Brown.

Clark, G. (1966), *A History of The Royal College of Physicians of London*. Vol. 1. Oxford: Clarendon Press.

Clark, S. (2007), *Vanities of the Eye in Early Modern Culture*. Oxford: Oxford University Press.

Colie, R. (1966), *Paradoxia Epidemica: The Renaissance Tradition of Paradox*. Princeton, New Jersey: Princeton University Press.

Comensoli, V. and Russell, A., eds. (1999), *Enacting Gender on the English Renaissance Stage*. Urbana, Illinois: University of Illinois Press.

Cox, C. I. (2008), "'Lord have mercy upon us': The King, the Pestilence, and Shakespeare's *Measure for Measure*," *Exemplaria* 20.4: 430–57.

Crane, M. T. (1998), "Male Pregnancy and Cognitive Permeability in *Measure for Measure*." *Shakespeare Quarterly* 49.3: 269–92.

—. (2001), *Shakespeare's Brain*. Princeton, New Jersey: Princeton University Press.

—. (2004), "The Physics of *King Lear*. Cognition in a Void," in G. Bradshaw, T. Bishop, and M. Turner, eds., *Shakespeare International Yearbook* 4. Bodmin, Cornwall: Ashgate, pp. 3–23.

Crawfurd, R. (1911), *The King's Evil.* Oxford: Clarendon Press.

Cregan, K. (2009), *The Theatre of the Body: Staging Death and Embodying Life in Early Modern London.* Turnout, Belgium, Brepols.

Cressy, D. (1997), *Birth, Marriage, and Death: Ritual, Religion, and the Life-cycle in Tudor and Stuart England.* Oxford: Oxford University Press.

Crystal, D. (2003), "Shakespeare's False Friends: Ecstasy." *e magazine* 20, April: 54–5, [online] <www.davidcrystal.com/David_Crystal/Shakespeare.htm> [Accessed September 7, 2010].

Daalder, J. (1997), "Perspectives of Madness in *Twelfth Night.*" *English Studies* 78: 105–10.

Dabydeen, D., ed. (1985), *The Black Presence in English Literature.* Manchester: Manchester University Press.

Daigle, E. N. (2010), *Reconciling Matter and Spirit: The Galenic Brain in Early Modern Literature.* Ph.D., University of Iowa.

D'Amico, J. (1991), *The Moor in English Renaissance Drama.* Tampa: University of South Florida Press.

Dannenfeldt, K. (1985), "Egyptian Mumia: The Sixteenth Century Experience and Debate." *Sixteenth Century Journal* 16: 163–80.

Daston, L. and Park, K. (1995), "The Hermaphrodite and the Orders of Nature: Sexual Ambiguity in Early Modern France." *GLQ* 1: 419–38.

—. (1998), *Wonders and the Order of Nature, 1150–1750.* New York and Cambridge, Massachussetts: Zone/MIT Press.

Davis, P. (2007), *Shakespeare Thinking.* London: Continuum.

Dawson, L. (2008), *Lovesickness and Gender in Early Modern English Literature.* Oxford: Oxford University Press.

Debus, A. (1965; American ed., 1968), *The English Paracelsians.* London: Oldbourne.

—. (1977), *The Chemical Philosophy: Paracelsian Science and Medicine in the Sixteenth and Seventeenth Centuries.* Two volumes. New York: Science History Publications/Neale Watson Academic Publications.

Dekker, T. (1998), *The Honest Whore, Part 1.* N. Somogyi, ed. London: Globe Education.

Deleuze, G. and Guattari, F. (1983), *Anti-Oedipus.* Preface by Michel Foucault. Minneapolis: University of Minnesota Press.

Detmer, E. (1997), "Civilizing Subordination: Domestic Violence and *The Taming of the Shrew.*" *Shakespeare Quarterly* 48.3: 273–94.

Diede, M. K. (2008), *Shakespeare's Knowledgeable Body.* New York: Lang.

DiGangi, M. (1993), "Pleasure and Danger: Measuring Female Sexuality in *Measure for Measure.*" *ELH* 60.3: 589–60.

Dimmock, M. (2005), *New Turkes: Dramatizing Islam and the Ottomans in Early Modern England.* Aldershot, United Kingdom: Ashgate.

Dobranski, S. (1998), "Children of the Mind: Miscarried Narratives in *Much Ado About Nothing.*" *Studies in English Literature, 1500–1900,* 38.2: 233–50.

Dobson, J. and Walker, R. M. (1979), *Barbers and Barber-Surgeons of London.* Oxford: Blackwell Scientific Publications.

Dobson, M. J. (1994), "Malaria in England: A Geographical and Historical Perspective." *Parassitologia* 36.1–2: 35–60.

—. (2003), *Contours of Death and Disease in Early Modern England.* Cambridge, England: Cambridge University Press.

Doebler, B. A. (1994), *"Rooted Sorrow": Dying in Early Modern England.* London and Toronto: Associated University Presses.

Dollimore, J. (2001), *Death, Desire and Loss in Western Culture.* London and New York: Routledge.

Doyle, C. (1981), "The Hair and Beard of Thomas More." *Moreana* 18: 5–14.

Drake-Brockman, J. (1973), "Shakespeare's *Hamlet,* I, iv, 24." *Explicator* 32.4: Item 31.

Draper, J. W. (1964), "The Humors: Some Psychological Aspects of Shakespeare's Tragedies." *Journal of the American Medical Association* 188: 259–62.

Drey, R. (1978), *Apothecary Jars: Pharmaceutical Pottery and Porcelain in Europe and the East 1150–1850.* London: Faber.

Dugan, H. (2011), *The Ephemeral History of Perfume.* Baltimore, Md: Johns Hopkins University Press.

Duncan-Jones, K. (1995), "Deep-dyed Canker Blooms: Botanical Reference in Shakespeare's Sonnet 54." *Review of English Studies* 46: 521–25.

Dyer, A. (1997), "The English Sweating Sickness of 1551: An Epidemic Anatomized," *Medical History* 41.3: 362–84.

Eccles, A. (1982), *Obstetrics and Gynaecology in Tudor and Stuart England.* Kent, Ohio: Kent State University Press.

Ehrenreich, B. and English, D. (1973), *Witches, Midwives and Nurses: A History of Women Healers.* Old Westbury, New York: Feminist Press.

Elam, K. (1996), "The Fertile Eunuch: Twelfth Night, Early Modern Intercourse, and the Fruits of Castration." *Shakespeare Quarterly* 47.1: 1–36.

Evans, G. B. et al., eds. (1974), *The Riverside Shakespeare.* Rev. ed., 1997. Boston, Massachusetts: Houghton Mifflin.

Evenden, D. (1993), "Mothers and their Midwives in Seventeenth-century London," in H. Marland, ed., *The Art of Midwifery: Early Modern Midwives in Europe.* London: Routledge, pp. 9–26.

—. (2000), *The Midwives of Seventeenth-Century London.* Cambridge: Cambridge University Press.

Fabricius, J. (1994), *Syphilis in Shakespeare's England.* Bristol, Pennsylvania: Jessica Kingsley.

Fadiman, A. (1998), *The Spirit Catches You and You Fall Down: A Hmong Child, Her American Doctors, and the Collision of Two Cultures.* New York: Macmillan.

Ferguson, L. and Yachnin, P. (1981), "The Name of Juliet's Nurse." *Shakespeare Quarterly* 32.1 (Spring): 95–6.

Fernie, E. (2002), *Shame in Shakespeare.* Series: *Accents on Shakespeare.* London: Routledge.

Fildes, V. A. (1986), *Breasts, Bottles and Babies: A History of Infant Feeding.* Edinburgh: Edinburgh University Press.

—. (1988), *A History of Wet-Nursing.* Oxford: Blackwell.

—, ed. (1990), *Women as Mothers in Pre-industrial England.* London: Routledge.

Fineman, J. (1986), *Shakespeare's Perjured Eye: The Invention of Poetic Subjectivity in the Sonnets*. Berkeley, California and London: University of California Press.

—. (1989), "Shakespeare's Ear." *Representations* 28: 6–13.

Fisher, W. (2001), "The Renaissance Beard: Masculinity in Early Modern England." *Renaissance Quarterly* 54.1: 155–87.

—. (2006), *Materializing Gender in Early Modern English Literature and Culture. Cambridge Studies in Renaissance Literature and Culture* 52. Cambridge: Cambridge University Press.

Fissell, M. (2004), *Vernacular Bodies: The Politics of Reproduction in Early Modern England*. Oxford: Oxford University Press.

—, ed. and introd. (2008), *Women, Health, and Healing in Early Modern Europe*. Special Issue of the *Bulletin of the History of Medicine* 82.1.

Fitzpatrick, J. (2007), *Food in Shakespeare: Early Modern Dietaries and the Plays*. Aldershot, England: Ashgate.

—. (2011), *Shakespeare and the Language of Food*. London: Continuum (in press).

Fleissner, R. F. (1961), "Falstaff's Green Sickness unto Death." *Shakespeare Quarterly* 12: 47–55.

—. (1983), "Putting Falstaff to Rest: 'Tabulating' the Facts." *Shakespeare Studies* 16: 57–74.

Fletcher, J. (1907), *The Pilgrim*. In A. R. Waller, ed., *The Complete Works of Beaumont and Fletcher*. 10 Vols. Vol. 5. pp. 153–229.

Floyd-Wilson, M. (2003), *English Ethnicity and Race in Early Modern English Drama*. Cambridge: Cambridge University Press.

—. (2004), "English Mettle." In G. Paster et al., eds., *Reading the Early Modern Passions*. Philadelphia: University of Pennsylvania Press, pp. 130–45.

Fogan, L. (1989), "The Neurology in Shakespeare," *Archives of Neurology* 46: 922–24.

Folkerth, W. (2002), *The Sound of Shakespeare*. London and New York: Routledge.

Ford, J. (1995), *Lovers' Melancholy*. R. F. Hill, ed. Manchester: Revels.

Foucault, M. (1994), *The Birth of the Clinic: An Archaeology of Medical Perception*. New York: Vintage.

—. (1995), *Discipline and Punish*. New York: Vintage.

—. (2001), *Madness and Civilization*. London: Routledge.

Fox, J. (1973), "'Clapperclaw' in Shakespeare." *American Notes & Queries*, Vol. 12. 4: 50–1.

Fraser-Harris, D. (1932), "Biology in Shakespeare." *The Scientific Monthly* 34.1: 54–68.

Freeman, D. (2004), "Othello and the 'Ocular Proof'" in G. Bradshaw, T. Bishop, and M. Turner, eds., *Shakespeare International Yearbook 4*. Bodmin, Cornwall: Ashgate, pp. 56–71.

Fryer, P. (1984), *Staying Power: The History of Black People in Britain*. London: Pluto Press.

Furman, Y., Wolf, S. M., and Rosenfeld, D. S. (1997), "Shakespeare and Sleep Disorders," *Neurology* 49: 1171–72.

Furnivall, F.J., ed., *The First Boke...by Andrew Borde*. London: Trübner, 1870.

Furst, Lilian R. (ed.) (1997), *Women Healers and Physicians: Climbing a Long Hill*. Lexington: University of Kentucky Press.

Fusch, D. (2008), "The Discourse of the Unmiraculous Miracle: Touching for the King's Evil in Stuart England." *Appositions: Studies in Renaissance/Early Modern Literature and Culture* 1 [online]. <http://appositions.blogspot.com> [Accessed July 31, 2010]

Garber, M. (1980), "The Healer in Shakespeare," in E. R. Peschel, ed., *Medicine and Literature*, New York: Neale Watson Academic Publications, pp. 103–9.

Garcia-Ballester, L. (2002), *Galen and Galenism: Theory and Medical Practice from Antiquity to the European Renaissance*, J. Arrizabalaga et al., eds. Burlington, Vermont: Ashgate.

Ginsberg, M. (1996), *Reconceiving Melancholy: Gynecological Moles of Difference in Shakespeare's* Hamlet *and* Richard II. Ph.D., SUNY-Buffalo.

Gittings, C. (1988), *Death, Burial, and the Individual in Early Modern England*. London: Routledge.

Gordon-Grube, K. (1988), "Anthropophagy in Post-Renaissance Europe: The Tradition of Medicinal Cannibalism." *American Anthropologist*, New Series, 90.2: 405–9.

Gouk, P. (2005), "Harmony, Health, and Healing: Music's Role in Early Modern Paracelsian Thought," in M. Pelling, and S. Mandelbrote, eds., *The Practice of Reform in Health, Medicine and Science, 1500–2000: Essays for Charles Webster*. London: Ashgate, pp. 23–42.

Grafton, A. and Siraisi, N. (2001), "Between the Election and My Hopes: Girolamo Cardano and Medical Astrology," in W. R. Newman, and A. Grafton, eds., *Secrets of Nature: Astrology and Alchemy in Early Modern Europe*. Cambridge: Massachusetts: MIT Press, pp. 69–131.

Gray, R. (2006), "Will in the Universe: Shakespeare's Sonnets, Plato's Symposium, Alchemy, and Renaissance Neoplatonism." *Shakespeare Survey* 59: 225–38.

Green, B. (1979), "Shakespeare's Heroic Elixir: A New Context for *The Phoenix and Turtle*." *Studia Neophilologica* 51: 215–23.

Greenberg, S. (2004), "Plague, the Printing Press, and Public Health in Seventeenth-Century London." *The Huntington Library Quarterly* 67. 4: 509–27.

Grigsby, B. L. (2000), '*The Doctour Maketh this Descriptioun*': The Moral and Social Meaning of Leprosy and Bubonic Plague in Literary, Theological, and Medical Texts of the English Middle Ages and Renaissance. Ph.D. Loyola University, Chicago.

—. (2004), *Pestilence in Medieval and Early Modern English Literature*. London: Routledge.

Habib, I. (2004), "Elizabethan Racial Medical Psychology, Popular Drama, and the Social Programming of the Late-Tudor Black: Sketching an Exploratory Postcolonial Hypothesis," in S. Moss and K. Peterson, eds., *Disease, Diagnosis, and Cure on the Early Modern Stage*. Aldershot, England: Ashgate, pp. 93–112.

Hadhazy, A. (2010), "Think Twice: How the Gut's 'Second Brain' Influences Mood and Well-Being," *Scientific American Online*. February 12, 2010. <www.scientificamerican.com/article.cfm?id=gut-second-brain>. [Accessed May 15, 2010]

Hale, D. (1971), "*Coriolanus*: The Death of a Political Metaphor." *Shakespeare Quarterly* 22.3: 197–202.

Halio, J., ed. (1996), *The First Quarto of* King Lear. Cambridge: Cambridge University Press.

Hall, E. (1980), *Shakespeare's Pharmacy*. Typescript at Folger Shakespeare Library, Washington, D.C. Austin, Texas: University of Texas at Austin College of Pharmacy.

Hall, K. F. (1995), *Things of Darkness: Economies of Race and Gender in Early Modern England*. Cornell: Cornell University Press.

Hall, J. (1998), "The Evacuations of Falstaff (*The Merry Wives of Windsor*)," in R. Knowles, ed., *Shakespeare and Carnival: After Bakhtin*. New York: St. Martin's, pp. 123–51.

Hankinson, R. J., ed. (2008), *The Cambridge Companion to Galen*. Cambridge: Cambridge University Press.

Hardin, R. F. (2002), "Playhouse Calls: Folk Play Doctors on the Elizabethan Stage." *Early Theatre* 5.1: 59–76.

Hardy, B. (1990), "The Talkative Woman in Shakespeare, Dickens, and George Eliot," in S. Minogue, ed., *Problems for Feminist Criticism*. London: Routledge, pp. 15–45.

Harkness, A. (2003), *The Rose: An Illustrated History*. London: Firefly.

Harkness, D. E. (2008), "A View from the Streets: Women and Medical Work in Elizabethan London." *Bulletin of the History of Medicine* 82.1: 52–85.

Harley, D. (1994), "Provincial Midwives in England: Lancashire and Cheshire, 1660–1760," in H. Marland, ed., *The Art of Midwifery: Early Modern Midwives in Europe*. London: Routledge, pp. 27–48.

Harris, J. G. (1998), "'The enterprise is sick': Pathologies of Value and Transnationality in *Troilus and Cressida*." *Renaissance Drama* new series 29: 3–37.

—. (2001), "Shakespeare's Hair: Staging the Object of Material Culture." *Shakespeare Quarterly* 52.4: 479–91.

—. (2004), *Sick Economies: Drama, Mercantilism, and Disease in Shakespeare's England*. Philadelphia: University of Pennsylvania Press.

—. (2007), "The Smell of *Macbeth*." *Shakespeare Quarterly* 58.4: 465–86.

Harrison, G. B., ed. (1924), *Daemonologie and Newes from Scotland*. London: Bodley Head.

Hart, F. E. (2000), "Cerimon's 'Rough' Music in *Pericles*, 3.2." *Shakespeare Quarterly* 51: 313–31.

Harvey, E. D. (2003), "The Touching Organ: Allegory, Anatomy, and the Renaissance Skin Envelope." in E. D. Harvey, ed., *Sensible Flesh: On Touch in Early Modern Culture*. Philadelphia: University of Pennsylvania Press, pp. 81–102.

Harvey, R. (1998), "The Judgements of Urine." *Canadian Medical Association Journal* 159.12: 1482. University of Georgia Libraries <www.libs.uga.edu> [Accessed August 17, 2005].

Haslem, L. S. (1996), "Tongue-Tied Women and Embarrassed Men in *Much Ado about Nothing* and *The Winter's Tale*," *Shakespeare Yearbook* 7: 381–401.

Hatchuel, S. (2005), "'Prithee, see there! Behold! Look!' (3.4.69): The Gift or the Denial of Sight in Screen Adaptations of Shakespeare's Macbeth," *Borrowers and Lenders: The Journal of Shakespeare and Appropriation* 1.2 (Fall/Winter). <www.borrowers.uga.edu/cocoon/borrowers/request?id=781443> [Accessed November 25, 2010]

Healy, M. (2001), *Fictions of Disease in Early Modern England.* New York: Palgrave.

—. (2003), "Anxious and Fatal Contacts: Taming the Contagious Touch," in E. D. Harvey, ed. *Sensible Flesh: On Touch in Early Modern Culture.* Philadelphia: University of Pennsylvania Press, pp. 22–38.

—. (2004), "Curing the 'Frenzy': Humanism, Medical Idiom, and 'Crises' of Counsel in Sixteenth-Century England." *Textual Practice* 18: 333–50.

—. (2007), "'Making the quadrangle round': Alchemy's Protean Forms in Shakespeare's Sonnets and *A Lover's Complaint,* in M. Schoenfeldt, ed. *A Companion to Shakespeare's Sonnets.* Oxford: Blackwell, pp. 405–25.

Heffernan, C. (1995), *The Melancholy Muse: Chaucer, Shakespeare, and Early Medicine.* Pittsburgh, Pennsylvania: Duquesne University Press.

Hendricks, M. (1996), "'Obscured by Dreams': Race, Empire, and Shakespeare's *A Midsummer Night's Dream.*" *Shakespeare Quarterly* 47: 37–60.

Hendricks, M. and Parker, P., eds. ,(1994) *Women, "Race" and Writing in the Early Modern Period.* London: Routledge.

Henning, S. (2000), "Branding Harlots on the Brow." *Shakespeare Quarterly* 51.1: 86–9.

Hibbard, G. R., ed., (2002), *Love's Labor's Lost.* By W. Shakespeare. Oxford: World's Classics.

Hillman, D. (2007), *Shakespeare's Entrails: Belief, Scepticism and the Interior of the Body.* London: Palgrave.

Hillman, D. and C. Mazzio, eds. (1997), *The Body in Parts: Fantasies of Corporeality in Early Modern Europe.* London: Routledge.

Hindson, B. (2009), "Attitudes towards Menstruation and Menstrual Blood in Elizabethan England." *Journal of Social History* 43.1: 89–114.

Hobgood, A. P. (2006), "*Twelfth Night's* 'notorious abuse' of Malvolio: Shame, Humorality, and Early Modern Spectatorship." *Shakespeare Bulletin* 24.3: 1–22.

Hockey, D. C. (1965), "Wormwood! Wormwood!" *ELN* 2: 174–7.

Hodgkin, K. (2007), *Madness in Seventeenth-century Autobiography.* London: Palgrave.

Hoeniger, F. (1992), *Medicine and Shakespeare in the English Renaissance.* Newark, Delaware: University of Delaware Press.

Holstun, J. (1983), "Tragic Superfluity in *Coriolanus.*" *ELH* 50.3: 485–507.

Horan, J. (1996), *The Porcelain God: A Social History of the Toilet.* Secaucus, New Jersey: Carol Publishing Group.

Howard, S. (2003), "Imagining the Pain and Peril of Seventeenth-century Childbirth: Danger and Deliverance in the Making of an Early Modern World." *Social History of Medicine* 16: 367–82.

Hudson, R. (1977), "The Biography of Disease: Lessons from Chlorosis." *Bulletin of the History of Medicine* 51: 448–63.

Hunt, M. (1988), "Homeopathy in Shakespearean Comedy and Romance." *Ball State University Forum* 29.3: 45–57.

—. (1989), "Shakespeare's Tragic Homeopathy," in R. Dotterer, ed. *Shakespeare: Text, Subtext, and Context.* Series: Susquehanna University Studies. Selinsgrove, Pennsylvania: Susquehanna University Press/ London and Toronto: Associated University Presses, pp. 77–84.

—. (2002), "Dismemberment, Corporal Reconstitution, and the Body Politic in *Cymbeline.*" *Studies in Philology* 99.4: 404–31.

Hunter, G. K. (1967), *Othello and Colour-Prejudice.* Oxford: British Academy Lecture.

Hunter, L. (2004), "Cankers in *Romeo and Juliet*: Sixteenth-century Medicine at a Figural/literal Cusp," in S. Moss and K. Peterson, eds., *Disease, Diagnosis, and Cure on the Early Modern Stage.* London: Ashgate, pp. 171–86.

Hunter, L. and Hutton, S., eds. (1997), *Women, Science and Medicine 1500–1700.* Stroud, Gloucester: Sutton.

Hunter, P. R. (1991), "The English Sweating Sickness, with Particular Reference to the 1551 Outbreak in Chester." *Reviews of Infectious Diseases,* 13.2: 303–6.

Hurd-Mead, K. (1938), *A History of Women in Medicine.* Repr. 1977. New York: AMS.

Iyengar, S. (2003), "'Handling Soft the Hurts': Female Healers and Manual Contact in Spenser, Ariosto and Shakespeare," in E. D. Harvey, ed., *Sensible Flesh: Renaissance Representations of the Tactile.* Philadelphia: University of Pennsylvania Press, pp. 39–61.

—. (2005), *Shades of Difference: Mythologies of Skin Color and Race in Early Modern England.* Philadelphia: University of Pennsylvania Press.

Jackson, K. (2005), *Separate Theaters: Bethlem ("Bedlam") Hospital and the Shakespearean Stage.* Newark, Delaware: University of Delaware Press.

Jankowski, T. (2000), *Pure Resistance: Queer Virginity in Early Modern Drama.* Philadelphia: University of Pennsylvania Press.

—. (2003), "Hymeneal Blood, Interchangeable Women, and the Early Modern Marriage Economy in *Measure for Measure* and *All's Well That Ends Well,*" in R. Dutton and J. E. Howard, eds., *Oxford Companion to Shakespeare's Works,* Volume 4. Oxford: Blackwell, pp. 89–105.

Jarcho, S. (1987), "Falstaff, Kittredge, and Galen." *Perspectives in Biology and Medicine* 30: 197–200.

Jenner, M. S. R. and Wallis, P., eds. (2007), *Medicine and the Market England and its Colonies, c.1450–c.1850.* Basingstoke: Palgrave.

Johnson, B. W. (1995), *Birthed Effects: Shakespeare's Generation of Monsters.* Ph.D., University of California–Berkeley.

Johnston, I., trans. (2006), *Galen: On Diseases and Symptoms.* Cambridge: Cambridge University Press.

Jones, E. (1949), *Hamlet and Oedipus.* London: Gollancz.

—. (1980), "Richard III's Disfigurement." *Folklore* 91: 211–27.

Jones, V. A. (1977), "John Hall: Seventeenth-Century Physician of Stratford upon Avon." *Proceedings of the Royal Society of Medicine* 70: 709–14.

Jordan, W. (1968), *White Over Black: American Attitudes Towards the Negro, 1550–1812.* Chapel Hill, North Carolina: University of North Carolina Press.

Joseph, H. (1964), *Shakespeare's Son-in-Law: John Hall, Man and Physician.* London: Bailey Brothers.

Jung, C. G. (1953, rpt. 1968 and 1989), *Psychology and Alchemy.* Translated by R. F. C. Hull, trans., and Sir H. Read. M. Fordham, G. Adler, W. McGuire, eds., *Collected Works of C. G. Jung,* Volume 12. London: Routledge.

Kahn, C. (1983), "Coming of Age in Verona," in C. Lenz, G. Greene, and C. T. Neely, eds., *The Woman's Part: Feminist Criticism of Shakespeare.* Urbana, Illinois: University of Illinois Press, pp. 171–93.

—. (1997), *Roman Shakespeare: Warriors, Wounds, and Women.* New York: Routledge.

Kaiser, P. (1963), *Praisers of Folly.* Harvard: Harvard University Press.

Kallendorf, H. (2003), *Exorcism and Its Texts: Subjectivity in Early Modern Literature of England and Spain.* Toronto and Buffalo: University of Toronto Press.

Kassell, L. (2001), "'The Food of Angels': Simon Forman's Alchemical Medicine," in W. R. Newman, and A. Grafton, eds., *Secrets of Nature: Astrology and Alchemy in Early Modern Europe.* Cambridge: Massachusetts: MIT Press, pp. 345–84.

—. (2007), *Medicine and Magic in Elizabethan London : Simon Forman, Astrologer, Alchemist and Physician.* Oxford: Oxford University Press.

Keirsey, D. and Bates, M. (1984), *Please Understand Me: Character and Temperament Types.* Del Mar, California: Prometheus Nemesis.

Keller, E. (2006), *Generating Bodies and Gendered Selves: The Rhetoric of Reproduction in Early Modern England.* Seattle: University of Washington Press.

Kelley, S. (2006), "Shakespeare's *The Winter's Tale.*" *Explicator,* Spring; 64. 140–1.

Kennedy, G. (2000), *Just Anger.* Carbondale: Southern Illinois University Press.

Kerwin, W. (1997), "Where Have You Gone, Margaret Kennix? Seeking the Tradition of Healing Women in English Renaissance Drama," in L. Furst, ed., *Women Healers and Physicians: Climbing a Long Hill.* Lexington, Kentucky: University of Kentucky Press, pp. 93–113.

—. (2005), *Beyond the Body: The Boundaries of Medicine and English Renaissance Drama.* Amherst, Massachussetts: University of Massachussetts Press.

King, H. (1993), "The Politick Midwife: Models of Midwifery in the Work of Elizabeth Cellier," in H. Marland, ed., *The Art of Midwifery: Early Modern Midwives in Europe.* London: Routledge, pp. 115–30.

—. (2007), *Midwifery, Obstetrics and the Rise of Gynaecology: The Uses of a Sixteenth-century Compendium.* Aldershot, England: Ashgate.

King, R. (1997), *The History of Dentistry: Technique and Demand.* [Exhibition Catalogue.] Cambridge: Wellcome Unit for the History of Medicine.

Kirschbaum, L. (1949), "Shakespeare's Stage Blood and Its Critical Significance." *PMLA* 64.3: 517–29.

Knapp, J. (1993), "Preachers and Players in Shakespeare's England." *Representations* 44: 29–59.

Knoepflmacher, U. C. (1963), "The Humors as Symbolic Nucleus in *Henry IV, Part I.*" *College English* 24: 497–501.

Knowles, R., ed. (1998), *Shakespeare and Carnival: After Bakhtin.* New York: St. Martin's.

La Belle, Jenijoy (1980), "'A Strange Infirmity': Lady Macbeth's Amenorrhea." *Shakespeare Quarterly* 31: 381–86.

Lane, J. (2000), *The Making of the English Patient: A Guide to Sources for the Social History of Medicine.* Stroud, Gloucestershire: Sutton Publishing.

Lane, J., and Earles, M., eds. (1996), *John Hall and His Patients: The Medical Practice of Shakespeare's Son-in-Law.* London: Shakespeare Birthplace Trust.

Laqueur, T. (1990), *Making Sex: Body and Gender from the Greeks to Freud.* Cambridge, Massachussetts: Harvard University Press.

Laroche, R. (2009), *Medical Authority and Englishwomen's Herbal Texts, 1550–1650.* Farnham, Surrey, England: Ashgate.

Laroque, F. (1998), "Shakespeare's Battle of Carnival and Lent: The Falstaff Scenes Reconsidered (*1 and 2 Henry IV*)" in R. Knowles, ed., *Shakespeare and Carnival: After Bakhtin.* New York: St. Martin's, pp. 83–96.

Lecercle, A. (1985), "Anatomy of a Fistula, Anomaly of a Drama," in J. Fuzier, and F. Laroque, eds., *All's Well That Ends Well: Nouvelles Perspectives Critiques.* Montpellier: University de Paul Valéry, pp. 105–24.

Lehnhof, K. (2007), "Performing Woman: Female Theatricality in *All's Well That Ends Well*," in G. Waller, ed., All's Well, That Ends Well: *New Critical Essays.* London: Routledge, pp. 111–24.

Leong, E. (2008), "Making Medicines in the Early Modern Household." *Bulletin of the History of Medicine* 82.1: 145–68.

Levin, C. (1999), "'Murder not then the fruit within my womb': Shakespeare's Joan, Foxe's Guernsey Martyr, and Women Pleading Pregnancy in Early Modern English History and Culture." *Quidditas* 20: 75–93.

Levin, J. (2002), "Lady Macbeth and the Daemonologie of Hysteria." *ELH* 69: 21–55.

Levin, R. (1996), "Flower Maidens, Wise Women, Witches, and the Gendering of Knowledge in English Renaissance Drama," in J. M. Mucciolo, ed., *Shakespeare's Universe: Renaissance Ideas and Conventions: Essays in Honour of W. R. Elton.* Aldershot: Scolar, pp. 95–107.

Lewin, J. (2002), *Wailing Eloquence: Sleep and Dreams in Early Modern English Literature.* Ph.D., Yale University.

—. (2003), "'Your Actions are My Dreams': Sleepy Minds in Shakespeare's Last Plays," *Shakespeare Studies* 31: 184–206.

—. (2005), "Murdering Sleep in Macbeth: the Mental World of the Protagonist," in G. Bradshaw, T. Bishop, R. H. Wells, M. Neill, eds., *Shakespearean International Yearbook* 5. Bodmin, Cornwall: Ashgate, pp. 181–8.

Linden, S. J. (1996), *Darke Hierogliphicks: Alchemy in English Literature from Chaucer to the Restoration.* Lexington, Kentucky: University of Kentucky Press.

Little, A. B. (2000), *Shakespeare Jungle Fever: National-Imperial Re-Visions of Race, Rape, and Sacrifice.* Stanford, California: Stanford University Press.

Lobanov-Rostovsky, S. (1997), "Taming the Basilisk," in D. Hillman, and C. Mazzio, eds., *The Body in Parts: Fantasies of Corporeality in Early Modern Europe.* London: Routledge, pp. 195–219.

Loomba, A. (1989), *Gender, Race, Renaissance Drama.* Manchester: Manchester University Press.

Loughlin, M. (1997), *Hymeneutics: Interpreting Virginity on the Early Modern Stage.* Cranbury, New Jersey, and London: Associated University Presses.

Lucking, D. (1997), "Bringing Deformed Forth: Engendering Meaning in *Much Ado About Nothing*," *Renaissance Forum* 2.1: <www.hull.ac.uk/renforum/v2no1/lucking.htm> [Accessed May 24, 2010]

Lupton, J. (1997), "Othello Circumcised: Shakespeare and the Pauline Discourse of Nations." *Representations* 57: 73–89.

Lux, M. (2002), "'Work on My Medicine': Physiologies and Anatomies in *Othello*," in P. Kolin, ed., *Othello: New Critical Essays*. New York: Routledge, pp. 379–90.

Lyons, B. G. (1971), *Voices of Melancholy: Studies in Literary Treatments of Melancholy in Renaissance England*. New York: Barnes and Noble.

MacDonald, J. G. (2002), *Women and Race in Early Modern Texts*. Cambridge: Cambridge University Press.

MacDonald, M. (1981), *Mystical Bedlam: Madness, Anxiety and Healing in Seventeenth-Century England*. Cambridge: Cambridge University Press.

Maclean, I. (1980), *The Renaissance Notion of Woman: A Study in the Fortunes of Scholasticism and Medical Science in European Intellectual Life*. Cambridge: Cambridge University Press.

Madelaine, R. (1982), "Oranges and Lemans: *Much Ado About Nothing*, IV, 1, 31." *Shakespeare Quarterly* 33.4: 491–92.

—. (1983), "Boys' Beards and Balurdo." *Notes and Queries* 228: 148–50.

Marland, H., ed., (1993), *The Art of Midwifery: Early Modern Midwives in Europe*. London: Routledge.

Marowitz, C. (1963), "Lear Log," *Drama Review* 8: 103–21.

Marshall, B., ed., (2002), *Helicobacter Pioneers: Firsthand Accounts from the Scientists who Discovered Helicobacters, 1892–1982*. Oxford and Victoria, Australia: Blackwell Science Asia.

Marshall, C. (1994), "Portia's Wound, Calphurnia's Dream: Reading Character in *Julius Caesar*." *English Literary Renaissance* 24: 471–88.

—. (1996), "Wound-Man: *Coriolanus*, Gender, and the Theatrical Construction of Interiority," in V. Traub, ed., *Feminist Readings of Early Modern Culture*. Cambridge: Cambridge University Press, pp. 93–118.

—. (2001), "Bodies in the Audience." *Shakespeare Studies* 29: 51–56.

Martin, E. (1994), *Flexible Bodies: Tracking Immunity in American Culture from the Days of Polio to the Age of AIDS*. Boston: Beacon.

Masten, J. (1997), "Is the Fundament a Grave?" in D. Hillman, and C. Mazzio, eds., *The Body in Parts: Fantasies of Corporeality in Early Modern Europe*. London: Routledge, pp. 129–46.

Mattern, S. (2008), *Galen and the Rhetoric of Healing*. Baltimore, Maryland: Johns Hopkins University Press.

Matthews, P. M. and McQuain, J., eds. (2003), *The Bard on the Brain: Understanding the Mind through the Art of Shakespeare and the Science of Brain Imaging*. New York: Dana Press.

Maus, K. (1995), *Inwardness and Theater in the English Renaissance*. Chicago: University of Chicago Press.

Mazzio, C. (1998), *Sins of the Tongue: Rhetoric, Print, and Speech in Early Modern England*. Ph.D., Harvard University.

—. (2009), "The History of Air: *Hamlet* and the Trouble with Instruments." *South Central Review* 26.1–2: 153–96.

McBride, C. (2002). *Places of Madness: The Role of the Early Modern Theatre in the Construction and Reinforcement of the Notion of Bedlam with Particular Reference to the*

Bethlem Hospital, and to Plays by Thomas Dekker, John Fletcher, Thomas Middleton, William Rowley, William Shakespeare, and John Webster. Ph.D., University of Wales (Cardiff).

McCullen, J. T., Jr. (1965), "Shakespeare's *Othello* I.iii.322–337." *Explicator* 23.6: 47.

McEachern, C. (1994), "*Henry V* and the Paradox of the Body Politic." *Shakespeare Quarterly* 45.1: 33–56.

McGeoch, A. H. (1955), "Shakespeare, the Dermatologist." *Australasian Journal of Dermatology* 3.2: 53–64. Repr. 2007.

McKeithen, A. [n.d.], "Dating the First English Plague Orders" <http://historical.hsl.virginia.edu/plague/mckeithen.cfm> [Accessed January 24, 2010].

McLaren, A. (1984), *Reproductive Rituals: The Perception of Fertility in England from the Sixteenth Century to the Nineteenth Century.* London: Methuen.

McSweegan E. (2004), "Anthrax and the Etiology of the English Sweating Sickness." *Medical Hypotheses* 62.1: 155–7.

McTavish, L. (2006), "Blame and Vindication in the Early Modern Birthing Chamber." *Medical History* October 1; 50(4): 447–64.

Melchiori, G., ed. (2007), *The Second Part of King Henry IV.* Cambridge: Cambridge University Press.

Middleton, T. and Rowley, T. (2007), *The Changeling.* M. Neill, ed. London: New Mermaid.

Moran, B. (2005), *Distilling Knowledge: Alchemy, Chemistry, and the Scientific Revolution.* Cambridge, Massachusetts: Harvard University Press.

Morgan, S. (1904) ed., *John Howe's ms., 1582.* London: [n.p.].

Moss, S. (1997), "Reading Epilepsy in *Othello,*" Ph.D., University of South Florida.

Moss, S. and Peterson, K., eds. (2004), *Disease, Diagnosis, and Cure on the Early Modern Stage.* Aldershot, England: Ashgate.

Muir, K. (1960), "Madness in *King Lear.*" *Shakespeare Survey* 13: 30–40.

Murphy-Lawless, J. (1998), *Reading Birth and Death.* Cork, Ireland: Cork University Press.

Murray, W. (1967), "Why Was Duncan's Blood Golden?" *Shakespeare Survey* 19: 34–44.

Myers, I. B. (1995), *Gifts Differing: Understanding Personality Type.* Mountain View, California: Davies-Black.

Neely, C. T. (2000), "Lovesickness, Gender, and Subjectivity: *Twelfth Night* and *As You Like It,*" in D. Callaghan, et al., ed., *A Feminist Companion to Shakespeare.* Oxford: Blackwell, pp. 276–98.

—. (2004), *Distracted Subjects: Madness and Gender in Shakespeare and Early Modern Culture.* Cornell, New York: Cornell University Press.

Newman, K. (1991), *Fashioning Femininity and English Renaissance Drama.* Chicago and London: University of Chicago Press.

Newman, L. (1979), "Ophelia's Herbal." *Economic Botany* 33.2: 227–32.

Newman, W. R. and Grafton, A. eds. (2001), *Secrets of Nature: Astrology and Alchemy in Early Modern Europe.* Cambridge, Massachusetts: MIT Press.

Nicholl, C. (1980), *The Chemical Theatre.* London: Routledge.

Noble, L. (2003), "'And Make Two Pasties of Your Shameful Heads': Medicinal Cannibalism and Healing the Body Politic in *Titus Andronicus.*" *ELH* 70.3: 677–708.

—. (2004), "The *Fille Vièrge* as *Pharmakon*: The Therapeutic Value of Desdemona's Corpse," in S. Moss, and K. Peterson, eds., *Disease, Diagnosis, and Cure on the Early Modern Stage*. Aldershot, England: Ashgate, pp. 135–50.

Nunn, H. M. (2005), *Staging Anatomies: Dissection and Spectacle in Early Stuart Tragedy*. Aldershot, England: Ashgate.

Nutton, V. (1987), *John Caius and the Manuscripts of Galen*. Cambridge: Cambridge Philological Society.

—. (1988), *From Democedes to Harvey*. London: Variorum Reprints.

—. (2004), *Ancient Medicine*. London: Taylor and Francis.

O'Brien, G. (1969), "*Hamlet* IV. iv. 26–29." *Shakespeare Quarterly* 20.1: 88–90.

O'Connell, M. (2000), *The Idolatrous Eye: Iconoclasm and Theater in Early Modern England*. New York and Oxford: Oxford University Press.

O'Donoghue, E. (1914), *The Story of Bethlehem Hospital*. London: Fisher Unwin.

Olivier, L., dir. (1955), *Richard III*. London Films.

Orgel, S. (1989), "Nobody's Perfect: Or, Why Did the English Stage Take Boys for Women?" *South Atlantic Quarterly* 88: 7–29.

—. (1996), *Impersonations: The Performance of Gender in Shakespeare's England*. Cambridge: Cambridge University Press.

—. ed., (1999), *King Lear*. London: Penguin.

Orme, N. and Webster, M. (1995), *The English Hospital, 1070–1570*. New Haven, Connecticut: Yale University Press.

Osler, W. (1916), *Creators, Transmuters, and Transmitters, as Illustrated by Shakespeare, Bacon, and Burton*. Nuneham (M. adds. 36e.13). Oxford: Bodleian Library.

Overton, D. A. (2006). *The Actor's Physical Articulation of Character Text in Shakespeare's Richard III: Performing Deformity*, Ph.D., University of Colorado-Boulder.

Pagel, W. (1958, rev. ed. 1982), *Paracelsus: An Introduction to Philosophical Medicine in the Era of the Renaissance*. 2nd rev. ed. Basel: Karger.

Park, K. (1997), "The Rediscovery of the Clitoris." in Hillman, D., and Mazzio, C., eds., *The Body in Parts: Fantasies of Corporeality in Early Modern Europe*. London: Routledge, pp. 171–94.

—. (2008), "The Death of Isabella Della Volpe: Four Eyewitness Accounts of a Postmortem Caesarean Section in 1545." *Bulletin of the History of Medicine* 82.1: 169–87.

Parker, P. (1993), "Gender Ideology, Gender Change: The Case of Marie-Germain," *Critical Inquiry* 19: 337–65.

—. (1994), "Fantasies of 'Race' and 'Gender': Africa, *Othello*, and Bringing to Light." Hendricks and Parker, *Women, "Race," and Writing*, pp. 84–100.

—. (2003), "Black *Hamlet*: Battening on the Moor." *Shakespeare Studies* 31: 127–64.

—. (2004), "Barbers and Barbary: Early Modern Cultural Semantics." *Renaissance Drama* 33: 201–44.

—. (2008), "Cutting Both Ways: Bloodletting, Castration/Circumscision, and the 'Lancelet' of *The Merchant of Venice*," in D. Henderson, ed., *Alternative Shakespeares 3*. London: Routledge, pp. 95–118.

Paster, G. K. (1993), *The Body Embarrassed: Drama and the Disciplines of Shame in Early Modern England*. Ithaca, New York: Cornell University Press.

Bibliography

—. (2004a), *Humoring the Body: Emotions and the Shakespearean Stage*. Chicago: University of Chicago Press.

—. (2004b), "Melancholy Cats, Lugged Bears, and Early Modern Cosmology: Reading Shakespeare's Psychological Materialism across the Species Barrier," in G. K. Paster, K. Rowe, and M. Floyd-Wilson, eds., *Reading the Early Modern Passions: Essays in the Cultural History of Emotion*. Philadelphia: University of Pennsylvania Press, pp. 113–29.

Paster, G. K., Rowe, K. and Floyd-Wilson, M., eds. (2004), *Reading the Early Modern Passions: Essays in the Cultural History of Emotion*. Philadelphia: University of Pennsylvania Press.

Patrick, A. (1965), "A Consideration of The Nature of The English Sweating Sickness." *Medical History* 9: 272–9.

Pearce, J. M. S. (2006), "Dr. John Hall (1575–1635) and Shakespeare's Medicine," *Journal of Medical Biography* 14: 187–91.

Peat, D. (2004), "Mad for Shakespeare: A Reconsideration for the Importance of Bedlam." *Parergon* 21.1: 113–32.

Pelling, M. and Mandelbrote, S., eds. (2005), *The Practice of Reform in Health, Medicine and Science, 1500–2000: Essays for Charles Webster*. Aldershot, England: Ashgate.

Pelling, M. and Webster, C., eds. (1977), *Essays on the Life and Work of Thomas Linacre, 1460–1524*. Oxford: Clarendon Press.

—. (1979), "Medical Practitioners," in C. Webster, ed., *Health, Medicine, and Mortality in the Sixteenth Century*. Cambridge: Cambridge University Press, pp. 165–236.

Pelling, M. and White, F. (2003), *Medical Conflicts in Early Modern London: Patronage, Physicians, and Irregular Practitioners, 1550–1640*. Oxford: Clarendon Press.

Persels, J. and Ganim, R., eds. (2004), *Fecal Matters in Early Modern Literature and Art*. Aldershot, England: Ashgate.

Pesta, J. D. (1999), *"My Well-known Body to Anatomize": Shakespeare and the Drama of Dissection*, Ph.D., Purdue University.

Peterson, Kaara L. "Historica Passio: *King Lear*, Early Modern Medicine, and Editorial Practice." *Shakespeare Quarterly* 57.1 (Spring 2006): 1–22.

Pettigrew, T. (2007), *Shakespeare and the Practice of Physic*. Newark, Delaware: University of Delaware Press/Associated University Presses.

Phillippy, P. (2002), *Women, Death and Literature in Post-Reformation England*. Cambridge: Cambridge University Press.

Phillis, R (2001), "The Stained Blood of Rape," in P.C. Collins et al., eds., *Shakespeare's Theories of Blood, Character, and Class*. New York: Lang, pp. 123–30.

Pollard, T. (2005), *Drugs and Theater in Early Modern England*. Oxford: Oxford University Press.

Poole, A. (2002), "Shakespeare and the Risk of Contagion." *Shakespeare Studies* (Shakespeare Society of Japan) 40: 93–115.

Porter, R. (1988), "A Touch of Danger: The Man-Midwife as Sexual Predator," in G. Rousseau and R. Porter, eds., *Sexual Underworlds of the Enlightenment*. Chapel Hill, North Carolina: University of North Carolina Press, pp. 206–32.

—. (1995), *Disease, Medicine and Society in England, 1550–1860*. 2nd edition. Cambridge: Cambridge University Press.

—. (2002), *Madness: A Brief History*. Oxford: Oxford University Press.

—, ed., (2003) *Patients and Practitioners: Lay Perceptions of Medicine in Pre-Industrial Society*. Cambridge: Cambridge University Press.

Principe, L. M. and Newman, W. R. (2001), "Some Problems with the Historiography of Alchemy," in W. R. Newman, and A. Grafton, eds., *Secrets of Nature: Astrology and Alchemy in Early Modern Europe*. Cambridge: Massachusetts: MIT Press, pp. 385–431.

Qualtiere, L. F., and Slights, W.W. E. (2003), "Contagion and Blame in Early Modern England: The Case of the French Pox," *Literature and Medicine* 22.1: 1–24.

Rackin, P. (1999), "Staging the Female Body: Maternal Breastfeeding and Lady Macbeth's 'Unsex me here,'" in C. Nesci, ed., *Corps/décors: Femmes, orgie, parodie*. Amsterdam: Rodopi, pp. 17–29.

Ramachandran, V. S. and Blakeslee, S. (1999), *Phantoms in the Brain: Probing the Mysteries of the Human Mind*. New York: William Morrow.

Ray, S. (1998), "'Rape, I fear, was root of thy annoy': The Politics of Consent in *Titus Andronicus*." *Shakespeare Quarterly* 49: 22–39.

Reed, R. (1952), *Bedlam on the Jacobean Stage*. Cambridge: Harvard University Press.

Reeve, M. (1989), "Conceptions." *Proceedings of the Cambridge Philological Society: Supplement* new series 36.215: 81–112.

Reid, P. (2010), "Giddy Lies the Head: Falling Sicknesses and the Body Politic in Shakespeare's *Henry IV* Plays," unpublished seminar paper, University of Georgia.

Reiter, P. (2000), "From Shakespeare to Defoe: Malaria in England in the Little Ice Age." *Emerging Infectious Diseases* 6.1 (Jan–Feb.): 1–11.

Rennard, B. O. et al. (2000), "Chicken Soup Inhibits Neutrophil Chemotaxis In Vitro*," *CHEST* 118.4: 1150–7.

Reno, R. H. (1961), "Hamlet's Quintessence of Dust." *Shakespeare Quarterly* 12: 107–13.

Rhodes, P. (1977), "Physical Deformity of Richard III," *British Medical Journal* 2/6103 (24–31 December): 1650–52.

Riddle, J. (1992), *Contraception and Abortion from the Ancient World to the Renaissance*. Cambridge, Massachusetts: Harvard University Press.

Ring, M. (1996), "Shakespeare and Dentistry: Teeth and Oral Care in the Writings of the Bard." *Journal of the California Dental Association* 24.4: 17–22.

Riss, A. (1992), "The Belly Politic: *Coriolanus* and the Revolt of Language." *ELH* 59.1: 53–75.

Roberts, G. (1983), "Shakespeare and 'Scratching.'" *Notes and Queries* 30: 111–14.

Roberts, J. A. (1992), "Shakespeare's Maimed Birth Rites," in L. Woodbridge, and E. Berry, eds., *True Rites and Maimed Rites*. Urbana, Illinois: University of Illinois Press, pp. 123–146.

Roberts, K. (1995), "The Wandering Womb: Classical Medical Theory and the Formation of Female Characters in *Hamlet*." *Classical and Modern Literature* 15: 223–32.

Roberts, R. S. (1965), "A Consideration of the Nature of the English Sweating Sickness." *Medical History* 9.4: 385–9.

Robson, M. (2001), "Looking with Ears, Hearing with Eyes: Shakespeare and the Ear of the Early Modern." *EMLS* 7.1. <http://extra.shu.ac.uk/emls/07–1/robsears.htm> [Accessed May 15, 2010].

Rolfe, R. (2002), *The Four Temperaments: A Rediscovery of the Ancient Way of Understanding Health and Character.* New York: Da Capo.

Rollins, P. and Smith, A., eds., (2001), *Shakespeare's Theories of Blood, Character, and Class: A Festschrift in Honor of David Shelley Berkeley.* New York: Lang.

Ross, J. J. (2005), "Shakespeare's Chancre: Did the Bard Have Syphilis?" *Clinical Infectious Diseases* 40: 399–404.

Royster, F. (2000), "White-Limed Walls: Whiteness and Gothic Extremism in Shakespeare's *Titus Andronicus.*" *Shakespeare Quarterly* 51: 432–55.

Salkeld, D. (1993), *Madness and Drama in the Age of Shakespeare.* Manchester and New York: Manchester University Press.

Saunders, B. (2004), "Iago's Clyster: Purgation, Anality, and the Civilizing Process." *Shakespeare Quarterly* 55: 148–76.

Sawday, J. (1996), *The Body Emblazoned: Dissection and the Human Body in Renaissance Culture.* London: Routledge.

Schaar, C. (1970), " 'Lunatic' and 'lunacy' in Shakespeare: A Pre-Psychiatric Note." *Acta Psychiatrica Scandinavica: Supplementum* S219: 190–7.

Schanzer, E. (1957), "Four Notes on *Macbeth,*" *Modern Language Review* 52: 223–7.

Schiebinger, L. (1991), *The Mind Has No Sex? Women in the Origins of Modern Science.* Cambridge: Harvard University Press.

Schleiner, W. (1991), *Melancholy, Genius, and Utopia in the Renaissance.* Wolfenbütteler Abhandlungen zur Renaissanceforschung 10. Wiesbaden: Harrassowitz.

—. (2000), "Early Modern Controversies About the One-Sex Model," *Renaissance Quarterly* 53: 180–91.

Schoenfeldt, M. (1999), *Bodies and Selves in Early Modern England.* Cambridge: Cambridge University Press.

Schwartz, R. B. (1990), *Shakespeare's Parted Eye: Perception, Knowledge, and Meaning in the Sonnets and Plays.* New York: Lang.

Schwarz, K. (2000), *Tough Love: Amazon Encounters in the English Renaissance.* Durham, North Carolina: Duke University Press.

Scott, W.O. (1988), "The Speculative Eye: Problematic Self-Knowledge in *Julius Caesar.*" *Shakespeare Survey* 40: 77–89.

Scott-Warren, J. (2001), *Sir John Harington and the Book as Gift.* Oxford: Oxford University Press.

Shenk, R. (1978), *The Sinner's Progress: A Study of Madness in English Renaissance Drama.* Salzburg: Institut für Englische Sprache und Literatur, Universität Salzburg.

Showalter, E. (1985), "Representing Ophelia: Women, Madness, and the Responsibilities of Feminist Criticism," in P. Parker and G. Hartman, eds., *Shakespeare and the Question of Theory.* New York and London: Methuen, pp. 77–94.

Siena, K. P. (1998), "Pollution, Promiscuity, and the Pox: English Venereology and the Early Modern Medical Discourse on Social and Sexual Danger." *Journal of the History of Sexuality* 8.4: 553–74.

—. (2004), *Venereal Disease, Hospitals, and the Urban Poor ; London's "foul wards," 1600–1800.* Rochester, New York: University of Rochester Press.

Silvette, H. (1967), *The Doctor on the Stage: Medicine and Medical Men in Seventeenth-century England.* Knoxville, Tennessee: University of Tennessee Press.

Simonds, P. M. (1999), "Sex in a Bottle: The Alchemical Distillation of Shakespeare's Hermaphrodite in Sonnet 20." *Renaissance Papers* 1999: 97–105.

Simpson, R. (1959), *Shakespeare and Medicine*. Edinburgh: Livingstone.

Siraisi, N. (1990), *Medieval and Early Renaissance Medicine*. Chicago: University of Chicago Press.

Skwire, S. (2000). *"No Health in us": Representations of Illness in Early Modern Literature*. Ph.D., University of Chicago.

Slack, P. (1979), "Mirrors of Health and Treasures of Poor Men: The Uses of the Vernacular Medical Literature of Tudor England," in C. Webster, ed., *Health, Medicine and Mortality in the Sixteenth Century*. Cambridge: Cambridge University Press. pp. 237–74.

Slack, P. (1985), *The Impact of Plague in Tudor and Stuart England*. London: Routledge.

Slights, W. W. E. (2008), *The Heart in the Age of Shakespeare*. Cambridge: Cambridge University Press.

Sloan, A. W. (1996), *English Medicine in the Seventeenth Century*. Durham: Durham Academic Press.

Sloan, L. L. (2002), "Trumpeting and 'Seeled' Eyes: A Semiotics of [Eye]conography in *Othello*," in P. Kolin, ed., *Othello: New Critical Essays*. New York: Routledge, pp. 363–77.

Smith, A. (1994). *Shakespeare and Renaissance Blood Lore*. Ph.D., University of Oklahoma.

Smith, B. R. (1999), *The Acoustic World of Early Modern England*. Chicago: University of Chicago Press.

—. (2008), *The Key of Green*. Chicago: University of Chicago Press.

Smith, H. (2004), "Gynecology and Ideology in Seventeenth-century England," in B. Carroll, ed., *Liberating Women's History*. Urbana, Illinois: University of Illinois Press, pp. 97–114.

Smith, P. (2004), *The Body of the Artisan: Art and Experience in the Scientific Revolution*. Chicago: University of Chicago Press.

Smith, P. J. (1996), "Ajax by Any Other Name Would Smell as Sweet: Shakespeare, Harington, and Onomastic Scatology," in *Tudor Theatre: Emotion in the Theatre*. Bern, Switzerland: Lang, pp. 125–58.

Starobinski, J. (1981), "Chlorosis—the 'Green Sickness.'" *Psychological Medicine* 11: 459–68.

Starks, L. S. (2007), "That's *Amores*! Latin Love and Lovesickness in Shakespeare's *Venus and Adonis*." *Shakespearean International Yearbook* 7: 75–91.

Stearns, C. (1865), *Shakespeare's Medical Knowledge*. New York: Appleton.

Stensgaard, R. K. (1972), "*All's Well That Ends Well* and the Galenico-Paracelsian Controversy," *Renaissance Quarterly* 25: 173–88.

Stone, L. (1983), *The Family, Sex and Marriage in England 1500–1800*. London: HarperPerennial.

Stransky, E. (1974), "On the History of Chlorosis." *Episteme* 8.1: 26–45.

Sugg, R. (2006), "Good Physic But Bad Food: Early Modern Attitudes to Medicinal Cannibalism and its Suppliers." *Social History of Medicine* 19.2: 225–40.

Sutherland, J. (2000), *Henry V, War Criminal?* Oxford: Oxford University Press.

Swain, D. W. (2004), *Language of the Soul: Galenism and the Medical Disciplines in Elyot, Huarte, and Shakespeare.* Ph.D. University of Massachusetts—Amherst.

Sweetser, E. (2004), "'The Suburbs of your good pleasure': Cognition, Culture, and the Bases of Metaphoric Structure." In G. Bradshaw, W. G. Bishop, and M. Turner, eds., *Shakespeare International Yearbook 4.* Bodmin, Cornwall: Ashgate, pp. 24–55.

Tate, J. (2004), "Tamburlaine's Urine," in Ganim, R., and Persels, J., eds., *Fecal Matters in Early Modern Literature and Art: Studies in Scatology.* Burlington, Vermont: Ashgate Publishers, pp. 138–53.

—. (2005), "Uroscopy in Early Modern England." Online [no longer available]. 2004. <http://students.washington.edu/jtate/uroscopy.html> [Accessed August 17, 2005].

Taylor, G. (2000), *Castration: An Abbreviated History of Western Manhood.* New York: Routledge.

Totaro, R. (2005), *Suffering in Paradise: The Bubonic Plague in English Literature from More to Milton.* Pittsburgh: Duquesne University Press.

Temkin, O. (1945), *The Falling Sickness: A History of Epilepsy.* Baltimore, Maryland: Johns Hopkins University Press.

—. (1973), *Galenism: Rise and Decline of A Medical Philosophy.* Ithaca, NY: Cornell University Press.

Thiher, A. (1999), *Revels in Madness: Insanity in Medicine and Literature.* Ann Arbor, Michigan: University of Michigan Press.

Thompson, A. and Thompson, J. O. (1991), "Sight Unseen: Problems with 'Imagery' in Macbeth," in L. Hunter, ed., *Toward a Definition of Topos.* London: Macmillan, pp. 45–65.

Thoren, V. E. (1990), *The Lord of Uraniborg: A Biography of Tycho Brahe.* Cambridge: Cambridge University Press.

Thwaites, G., Taviner, M., and Gant, V. (1997), "The English Sweating Sickness, 1485 to 1551." *The New England Journal of Medicine* 336.8, February 20. [online] Available through the University of Georgia Libraries <www.libs.uga.edu> [Accessed July 31, 2010].

Tidy, H. (1945), "Sweating Sickness and Picardy Sweat." *The British Medical Journal,* 2.4410: 63–4.

Tognotti E. (2007), "Camillo Golgi and the Contribution of the Italian Scientists to the Development of the Malariology in the Last Quarter of the Nineteenth Century," Abstract, *Med Secoli* 19.1: 101–17. [online] Available through the University of Georgia Libraries <www.libs.uga.edu>. [Accessed July 31, 2010].

Torrey, M. (2000), "'The plain devil and dissembling looks': Ambivalent Physiognomy and Shakespeare's *Richard III.*" *ELR* 30: 123–53.

Traister, B. (2004), "'Note her a little farther': Doctors and Healers in the Drama of Shakespeare," in S. Moss, and K. Petersen, eds., *Disease, Diagnosis, and Cure on the Early Modern Stage.* Aldershot, England: Ashgate, pp. 43–52.

Travitsky, B. (1990), "Placing Women in the English Renaissance." *The Renaissance Englishwoman in Print.* Amherst, Massachusetts: University of Massachusetts Press, pp. 3–41.

Trevor, D. (2004), *The Poetics of Melancholy in Early Modern England.* Cambridge: Cambridge University Press.

Turner, M. (2004), "The Ghost of Anyone's Father," in G. Bradshaw, W. G. Bishop and M. Turner, eds., *Shakespeare International Yearbook* 4. Bodmin, Cornwall: Ashgate, pp. 72–97.

Urkowitz, S. (1980), *Shakespeare's Revision of* King Lear. Princeton, New Jersey Princeton University Press.

Van Dijkhuizen, J. F. (2007), *Devil Theatre: Demonic Possession and Exorcism in English Renaissance Drama, 1558–1642.* Woodbridge, Suffolk: Brewer.

Vaught, J. (2008), *Masculinity and Emotion in Early Modern English Literature.* Aldershot, England, and Burlington, Vermont: Ashgate.

Vendler, H. (1997), *The Art of Shakespeare's Sonnets.* Cambridge, Massachusetts: Harvard University Press.

Verity, A., and S. Instone, eds. (2007), *Pindar: The Complete Odes.* Oxford: Oxford University Press.

Vickers, N. (1985), "The Blazon of Sweet Beauty's Best: Shakespeare's *Lucrece*," in Parker, P. and Hartman, G., eds., *Shakespeare and the Question of Theory.* New York and London: Methuen, pp. 95–115.

Vinge, L. (1975), *The Five Senses: Studies in a Literary Tradition.* Lund: Acta Regiae Societatis Humaniorum Litterarum Lundensis.

Wack, M. (1990), *Lovesickness in the Middle Ages: The Viaticum and its Commentaries.* Philadelphia: University of Pennsylvania Press.

Wall, W. (2002), *Staging Domesticity: Household World and English Identity in Early Modern Drama.* Cambridge: Cambridge University Press.

—. (2006), "Shakespearean Jell-O: Morality and Malleability in the Kitchen." *Gastronomica: The Journal of Food and Culture* 6: 41–50.

Wallace, D. F. (1998), "The Depressed Person." *Harper's Magazine.* January. 57–64.

Wallis, P. (2006), "Plagues, Morality and the Place of Medicine in Early Modern England." *The English Historical Review* 121.490: 1–24.

Watt, R. J. C. (1997), "Neither parti-eyed nor poorly led: Edgar Meets the Blind Gloucester." *The Review of English Studies* 48.189 (February 1): 51.

Webster, C., ed., (1979), *Health, Medicine and Mortality in the Sixteenth Century.* Cambridge: Cambridge University Press.

—. (1979), "Alchemical and Paracelsian Medicine," in C. Webster, ed., *Health, Medicine and Mortality in the Sixteenth Century.* Cambridge: Cambridge University Press, pp. 301–34.

Webster, J. (1993), *The Duchess of Malfi.* E. Brennan, ed. London: New Mermaids.

Weil, J. (2005), *Service and Dependency in Shakespeare's Plays.* Cambridge: Cambridge University Press.

Wheatley, E. (2009), "Voices of Violence: Medieval French Farce and the Dover Cliff Scene in *King Lear.*" *Comparative Drama* 43.4: 455–71.

Wheeler, R. (2000), *The Complexion of Race: Categories of Difference in Eighteenth-century British Culture.* Philadelphia: University of Pennsylvania Press.

Williams, G. (1994), *A Dictionary of Sexual Language and Imagery in Shakespearean and Stuart Literature.* London: Athlone.

Williams, G. S. and Gunnoe, C. D., Jr., eds. (2002), *Paracelsian Moments: Science, Medicine and Astrology in Early Modern Europe*. Kirksville, Missouri: Truman State University Press/Sixteenth-Century Journal.

Williams, X. (1996), *The Four Temperaments: How to Achieve Love, Health, and Happiness by Understanding Yourself and the People Around You*. New York: St. Martin's.

Willis, D. (1992), "The Monarch and the Sacred: Shakespeare and the Ceremony for the Healing of the King's Evil," in L. Woodbridge, ed., *True Rites and Maimed Rites*. Urbana and Chicago: University of Illinois Press, pp. 147–68.

Wilson, A. (1990), "The Ceremony of Childbirth and its Interpretation," in V. Fildes, ed., *Women as Mothers in Pre-industrial England*. London: Routledge, pp. 70–83.

—. (1995), *The Making of Man-Midwifery: Childbirth in England, 1660–1770*. Cambridge: Harvard University Press.

Wilson, D. (1993), *Signs and Portents: Monstrous Births from the Middle Ages to the Enlightenment*. London: Routledge.

Wilson, J. D. (1936, repr. 1951), *What Happens in Hamlet*. New York: Macmillan.

—. (1979), *The Fortunes of Falstaff*. Cambridge: Cambridge University Press.

Winston, J. (2002), "Richard III's Teeth." *Rendezvous: Idaho State University Journal of Arts and Letters* 36.2: 43–6.

Woodbridge, L. (1984), *Women in the English Renaissance: Literature and the Nature of Womankind 1540–1620*. Urbana and Chicago, Illinois: University of Illinois Press.

—. (2001), *Vagrancy, Homelessness, and the English Renaissance*. Urbana and Chicago, Illinois: University of Illinois Press.

—. ed. (1992), *True Rites and Maimed Rites*. Urbana and Chicago, Illinois: University of Illinois Press.

Woodforde, J. (1983), *The Strange Story of False Teeth*. London: Routledge.

Wright, L. (1960), *Clean and Decent: The Fascinating History of the Bathroom and the Water Closet and of Sundry Habits, Fashions & Accessories of the Toilet*. New York: Viking.

Wynne-Davies, M. (1991), "'The swallowing womb': Consumed and Consuming Women in *Titus Andronicus*," in V. Wayne, ed., *The Matter of Difference: Materialist Feminist Criticism of Shakespeare*. Ithaca, New York: Cornell University Press, pp. 129–51.

Yalom, M. (1997), *A History of the Breast*. New York: Ballantine.

Yates, Dame F. (1979), *The Occult Philosophy in the Elizabethan Age*. London: Routledge.

Index

Page numbers in **bold** denote table.

1H4 (*King Henry IV, Part 1*) 17, 21, 32, 37,
   42, 46, 48, 53, 58, 64, 66, 71, 80, 85,
   97, 109–10, 131–2, 134, 148, 155,
   157–9, 169, 178, 189, 194, 205, 212,
   219, 232, 247, 258, 263, 265, 274,
   276, 279, 281–2, 292, 297–8, 307,
   311, 315–17, 319–20, 341, 346, 352
1H6 (*King Henry VI, Part 1*) 38, 42, 53, 64,
   87–8, 91, 106, 133, 141, 147, 150, 224,
   230, 244, 264, 268, 292, 298, 304,
   307–8, 310, 317, 325, 340, 358, 362
2H4 (*King Henry IV, Part 2*) 15, 19, 22, 27,
   31, 39, 42, 46, 58, 65, 70, 76, 80–1,
   92–3, 98–9, 101, 105–6, 135, 137,
   145, 147, 151, 153–4, 158, 163,
   169–70, 174, 176, 179–80, 192, 194,
   201, 210, 214, 247, 250–1, 256, 259,
   266, 274, 276, 278–82, 292, 295, 299,
   301, 308, 315, 323, 328, 330, 334,
   336, 349, 352, 354, 356, 358, 361
2H6 (*King Henry VI, Part 2*) 12, 24, 29, 37,
   53, 64–5, 92, 106, 111, 123, 142,
   147–8, 157–8, 161, 168, 176, 178,
   189, 210, 221, 244, 281, 290, 307–8,
   312–13, 320, 324
3H6 (*King Henry VI, Part 3*) 13, 15, 26,
   38–9, 58, 71, 87, 92, 93, 133, 157,
   161, 176, 188, 205, 210, 222, 240,
   264, 278–9, 282, 297, 304, 310, 312,
   317, 330, 341, 362

abhorson (abortion) 11–12, 164
abortifacient 27–8, 85, 164, 187, 210, 279,
   296
abortive 11–13, 18, 164, 225, 248, 279, 296
   see also abhorson (abortion),
   deformed, hare-lip, legs forward, mole

ache 13–14 *see also* bone-ache,
   tooth-ache
   headache 13–14, 72, 119, 121, 183, 187,
   210, 271, 327, 347
Ackerman, D. 46
aconitum 15
acrophobia 105
Adams, T. 208, 231
Adelman, J. 41, 138, 306
ADO (*Much Ado About Nothing*) 12, 14, 16,
   53, 55, 57, 68–9, 73, 81, 97, 116,
   127, 130, 132, 158, 167–8, 178–9,
   184, 193, 212–13, 218, 242, 248,
   250–1, 253, 292, 294, 299, 304, 313,
   319, 333
adust, adustion 65, 83, 100, 135, 140, 163,
   201, 275, 358
   melancholy adust 52, 66, 216, 226, 270
Aesculapius 15, 51, 144
agony 15–16, 172
ague 16–17 *see also* fever, quotidian,
   tertian
alchemist, alchemy, alcumist 17–19, 51,
   103, 105, 118, 214, 245–6, 267,
   337–8 *see also* med'cine potable,
   Paracelsus, tincture
   spiritual alchemy 19
almshouse *see* hospital
alopecia 158
amenorrhea 36, 47, 357
anatomy, atomy
   as skeleton 19–20
   anatomical dissection 51, 145, 258,
   324, 326
Anderson, M. 114
Anderson, T. P. 87, 130
Andrews, J. 29

angelica 20–1, 263
  as remedy for plague 21, 55
ANT (Antony and Cleopatra) 22, 45, 58, 71,
    85, 98–9, 110, 113–14, 117, 123,
    134, 137, 153, 157, 158, 162, 180,
    189, 194, 209, 214, 227, 230, 236,
    241, 250, 252, 268, 277, 290, 292–3,
    306–7, 313, 318, 323, 330, 333, 337,
    343, 345, 350, 359–61
anthrax 174, 328
apoplexy 21, 55–6, 70, 92–3, 105–6,
    119–20, 122, 145, 172, 243, 251,
    308, 329–30 *see also* epilepsy, fit,
    swoon
apothecary 5, 20, 22–3, 32, 68, 78, 80,
    92, 108–9, 118, 253–4, 257, 278,
    280, 309
  Apoticaries Rules 22
  apothecary weights 108
  in *ROM* 228, 309
  relation to physician 254, 278
apple 23 *see also* eye
Appleby, A. B. 98
aqua vitae 23, 26, 86, 263, 287–8, 293, 295,
    342, 361
Arcaeus, F. 138
Arderne, J. 138
Ariès, P. 94
Arikha, N. 78
Aristotle 2, 47, 68, 117, 127, 146, 246,
    334
Armin, R. 192
Aronson, A. 130
artery 23–4 *see also* blood, heart, spirit,
    vein
Ascham, A. 50, 190, 273, 279, 361
ashy 24–5 *see also* blood, cheek
astrological medicine 55, 245, 267–9, 299,
    332 *see also* planet, Saturn, Taurus
atomy *see* anatomy
Austen, J. 167
Avicenna 40, 126, 172, 302, 341, 346
AWW (All's Well That Ends Well) 50, 67, 73,
    86, 88, 98–9, 104, 107–8, 123, 130,
    138, 145, 164, 196, 205, 210, 212,
    215, 224, 242, 245, 248, 254, 256,
    258, 260, 264–5, 268, 272, 276,
    278, 280, 292, 300, 305, 308–9,
    319, 323, 337

Helena as healer in 88, 99
  King's fistula in 99, 245
AYL (As You Like It) 29, 31, 33, 45, 49, 57,
    67, 68–70, 82, 85–6, 99, 111, 130–1,
    134, 140–1, 151, 154, 158, 168, 171,
    176, 179, 182, 192–3, 199, 201, 209,
    217–18, 238, 279, 305, 315–16, 318,
    330, 333, 362

Babb, L. 219
Bacon, R. 34, 114, 337
Baker, G. 104, 191, 287, 331
Baley, W. 34, 102, 130, 139, 356
Balizet, A. M. 41, 171
bald *see* hair
  baldness as symptom of pox 275, 326
Ball, P. 246, 343
Banckes, R. 361
Banister, J. 7, 15, 27, 54, 67, 163, 344
Banister, R. 130, 132
balm, balsam, balsamum 26–8, 40, 95,
    160, 228–9, 233, 244, 315
  gentle balm 27
Barclay, W. 106
Barker, F. 1
barley-broth 27–8, 95, 140, 244
Barroll, L. 266
Barrough, P. 13–14, 21, 54, 72, 81, 100,
    102, 119, 120, 121–2, 164, 207, 209,
    211, 213, 244, 256, 288, 336, 338,
    342, 357, 360
Bartolomeus Anglicus 141, 163, 166,
    200, 299 *see also* Batman, S.
Bassi, S. 46
Bate, J. 231
baths 28–9 *see also* tub-fast
Batman, S. 14, 49, 109, 132, 141, 163, 166,
    184, 186, 200, 299
Baumbach, S. 59, 252
Beaumont, F. 29
Becker, L. M. 63, 94
Bedlam 29–30, 86, 114, 140, 166, 198, 202
    see also hospital, insane, lunacy,
    madness
Bellamy, E. 171
belch
  as bodily function 30, 201, 240
  as name of character 20, 23, 30, 49,
    222, 260, 332, 348

Belling, C. 20, 41
belly 30–1
Bennett, J. W. 209
Bentley, J. S. 246
Bergeron, J. 139, 259
Berkeley, D.S. 41
Berry, P. 114
Best, G. 291
Bevington, D. 213
Bicks, C. 188, 198, 223, 286, 345, 360
Black Death, the *see* plague
bladder 31–2 *see also* imposthume
    animal bladders 32
blain 32, 185, 189 *see also* carbuncle,
        itch, kibe, plague
blind 32–5 *see also* eye, eye-string,
        high-gravel-blind, pearl, pin and
        web, sand-blind
    literal and figurative blindness 34
blood 35–41 *see also* artery, heart, liver,
        spirit, vein
    "blood and death" 39
    blood-letting 35–6
    heart-blood 40, 160
    life-blood 37
    menstrual blood 36–7, 41, 151–2, 172,
        225
blushing 24–5, 56–8, 280, 289, 292, 298
    see also cheek, race, sanguine
Bodin, J. 78, 170
bone-ache 41–2, 232, 275 *see also* pox
Bonelli, E. 154
Boorde, A. 98, 138, 145, 312, 319, 328
Boseley, S. 9
Bosman, A. 130
Bostocke, R. 118, 177, 215, 245, 246
Bovilsky, L. 41, 78, 292
bowels 42–3
    as organs 42–3
    voiding of *see* jakes
Boyle, R. 23
Brahe, T. 84
brain 43–6 *see also* fume
    as metaphor for ideas 45
    as comparable to womb 253, 286
Brasbridge, T. 21, 55, 269
brawn 46–7, 50, 311
breast 47–8 *see also* dug, pap, milk-pap,
        nipple

Aristotle on the location of 47
    debate between Hippocratic and
        Galenic texts on its function 47–8
    function and working of 48
    as sex-specific organ 47
Briggs, K. 269
Bright, T. 55, 66, 208, 213, 269, 316, 318
brimstone 48–9 *see also* sulphur
    in baths 29
    as cure for lice 196
    as hellfire 49
Brody, S.N. 190
Brotherston, R. P. 316
Browne, T. 261, 291
Brunschwig, H. 314
Bruun, E. 296
bubukle 49, 54, 261 *see also* carbuncle
Bullein, W. 15, 22, 27, 28, 50, 72, 81, 100,
        114, 118, 137, 163, 190, 200, 213,
        244, 253, 257, 261, 272, 273, 283,
        309, 310, 324, 334, 335, 337
burdock 49, 143
    confused with dock 106
burnet 49–50, 185
Burnett, M.T. 227
Burns, E. 227
Burton, R. 55, 66, 78, 86, 208, 218–19,
        315, 318
Butler, J. 1
    Gender Trouble 1
buttock 49–50
    brawn buttock 50
    pin-buttock 50
    quat 284
    quatch-buttock 50

cacophagy 36, 83, 229, 255
caduceus 51
Caesarian section 345 *see* untimely
        ripp'd
Caius (character in Shakespeare) 15, 51,
        145, 165, 235, 248, 253, 254, 258,
        274, 309
Caius, J. (historical physician) 6, 51, 146,
        165, 250, 258, 327, 328
Campbell, L. B. 1, 170
cancer (carcinoma) *see* canker
canker 51–4
    carcinoma 52, 54

carbuncle 32, 49, 54–5, 150, 174, 265
  see also bubukle
Cardolano, G. 269
carduus benedictus 55
Carey, M. 248
Carroll, W. 30
Cartwright, T. 50, 85, 337
cataplasm 55 *see also* plaster, poultice
cataract 34, 127, 129, 356 *see also* pearl
  operation for cataract 130
catarrhs 55–6, 293
Cellier, E. 222
Cerimon 5, 15, 22, 30, 192, 213, 229, 233,
  244–5, 255, 258, 353, 357
Chakravarti, P. 209
Chamberlain, S. 345
Chapman, A. 269
Chapman, A. A. 209
Chapman, G. 34
  The Blinde Beggar of Alexandria 34
Charron, P. 233, 361
cheek 56–9 *see also* ashy, complexion,
    humor, perturbation, tawny
  blushing cheeks 56
  lank and wrinkled cheeks 58
  pale and dark cheeks 57
chilblains *see* blain, kibe
childbed 59–64 *see also* midwife
  beginning of fetal life
      ("quickening") 284, 286
  breech presentation of fetus
      see legs forward
  Caesarian birth 345
  "churching" after childbed 223
  Shakespeare's birth scenes 63
  signs of imminent delivery 59
  strength of limit 61
childbirth *see* childbed
childhood illnesses
  colic 72, 109
  lice 190, 195–6
  measles 83, 142, 210–11, 286, 336
choler, choleric 3–4, 6, 13, 16, 30–2, 35–9,
    40, 56, 64–7, 72, **74**, 75, 80, 83,
    91–2, 97, 101, 110, 119, 135, 140–1,
    146–8, 151, 155–6, 158–9, 163–4,
    167–8, 170, 174–6, 183, 191–3, 203,
    205–7, 210, 215, 223, 240–1, 251–3,
    254–7, 259, 261, 267, 272, 275,

    278–80, 282, 289, 293, 295–6, 299,
    306–7, 316–17, 332, 335, 338, 341,
    347, 353, 358 *see also* complexion,
    gall, humor
Christakis, N. 82, 84
cicatrice 67–8 *see also* skin
civet 22, 68, 140 *see also* perfume
clapperclaw 68 *see also* leprosy
Clark, G. 73, 118, 146, 259, 326
Clarke, J. 300
Clark, S. 34, 130
cleft palate 159 *see also* hare-lip
  cleft lip 159
close-stool *see* jakes
cloves 68
  as cure for tooth-ache 68
  in pomander 68, 272, 328
Clowes, W. 124, 277, 287, 335, 326, 343
clyster 16, 21, 28, 52, 54, 68, 72, 81, 87,
    105, 139, 151–2, 209, 271, 281, 297,
    300, 321, 335, 347, 358
clyster-pipes 68–9
cod, cods, codpiece 69
Cogan, T. 342
cold 69–72
  as quality of humor 70
  as rhinovirus 70, 72
  as sign of temperance or chastity 71
colic 72, 109 *see also* guts-griping
Colie, R. 34
college 7, 73 *see also* physician, surgeon
  call for midwives' college 222
  foundation of Royal College of
      Physicians 2, 18, 22, 73, 107, 118,
      138, 146, 228, 254, 326
coloquintida 73
complexion 73–8 *see also* humor, race
  as humoral temperament **74–5**
  as skin color 77
compound 78–80
  apothecaries' monopoly on
      compounding 254
  midwives' powders 220
consumption 26, 53, 80–1, 88, 99, 104,
    114, 139, 164, 195, 273, 338
  see also hectic, tisick
contagion 81–4 *see also* infection
  miasma theory 83, 176, 352
Copland, W. 143

copper nose 84, 234
  as flushed from drinking 234
  as prosthesis 84
COR (*Coriolanus*) 20, 21, 27–8, 31,
        42, 46–8, 50, 54, 57, 65, 67, 72,
        82, 99, 113, 119, 123, 145, 178,
        180, 201, 205, 211, 223, 231, 235–6,
        244, 250, 252, 256–7, 264, 268,
        270, 278, 281, 294, 297, 299,
        310, 313, 317, 323, 330, 333,
        334, 338, 361
corns 84–5, 356 *see also* warts
Cotta, J. 107, 118
cough, coughing, Hem! 85 *see also*
        consumption, tisick
cowslip 48, 58, 85–6, 185
Cox, C. I. 253
cramp 21, 85–6, 110, 155, 311
Crane, M. T. 46, 253, 260, 278, 286
crazed, crazy 86–7 *see also* Bedlam,
        distracted, ecstasy, frenzy, lunacy,
        madness
Cregan, K. 20
Cressy, D. 63, 94
Croll, O. 229
crookback 87 *see also* legs forward,
        monster
Crooke, H. 7, 20, 29, 32, 46, 47, 48, 63,
        68, 69, 131, 132, 146, 171, 193, 226,
        234, 258, 296, 302, 306, 339, 341,
        345, 355, 357
  Microcosmographia 20, 63, 131, 146,
        306, 357
Crystal, D. 117
Culpeper, N. 49, 114, 154, 163, 164, 253,
        308
cupping 21, 36, 92, 127, 165, 175, 187,
        243, 271, 283, 326–7, 341, 357 *see
        also* surgeon's box
cure 87–9
  weapon-salve 88
CYM (*Cymbeline*) 22–3, 30, 38, 40, 47–8,
        54, 57, 71, 78, 86, 98, 100, 104, 106,
        108–9, 123, 129, 132–3, 136, 141–2,
        147, 151, 174, 179, 193, 197, 201,
        206, 213–14, 226, 233, 238, 248,
        250–1, 258–9, 277, 298–9, 305, 307,
        320, 335, 343–5, 359
cyme 89–90, 295, 349

Daalder, J. 209
Dabydeen, D. 292
Daigle, E. N. 46
D'Amico, J. 292
Dannenfeldt, K. 229
darnel 91, 185
Daston, L. 13, 227
Davis, P. 46
Dawson, L. 154
deaf 91–2 *see also* ear, earwax
death 92–5
  embalming 26, 228–9
  facies Hippocratica (Hippocratic
        face) 234
Debus, A. 5, 19, 245–6, 260
de Chauliac, G. (Guy de Chauliac) 137
decoct 95 *see also* barley-broth
deform, deformed, deformity 95–7
        see also hare-lip, mole, monster,
        prodigy, stigmatical
degree 117
  of cold, heat, moisture, or aridity in
        plants 73, 85, 90, 272
Dekker, T. 29, 180, 253, 266
Deleuze, G. 242
depression 217 *see also* melancholy
diabetes ("the pissing evil") 347
diet 97–9 *see also* complexion, excrement,
        humor, purge, stomach, surfeit
  Boorde's *Dyetary* 319
  Regimen Sanitatem Salernii ("The
        Salernian regimen") 30, 98, 170
DiGangi, M. 11–12, 279
Digges, L. 332
Dimmock, M. 122
disability
  mental 202 *see also* natural
  physical *see* blind, crookback, deaf,
        tongue-tied
disease 99–100
Diseases of Children 196
distemper, distemperature, distempered,
        mistempered 100–2
distil, distilled, distillation 103–5
        see also alchemy, limbeck
distraction 105–6 *see also* apoplexy, dizzy,
        epilepsy, giddy, lunacy, madness
diuretic 143, 187, 281
dizzy 105–6, 108, 318

Dobranski, S. 12
Dobson, J. 20, 326
Dobson, M. J. 17, 95
dock 106–7 *see also* burdock, burr
Doctor She 4, 107–8, 138, 145
Dodoens, R. 15, 55, 73, 86, 90, 135, 139,
    171, 187, 190, 195, 197, 210, 232,
    270, 296, 310, 316, 361
Doebler, B. A. 94
Dollimore, J. 95
Doyle, C. 159
Drake-Brockman, J. 226
dram 5, 108, 247, 274, 278, 300, 320
Draper, J. W. 67, 170
Drey, R. 23
dropsies, dropsy 86, 108–9, 142, 210, 347
Drouet, P. 55, 83
drug, drugs 109–10 *see also* compound,
    death, medicine, physic
dry, dryness 110 *see also* heat, humor, cold,
    complexion, moisture
Du Chesne, J. 278, 287
Du Laurens, A. 125, 219
Dugan, H. E. 234, 250
dug 110–11 *see also* breast, nurse, pap
Dyer, A. 328
dysentery *see also* flux 72, 139
    opium poppy as cure for symptoms
        of 273

ear 112–14
earwax 114
Eccles, A. 222
ecstasy 114–17 *see also* Bedlam, crazed,
    distracted, frenzy, lunacy, madness
eczema 299
Elam, K. 123, 242, 345
element *see also* complexion
    classical elements, four 35, 117–8
    fifth element 18, 60, 117
    Paracelsian elements 117, 350 *see also*
        salt, sulphur (brimstone), mercury
        (quicksilver)
Elizabeth I of England 2
Elyot, T. 23, 66, 68, 78, 98, 111, 125, 170,
    196, 253, 279, 280, 298, 354
    The Castel of Helthe (1539) 196
    The Castel of Helthe (1595) 23, 295
    Dictionary 125

emetic 16, 81, 135, 281, 282, 288, 321,
    347, 353–4
emmenagogue 11, 52, 55, 152, 164, 187,
    210, 296
empirics 118–19 *see also* alchemist,
    apothecary, herb-woman,
    mountebank, midwife, Paracelsus,
    physician, surgeon
    as trusted figure 127
    John Hall as 247
empiricutic 119 *see also* empiric
epilepsy, epileptic 119–22
    as the retention of phlegm in the
        brain 121
erection 122
ERR (*The Comedy of Errors*) 20, 23, 55, 58,
    65, 70, 82, 92, 96, 98, 110, 115, 125,
    134, 136, 141, 158, 174, 180, 203,
    209, 218, 226, 230, 238, 248, 280,
    295, 313, 318, 331, 351, 356
eryngo, eringoes 122
erysipelas 174
eunuch 122–3, 148, 151, 344–5
Evenden, D. 222
evil, the 3, 7, 27, 85, 89, 91, 123–5, 174
excrement 125–6 *see also* fume, hair, vapor
eye, eyne 126–30 *see also* apple, blind,
    eye-strings
    Aristotle's theory of vision 127
    eye-spirit 23, 33, 96, 105, 113, 126–9,
        131, 251, 284, 314
eyebrow 130–1
eyelid 131–2
eye-string 132 *see also* eye, heart-string,
    sinew

Fadiman, A. 8
    The Spirit Catches You 8
faint 133–5 *see also* swoon
falling sickness *see* epilepsy
femiter *see* fumiter
fennel 72, 85, 134–5, 211, 288, 356
Ferguson, L. 20–1
Fernie, E. 24, 58
fever 135–7 *see also* ague, frenzy,
    quotidian, tertian
    phlebotomy to reduce elevated
        temperature 36
Ficino, M. 126

Fildes, V. A. 224
Fine, O. 332
Fineman, J. 114, 130
Fisher, W. 69, 159
Fissell, M. 2, 12–13, 107, 118
fistula 137–9
Fitzpatrick, J. 67, 99, 105, 122, 135, 224,
    273, 319
flax 139 *see also* linen
  with whites of eggs, as remedy for
    eyes 6
Fleissner, R. F. 93, 154, 234
Fletcher, J. 29, 346, 350
Floyd-Wilson, M. 3, 67, 78, 134, 170, 220,
    241, 252–3, 292, 352
Fludd, R. 298
flux 139–40
  belly 139
  menstrual 37, 163, 357
Fogan, L. 316
Folkerth, W. 114
folly *see* madness, natural
Ford, J. 29
Forman, S. 18, 269
Foster, W. 298
Foucault, M. 1, 208
  Discipline and Punish 1
Fowler, J. H. 82, 84
Fox, J. 68
frantic *see* frenzy
Frascatoro, G. 277
Freeman, D. 46, 130
frenzy 140–1 *see also* Bedlam, crazed,
    lunacy, madness
Fryer, P. 291
fume 142
  as therapy for syphilis 343
  as vapor or excrement 89, 156
fumiter, fumitory, fumitor 142–3
Furman, Y. 316
Furnivall, F. 98
Fusch, D. 125

Gale, T. 326
Galen 2, 4–5, 47, 78, 108, 119, 120, 126,
    144–6, 163, 165, 167, 195, 200, 209,
    246, 253, 257, 259, 271, 286, 326
  see also complexion, humor
Galen's wax 84, 175, 297, 327

gall 3, 64, 66, **74**, 146–8, 167, 224
  see also choler
gangrened 148
Garber, M. 326
Garcia-Ballester, L. 144, 146
Gardiner, E. 255, 310
Garzoni, T. 208, 231
geld, gelded 148–9 *see also* eunuch,
  glib, splay, unseminar'd
Gerard, J. 27, 28, 73, 86, 90, 143, 164, 187,
    209, 210, 270, 279, 296, 310, 316,
    361, 363
Gesner, K. 14, 17, 19, 23, 68, 86, 103,
    104, 142, 191, 247, 287, 331,
    340, 362
Gibson, M. 269
Ginsberg, M. 226
Gittings, C. 94
glib 149 *see also* geld
Goeurot, J. 72, 83, 86, 102, 140, 180, 196,
    211, 272
goiter 245
gonorrhea 154, 275 *see also* pox
Goose of Winchester 149
Gordon-Grube, K. 41
gore 149–50 *see also* blood
gout 85, 151, 158, 192, 244, 276, 298, 347
Grafton, A. 19, 269
gravel i' th'back 151–2, 347
gravel-blind, high-gravel-blind
    see sand-blind
Gray, R. 19
Greenberg, S. 266
Greene, R. 41
green-sickness 1, 76, 152–4, 172, 202, 208,
    217 *see also* love-sick
Grigsby, B. L. 190, 253, 266, 277
groin 154
Guattari, F. 242
Guibert, P. 27, 229
Guillemeau, J. 12, 55, 130, 160, 166,
    171, 175, 187, 222, 226, 235,
    238, 247, 301, 316, 327, 341,
    342, 345, 360, 362
gum, gums 154
gut 154–5
guts-griping 72, 155, 183
Gyer, N. 6, 21, 40–1, 176, 195
  English Phlebotomy 6

Habib, I. 41
Hadhazy, A. 9
hair 156–9
  baldness 156, 158, 275, 326
  as secondary sexual characteristic 159
Hakewell, G. 34
  Vanity of the Eie 34
Hale, D. 31
Halio, J. 247
Hall, E. 215
Hall, J. (Shakespeare's son-in-law) 1, 5,
    89, 139, 247, 259, 260, 274, 275,
    328, 354
Hall, J(onathan) 186
Hall, K. F. 292
HAM (*Hamlet*) 13, 20–1, 24, 33, 34, 42,
    45–6, 55, 67, 71, 82–3, 95, 97–9,
    104, 106, 110, 112, 114–15, 125,
    127, 129–30, 146, 147, 150, 154,
    161–4, 178–9, 192, 195, 203, 206,
    208–9, 217, 227, 238, 242, 250–2,
    256, 261, 264, 268, 272, 274, 277,
    280, 294, 296, 300, 307–9, 311–12,
    337, 344, 356, 359, 361
Hardy, B. 238
hare-brain'd 158–9 *see also* brain
hare-lip 12, 95, 159–60, 225 *see also*
    deformed, mole, monster
Harington, J. 182–3
Harkness, A. 59
Harkness, D. E. 2, 107, 118, 192, 223
Harman, T. 29
Harris, J. G. 4–5, 54, 83, 149, 159, 180,
    234, 277, 299, 309
Harsnett, S. 172, 208
Hart, F. E. 350
Hart, J. 353
Harvey, E. D. 314
Harvey, G. 318
Harward, S. 40
Haslem, L. S. 341
Healy, M. 4–5, 19, 83, 180, 253, 266, 277,
    309
heart 160–2 *see also* blood, brain, eye,
    liver, lung, heart-string
heart-string 132, 160, 162, 311, 321
heat 4, 13, 16, 26, 35, 45, 52, 64, 70, 82–4,
    103, 105, 110, 119, 121, 134–5, 139,
    152, 162–3

as cause of "adustion" 201, 216, 226,
    270, 275
as cause of jaundice 183
as cause of plague 176
as cause of pox 275
as characteristic of men 153
as characteristic of women 37
as quality of element 77, 117
hebenon *see* hebona
hebona 163, 286, 352
hectic 163–4 *see also* fever
Heffernan, C. 219
hemlock 164
henbane 70, 163, 287
Hendricks, M. 290, 292
Henning, S. 314
H5 (*King Henry V*) 27–8, 33, 39, 42, 49–50,
    58, 64, 65, 71, 80, 86, 91, 93, 95, 98,
    104, 106–7, 117, 137, 147, 150, 155,
    157, 161–2, 166, 169, 174, 187, 189,
    196, 205, 219, 230, 234, 236, 241–2,
    276, 282, 294–5, 301–2, 308, 310,
    319, 325, 333, 336, 343, 352, 360
H8 (*King Henry VIII, or All is True*) 14,
    16–17, 32, 38, 41, 57, 63, 65, 71, 89,
    130, 134, 147, 157, 159, 161–2, 180,
    238, 252, 259, 278, 281, 304, 307–8,
    316
herb-grace, herb of grace 164, 296 *see also*
    marjoram and rue
herb-woman 164 *see also* empiric
herpes 336 *see also* pox, sapego
Herring, F. 118
Hester, J. 245, 287, 309
Hibbard, G. R. 181
Hibocrates 165
high-gravel-blind *see* sand-blind
Hill, T. 87, 159, 192, 226, 340–1
Hillman, D. 1–2, 43, 242, 314
Hindson, B. 41
Hippocrates 2, 34, 36, 47, 64, 93–4, 118,
    120, 130, 135, 139, 146, 152, 163,
    165, 172, 222, 229, 255, 257, 271,
    306, 356, 358, 362
  mistakenly pronounced as
    Hibocrates 165
  as model for good physician 165
Hobgood, A. P. 170
Hockey, D. C. 361

Hoeniger, F. D. 3–4, 51, 67, 78, 100,
    120–1, 124, 138, 172, 190, 213,
    242, 246, 259–61, 269, 309, 318,
    326, 362
  *Medicine and Shakespeare in the English
    Renaissance* 3
Holinshed, R. 56, 328
Holland, P. 151
Holstun, J. 31
Horan, J. 183
hor-dock *see* burdock
horse-leech *see also* leech 165–6
hospital, 'spital, 'spital-house 166–7
    see also Bedlam, lazar
Howard, S. 63, 248
Howe, J. 167
Huloet, R. 111, 298
humor 167–70 *see also* blood, complexion,
    gall, liver, spleen
  choleric 64–7 *see also* choler *under*
    individual entries
  melancholic 21, 56, 64, 66, 72, **74**, 77,
    83, 156, 182, 201, 215–19, 251, 267,
    280, 316–17, 332
  phlegmatic 3, 4, 43, 56, 66–7, 72, 74,
    80, 83–4, 98, 103, 123–4, 156, 167,
    191, 193, 224, 253–4, 267, 280,
    294, 347
  sanguine 3, 35, 37, 49, 56, 67, **74**, 76–7,
    147, 156, 169, 224, 254, 280, 282,
    289, 298, 306, 338, 339, 347
Hunt, M. 226, 246
Hunter, G. K. 291
Hunter, L. 2, 4, 54, 180
Hunter, P. R. 328
Hutten, U. von 277
Hutton, S. 2
hymen, maidenhead, virgin-knot 170–1
hyssop 171
hysterica passio 37, 92, 142, 172–3, 202,
    208, 215, 227, 241, 249, 357–8 *see
    also* madness, womb

illness 174
impetigo 336
imposthume 174–5 *see also* ulcer
incision 35, 84, 131, 175–6, 345 *see also*
    blood
indigested 176 *see also* deformed

infect, infected, infects, infectious,
    infection 176–80 *see also* contagion,
    Paracelsus, plague, pox
  Paracelsian theories of disease 177
inflammation 180–1
insane 181 *see also* Bedlam, crazed, ecstasy,
    frenzy, lunacy, madness
insanie 181
Instone, S. 15
Iyengar, S. 25, 78, 138, 154, 227, 292

Jackson, K. 29, 209
jakes, close-stool, stool 182–3
Jankowski, T. 41, 171
Jarcho, S. 288, 336
jaundice, jaundies 155, 183–4, 215, 279,
    295
JC (*Julius Caesar*) 17, 38, 42, 44, 58, 61, 65,
    82–4, 92, 117, 120, 134, 137, 157,
    168, 219, 257, 306–8, 310, 317, 326,
    337, 340, 362
JN (*King John*) 12, 14, 17–18, 20, 33, 38–9,
    42, 44, 53, 88–9, 100, 102, 113, 129,
    141, 157–8, 170, 178, 204, 218, 225,
    265, 270–1, 280, 294, 304, 307, 311,
    313–14, 330, 355, 359
Johnson, S. 298
Johnson, T. 227
Johnston, I. 78
Jones, E. 209
Jones, V. A. 259
Jonson, B. 132, 167, 170, 283, 350
Jordan, W. 291
Jorden, E. 121, 172–3, 203, 207
Jung, C. G. 19

Kahn, C. 238, 362
Kaiser, P. 231
Kallendorf, H. 30, 209
Kassell, L. 18, 119, 269
kecksies 185
Keller, E. 7, 63, 146
Kellwaye, S. 50, 83, 180, 253, 266
Kennedy, G. 252
Kerwin, W. 3, 23, 107, 108, 248, 257, 260,
    326, 338
kibe 32, 185 *see also* blain
kidney 185–6
  stones 151–2, 347

King, H. 2, 7, 64, 163, 165, 220, 222, 302, 306
Kirschbaum, L. 150
Knapp, J. 242
Knoepflmacher, U. C. 170

Landi, O. 121
Lane, J. 5, 89, 249, 259, 354
Lanfranco (of Milan) 163, 184, 288, 298, 344, 360
Lange, J. 154
Langham, W. 164
Langton, C. 28, 354
La Primaudaye, P. de 50
Laqueur, T. 1–2, 146, 163, 222, 302, 306
Laroche, R. 164
Laroque, F. 186
Lavater, L. 315
lavender 187, 329
lazar *see* leprosy
LC (*A Lover's Complaint*) 224
Lecercle, A. 138
leech 165, 187, 283
legs forward 188
Lehnhof, K. 228
Lemnius, L. 66, 77–8, 122, 125, 134, 143, 155, 170, 184, 251, 315
Leong, E. 2, 107
leprosy, lazar 5, 68, 82, 91, 107, 142, 156, 166, 171, 178, 187, 188–90, 210–11, 215, 275, 286, 337
lethargy, lethargies 21, 91, 119, 140, 190, 197, 202, 215–16, 240, 243 *see also* apoplexy
lettuce 4, 28, 64, 97, 135, 183, 190, 335, 347
Levin, C. 360
Levin, R. 148, 164
lice *see* louse
lily-liver'd 190–1 *see also* pigeon-liver'd
limbeck 45, 103, 142, 191–2, 274, 293, 315 *see also* distil
lime-kills i'th' palm *see* lime-kilns i'th' palm
lime-kilns i'th' palm 192
Linacre, T. 146, 257
Linche, R. 198
linen 139, 192 *see also* flax
  as material for bandages 192
  as material for probes ("tent") 192

as midwifery supply 192
lisp, lisping 192–3 *see also* tongue-tied, stammer
Little, A. B. 292
liver 30, 35, 38–9, 42–9, 52–64, 70–1, **74**, 77, 94, 108–9, 126, 142, 146, 153–5, 161, 185, 193–4 *see also* lily-liver'd, liver-vein
  hot liver and spotted liver 194
  lily-liver'd 20, 190–1
  milk-liver'd 224
  pigeon-liver'd 224
liver-vein 194–5
LLL (*Love's Labour's Lost*) 12, 16, 23–4, 31, 33, 48, 57, 68, 76, 85, 88, 96, 114, 125, 129, 131, 146, 148, 158, 161, 166, 168, 176, 181–2, 192, 195–6, 201, 217–18, 224, 244, 260, 264, 270, 297, 315, 317, 330, 333, 338–9, 342, 351, 359
Lloyd, G. 288
Lobanov-Rostovsky 130
Lodge, T. 180, 253, 266, 272
Loe, W. 261
long purples, dead men's fingers 195
Loomba, A. 292
Loughlin, M. 171
louse, lousy, lice, nit 195–6, 232
love-in-idleness 23, 128, 131, 197, 274, 315, 322, 362
love-sick 197 *see also* green-sick, melancholy
Lowe, P. 24, 54, 67–8, 94, 122, 145, 165, 175, 185, 271, 315, 327
LR (*King Lear*) 17, 20, 34, 46, 53, 68–71, 81, 84, 87, 91, 93, 99, 105, 110, 121, 129, 139, 160, 172, 178, 185, 190, 200, 203, 206, 208–10, 212, 224, 230–1, 235, 241, 247, 259–60, 265, 268–9, 277, 292, 301, 308–9, 314, 316, 323, 325, 356
LUC (*The Rape of Lucrece*) 159, 297, 304
Lucina 197–8, 221
Lucking, D. 97
lunacy, lunatic 198–200 *see also* Bedlam, crazed, madness
lungs 200–1
Lupton, D. 29, 160
lupus 52–3

Lux, M. 213, 273
lymph nodes 154
Lyons, B. G. 219

MAC (*Macbeth*) 28, 39, 45, 87, 89, 99–100,
   121, 124, 130, 134, 147–8, 150, 154,
   163, 174, 181, 191, 194, 198, 209,
   212, 223, 232, 234, 241, 250–1, 256,
   260, 268, 293, 302, 306, 308, 312,
   314–16, 325, 330, 345, 349, 363
MacDonald, J. G. 292
MacDonald, M. 29, 208
Maclean, I. 2, 146
Madeleine, R. 184
madness 202–9 *see also* Bedlam, crazed,
   ecstasy, frenzy, *hysterica passio*,
   insane, love-sick, lunacy,
   melancholy, natural
magical healing
   through astrology 101, 117–18, 146,
      215, 266–9, 328
   in *AWW* 107, 215
   in *ERR* 203, 228
   through mummy 228
   through natural magic 245
   in *PER* 180, 245, 254
   for plague 118
   through sleep 131
   through the weapon-salve 88
malady of France 166 *see also* pox
malady *see* disease
Malapropisms, medical 16, 99, 135, 163,
   165, 198, 218, 280, 288, 293–5,
   334, 336
mandragora, mandrake 209–10, 212,
   273, 287
mare *see* sleep
marjoram 72, 164, 187, 209–10
Marland, H. 222
Marlowe, C. 350
Marowitz, C. 139
marrow 46, 80, 99, 210, 228, 243, 355
Marshall, B. 8–9, 252, 257, 362
Mary of Guise 2
Masten, J. 138
matter
   as pus 50, 179, 270
   as raw material of conception 30, 77,
      95, 171, 225, 285, 303, 359, 367

Mattern, S. 146
Matthews, P. M. 46
Maus, K. 1, 43, 162, 319
Mazzio, C. 1–2, 130, 234, 242, 339
McBride, C. 29
McEachern, C. 242
McGeoch, A. H. 192
McKeithen, A. 266
McLaren, A. 12
McQuain, J. 46
McSweegan, E. 328
measles 83, 142, 201, 210–11, 286,
   336
med'cine potable 17, 211, 214–15
   see also alchemy
medicinable 213–14
medicine, medicinal 211–13 *see also*
   med'cine potable, physic, tincture
Mediolano, J. de (Johannes de
   Mediolano)
   Regimen Sanitatis 109, 122, 195, 301
megrim *see* ache
melancholy 215–19 *see also* complexion,
   love-sickness, madness, spleen
   as affectation 217
   as cause of canker 52
   as cause of madness 216
   as love-melancholy 115–16, 122, 197,
      207, 216–17, 219
menstruation 12, 37, 40–1, 47, 52, 67,
   163–4, 232, 357 *see also* blood
   male 37
   medicines and therapies to induce
      (emmenagogues) 164, 232, 12
   in women 37, 163, 357
mercury *see* quicksilver
   in cure for syphilis *see* tub-fast
mettle 219–20
Middleton, T. 29, 149, 350
midwife 220–3 *see also* childbed
   male midwives 222
   proposed college for midwives 222
migraine 13–14 *see* ache
milk-liver'd *see* lily-liver'd, pigeon-liver'd
milk-pap *see* pap
milk 223–4 *see also* breast, dug, nurse,
   pap, sex
   cows' milk 223–4
   breast-milk as remedy 80, 127, 338

MM (*Measure for Measure*) 11, 12, 14, 42,
    46, 49, 66, 71, 77, 89, 98, 114, 137,
    149, 151, 180, 212, 236, 244, 253,
    276, 278–9, 291, 295–6, 298, 300–1,
    311–2, 317, 322, 328–9, 343, 360
MND (*Midsummer Night's Dream*) 23, 33,
    49, 58, 85–7, 99, 113, 123, 128,
    130–1, 134, 141, 149, 158, 160,
    197–8, 203, 224–5, 230, 232, 244,
    274, 281, 295, 305, 307, 312,
    315, 317, 322, 326, 330, 333,
    340, 360, 362
moist, moisture 3, 13, 26, 35–6, 43, 45–6,
    48, 54, 67, 69, 70, 77, 80–2, 86, 91,
    97, 108–10, 117–8, 135, 151, 163,
    197, 201, 224
molar pregnancy 225–6, 358
mole 225–6 *see also* hare-lip, monster
Monardes, N. 213
monster 226–7 *see also* prodigy
Moore, P. 50, 118
Moran, B. 105
More, T. 29, 87, 231
Morgan, S. 167
Moss, S. 4, 41, 73, 121–2, 229, 247, 273
mother *see hysterica passio*, womb
Moulton, T. 269, 309
mountebank 227–8 *see also* empiric
Muir, K. 209
mummy 228–9
Murphy-Lawless, J. 63
Murray, W. 246
MV (*The Merchant of Venice*) 17, 33, 37, 76,
    99, 108, 125, 157–8, 170, 176–7,
    180, 184, 194, 201, 217, 224, 252,
    294, 298, 300, 322–3, 325, 348

nail 230
    used to "scratch" a witch 36
Nashe, T. 283
natural 231 *see also* madness
navel 231
    midwife's job to cut the navel-
        string 220, 231
Neely, C. T. 29–30, 41, 154, 195, 202, 209,
    219, 273
neeze 232
Neopolitan bone-ache *see* bone-ache, pox,
    sciatica

nettle 190, 232
Newman, L. 12, 130, 164, 296
Newman, W. R. 19, 269
Newton, T. 84
night-mare *see* sleep
nipple 232–3 *see also* dug, milk-pap,
        pap, breast
nit *see* louse
Noble, L. 41, 84, 122, 229, 247
nose, nostril 233–4 *see also* fume, perfume
Nose-herb *see* pomander
nostril *see* nose
Nunn, H. M. 20, 34
nurse, nursery, nursing 234–9 *see also* milk
    sick-nurse 220, 234–5, 239
    wet-nurse 72, 211, 223–4, 234–5,
        236–8, 275
    dry-nurse 234, 237
Nutton, V. 7, 146

Oberndorf, J. 228
O'Connell, M. 130
O'Donoghue, E. 29
o'ercharged, o'erfraught 240–1
oophorectomy 148–9
orchiectomy 148
organ 241–2 *see also hysterica passio*
Orgel, S. 123, 242, 247
Orme, N. 167
Osler, W. 218–19
OTH (*Othello*) 14, 30, 46, 49, 65, 68–9, 71,
    77, 85, 89, 98, 108, 114–15, 117,
    120–1, 130, 134, 147, 154, 158, 190,
    210, 212–13, 227, 229, 234, 245,
    250, 252, 259, 273, 277–8, 283, 292,
    294, 317, 319, 331, 341, 351, 353
Overton, D. A. 87
Ovid 197
    Metamorphoses 197

Pagel, W. 180, 246, 287
palmar psoriasis 192
palsy 243–4
pap, milk-pap 244 *see also* breast
Paracelsus 4–6, 108, 117, 151, 177, 228,
    245–7, 259, 287, 343 *see also*
        alchemy, contagion, distil, element,
        empiric, infection
    belief in natural magic 245

three elements of 18, 342
works of 245–6
Paré, A. 68, 97, 152, 154, 160, 208, 226, 227, 279, 287, 288, 302
Parker, P. 41, 219, 292
Park, K. 13, 227, 302, 306, 345, 360
parmaceti 247
parti-ey'd 247
Paster, G. K. 1–3, 67, 134, 170, 183, 219, 238, 241–2, 252, 273, 279, 283, 302, 306, 309, 350
patient 247–9
Patrick, A. 328
Pearce, J. M. S. 164
pearl 126, 249, 356 *see also* web and pin, eye
Peat, D. 30
Pechey, J. 49, 91
pediculosis 195–6
Pelling, M. 2, 107, 118, 146, 222, 239, 248, 253, 259, 326
PER (*Pericles*) 22–3, 30, 60, 66, 92, 99, 148, 153, 164, 171, 180, 192, 197, 201, 213, 218, 221, 224, 229, 233, 235, 237, 240, 245, 248, 254–5, 258, 260, 274, 278, 282, 290, 326, 353, 358
perfume 249–50 *see also* fume
perniosis (chilblains) 185 *see* blain, kibe
perturbation 4, 21, 24, 35, 41, 56, 82, 100, 135, 145, 160–2, 176, 179, 194, 200, 216, 250–2, 271, 280, 314–5, 328–9
Pesta, J. D. 20
pestilence 20, 99, 178, 189, 211, 252–3, 266, 307, 309, 351 *see also* plague
Peterson, K. 4, 41, 172, 360
Pettigrew, T. 3, 23, 51, 108, 213, 257, 260, 326
Phillippy, P. 95
Phillis, R. 41
phlebotomy 36–7, 40, 52, 82, 135, 176, 183, 244, 257, 271, 281–2, 324, 347, 353
phlegmatic 253–4 *see also* complexion
physic 254–7
physical 257
physician 257–60 *see also* college, surgeon
pia mater 260
pica 152

pigeon-liver'd 261 *see also* lily-liver'd, milk-liver'd, white-liver'd
pills 261 *see also* drug, medicine, physic, potion
pin and web *see* web and pin
piss 349 *see* urine
pissing evil 347
plague 261–6 *see also* bubukle, contagion, infection, pestilence
planet, star 55, 245, 266–9, 299, 332
as cause of plague 266
plantain 269–70, 288, 296, 357
plaster 270–1 *see also* cataplasm, poultice
Platt, H. 105
Plato 32, 126
pleurisy *see* plurisy
Pliny 32, 163, 355
plurisy 271–2
bloodletting as cure for 271
pneumonia 201
Pollard, T. 114, 257
pomander, nose-herbs 272 *see also* cloves, perfume
Poole, A. 83
poppy 139–40, 209, 212, 272–3, 287, 293, 331
Porter, R. 248
potato 122, 273
pothecary *see* apothecary
potion 273–4
poultice 274–5 *see also* cataplasm, plaster
powdering-tub *see* salt, tub-fast
pox 5, 13, 36, 41, 76, 80, 83–4, 87, 110, 123, 142, 147, 149, 151, 153, 156, 158, 166, 174, 176–7, 179, 210–11, 266, 275–7, 286–7, 298–9, 306–7, 326, 328, 342–3 *see also* infection, plague, bone-ache, nose
pregnant 277–8 *see also* brain, womb
prescription 278–9 *see also* apothecary
Principe, L. M. 19
prodigy 279 *see also* monster
prunes, stewed 11–2, 72, 279 *see also* Abhorson, abortive
P's ("pees") 349 *see* urine
puking 279 *see also* vomit
pulse 279–80 *see also* heart
pulsidge 280

purge 281–3 *see also* blood, clyster-pipe, humor, puke, sweat, vomit
  through diet 175
  through phlebotomy 353
  "by siege" 353–4

qualm 284 *see also* stomach-qualmed
Qualtiere, L. F. 83, 180, 276
quick, quickens, quickening 284–6
  see also pregnant
Quickly, Mistress
  Housekeeper of Dr. Caius 19, 93, 122, 154, 161, 166, 234–5, 250, 253, 276, 280, 288, 295, 314, 334, 336, 338
  medical malapropisms 253, 280, 288, 334, 336
  outlining signs of imminent death 93
quicksilver *see also* tub-fast 88, 163, 195–6, 245, 276–7, 286–7, 328, 342–3
quintessence 18, 117, 247, 287, 337, 362
quotidian 16, 99, 135, 163–4, 176, 281, 287–8, 336 *see also* ague, tertian

R2 (*King Richard II*) 17, 21, 27, 39, 45, 48, 92, 111, 141, 148, 161, 174, 176, 178, 200, 230, 236, 244, 252, 259, 279, 282, 296, 315, 323, 338, 353, 359, 362–3
R3 (*King Richard III*) 12–13, 16, 27, 30, 37, 39–40, 42, 58, 87, 98, 106, 111, 133, 141, 157, 178, 179, 200, 224, 236, 244, 251, 258, 290, 308, 315, 317, 323, 340–1, 354, 358–9, 361–2
race 289–92 *see also* complexion
Rackin, P. 238
Ramachandran, V. S. 46
ratsbane 148, 224, 292
raw eyes 292 *see also* inflammation
Ray, S. 339
Raynalde, J. 63, 171, 188, 222, 306
  The Birth of Mankynde 63
Read, J. 138
receipt 292–3 *see also* prescription
Record, R. 350
Reed, R. 29
Regimen Sanitatis Salerni 30
Reid, P. 6
Reiter, P. 17
reins 293 *see also* kidney

Rennard, B. O. 72
Reno, R. H. 287
rheum, rheumatic 293–5 *see also* catarrh, neeze
Rhodes, P. 87
rhubarb 90, 282, 295–6, 341, 347
  see also cyme
Riddle, J. 12
ringworm 107, 299, 336
Ripley, T. 18, 337
ripp'd *see* untimely ripp'd 296
Riss, A. 31
Rivière, L. 171
Roberts, G. 41, 154, 328
Roberts, J. A. 63, 198
Robson, M. 114, 162
Rolfe, R. 77
ROM (*Romeo and Juliet*) 14, 20, 23, 41, 44, 54, 57–8, 66, 71, 80, 84–5, 88, 92, 94, 102, 108, 110, 113, 134, 142, 146, 149, 153, 168, 170–1, 178–80, 192, 210, 221, 224, 228, 231, 253, 256, 265, 269–70, 273–4, 276, 280–1, 301, 304, 309, 317, 333, 360–1, 363
  apothecary in 20, 22, 228, 309
  plague-searchers in 253
rose
  damask rose 53, 57–9
  as rose-oil 59, 139, 151, 175, 297, 327
  as rosed honey to cure a bleeding tongue 339
  as rose-water 13, 67, 175, 211, 250, 328, 334
Ross, J. 277
Rous, F. 342
Roussat, R. 332
Rowe, K. 134, 170, 241, 252
Royal College of Physicians 2, 18, 22, 118, 138, 146, 254, 326
Royster, F. 25, 78
Rüff, J. 12, 188, 360
rue 296 *see also* herb-grace
ruptures 296
Rusceli 50, 72, 163, 200, 215, 272, 283

St. John's wort
  for palsy 244
  for postpartum contractions 60

Salkeld, D. 208
salt 54, 148, 177, 185, 195, 245–6, 286,
    297, 335, 337, 350 *see also* tub-fast
salve 297–8 *see also* balsam, plantain,
    wound
sand-blind 298 *see also* blind, eye
sanguine 3, 35, 37, 49, 56, 67, **74**, 76–7,
    147, 156, 169, 224, 254, 280, 282,
    289, 298, 306, 338, 339, 347
sapego, suppeago 298–9
Saturn 215, 218, 299 *see also* melancholy,
    planet
    as cause of plague 262
Saunders, B. 69, 283
Sawday, J. 20, 248, 326
scab 299 *see also* cicatrice, skin
scabies 299, 336
scar *see* cicatrice, skin
scarification 21, 84, 105, 148, 175, 187,
    244, 313, 327, 341, 356
Schaar, C. 200
Schanzer, E, 192
Schiebinger, L. 222, 306
Schleiner, W. 208, 306
Schoenfeldt, M. 1, 43, 162, 170, 252, 319
Schwartz, R. B. 130
Schwarz, K. 48
sciatica, hip-gout 10, 299–300, 323
Scott, W. O. 130
Scot, R. 203
Scott-Warren, J. 183
scrofula 89, 123, *see* evil
scruple 300 *see also* dram
scurvy 215, 281, 300–1
searchers 253, 262 *see also* plague
sea-sick 100, 284, 301, 307, 319–20
seed 301–2 *see also* sex
senna *see* cyme
Sennert, D. 298
serpigo *see* sapego
sex, unsex 302–7
    one-sex model 2, 41, 146, 148, 222, 242,
        302, 306
    sexual relations 49, 82, 151
    sexuality 49, 138, 153, 237, 254, 285,
        292
Seynge of Urines 346, 350
Sharp, J. 222
shingles (St. Anthony's fire) 272

shins
    aching from syphilis 80, 276
    broken 270, 298
SHR (*The Taming of the Shrew*) 58, 66, 70,
    80, 106, 141–2, 196, 198, 203, 250,
    315, 317, 319, 338
sickness, sick 307–9 *see also* infection,
    green-sick, love-sick, plague,
    seasick, vomit
Siena, K. 277
Shenk, R. 208
Simonds, P. M. 19, 105
simple 2, 5, 22, 49, 54–5, 70, 73, 78–80,
    218, 273, 309–10, 339
Simpson, R. R. 259
Sincklo, J. 19, 20
sinew 86, 132, 175, 310–12, 341
sinows *see* sinew
Siraisi, N. 3, 78, 269, 309
skin 312–14
Skwire, S. 138
Slack, P. 266
sleep, mare, night-mare 314–16
Slights, W. W. E. 83, 162, 180
Sloan, L. L. 130
smallpox
    caused by planetary aspects 266
    as childhood disease 142
    as communicable disease 177
    confused with measles 211
    as distinct from great pox or
        measles 277
Smith, A. 41
Smith, B. R. 34, 46, 114, 130, 252
Smith, P. 118
Smith, P. J. 183
SON (*Sonnets*) 45, 178, 258, 274, 281,
    309, 324, 337, 361
Soranus 120
sound *see* swoon
spear-grass 316
spectacles 126, 129–30
    Worshipful Company of
        Spectacle-Makers 129
Spenser, E. 102
    Faerie Queene 102
'spital *see* hospital, lazar
spleen 316–18
squint *see* web and pin

staggers, the 106 *see also* dizzy
stale *see* urine
stammer 318 *see also* tongue-tied
star *see* planet
Starks, L. S. 154
Starobinski, J. 1, 154
Stensgaard, R. K. 108
stigmatical 95–6, 318 *see also* deformed,
    hare-lip, mole, monster
stomach 318–19
stomach-qualmed 320 *see also* seasick
Stone, L. 94
strangle, strangled 320–1
strings *see* heart-strings
Stubbes, P. 269
Sugg, R. 229
sulphur 117, 177, 246, 286, 297, 350
    see also brimstone
suppeago *see* sapego
surfeit 321–4
surgeon 1–4, 6–7, 16, 20, 34, 36, 40, 52,
    54–5, 59–64, 67, 73, 84–5, 89, 112,
    118, 123–4, 138, 148–9, 152,
    159–60, 175–7, 220, 225, 254,
    257–8, 271, 287, 297, 324–7, 334–6,
    340, 342–3, 345, 358
surgeon's box 21, 36, 92, 120, 127, 140,
    152, 165, 175, 187, 244, 283, 326–7,
    334, 356–7 *see also* tent
Sutherland, J. 331
Swain, D. W. 148, 224, 306
sweat
    dissipated through hair 130
    as symptom of fever 288, 335
    as symptom of sweating sickness 327–8
    as treatment for syphilis 98–9, 286,
        343
    as vapor or excrement 24, 35, 125, 281
Sweetser, E. 46
swoon, swooning, swooned 328–31
    see also faint
swound *see* swoon
syphilis 4–5, 41, 55, 68, 80–1, 83–4, 87–8,
    98, 122, 137, 149, 153, 156, 158,
    166, 177, 180, 189–90, 197, 233–4,
    238, 245–6, 258–65, 275–6, 286–7,
    299–300, 309, 325, 328, 342, 359
    see also pox
syrup 331

Tate, J. 350
Taurus 175, 267–8, 332 *see also* planet
tawny 332–3 *see also* cheek, complexion,
    race
Taylor, G. 123, 149
teeth 333–4 *see also* tooth-ache,
    tooth-drawer
Temkin, O. 122, 145
temperality 334 *see also* pulsidge
tent 334–5
tertian, burning fever 16, 135, 163, 288,
    335–6 *see also* ague, fever, quotidian
tetter 107, 189, 201, 211, 286, 336–7
TGV (*The Two Gentlemen of Verona*) 53, 70,
    96, 98, 158, 163, 218, 236, 249, 253,
    261, 264, 311, 315, 324, 334, 337
Thiher, A. 209
Thoren, V. E. 84
Thwaites, G. 328
Tidy, H. 328
TIM (*Timon of Athens*) 14, 17–18, 27, 32,
    64, 81, 83, 98, 108, 122, 133, 137,
    150, 154, 171, 178, 180, 189, 210,
    244, 250, 258, 265–6, 276, 290, 317,
    323, 343, 348, 355
tinct, tincture 17, 211, 214–15, 287,
    337–8
tisick 80, 338 *see also* consumption
TIT (*Titus Andronicus*) 38–9, 42, 48, 58,
    61, 84, 87, 92, 103, 116, 123, 134,
    141, 148, 197, 199, 218, 223, 227,
    245, 249, 250, 256, 298, 313, 319,
    323, 329, 333, 339, 353, 355, 359,
    360, 363
TMP (*The Tempest*) 17, 30, 40, 54, 71, 86,
    88, 102, 107, 109–10, 116–17, 127,
    131–2, 136, 142, 158, 171, 178–9,
    185, 193, 201, 214, 227, 230–1, 245,
    250, 270, 276, 280, 290, 301–2, 305,
    311, 349, 357, 359
TN (*Twelfth Night*) 17, 20, 23, 38, 49, 58,
    77, 83–4, 97, 101, 116, 123, 141,
    154, 161, 170, 179, 184, 193, 203,
    209, 217, 220, 222, 224, 226, 242,
    250, 252, 260, 268, 277, 299–300,
    311, 317, 321, 326, 332, 348–9, 363
TNK (*The Two Noble Kinsmen*) 108, 154,
    203, 207, 209, 213, 217, 219, 271–2
Tognotti, E. 336

tongue 338–40 *see also* tongue-tied
  relation to umbilical cord 220, 338
  in *TIT* 339, 353
tongue-tied 340–1 *see also* stammer, lisp
Tomkiss, T. 339
Tooker, W. 7, 124–5
tooth-ache 341–2 *see also* teeth,
  tooth-drawer
tooth-drawer 342 *see also* surgeon,
  tooth-ache, teeth
Topsell, E. 163
Torrey, M. 87
Totaro, R. 266
Traister, B. 260
tremor cordis 342
Trevor, D. 3, 219
TRO (*Troilus and Cressida*) 17, 27, 32,
  39, 41–2, 45–6, 51, 55, 68, 70, 72,
  84–5, 99, 101, 106, 114, 134, 137,
  141, 147, 149, 155, 161, 175,
  179–80, 182, 184, 192, 194, 196,
  201, 205, 214, 227, 242, 244, 248,
  252, 259–60, 264–5, 273, 280, 283,
  292, 294, 296, 299–300, 302, 311,
  317, 327, 329, 334, 337–8, 340, 344,
  356, 362
  Thersites' catalog of ailments in
  TRO 5.1 41, 151, 192, 292, 296
tub-fast 6, 28, 98, 275–7, 286, 297, 325,
  328, 342–3 *see also* pox, quicksilver
Turner, M. 46
Turner, W. 27–9, 210, 296
  Book of Baths 29
typhus 195, 252

ulcer 8, 27, 31–2, 51–2, 67, 84–5, 91, 100,
  124, 137, 139, 146, 156, 163, 166,
  174–5, 232, 269–71, 276, 278,
  285–6, 300, 312–16, 338, 340, 344,
  355, 358 *see also* evil
umbilical cord 59, 220, 231
  length of as indicator of woman's
  tongue 220, 338
unpaved 344–5 *see also* eunuch, geld,
  splay, unseminar'd
untimely ripp'd 6, 59, 197, 220, 296, 345
urinal, jordan 346 *see also* urine
urine, piss, stale 346–50 *see also* urinal
  as breeder of fleas 346

of child as cure for cancer 52
colored, as prognostic of pleurisy 271
malodorous, as prognostic of
  plague 261
of man as cure for gout 347
Urkowitz, S. 139

Van Dijkhuizen, J. F. 209
vapor 351–2
Varandaeus, J. 154
Vaughan, W. 114
Vaught, J. 252
VEN (*Venus and Adonis*) 99, 111,
  140, 153–4, 159, 162, 175, 210,
  224, 297
ventricle
  of brain, 163, 315 *see also* pia mater
  of heart, 160
Verity, A. 15
Vesalius, A. 20
  De Humani Corporis Fabrica 20
vial 352–3
Vicary, T. 24, 43, 58, 69, 107, 114, 130–2,
  140, 148, 155, 162, 186, 200, 234,
  244, 260, 297, 298, 300, 312, 314,
  318–19, 326, 342, 362
Vickers, N. 48
Vigo, J. 28, 32, 175, 342
Vinge, L. 46
viol 353
vomit 353–4 *see also* purge, puking

Wall, W. 105, 224, 239
Wallace, D. F. 219
wall-eyed 355
Wallis, P. 266
wappen'd 355
wart 48, 84, 355–6 *see also* corn
Watt, R. J. C. 247
weapon-salve 88, 298
web and pin, pin and web 160, 249, 261,
  318, 356–7 *see also* pearl
Webster, C. 2, 29, 146, 149, 167, 248,
  326
Wecker, J. 84, 278, 356
Weil, J. 239
Weyer, J. 301
wezand 357
Wheatley, E. 35

Wheeler, R. 78
White, F. 2, 118, 222, 239, 259
whites of eggs 34, 259, 335 *see also* flax
    and eye
Willet, A. 274
Williams, G. 122
Willis, D. 125
Wilson, A. 63, 222
Wilson, D. 186
Wilson, J. D. 209
WIV (*The Merry Wives of Windsor*) 15, 23,
    27–8, 51, 68, 78, 101, 104, 122, 141,
    145, 155, 161, 165, 167, 169, 177,
    185–6, 193–4, 196, 199, 201, 209,
    229, 233, 235, 241, 248, 253–4, 258,
    273–4, 279, 293, 295, 309, 312, 346,
    349–50, 356
womb 357–61 *see also* blood, *hysterica*
    passio, pregnant, sex
women
  as doctors *see* Doctor She
  as nurses 72, 107, 110, 211, 220, 221,
    223–4, 234–9, 275
  as midwives 2, 12, 59, 60, 63, 107,
    220–2

as subject to hysteria *see hysterica passio*,
    womb
Woodall, J. 32
Woodbridge, L. 34
wooden legs 32
Woodforde, J. 342
wound 361–2 *see also* tent
Wright, T. 24, 58, 66, 78, 134, 170, 183,
    241, 251
WT (*The Winter's Tale*) 23, 60–2, 69, 92,
    101, 108, 125, 131, 149, 163, 178–9,
    187, 194, 206, 210, 213, 222, 233–4,
    238, 241, 250, 255, 259, 268, 272,
    274, 278, 282, 291, 295–6, 301, 304,
    315–16, 330, 333, 337, 340–2, 353,
    356, 359–60
Wynne-Davies, M. 360

Yachnin, P. 20–1
Yalom, M. 48
Yates, Dame F. 19, 338
Yersinia pestis 49, 261 *see* plague
yew 363

zany 231 *see* natural